In Praise of *Computer Organization and Design: The Hardware/ Software Interface*, Revised Fourth Edition

"Patterson and Hennessy not only improve the pedagogy of the traditional material on pipelined processors and memory hierarchies, but also greatly expand the multiprocessor coverage to include emerging multicore processors and GPUs. The fourth edition of *Computer Organization and Design* sets a new benchmark against which all other architecture books must be compared."

—David A. Wood, *University of Wisconsin-Madison*

"Patterson and Hennessy have greatly improved what was already the gold standard of textbooks. In the rapidly evolving field of computer architecture, they have woven an impressive number of recent case studies and contemporary issues into a framework of time-tested fundamentals."

—Fred Chong, *University of California at Santa Barbara*

"Since the publication of the first edition in 1994, *Computer Organization and Design* has introduced a generation of computer science and engineering students to computer architecture. Now, many of those students have become leaders in the field. In academia, the tradition continues as faculty use the latest edition of the book that inspired them to engage the next generation. With the fourth edition, readers are prepared for the next era of computing."

—David I. August, *Princeton University*

"The new coverage of multiprocessors and parallelism lives up to the standards of this well-written classic. It provides well-motivated, gentle introductions to the new topics, as well as many details and examples drawn from current hardware."

—John Greiner, *Rice University*

"As computer hardware architecture moves from uniprocessor to multicores, the parallel programming environments used to take advantage of these cores will be a defining challenge to the success of these new systems. In the multicore systems, the interface between the hardware and software is of particular importance. This new edition of *Computer Organization and Design* is mandatory for any student who wishes to understand multicore architecture including the interface between programming it and its architecture."

—Jesse Fang, *Director of Programming System Lab at Intel*

"The fourth edition of *Computer Organization and Design* continues to improve the high standards set by the previous editions. The new content, on trends that are reshaping computer systems including multicores, Flash memory, GPUs, etc., makes this edition a must read—even for all of those who grew up on previous editions of the book."

—Parthasarathy Ranganathan, *Principal Research Scientist, HP Labs*

REVISED FOURTH EDITION

Computer Organization and Design

THE HARDWARE/SOFTWARE INTERFACE

ACKNOWLEDGMENTS

Figures 1.7, 1.8 Courtesy of Other World Computing (*www.macsales.com*).

Figures 1.9, 1.19, 5.37 Courtesy of AMD.

Figure 1.10 Courtesy of Storage Technology Corp.

Figures 1.10.1, 1.10.2, 4.15.2 Courtesy of the Charles Babbage Institute, University of Minnesota Libraries, Minneapolis.

Figures 1.10.3, 4.15.1, 4.15.3, 5.12.3, 6.14.2 Courtesy of IBM.

Figure 1.10.4 Courtesy of Cray Inc.

Figure 1.10.5 Courtesy of Apple Computer, Inc.

Figure 1.10.6 Courtesy of the Computer History Museum.

Figures 5.12.1, 5.12.2 Courtesy of Museum of Science, Boston.

Figure 5.12.4 Courtesy of MIPS Technologies, Inc.

Figures 6.15, 6.16, 6.17 Courtesy of Sun Microsystems, Inc.

Figure 6.4 © Peg Skorpinski.

Figure 6.14.1 Courtesy of the Computer Museum of America.

Figure 6.14.3 Courtesy of the Commercial Computing Museum.

Figures 7.13.1 Courtesy of NASA Ames Research Center.

REVISED FOURTH EDITION

Computer Organization and Design

THE HARDWARE/SOFTWARE INTERFACE

David A. Patterson
University of California, Berkeley

John L. Hennessy
Stanford University

With contributions by

Perry Alexander
The University of Kansas

Peter J. Ashenden
Ashenden Designs Pty Ltd

Javier Bruguera
Universidade de Santiago de Compostela

Jichuan Chang
Hewlett-Packard

Matthew Farrens
University of California, Davis

David Kaeli
Northeastern University

Nicole Kaiyan
University of Adelaide

David Kirk
NVIDIA

James R. Larus
Microsoft Research

Jacob Leverich
Hewlett-Packard

Kevin Lim
Hewlett-Packard

John Nickolls
NVIDIA

John Oliver
Cal Poly, San Luis Obispo

Milos Prvulovic
Georgia Tech

Partha Ranganathan
Hewlett-Packard

AMSTERDAM · BOSTON · HEIDELBERG · LONDON
NEW YORK · OXFORD · PARIS · SAN DIEGO
SAN FRANCISCO · SINGAPORE · SYDNEY · TOKYO
Morgan Kaufmann is an imprint of Elsevier

Acquiring Editor: Todd Green
Development Editor: Nate McFadden
Project Manager: Jessica Vaughan
Designer: Eric DeCicco

Morgan Kaufmann is an imprint of Elsevier
225 Wyman Street, Waltham, MA 02451, USA

Library of Congress Cataloging-in-Publication Data
Patterson, David A.
  Computer organization and design: the hardware/software interface / David A. Patterson, John L. Hennessy. — 4th ed.
      p. cm. — (The Morgan Kaufmann series in computer architecture and design)
  Rev. ed. of: Computer organization and design / John L. Hennessy, David A. Patterson. 1998.
  Summary: "Presents the fundamentals of hardware technologies, assembly language, computer arithmetic, pipelining, memory hierarchies and I/O"— Provided by publisher.
  ISBN 978-0-12-374750-1 (pbk.)
  1. Computer organization.   2. Computer engineering.   3. Computer interfaces.   I. Hennessy, John L.   II. Hennessy, John L.
Computer organization and design.   III. Title.
  QA76.9.C643H46 2011
  004.2′2—dc23

                                                                    2011029199

British Library Cataloguing-in-Publication Data
A catalogue record for this book is available from the British Library.

ISBN: 978-0-12-374750-1

Printed in the United States of America

12   13   14   15   16   10 9 8 7 6 5 4 3 2 1

To Linda,
who has been, is, and always will be the love of my life

Contents

3 Arithmetic for Computers   222

4 The Processor   298

APPENDICES

A   Graphics and Computing GPUs   A-2

B   Assemblers, Linkers, and the SPIM Simulator   B-2

CD - ROM   CONTENT

The Basics of Logic Design   C-2

Mapping Control to Hardware   D-2

A Survey of RISC Architectures for Desktop, Server, and Embedded Computers   E-2

Preface

*The most beautiful thing we can experience is the mysterious.
It is the source of all true art and science.*

Albert Einstein, *What I Believe*, 1930

About This Book

We believe that learning in computer science and engineering should reflect the current state of the field, as well as introduce the principles that are shaping computing. We also feel that readers in every specialty of computing need to appreciate the organizational paradigms that determine the capabilities, performance, and, ultimately, the success of computer systems.

Modern computer technology requires professionals of every computing specialty to understand both hardware and software. The interaction between hardware and software at a variety of levels also offers a framework for understanding the fundamentals of computing. Whether your primary interest is hardware or software, computer science or electrical engineering, the central ideas in computer organization and design are the same. Thus, our emphasis in this book is to show the relationship between hardware and software and to focus on the concepts that are the basis for current computers.

The recent switch from uniprocessor to multicore microprocessors confirmed the soundness of this perspective, given since the first edition. While programmers could ignore the advice and rely on computer architects, compiler writers, and silicon engineers to make their programs run faster without change, that era is over. For programs to run faster, they must become parallel. While the goal of many researchers is to make it possible for programmers to be unaware of the underlying parallel nature of the hardware they are programming, it will take many years to realize this vision. Our view is that for at least the next decade, most programmers are going to have to understand the hardware/software interface if they want programs to run efficiently on parallel computers.

The audience for this book includes those with little experience in assembly language or logic design who need to understand basic computer organization as well as readers with backgrounds in assembly language and/or logic design who want to learn how to design a computer or understand how a system works and why it performs as it does.

About the Other Book

Some readers may be familiar with *Computer Architecture: A Quantitative Approach*, popularly known as Hennessy and Patterson. (This book in turn is often called Patterson and Hennessy.) Our motivation in writing the earlier book was to describe the principles of computer architecture using solid engineering fundamentals and quantitative cost/performance tradeoffs. We used an approach that combined examples and measurements, based on commercial systems, to create realistic design experiences. Our goal was to demonstrate that computer architecture could be learned using quantitative methodologies instead of a descriptive approach. It was intended for the serious computing professional who wanted a detailed understanding of computers.

A majority of the readers for this book do not plan to become computer architects. The performance and energy efficiency of future software systems will be dramatically affected, however, by how well software designers understand the basic hardware techniques at work in a system. Thus, compiler writers, operating system designers, database programmers, and most other software engineers need a firm grounding in the principles presented in this book. Similarly, hardware designers must understand clearly the effects of their work on software applications.

Thus, we knew that this book had to be much more than a subset of the material in *Computer Architecture*, and the material was extensively revised to match the different audience. We were so happy with the result that the subsequent editions of *Computer Architecture* were revised to remove most of the introductory material; hence, there is much less overlap today than with the first editions of both books.

Changes for the Fourth Edition

We had five major goals for the fourth edition of *Computer Organization and Design:* given the multicore revolution in microprocessors, highlight parallel hardware and software topics throughout the book; streamline the existing material to make room for topics on parallelism; enhance pedagogy in general; update the technical content to reflect changes in the industry since the publication of the third edition in 2004; and restore the usefulness of exercises in this Internet age.

Before discussing the goals in detail, let's look at the table on the next page. It shows the hardware and software paths through the material. Chapters 1, 4, 5, and 7 are found on both paths, no matter what the experience or the focus. Chapter 1 is a new introduction that includes a discussion on the importance of power and how it motivates the switch from single core to multicore microprocessors. It also includes performance and benchmarking material that was a separate chapter in the third edition. Chapter 2 is likely to be review material for the hardware-oriented, but it is essential reading for the software-oriented, especially for those readers interested in learning more about compilers and object-oriented programming

Chapter or appendix	Sections	Software focus	Hardware focus
1. Computer Abstractions and Technology	1.1 to 1.9	Read carefully	Read carefully
	● 1.10 (History)	Read for culture	Read for culture
2. Instructions: Language of the Computer	2.1 to 2.14	Read carefully	Read carefully
	● 2.15 (Compilers & Java)	Read for culture	
	2.16 to 2.19	Read carefully	Read carefully
	● 2.20 (History)	Read for culture	Read for culture
E. RISC Instruction-Set Architectures	● E.1 to E.19	Read for culture	
3. Arithmetic for Computers	3.1 to 3.9	Read carefully	Read carefully
	● 3.10 (History)	Read for culture	Read for culture
C. The Basics of Logic Design	● C.1 to C.13		Read carefully
4. The Processor	4.1 (Overview)	Read carefully	Read carefully
	4.2 (Logic Conventions)		Read carefully
	4.3 to 4.4 (Simple Implementation)	Review or read	Read carefully
	4.5 (Pipelining Overview)	Read carefully	Read carefully
	4.6 (Pipelined Datapath)	Review or read	Read carefully
	4.7 to 4.9 (Hazards, Exceptions)		Read carefully
	4.10 to 4.11 (Parallel, Real Stuff)	Read for culture	Read carefully
	● 4.12 (Verilog Pipeline Control)		Read for culture
	4.13 to 4.14 (Fallacies)	Read for culture	Read carefully
	● 4.15 (History)	Read for culture	Read for culture
D. Mapping Control to Hardware	● D.1 to D.6		Read for culture
5. Large and Fast: Exploiting Memory Hierarchy	5.1 to 5.8	Review or read	Read carefully
	● 5.9 (Verilog Cache Controller)		Read for culture
	5.10 to 5.12	Read for culture	Read carefully
	● 5.13 (History)	Read for culture	Read if have time
6. Storage and Other I/O Topics	6.1 to 6.10	Read for culture	Read for culture
	● 6.11 (Networks)	Read for culture	Read for culture
	6.12 to 6.13	Read carefully	Read for culture
	● 6.14 (History)	Read for culture	Read for culture
7. Multicores, Multiprocessors, and Clusters	7.1 to 7.13	Read carefully	Read carefully
	● 7.14 (History)	Read for culture	Read for culture
A. Graphics Processor Units	A.1 to A.12	Read for culture	Read for culture
B. Assemblers, Linkers, and the SPIM Simulator	B.1 to B.12	Reference	Reference

Read carefully		Read if have time	Reference
Review or read		Read for culture	

languages. It includes material from Chapter 3 in the third edition so that the complete MIPS architecture is now in a single chapter, minus the floating-point instructions. Chapter 3 is for readers interested in constructing a datapath or in learning more about floating-point arithmetic. Some will skip Chapter 3, either because they don't need it or because it is a review. Chapter 4 combines two chapters from the third edition to explain pipelined processors. Sections 4.1, 4.5, and 4.10 give overviews for those with a software focus. Those with a hardware focus, however, will find that this chapter presents core material; they may also, depending on their background, want to read Appendix C on logic design first. Chapter 6 on storage is critical to readers with a software focus, and should be read by others if time permits. The last chapter on multicores, multiprocessors, and clusters is mostly new content and should be read by everyone.

The first goal was to make parallelism a first class citizen in this edition, as it was a separate chapter on the CD in the last edition. The most obvious example is Chapter 7. In particular, this chapter introduces the Roofline performance model, and shows its value by evaluating four recent multicore architectures on two kernels. This model could prove to be as insightful for multicore microprocessors as the 3Cs model is for caches.

Given the importance of parallelism, it wasn't wise to wait until the last chapter to talk about, so there is a section on parallelism in each of the preceding six chapters:

- *Chapter 1: Parallelism and Power.* It shows how power limits have forced the industry to switch to parallelism, and why parallelism helps.

- *Chapter 2: Parallelism and Instructions: Synchronization.* This section discusses locks for shared variables, specifically the MIPS instructions Load Linked and Store Conditional.

- *Chapter 3: Parallelism and Computer Arithmetic: Floating-Point Associativity.* This section discusses the challenges of numerical precision and floating-point calculations.

- *Chapter 4: Parallelism and Advanced Instruction-Level Parallelism.* It covers advanced ILP—superscalar, speculation, VLIW, loop-unrolling, and OOO—as well as the relationship between pipeline depth and power consumption.

- *Chapter 5: Parallelism and Memory Hierarchies: Cache Coherence.* It introduces coherency, consistency, and snooping cache protocols.

- *Chapter 6: Parallelism and I/O: Redundant Arrays of Inexpensive Disks.* It describes RAID as a parallel I/O system as well as a highly available ICO system.

Chapter 7 concludes with reasons for optimism why this foray into parallelism should be more successful than those of the past.

I am particularly excited about the addition of an appendix on Graphical Processing Units written by NVIDIA's chief scientist, David Kirk, and chief architect, John Nickolls. Appendix A is the first in-depth description of GPUs, which is a new and interesting thrust in computer architecture. The appendix builds upon the parallel themes of this edition to present a style of computing that allows the programmer to think MIMD yet the hardware tries to execute in SIMD-style whenever possible. As GPUs are both inexpensive and widely available—they are even found in many laptops—and their programming environments are freely available, they provide a parallel hardware platform that many could experiment with.

The second goal was to streamline the book to make room for new material in parallelism. The first step was simply going through all the paragraphs accumulated over three editions with a fine-toothed comb to see if they were still necessary. The coarse-grained changes were the merging of chapters and dropping of topics. Mark Hill suggested dropping the multicycle processor implementation and instead adding a multicycle cache controller to the memory hierarchy chapter. This allowed the processor to be presented in a single chapter instead of two, enhancing the processor material by omission. The performance material from a separate chapter in the third edition is now blended into the first chapter.

The third goal was to improve the pedagogy of the book. Chapter 1 is now meatier, including performance, integrated circuits, and power, and it sets the stage for the rest of the book. Chapters 2 and 3 were originally written in an evolutionary style, starting with a "single celled" architecture and ending up with the full MIPS architecture by the end of Chapter 3. This leisurely style is not a good match to the modern reader. This edition merges all of the instruction set material for the integer instructions into Chapter 2—making Chapter 3 optional for many readers—and each section now stands on its own. The reader no longer needs to read all of the preceding sections. Hence, Chapter 2 is now even better as a reference than it was in prior editions. Chapter 4 works better since the processor is now a single chapter, as the multicycle implementation is a distraction today. Chapter 5 has a new section on building cache controllers, along with a new CD section containing the Verilog code for that cache.

The accompanying CD-ROM introduced in the third edition allowed us to reduce the cost of the book by saving pages as well as to go into greater depth on topics that were of interest to some but not all readers. Alas, in our enthusiasm to save pages, readers sometimes found themselves going back and forth between the CD and book more often than they liked. This should not be the case in this edition. Each chapter now has the Historical Perspectives section on the CD and four chapters also have one advanced material section on the CD. Additionally, all exercises are in the printed book, so flipping between book and CD should be rare in this edition.

For those of you who wonder why we include a CD-ROM with the book, the answer is simple: the CD contains content that we feel should be easily and immediately accessible to the reader no matter where they are. If you are interested in the advanced content, or would like to review a VHDL tutorial (for example), it is on the CD, ready for you to use. The CD-ROM also includes a feature that should greatly enhance your study of the material: a search engine is included that allows you to search for any string of text, in the printed book or on the CD itself. If you are hunting for content that may not be included in the book's printed index, you can simply enter the text you're searching for and the page number it appears on will be displayed in the search results. This is a very useful feature that we hope you make frequent use of as you read and review the book.

This is a fast-moving field, and as is always the case for our new editions, an important goal is to update the technical content. The AMD Opteron X4 model 2356 (code named "Barcelona") serves as a running example throughout the book, and is found in Chapters 1, 4, 5, and 7. Chapters 1 and 6 add results from the new power benchmark from SPEC. Chapter 2 adds a section on the ARM architecture, which is currently the world's most popular 32-bit ISA. Chapter 5 adds a new section on Virtual Machines, which are resurging in importance. Chapter 5 has detailed cache performance measurements on the Opteron X4 multicore and a few details on its rival, the Intel Nehalem, which will not be announced until after this edition is published. Chapter 6 describes Flash Memory for the first time as well as a remarkably compact server from Sun, which crams 8 cores, 16 DIMMs, and 8 disks into a single 1U bit. It also includes the recent results on long-term disk failures. Chapter 7 covers a wealth of topics regarding parallelism—including multithreading, SIMD, vector, GPUs, performance models, benchmarks, multiprocessor networks—and describes three multicores plus the Opteron X4: Intel Xeon model e5345 (Clovertown), IBM Cell model QS20, and the Sun Microsystems T2 model 5120 (Niagara 2).

The final goal was to try to make the exercises useful to instructors in this Internet age, for homework assignments have long been an important way to learn material. Alas, answers are posted today almost as soon as the book appears. We have a two-part approach. First, expert contributors have worked to develop entirely new exercises for each chapter in the book. Second, most exercises have a qualitative description supported by a table that provides several alternative quantitative parameters needed to answer this question. The sheer number plus flexibility in terms of how the instructor can choose to assign variations of exercises will make it hard for students to find the matching solutions online. Instructors will also be able to change these quantitative parameters as they wish, again frustrating those students who have come to rely on the Internet to provide solutions for a static and unchanging set of exercises. We feel this new approach is a valuable new addition to the book—please let us know how well it works for you, either as a student or instructor!

We have preserved useful book elements from prior editions. To make the book work better as a reference, we still place definitions of new terms in the margins at their first occurrence. The book element called "Understanding Program Performance" sections helps readers understand the performance of their programs and how to improve it, just as the "Hardware/Software Interface" book element helped readers understand the tradeoffs at this interface. "The Big Picture" section remains so that the reader sees the forest even despite all the trees. "Check Yourself" sections help readers to confirm their comprehension of the material on the first time through with answers provided at the end of each chapter. This edition also includes the green MIPS reference card, which was inspired by the "Green Card" of the IBM System/360. The removable card has been updated and should be a handy reference when writing MIPS assembly language programs.

Instructor Support

We have collected a great deal of material to help instructors teach courses using this book. Solutions to exercises, chapter quizzes, figures from the book, lecture notes, lecture slides, and other materials are available to adopters from the publisher. Check the publisher's Web site for more information:

textbooks.elsevier.com/9780123744937

Concluding Remarks

If you read the following acknowledgments section, you will see that we went to great lengths to correct mistakes. Since a book goes through many printings, we have the opportunity to make even more corrections. If you uncover any remaining, resilient bugs, please contact the publisher by electronic mail at *cod4bugs@mkp.com* or by low-tech mail using the address found on the copyright page.

This edition marks a break in the long-standing collaboration between Hennessy and Patterson, which started in 1989. The demands of running one of the world's great universities meant that President Hennessy could no longer make the substantial commitment to create a new edition. The remaining author felt like a juggler who had always performed with a partner who suddenly is thrust on the stage as a solo act. Hence, the people in the acknowledgments and Berkeley colleagues played an even larger role in shaping the contents of this book. Nevertheless, this time around there is only one author to blame for the new material in what you are about to read.

Acknowledgments for the Fourth Edition

I'd like to thank **David Kirk**, **John Nickolls**, and their colleagues at NVIDIA (Michael Garland, John Montrym, Doug Voorhies, Lars Nyland, Erik Lindholm, Paulius Micikevicius, Massimiliano Fatica, Stuart Oberman, and Vasily Volkov) for writing the first in-depth appendix on GPUs. I'd like to express again my appreciation to **Jim Larus** of Microsoft Research for his willingness in contributing his expertise on assembly language programming, as well as for welcoming readers of this book to use the simulator he developed and maintains.

I am also very grateful for the contributions of the many experts who developed the new exercises for this new edition. Writing good exercises is not an easy task, and each contributor worked long and hard to develop problems that are both challenging and engaging:

- *Chapter 1:* **Javier Bruguera** (Universidade de Santiago de Compostela)

- *Chapter 2:* **John Oliver** (Cal Poly, San Luis Obispo), with contributions from **Nicole Kaiyan** (University of Adelaide) and **Milos Prvulovic** (Georgia Tech)

- *Chapter 3:* **Matthew Farrens** (University of California, Davis)

- *Chapter 4:* **Milos Prvulovic** (Georgia Tech)

- *Chapter 5:* **Jichuan Chang, Jacob Leverich, Kevin Lim**, and **Partha Ranganathan** (all from Hewlett-Packard), with contributions from Nicole Kaiyan (University of Adelaide)

- *Chapter 6:* **Perry Alexander** (The University of Kansas)

- *Chapter 7:* **David Kaeli** (Northeastern University)

Peter Ashenden took on the Herculean task of editing and evaluating *all* of the new exercises. Moreover, he even added the substantial burden of developing the companion CD and new lecture slides.

Thanks to **David August** and **Prakash Prabhu** of Princeton University for their work on the chapter quizzes that are available for instructors on the publisher's Web site.

I relied on my Silicon Valley colleagues for much of the technical material that this book relies upon:

- **AMD**—for the details and measurements of the Opteron X4 (Barcelona): **William Brantley, Vasileios Liaskovitis, Chuck Moore**, and **Brian Waldecker.**

- **Intel**—for the prereleased information on the Intel Nehalem: **Faye Briggs.**

- **Micron**—for background on Flash Memory in Chapter 6: **Dean Klein.**

- **Sun Microsystems**—for the measurements of the instruction mixes for the SPEC CPU2006 benchmarks in Chapter 2 and details and measurements of the Sun Server x4150 in Chapter 6: **Yan Fisher, John Fowler, Darryl Gove, Paul Joyce, Shenik Mehta, Pierre Reynes, Dimitry Stuve, Durgam Vahia,** and **David Weaver.**

- **U.C. Berkeley**—**Krste Asanovic** (who supplied the idea for software concurrency versus hardware parallelism in Chapter 7), **James Demmel** and **Velvel Kahan** (who commented on parallelism and floating-point calculations), **Zhangxi Tan** (who designed the cache controller and wrote the Verilog for it in Chapter 5), **Sam Williams** (who supplied the roofline model and the multicore measurements in Chapter 7), and the rest of my colleagues in the **Par Lab** who gave extensive suggestions and feedback on parallelism topics found throughout the book.

I am grateful to the many instructors who answered the publisher's surveys, reviewed our proposals, and attended focus groups to analyze and respond to our plans for this edition. They include the following individuals: *Focus Group:* Mark Hill (University of Wisconsin, Madison), E.J. Kim (Texas A&M University), Jihong Kim (Seoul National University), Lu Peng (Louisiana State University), Dean Tullsen (UC San Diego), Ken Vollmar (Missouri State University), David Wood (University of Wisconsin, Madison), Ki Hwan Yum (University of Texas, San Antonio); *Surveys and Reviews:* Mahmoud Abou-Nasr (Wayne State University), Perry Alexander (The University of Kansas), Hakan Aydin (George Mason University), Hussein Badr (State University of New York at Stony Brook), Mac Baker (Virginia Military Institute), Ron Barnes (George Mason University), Douglas Blough (Georgia Institute of Technology), Kevin Bolding (Seattle Pacific University), Miodrag Bolic (University of Ottawa), John Bonomo (Westminster College), Jeff Braun (Montana Tech), Tom Briggs (Shippensburg University), Scott Burgess (Humboldt State University), Fazli Can (Bilkent University), Warren R. Carithers (Rochester Institute of Technology), Bruce Carlton (Mesa Community College), Nicholas Carter (University of Illinois at Urbana-Champaign), Anthony Cocchi (The City University of New York), Don Cooley (Utah State University), Robert D. Cupper (Allegheny College), Edward W. Davis (North Carolina State University), Nathaniel J. Davis (Air Force Institute of Technology), Molisa Derk (Oklahoma City University), Derek Eager (University of Saskatchewan), Ernest Ferguson (Northwest Missouri State University), Rhonda Kay Gaede (The University of Alabama), Etienne M. Gagnon (UQAM), Costa Gerousis (Christopher Newport University), Paul Gillard (Memorial University of Newfoundland), Michael Goldweber (Xavier University), Georgia Grant (College of San Mateo), Merrill Hall (The Master's College), Tyson Hall (Southern Adventist University), Ed Harcourt (Lawrence University), Justin E. Harlow (University of South Florida), Paul F. Hemler (Hampden-Sydney College), Martin Herbordt (Boston University), Steve J. Hodges (Cabrillo College), Kenneth Hopkinson (Cornell University), Dalton Hunkins (St. Bonaventure University), Baback Izadi (State University of New York—New Paltz), Reza Jafari, Robert W. Johnson (Colorado Technical University), Bharat Joshi (University of North Carolina, Charlotte), Nagarajan Kandasamy (Drexel University), Rajiv Kapadia, Ryan Kastner (University of California, Santa Barbara), Jim Kirk (Union University), Geoffrey S. Knauth (Lycoming College), Manish M. Kochhal (Wayne State), Suzan Koknar-Tezel (Saint Joseph's University), Angkul Kongmunvattana (Columbus State University), April Kontostathis (Ursinus College), Christos Kozyrakis (Stanford University), Danny Krizanc (Wesleyan University), Ashok Kumar, S. Kumar (The University of Texas), Robert N. Lea (University of Houston),

Baoxin Li (Arizona State University), Li Liao (University of Delaware), Gary Livingston (University of Massachusetts), Michael Lyle, Douglas W. Lynn (Oregon Institute of Technology), Yashwant K Malaiya (Colorado State University), Bill Mark (University of Texas at Austin), Ananda Mondal (Claflin University), Alvin Moser (Seattle University), Walid Najjar (University of California, Riverside), Danial J. Neebel (Loras College), John Nestor (Lafayette College), Joe Oldham (Centre College), Timour Paltashev, James Parkerson (University of Arkansas), Shaunak Pawagi (SUNY at Stony Brook), Steve Pearce, Ted Pedersen (University of Minnesota), Gregory D Peterson (The University of Tennessee), Dejan Raskovic (University of Alaska, Fairbanks) Brad Richards (University of Puget Sound), Roman Rozanov, Louis Rubinfield (Villanova University), Md Abdus Salam (Southern University), Augustine Samba (Kent State University), Robert Schaefer (Daniel Webster College), Carolyn J. C. Schauble (Colorado State University), Keith Schubert (CSU San Bernardino), William L. Schultz, Kelly Shaw (University of Richmond), Shahram Shirani (McMaster University), Scott Sigman (Drury University), Bruce Smith, David Smith, Jeff W. Smith (University of Georgia, Athens), Philip Snyder (Johns Hopkins University), Alex Sprintson (Texas A&M), Timothy D. Stanley (Brigham Young University), Dean Stevens (Morningside College), Nozar Tabrizi (Kettering University), Yuval Tamir (UCLA), Alexander Taubin (Boston University), Will Thacker (Winthrop University), Mithuna Thottethodi (Purdue University), Manghui Tu (Southern Utah University), Rama Viswanathan (Beloit College), Guoping Wang (Indiana-Purdue University), Patricia Wenner (Bucknell University), Kent Wilken (University of California, Davis), David Wolfe (Gustavus Adolphus College), David Wood (University of Wisconsin, Madison), Mohamed Zahran (City College of New York), Gerald D. Zarnett (Ryerson University), Nian Zhang (South Dakota School of Mines & Technology), Jiling Zhong (Troy University), Huiyang Zhou (The University of Central Florida), Weiyu Zhu (Illinois Wesleyan University).

I would especially like to thank the Berkeley people who gave key feedback for Chapter 7 and Appendix A, which were the most challenging pieces to write for this edition: **Krste Asanovic**, **Christopher Batten**, **Rastilav Bodik**, **Bryan Catanzaro**, **Jike Chong**, **Kaushik Data**, **Greg Giebling**, **Anik Jain**, **Jae Lee**, **Vasily Volkov**, and **Samuel Williams.**

A special thanks also goes to **Mark Smotherman** for making multiple passes to find technical and writing glitches that significantly improved the quality of this edition. He played an even more important role this time given that this edition was done as a solo act.

We wish to thank the extended Morgan Kaufmann family for agreeing to publish this book again under the able leadership of **Denise Penrose**. **Nathaniel McFadden** was the developmental editor for this edition and worked with me weekly on the contents of the book. **Kimberlee Honjo** coordinated the surveying of users and their responses.

Dawnmarie Simpson managed the book production process. We thank also the many freelance vendors who contributed to this volume, especially Alan Rose of Multiscience Press and diacriTech, our compositor.

The contributions of the nearly 200 people we mentioned here have helped make this fourth edition what I hope will be our best book yet. Enjoy!

David A. Patterson

1

Computer Abstractions and Technology

Civilization advances by extending the number of important operations which we can perform without thinking about them.

Alfred North Whitehead
An Introduction to Mathematics, 1911

1.1   Introduction

Welcome to this book! We're delighted to have this opportunity to convey the excitement of the world of computer systems. This is not a dry and dreary field, where progress is glacial and where new ideas atrophy from neglect. No! Computers are the product of the incredibly vibrant information technology industry, all aspects of which are responsible for almost 10% of the gross national product of the United States, and whose economy has become dependent in part on the rapid improvements in information technology promised by Moore's law. This unusual industry embraces innovation at a breathtaking rate. In the last 25 years, there have been a number of new computers whose introduction appeared to revolutionize the computing industry; these revolutions were cut short only because someone else built an even better computer.

This race to innovate has led to unprecedented progress since the inception of electronic computing in the late 1940s. Had the transportation industry kept pace with the computer industry, for example, today we could travel from New York to London in about a second for roughly a few cents. Take just a moment to contemplate how such an improvement would change society—living in Tahiti while working in San Francisco, going to Moscow for an evening at the Bolshoi Ballet—and you can appreciate the implications of such a change.

Computers have led to a third revolution for civilization, with the information revolution taking its place alongside the agricultural and the industrial revolutions. The resulting multiplication of humankind's intellectual strength and reach naturally has affected our everyday lives profoundly and changed the ways in which the search for new knowledge is carried out. There is now a new vein of scientific investigation, with computational scientists joining theoretical and experimental scientists in the exploration of new frontiers in astronomy, biology, chemistry, and physics, among others.

The computer revolution continues. Each time the cost of computing improves by another factor of 10, the opportunities for computers multiply. Applications that were economically infeasible suddenly become practical. In the recent past, the following applications were "computer science fiction."

- *Computers in automobiles:* Until microprocessors improved dramatically in price and performance in the early 1980s, computer control of cars was ludicrous. Today, computers reduce pollution, improve fuel efficiency via engine controls, and increase safety through the prevention of dangerous skids and through the inflation of air bags to protect occupants in a crash.

- *Cell phones:* Who would have dreamed that advances in computer systems would lead to mobile phones, allowing person-to-person communication almost anywhere in the world?

- *Human genome project:* The cost of computer equipment to map and analyze human DNA sequences is hundreds of millions of dollars. It's unlikely that anyone would have considered this project had the computer costs been 10 to 100 times higher, as they would have been 10 to 20 years ago. Moreover, costs continue to drop; you may be able to acquire your own genome, allowing medical care to be tailored to you.

- *World Wide Web:* Not in existence at the time of the first edition of this book, the World Wide Web has transformed our society. For many, the WWW has replaced libraries.

- *Search engines:* As the content of the WWW grew in size and in value, finding relevant information became increasingly important. Today, many people rely on search engines for such a large part of their lives that it would be a hardship to go without them.

Clearly, advances in this technology now affect almost every aspect of our society. Hardware advances have allowed programmers to create wonderfully useful software, which explains why computers are omnipresent. Today's science fiction suggests tomorrow's killer applications: already on their way are virtual worlds, practical speech recognition, and personalized health care.

Classes of Computing Applications and Their Characteristics

Although a common set of hardware technologies (see Sections 1.3 and 1.7) is used in computers ranging from smart home appliances to cell phones to the largest supercomputers, these different applications have different design requirements and employ the core hardware technologies in different ways. Broadly speaking, computers are used in three different classes of applications.

Desktop computers are possibly the best-known form of computing and are characterized by the personal computer, which readers of this book have likely used extensively. Desktop computers emphasize delivery of good performance to single users at low cost and usually execute third-party software. The evolution of many computing technologies is driven by this class of computing, which is only about 30 years old!

Servers are the modern form of what were once mainframes, minicomputers, and supercomputers, and are usually accessed only via a network. Servers are oriented to carrying large workloads, which may consist of either single complex applications—usually a scientific or engineering application—or handling many small jobs, such as would occur in building a large Web server. These applications are usually based on software from another source (such as a database or simulation system), but are often modified or customized for a particular function. Servers are built from the same basic technology as desktop computers, but provide for greater expandability of both computing and input/output capacity. In general, servers also place a greater emphasis on dependability, since a crash is usually more costly than it would be on a single-user desktop computer.

Servers span the widest range in cost and capability. At the low end, a server may be little more than a desktop computer without a screen or keyboard and cost a thousand dollars. These low-end servers are typically used for file storage, small business applications, or simple Web serving (see Section 6.10). At the other extreme are **supercomputers**, which at the present consist of hundreds to thousands of processors and usually **terabytes** of memory and **petabytes** of storage, and cost millions to hundreds of millions of dollars. Supercomputers are usually used for high-end scientific and engineering calculations, such as weather forecasting, oil exploration, protein structure determination, and other large-scale problems. Although such supercomputers represent the peak of computing capability, they represent a relatively small fraction of the servers and a relatively small fraction of the overall computer market in terms of total revenue.

Although not called supercomputers, Internet **datacenters** used by companies like eBay and Google also contain thousands of processors, terabytes of memory, and petabytes of storage. These are usually considered as large clusters of computers (see Chapter 7).

Embedded computers are the largest class of computers and span the widest range of applications and performance. Embedded computers include the

desktop computer A computer designed for use by an individual, usually incorporating a graphics display, a keyboard, and a mouse.

server A computer used for running larger programs for multiple users, often simultaneously, and typically accessed only via a network.

supercomputer A class of computers with the highest performance and cost; they are configured as servers and typically cost millions of dollars.

terabyte Originally 1,099,511,627,776 (2^{40}) bytes, although some communications and secondary storage systems have redefined it to mean 1,000,000,000,000 (10^{12}) bytes.

petabyte Depending on the situation, either 1000 or 1024 terabytes.

datacenter A room or building designed to handle the power, cooling, and networking needs of a large number of servers.

embedded computer A computer inside another device used for running one predetermined application or collection of software.

microprocessors found in your car, the computers in a cell phone, the computers in a video game or television, and the networks of processors that control a modern airplane or cargo ship. Embedded computing systems are designed to run one application or one set of related applications, that are normally integrated with the hardware and delivered as a single system; thus, despite the large number of embedded computers, most users never really see that they are using a computer!

Figure 1.1 shows that during the last several years, the growth in cell phones that rely on embedded computers has been much faster than the growth rate of desktop computers. Note that the embedded computers are also found in digital TVs and set-top boxes, automobiles, digital cameras, music players, video games, and a variety of other such consumer devices, which further increases the gap between the number of embedded computers and desktop computers.

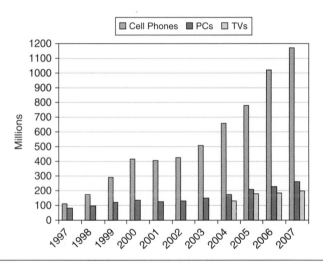

FIGURE 1.1   The number of cell phones, personal computers, and televisions manufactured per year between 1997 and 2007. (We have television data only from 2004.) More than a billion new cell phones were shipped in 2006. Cell phones sales exceeded PCs by only a factor of 1.4 in 1997, but the ratio grew to 4.5 in 2007. The total number in use in 2004 is estimated to be about 2.0B televisions, 1.8B cell phones, and 0.8B PCs. As the world population was about 6.4B in 2004, there were approximately one PC, 2.2 cell phones, and 2.5 televisions for every eight people on the planet. A 2006 survey of U.S. families found that they owned on average 12 gadgets, including three TVs, 2 PCs, and other devices such as game consoles, MP3 players, and cell phones.

Embedded applications often have unique application requirements that combine a minimum performance with stringent limitations on cost or power. For example, consider a music player: the processor need only be as fast as necessary to handle its limited function, and beyond that, minimizing cost and power are the most important objectives. Despite their low cost, embedded computers often have lower tolerance for failure, since the results can vary from upsetting (when your new television crashes) to devastating (such as might occur when the computer in a plane or cargo ship crashes). In consumer-oriented embedded applications, such as a digital home appliance, dependability is achieved primarily through simplicity—the emphasis is on doing one function as perfectly as possible. In large embedded systems, techniques of redundancy from the server world are often employed (see Section 6.9). Although this book focuses on general-purpose computers, most concepts apply directly, or with slight modifications, to embedded computers.

Elaboration: Elaborations are short sections used throughout the text to provide more detail on a particular subject that may be of interest. Disinterested readers may skip over an elaboration, since the subsequent material will never depend on the contents of the elaboration.

Many embedded processors are designed using *processor cores*, a version of a processor written in a hardware description language, such as Verilog or VHDL (see Chapter 4). The core allows a designer to integrate other application-specific hardware with the processor core for fabrication on a single chip.

What You Can Learn in This Book

Successful programmers have always been concerned about the performance of their programs, because getting results to the user quickly is critical in creating successful software. In the 1960s and 1970s, a primary constraint on computer performance was the size of the computer's memory. Thus, programmers often followed a simple credo: minimize memory space to make programs fast. In the last decade, advances in computer design and memory technology have greatly reduced the importance of small memory size in most applications other than those in embedded computing systems.

Programmers interested in performance now need to understand the issues that have replaced the simple memory model of the 1960s: the parallel nature of processors and the hierarchical nature of memories. Programmers who seek to build competitive versions of compilers, operating systems, databases, and even applications will therefore need to increase their knowledge of computer organization.

We are honored to have the opportunity to explain what's inside this revolutionary machine, unraveling the software below your program and the hardware under the covers of your computer. By the time you complete this book, we believe you will be able to answer the following questions:

- How are programs written in a high-level language, such as C or Java, translated into the language of the hardware, and how does the hardware execute the resulting program? Comprehending these concepts forms the basis of understanding the aspects of both the hardware and software that affect program performance.

- What is the interface between the software and the hardware, and how does software instruct the hardware to perform needed functions? These concepts are vital to understanding how to write many kinds of software.

- What determines the performance of a program, and how can a programmer improve the performance? As we will see, this depends on the original program, the software translation of that program into the computer's language, and the effectiveness of the hardware in executing the program.

- What techniques can be used by hardware designers to improve performance? This book will introduce the basic concepts of modern computer design. The interested reader will find much more material on this topic in our advanced book, *Computer Architecture: A Quantitative Approach*.

- What are the reasons for and the consequences of the recent switch from sequential processing to parallel processing? This book gives the motivation, describes the current hardware mechanisms to support parallelism, and surveys the new generation of **"multicore" microprocessors** (see Chapter 7).

multicore microprocessor A microprocessor containing multiple processors ("cores") in a single integrated circuit.

Without understanding the answers to these questions, improving the performance of your program on a modern computer, or evaluating what features might make one computer better than another for a particular application, will be a complex process of trial and error, rather than a scientific procedure driven by insight and analysis.

This first chapter lays the foundation for the rest of the book. It introduces the basic ideas and definitions, places the major components of software and hardware in perspective, shows how to evaluate performance and power, introduces integrated circuits (the technology that fuels the computer revolution), and explains the shift to multicores.

In this chapter and later ones, you will likely see many new words, or words that you may have heard but are not sure what they mean. Don't panic! Yes, there is a lot of special terminology used in describing modern computers, but the terminology actually helps, since it enables us to describe precisely a function or capability. In addition, computer designers (including your authors) *love* using **acronyms**, which are *easy* to understand once you know what the letters stand for! To help you remember and locate terms, we have included a **highlighted** definition of every term in the margins the first time it appears in the text. After a short time of working with the terminology, you will be fluent, and your friends will be impressed as you correctly use acronyms such as BIOS, CPU, DIMM, DRAM, PCIE, SATA, and many others.

acronym A word constructed by taking the initial letters of a string of words. For example: RAM is an acronym for Random Access Memory, and CPU is an acronym for Central Processing Unit.

To reinforce how the software and hardware systems used to run a program will affect performance, we use a special section, *Understanding Program Performance*, throughout the book to summarize important insights into program performance. The first one appears below.

Understanding Program Performance

The performance of a program depends on a combination of the effectiveness of the algorithms used in the program, the software systems used to create and translate the program into machine instructions, and the effectiveness of the computer in executing those instructions, which may include input/output (I/O) operations. This table summarizes how the hardware and software affect performance.

Hardware or software component	How this component affects performance	Where is this topic covered?
Algorithm	Determines both the number of source-level statements and the number of I/O operations executed	Other books!
Programming language, compiler, and architecture	Determines the number of computer instructions for each source-level statement	Chapters 2 and 3
Processor and memory system	Determines how fast instructions can be executed	Chapters 4, 5, and 7
I/O system (hardware and operating system)	Determines how fast I/O operations may be executed	Chapter 6

Check Yourself

Check Yourself sections are designed to help readers assess whether they comprehend the major concepts introduced in a chapter and understand the implications of those concepts. Some *Check Yourself* questions have simple answers; others are for discussion among a group. Answers to the specific questions can be found at the end of the chapter. *Check Yourself* questions appear only at the end of a section, making it easy to skip them if you are sure you understand the material.

1. Section 1.1 showed that the number of embedded processors sold every year greatly outnumbers the number of desktop processors. Can you confirm or deny this insight based on your own experience? Try to count the number of embedded processors in your home. How does it compare with the number of desktop computers in your home?

2. As mentioned earlier, both the software and hardware affect the performance of a program. Can you think of examples where each of the following is the right place to look for a performance bottleneck?

   - The algorithm chosen
   - The programming language or compiler
   - The operating system
   - The processor
   - The I/O system and devices

In Paris they simply stared when I spoke to them in French; I never did succeed in making those idiots understand their own language.

Mark Twain, *The Innocents Abroad*, 1869

systems software
Software that provides services that are commonly useful, including operating systems, compilers, loaders, and assemblers.

operating system
Supervising program that manages the resources of a computer for the benefit of the programs that run on that computer.

1.2   Below Your Program

A typical application, such as a word processor or a large database system, may consist of millions of lines of code and rely on sophisticated software libraries that implement complex functions in support of the application. As we will see, the hardware in a computer can only execute extremely simple low-level instructions. To go from a complex application to the simple instructions involves several layers of software that interpret or translate high-level operations into simple computer instructions.

Figure 1.2 shows that these layers of software are organized primarily in a hierarchical fashion, with applications being the outermost ring and a variety of **systems software** sitting between the hardware and applications software.

There are many types of systems software, but two types of systems software are central to every computer system today: an operating system and a compiler. An **operating system** interfaces between a user's program and the hardware and provides a variety of services and supervisory functions. Among the most important functions are

- Handling basic input and output operations

- Allocating storage and memory

- Providing for protected sharing of the computer among multiple applications using it simultaneously.

Examples of operating systems in use today are Linux, MacOS, and Windows.

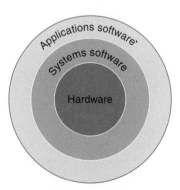

FIGURE 1.2   A simplified view of hardware and software as hierarchical layers, shown as concentric circles with hardware in the center and applications software outermost. In complex applications, there are often multiple layers of application software as well. For example, a database system may run on top of the systems software hosting an application, which in turn runs on top of the database.

Compilers perform another vital function: the translation of a program written in a high-level language, such as C, C++, Java, or Visual Basic into instructions that the hardware can execute. Given the sophistication of modern programming languages and the simplicity of the instructions executed by the hardware, the translation from a high-level language program to hardware instructions is complex. We give a brief overview of the process here and then go into more depth in Chapter 2 and Appendix B.

compiler A program that translates high-level language statements into assembly language statements.

From a High-Level Language to the Language of Hardware

To actually speak to electronic hardware, you need to send electrical signals. The easiest signals for computers to understand are *on* and *off*, and so the computer alphabet is just two letters. Just as the 26 letters of the English alphabet do not limit how much can be written, the two letters of the computer alphabet do not limit what computers can do. The two symbols for these two letters are the numbers 0 and 1, and we commonly think of the computer language as numbers in base 2, or *binary numbers.* We refer to each "letter" as a **binary digit** or **bit**. Computers are slaves to our commands, which are called **instructions**. Instructions, which are just collections of bits that the computer understands and obeys, can be thought of as numbers. For example, the bits

binary digit Also called a **bit**. One of the two numbers in base 2 (0 or 1) that are the components of information.

instruction A command that computer hardware understands and obeys.

    1000110010100000

tell one computer to add two numbers. Chapter 2 explains why we use numbers for instructions *and* data; we don't want to steal that chapter's thunder, but using numbers for both instructions and data is a foundation of computing.

The first programmers communicated to computers in binary numbers, but this was so tedious that they quickly invented new notations that were closer to the way humans think. At first, these notations were translated to binary by hand, but this process was still tiresome. Using the computer to help program the computer, the pioneers invented programs to translate from symbolic notation to binary. The first of these programs was named an **assembler**. This program translates a symbolic version of an instruction into the binary version. For example, the programmer would write

assembler A program that translates a symbolic version of instructions into the binary version.

    add A,B

and the assembler would translate this notation into

    1000110010100000

This instruction tells the computer to add the two numbers A and B. The name coined for this symbolic language, still used today, is **assembly language**. In contrast, the binary language that the machine understands is the **machine language**.

Although a tremendous improvement, assembly language is still far from the notations a scientist might like to use to simulate fluid flow or that an accountant might use to balance the books. Assembly language requires the programmer

assembly language A symbolic representation of machine instructions.

machine language A binary representation of machine instructions.

to write one line for every instruction that the computer will follow, forcing the programmer to think like the computer.

The recognition that a program could be written to translate a more powerful language into computer instructions was one of the great breakthroughs in the early days of computing. Programmers today owe their productivity—and their sanity—to the creation of **high-level programming languages** and compilers that translate programs in such languages into instructions. Figure 1.3 shows the relationships among these programs and languages.

high-level programming language A portable language such as C, C++, Java, or Visual Basic that is composed of words and algebraic notation that can be translated by a compiler into assembly language.

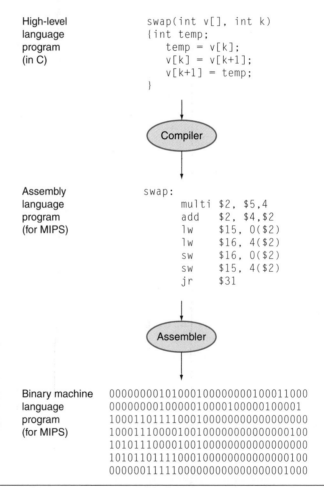

High-level language program (in C)

```
swap(int v[], int k)
{int temp;
    temp = v[k];
    v[k] = v[k+1];
    v[k+1] = temp;
}
```

Compiler

Assembly language program (for MIPS)

```
swap:
        multi $2, $5,4
        add   $2, $4,$2
        lw    $15, 0($2)
        lw    $16, 4($2)
        sw    $16, 0($2)
        sw    $15, 4($2)
        jr    $31
```

Assembler

Binary machine language program (for MIPS)

```
00000000101000100000000100011000
00000000100000100001000000100001
10001101111000100000000000000000
10001110000010010000000000000100
10101110000010010000000000000000
10101101111000100000000000000100
00000011111000000000000000001000
```

FIGURE 1.3 C program compiled into assembly language and then assembled into binary machine language. Although the translation from high-level language to binary machine language is shown in two steps, some compilers cut out the middleman and produce binary machine language directly. These languages and this program are examined in more detail in Chapter 2.

A compiler enables a programmer to write this high-level language expression:

```
A + B
```

The compiler would compile it into this assembly language statement:

```
add A,B
```

As shown above, the assembler would translate this statement into the binary instructions that tell the computer to add the two numbers A and B.

High-level programming languages offer several important benefits. First, they allow the programmer to think in a more natural language, using English words and algebraic notation, resulting in programs that look much more like text than like tables of cryptic symbols (see Figure 1.3). Moreover, they allow languages to be designed according to their intended use. Hence, Fortran was designed for scientific computation, Cobol for business data processing, Lisp for symbol manipulation, and so on. There are also domain-specific languages for even narrower groups of users, such as those interested in simulation of fluids, for example.

The second advantage of programming languages is improved programmer productivity. One of the few areas of widespread agreement in software development is that it takes less time to develop programs when they are written in languages that require fewer lines to express an idea. Conciseness is a clear advantage of high-level languages over assembly language.

The final advantage is that programming languages allow programs to be independent of the computer on which they were developed, since compilers and assemblers can translate high-level language programs to the binary instructions of any computer. These three advantages are so strong that today little programming is done in assembly language.

1.3 Under the Covers

Now that we have looked below your program to uncover the underlying software, let's open the covers of your computer to learn about the underlying hardware. The underlying hardware in any computer performs the same basic functions: inputting data, outputting data, processing data, and storing data. How these functions are performed is the primary topic of this book, and subsequent chapters deal with different parts of these four tasks.

When we come to an important point in this book, a point so important that we hope you will remember it forever, we emphasize it by identifying it as a *Big Picture* item. We have about a dozen Big Pictures in this book, the first being the five components of a computer that perform the tasks of inputting, outputting, processing, and storing data.

The BIG Picture

The five classic components of a computer are input, output, memory, datapath, and control, with the last two sometimes combined and called the processor. Figure 1.4 shows the standard organization of a computer. This organization is independent of hardware technology: you can place every piece of every computer, past and present, into one of these five categories. To help you keep all this in perspective, the five components of a computer are shown on the front page of each of the following chapters, with the portion of interest to that chapter highlighted.

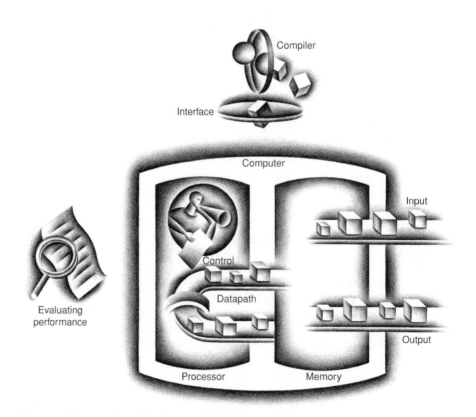

FIGURE 1.4 The organization of a computer, showing the five classic components. The processor gets instructions and data from memory. Input writes data to memory, and output reads data from memory. Control sends the signals that determine the operations of the datapath, memory, input, and output.

FIGURE 1.5 A desktop computer. The liquid crystal display (LCD) screen is the primary output device, and the keyboard and mouse are the primary input devices. On the right side is an Ethernet cable that connected the laptop to the network and the Web. The laptop contains the processor, memory, and additional I/O devices. This system is a Macbook Pro 15" laptop connected to an external display.

Figure 1.5 shows a computer with keyboard, wireless mouse, and screen. This photograph reveals two of the key components of computers: **input devices**, such as the keyboard and mouse, and **output devices**, such as the screen. As the names suggest, input feeds the computer, and output is the result of computation sent to the user. Some devices, such as networks and disks, provide both input and output to the computer.

Chapter 6 describes input/output (I/O) devices in more detail, but let's take an introductory tour through the computer hardware, starting with the external I/O devices.

input device
A mechanism through which the computer is fed information, such as the keyboard or mouse.

output device
A mechanism that conveys the result of a computation to a user or another computer.

I got the idea for the mouse while attending a talk at a computer conference. The speaker was so boring that I started daydreaming and hit upon the idea.

Doug Engelbart

Through computer displays I have landed an airplane on the deck of a moving carrier, observed a nuclear particle hit a potential well, flown in a rocket at nearly the speed of light and watched a computer reveal its innermost workings.

Ivan Sutherland, the "father" of computer graphics, *Scientific American*, 1984

liquid crystal display
A display technology using a thin layer of liquid polymers that can be used to transmit or block light according to whether a charge is applied.

active matrix display
A liquid crystal display using a transistor to control the transmission of light at each individual pixel.

pixel The smallest individual picture element. Screens are composed of hundreds of thousands to millions of pixels, organized in a matrix.

Anatomy of a Mouse

Although many users now take mice for granted, the idea of a pointing device such as a mouse was first shown by Doug Engelbart using a research prototype in 1967. The Alto, which was the inspiration for all workstations as well as for the Macintosh and Windows OS, included a mouse as its pointing device in 1973. By the 1990s, all desktop computers included this device, and new user interfaces based on graphics displays and mice became the norm.

The original mouse was electromechanical and used a large ball that when rolled across a surface would cause an *x* and *y* counter to be incremented. The amount of increase in each counter told how far the mouse had been moved.

The electromechanical mouse has largely been replaced by the newer all-optical mouse. The optical mouse is actually a miniature optical processor including an LED to provide lighting, a tiny black-and-white camera, and a simple optical processor. The LED illuminates the surface underneath the mouse; the camera takes 1500 sample pictures a second under the illumination. Successive pictures are sent to a simple optical processor that compares the images and determines whether the mouse has moved and how far. The replacement of the electromechanical mouse by the electro-optical mouse is an illustration of a common phenomenon where the decreasing costs and higher reliability of electronics cause an electronic solution to replace the older electromechanical technology. On page 22 we'll see another example: flash memory.

Through the Looking Glass

The most fascinating I/O device is probably the graphics display. All laptop and handheld computers, calculators, cellular phones, and almost all desktop computers now use **liquid crystal displays (LCDs)** to get a thin, low-power display. The LCD is not the source of light; instead, it controls the transmission of light. A typical LCD includes rod-shaped molecules in a liquid that form a twisting helix that bends light entering the display, from either a light source behind the display or less often from reflected light. The rods straighten out when a current is applied and no longer bend the light. Since the liquid crystal material is between two screens polarized at 90 degrees, the light cannot pass through unless it is bent. Today, most LCD displays use an **active matrix** that has a tiny transistor switch at each pixel to precisely control current and make sharper images. A red-green-blue mask associated with each dot on the display determines the intensity of the three color components in the final image; in a color active matrix LCD, there are three transistor switches at each point.

The image is composed of a matrix of picture elements, or **pixels**, which can be represented as a matrix of bits, called a *bit map*. Depending on the size of the screen and the resolution, the display matrix ranges in size from 640×480 to 2560×1600 pixels in 2008. A color display might use 8 bits for each of the three colors (red, blue, and green), for 24 bits per pixel, permitting millions of different colors to be displayed.

The computer hardware support for graphics consists mainly of a *raster refresh buffer*, or *frame buffer*, to store the bit map. The image to be represented onscreen is stored in the frame buffer, and the bit pattern per pixel is read out to the graphics display at the refresh rate. Figure 1.6 shows a frame buffer with a simplified design of just 4 bits per pixel.

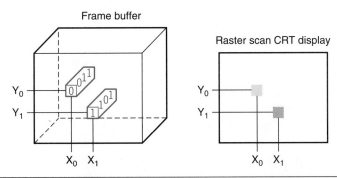

FIGURE 1.6 Each coordinate in the frame buffer on the left determines the shade of the corresponding coordinate for the raster scan CRT display on the right. Pixel (X_0, Y_0) contains the bit pattern 0011, which is a lighter shade on the screen than the bit pattern 1101 in pixel (X_1, Y_1).

The goal of the bit map is to faithfully represent what is on the screen. The challenges in graphics systems arise because the human eye is very good at detecting even subtle changes on the screen.

Opening the Box

If we open the box containing the computer, we see a fascinating board of thin plastic, covered with dozens of small gray or black rectangles. Figure 1.7 shows the contents of the laptop computer in Figure 1.5. The **motherboard** is shown in the upper part of the photo. Two disk drives are in front—the hard drive on the left and a DVD drive on the right. The hole in the middle is for the laptop battery.

The small rectangles on the motherboard contain the devices that drive our advancing technology, called **integrated circuits** and nicknamed **chips**. The board is composed of three pieces: the piece connecting to the I/O devices mentioned earlier, the memory, and the processor.

The **memory** is where the programs are kept when they are running; it also contains the data needed by the running programs. Figure 1.8 shows that memory is found on the two small boards, and each small memory board contains eight integrated circuits. The memory in Figure 1.8 is built from DRAM chips. *DRAM*

motherboard A plastic board containing packages of integrated circuits or chips, including processor, cache, memory, and connectors for I/O devices such as networks and disks.

integrated circuit Also called a **chip**. A device combining dozens to millions of transistors.

memory The storage area in which programs are kept when they are running and that contains the data needed by the running programs.

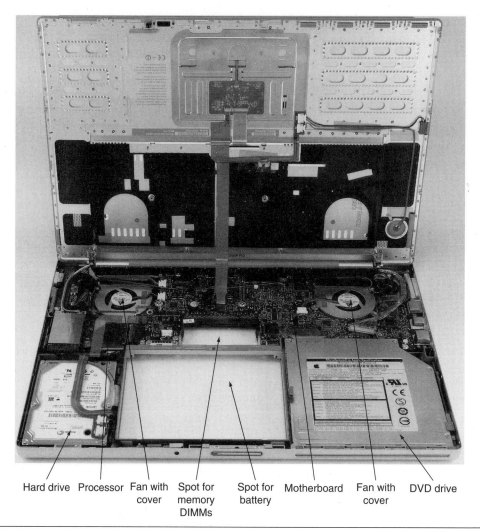

Hard drive   Processor   Fan with   Spot for   Spot for   Motherboard   Fan with   DVD drive
                          cover   memory   battery   cover
                                     DIMMs

FIGURE 1.7   Inside the laptop computer of Figure 1.5. The shiny box with the white label on the lower left is a 100 GB SATA hard disk drive, and the shiny metal box on the lower right side is the DVD drive. The hole between them is where the laptop battery would be located. The small hole above the battery hole is for memory DIMMs. Figure 1.8 is a close-up of the DIMMs, which are inserted from the bottom in this laptop. Above the battery hole and DVD drive is a printed circuit board (PC board), called the *motherboard*, which contains most of the electronics of the computer. The two shiny circles in the upper half of the picture are two fans with covers. The processor is the large raised rectangle just below the left fan. Photo courtesy of OtherWorldComputing.com.

stands for **dynamic random access memory**. Several DRAMs are used together to contain the instructions and data of a program. In contrast to sequential access memories, such as magnetic tapes, the *RAM* portion of the term DRAM means that memory accesses take basically the same amount of time no matter what portion of the memory is read.

dynamic random access memory (DRAM) Memory built as an integrated circuit; it provides random access to any location.

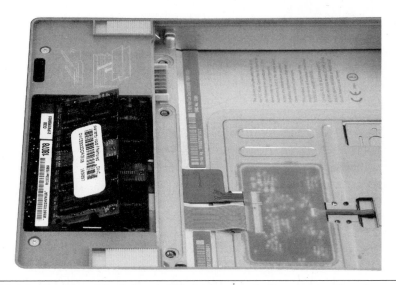

FIGURE 1.8   Close-up of the bottom of the laptop reveals the memory. The main memory is contained on one or more small boards shown on the left. The hole for the battery is to the right. The DRAM chips are mounted on these boards (called **DIMMs**, for dual inline memory modules) and then plugged into the connectors. Photo courtesy of OtherWorldComputing.com.

dual inline memory module (DIMM) A small board that contains DRAM chips on both sides. (SIMMs have DRAMs on only one side.)

central processor unit (CPU) Also called processor. The active part of the computer, which contains the datapath and control and which adds numbers, tests numbers, signals I/O devices to activate, and so on.

The *processor* is the active part of the board, following the instructions of a program to the letter. It adds numbers, tests numbers, signals I/O devices to activate, and so on. The processor is under the fan and covered by a heat sink on the left side of Figure 1.7. Occasionally, people call the processor the **CPU**, for the more bureaucratic-sounding **central processor unit**.

Descending even lower into the hardware, Figure 1.9 reveals details of a microprocessor. The processor logically comprises two main components: datapath and control, the respective brawn and brain of the processor. The **datapath** performs the arithmetic operations, and **control** tells the datapath, memory, and I/O devices what to do according to the wishes of the instructions of the program. Chapter 4 explains the datapath and control for a higher-performance design.

datapath The component of the processor that performs arithmetic operations

control The component of the processor that commands the datapath, memory, and I/O devices according to the instructions of the program.

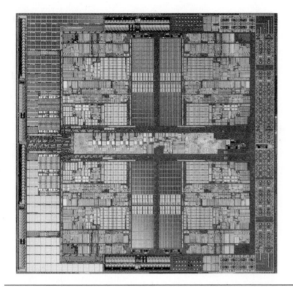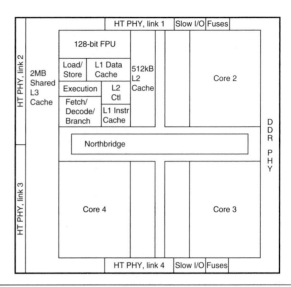

FIGURE 1.9   Inside the AMD Barcelona microprocessor. The left-hand side is a microphotograph of the AMD Barcelona processor chip, and the right-hand side shows the major blocks in the processor. This chip has four processors or "cores". The microprocessor in the laptop in Figure 1.7 has two cores per chip, called an Intel Core 2 Duo.

cache memory A small, fast memory that acts as a buffer for a slower, larger memory.

static random access memory (SRAM) Also memory built as an integrated circuit, but faster and less dense than DRAM.

abstraction A model that renders lower-level details of computer systems temporarily invisible to facilitate design of sophisticated systems.

Descending into the depths of any component of the hardware reveals insights into the computer. Inside the processor is another type of memory—cache memory. **Cache memory** consists of a small, fast memory that acts as a buffer for the DRAM memory. (The nontechnical definition of *cache* is a safe place for hiding things.) Cache is built using a different memory technology, **static random access memory (SRAM)**. SRAM is faster but less dense, and hence more expensive, than DRAM (see Chapter 5).

You may have noticed a common theme in both the software and the hardware descriptions: delving into the depths of hardware or software reveals more information or, conversely, lower-level details are hidden to offer a simpler model at higher levels. The use of such layers, or **abstractions**, is a principal technique for designing very sophisticated computer systems.

One of the most important abstractions is the interface between the hardware and the lowest-level software. Because of its importance, it is given a special name: the **instruction set architecture**, or simply **architecture**, of a computer. The instruction set architecture includes anything programmers need to know to make a binary machine language program work correctly, including instructions, I/O devices, and so on. Typically, the operating system will encapsulate the details of doing I/O, allocating memory, and other low-level system functions so that application programmers do not need to worry about such details. The combination of the basic instruction set and the operating system interface provided for application programmers is called the **application binary interface (ABI)**.

An instruction set architecture allows computer designers to talk about functions independently from the hardware that performs them. For example, we can talk about the functions of a digital clock (keeping time, displaying the time, setting the alarm) independently from the clock hardware (quartz crystal, LED displays, plastic buttons). Computer designers distinguish architecture from an **implementation** of an architecture along the same lines: an implementation is hardware that obeys the architecture abstraction. These ideas bring us to another Big Picture.

instruction set architecture Also called **architecture**. An abstract interface between the hardware and the lowest-level software that encompasses all the information necessary to write a machine language program that will run correctly, including instructions, registers, memory access, I/O, ...

application binary interface (ABI) The user portion of the instruction set plus the operating system interfaces used by application programmers. Defines a standard for binary portability across computers.

implementation Hardware that obeys the architecture abstraction.

The BIG Picture

Both hardware and software consist of hierarchical layers, with each lower layer hiding details from the level above. This principle of *abstraction* is the way both hardware designers and software designers cope with the complexity of computer systems. One key interface between the levels of abstraction is the *instruction set architecture*—the interface between the hardware and low-level software. This abstract interface enables many *implementations* of varying cost and performance to run identical software.

volatile memory Storage, such as DRAM, that retains data only if it is receiving power.

nonvolatile memory A form of memory that retains data even in the absence of a power source and that is used to store programs between runs. Magnetic disk is nonvolatile.

main memory Also called **primary memory**. Memory used to hold programs while they are running; typically consists of DRAM in today's computers.

A Safe Place for Data

Thus far, we have seen how to input data, compute using the data, and display data. If we were to lose power to the computer, however, everything would be lost because the memory inside the computer is **volatile**—that is, when it loses power, it forgets. In contrast, a DVD doesn't forget the recorded film when you turn off the power to the DVD player and is thus a **nonvolatile memory** technology.

To distinguish between the volatile memory used to hold data and programs while they are running and this nonvolatile memory used to store data and programs between runs, the term **main memory** or **primary memory** is used for the

secondary memory
Nonvolatile memory used to store programs and data between runs; typically consists of magnetic disks in today's computers.

magnetic disk Also called **hard disk**. A form of nonvolatile secondary memory composed of rotating platters coated with a magnetic recording material.

flash memory
A nonvolatile semiconductor memory. It is cheaper and slower than DRAM but more expensive and faster than magnetic disks.

former, and **secondary memory** for the latter. DRAMs have dominated main memory since 1975, but **magnetic disks** have dominated secondary memory since 1965. The primary nonvolatile storage used in all server computers and workstations is the magnetic **hard disk**. **Flash memory**, a nonvolatile semiconductor memory, is used instead of disks in mobile devices such as cell phones and is increasingly replacing disks in music players and even laptops.

As Figure 1.10 shows, a magnetic hard disk consists of a collection of platters, which rotate on a spindle at 5400 to 15,000 revolutions per minute. The metal platters are covered with magnetic recording material on both sides, similar to the material found on a cassette or videotape. To read and write information on a hard disk, a movable *arm* containing a small electromagnetic coil called a *read-write head* is located just above each surface. The entire drive is permanently sealed to control the environment inside the drive, which, in turn, allows the disk heads to be much closer to the drive surface.

FIGURE 1.10   A disk showing 10 disk platters and the read/write heads.

Diameters of hard disks vary by more than a factor of 3 today, from 1 inch to 3.5 inches, and have been shrunk over the years to fit into new products; workstation servers, personal computers, laptops, palmtops, and digital cameras have all inspired new disk form factors. Traditionally, the widest disks have the highest performance and the smallest disks have the lowest unit cost. The best cost per **gigabyte** varies. Although most hard drives appear inside computers, as in Figure 1.7, hard drives can also be attached using external interfaces such as universal serial bus (USB).

The use of mechanical components means that access times for magnetic disks are much slower than for DRAMs: disks typically take 5–20 milliseconds, while DRAMs take 50–70 nanoseconds—making DRAMs about 100,000 times faster. Yet disks have much lower costs than DRAM for the same storage capacity, because the production costs for a given amount of disk storage are lower than for the same amount of integrated circuit. In 2008, the cost per gigabyte of disk is 30 to 100 times less expensive than DRAM.

Thus, there are three primary differences between magnetic disks and main memory: disks are nonvolatile because they are magnetic; they have a slower access time because they are mechanical devices; and they are cheaper per gigabyte because they have very high storage capacity at a modest cost.

Many have tried to invent a technology cheaper than DRAM but faster than disk to fill that gap, but many have failed. Challengers have never had a product to market at the right time. By the time a new product would ship, DRAMs and disks had continued to make rapid advances, costs had dropped accordingly, and the challenging product was immediately obsolete.

Flash memory, however, is a serious challenger. This semiconductor memory is nonvolatile like disks and has about the same bandwidth, but latency is 100 to 1000 times faster than disk. Flash is popular in cameras and portable music players because it comes in much smaller capacities, it is more rugged, and it is more power efficient than disks, despite the cost per gigabyte in 2008 being about 6 to 10 times higher than disk. Unlike disks and DRAM, flash memory bits wear out after 100,000 to 1,000,000 writes. Thus, file systems must keep track of the number of writes and have a strategy to avoid wearing out storage, such as by moving popular data. Chapter 6 describes flash in more detail.

Although hard drives are not removable, there are several storage technologies in use that include the following:

■ Optical disks, including both compact disks (CDs) and digital video disks (DVDs), constitute the most common form of removable storage. The Blu-Ray (BD) optical disk standard is the heir-apparent to DVD.

■ Flash-based removable memory cards typically attach to a USB connection and are often used to transfer files.

■ Magnetic tape provides only slow serial access and has been used to back up disks, a role now often replaced by duplicate hard drives.

gigabyte Traditionally 1,073,741,824 (2^{30}) bytes, although some communications and secondary storage systems have redefined it to mean 1,000,000,000 (10^9) bytes. Similarly, depending on the context, megabyte is either 2^{20} or 10^6 bytes.

Optical disk technology works differently than magnetic disk technology. In a CD, data is recorded in a spiral fashion, with individual bits being recorded by burning small pits—approximately 1 micron (10^{-6} meters) in diameter—into the disk surface. The disk is read by shining a laser at the CD surface and determining by examining the reflected light whether there is a pit or flat (reflective) surface. DVDs use the same approach of bouncing a laser beam off a series of pits and flat surfaces. In addition, there are multiple layers that the laser beam can focus on, and the size of each bit is much smaller, which together increase capacity significantly. Blu-Ray uses shorter wavelength lasers that shrink the size of the bits and thereby increase capacity.

Optical disk writers in personal computers use a laser to make the pits in the recording layer on the CD or DVD surface. This writing process is relatively slow, taking from minutes (for a full CD) to tens of minutes (for a full DVD). Thus, for large quantities a different technique called *pressing* is used, which costs only pennies per optical disk.

Rewritable CDs and DVDs use a different recording surface that has a crystalline, reflective material; pits are formed that are not reflective in a manner similar to that for a write-once CD or DVD. To erase the CD or DVD, the surface is heated and cooled slowly, allowing an annealing process to restore the surface recording layer to its crystalline structure. These rewritable disks are the most expensive, with write-once being cheaper; for read-only disks—used to distribute software, music, or movies—both the disk cost and recording cost are much lower.

Communicating with Other Computers

We've explained how we can input, compute, display, and save data, but there is still one missing item found in today's computers: computer networks. Just as the processor shown in Figure 1.4 is connected to memory and I/O devices, networks interconnect whole computers, allowing computer users to extend the power of computing by including communication. Networks have become so popular that they are the backbone of current computer systems; a new computer without an optional network interface would be ridiculed. Networked computers have several major advantages:

- *Communication:* Information is exchanged between computers at high speeds.

- *Resource sharing:* Rather than each computer having its own I/O devices, devices can be shared by computers on the network.

- *Nonlocal access:* By connecting computers over long distances, users need not be near the computer they are using.

Networks vary in length and performance, with the cost of communication increasing according to both the speed of communication and the distance that information travels. Perhaps the most popular type of network is *Ethernet*. It can be up to a kilometer long and transfer at upto 10 gigabits per second. Its length and speed make Ethernet useful to connect computers on the same floor of a building; hence, it is an example of what is generically called a **local area network**. Local area networks are interconnected with switches that can also provide routing services and security. **Wide area networks** cross continents and are the backbone of the Internet, which supports the World Wide Web. They are typically based on optical fibers and are leased from telecommunication companies.

Networks have changed the face of computing in the last 25 years, both by becoming much more ubiquitous and by making dramatic increases in performance. In the 1970s, very few individuals had access to electronic mail, the Internet and Web did not exist, and physically mailing magnetic tapes was the primary way to transfer large amounts of data between two locations. Local area networks were almost nonexistent, and the few existing wide area networks had limited capacity and restricted access.

As networking technology improved, it became much cheaper and had a much higher capacity. For example, the first standardized local area network technology, developed about 25 years ago, was a version of Ethernet that had a maximum capacity (also called bandwidth) of 10 million bits per second, typically shared by tens of, if not a hundred, computers. Today, local area network technology offers a capacity of from 100 million bits per second to 10 gigabits per second, usually shared by at most a few computers. Optical communications technology has allowed similar growth in the capacity of wide area networks, from hundreds of kilobits to gigabits and from hundreds of computers connected to a worldwide network to millions of computers connected. This combination of dramatic rise in deployment of networking combined with increases in capacity have made network technology central to the information revolution of the last 25 years.

For the last decade another innovation in networking is reshaping the way computers communicate. Wireless technology is widespread, and laptops now incorporate this technology. The ability to make a radio in the same low-cost semiconductor technology (CMOS) used for memory and microprocessors enabled a significant improvement in price, leading to an explosion in deployment. Currently available wireless technologies, called by the IEEE standard name 802.11, allow for transmission rates from 1 to nearly 100 million bits per second. Wireless technology is quite a bit different from wire-based networks, since all users in an immediate area share the airwaves.

■ Semiconductor DRAM and disk storage differ significantly. Describe the fundamental difference for each of the following: volatility, access time, and cost.

local area network (LAN) A network designed to carry data within a geographically confined area, typically within a single building.

wide area network (WAN) A network extended over hundreds of kilometers that can span a continent.

Check Yourself

Technologies for Building Processors and Memory

Processors and memory have improved at an incredible rate, because computer designers have long embraced the latest in electronic technology to try to win the race to design a better computer. Figure 1.11 shows the technologies that have been used over time, with an estimate of the relative performance per unit cost for each technology. Section 1.7 explores the technology that has fueled the computer industry since 1975 and will continue to do so for the foreseeable future. Since this technology shapes what computers will be able to do and how quickly they will evolve, we believe all computer professionals should be familiar with the basics of integrated circuits.

vacuum tube An electronic component, predecessor of the transistor, that consists of a hollow glass tube about 5 to 10 cm long from which as much air has been removed as possible and that uses an electron beam to transfer data.

Year	Technology used in computers	Relative performance/unit cost
1951	Vacuum tube	1
1965	Transistor	35
1975	Integrated circuit	900
1995	Very large-scale integrated circuit	2,400,000
2005	Ultra large-scale integrated circuit	6,200,000,000

FIGURE 1.11 Relative performance per unit cost of technologies used in computers over time. Source: Computer Museum, Boston, with 2005 extrapolated by the authors. See Section 1.10 on the CD.

transistor An on/off switch controlled by an electric signal.

A **transistor** is simply an on/off switch controlled by electricity. The *integrated circuit* (IC) combined dozens to hundreds of transistors into a single chip. To describe the tremendous increase in the number of transistors from hundreds to millions, the adjective *very large scale* is added to the term, creating the abbreviation *VLSI*, for **very large-scale integrated circuit**.

very large-scale integrated (VLSI) circuit A device containing hundreds of thousands to millions of transistors.

This rate of increasing integration has been remarkably stable. Figure 1.12 shows the growth in DRAM capacity since 1977. For 20 years, the industry has consistently quadrupled capacity every 3 years, resulting in an increase in excess of 16,000 times! This increase in transistor count for an integrated circuit is popularly known as Moore's law, which states that transistor capacity doubles every 18–24 months. Moore's law resulted from a prediction of such growth in IC capacity made by Gordon Moore, one of the founders of Intel during the 1960s.

Sustaining this rate of progress for almost 40 years has required incredible innovation in manufacturing techniques. In Section 1.7, we discuss how to manufacture integrated circuits.

1.4 Performance

Assessing the performance of computers can be quite challenging. The scale and intricacy of modern software systems, together with the wide range of performance improvement techniques employed by hardware designers, have made performance assessment much more difficult.

When trying to choose among different computers, performance is an important attribute. Accurately measuring and comparing different computers is critical to

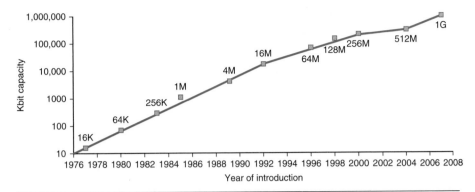

FIGURE 1.12 Growth of capacity per DRAM chip over time. The y-axis is measured in Kilobits, where K = 1024 (2^{10}). The DRAM industry quadrupled capacity almost every three years, a 60% increase per year, for 20 years. In recent years, the rate has slowed down and is somewhat closer to doubling every two years to three years.

purchasers and therefore to designers. The people selling computers know this as well. Often, salespeople would like you to see their computer in the best possible light, whether or not this light accurately reflects the needs of the purchaser's application. Hence, understanding how best to measure performance and the limitations of performance measurements is important in selecting a computer.

The rest of this section describes different ways in which performance can be determined; then, we describe the metrics for measuring performance from the viewpoint of both a computer user and a designer. We also look at how these metrics are related and present the classical processor performance equation, which we will use throughout the text.

Defining Performance

When we say one computer has better performance than another, what do we mean? Although this question might seem simple, an analogy with passenger airplanes shows how subtle the question of performance can be. Figure 1.13 shows some typical passenger airplanes, together with their cruising speed, range, and capacity. If we wanted to know which of the planes in this table had the best performance, we would first need to define performance. For example, considering different measures of performance, we see that the plane with the highest cruising speed is the Concorde, the plane with the longest range is the DC-8, and the plane with the largest capacity is the 747.

Let's suppose we define performance in terms of speed. This still leaves two possible definitions. You could define the fastest plane as the one with the highest cruising speed, taking a single passenger from one point to another in the least time. If you

Airplane	Passenger capacity	Cruising range (miles)	Cruising speed (m.p.h.)	Passenger throughput (passengers × m.p.h.)
Boeing 777	375	4630	610	228,750
Boeing 747	470	4150	610	286,700
BAC/Sud Concorde	132	4000	1350	178,200
Douglas DC-8-50	146	8720	544	79,424

FIGURE 1.13   The capacity, range, and speed for a number of commercial airplanes. The last column shows the rate at which the airplane transports passengers, which is the capacity times the cruising speed (ignoring range and takeoff and landing times).

response time Also called **execution time**. The total time required for the computer to complete a task, including disk accesses, memory accesses, I/O activities, operating system over-head, CPU execution time, and so on.

throughput Also called **bandwidth**. Another measure of performance, it is the number of tasks completed per unit time.

were interested in transporting 450 passengers from one point to another, however, the 747 would clearly be the fastest, as the last column of the figure shows. Similarly, we can define computer performance in several different ways.

If you were running a program on two different desktop computers, you'd say that the faster one is the desktop computer that gets the job done first. If you were running a datacenter that had several servers running jobs submitted by many users, you'd say that the faster computer was the one that completed the most jobs during a day. As an individual computer user, you are interested in reducing **response time**—the time between the start and completion of a task—also referred to as **execution time**. Datacenter managers are often interested in increasing **throughput** or **bandwidth**—the total amount of work done in a given time. Hence, in most cases, we will need different performance metrics as well as different sets of applications to benchmark embedded and desktop computers, which are more focused on response time, versus servers, which are more focused on throughput.

Throughput and Response Time

Do the following changes to a computer system increase throughput, decrease response time, or both?

1. Replacing the processor in a computer with a faster version

2. Adding additional processors to a system that uses multiple processors for separate tasks—for example, searching the World Wide Web

Decreasing response time almost always improves throughput. Hence, in case 1, both response time and throughput are improved. In case 2, no one task gets work done faster, so only throughput increases.

If, however, the demand for processing in the second case was almost as large as the throughput, the system might force requests to queue up. In this case, increasing the throughput could also improve response time, since it would reduce the waiting time in the queue. Thus, in many real computer systems, changing either execution time or throughput often affects the other.

In discussing the performance of computers, we will be primarily concerned with response time for the first few chapters. To maximize performance, we want to minimize response time or execution time for some task. Thus, we can relate performance and execution time for a computer X:

$$\text{Performance}_X = \frac{1}{\text{Execution time}_X}$$

This means that for two computers X and Y, if the performance of X is greater than the performance of Y, we have

$$\text{Performance}_X > \text{Performance}_Y$$

$$\frac{1}{\text{Execution time}_X} > \frac{1}{\text{Execution time}_Y}$$

$$\text{Execution time}_Y > \text{Execution time}_X$$

That is, the execution time on Y is longer than that on X, if X is faster than Y.

In discussing a computer design, we often want to relate the performance of two different computers quantitatively. We will use the phrase "X is n times faster than Y"—or equivalently "X is n times as fast as Y"—to mean

$$\frac{\text{Performance}_X}{\text{Performance}_Y} = n$$

If X is n times faster than Y, then the execution time on Y is n times longer than it is on X:

$$\frac{\text{Performance}_X}{\text{Performance}_Y} = \frac{\text{Execution time}_Y}{\text{Execution time}_X} = n$$

Relative Performance

If computer A runs a program in 10 seconds and computer B runs the same program in 15 seconds, how much faster is A than B?

EXAMPLE

We know that A is n times faster than B if

$$\frac{\text{Performance}_A}{\text{Performance}_B} = \frac{\text{Execution time}_B}{\text{Execution time}_A} = n$$

ANSWER

Thus the performance ratio is

$$\frac{15}{10} = 1.5$$

and A is therefore 1.5 times faster than B.

In the above example, we could also say that computer B is 1.5 times *slower than* computer A, since

$$\frac{\text{Performance}_A}{\text{Performance}_B} = 1.5$$

means that

$$\frac{\text{Performance}_A}{1.5} = \text{Performance}_B$$

For simplicity, we will normally use the terminology *faster than* when we try to compare computers quantitatively. Because performance and execution time are reciprocals, increasing performance requires decreasing execution time. To avoid the potential confusion between the terms *increasing* and *decreasing*, we usually say "improve performance" or "improve execution time" when we mean "increase performance" and "decrease execution time."

Measuring Performance

Time is the measure of computer performance: the computer that performs the same amount of work in the least time is the fastest. Program *execution time* is measured in seconds per program. However, time can be defined in different ways, depending on what we count. The most straightforward definition of time is called *wall clock time, response time,* or *elapsed time.* These terms mean the total time to complete a task, including disk accesses, memory accesses, input/output (I/O) activities, operating system overhead—everything.

Computers are often shared, however, and a processor may work on several programs simultaneously. In such cases, the system may try to optimize through-put rather than attempt to minimize the elapsed time for one program. Hence, we often want to distinguish between the elapsed time and the time that the processor is working on our behalf. **CPU execution time** or simply **CPU time**, which recognizes this distinction, is the time the CPU spends computing for this task and does not include time spent waiting for I/O or running other programs. (Remember, though, that the response time experienced by the user will be the elapsed time of the program, not the CPU time.) CPU time can be further divided into the CPU time spent in the program, called **user CPU time**, and the CPU time spent in the operating system performing tasks on behalf of the program, called **system CPU time**. Differentiating between system and user CPU time is difficult to

CPU execution time Also called **CPU time**. The actual time the CPU spends computing for a specific task.

user CPU time The CPU time spent in a program itself.

system CPU time The CPU time spent in the operating system performing tasks on behalf of the program.

do accurately, because it is often hard to assign responsibility for operating system activities to one user program rather than another and because of the functionality differences among operating systems.

For consistency, we maintain a distinction between performance based on elapsed time and that based on CPU execution time. We will use the term *system performance* to refer to elapsed time on an unloaded system and *CPU performance* to refer to user CPU time. We will focus on CPU performance in this chapter, although our discussions of how to summarize performance can be applied to either elapsed time or CPU time measurements.

Understanding Program Performance

Different applications are sensitive to different aspects of the performance of a computer system. Many applications, especially those running on servers, depend as much on I/O performance, which, in turn, relies on both hardware and software. Total elapsed time measured by a wall clock is the measurement of interest. In some application environments, the user may care about throughput, response time, or a complex combination of the two (e.g., maximum throughput with a worst-case response time). To improve the performance of a program, one must have a clear definition of what performance metric matters and then proceed to look for performance bottlenecks by measuring program execution and looking for the likely bottlenecks. In the following chapters, we will describe how to search for bottlenecks and improve performance in various parts of the system.

Although as computer users we care about time, when we examine the details of a computer it's convenient to think about performance in other metrics. In particular, computer designers may want to think about a computer by using a measure that relates to how fast the hardware can perform basic functions. Almost all computers are constructed using a clock that determines when events take place in the hardware. These discrete time intervals are called **clock cycles** (or **ticks, clock ticks, clock periods, clocks, cycles**). Designers refer to the length of a **clock period** both as the time for a complete *clock cycle* (e.g., 250 picoseconds, or 250 ps) and as the *clock rate* (e.g., 4 gigahertz, or 4 GHz), which is the inverse of the clock period. In the next subsection, we will formalize the relationship between the clock cycles of the hardware designer and the seconds of the computer user.

clock cycle Also called tick, clock tick, clock period, clock, cycle. The time for one clock period, usually of the processor clock, which runs at a constant rate.

clock period The length of each clock cycle.

Check Yourself

1. Suppose we know that an application that uses both a desktop client and a remote server is limited by network performance. For the following changes, state whether only the throughput improves, both response time and throughput improve, or neither improves.

   a. An extra network channel is added between the client and the server, increasing the total network throughput and reducing the delay to obtain network access (since there are now two channels).

     b. The networking software is improved, thereby reducing the network communication delay, but not increasing throughput.

     c. More memory is added to the computer.

2. Computer C's performance is 4 times faster than the performance of computer B, which runs a given application in 28 seconds. How long will computer C take to run that application?

CPU Performance and Its Factors

Users and designers often examine performance using different metrics. If we could relate these different metrics, we could determine the effect of a design change on the performance as experienced by the user. Since we are confining ourselves to CPU performance at this point, the bottom-line performance measure is CPU execution time. A simple formula relates the most basic metrics (clock cycles and clock cycle time) to CPU time:

$$\frac{\text{CPU execution time}}{\text{for a program}} = \frac{\text{CPU clock cycles}}{\text{for a program}} \times \text{Clock cycle time}$$

Alternatively, because clock rate and clock cycle time are inverses,

$$\frac{\text{CPU execution time}}{\text{for a program}} = \frac{\text{CPU clock cycles for a program}}{\text{Clock rate}}$$

This formula makes it clear that the hardware designer can improve performance by reducing the number of clock cycles required for a program or the length of the clock cycle. As we will see in later chapters, the designer often faces a trade-off between the number of clock cycles needed for a program and the length of each cycle. Many techniques that decrease the number of clock cycles may also increase the clock cycle time.

EXAMPLE

Improving Performance

Our favorite program runs in 10 seconds on computer A, which has a 2 GHz clock. We are trying to help a computer designer build a computer, B, which will run this program in 6 seconds. The designer has determined that a substantial increase in the clock rate is possible, but this increase will affect the rest of the CPU design, causing computer B to require 1.2 times as many clock cycles as computer A for this program. What clock rate should we tell the designer to target?

Let's first find the number of clock cycles required for the program on A:

$$\text{CPU time}_A = \frac{\text{CPU clock cycles}_A}{\text{Clock rate}_A}$$

$$10 \text{ seconds} = \frac{\text{CPU clock cycles}_A}{2 \times 10^9 \frac{\text{cycles}}{\text{second}}}$$

$$\text{CPU clock cycles}_A = 10 \text{ seconds} \times 2 \times 10^9 \frac{\text{cycles}}{\text{second}} = 20 \times 10^9 \text{ cycles}$$

CPU time for B can be found using this equation:

$$\text{CPU time}_B = \frac{1.2 \times \text{CPU clock cycles}_A}{\text{Clock rate}_B}$$

$$6 \text{ seconds} = \frac{1.2 \times 20 \times 10^9 \text{ cycles}}{\text{Clock rate}_B}$$

$$\text{Clock rate}_B = \frac{1.2 \times 20 \times 10^9 \text{ cycles}}{6 \text{ seconds}} = \frac{0.2 \times 20 \times 10^9 \text{ cycles}}{\text{second}} = \frac{4 \times 10^9 \text{ cycles}}{\text{second}} = 4 \text{ GHz}$$

To run the program in 6 seconds, B must have twice the clock rate of A.

Instruction Performance

The performance equations above did not include any reference to the number of instructions needed for the program. (We'll see what the instructions that make up a program look like in the next chapter.) However, since the compiler clearly generated instructions to execute, and the computer had to execute the instructions to run the program, the execution time must depend on the number of instructions in a program. One way to think about execution time is that it equals the number of instructions executed multiplied by the average time per instruction. Therefore, the number of clock cycles required for a program can be written as

$$\text{CPU clock cycles} = \text{Instructions for a program} \times \frac{\text{Average clock cycles}}{\text{per instruction}}$$

clock cycles per instruction (CPI) Average number of clock cycles per instruction for a program or program fragment.

The term **clock cycles per instruction**, which is the average number of clock cycles each instruction takes to execute, is often abbreviated as **CPI**. Since different instructions may take different amounts of time depending on what they do, CPI is an average of all the instructions executed in the program. CPI provides one way of comparing two different implementations of the same instruction set architecture, since the number of instructions executed for a program will, of course, be the same.

Using the Performance Equation

EXAMPLE

Suppose we have two implementations of the same instruction set architecture. Computer A has a clock cycle time of 250 ps and a CPI of 2.0 for some program, and computer B has a clock cycle time of 500 ps and a CPI of 1.2 for the same program. Which computer is faster for this program and by how much?

ANSWER

We know that each computer executes the same number of instructions for the program; let's call this number I. First, find the number of processor clock cycles for each computer:

$$\text{CPU clock cycles}_A = I \times 2.0$$

$$\text{CPU clock cycles}_B = I \times 1.2$$

Now we can compute the CPU time for each computer:

$$\text{CPU time}_A = \text{CPU clock cycles}_A \times \text{Clock cycle time}$$

$$= I \times 2.0 \times 250 \text{ ps} = 500 \times I \text{ ps}$$

Likewise, for B:

$$\text{CPU time}_B = I \times 1.2 \times 500 \text{ ps} = 600 \times I \text{ ps}$$

Clearly, computer A is faster. The amount faster is given by the ratio of the execution times:

$$\frac{\text{CPU performance}_A}{\text{CPU performance}_B} = \frac{\text{Execution time}_B}{\text{Execution time}_A} = \frac{600 \times I \text{ ps}}{500 \times I \text{ ps}} = 1.2$$

We can conclude that computer A is 1.2 times as fast as computer B for this program.

The Classic CPU Performance Equation

We can now write this basic performance equation in terms of **instruction count** (the number of instructions executed by the program), CPI, and clock cycle time:

$$\text{CPU time} = \text{Instruction count} \times \text{CPI} \times \text{Clock cycle time}$$

instruction count The number of instructions executed by the program.

or, since the clock rate is the inverse of clock cycle time:

$$\text{CPU time} = \frac{\text{Instruction count} \times \text{CPI}}{\text{Clock rate}}$$

These formulas are particularly useful because they separate the three key factors that affect performance. We can use these formulas to compare two different implementations or to evaluate a design alternative if we know its impact on these three parameters.

Comparing Code Segments

A compiler designer is trying to decide between two code sequences for a particular computer. The hardware designers have supplied the following facts:

EXAMPLE

	CPI for each instruction class		
	A	B	C
CPI	1	2	3

For a particular high-level language statement, the compiler writer is considering two code sequences that require the following instruction counts:

Code sequence	Instruction counts for each instruction class		
	A	B	C
1	2	1	2
2	4	1	1

Which code sequence executes the most instructions? Which will be faster? What is the CPI for each sequence?

ANSWER

Sequence 1 executes $2 + 1 + 2 = 5$ instructions. Sequence 2 executes $4 + 1 + 1 = 6$ instructions. Therefore, sequence 1 executes fewer instructions.

We can use the equation for CPU clock cycles based on instruction count and CPI to find the total number of clock cycles for each sequence:

$$\text{CPU clock cycles} = \sum_{i=1}^{n} (\text{CPI}_i \times \text{C}_i)$$

This yields

$$\text{CPU clock cycles}_1 = (2 \times 1) + (1 \times 2) + (2 \times 3) = 2 + 2 + 6 = 10 \text{ cycles}$$

$$\text{CPU clock cycles}_2 = (4 \times 1) + (1 \times 2) + (1 \times 3) = 4 + 2 + 3 = 9 \text{ cycles}$$

So code sequence 2 is faster, even though it executes one extra instruction. Since code sequence 2 takes fewer overall clock cycles but has more instructions, it must have a lower CPI. The CPI values can be computed by

$$\text{CPI} = \frac{\text{CPU clock cycles}}{\text{Instruction count}}$$

$$\text{CPI}_1 = \frac{\text{CPU clock cycles}_1}{\text{Instruction count}_1} = \frac{10}{5} = 2.0$$

$$\text{CPI}_2 = \frac{\text{CPU clock cycles}_2}{\text{Instruction count}_2} = \frac{9}{6} = 1.5$$

The BIG Picture

Figure 1.14 shows the basic measurements at different levels in the computer and what is being measured in each case. We can see how these factors are combined to yield execution time measured in seconds per program:

$$\text{Time} = \text{Seconds/Program} = \frac{\text{Instructions}}{\text{Program}} \times \frac{\text{Clock cycles}}{\text{Instruction}} \times \frac{\text{Seconds}}{\text{Clock cycle}}$$

Always bear in mind that the only complete and reliable measure of computer performance is time. For example, changing the instruction set to lower the instruction count may lead to an organization with a slower clock cycle time or higher CPI that offsets the improvement in instruction count. Similarly, because CPI depends on type of instructions executed, the code that executes the fewest number of instructions may not be the fastest.

Components of performance	Units of measure
CPU execution time for a program	Seconds for the program
Instruction count	Instructions executed for the program
Clock cycles per instruction (CPI)	Average number of clock cycles per instruction
Clock cycle time	Seconds per clock cycle

FIGURE 1.14   The basic components of performance and how each is measured.

How can we determine the value of these factors in the performance equation? We can measure the CPU execution time by running the program, and the clock cycle time is usually published as part of the documentation for a computer. The instruction count and CPI can be more difficult to obtain. Of course, if we know the clock rate and CPU execution time, we need only one of the instruction count or the CPI to determine the other.

We can measure the instruction count by using software tools that profile the execution or by using a simulator of the architecture. Alternatively, we can use hardware counters, which are included in most processors, to record a variety of measurements, including the number of instructions executed, the average CPI, and often, the sources of performance loss. Since the instruction count depends on the architecture, but not on the exact implementation, we can measure the instruction count without knowing all the details of the implementation. The CPI, however, depends on a wide variety of design details in the computer, including both the memory system and the processor structure (as we will see in Chapters 4 and 5), as well as on the mix of instruction types executed in an application. Thus, CPI varies by application, as well as among implementations with the same instruction set.

The above example shows the danger of using only one factor (instruction count) to assess performance. When comparing two computers, you must look at all three components, which combine to form execution time. If some of the factors are identical, like the clock rate in the above example, performance can be determined by comparing all the nonidentical factors. Since CPI varies by **instruction mix**, both instruction count and CPI must be compared, even if clock rates are identical. Several exercises at the end of this chapter ask you to evaluate a series of computer and compiler enhancements that affect clock rate, CPI, and instruction count. In Section 1.8, we'll examine a common performance measurement that does not incorporate all the terms and can thus be misleading.

instruction mix A measure of the dynamic frequency of instructions across one or many programs.

Understanding Program Performance

The performance of a program depends on the algorithm, the language, the compiler, the architecture, and the actual hardware. The following table summarizes how these components affect the factors in the CPU performance equation.

Hardware or software component	Affects what?	How?
Algorithm	Instruction count, possibly CPI	The algorithm determines the number of source program instructions executed and hence the number of processor instructions executed. The algorithm may also affect the CPI, by favoring slower or faster instructions. For example, if the algorithm uses more floating-point operations, it will tend to have a higher CPI.
Programming language	Instruction count, CPI	The programming language certainly affects the instruction count, since statements in the language are translated to processor instructions, which determine instruction count. The language may also affect the CPI because of its features; for example, a language with heavy support for data abstraction (e.g., Java) will require indirect calls, which will use higher CPI instructions.
Compiler	Instruction count, CPI	The efficiency of the compiler affects both the instruction count and average cycles per instruction, since the compiler determines the translation of the source language instructions into computer instructions. The compiler's role can be very complex and affect the CPI in complex ways.
Instruction set architecture	Instruction count, clock rate, CPI	The instruction set architecture affects all three aspects of CPU performance, since it affects the instructions needed for a function, the cost in cycles of each instruction, and the overall clock rate of the processor.

Elaboration: Although you might expect that the minimum CPI is 1.0, as we'll see in Chapter 4, some processors fetch and execute multiple instructions per clock cycle. To reflect that approach, some designers invert CPI to talk about *IPC*, or *instructions per clock cycle*. If a processor executes on average 2 instructions per clock cycle, then it has an IPC of 2 and hence a CPI of 0.5.

Check Yourself

A given application written in Java runs 15 seconds on a desktop processor. A new Java compiler is released that requires only 0.6 as many instructions as the old compiler. Unfortunately, it increases the CPI by 1.1. How fast can we expect the application to run using this new compiler? Pick the right answer from the three choices below

a. $\dfrac{15 \times 0.6}{1.1} = 8.2$ sec

b. $15 \times 0.6 \times 1.1 = 9.9$ sec

c. $\dfrac{15 \times 1.1}{0.6} = 27.5$ sec

1.5 The Power Wall

Figure 1.15 shows the increase in clock rate and power of eight generations of Intel microprocessors over 25 years. Both clock rate and power increased rapidly for decades, and then flattened off recently. The reason they grew together is that they are correlated, and the reason for their recent slowing is that we have run into the practical power limit for cooling commodity microprocessors.

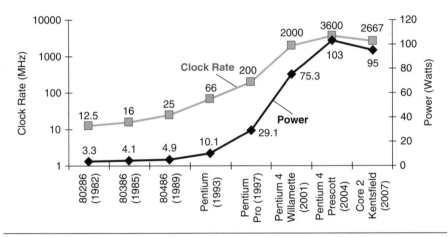

FIGURE 1.15 Clock rate and Power for Intel x86 microprocessors over eight generations and 25 years. The Pentium 4 made a dramatic jump in clock rate and power but less so in performance. The Prescott thermal problems led to the abandonment of the Pentium 4 line. The Core 2 line reverts to a simpler pipeline with lower clock rates and multiple processors per chip.

The dominant technology for integrated circuits is called CMOS (complementary metal oxide semiconductor). For CMOS, the primary source of power dissipation is so-called dynamic power—that is, power that is consumed during switching. The dynamic power dissipation depends on the capacitive loading of each transistor, the voltage applied, and the frequency that the transistor is switched:

$$\text{Power} = \text{Capacitive load} \times \text{Voltage}^2 \times \text{Frequency switched}$$

Frequency switched is a function of the clock rate. The capacitive load per transistor is a function of both the number of transistors connected to an output (called the *fanout*) and the technology, which determines the capacitance of both wires and transistors.

How could clock rates grow by a factor of 1000 while power grew by only a factor of 30? Power can be reduced by lowering the voltage, which occurred with each new generation of technology, and power is a function of the voltage squared. Typically, the voltage was reduced about 15% per generation. In 20 years, voltages have gone from 5V to 1V, which is why the increase in power is only 30 times.

Relative Power

EXAMPLE

Suppose we developed a new, simpler processor that has 85% of the capacitive load of the more complex older processor. Further, assume that it has adjustable voltage so that it can reduce voltage 15% compared to processor B, which results in a 15% shrink in frequency. What is the impact on dynamic power?

ANSWER

$$\frac{\text{Power}_{\text{new}}}{\text{Power}_{\text{old}}} = \frac{\langle\text{Capacitive load} \times 0.85\rangle \times \langle\text{Voltage} \times 0.85\rangle^2 \times \langle\text{Frequency switched} \times 0.85\rangle}{\text{Capacitive load} \times \text{Voltage}^2 \times \text{Frequency switched}}$$

Thus the power ratio is

$$0.85^4 = 0.52$$

Hence, the new processor uses about half the power of the old processor.

The problem today is that further lowering of the voltage appears to make the transistors too leaky, like water faucets that cannot be completely shut off. Even today about 40% of the power consumption is due to leakage. If transistors started leaking more, the whole process could become unwieldy.

To try to address the power problem, designers have already attached large devices to increase cooling, and they turn off parts of the chip that are not used in a given clock cycle. Although there are many more expensive ways to cool chips and thereby raise their power to, say, 300 watts, these techniques are too expensive for desktop computers.

Since computer designers slammed into a power wall, they needed a new way forward. They chose a different way from the way they designed microprocessors for their first 30 years.

Elaboration: Although dynamic power is the primary source of power dissipation in CMOS, static power dissipation occurs because of leakage current that flows even when a transistor is off. As mentioned above, leakage is typically responsible for 40% of the power consumption in 2008. Thus, increasing the number of transistors increases power dissipation, even if the transistors are always off. A variety of design techniques and technology innovations are being deployed to control leakage, but it's hard to lower voltage further.

1.6 The Sea Change: The Switch from Uniprocessors to Multiprocessors

The power limit has forced a dramatic change in the design of microprocessors. Figure 1.16 shows the improvement in response time of programs for desktop microprocessors over time. Since 2002, the rate has slowed from a factor of 1.5 per year to less than a factor of 1.2 per year.

Rather than continuing to decrease the response time of a single program running on the single processor, as of 2006 all desktop and server companies are shipping microprocessors with multiple processors per chip, where the benefit is often more on throughput than on response time. To reduce confusion between the words processor and microprocessor, companies refer to processors as "cores," and such microprocessors are generically called multicore microprocessors. Hence, a "quadcore" microprocessor is a chip that contains four processors or four cores.

Figure 1.17 shows the number of processors (cores), power, and clock rates of recent microprocessors. The official plan of record for many companies is to double the number of cores per microprocessor per semiconductor technology generation, which is about every two years (see Chapter 7).

In the past, programmers could rely on innovations in hardware, architecture, and compilers to double performance of their programs every 18 months without having to change a line of code. Today, for programmers to get significant improvement in response time, they need to rewrite their programs to take advantage of multiple processors. Moreover, to get the historic benefit of running faster on new microprocessors, programmers will have to continue to improve performance of their code as the number of cores doubles.

To reinforce how the software and hardware systems work hand in hand, we use a special section, *Hardware/Software Interface*, throughout the book, with the first one appearing below. These elements summarize important insights at this critical interface.

"Up to now, most software has been like music written for a solo performer; with the current generation of chips we're getting a little experience with duets and quartets and other small ensembles; but scoring a work for large orchestra and chorus is a different kind of challenge."

Brian Hayes, *Computing in a Parallel Universe,* 2007.

Hardware/ Software Interface

Parallelism has always been critical to performance in computing, but it was often hidden. Chapter 4 will explain pipelining, an elegant technique that runs programs faster by overlapping the execution of instructions. This is one example of *instruction-level parallelism*, where the parallel nature of the hardware is abstracted away so the programmer and compiler can think of the hardware as executing instructions sequentially.

Forcing programmers to be aware of the parallel hardware and to explicitly rewrite their programs to be parallel had been the "third rail" of computer architecture, for companies in the past that depended on such a change in behavior failed (see Section 7.14 on the CD). From this historical perspective, it's startling that the whole IT industry has bet its future that programmers will finally successfully switch to explicitly parallel programming.

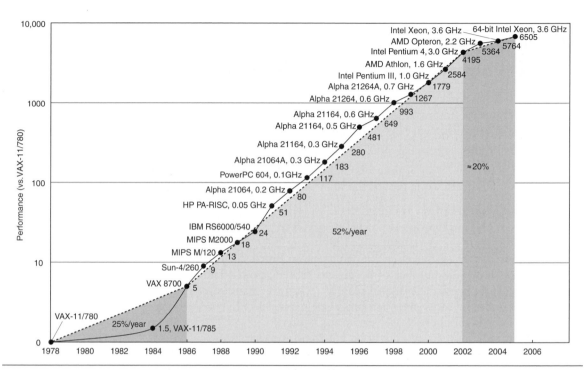

FIGURE 1.16   Growth in processor performance since the mid-1980s. This chart plots performance relative to the VAX 11/780 as measured by the SPECint benchmarks (see Section 1.8). Prior to the mid-1980s, processor performance growth was largely technology-driven and averaged about 25% per year. The increase in growth to about 52% since then is attributable to more advanced architectural and organizational ideas. By 2002, this growth led to a difference in performance of about a factor of seven. Performance for floating-point-oriented calculations has increased even faster. Since 2002, the limits of power, available instruction-level parallelism, and long memory latency have slowed uniprocessor performance recently, to about 20% per year.

Product	AMD Opteron X4 (Barcelona)	Intel Nehalem	IBM Power 6	Sun Ultra SPARC T2 (Niagara 2)
Cores per chip	4	4	2	8
Clock rate	2.5 GHz	~ 2.5 GHz ?	4.7 GHz	1.4 GHz
Microprocessor power	120 W	~ 100 W ?	~ 100 W ?	94 W

FIGURE 1.17   Number of cores per chip, clock rate, and power for 2008 multicore microprocessors.

Why has it been so hard for programmers to write explicitly parallel programs? The first reason is that parallel programming is by definition performance programming, which increases the difficulty of programming. Not only does the program need to be correct, solve an important problem, and provide a useful interface to the people or other programs that invoke it, the program must also be fast. Otherwise, if you don't need performance, just write a sequential program.

The second reason is that fast for parallel hardware means that the programmer must divide an application so that each processor has roughly the same amount to do at the same time, and that the overhead of scheduling and coordination doesn't fritter away the potential performance benefits of parallelism.

As an analogy, suppose the task was to write a newspaper story. Eight reporters working on the same story could potentially write a story eight times faster. To achieve this increased speed, one would need to break up the task so that each reporter had something to do at the same time. Thus, we must *schedule* the sub-tasks. If anything went wrong and just one reporter took longer than the seven others did, then the benefits of having eight writers would be diminished. Thus, we must *balance the load* evenly to get the desired speedup. Another danger would be if reporters had to spend a lot of time talking to each other to write their sections. You would also fall short if one part of the story, such as the conclusion, couldn't be written until all of the other parts were completed. Thus, care must be taken to *reduce communication and synchronization overhead*. For both this analogy and parallel programming, the challenges include scheduling, load balancing, time for synchronization, and overhead for communication between the parties. As you might guess, the challenge is stiffer with more reporters for a newspaper story and more processors for parallel programming.

To reflect this sea change in the industry, the next five chapters in this edition of the book each have a section on the implications of the parallel revolution to that chapter:

- *Chapter 2, Section 2.11: Parallelism and Instructions: Synchronization.* Usually independent parallel tasks need to coordinate at times, such as to say when they have completed their work. This chapter explains the instructions used by multicore processors to synchronize tasks.

- *Chapter 3, Section 3.6: Parallelism and Computer Arithmetic: Associativity.* Often parallel programmers start from a working sequential program. A natural question to learn if their parallel version works is, "does it get the same answer?" If not, a logical conclusion is that there are bugs in the new version. This logic assumes that computer arithmetic is associative: you get the same sum when adding a million numbers, no matter what the order. This chapter explains that while this logic holds for integers, it doesn't hold for floating-point numbers.

- *Chapter 4, Section 4.10: Parallelism and Advanced Instruction-Level Parallelism.* Given the difficulty of explicitly parallel programming, tremendous effort was invested in the 1990s in having the hardware and the compiler uncover implicit parallelism. This chapter describes some of these aggressive techniques, including fetching and executing multiple instructions simultaneously and guessing on the outcomes of decisions, and executing instructions speculatively.

■ *Chapter 5, Section 5.8: Parallelism and Memory Hierarchies: Cache Coherence.* One way to lower the cost of communication is to have all processors use the same address space, so that any processor can read or write any data. Given that all processors today use caches to keep a temporary copy of the data in faster memory near the processor, it's easy to imagine that parallel programming would be even more difficult if the caches associated with each processor had inconsistent values of the shared data. This chapter describes the mechanisms that keep the data in all caches consistent.

■ *Chapter 6, Section 6.9: Parallelism and I/O: Redundant Arrays of Inexpensive Disks.* If you ignore input and output in this parallel revolution, the unintended consequence of parallel programming may be to make your parallel program spend most of its time waiting for I/O. This chapter describes RAID, a technique to accelerate the performance of storage accesses. RAID points out another potential benefit of parallelism: by having many copies of resources, the system can continue to provide service despite a failure of one resource. Hence, RAID can improve both I/O performance and availability.

In addition to these sections, there is a full chapter on parallel processing. Chapter 7 goes into more detail on the challenges of parallel programming; presents the two contrasting approaches to communication of shared addressing and explicit message passing; describes a restricted model of parallelism that is easier to program; discusses the difficulty of benchmarking parallel processors; introduces a new simple performance model for multicore microprocessors and finally describes and evaluates four examples of multicore microprocessors using this model.

Starting with this edition of the book, Appendix A describes an increasingly popular hardware component that is included with desktop computers, the graphics processing unit (GPU). Invented to accelerate graphics, GPUs are becoming programming platforms in their own right. As you might expect, given these times, GPUs are highly parallel. Appendix A describes the NVIDIA GPU and highlights parts of its parallel programming environment.

> *I thought [computers] would be a universally applicable idea, like a book is. But I didn't think it would develop as fast as it did, because I didn't envision we'd be able to get as many parts on a chip as we finally got. The transistor came along unexpectedly. It all happened much faster than we expected.*
>
> J. Presper Eckert, coinventor of ENIAC, speaking in 1991

1.7   Real Stuff: Manufacturing and Benchmarking the AMD Opteron X4

Each chapter has a section entitled "Real Stuff" that ties the concepts in the book with a computer you may use every day. These sections cover the technology underlying modern computers. For this first "Real Stuff" section, we look at how integrated circuits are manufactured and how performance and power are measured, with the AMD Opteron X4 as the example.

Let's start at the beginning. The manufacture of a chip begins with **silicon**, a substance found in sand. Because silicon does not conduct electricity well, it is called a **semiconductor**. With a special chemical process, it is possible to add materials to silicon that allow tiny areas to transform into one of three devices:

- Excellent conductors of electricity (using either microscopic copper or aluminum wire)

- Excellent insulators from electricity (like plastic sheathing or glass)

- Areas that can conduct *or* insulate under special conditions (as a switch)

Transistors fall in the last category. A VLSI circuit, then, is just billions of combinations of conductors, insulators, and switches manufactured in a single small package.

The manufacturing process for integrated circuits is critical to the cost of the chips and hence important to computer designers. Figure 1.18 shows that process. The process starts with a **silicon crystal ingot**, which looks like a giant sausage. Today, ingots are 8–12 inches in diameter and about 12–24 inches long. An ingot is finely sliced into **wafers** no more than 0.1 inch thick. These wafers then go through a series of processing steps, during which patterns of chemicals are placed on

silicon A natural element that is a semiconductor.

semiconductor A substance that does not conduct electricity well.

silicon crystal ingot A rod composed of a silicon crystal that is between 8 and 12 inches in diameter and about 12 to 24 inches long.

wafer A slice from a silicon ingot no more than 0.1 inch thick, used to create chips.

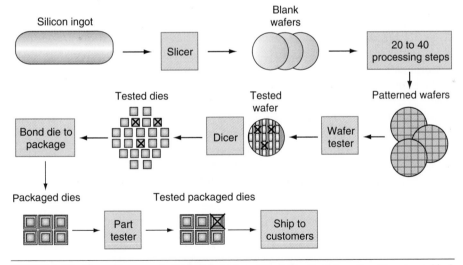

FIGURE 1.18 The chip manufacturing process. After being sliced from the silicon ingot, blank wafers are put through 20 to 40 steps to create patterned wafers (see Figure 1.19). These patterned wafers are then tested with a wafer tester, and a map of the good parts is made. Then, the wafers are diced into dies (see Figure 1.9). In this figure, one wafer produced 20 dies, of which 17 passed testing. (*X* means the die is bad.) The yield of good dies in this case was 17/20, or 85%. These good dies are then bonded into packages and tested one more time before shipping the packaged parts to customers. One bad packaged part was found in this final test.

each wafer, creating the transistors, conductors, and insulators discussed earlier. Today's integrated circuits contain only one layer of transistors but may have from two to eight levels of metal conductor, separated by layers of insulators.

A single microscopic flaw in the wafer itself or in one of the dozens of patterning steps can result in that area of the wafer failing. These **defects**, as they are called, make it virtually impossible to manufacture a perfect wafer. To cope with imperfection, several strategies have been used, but the simplest is to place many independent components on a single wafer. The patterned wafer is then chopped up, or *diced,* into these components, called **dies** and more informally known as **chips**. Figure 1.19 is a photograph of a wafer containing microprocessors before they have been diced; earlier, Figure 1.9 on page 20 shows an individual microprocessor die and its major components.

Dicing enables you to discard only those dies that were unlucky enough to contain the flaws, rather than the whole wafer. This concept is quantified by the **yield** of a process, which is defined as the percentage of good dies from the total number of dies on the wafer.

The cost of an integrated circuit rises quickly as the die size increases, due both to the lower yield and the smaller number of dies that fit on a wafer. To reduce the cost, a large die is often "shrunk" by using the next generation process, which incorporates smaller sizes for both transistors and wires. This improves the yield and the die count per wafer.

Once you've found good dies, they are connected to the input/output pins of a package, using a process called *bonding*. These packaged parts are tested a final time, since mistakes can occur in packaging, and then they are shipped to customers.

As mentioned above, an increasingly important design constraint is power. Power is a challenge for two reasons. First, power must be brought in and distributed around the chip; modern microprocessors use hundreds of pins just for power and ground! Similarly, multiple levels of interconnect are used solely for power and ground distribution to portions of the chip. Second, power is dissipated as heat and must be removed. An AMD Opteron X4 model 2356 2.0 GHz burns 120 watts in 2008, which must be removed from a chip whose surface area is just over 1 cm²!

defect A microscopic flaw in a wafer or in patterning steps that can result in the failure of the die containing that defect.

die The individual rectangular sections that are cut from a wafer, more informally known as **chips**.

yield The percentage of good dies from the total number of dies on the wafer.

Elaboration: The cost of an integrated circuit can be expressed in three simple equations:

$$\text{Cost per die} = \frac{\text{Cost per wafer}}{\text{Dies per wafer} \times \text{yield}}$$

$$\text{Dies per wafer} \approx \frac{\text{Wafer area}}{\text{Die area}}$$

$$\text{Yield} = \frac{1}{(1 + (\text{Defects per area} \times \text{Die area}/2))^2}$$

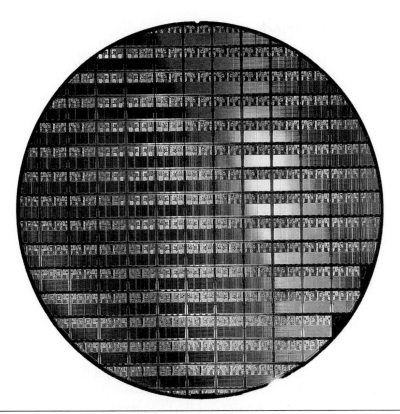

FIGURE 1.19 A 12-inch (300mm) wafer of AMD Opteron X2 chips, the predecessor of Opteron X4 chips (Courtesy AMD). The number of dies per wafer at 100% yield is 117. The several dozen partially rounded chips at the boundaries of the wafer are useless; they are included because it's easier to create the masks used to pattern the silicon. This die uses a 90-nanometer technology, which means that the smallest transistors are approximately 90 nm in size, although they are typically somewhat smaller than the actual feature size, which refers to the size of the transistors as "drawn" versus the final manufactured size.

The first equation is straightforward to derive. The second is an approximation, since it does not subtract the area near the border of the round wafer that cannot accommodate the rectangular dies (see Figure 1.19). The final equation is based on empirical observations of yields at integrated circuit factories, with the exponent related to the number of critical processing steps.

Hence, depending on the defect rate and the size of the die and wafer, costs are generally not linear in die area.

SPEC CPU Benchmark

workload A set of programs run on a computer that is either the actual collection of applications run by a user or constructed from real programs to approximate such a mix. A typical workload specifies both the programs and the relative frequencies.

benchmark A program selected for use in comparing computer performance.

A computer user who runs the same programs day in and day out would be the perfect candidate to evaluate a new computer. The set of programs run would form a **workload**. To evaluate two computer systems, a user would simply compare the execution time of the workload on the two computers. Most users, however, are not in this situation. Instead, they must rely on other methods that measure the performance of a candidate computer, hoping that the methods will reflect how well the computer will perform with the user's workload. This alternative is usually followed by evaluating the computer using a set of **benchmarks**—programs specifically chosen to measure performance. The benchmarks form a workload that the user hopes will predict the performance of the actual workload.

SPEC (System Performance Evaluation Cooperative) is an effort funded and supported by a number of computer vendors to create standard sets of benchmarks for modern computer systems. In 1989, SPEC originally created a benchmark set focusing on processor performance (now called SPEC89), which has evolved through five generations. The latest is SPEC CPU2006, which consists of a set of 12 integer benchmarks (CINT2006) and 17 floating-point benchmarks (CFP2006). The integer benchmarks vary from part of a C compiler to a chess program to a quantum computer simulation. The floating-point benchmarks include structured grid codes for finite element modeling, particle method codes for molecular dynamics, and sparse linear algebra codes for fluid dynamics.

Figure 1.20 describes the SPEC integer benchmarks and their execution time on the Opteron X4 and shows the factors that explain execution time: instruction count, CPI, and clock cycle time. Note that CPI varies by a factor of 13.

To simplify the marketing of computers, SPEC decided to report a single number to summarize all 12 integer benchmarks. The execution time measurements are first normalized by dividing the execution time on a reference processor by the execution time on the measured computer; this normalization yields a measure, called the *SPECratio*, which has the advantage that bigger numeric results indicate faster performance (i.e., the SPECratio is the inverse of execution time). A CINT2006 or CFP2006 summary measurement is obtained by taking the geometric mean of the SPECratios.

Elaboration: When comparing two computers using SPECratios, use the geometric mean so that it gives the same relative answer no matter what computer is used to normalize the results. If we averaged the normalized execution time values with an arithmetic mean, the results would vary depending on the computer we choose as the reference.

Description	Name	Instruction Count × 10⁹	CPI	Clock cycle time (seconds × 10⁻⁹)	Execution Time (seconds)	Reference Time (seconds)	SPECratio
Interpreted string processing	perl	2,118	0.75	0.4	637	9,770	15.3
Block-sorting compression	bzip2	2,389	0.85	0.4	817	9,650	11.8
GNU C compiler	gcc	1,050	1.72	0.4	724	8,050	11.1
Combinatorial optimization	mcf	336	10.00	0.4	1,345	9,120	6.8
Go game (AI)	go	1,658	1.09	0.4	721	10,490	14.6
Search gene sequence	hmmer	2,783	0.80	0.4	890	9,330	10.5
Chess game (AI)	sjeng	2,176	0.96	0.4	837	12,100	14.5
Quantum computer simulation	libquantum	1,623	1.61	0.4	1,047	20,720	19.8
Video compression	h264avc	3,102	0.80	0.4	993	22,130	22.3
Discrete event simulation library	omnetpp	587	2.94	0.4	690	6,250	9.1
Games/path finding	astar	1,082	1.79	0.4	773	7,020	9.1
XML parsing	xalancbmk	1,058	2.70	0.4	1,143	6,900	6.0
Geometric Mean							11.7

FIGURE 1.20   SPECINTC2006 benchmarks running on AMD Opteron X4 model 2356 (Barcelona). As the equation on page 35 explains, execution time is the product of the three factors in this table: instruction count in billions, clocks per instruction (CPI), and clock cycle time in nanoseconds. SPECratio is simply the reference time, which is supplied by SPEC, divided by the measured execution time. The single number quoted as SPECINTC2006 is the geometric mean of the SPECratios. Figure 5.40 on page 542 shows that mcf, libquantum, omnetpp, and xalancbmk have relatively high CPIs because they have high cache miss rates.

The formula for the geometric mean is

$$\sqrt[n]{\prod_{i=1}^{n} \text{Execution time ratio}_i}$$

where Execution time ratio$_i$ is the execution time, normalized to the reference computer, for the ith program of a total of n in the workload, and

$$\prod_{i=1}^{n} a_i \text{ means the product } a_1 \times a_2 \times \ldots \times a_n$$

SPEC Power Benchmark

Today, SPEC offers a dozen different benchmark sets designed to test a wide variety of computing environments using real applications and strictly specified execution rules and reporting requirements. The most recent is SPECpower. It reports power consumption of servers at different workload levels, divided into 10% increments, over a period of time. Figure 1.21 shows the results for a server using Barcelona.

SPECpower started with the SPEC benchmark for Java business applications (SPECJBB2005), which exercises the processors, caches, and main memory as well as the Java virtual machine, compiler, garbage collector, and pieces of the operating

Target Load %	Performance (ssj_ops)	Average Power (Watts)
100%	231,867	295
90%	211,282	286
80%	185,803	275
70%	163,427	265
60%	140,160	256
50%	118,324	246
40%	92,035	233
30%	70,500	222
20%	47,126	206
10%	23,066	180
0%	0	141
Overall Sum	1,283,590	2,605
Σ ssj_ops / Σ power =		493

FIGURE 1.21   SPECpower_ssj2008 running on dual socket 2.3 GHz AMD Opteron X4 2356 (Barcelona) with 16 GB Of DDR2-667 DRAM and one 500 GB disk.

system. Performance is measured in throughput, and the units are business operations per second. Once again, to simplify the marketing of computers, SPEC boils these numbers down to a single number, called "overall ssj_ops per Watt." The formula for this single summarizing metric is

$$\text{overall ssj\_ops per Watt} = \left(\sum_{i=0}^{10} \text{ssj\_ops}_i \right) / \left(\sum_{i=0}^{10} \text{power}_i \right)$$

where ssj_ops$_i$ is performance at each 10% increment and power$_i$ is power consumed at each performance level.

Check Yourself
A key factor in determining the cost of an integrated circuit is volume. Which of the following are reasons why a chip made in high volume should cost less?

1. With high volumes, the manufacturing process can be tuned to a particular design, increasing the yield.

2. It is less work to design a high-volume part than a low-volume part.

3. The masks used to make the chip are expensive, so the cost per chip is lower for higher volumes.

4. Engineering development costs are high and largely independent of volume; thus, the development cost per die is lower with high-volume parts.

5. High-volume parts usually have smaller die sizes than low-volume parts and therefore have higher yield per wafer.

Science must begin with myths, and the criticism of myths.

Sir Karl Popper, *The Philosophy of Science,* 1957

1.8 Fallacies and Pitfalls

The purpose of a section on fallacies and pitfalls, which will be found in every chapter, is to explain some commonly held misconceptions that you might encounter. We call such misbeliefs *fallacies.* When discussing a fallacy, we try to give a counterexample. We also discuss *pitfalls,* or easily made mistakes. Often pitfalls are generalizations of principles that are true in a limited context. The purpose of these sections is to help you avoid making these mistakes in the computers you may design or use. Cost/performance fallacies and pitfalls have ensnared many a computer architect, including us. Accordingly, this section suffers no shortage of relevant examples. We start with a pitfall that traps many designers and reveals an important relationship in computer design.

Pitfall: Expecting the improvement of one aspect of a computer to increase overall performance by an amount proportional to the size of the improvement.

This pitfall has visited designers of both hardware and software. A simple design problem illustrates it well. Suppose a program runs in 100 seconds on a computer, with multiply operations responsible for 80 seconds of this time. How much do I have to improve the speed of multiplication if I want my program to run five times faster?

The execution time of the program after making the improvement is given by the following simple equation known as **Amdahl's law:**

$$\text{Execution time after improvement} =$$

$$\frac{\text{Execution time affected by improvement}}{\text{Amount of improvement}} + \text{Execution time unaffected}$$

Amdahl's law A rule stating that the performance enhancement possible with a given improvement is limited by the amount that the improved feature is used. It is a quantitative version of the law of diminishing returns.

For this problem:

$$\text{Execution time after improvement} = \frac{80 \text{ seconds}}{n} + (100 - 80 \text{ seconds})$$

Since we want the performance to be five times faster, the new execution time should be 20 seconds, giving

$$20 \text{ seconds} = \frac{80 \text{ seconds}}{n} + 20 \text{ seconds}$$

$$0 = \frac{80 \text{ seconds}}{n}$$

That is, there is *no amount* by which we can enhance-multiply to achieve a fivefold increase in performance, if multiply accounts for only 80% of the workload.

The performance enhancement possible with a given improvement is limited by the amount that the improved feature is used. This concept also yields what we call the law of diminishing returns in everyday life.

We can use Amdahl's law to estimate performance improvements when we know the time consumed for some function and its potential speedup. Amdahl's law, together with the CPU performance equation, is a handy tool for evaluating potential enhancements. Amdahl's law is explored in more detail in the exercises.

A common theme in hardware design is a corollary of Amdahl's law: *Make the common case fast.* This simple guideline reminds us that in many cases the frequency with which one event occurs may be much higher than the frequency of another. Amdahl's law reminds us that the opportunity for improvement is affected by how much time the event consumes. Thus, making the common case fast will tend to enhance performance better than optimizing the rare case. Ironically, the common case is often simpler than the rare case and hence is often easier to enhance.

Amdahl's law is also used to argue for practical limits to the number of parallel processors. We examine this argument in the Fallacies and Pitfalls section of Chapter 7.

Fallacy: Computers at low utilization use little power.

Power efficiency matters at low utilizations because server workloads vary. CPU utilization for servers at Google, for example, is between 10% and 50% most of the time and at 100% less than 1% of the time. Figure 1.22 shows power for servers with the best SPECpower results at 100% load, 50% load, 10% load, and idle. Even servers that are only 10% utilized burn about two-thirds of their peak power.

Since servers' workloads vary but use a large fraction of peak power, Luiz Barroso and Urs Hölzle [2007] argue that we should redesign hardware to achieve "energy-proportional computing." If future servers used, say, 10% of peak power at 10% workload, we could reduce the electricity bill of datacenters and become good corporate citizens in an era of increasing concern about CO_2 emissions.

Server Manufacturer	Micro-processor	Total Cores/ Sockets	Clock Rate	Peak Performance (ssj_ops)	100% Load Power	50% Load Power	50% Load/ 100% Power	10% Load Power	10% Load/ 100% Power	Active Idle Power	Active Idle/ 100% Power
HP	Xeon E5440	8/2	3.0 GHz	308,022	269 W	227 W	84%	174 W	65%	160 W	59%
Dell	Xeon E5440	8/2	2.8 GHz	305,413	276 W	230 W	83%	173 W	63%	157 W	57%
Fujitsu Seimens	Xeon X3220	4/1	2.4 GHz	143,742	132 W	110 W	83%	85 W	65%	80 W	60%

FIGURE 1.22   SPECPower results for three servers with the best overall ssj_ops per watt in the fourth quarter of 2007. The overall ssj_ops per watt of the three servers are 698, 682, and 667, respectively. The memory of the top two servers is 16 GB and the bottom is 8 GB.

Pitfall: Using a subset of the performance equation as a performance metric.

We have already shown the fallacy of predicting performance based on simply one of clock rate, instruction count, or CPI. Another common mistake is to use only two of the three factors to compare performance. Although using two of the three factors may be valid in a limited context, the concept is also easily misused. Indeed, nearly all proposed alternatives to the use of time as the performance metric have led eventually to misleading claims, distorted results, or incorrect interpretations.

One alternative to time is **MIPS (million instructions per second)**. For a given program, MIPS is simply

$$\text{MIPS} = \frac{\text{Instruction count}}{\text{Execution time} \times 10^6}$$

Since MIPS is an instruction execution rate, MIPS specifies performance inversely to execution time; faster computers have a higher MIPS rating. The good news about MIPS is that it is easy to understand, and faster computers mean bigger MIPS, which matches intuition.

There are three problems with using MIPS as a measure for comparing computers. First, MIPS specifies the instruction execution rate but does not take into account the capabilities of the instructions. We cannot compare computers with different instruction sets using MIPS, since the instruction counts will certainly differ. Second, MIPS varies between programs on the same computer; thus, a computer cannot have a single MIPS rating. For example, by substituting for execution time, we see the relationship between MIPS, clock rate, and CPI:

$$\text{MIPS} = \frac{\text{Instruction count}}{\dfrac{\text{Instruction count} \times \text{CPI}}{\text{Clock rate}} \times 10^6} = \frac{\text{Clock rate}}{\text{CPI} \times 10^6}$$

Recall that CPI varied by 13× for SPEC CPU2006 on Opteron X4, so MIPS does as well. Finally, and most importantly, if a new program executes more instructions but each instruction is faster, MIPS can vary independently from performance!

million instructions per second (MIPS) A measurement of program execution speed based on the number of millions of instructions. MIPS is computed as the instruction count divided by the product of the execution time and 10^6.

Consider the following performance measurements for a program:

Check Yourself

Measurement	Computer A	Computer B
Instruction count	10 billion	8 billion
Clock rate	4 GHz	4 GHz
CPI	1.0	1.1

a. Which computer has the higher MIPS rating?

b. Which computer is faster?

1.9 Concluding Remarks

Although it is difficult to predict exactly what level of cost/performance computers will have in the future, it's a safe bet that they will be much better than they are today. To participate in these advances, computer designers and programmers must understand a wider variety of issues.

Both hardware and software designers construct computer systems in hierarchical layers, with each lower layer hiding details from the level above. This principle of abstraction is fundamental to understanding today's computer systems, but it does not mean that designers can limit themselves to knowing a single abstraction. Perhaps the most important example of abstraction is the interface between hardware and low-level software, called the *instruction set architecture*. Maintaining the instruction set architecture as a constant enables many implementations of that architecture—presumably varying in cost and performance—to run identical software. On the downside, the architecture may preclude introducing innovations that require the interface to change.

There is a reliable method of determining and reporting performance by using the execution time of real programs as the metric. This execution time is related to other important measurements we can make by the following equation:

$$\frac{\text{Seconds}}{\text{Program}} = \frac{\text{Instructions}}{\text{Program}} \times \frac{\text{Clock cycles}}{\text{Instruction}} \times \frac{\text{Seconds}}{\text{Clock cycle}}$$

We will use this equation and its constituent factors many times. Remember, though, that individually the factors do not determine performance: only the product, which equals execution time, is a reliable measure of performance.

The BIG Picture

Execution time is the only valid and unimpeachable measure of performance. Many other metrics have been proposed and found wanting. Sometimes these metrics are flawed from the start by not reflecting execution time; other times a metric that is valid in a limited context is extended and used beyond that context or without the additional clarification needed to make it valid.

The key hardware technology for modern processors is silicon. Equal in importance to an understanding of integrated circuit technology is an understanding of the expected rates of technological change. While silicon fuels the rapid advance of hardware, new ideas in the organization of computers have improved price/performance. Two of the key ideas are exploiting parallelism in the program, typically today via multiple processors, and exploiting locality of accesses to a memory hierarchy, typically via caches.

Power has replaced die area as the most critical resource of microprocessor design. Conserving power while trying to increase performance has forced the hardware industry to switch to multicore microprocessors, thereby forcing the software industry to switch to programming parallel hardware.

Computer designs have always been measured by cost and performance, as well as other important factors such as power, reliability, cost of ownership, and scalability. Although this chapter has focused on cost, performance, and power, the best designs will strike the appropriate balance for a given market among all the factors.

Road Map for This Book

At the bottom of these abstractions are the five classic components of a computer: datapath, control, memory, input, and output (refer to Figure 1.4). These five components also serve as the framework for the rest of the chapters in this book:

- *Datapath:* Chapters 3, 4, 7, and Appendix A

- *Control:* Chapters 4, 7, and Appendix A

- *Memory:* Chapter 5

- *Input:* Chapter 6

- *Output:* Chapter 6

As mentioned above, Chapter 4 describes how processors exploit implicit parallelism, Chapter 7 describes the explicitly parallel multicore microprocessors that are at the heart of the parallel revolution, and Appendix A describes the highly parallel graphics processor chip. Chapter 5 describes how a memory hierarchy exploits locality. Chapter 2 describes instruction sets—the interface between compilers and the computer—and emphasizes the role of compilers and programming languages in using the features of the instruction set. Appendix B provides a reference for the instruction set of Chapter 2. Chapter 3 describes how computers handle arithmetic data. ⊚ **Appendix C**, on the CD, introduces logic design.

Historical Perspective and Further Reading

For each chapter in the text, a section devoted to a historical perspective can be found on the CD that accompanies this book. We may trace the development of an idea through a series of computers or describe some important projects, and we provide references in case you are interested in probing further.

An active field of science is like an immense anthill; the individual almost vanishes into the mass of minds tumbling over each other, carrying information from place to place, passing it around at the speed of light.

Lewis Thomas, "Natural Science," in *The Lives of a Cell,* 1974

The historical perspective for this chapter provides a background for some of the key ideas presented in this opening chapter. Its purpose is to give you the human story behind the technological advances and to place achievements in their historical context. By understanding the past, you may be better able to understand the forces that will shape computing in the future. Each historical perspectives section on the CD ends with suggestions for further reading, which are also collected separately on the CD under the section "**Further Reading**." The rest of **Section 1.10** is found on the CD.

1.11 Exercises

Contributed by Javier Bruguera of Universidade de Santiago de Compostela

Most of the exercises in this edition are designed so that they feature a qualitative description supported by a table that provides alternative quantitative parameters. These parameters are needed to solve the questions that comprise the exercise. Individual questions can be solved using any or all of the parameters—you decide how many of the parameters should be considered for any given exercise question. For example, it is possible to say "complete Question 4.1.1 using the parameters given in row A of the table." Alternately, instructors can customize these exercises to create novel solutions by replacing the given parameters with your own unique values.

The number of quantitative exercises varies from chapter to chapter and depends largely on the topics covered. More conventional exercises are provided where the quantitative approach does not fit.

The relative time ratings of exercises are shown in square brackets after each exercise number. On average, an exercise rated [10] will take you twice as long as one rated [5]. Sections of the text that should be read before attempting an exercise will be given in angled brackets; for example, <1.3> means you should have read Section 1.3, Under the Covers, to help you solve this exercise.

Exercise 1.1

Find the word or phrase from the list below that best matches the description in the following questions. Use the numbers to the left of words in the answer. Each answer should be used only once.

1.	virtual worlds	**14.**	operating system
2.	desktop computers	**15.**	compiler
3.	servers	**16.**	bit
4.	low-end servers	**17.**	instruction
5.	supercomputers	**18.**	assembly language
6.	terabyte	**19.**	machine language
7.	petabyte	**20.**	C
8.	data centers	**21.**	assembler
9.	embedded computers	**22.**	high-level language
10.	multicore processors	**23.**	system software
11.	VHDL	**24.**	application software
12.	RAM	**25.**	Cobol
13.	CPU	**26.**	Fortran

1.1.1 [2] <1.1> Computer used to run large problems and usually accessed via a network

1.1.2 [2] <1.1> 10^{15} or 2^{50} bytes

1.1.3 [2] <1.1> A class of computers composed of hundred to thousand processors and terabytes of memory and having the highest performance and cost

1.1.4 [2] <1.1> Today's science fiction application that probably will be available in the near future

1.1.5 [2] <1.1> A kind of memory called random access memory

1.1.6 [2] <1.1> Part of a computer called central processor unit

1.1.7 [2] <1.1> Thousands of processors forming a large cluster

1.1.8 [2] <1.1> Microprocessors containing several processors in the same chip

1.1.9 [2] <1.1> Desktop computer without a screen or keyboard usually accessed via a network

1.1.10 [2] <1.1> A computer used to running one predetermined application or collection of software

1.1.11 [2] <1.1> Special language used to describe hardware components

1.1.12 [2] <1.1> Personal computer delivering good performance to single users at low cost

1.1.13 [2] <1.2> Program that translates statements in high-level language to assembly language

1.1.14 [2] <1.2> Program that translates symbolic instructions to binary instructions

1.1.15 [2] <1.2> High-level language for business data processing

1.1.16 [2] <1.2> Binary language that the processor can understand

1.1.17 [2] <1.2> Commands that the processors understand

1.1.18 [2] <1.2> High-level language for scientific computation

1.1.19 [2] <1.2> Symbolic representation of machine instructions

1.1.20 [2] <1.2> Interface between user's program and hardware providing a variety of services and supervision functions

1.1.21 [2] <1.2> Software/programs developed by the users

1.1.22 [2] <1.2> Binary digit (value 0 or 1)

1.1.23 [2] <1.2> Software layer between the application software and the hardware that includes the operating system and the compilers

1.1.24 [2] <1.2> High-level language used to write application and system software

1.1.25 [2] <1.2> Portable language composed of words and algebraic expressions that must be translated into assembly language before run in a computer

1.1.26 [2] <1.2> 10^{12} or 2^{40} bytes

Exercise 1.2

Consider the different configurations shown in the table

	Configuration	Resolution	Main Memory	Ethernet Network
a.	1	640 × 480	2 Gbytes	100 Mbit
	2	1280 × 1024	4 Gbytes	1 Gbit
b.	1	1024 × 768	2 Gbytes	100 Mbit
	2	2560 × 1600	4 Gbytes	1Gbit

1.2.1 [10] <1.3> For a color display using 8 bits for each of the primary colors (red, green, blue) per pixel, what should be the minimum size in bytes of the frame buffer to store a frame?

1.2.2 [5] <1.3> How many frames could it store, assuming the memory contains no other information?

1.2.3 [5] <1.3> If a 256 Kbytes file is sent through the Ethernet connection, how long it would take?

For problems below, use the information about access time for every type of memory in the following table.

	Cache	DRAM	Flash Memory	Magnetic Disk
a.	5 ns	50 ns	5 µs	5 ms
b.	7 ns	70 ns	15 µs	20 ms

1.2.4 [5] <1.3> Find how long it takes to read a file from a DRAM if it takes 2 microseconds from the cache memory.

1.2.5 [5] <1.3> Find how long it takes to read a file from a disk if it takes 2 microseconds from the cache memory.

1.2.6 [5] <1.3> Find how long it takes to read a file from a flash memory if it takes 2 microseconds from the cache memory.

Exercise 1.3

Consider three different processors P1, P2, and P3 executing the same instruction set with the clock rates and CPIs given in the following table.

	Processor	Clock Rate	CPI
a.	P1	3 GHz	1.5
	P2	2.5 GHz	1.0
	P3	4 GHz	2.2
b.	P1	2 GHz	1.2
	P2	3 GHz	0.8
	P3	4 GHz	2.0

1.3.1 [5] <1.4> Which processor has the highest performance expressed in instructions per second?

1.3.2 [10] <1.4> If the processors each execute a program in 10 seconds, find the number of cycles and the number of instructions.

1.3.3 [10] <1.4> We are trying to reduce the time by 30% but this leads to an increase of 20% in the CPI. What clock rate should we have to get this time reduction?

For problems below, use the information in the following table.

	Processor	Clock Rate	No. Instructions	Time
a.	P1	3 GHz	20.00E+09	7 s
	P2	2.5 GHz	30.00E+09	10 s
	P3	4 GHz	90.00E+09	9 s
b.	P1	2 GHz	20.00E+09	5 s
	P2	3 GHz	30.00E+09	8 s
	P3	4 GHz	25.00E+09	7 s

1.3.4 [10] <1.4> Find the IPC (instructions per cycle) for each processor.

1.3.5 [5] <1.4> Find the clock rate for P2 that reduces its execution time to that of P1.

1.3.6 [5] <1.4> Find the number of instructions for P2 that reduces its execution time to that of P3.

Exercise 1.4

Consider two different implementations of the same instruction set architecture. There are four classes of instructions, A, B, C, and D. The clock rate and CPI of each implementation are given in the following table.

		Clock Rate	CPI Class A	CPI Class B	CPI Class C	CPI Class D
a.	P1	2.5 GHz	1	2	3	3
	P2	3 GHz	2	2	2	2
b.	P1	2.5 GHz	2	1.5	2	1
	P2	3 GHz	1	2	1	1

1.4.1 [10] <1.4> Given a program with 10^6 instructions divided into classes as follows: 10% class A, 20% class B, 50% class C, and 20% class D, which implementation is faster?

1.4.2 [5] <1.4> What is the global CPI for each implementation?

1.4.3 [5] <1.4> Find the clock cycles required in both cases.

The following table shows the number of instructions for a program.

	Arith	Store	Load	Branch	Total
a.	650	100	600	50	1400
b.	750	250	500	500	2000

1.4.4 [5] <1.4> Assuming that arith instructions take 1 cycle, load and store 5 cycles, and branches 2 cycles, what is the execution time of the program in a 2 GHz processor?

1.4.5 [5] <1.4> Find the CPI for the program.

1.4.6 [10] <1.4> If the number of load instructions can be reduced by one half, what is the speedup and the CPI?

Exercise 1.5

Consider two different implementations, P1 and P2, of the same instruction set. There are five classes of instructions (A, B, C, D, and E) in the instruction set. The clock rate and CPI of each class is given below.

		Clock Rate	CPI Class A	CPI Class B	CPI Class C	CPI Class D	CPI Class E
a.	P1	2.0 GHz	1	2	3	4	3
	P2	4.0 GHz	2	2	2	4	4
b.	P1	2.0 GHz	1	1	2	3	2
	P2	3.0 GHz	1	2	3	4	3

1.5.1 [5] <1.4> Assume that peak performance is defined as the fastest rate that a computer can execute any instruction sequence. What are the peak performances of P1 and P2 expressed in instructions per second?

1.5.2 [10] <1.4> If the number of instructions executed in a certain program is divided equally among the classes of instructions except for class A, which occurs twice as often as each of the others, which computer is faster? How much faster is it?

1.5.3 [10] <1.4> If the number of instructions executed in a certain program is divided equally among the classes of instructions except for class E, which occurs twice as often as each of the others, which computer is faster? How much faster is it?

The table below shows instruction-type breakdown for different programs. Using this data, you will be exploring the performance trade-offs for different changes made to an MIPS processor.

		No. Instructions				
		Compute	Load	Store	Branch	Total
a.	Program1	600	600	200	50	1450
b.	Program 2	900	500	100	200	1700

1.5.4 [5] <1.4> Assuming that computes take 1 cycle, loads and store instructions take 10 cycles, and branches take 3 cycles, find the execution time on a 3 GHz MIPS processor.

1.5.5 [5] <1.4> Assuming that computes take 1 cycle, loads and store instructions take 2 cycles, and branches take 3 cycles, find the execution time on a 3 GHz MIPS processor.

1.5.6 [5] <1.4> Assuming that computes take 1 cycle, loads and store instructions take 2 cycles, and branches take 3 cycles, what is the speedup if the number of compute instruction can be reduced by one-half?

Exercise 1.6

Compilers can have a profound impact on the performance of an application on given a processor. This problem will explore the impact compilers have on execution time.

	Compiler A		Compiler B	
	No. Instructions	Execution Time	No. Instructions	Execution Time
a.	1.00E+09	1.8 s	1.20E+09	1.8 s
b.	1.00E+09	1.1 s	1.20E+09	1.5 s

1.6.1 [5] <1.4> For the same program, two different compilers are used. The table above shows the execution time of the two different compiled programs. Find the average CPI for each program given that the processor has a clock cycle time of 1 ns.

1.6.2 [5] <1.4> Assume the average CPIs found in 1.6.1, but that the compiled programs run on two different processors. If the execution times on the two processors are the same, how much faster is the clock of the processor running compiler A's code versus the clock of the processor running compiler B's code?

1.6.3 [5] <1.4> A new compiler is developed that uses only 600 million instructions and has an average CPI of 1.1. What is the speedup of using this new compiler versus using Compiler A or B on the original processor of 1.6.1?

Consider two different implementations, P1 and P2, of the same instruction set. There are five classes of instructions (A, B, C, D, and E) in the instruction set. P1 has a clock rate of 4 GHz, and P2 has a clock rate of 6 GHz. The average number of cycles for each instruction class for P1 and P2 are listed in the following table.

		CPI Class A	CPI Class B	CPI Class C	CPI Class D	CPI Class E
a.	P1	1	2	3	4	5
	P2	3	3	3	5	5
b.	P1	1	2	3	4	5
	P2	2	2	2	2	6

1.6.4 [5] <1.4> Assume that peak performance is defined as the fastest rate that a computer can execute any instruction sequence. What are the peak performances of P1 and P2 expressed in instructions per second?

1.6.5 [5] <1.4> If the number of instructions executed in a certain program is divided equally among the five classes of instructions except for class A, which occurs twice as often as each of the others, how much faster is P2 than P1?

1.6.6 [5] <1.4> At what frequency does P1 have the same performance of P2 for the instruction mix given in 1.6.5?

Exercise 1.7

The following table shows the increase in clock rate and power of eight generations of Intel processors over 28 years.

Processor	Clock Rate	Power
80286 (1982)	12.5 MHz	3.3 W
80386 (1985)	16 MHz	4.1 W
80486 (1989)	25 MHz	4.9 W
Pentium (1993)	66 MHz	10.1 W
Pentium Pro (1997)	200 MHz	29.1 W
Pentium 4 Willamette (2001)	2 GHz	75.3 W
Pentium 4 Prescott (2004)	3.6 GHz	103 W
Core 2 Ketsfield (2007)	2.667 GHz	95 W

1.7.1 [5] <1.5> What is the geometric mean of the ratios between consecutive generations for both clock rate and power? (The geometric mean is described in Section 1.7.)

1.7.2 [5] <1.5> What is the largest relative change in clock rate and power between generations?

1.7.3 [5] <1.5> How much larger is the clock rate and power of the last generation with respect to the first generation?

Consider the following values for voltage in each generation.

Processor	Voltage
80286 (1982)	5
80386 (1985)	5
80486 (1989)	5
Pentium (1993)	5
Pentium Pro (1997)	3.3
Pentium 4 Willamette (2001)	1.75
Pentium 4 Prescott (2004)	1.25
Core 2 Ketsfield (2007)	1.1

1.7.4 [5] <1.5> Find the average capacitive loads, assuming a negligible static power consumption.

1.7.5 [5] <1.5> Find the largest relative change in voltage between generations.

1.7.6 [5] <1.5> Find the geometric mean of the voltage ratios in the generations since the Pentium.

Exercise 1.8

Suppose we have developed new versions of a processor with the following characteristics.

	Version	Voltage	Clock Rate
a.	Version 1	1.75 V	1.5 GHz
	Version 2	1.2 V	2 GHz
b.	Version 1	1.1 V	3 GHz
	Version 2	0.8 V	4 GHz

1.8.1 [5] <1.5> How much has the capacitive load varied between versions if the dynamic power has been reduced by 10%?

1.8.2 [5] <1.5> How much has the dynamic power been reduced if the capacitive load does not change?

1.8.3 [10] <1.5> Assuming that the capacitive load of version 2 is 80% the capacitive load of version 1, find the voltage for version 2 if the dynamic power of version 2 is reduced by 40% from version 1.

Suppose that the industry trends show that a new process generation varies as follows.

	Capacitance	Voltage	Clock Rate	Area
a.	1	$1/2^{1/2}$	1.15	$1/2^{1/2}$
b.	1	$1/2^{1/4}$	1.2	$1/2^{1/4}$

1.8.4 [5] <1.5> Find the scaling factor for the dynamic power.

1.8.5 [5] <1.5> Find the scaling of the capacitance per unit area unit.

1.8.6 [5] <1.5> Assuming a Core 2 processor with a clock rate of 2.667 GHz, a power consumption of 95 W, and a voltage of 1.1 V, find the voltage and clock rate of this processor for the next process generation.

Exercise 1.9

Although the dynamic power is the primary source of power dissipation in CMOS, leakage current produces a static power dissipation $V \times I_{leak}$. The smaller the on-chip dimensions, the more significant is the static power. Assume the figures shown in the following table for static and dynamic power dissipation for several generations of processors.

	Technology	Dynamic Power (W)	Static Power (W)	Voltage (V)
a.	180 nm	50	10	1.2
b.	70 nm	90	60	0.9

1.9.1 [5] <1.5> Find the percentage of the total dissipated power comprised by static power.

1.9.2 [5] <1.5> If the total dissipated power is reduced by 10% while maintaining the static to total power rate of problem 1.9.1, how much should the voltage be reduced to maintain the same leakage current?

1.9.3 [5] <1.5> Determine the ratio of static power to dynamic power for each technology.

Consider now the dynamic power dissipation of different versions of a given processor for three different voltages given in the following table.

	1.2 V	1.0 V	0.8 V
a.	75 W	60 W	35 W
b.	62 W	50 W	30 W

1.9.4 [5] <1.5> Determine the static power at 0.8 V, assuming a static to dynamic power ratio of 0.6.

1.9.5 [5] <1.5> Determine the static and dynamic power dissipation assuming the rates obtained in problem 1.9.1.

1.9.6 [10] <1.5> Determine the geometric mean of the power variations between versions.

Exercise 1.10

The table below shows the instruction type breakdown of a given application executed on 1, 2, 4, or 8 processors. Using this data, you will be exploring the speed-up of applications on parallel processors.

	Processors	No. Instructions per Processor			CPI		
		Arithmetic	Load/Store	Branch	Arithmetic	Load/Store	Branch
a.	1	2560	1280	256	1	4	2
	2	1280	640	128	1	5	2
	4	640	320	64	1	7	2
	8	320	160	32	1	12	2

	Processors	No. Instructions per Processor			CPI		
		Arithmetic	Load/Store	Branch	Arithmetic	Load/Store	Branch
b.	1	2560	1280	256	1	4	2
	2	1280	640	128	1	6	2
	4	640	320	64	1	8	2
	8	320	160	32	1	10	2

1.10.1 [5] <1.4, 1.6> The table above shows the number of instructions required per processor to complete a program on a multiprocessor with 1, 2, 4, or 8 processors. What is the total number of instructions executed per processor? What is the aggregate number of instructions executed across all processors?

1.10.2 [5] <1.4, 1.6> Given the CPI values on the right of the table above, find the total execution time for this program on 1, 2, 4, and 8 processors. Assume that each processor has a 2 GHz clock frequency.

1.10.3 [10] <1.4, 1.6> If the CPI of the arithmetic instructions was doubled, what would the impact be on the execution time of the program on 1, 2, 4, or 8 processors?

The table below shows the number of instructions per processor core on a multicore processor as well as the average CPI for executing the program on 1, 2, 4, or 8 cores. Using this data, you will be exploring the speedup of applications on multicore processors.

	Cores per Processor	Instructions per Core	Average CPI
a.	1	1.00E+10	1.2
	2	5.00E+09	1.4
	4	2.50E+09	1.8
	8	1.25E+09	2.6

	Cores per Processor	Instructions per Core	Average CPI
b.	1	1.00E+10	1.0
	2	5.00E+09	1.2
	4	2.50E+09	1.4
	8	1.25E+09	1.7

1.10.4 [10] <1.4, 1.6> Assuming a 3 GHz clock frequency, what is the execution time of the program using 1, 2, 4, or 8 cores?

1.10.5 [10] <1.5, 1.6> Assume that the power consumption of a processor core can be described by the following equation:

$$\text{Power} = \frac{5.0\text{mA}}{\text{MHz}}\,\text{Voltage}^2$$

where the operation voltage of the processor is described by the following equation:

$$\text{Voltage} = \frac{1}{5}\text{Frequency} + 0.4$$

with the frequency measured in GHz. So, at 5 GHz, the voltage would be 1.4 V. Find the power consumption of the program executing on 1, 2, 4, and 8 cores assuming that each core is operating at a 3 GHz clock frequency. Likewise, find the power consumption of the program executing on 1, 2, 4, or 8 cores assuming that each core is operating at 500 MHz.

1.10.6 [10] <1.5, 1.6> If using a single core, find the required CPI for this core to get an execution time equal to the time obtained by using the number of cores in the table above (execution times in problem 1.10.4). Note that the number of instructions should be the aggregate number of instructions executed across all the cores.

Exercise 1.11

The following table shows manufacturing data for various processors.

	Wafer Diameter	Dies per Wafer	Defects per Unit Area	Cost per Wafer
a.	15 cm	84	0.020 defects/cm²	12
b.	20 cm	100	0.031 defects/cm²	15

1.11.1 [10] <1.7> Find the yield.

1.11.2 [5] <1.7> Find the cost per die.

1.11.3 [10] <1.7> If the number of dies per wafer is increased by 10% and the defects per area unit increases by 15%, find the die area and yield.

Suppose that, with the evolution of the electronic devices manufacturing technology, the yield varies as shown in the following table.

	T1	T2	T3	T4
Yield	0.85	0.89	0.92	0.95

1.11.4 [10] <1.7> Find the defects per area unit for each technology given a die area of 200 mm².

1.11.5 [5] <1.7> Represent graphically the variation of the yield together with the variation of defects per unit area.

Exercise 1.12

The following table shows results for SPEC CPU2006 benchmark programs running on an AMD Barcelona.

	Name	Intr. Count × 10⁹	Execution Time (seconds)	Reference Time (seconds)
a.	bzip2	2389	750	9650
b.	go	1658	700	10,490

1.12.1 [5] <1.7> Find the CPI if the clock cycle time is 0.333 ns.

1.12.2 [5] <1.7> Find the SPECratio.

1.12.3 [5] <1.7> For these two benchmarks, find the geometric mean of the SPECratio.

The following table shows data for further benchmarks.

	Name	CPI	Clock Rate	SPECratio
a.	libquantum	1.61	4 GHz	19.8
b.	astar	1.79	4 GHz	9.1

1.12.4 [5] <1.7> Find the increase in CPU time if the number of instructions of the benchmark is increased by 10% without affecting the CPI.

1.12.5 [5] <1.7> Find the increase in CPU time if the number of instructions of the benchmark is increased by 10% and the CPI is increased by 5%.

1.12.6 [5] <1.7> Find the change in the SPECratio for the change described in 1.12.5.

Exercise 1.13

Suppose that we are developing a new version of the AMD Barcelona processor with a 4 GHz clock rate. We have added some additional instructions to the instruction set in such a way that the number of instructions has been reduced by 15% from the values shown for each benchmark in Exercise 1.12. The execution times obtained are shown in the following table.

	Name	Execution Time (seconds)	Reference Time (seconds)	SPECratio
a.	bzip2	700	9650	13.7
b.	go	620	10490	16.9

1.13.1 [10] <1.8> Find the new CPI.

1.13.2 [10] <1.8> In general, these CPI values are larger than those obtained in previous exercises for the same benchmarks. This is due mainly to the clock rate used in both cases, 3 GHz and 4 GHz. Determine whether the increase in the CPI is similar to that of the clock rate. If they are dissimilar, why?

1.13.3 [5] <1.8> How much has the CPU time been reduced?

The following table shows data for further benchmarks.

	Name	Execution Time (seconds)	CPI	Clock Rate
a.	libquantum	960	1.61	3 GHz
b.	astar	690	1.79	3 GHz

1.13.4 [10] <1.8> If the execution time is reduced by an additional 10% without affecting to the CPI and with a clock rate of 4 GHz, determine the number of instructions.

1.13.5 [10] <1.8> Determine the clock rate required to give a further 10% reduction in CPU time while maintaining the number of instructions and with the CPI unchanged.

1.13.6 [10] <1.8> Determine the clock rate if the CPI is reduced by 15% and the CPU time by 20% while the number of instructions is unchanged.

Exercise 1.14

Section 1.8 cites as a pitfall the utilization of a subset of the performance equation as a performance metric. To illustrate this, consider the following data for the execution of a program in different processors.

	Processor	Clock Rate	CPI	No. Instr.
a.	P1	4 GHz	0.9	5.00E+06
	P2	3 GHz	0.75	1.00E+06
b.	P1	3 GHz	1.1	3.00E+06
	P2	2.5 GHz	1.0	0.50E+06

1.14.1 [5] <1.8> One usual fallacy is to consider the computer with the largest clock rate as having the largest performance. Check if this is true for P1 and P2.

1.14.2 [10] <1.8> Another fallacy is to consider that the processor executing the largest number of instructions will need a larger CPU time. Considering that processor P1 is executing a sequence of 10^6 instructions and that the CPI of processors P1 and P2 do not change, determine the number of instructions that P2 can execute in the same time that P1 needs to execute 10^6 instructions.

1.14.3 [10] <1.8> A common fallacy is to use MIPS (millions of instructions per second) to compare the performance of two different processors, and consider that the processor with the largest MIPS has the largest performance. Check if this is true for P1 and P2.

Another common performance figure is MFLOPS (million of floating-point operations per second), defined as

MFLOPS = No. FP operations / (execution time × 10^6)

but this figure has the same problems as MIPS. Consider the program in the following table, running on the two processors below.

	Processor	Instr. Count	No. Instructions			CPI			Clock Rate
			L/S	FP	Branch	L/S	FP	Branch	
a.	P1	1.00E+06	50%	40%	10%	0.75	1.0	1.5	4 GHz
	P2	5.00E+06	40%	40%	20%	1.25	0.8	1.25	3 GHz
b.	P1	5.00E+06	30%	30%	40%	1.5	1.0	2.0	4 GHz
	P2	2.00E+06	40%	30%	30%	1.25	1.0	2.5	3 GHz

1.14.4 [10] <1.8> Find the MFLOPS figures for the programs.

1.14.5 [10] <1.8> Find the MIPS figures for the programs.

1.14.6 [10] <1.8> Find the performance for the programs and compare it with MIPS and MFLOPS.

Exercise 1.15

Another pitfall cited in Section 1.8 is expecting to improve the overall performance of a computer by improving only one aspect of the computer. This might be true, but not always. Consider a computer running programs with CPU times shown in the following table.

	FP Instr.	INT Instr.	L/S Instr.	Branch Instr.	Total Time
a.	70 s	85 s	55 s	40 s	250 s
b.	40 s	90 s	60 s	20 s	210 s

1.15.1 [5] <1.8> How much is the total time reduced if the time for FP operations is reduced by 20%?

1.15.2 [5] <1.8> How much is the time for INT operations reduced if the total time is reduced by 20%?

1.15.3 [5] <1.8> Can the total time can be reduced by 20% by reducing only the time for branch instructions?

The following table shows the instruction type breakdown per processor of given applications executed in different numbers of processors.

	Processors	FP Instr.	INT Instr.	L/S Instr.	Branch Instr.	CPI (FP)	CPI (INT)	CPI (L/S)	CPI (Branch)
a.	2	280×10^6	1000×16^6	640×10^6	128×10^6	1	1	4	2
b.	16	50×10^6	110×10^6	80×10^6	16×10^6	1	1	4	2

Assume that each processor has a 2 GHz clock rate.

1.15.4 [10] <1.8> How much must we improve the CPI of FP instructions if we want the program to run two times faster?

1.15.5 [10] <1.8> How much must we improve the CPI of L/S instructions if we want the program to run two times faster?

1.15.6 [5] <1.8> How much is the execution time of the program improved if the CPI of INT and FP instructions is reduced by 40% and the CPI of L/S and Branch is reduced by 30%?

Exercise 1.16

Another pitfall, related to the execution of programs in multiprocessor systems, is expecting improvement in performance by improving only the execution time of part of the routines. The following table shows the execution time of five routines of a program running on different numbers of processors.

	No. Processors	Routine A (ms)	Routine B (ms)	Routine C (ms)	Routine D (ms)	Routine E (ms)
a.	4	12	45	6	36	3
b.	32	2	7	1	6	2

1.16.1 [10] <1.8> Find the total execution time and by how much it is reduced if the time of routines A, C, and E is improved by 15%.

1.16.2 [10] <1.8> How much is the total time reduced if routine B is improved by 10%?

1.16.3 [10] <1.8> How much is the total time reduced if routine D is improved by 10%?

Execution time in a multiprocessor system can be split into computing time for the routines plus routing time spent sending data from one processor to another. Consider the execution time and routing time given in the following table. In this case, the routing time is an important component of the total time.

No. Processors	Routine A (ms)	Routine B (ms)	Routine C (ms)	Routine D (ms)	Routine E (ms)	Routing Time (ms)
2	40	78	9	70	4	11
4	29	60	4	36	2	13
8	15	45	3	19	3	17
16	7	35	1	11	2	22
32	4	23	1	6	1	23
64	2	12	0.5	3	1	26

1.16.4 [10] <1.8> For each doubling of the number of processors, determine the ratio of new to old computing time and the ratio of new to old routing time.

1.16.5 [5] <1.8> Using the geometric means of the ratios, extrapolate to find the computing time and routing time in a 128-processor system.

1.16.6 [10] <1.8> Find the computing time and routing time for a system with one processor.

§1.1, page 9: Discussion questions: many answers are acceptable.
§1.3, page 25: Disk memory: nonvolatile, long access time (milliseconds), and cost $0.20–$2.00/GB. Semiconductor memory: volatile, short access time (nanoseconds), and cost $20–$75/GB.
§1.4, page 31: 1. a: both, b: latency, c: neither. 2. 7 seconds.
§1.4, page 38: b.
§1.7, page 50: 1, 3, and 4 are valid reasons. Answer 5 can be generally true because high volume can make the extra investment to reduce die size by, say, 10% a good economic decision, but it doesn't have to be true.
§1.8, page 53: a. Computer A has the higher MIPS rating. b. Computer B is faster.

Answers to Check Yourself

2

Instructions: Language of the Computer

I speak Spanish to God, Italian to women, French to men, and German to my horse.

Charles V, Holy Roman Emperor
(1500–1558)

The Five Classic Components of a Computer

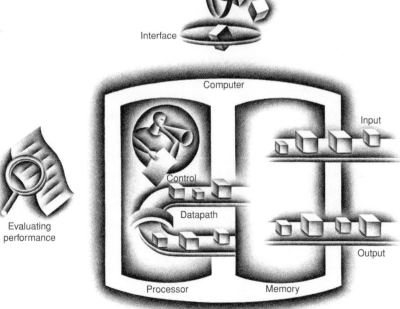

2.1   Introduction

instruction set The
vocabulary of commands
understood by a given
architecture.

To command a computer's hardware, you must speak its language. The words of a computer's language are called *instructions*, and its vocabulary is called an **instruction set**. In this chapter, you will see the instruction set of a real computer, both in the form written by people and in the form read by the computer. We introduce instructions in a top-down fashion. Starting from a notation that looks like a restricted programming language, we refine it step-by-step until you see the real language of a real computer. Chapter 3 continues our downward descent, unveiling the hardware for arithmetic and the representation of floating-point numbers.

You might think that the languages of computers would be as diverse as those of people, but in reality computer languages are quite similar, more like regional dialects than like independent languages. Hence, once you learn one, it is easy to pick up others. This similarity occurs because all computers are constructed from hardware technologies based on similar underlying principles and because there are a few basic operations that all computers must provide. Moreover, computer designers have a common goal: to find a language that makes it easy to build the hardware and the compiler while maximizing performance and minimizing cost and power. This goal is time honored; the following quote was written before you could buy a computer, and it is as true today as it was in 1947:

> *It is easy to see by formal-logical methods that there exist certain [instruction sets] that are in abstract adequate to control and cause the execution of any sequence of operations. . . . The really decisive considerations from the present point of view, in selecting an [instruction set], are more of a practical nature: simplicity of the equipment demanded by the [instruction set], and the clarity of its application to the actually important problems together with the speed of its handling of those problems.*

> Burks, Goldstine, and von Neumann, 1947

The "simplicity of the equipment" is as valuable a consideration for today's computers as it was for those of the 1950s. The goal of this chapter is to teach an instruction set that follows this advice, showing both how it is represented in hardware and the relationship between high-level programming languages and this more primitive one. Our examples are in the C programming language; ⊙ Section 2.15 on the CD shows how these would change for an object-oriented language like Java.

By learning how to represent instructions, you will also discover the secret of computing: the **stored-program concept**. Moreover, you will exercise your "foreign language" skills by writing programs in the language of the computer and running them on the simulator that comes with this book. You will also see the impact of programming languages and compiler optimization on performance. We conclude with a look at the historical evolution of instruction sets and an overview of other computer dialects.

The chosen instruction set comes from MIPS Technologies, which is an elegant example of the instruction sets designed since the 1980s. Later, we will take a quick look at two other popular instruction sets. ARM is quite similar to MIPS, and more than three billion ARM processors were shipped in embedded devices in 2008. The other example, the Intel x86, is inside almost all of the 330 million PCs made in 2008.

We reveal the MIPS instruction set a piece at a time, giving the rationale along with the computer structures. This top-down, step-by-step tutorial weaves the components with their explanations, making the computer's language more palatable. Figure 2.1 gives a sneak preview of the instruction set covered in this chapter.

> **stored-program concept** The idea that instructions and data of many types can be stored in memory as numbers, leading to the stored-program computer.

2.2   Operations of the Computer Hardware

Every computer must be able to perform arithmetic. The MIPS assembly language notation

```
add a, b, c
```

instructs a computer to add the two variables b and c and to put their sum in a.

This notation is rigid in that each MIPS arithmetic instruction performs only one operation and must always have exactly three variables. For example, suppose we want to place the sum of four variables b, c, d, and e into variable a. (In this section we are being deliberately vague about what a "variable" is; in the next section we'll explain in detail.)

The following sequence of instructions adds the four variables:

```
add a, b, c    # The sum of b and c is placed in a.
add a, a, d    # The sum of b, c, and d is now in a.
add a, a, e    # The sum of b, c, d, and e is now in a.
```

Thus, it takes three instructions to sum the four variables.

The words to the right of the sharp symbol (#) on each line above are *comments* for the human reader, and the computer ignores them. Note that unlike other programming languages, each line of this language can contain at most one instruction. Another difference from C is that comments always terminate at the end of a line.

> *There must certainly be instructions for performing the fundamental arithmetic operations.*
>
> Burks, Goldstine, and von Neumann, 1947

MIPS operands

Name	Example	Comments
32 registers	$s0-$s7, $t0-$t9, $zero, $a0-$a3, $v0-$v1, $gp, $fp, $sp, $ra, $at	Fast locations for data. In MIPS, data must be in registers to perform arithmetic, register $zero always equals 0, and register $at is reserved by the assembler to handle large constants.
2^{30} memory words	Memory[0], Memory[4], . . . , Memory[4294967292]	Accessed only by data transfer instructions. MIPS uses byte addresses, so sequential word addresses differ by 4. Memory holds data structures, arrays, and spilled registers.

MIPS assembly language

Category	Instruction	Example	Meaning	Comments
Arithmetic	add	add $s1,$s2,$s3	$s1 = $s2 + $s3	Three register operands
	subtract	sub $s1,$s2,$s3	$s1 = $s2 – $s3	Three register operands
	add immediate	addi $s1,$s2,20	$s1 = $s2 + 20	Used to add constants
Data transfer	load word	lw $s1,20($s2)	$s1 = Memory[$s2 + 20]	Word from memory to register
	store word	sw $s1,20($s2)	Memory[$s2 + 20] = $s1	Word from register to memory
	load half	lh $s1,20($s2)	$s1 = Memory[$s2 + 20]	Halfword memory to register
	load half unsigned	lhu $s1,20($s2)	$s1 = Memory[$s2 + 20]	Halfword memory to register
	store half	sh $s1,20($s2)	Memory[$s2 + 20] = $s1	Halfword register to memory
	load byte	lb $s1,20($s2)	$s1 = Memory[$s2 + 20]	Byte from memory to register
	load byte unsigned	lbu $s1,20($s2)	$s1 = Memory[$s2 + 20]	Byte from memory to register
	store byte	sb $s1,20($s2)	Memory[$s2 + 20] = $s1	Byte from register to memory
	load linked word	ll $s1,20($s2)	$s1 = Memory[$s2 + 20]	Load word as 1st half of atomic swap
	store condition. word	sc $s1,20($s2)	Memory[$s2+20]=$s1;$s1=0 or 1	Store word as 2nd half of atomic swap
	load upper immed.	lui $s1,20	$s1 = 20 * 2^{16}	Loads constant in upper 16 bits
Logical	and	and $s1,$s2,$s3	$s1 = $s2 & $s3	Three reg. operands; bit-by-bit AND
	or	or $s1,$s2,$s3	$s1 = $s2 | $s3	Three reg. operands; bit-by-bit OR
	nor	nor $s1,$s2,$s3	$s1 = ~ ($s2 | $s3)	Three reg. operands; bit-by-bit NOR
	and immediate	andi $s1,$s2,20	$s1 = $s2 & 20	Bit-by-bit AND reg with constant
	or immediate	ori $s1,$s2,20	$s1 = $s2 | 20	Bit-by-bit OR reg with constant
	shift left logical	sll $s1,$s2,10	$s1 = $s2 << 10	Shift left by constant
	shift right logical	srl $s1,$s2,10	$s1 = $s2 >> 10	Shift right by constant
Conditional branch	branch on equal	beq $s1,$s2,25	if ($s1 == $s2) go to PC + 4 + 100	Equal test; PC-relative branch
	branch on not equal	bne $s1,$s2,25	if ($s1!= $s2) go to PC + 4 + 100	Not equal test; PC-relative
	set on less than	slt $s1,$s2,$s3	if ($s2 < $s3) $s1 = 1; else $s1 = 0	Compare less than; for beq, bne
	set on less than unsigned	sltu $s1,$s2,$s3	if ($s2 < $s3) $s1 = 1; else $s1 = 0	Compare less than unsigned
	set less than immediate	slti $s1,$s2,20	if ($s2 < 20) $s1 = 1; else $s1 = 0	Compare less than constant
	set less than immediate unsigned	sltiu $s1,$s2,20	if ($s2 < 20) $s1 = 1; else $s1 = 0	Compare less than constant unsigned
Unconditional jump	jump	j 2500	go to 10000	Jump to target address
	jump register	jr $ra	go to $ra	For switch, procedure return
	jump and link	jal 2500	$ra = PC + 4; go to 10000	For procedure call

FIGURE 2.1 MIPS assembly language revealed in this chapter. This information is also found in Column 1 of the MIPS Reference Data Card at the front of this book.

The natural number of operands for an operation like addition is three: the two numbers being added together and a place to put the sum. Requiring every instruction to have exactly three operands, no more and no less, conforms to the philosophy of keeping the hardware simple: hardware for a variable number of operands is more complicated than hardware for a fixed number. This situation illustrates the first of four underlying principles of hardware design:

Design Principle 1: Simplicity favors regularity.

We can now show, in the two examples that follow, the relationship of programs written in higher-level programming languages to programs in this more primitive notation.

Compiling Two C Assignment Statements into MIPS

This segment of a C program contains the five variables a, b, c, d, and e. Since Java evolved from C, this example and the next few work for either high-level programming language:

EXAMPLE

```
a = b + c;
d = a - e;
```

The translation from C to MIPS assembly language instructions is performed by the *compiler*. Show the MIPS code produced by a compiler.

A MIPS instruction operates on two source operands and places the result in one destination operand. Hence, the two simple statements above compile directly into these two MIPS assembly language instructions:

ANSWER

```
add a, b, c
sub d, a, e
```

Compiling a Complex C Assignment into MIPS

A somewhat complex statement contains the five variables f, g, h, i, and j:

EXAMPLE

```
f = (g + h) - (i + j);
```

What might a C compiler produce?

ANSWER

The compiler must break this statement into several assembly instructions, since only one operation is performed per MIPS instruction. The first MIPS instruction calculates the sum of g and h. We must place the result somewhere, so the compiler creates a temporary variable, called t0:

```
add t0,g,h # temporary variable t0 contains g + h
```

Although the next operation is subtract, we need to calculate the sum of i and j before we can subtract. Thus, the second instruction places the sum of i and j in another temporary variable created by the compiler, called t1:

```
add t1,i,j # temporary variable t1 contains i + j
```

Finally, the subtract instruction subtracts the second sum from the first and places the difference in the variable f, completing the compiled code:

```
sub f,t0,t1 # f gets t0 - t1, which is (g + h) - (i + j)
```

Check Yourself

For a given function, which programming language likely takes the most lines of code? Put the three representations below in order.

1. Java

2. C

3. MIPS assembly language

Elaboration: To increase portability, Java was originally envisioned as relying on a software interpreter. The instruction set of this interpreter is called *Java bytecodes* (see ◉ Section 2.15 on the CD), which is quite different from the MIPS instruction set. To get performance close to the equivalent C program, Java systems today typically compile Java bytecodes into the native instruction sets like MIPS. Because this compilation is normally done much later than for C programs, such Java compilers are often called *Just In Time* (JIT) compilers. Section 2.12 shows how JITs are used later than C compilers in the start-up process, and Section 2.13 shows the performance consequences of compiling versus interpreting Java programs.

2.3   Operands of the Computer Hardware

Unlike programs in high-level languages, the operands of arithmetic instructions are restricted; they must be from a limited number of special locations built directly in hardware called *registers*. Registers are primitives used in hardware design that are also visible to the programmer when the computer is completed, so you can think of registers as the bricks of computer construction. The size of a register in the MIPS architecture is 32 bits; groups of 32 bits occur so frequently that they are given the name **word** in the MIPS architecture.

word The natural unit of access in a computer, usually a group of 32 bits; corresponds to the size of a register in the MIPS architecture.

One major difference between the variables of a programming language and registers is the limited number of registers, typically 32 on current computers, like MIPS. (See ⊙ **Section 2.20** on the CD for the history of the number of registers.) Thus, continuing in our top-down, stepwise evolution of the symbolic representation of the MIPS language, in this section we have added the restriction that the three operands of MIPS arithmetic instructions must each be chosen from one of the 32 32-bit registers.

The reason for the limit of 32 registers may be found in the second of our four underlying design principles of hardware technology:

Design Principle 2: Smaller is faster.

A very large number of registers may increase the clock cycle time simply because it takes electronic signals longer when they must travel farther.

Guidelines such as "smaller is faster" are not absolutes; 31 registers may not be faster than 32. Yet, the truth behind such observations causes computer designers to take them seriously. In this case, the designer must balance the craving of programs for more registers with the designer's desire to keep the clock cycle fast. Another reason for not using more than 32 is the number of bits it would take in the instruction format, as Section 2.5 demonstrates.

Chapter 4 shows the central role that registers play in hardware construction; as we shall see in this chapter, effective use of registers is critical to program performance.

Although we could simply write instructions using numbers for registers, from 0 to 31, the MIPS convention is to use two-character names following a dollar sign to represent a register. Section 2.8 will explain the reasons behind these names. For now, we will use $s0, $s1, . . . for registers that correspond to variables in C and Java programs and $t0, $t1, . . . for temporary registers needed to compile the program into MIPS instructions.

Compiling a C Assignment Using Registers

It is the compiler's job to associate program variables with registers. Take, for instance, the assignment statement from our earlier example:

```
f = (g + h) - (i + j);
```

The variables f, g, h, i, and j are assigned to the registers $s0, $s1, $s2, $s3, and $s4, respectively. What is the compiled MIPS code?

EXAMPLE

ANSWER

The compiled program is very similar to the prior example, except we replace the variables with the register names mentioned above plus two temporary registers, $t0 and $t1, which correspond to the temporary variables above:

```
add $t0,$s1,$s2 # register $t0 contains g + h
add $t1,$s3,$s4 # register $t1 contains i + j
sub $s0,$t0,$t1 # f gets $t0 - $t1, which is (g + h)-(i + j)
```

Memory Operands

Programming languages have simple variables that contain single data elements, as in these examples, but they also have more complex data structures—arrays and structures. These complex data structures can contain many more data elements than there are registers in a computer. How can a computer represent and access such large structures?

Recall the five components of a computer introduced in Chapter 1 and repeated on page 75. The processor can keep only a small amount of data in registers, but computer memory contains billions of data elements. Hence, data structures (arrays and structures) are kept in memory.

data transfer instruction A command that moves data between memory and registers.

address A value used to delineate the location of a specific data element within a memory array.

As explained above, arithmetic operations occur only on registers in MIPS instructions; thus, MIPS must include instructions that transfer data between memory and registers. Such instructions are called **data transfer instructions**. To access a word in memory, the instruction must supply the memory **address**. Memory is just a large, single-dimensional array, with the address acting as the index to that array, starting at 0. For example, in Figure 2.2, the address of the third data element is 2, and the value of Memory[2] is 10.

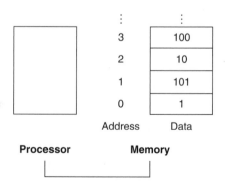

FIGURE 2.2   Memory addresses and contents of memory at those locations. If these elements were words, these addresses would be incorrect, since MIPS actually uses byte addressing, with each word representing four bytes. Figure 2.3 shows the memory addressing for sequential word addresses.

The data transfer instruction that copies data from memory to a register is traditionally called *load*. The format of the load instruction is the name of the operation followed by the register to be loaded, then a constant and register used to access memory. The sum of the constant portion of the instruction and the contents of the second register forms the memory address. The actual MIPS name for this instruction is lw, standing for *load word*.

Compiling an Assignment When an Operand Is in Memory

EXAMPLE

Let's assume that A is an array of 100 words and that the compiler has associated the variables g and h with the registers $s1 and $s2 as before. Let's also assume that the starting address, or *base address,* of the array is in $s3. Compile this C assignment statement:

```
g = h + A[8];
```

ANSWER

Although there is a single operation in this assignment statement, one of the operands is in memory, so we must first transfer A[8] to a register. The address of this array element is the sum of the base of the array A, found in register $s3, plus the number to select element 8. The data should be placed in a temporary register for use in the next instruction. Based on Figure 2.2, the first compiled instruction is

```
lw    $t0,8($s3) # Temporary reg $t0 gets A[8]
```

(On the next page we'll make a slight adjustment to this instruction, but we'll use this simplified version for now.) The following instruction can operate on the value in $t0 (which equals A[8]) since it is in a register. The instruction must add h (contained in $s2) to A[8] ($t0) and put the sum in the register corresponding to g (associated with $s1):

```
add   $s1,$s2,$t0 # g = h + A[8]
```

The constant in a data transfer instruction (8) is called the *offset,* and the register added to form the address ($s3) is called the *base register.*

**Hardware/
Software
Interface**

In addition to associating variables with registers, the compiler allocates data structures like arrays and structures to locations in memory. The compiler can then place the proper starting address into the data transfer instructions.

Since 8-bit *bytes* are useful in many programs, most architectures address individual bytes. Therefore, the address of a word matches the address of one of the 4 bytes within the word, and addresses of sequential words differ by 4. For example, Figure 2.3 shows the actual MIPS addresses for the words in Figure 2.2; the byte address of the third word is 8.

In MIPS, words must start at addresses that are multiples of 4. This requirement is called an **alignment restriction**, and many architectures have it. (Chapter 4 suggests why alignment leads to faster data transfers.)

alignment restriction
A requirement that data be aligned in memory on natural boundaries.

Computers divide into those that use the address of the leftmost or "big end" byte as the word address versus those that use the rightmost or "little end" byte. MIPS is in the *big-endian* camp. (Appendix B, shows the two options to number bytes in a word.)

Byte addressing also affects the array index. To get the proper byte address in the code above, *the offset to be added to the base register* $s3 *must be 4 × 8, or 32,* so that the load address will select A[8] and not A[8/4]. (See the related pitfall on page 175 of Section 2.18.)

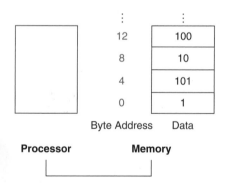

FIGURE 2.3   **Actual MIPS memory addresses and contents of memory for those words.**
The changed addresses are highlighted to contrast with Figure 2.2. Since MIPS addresses each byte, word addresses are multiples of 4: there are 4 bytes in a word.

The instruction complementary to load is traditionally called *store;* it copies data from a register to memory. The format of a store is similar to that of a load: the name of the operation, followed by the register to be stored, then offset to select the array element, and finally the base register. Once again, the MIPS address is specified in part by a constant and in part by the contents of a register. The actual MIPS name is sw, standing for *store word.*

Compiling Using Load and Store

Assume variable h is associated with register $s2 and the base address of the array A is in $s3. What is the MIPS assembly code for the C assignment statement below?

EXAMPLE

```
A[12] = h + A[8];
```

Although there is a single operation in the C statement, now two of the operands are in memory, so we need even more MIPS instructions. The first two instructions are the same as the prior example, except this time we use the proper offset for byte addressing in the load word instruction to select A[8], and the add instruction places the sum in $t0:

ANSWER

```
lw    $t0,32($s3)  # Temporary reg $t0 gets A[8]
add   $t0,$s2,$t0  # Temporary reg $t0 gets h + A[8]
```

The final instruction stores the sum into A[12], using 48 (4×12) as the offset and register $s3 as the base register.

```
sw    $t0,48($s3)  # Stores h + A[8] back into A[12]
```

Load word and store word are the instructions that copy words between memory and registers in the MIPS architecture. Other brands of computers use other instructions along with load and store to transfer data. An architecture with such alternatives is the Intel x86, described in Section 2.17.

**Hardware/
Software
Interface**

Many programs have more variables than computers have registers. Consequently, the compiler tries to keep the most frequently used variables in registers and places the rest in memory, using loads and stores to move variables between registers and memory. The process of putting less commonly used variables (or those needed later) into memory is called *spilling* registers.

The hardware principle relating size and speed suggests that memory must be slower than registers, since there are fewer registers. This is indeed the case; data accesses are faster if data is in registers instead of memory.

Moreover, data is more useful when in a register. A MIPS arithmetic instruction can read two registers, operate on them, and write the result. A MIPS data transfer instruction only reads one operand or writes one operand, without operating on it.

Thus, registers take less time to access *and* have higher throughput than memory, making data in registers both faster to access and simpler to use. Accessing registers also uses less energy than accessing memory. To achieve highest performance and conserve energy, compilers must use registers efficiently.

Constant or Immediate Operands

Many times a program will use a constant in an operation—for example, incrementing an index to point to the next element of an array. In fact, more than half of the MIPS arithmetic instructions have a constant as an operand when running the SPEC CPU2006 benchmarks.

Using only the instructions we have seen so far, we would have to load a constant from memory to use one. (The constants would have been placed in memory when the program was loaded.) For example, to add the constant 4 to register $s3, we could use the code

```
lw $t0, AddrConstant4($s1)   # $t0 = constant 4
add $s3,$s3,$t0              # $s3 = $s3 + $t0 ($t0 == 4)
```

assuming that $s1 + AddrConstant4 is the memory address of the constant 4.

An alternative that avoids the load instruction is to offer versions of the arithmetic instructions in which one operand is a constant. This quick add instruction with one constant operand is called *add immediate* or addi. To add 4 to register $s3, we just write

```
addi    $s3,$s3,4           # $s3 = $s3 + 4
```

Immediate instructions illustrate the third hardware design principle, first mentioned in the Fallacies and Pitfalls of Chapter 1:

Design Principle 3: Make the common case fast.

Constant operands occur frequently, and by including constants inside arithmetic instructions, operations are much faster and use less energy than if constants were loaded from memory.

The constant zero has another role, which is to simplify the instruction set by offering useful variations. For example, the move operation is just an add instruction where one operand is zero. Hence, MIPS dedicates a register $zero to be hard-wired to the value zero. (As you might expect, it is register number 0.)

Given the importance of registers, what is the rate of increase in the number of registers in a chip over time?

Check Yourself

1. Very fast: They increase as fast as Moore's law, which predicts doubling the number of transistors on a chip every 18 months.

2. Very slow: Since programs are usually distributed in the language of the computer, there is inertia in instruction set architecture, and so the number of registers increases only as fast as new instruction sets become viable.

Elaboration: Although the MIPS registers in this book are 32 bits wide, there is a 64-bit version of the MIPS instruction set with 32 64-bit registers. To keep them straight, they are officially called MIPS-32 and MIPS-64. In this chapter, we use a subset of MIPS-32. ◉ Appendix E shows the differences between MIPS-32 and MIPS-64.

The MIPS offset plus base register addressing is an excellent match to structures as well as arrays, since the register can point to the beginning of the structure and the offset can select the desired element. We'll see such an example in Section 2.13.

The register in the data transfer instructions was originally invented to hold an index of an array with the offset used for the starting address of an array. Thus, the base register is also called the *index register*. Today's memories are much larger and the software model of data allocation is more sophisticated, so the base address of the array is normally passed in a register since it won't fit in the offset, as we shall see.

Since MIPS supports negative constants, there is no need for subtract immediate in MIPS.

2.4 Signed and Unsigned Numbers

First, let's quickly review how a computer represents numbers. Humans are taught to think in base 10, but numbers may be represented in any base. For example, 123 base 10 = 1111011 base 2.

Numbers are kept in computer hardware as a series of high and low electronic signals, and so they are considered base 2 numbers. (Just as base 10 numbers are called *decimal* numbers, base 2 numbers are called *binary* numbers.)

A single digit of a binary number is thus the "atom" of computing, since all information is composed of **binary digits** or *bits*. This fundamental building block

binary digit Also called binary bit. One of the two numbers in base 2, 0 or 1, that are the components of information.

can be one of two values, which can be thought of as several alternatives: high or low, on or off, true or false, or 1 or 0.

Generalizing the point, in any number base, the value of ith digit d is

$$d \times \text{Base}^i$$

where i starts at 0 and increases from right to left. This leads to an obvious way to number the bits in the word: simply use the power of the base for that bit. We subscript decimal numbers with *ten* and binary numbers with *two*. For example,

$$1011_{two}$$

represents

$$
\begin{aligned}
(1 \times 2^3) &+ (0 \times 2^2) + (1 \times 2^1) + (1 \times 2^0)_{ten} \\
= (1 \times 8) &+ (0 \times 4) + (1 \times 2) + (1 \times 1)_{ten} \\
= \quad 8 \quad &+ \quad 0 \quad + \quad 2 \quad + \quad 1_{ten} \\
= 11_{ten}
\end{aligned}
$$

We number the bits 0, 1, 2, 3, . . . from *right to left* in a word. The drawing below shows the numbering of bits within a MIPS word and the placement of the number 1011_{two}:

31 30 29 28	27 26 25 24	23 22 21 20	19 18 17 16	15 14 13 12	11 10 9 8	7 6 5 4	3 2 1 0
0 0 0 0	0 0 0 0	0 0 0 0	0 0 0 0	0 0 0 0	0 0 0 0	0 0 0 0	1 0 1 1

(32 bits wide)

Since words are drawn vertically as well as horizontally, leftmost and rightmost may be unclear. Hence, the phrase **least significant bit** is used to refer to the right-most bit (bit 0 above) and **most significant bit** to the leftmost bit (bit 31).

least significant bit The rightmost bit in a MIPS word.

most significant bit The leftmost bit in a MIPS word.

The MIPS word is 32 bits long, so we can represent 2^{32} different 32-bit patterns. It is natural to let these combinations represent the numbers from 0 to $2^{32} - 1$ ($4{,}294{,}967{,}295_{ten}$):

$$
\begin{aligned}
0000\ 0000\ 0000\ 0000\ 0000\ 0000\ 0000\ 0000_{two} &= 0_{ten} \\
0000\ 0000\ 0000\ 0000\ 0000\ 0000\ 0000\ 0001_{two} &= 1_{ten} \\
0000\ 0000\ 0000\ 0000\ 0000\ 0000\ 0000\ 0010_{two} &= 2_{ten}
\end{aligned}
$$

. . .   . . .

$$
\begin{aligned}
1111\ 1111\ 1111\ 1111\ 1111\ 1111\ 1111\ 1101_{two} &= 4{,}294{,}967{,}293_{ten} \\
1111\ 1111\ 1111\ 1111\ 1111\ 1111\ 1111\ 1110_{two} &= 4{,}294{,}967{,}294_{ten} \\
1111\ 1111\ 1111\ 1111\ 1111\ 1111\ 1111\ 1111_{two} &= 4{,}294{,}967{,}295_{ten}
\end{aligned}
$$

That is, 32-bit binary numbers can be represented in terms of the bit value times a power of 2 (here xi means the ith bit of x):

$$(x31 \times 2^{31}) + (x30 \times 2^{30}) + (x29 \times 2^{29}) + \ldots + (x1 \times 2^1) + (x0 \times 2^0)$$

Keep in mind that the binary bit patterns above are simply *representatives* of numbers. Numbers really have an infinite number of digits, with almost all being 0 except for a few of the rightmost digits. We just don't normally show leading 0s.

Hardware can be designed to add, subtract, multiply, and divide these binary bit patterns. If the number that is the proper result of such operations cannot be represented by these rightmost hardware bits, *overflow* is said to have occurred. It's up to the programming language, the operating system, and the program to determine what to do if overflow occurs.

Computer programs calculate both positive and negative numbers, so we need a representation that distinguishes the positive from the negative. The most obvious solution is to add a separate sign, which conveniently can be represented in a single bit; the name for this representation is *sign and magnitude*.

Alas, sign and magnitude representation has several shortcomings. First, it's not obvious where to put the sign bit. To the right? To the left? Early computers tried both. Second, adders for sign and magnitude may need an extra step to set the sign because we can't know in advance what the proper sign will be. Finally, a separate sign bit means that sign and magnitude has both a positive and a negative zero, which can lead to problems for inattentive programmers. As a result of these shortcomings, sign and magnitude representation was soon abandoned.

In the search for a more attractive alternative, the question arose as to what would be the result for unsigned numbers if we tried to subtract a large number from a small one. The answer is that it would try to borrow from a string of leading 0s, so the result would have a string of leading 1s.

Given that there was no obvious better alternative, the final solution was to pick the representation that made the hardware simple: leading 0s mean positive, and leading 1s mean negative. This convention for representing signed binary numbers is called *two's complement* representation:

$$0000\ 0000\ 0000\ 0000\ 0000\ 0000\ 0000\ 0000_{two} = 0_{ten}$$
$$0000\ 0000\ 0000\ 0000\ 0000\ 0000\ 0000\ 0001_{two} = 1_{ten}$$
$$0000\ 0000\ 0000\ 0000\ 0000\ 0000\ 0000\ 0010_{two} = 2_{ten}$$

. . .   . . .

$$0111\ 1111\ 1111\ 1111\ 1111\ 1111\ 1111\ 1101_{two} = 2,147,483,645_{ten}$$
$$0111\ 1111\ 1111\ 1111\ 1111\ 1111\ 1111\ 1110_{two} = 2,147,483,646_{ten}$$
$$0111\ 1111\ 1111\ 1111\ 1111\ 1111\ 1111\ 1111_{two} = 2,147,483,647_{ten}$$
$$1000\ 0000\ 0000\ 0000\ 0000\ 0000\ 0000\ 0000_{two} = -2,147,483,648_{ten}$$
$$1000\ 0000\ 0000\ 0000\ 0000\ 0000\ 0000\ 0001_{two} = -2,147,483,647_{ten}$$
$$1000\ 0000\ 0000\ 0000\ 0000\ 0000\ 0000\ 0010_{two} = -2,147,483,646_{ten}$$

. . .   . . .

$$1111\ 1111\ 1111\ 1111\ 1111\ 1111\ 1111\ 1101_{two} = -3_{ten}$$
$$1111\ 1111\ 1111\ 1111\ 1111\ 1111\ 1111\ 1110_{two} = -2_{ten}$$
$$1111\ 1111\ 1111\ 1111\ 1111\ 1111\ 1111\ 1111_{two} = -1_{ten}$$

The positive half of the numbers, from 0 to $2{,}147{,}483{,}647_{ten}$ ($2^{31} - 1$), use the same representation as before. The following bit pattern ($1000 \ldots 0000_{two}$) represents the most negative number $-2{,}147{,}483{,}648_{ten}$ (-2^{31}). It is followed by a declining set of negative numbers: $-2{,}147{,}483{,}647_{ten}$ ($1000 \ldots 0001_{two}$) down to -1_{ten} ($1111 \ldots 1111_{two}$).

Two's complement does have one negative number, $-2{,}147{,}483{,}648_{ten}$, that has no corresponding positive number. Such imbalance was also a worry to the inattentive programmer, but sign and magnitude had problems for both the programmer *and* the hardware designer. Consequently, every computer today uses two's complement binary representations for signed numbers.

Two's complement representation has the advantage that all negative numbers have a 1 in the most significant bit. Consequently, hardware needs to test only this bit to see if a number is positive or negative (with the number 0 considered positive). This bit is often called the *sign bit*. By recognizing the role of the sign bit, we can represent positive and negative 32-bit numbers in terms of the bit value times a power of 2:

$$(x31 \times -2^{31}) + (x30 \times 2^{30}) + (x29 \times 2^{29}) + \ldots + (x1 \times 2^{1}) + (x0 \times 2^{0})$$

The sign bit is multiplied by -2^{31}, and the rest of the bits are then multiplied by positive versions of their respective base values.

Binary to Decimal Conversion

EXAMPLE

What is the decimal value of this 32-bit two's complement number?

$$1111\ 1111\ 1111\ 1111\ 1111\ 1111\ 1111\ 1100_{two}$$

ANSWER

Substituting the number's bit values into the formula above:

$$(1 \times -2^{31}) + (1 \times 2^{30}) + (1 \times 2^{29}) + \ldots + (1 \times 2^{2}) + (0 \times 2^{1}) + (0 \times 2^{0})$$
$$= -2^{31} \quad + \quad 2^{30} \quad + \quad 2^{29} \quad + \ldots + \quad 2^{2} \quad + \quad 0 \quad + \quad 0$$
$$= -2{,}147{,}483{,}648_{ten} + 2{,}147{,}483{,}644_{ten}$$
$$= -4_{ten}$$

We'll see a shortcut to simplify conversion from negative to positive soon.

Just as an operation on unsigned numbers can overflow the capacity of hardware to represent the result, so can an operation on two's complement numbers. Overflow occurs when the leftmost retained bit of the binary bit pattern is not the same as the infinite number of digits to the left (the sign bit is incorrect): a 0 on the left of the bit pattern when the number is negative or a 1 when the number is positive.

Unlike the numbers discussed above, memory addresses naturally start at 0 and continue to the largest address. Put another way, negative addresses make no sense. Thus, programs want to deal sometimes with numbers that can be positive or negative and sometimes with numbers that can be only positive. Some programming languages reflect this distinction. C, for example, names the former *integers* (declared as `int` in the program) and the latter *unsigned integers* (`unsigned int`). Some C style guides even recommend declaring the former as `signed int` to keep the distinction clear.

Hardware/ Software Interface

Let's examine two useful shortcuts when working with two's complement numbers. The first shortcut is a quick way to negate a two's complement binary number. Simply invert every 0 to 1 and every 1 to 0, then add one to the result. This shortcut is based on the observation that the sum of a number and its inverted representation must be $111 \ldots 111_{\text{two}}$, which represents -1. Since $x + \bar{x} = -1$, therefore $x + \bar{x} + 1 = 0$ or $\bar{x} + 1 = -x$.

Negation Shortcut

Negate 2_{ten}, and then check the result by negating -2_{ten}.

$2_{\text{ten}} = 0000\ 0000\ 0000\ 0000\ 0000\ 0000\ 0000\ 0010_{\text{two}}$

EXAMPLE

ANSWER

Negating this number by inverting the bits and adding one,

$$
\begin{aligned}
& \quad\ 1111\ 1111\ 1111\ 1111\ 1111\ 1111\ 1111\ 1101_{\text{two}} \\
+ & \quad\ 1_{\text{two}} \\
\hline
= & \quad\ 1111\ 1111\ 1111\ 1111\ 1111\ 1111\ 1111\ 1110_{\text{two}} \\
= & \quad\ -2_{\text{ten}}
\end{aligned}
$$

Going the other direction,

$$1111\ 1111\ 1111\ 1111\ 1111\ 1111\ 1111\ 1110_{two}$$

is first inverted and then incremented:

$$
\begin{aligned}
&\quad\ 0000\ 0000\ 0000\ 0000\ 0000\ 0000\ 0000\ 0001_{two} \\
+&\qquad\qquad\qquad\qquad\qquad\qquad\qquad\qquad\qquad\ 1_{two} \\
\hline
=&\quad\ 0000\ 0000\ 0000\ 0000\ 0000\ 0000\ 0000\ 0010_{two} \\
=&\quad\ 2_{ten}
\end{aligned}
$$

Our next shortcut tells us how to convert a binary number represented in n bits to a number represented with more than n bits. For example, the immediate field in the load, store, branch, add, and set on less than instructions contains a two's complement 16-bit number, representing $-32{,}768_{ten}$ (-2^{15}) to $32{,}767_{ten}$ ($2^{15} - 1$). To add the immediate field to a 32-bit register, the computer must convert that 16-bit number to its 32-bit equivalent. The shortcut is to take the most significant bit from the smaller quantity—the sign bit—and replicate it to fill the new bits of the larger quantity. The old bits are simply copied into the right portion of the new word. This shortcut is commonly called *sign extension*.

EXAMPLE

Sign Extension Shortcut

Convert 16-bit binary versions of 2_{ten} and -2_{ten} to 32-bit binary numbers.

ANSWER

The 16-bit binary version of the number 2 is

$$0000\ 0000\ 0000\ 0010_{two} = 2_{ten}$$

It is converted to a 32-bit number by making 16 copies of the value in the most significant bit (0) and placing that in the left-hand half of the word. The right half gets the old value:

$$0000\ 0000\ 0000\ 0000\ 0000\ 0000\ 0000\ 0010_{two} = 2_{ten}$$

Let's negate the 16-bit version of 2 using the earlier shortcut. Thus,

$$0000\ 0000\ 0000\ 0010_{two}$$

becomes

$$1111\ 1111\ 1111\ 1101_{two}$$
$$+\ 1_{two}$$
$$\overline{\ }$$
$$=\ 1111\ 1111\ 1111\ 1110_{two}$$

Creating a 32-bit version of the negative number means copying the sign bit 16 times and placing it on the left:

$$1111\ 1111\ 1111\ 1111\ 1111\ 1111\ 1111\ 1110_{two}\ =\ -2_{ten}$$

This trick works because positive two's complement numbers really have an infinite number of 0s on the left and negative two's complement numbers have an infinite number of 1s. The binary bit pattern representing a number hides leading bits to fit the width of the hardware; sign extension simply restores some of them.

Summary

The main point of this section is that we need to represent both positive and negative integers within a computer word, and although there are pros and cons to any option, the overwhelming choice since 1965 has been two's complement.

What is the decimal value of this 64-bit two's complement number?

Check Yourself

$$1111\ 1111\ 1111\ 1111\ 1111\ 1111\ 1111\ 1111\ 1111\ 1111\ 1111\ 1111\ 1111\ 1111\ 1111\ 1000_{two}$$

1) -4_{ten}

2) -8_{ten}

3) -16_{ten}

4) $18,446,744,073,709,551,609_{ten}$

Elaboration: Two's complement gets its name from the rule that the unsigned sum of an n-bit number and its negative is 2^n; hence, the complement or negation of a two's complement number x is $2^n - x$.

one's complement
A notation that represents
the most negative value
by $10 \ldots 000_{two}$ and the
most positive value by
$01 \ldots 11_{two}$, leaving
an equal number of
negatives and positives
but ending up with
two zeros, one positive
$(00 \ldots 00_{two})$ and one
negative $(11 \ldots 11_{two})$.
The term is also used to
mean the inversion of
every bit in a pattern: 0 to
1 and 1 to 0.

A third alternative representation to two's complement and sign and magnitude is called one's complement. The negative of a one's complement is found by inverting each bit, from 0 to 1 and from 1 to 0, which helps explain its name since the complement of x is $2^n - x - 1$. It was also an attempt to be a better solution than sign and magnitude, and several early scientific computers did use the notation. This representation is similar to two's complement except that it also has two 0s: $00 \ldots 00_{two}$ is positive 0 and $11 \ldots 11_{two}$ is negative 0. The most negative number, $10 \ldots 000_{two}$, represents $-2,147,483,647_{ten}$, and so the positives and negatives are balanced. One's complement adders did need an extra step to subtract a number, and hence two's complement dominates today.

A final notation, which we will look at when we discuss floating point in Chapter 3, is to represent the most negative value by $00 \ldots 000_{two}$ and the most positive value by $11 \ldots 11_{two}$, with 0 typically having the value $10 \ldots 00_{two}$. This is called a biased notation, since it biases the number such that the number plus the bias has a nonnegative representation.

biased notation
A notation that represents
the most negative value
by $00 \ldots 000_{two}$ and
the most positive value
by $11 \ldots 11_{two}$, with 0
typically having the value
$10 \ldots 00_{two}$, thereby
biasing the number such
that the number plus the
bias has a nonnegative
representation.

Elaboration: For signed decimal numbers, we used "−" to represent negative because there are no limits to the size of a decimal number. Given a fixed word size, binary and hexadecimal (see Figure 2.4) bit strings can encode the sign; hence we do not normally use "+" or "−" with binary or hexadecimal notation.

2.5   Representing Instructions in the Computer

We are now ready to explain the difference between the way humans instruct computers and the way computers see instructions.

Instructions are kept in the computer as a series of high and low electronic signals and may be represented as numbers. In fact, each piece of an instruction can be considered as an individual number, and placing these numbers side by side forms the instruction.

Since registers are referred to by almost all instructions, there must be a convention to map register names into numbers. In MIPS assembly language, registers $s0 to $s7 map onto registers 16 to 23, and registers $t0 to $t7 map onto registers 8 to 15. Hence, $s0 means register 16, $s1 means register 17, $s2 means register 18, …, $t0 means register 8, $t1 means register 9, and so on. We'll describe the convention for the rest of the 32 registers in the following sections.

Translating a MIPS Assembly Instruction into a Machine Instruction

Let's do the next step in the refinement of the MIPS language as an example. We'll show the real MIPS language version of the instruction represented symbolically as

EXAMPLE

```
add $t0,$s1,$s2
```

first as a combination of decimal numbers and then of binary numbers.

The decimal representation is

ANSWER

0	17	18	8	0	32

Each of these segments of an instruction is called a *field*. The first and last fields (containing 0 and 32 in this case) in combination tell the MIPS computer that this instruction performs addition. The second field gives the number of the register that is the first source operand of the addition operation (17 = $s1), and the third field gives the other source operand for the addition (18 = $s2). The fourth field contains the number of the register that is to receive the sum (8 = $t0). The fifth field is unused in this instruction, so it is set to 0. Thus, this instruction adds register $s1 to register $s2 and places the sum in register $t0.

This instruction can also be represented as fields of binary numbers as opposed to decimal:

000000	10001	10010	01000	00000	100000
6 bits	5 bits	5 bits	5 bits	5 bits	6 bits

This layout of the instruction is called the **instruction format**. As you can see from counting the number of bits, this MIPS instruction takes exactly 32 bits—the same size as a data word. In keeping with our design principle that simplicity favors regularity, all MIPS instructions are 32 bits long.

To distinguish it from assembly language, we call the numeric version of instructions **machine language** and a sequence of such instructions *machine code*.

It would appear that you would now be reading and writing long, tedious strings of binary numbers. We avoid that tedium by using a higher base than binary that converts easily into binary. Since almost all computer data sizes are multiples of 4, **hexadecimal** (base 16) numbers are popular. Since base 16 is a power of 2, we can trivially convert by replacing each group of four binary digits by a single hexadecimal digit, and vice versa. Figure 2.4 converts between hexadecimal and binary.

instruction format A form of representation of an instruction composed of fields of binary numbers.

machine language Binary representation used for communication within a computer system.

hexadecimal Numbers in base 16.

Hexadecimal	Binary	Hexadecimal	Binary	Hexadecimal	Binary	Hexadecimal	Binary
0_{hex}	0000_{two}	4_{hex}	0100_{two}	8_{hex}	1000_{two}	c_{hex}	1100_{two}
1_{hex}	0001_{two}	5_{hex}	0101_{two}	9_{hex}	1001_{two}	d_{hex}	1101_{two}
2_{hex}	0010_{two}	6_{hex}	0110_{two}	a_{hex}	1010_{two}	e_{hex}	1110_{two}
3_{hex}	0011_{two}	7_{hex}	0111_{two}	b_{hex}	1011_{two}	f_{hex}	1111_{two}

FIGURE 2.4   The hexadecimal-binary conversion table. Just replace one hexadecimal digit by the corresponding four binary digits, and vice versa. If the length of the binary number is not a multiple of 4, go from right to left.

Because we frequently deal with different number bases, to avoid confusion we will subscript decimal numbers with *ten*, binary numbers with *two*, and hexadecimal numbers with *hex*. (If there is no subscript, the default is base 10.) By the way, C and Java use the notation 0x*nnnn* for hexadecimal numbers.

EXAMPLE

Binary to Hexadecimal and Back

Convert the following hexadecimal and binary numbers into the other base:

eca8 6420_{hex}

0001 0011 0101 0111 1001 1011 1101 1111_{two}

ANSWER

Using Figure 2.4, the answer is just a table lookup one way:

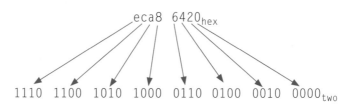

And then the other direction:

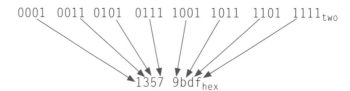

MIPS Fields

MIPS fields are given names to make them easier to discuss:

op	rs	rt	rd	shamt	funct
6 bits	5 bits	5 bits	5 bits	5 bits	6 bits

Here is the meaning of each name of the fields in MIPS instructions:

- *op:* Basic operation of the instruction, traditionally called the **opcode**.

- *rs:* The first register source operand.

- *rt:* The second register source operand.

- *rd:* The register destination operand. It gets the result of the operation.

- *shamt:* Shift amount. (Section 2.6 explains shift instructions and this term; it will not be used until then, and hence the field contains zero in this section.)

- *funct:* Function. This field, often called the *function code*, selects the specific variant of the operation in the op field.

opcode The field that denotes the operation and format of an instruction.

A problem occurs when an instruction needs longer fields than those shown above. For example, the load word instruction must specify two registers and a constant. If the address were to use one of the 5-bit fields in the format above, the constant within the load word instruction would be limited to only 2^5 or 32. This constant is used to select elements from arrays or data structures, and it often needs to be much larger than 32. This 5-bit field is too small to be useful.

Hence, we have a conflict between the desire to keep all instructions the same length and the desire to have a single instruction format. This leads us to the final hardware design principle:

Design Principle 4: Good design demands good compromises.

The compromise chosen by the MIPS designers is to keep all instructions the same length, thereby requiring different kinds of instruction formats for different kinds of instructions. For example, the format above is called *R-type* (for register) or *R-format.* A second type of instruction format is called *I-type* (for immediate) or *I-format* and is used by the immediate and data transfer instructions. The fields of I-format are

op	rs	rt	constant or address
6 bits	5 bits	5 bits	16 bits

The 16-bit address means a load word instruction can load any word within a region of $\pm 2^{15}$ or 32,768 bytes ($\pm 2^{13}$ or 8192 words) of the address in the base register rs. Similarly, add immediate is limited to constants no larger than $\pm 2^{15}$. We see that more than 32 registers would be difficult in this format, as the rs and rt fields would each need another bit, making it harder to fit everything in one word.

Let's look at the load word instruction from page 83:

```
lw    $t0,32($s3)   # Temporary reg $t0 gets A[8]
```

Here, 19 (for $s3) is placed in the rs field, 8 (for $t0) is placed in the rt field, and 32 is placed in the address field. Note that the meaning of the rt field has changed for this instruction: in a load word instruction, the rt field specifies the *destination* register, which receives the result of the load.

Although multiple formats complicate the hardware, we can reduce the complexity by keeping the formats similar. For example, the first three fields of the R-type and I-type formats are the same size and have the same names; the length of the fourth field in I-type is equal to the sum of the lengths of the last three fields of R-type.

In case you were wondering, the formats are distinguished by the values in the first field: each format is assigned a distinct set of values in the first field (op) so that the hardware knows whether to treat the last half of the instruction as three fields (R-type) or as a single field (I-type). Figure 2.5 shows the numbers used in each field for the MIPS instructions covered here.

Instruction	Format	op	rs	rt	rd	shamt	funct	address
add	R	0	reg	reg	reg	0	32_{ten}	n.a.
sub (subtract)	R	0	reg	reg	reg	0	34_{ten}	n.a.
add immediate	I	8_{ten}	reg	reg	n.a.	n.a.	n.a.	constant
lw (load word)	I	35_{ten}	reg	reg	n.a.	n.a.	n.a.	address
sw (store word)	I	43_{ten}	reg	reg	n.a.	n.a.	n.a.	address

FIGURE 2.5   MIPS instruction encoding. In the table above, "reg" means a register number between 0 and 31, "address" means a 16-bit address, and "n.a." (not applicable) means this field does not appear in this format. Note that add and sub instructions have the same value in the op field; the hardware uses the funct field to decide the variant of the operation: add (32) or subtract (34).

EXAMPLE

Translating MIPS Assembly Language into Machine Language

We can now take an example all the way from what the programmer writes to what the computer executes. If $t1 has the base of the array A and $s2 corresponds to h, the assignment statement

```
A[300] = h + A[300];
```

is compiled into

```
lw    $t0,1200($t1)# Temporary reg $t0 gets A[300]
add   $t0,$s2,$t0  # Temporary reg $t0 gets h + A[300]
sw    $t0,1200($t1) # Stores h + A[300] back into A[300]
```

What is the MIPS machine language code for these three instructions?

For convenience, let's first represent the machine language instructions using decimal numbers. From Figure 2.5, we can determine the three machine language instructions:

op	rs	rt	rd	address/ shamt	funct
35	9	8		1200	
0	18	8	8	0	32
43	9	8		1200	

The lw instruction is identified by 35 (see Figure 2.5) in the first field (op). The base register 9 ($t1) is specified in the second field (rs), and the destination register 8 ($t0) is specified in the third field (rt). The offset to select A[300] (1200 = 300 × 4) is found in the final field (address).

The add instruction that follows is specified with 0 in the first field (op) and 32 in the last field (funct). The three register operands (18, 8, and 8) are found in the second, third, and fourth fields and correspond to $s2, $t0, and $t0.

The sw instruction is identified with 43 in the first field. The rest of this final instruction is identical to the lw instruction.

Since $1200_{ten} = 0000\ 0100\ 1011\ 0000_{two}$, the binary equivalent to the decimal form is:

100011	01001	01000	0000 0100 1011 0000		
000000	10010	01000	01000	00000	100000
101011	01001	01000	0000 0100 1011 0000		

Note the similarity of the binary representations of the first and last instructions. The only difference is in the third bit from the left, which is highlighted here.

Figure 2.6 summarizes the portions of MIPS machine language described in this section. As we shall see in Chapter 4, the similarity of the binary representations of related instructions simplifies hardware design. These similarities are another example of regularity in the MIPS architecture.

MIPS machine language

Name	Format	Example						Comments
add	R	0	18	19	17	0	32	add $s1,$s2,$s3
sub	R	0	18	19	17	0	34	sub $s1,$s2,$s3
addi	I	8	18	17	100			addi $s1,$s2,100
lw	I	35	18	17	100			lw $s1,100($s2)
sw	I	43	18	17	100			sw $s1,100($s2)
Field size		6 bits	5 bits	5 bits	5 bits	5 bits	6 bits	All MIPS instructions are 32 bits long
R-format	R	op	rs	rt	rd	shamt	funct	Arithmetic instruction format
I-format	I	op	rs	rt	address			Data transfer format

FIGURE 2.6 MIPS architecture revealed through Section 2.5. The two MIPS instruction formats so far are R and I. The first 16 bits are the same: both contain an *op* field, giving the base operation; an *rs* field, giving one of the sources; and the *rt* field, which specifies the other source operand, except for load word, where it specifies the destination register. R-format divides the last 16 bits into an *rd* field, specifying the destination register; the *shamt* field, which Section 2.6 explains; and the *funct* field, which specifies the specific operation of R-format instructions. I-format combines the last 16 bits into a single *address* field.

The **BIG** Picture

Today's computers are built on two key principles:

1. Instructions are represented as numbers.

2. Programs are stored in memory to be read or written, just like numbers.

These principles lead to the *stored-program* concept; its invention let the computing genie out of its bottle. Figure 2.7 shows the power of the concept; specifically, memory can contain the source code for an editor program, the corresponding compiled machine code, the text that the compiled program is using, and even the compiler that generated the machine code.

One consequence of instructions as numbers is that programs are often shipped as files of binary numbers. The commercial implication is that computers can inherit ready-made software provided they are compatible with an existing instruction set. Such "binary compatibility" often leads industry to align around a small number of instruction set architectures.

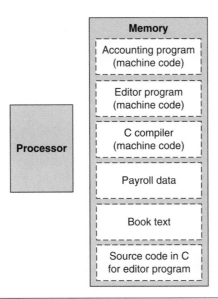

FIGURE 2.7 The stored-program concept. Stored programs allow a computer that performs accounting to become, in the blink of an eye, a computer that helps an author write a book. The switch happens simply by loading memory with programs and data and then telling the computer to begin executing at a given location in memory. Treating instructions in the same way as data greatly simplifies both the memory hardware and the software of computer systems. Specifically, the memory technology needed for data can also be used for programs, and programs like compilers, for instance, can translate code written in a notation far more convenient for humans into code that the computer can understand.

What MIPS instruction does this represent? Chose from one of the four options below.

Check Yourself

op	rs	rt	rd	shamt	funct
0	8	9	10	0	34

1. sub $t0, $t1, $t2
2. add $t2, $t0, $t1
3. sub $t2, $t1, $t0
4. sub $t2, $t0, $t1

"Contrariwise," continued Tweedledee, "if it was so, it might be; and if it were so, it would be; but as it isn't, it ain't. That's logic."

Lewis Carroll, *Alice's Adventures in Wonderland,* 1865

2.6 Logical Operations

Although the first computers operated on full words, it soon became clear that it was useful to operate on fields of bits within a word or even on individual bits. Examining characters within a word, each of which is stored as 8 bits, is one example of such an operation (see Section 2.9). It follows that operations were added to programming languages and instruction set architectures to simplify, among other things, the packing and unpacking of bits into words. These instructions are called logical operations. Figure 2.8 shows logical operations in C, Java, and MIPS.

Logical operations	C operators	Java operators	MIPS instructions
Shift left	<<	<<	`sll`
Shift right	>>	>>>	`srl`
Bit-by-bit AND	&	&	`and, andi`
Bit-by-bit OR	|	|	`or, ori`
Bit-by-bit NOT	~	~	`nor`

FIGURE 2.8 C and Java logical operators and their corresponding MIPS instructions. MIPS implements NOT using a NOR with one operand being zero.

The first class of such operations is called *shifts*. They move all the bits in a word to the left or right, filling the emptied bits with 0s. For example, if register `$s0` contained

$$0000\ 0000\ 0000\ 0000\ 0000\ 0000\ 0000\ 1001_{two} = 9_{ten}$$

and the instruction to shift left by 4 was executed, the new value would be:

$$0000\ 0000\ 0000\ 0000\ 0000\ 0000\ 1001\ 0000_{two} = 144_{ten}$$

The dual of a shift left is a shift right. The actual name of the two MIPS shift instructions are called *shift left logical* (`sll`) and *shift right logical* (`srl`). The following instruction performs the operation above, assuming that the original value was in register $s0 and the result should go in register $t2:

```
sll  $t2,$s0,4   # reg $t2 = reg $s0 << 4 bits
```

We delayed explaining the *shamt* field in the R-format. Used in shift instructions, it stands for *shift amount*. Hence, the machine language version of the instruction above is

op	rs	rt	rd	shamt	funct
0	0	16	10	4	0

The encoding of sll is 0 in both the op and funct fields, rd contains 10 (register $t2), rt contains 16 (register $s0), and shamt contains 4. The rs field is unused and thus is set to 0.

Shift left logical provides a bonus benefit. Shifting left by i bits gives the same result as multiplying by 2^i, just as shifting a decimal number by i digits is equivalent to multiplying by 10^i. For example, the above sll shifts by 4, which gives the same result as multiplying by 2^4 or 16. The first bit pattern above represents 9, and $9 \times 16 = 144$, the value of the second bit pattern.

Another useful operation that isolates fields is **AND**. (We capitalize the word to avoid confusion between the operation and the English conjunction.) AND is a bit-by-bit operation that leaves a 1 in the result only if both bits of the operands are 1. For example, if register $t2 contains

AND A logical bit-by-bit operation with two operands that calculates a 1 only if there is a 1 in *both* operands.

0000 0000 0000 0000 0000 1101 1100 0000$_{two}$

and register $t1 contains

0000 0000 0000 0000 0011 1100 0000 0000$_{two}$

then, after executing the MIPS instruction

```
and $t0,$t1,$t2     # reg $t0 = reg $t1 & reg $t2
```

the value of register $t0 would be

0000 0000 0000 0000 0000 1100 0000 0000$_{two}$

As you can see, AND can apply a bit pattern to a set of bits to force 0s where there is a 0 in the bit pattern. Such a bit pattern in conjunction with AND is traditionally called a *mask*, since the mask "conceals" some bits.

OR A logical bit-by-bit operation with two operands that calculates a 1 if there is a 1 in *either* operand.

To place a value into one of these seas of 0s, there is the dual to AND, called **OR**. It is a bit-by-bit operation that places a 1 in the result if *either* operand bit is a 1. To elaborate, if the registers $t1 and $t2 are unchanged from the preceding example, the result of the MIPS instruction

```
or $t0,$t1,$t2 # reg $t0 = reg $t1 | reg $t2
```

is this value in register $t0:

0000 0000 0000 0000 0011 1101 1100 0000$_{two}$

NOT A logical bit-by-bit operation with one operand that inverts the bits; that is, it replaces every 1 with a 0, and every 0 with a 1.

The final logical operation is a contrarian. **NOT** takes one operand and places a 1 in the result if one operand bit is a 0, and vice versa. In keeping with the three-operand format, the designers of MIPS decided to include the instruction **NOR** (NOT OR) instead of NOT. If one operand is zero, then it is equivalent to NOT: A NOR 0 = NOT (A OR 0) = NOT (A).

If the register $t1 is unchanged from the preceding example and register $t3 has the value 0, the result of the MIPS instruction

NOR A logical bit-by-bit operation with two operands that calculates the NOT of the OR of the two operands. That is, it calculates a 1 only if there is a 0 in *both* operands.

```
nor $t0,$t1,$t3 # reg $t0 = ~ (reg $t1 | reg $t3)
```

is this value in register $t0:

1111 1111 1111 1111 1100 0011 1111 1111$_{two}$

Figure 2.8 above shows the relationship between the C and Java operators and the MIPS instructions. Constants are useful in AND and OR logical operations as well as in arithmetic operations, so MIPS also provides the instructions *and immediate* (andi) and *or immediate* (ori). Constants are rare for NOR, since its main use is to invert the bits of a single operand; thus, the MIPS instruction set architecture has no immediate version.

Elaboration: The full MIPS instruction set also includes exclusive or (XOR), which sets the bit to 1 when two corresponding bits differ, and to 0 when they are the same. C allows *bit fields* or *fields* to be defined within words, both allowing objects to be packed within a word and to match an externally enforced interface such as an I/O device. All fields must fit within a single word. Fields are unsigned integers that can be as short as 1 bit. C compilers insert and extract fields using logical instructions in MIPS: `and`, `or`, `sll`, and `srl`.

Which operations can isolate a field in a word?

1. AND

2. A shift left followed by a shift right

Check Yourself

2.7 Instructions for Making Decisions

What distinguishes a computer from a simple calculator is its ability to make decisions. Based on the input data and the values created during computation, different instructions execute. Decision making is commonly represented in programming languages using the *if* statement, sometimes combined with *go to* statements and labels. MIPS assembly language includes two decision-making instructions, similar to an *if* statement with a *go to*. The first instruction is

```
beq register1, register2, L1
```

This instruction means go to the statement labeled L1 if the value in `register1` equals the value in `register2`. The mnemonic `beq` stands for *branch if equal*. The second instruction is

```
bne register1, register2, L1
```

It means go to the statement labeled L1 if the value in `register1` does *not* equal the value in `register2`. The mnemonic `bne` stands for *branch if not equal*. These two instructions are traditionally called **conditional branches**.

The utility of an automatic computer lies in the possibility of using a given sequence of instructions repeatedly, the number of times it is iterated being dependent upon the results of the computation. ...This choice can be made to depend upon the sign of a number (zero being reckoned as plus for machine purposes). Consequently, we introduce an [instruction] (the conditional transfer [instruction]) which will, depending on the sign of a given number, cause the proper one of two routines to be executed.

Burks, Goldstine, and von Neumann, 1947

conditional branch An instruction that requires the comparison of two values and that allows for a subsequent transfer of control to a new address in the program based on the outcome of the comparison.

Compiling *if-then-else* into Conditional Branches

EXAMPLE

In the following code segment, f, g, h, i, and j are variables. If the five variables f through j correspond to the five registers $s0 through $s4, what is the compiled MIPS code for this C *if* statement?

```
if (i == j) f = g + h; else f = g - h;
```

ANSWER

Figure 2.9 is a flowchart of what the MIPS code should do. The first expression compares for equality, so it would seem that we would want the branch if registers are equal instruction (beq). In general, the code will be more efficient if we test for the opposite condition to branch over the code that performs the subsequent *then* part of the *if* (the label Else is defined below) and so we use the branch if registers are *not* equal instruction (bne):

```
bne $s3,$s4,Else   # go to Else if i ≠ j
```

The next assignment statement performs a single operation, and if all the operands are allocated to registers, it is just one instruction:

```
add $s0,$s1,$s2    # f = g + h (skipped if i ≠ j)
```

We now need to go to the end of the *if* statement. This example introduces another kind of branch, often called an *unconditional branch*. This instruction says that the processor always follows the branch. To distinguish between conditional and unconditional branches, the MIPS name for this type of instruction is *jump*, abbreviated as j (the label Exit is defined below).

```
j Exit     # go to Exit
```

The assignment statement in the *else* portion of the *if* statement can again be compiled into a single instruction. We just need to append the label Else to this instruction. We also show the label Exit that is after this instruction, showing the end of the *if-then-else* compiled code:

```
Else:sub $s0,$s1,$s2   # f = g - h (skipped if i = j)
Exit:
```

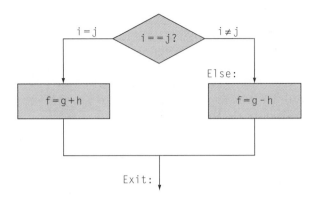

FIGURE 2.9 Illustration of the options in the *if* statement above. The left box corresponds to the *then* part of the *if* statement, and the right box corresponds to the *else* part.

Notice that the assembler relieves the compiler and the assembly language programmer from the tedium of calculating addresses for branches, just as it does for calculating data addresses for loads and stores (see Section 2.12).

Compilers frequently create branches and labels where they do not appear in the programming language. Avoiding the burden of writing explicit labels and branches is one benefit of writing in high-level programming languages and is a reason coding is faster at that level.

Hardware/ Software Interface

Loops

Decisions are important both for choosing between two alternatives—found in *if* statements—and for iterating a computation—found in loops. The same assembly instructions are the building blocks for both cases.

Compiling a *while* Loop in C

Here is a traditional loop in C:

```
while (save[i] == k)
        i += 1;
```

EXAMPLE

Assume that i and k correspond to registers $s3 and $s5 and the base of the array save is in $s6. What is the MIPS assembly code corresponding to this C segment?

ANSWER

The first step is to load save[i] into a temporary register. Before we can load save[i] into a temporary register, we need to have its address. Before we can add i to the base of array save to form the address, we must multiply the index i by 4 due to the byte addressing problem. Fortunately, we can use shift left logical, since shifting left by 2 bits multiplies by 2^2 or 4 (see page 103 in the prior section). We need to add the label Loop to it so that we can branch back to that instruction at the end of the loop:

```
Loop: sll  $t1,$s3,2    # Temp reg $t1 = i * 4
```

To get the address of save[i], we need to add $t1 and the base of save in $s6:

```
      add $t1,$t1,$s6    # $t1 = address of save[i]
```

Now we can use that address to load save[i] into a temporary register:

```
      lw  $t0,0($t1)     # Temp reg $t0 = save[i]
```

The next instruction performs the loop test, exiting if save[i] ≠ k:

```
      bne $t0,$s5, Exit  # go to Exit if save[i] ≠ k
```

The next instruction adds 1 to i:

```
      addi  $s3,$s3,1    # i = i + 1
```

The end of the loop branches back to the *while* test at the top of the loop. We just add the Exit label after it, and we're done:

```
      j    Loop          # go to Loop
  Exit:
```

(See the exercises for an optimization of this sequence.)

Hardware/ Software Interface

Such sequences of instructions that end in a branch are so fundamental to compiling that they are given their own buzzword: a **basic block** is a sequence of instructions without branches, except possibly at the end, and without branch targets or branch labels, except possibly at the beginning. One of the first early phases of compilation is breaking the program into basic blocks.

---

basic block A sequence of instructions without branches (except possibly at the end) and without branch targets or branch labels (except possibly at the beginning).

The test for equality or inequality is probably the most popular test, but sometimes it is useful to see if a variable is less than another variable. For example, a *for* loop may want to test to see if the index variable is less than 0. Such comparisons are accomplished in MIPS assembly language with an instruction that compares two registers and sets a third register to 1 if the first is less than the second; otherwise, it is set to 0. The MIPS instruction is called *set on less than*, or slt. For example,

```
slt     $t0, $s3, $s4   # $t0 = 1 if $s3 < $s4
```

means that register $t0 is set to 1 if the value in register $s3 is less than the value in register $s4; otherwise, register $t0 is set to 0.

Constant operands are popular in comparisons, so there is an immediate version of the set on less than instruction. To test if register $s2 is less than the constant 10, we can just write

```
slti    $t0,$s2,10      # $t0 = 1 if $s2 < 10
```

MIPS compilers use the slt, slti, beq, bne, and the fixed value of 0 (always available by reading register $zero) to create all relative conditions: equal, not equal, less than, less than or equal, greater than, greater than or equal.

Hardware/ Software Interface

Heeding von Neumann's warning about the simplicity of the "equipment," the MIPS architecture doesn't include branch on less than because it is too complicated; either it would stretch the clock cycle time or it would take extra clock cycles per instruction. Two faster instructions are more useful.

Comparison instructions must deal with the dichotomy between signed and unsigned numbers. Sometimes a bit pattern with a 1 in the most significant bit represents a negative number and, of course, is less than any positive number, which must have a 0 in the most significant bit. With unsigned integers, on the other hand, a 1 in the most significant bit represents a number that is *larger* than any that begins with a 0. (We'll soon take advantage of this dual meaning of the most significant bit to reduce the cost of the array bounds checking.)

MIPS offers two versions of the set on less than comparison to handle these alternatives. *Set on less than* (slt) and *set on less than immediate* (slti) work with signed integers. Unsigned integers are compared using *set on less than unsigned* (sltu) and *set on less than immediate unsigned* (sltiu).

Hardware/ Software Interface

EXAMPLE

Signed versus Unsigned Comparison

Suppose register $\$s0$ has the binary number

    1111 1111 1111 1111 1111 1111 1111 1111$_{two}$

and that register $\$s1$ has the binary number

    0000 0000 0000 0000 0000 0000 0000 0001$_{two}$

What are the values of registers $\$t0$ and $\$t1$ after these two instructions?

```
slt      $t0, $s0, $s1 # signed comparison
sltu     $t1, $s0, $s1 # unsigned comparison
```

ANSWER

The value in register $\$s0$ represents -1_{ten} if it is an integer and $4{,}294{,}967{,}295_{ten}$ if it is an unsigned integer. The value in register $\$s1$ represents 1_{ten} in either case. Then register $\$t0$ has the value 1, since $-1_{ten} < 1_{ten}$, and register $\$t1$ has the value 0, since $4{,}294{,}967{,}295_{ten} > 1_{ten}$.

Treating signed numbers as if they were unsigned gives us a low cost way of checking if $0 \leq x < y$, which matches the index out-of-bounds check for arrays. The key is that negative integers in two's complement notation look like large numbers in unsigned notation; that is, the most significant bit is a sign bit in the former notation but a large part of the number in the latter. Thus, an unsigned comparison of $x < y$ also checks if x is negative as well as if x is less than y.

EXAMPLE

Bounds Check Shortcut

Use this shortcut to reduce an index-out-of-bounds check: jump to IndexOutOfBounds if $\$s1 \geq \$t2$ or if $\$s1$ is negative.

ANSWER

The checking code just uses sltu to do both checks:

```
sltu $t0,$s1,$t2 # $t0=0 if $s1>=length or $s1<0
beq  $t0,$zero,IndexOutOfBounds #if bad, goto Error
```

Case/Switch Statement

Most programming languages have a *case* or *switch* statement that allows the programmer to select one of many alternatives depending on a single value. The simplest way to implement *switch* is via a sequence of conditional tests, turning the *switch* statement into a chain of *if-then-else* statements.

Sometimes the alternatives may be more efficiently encoded as a table of addresses of alternative instruction sequences, called a **jump address table** or **jump table**, and the program needs only to index into the table and then jump to the appropriate sequence. The jump table is then just an array of words containing addresses that correspond to labels in the code. The program loads the appropriate entry from the jump table into a register. It then needs to jump using the address in the register. To support such situations, computers like MIPS include a *jump register* instruction (jr), meaning an unconditional jump to the address specified in a register. Then it jumps to the proper address using this instruction, which is described in the next section.

jump address table Also called jump table. A table of addresses of alternative instruction sequences.

Although there are many statements for decisions and loops in programming languages like C and Java, the bedrock statement that implements them at the instruction set level is the conditional branch.

Hardware/ Software Interface

Elaboration: If you have heard about *delayed branches*, covered in Chapter 4, don't worry: the MIPS assembler makes them invisible to the assembly language programmer.

I. C has many statements for decisions and loops, while MIPS has few. Which of the following do or do not explain this imbalance? Why?

Check Yourself

1. More decision statements make code easier to read and understand.

2. Fewer decision statements simplify the task of the underlying layer that is responsible for execution.

3. More decision statements mean fewer lines of code, which generally reduces coding time.

4. More decision statements mean fewer lines of code, which generally results in the execution of fewer operations.

II. Why does C provide two sets of operators for AND (& and &&) and two sets of operators for OR (| and ||), while MIPS doesn't?

1. Logical operations AND and OR implement & and |, while conditional branches implement && and ||.

2. The previous statement has it backwards: && and || correspond to logical operations, while & and | map to conditional branches.

3. They are redundant and mean the same thing: && and || are simply inherited from the programming language B, the predecessor of C.

2.8   Supporting Procedures in Computer Hardware

procedure A stored subroutine that performs a specific task based on the parameters with which it is provided.

A **procedure** or function is one tool programmers use to structure programs, both to make them easier to understand and to allow code to be reused. Procedures allow the programmer to concentrate on just one portion of the task at a time; parameters act as an interface between the procedure and the rest of the program and data, since they can pass values and return results. We describe the equivalent to procedures in Java in Section 2.15 on the CD, but Java needs everything from a computer that C needs.

You can think of a procedure like a spy who leaves with a secret plan, acquires resources, performs the task, covers his or her tracks, and then returns to the point of origin with the desired result. Nothing else should be perturbed once the mission is complete. Moreover, a spy operates on only a "need to know" basis, so the spy can't make assumptions about his employer.

Similarly, in the execution of a procedure, the program must follow these six steps:

1. Put parameters in a place where the procedure can access them.

2. Transfer control to the procedure.

3. Acquire the storage resources needed for the procedure.

4. Perform the desired task.

5. Put the result value in a place where the calling program can access it.

6. Return control to the point of origin, since a procedure can be called from several points in a program.

As mentioned above, registers are the fastest place to hold data in a computer, so we want to use them as much as possible. MIPS software follows the following convention for procedure calling in allocating its 32 registers:

- $a0–$a3: four argument registers in which to pass parameters
- $v0–$v1: two value registers in which to return values
- $ra: one return address register to return to the point of origin

In addition to allocating these registers, MIPS assembly language includes an instruction just for the procedures: it jumps to an address and simultaneously saves the address of the following instruction in register $ra. The **jump-and-link instruction** (jal) is simply written

```
jal ProcedureAddress
```

The *link* portion of the name means that an address or link is formed that points to the calling site to allow the procedure to return to the proper address. This "link," stored in register $ra (register 31), is called the **return address**. The return address is needed because the same procedure could be called from several parts of the program.

To support such situations, computers like MIPS use *jump register* instruction (jr), introduced above to help with case statements, meaning an unconditional jump to the address specified in a register:

```
jr   $ra
```

Jump register instruction jumps to the address stored in register $ra—which is just what we want. Thus, the calling program, or **caller**, puts the parameter values in $a0–$a3 and uses jal X to jump to procedure X (sometimes named the **callee**). The callee then performs the calculations, places the results in $v0 and $v1, and returns control to the caller using jr $ra.

Implicit in the stored-program idea is the need to have a register to hold the address of the current instruction being executed. For historical reasons, this register is almost always called the **program counter**, abbreviated *PC* in the MIPS architecture, although a more sensible name would have been *instruction address register*. The jal instruction actually saves PC + 4 in register $ra to link to the following instruction to set up the procedure return.

jump-and-link instruction An instruction that jumps to an address and simultaneously saves the address of the following instruction in a register ($ra in MIPS).

return address A link to the calling site that allows a procedure to return to the proper address; in MIPS it is stored in register $ra.

caller The program that instigates a procedure and provides the necessary parameter values.

callee A procedure that executes a series of stored instructions based on parameters provided by the caller and then returns control to the caller.

program counter (PC) The register containing the address of the instruction in the program being executed.

Using More Registers

Suppose a compiler needs more registers for a procedure than the four argument and two return value registers. Since we must cover our tracks after our mission is complete, any registers needed by the caller must be restored to the values that they contained *before* the procedure was invoked. This situation is an example in which we need to spill registers to memory, as mentioned in the *Hardware/Software Interface* section.

The ideal data structure for spilling registers is a **stack**—a last-in-first-out queue. A stack needs a pointer to the most recently allocated address in the stack to show where the next procedure should place the registers to be spilled or where old register values are found. The **stack pointer** is adjusted by one word for each register that is saved or restored. MIPS software reserves register 29 for the stack pointer, giving it the obvious name $sp. Stacks are so popular that they have their own buzzwords for transferring data to and from the stack: placing data onto the stack is called a **push**, and removing data from the stack is called a **pop**.

By historical precedent, stacks "grow" from higher addresses to lower addresses. This convention means that you push values onto the stack by subtracting from the stack pointer. Adding to the stack pointer shrinks the stack, thereby popping values off the stack.

stack A data structure for spilling registers organized as a last-in-first-out queue.

stack pointer A value denoting the most recently allocated address in a stack that shows where registers should be spilled or where old register values can be found. In MIPS, it is register $sp.

push Add element to stack.

pop Remove element from stack.

EXAMPLE

Compiling a C Procedure That Doesn't Call Another Procedure

Let's turn the example on page 79 from Section 2.2 into a C procedure:

```
int leaf_example (int g, int h, int i, int j)
{
    int f;

    f = (g + h) - (i + j);
    return f;
}
```

What is the compiled MIPS assembly code?

ANSWER

The parameter variables g, h, i, and j correspond to the argument registers $a0, $a1, $a2, and $a3, and f corresponds to $s0. The compiled program starts with the label of the procedure:

```
leaf_example:
```

The next step is to save the registers used by the procedure. The C assignment statement in the procedure body is identical to the example on page 79, which uses two temporary registers. Thus, we need to save three registers: $s0, $t0, and $t1. We "push" the old values onto the stack by creating space for three words (12 bytes) on the stack and then store them:

```
addi $sp, $sp, -12    # adjust stack to make room for 3 items
sw   $t1, 8($sp)      # save register $t1 for use afterwards
sw   $t0, 4($sp)      # save register $t0 for use afterwards
sw   $s0, 0($sp)      # save register $s0 for use afterwards
```

Figure 2.10 shows the stack before, during, and after the procedure call.

The next three statements correspond to the body of the procedure, which follows the example on page 79:

```
add $t0,$a0,$a1 # register $t0 contains g + h
add $t1,$a2,$a3 # register $t1 contains i + j
sub $s0,$t0,$t1 # f = $t0 - $t1, which is (g + h)-(i + j)
```

To return the value of f, we copy it into a return value register:

```
add $v0,$s0,$zero # returns f ($v0 = $s0 + 0)
```

Before returning, we restore the three old values of the registers we saved by "popping" them from the stack:

```
lw   $s0, 0($sp)  # restore register $s0 for caller
lw   $t0, 4($sp)  # restore register $t0 for caller
lw   $t1, 8($sp)  # restore register $t1 for caller
addi $sp,$sp,12   # adjust stack to delete 3 items
```

The procedure ends with a jump register using the return address:

```
jr  $ra     # jump back to calling routine
```

In the previous example, we used temporary registers and assumed their old values must be saved and restored. To avoid saving and restoring a register whose value is never used, which might happen with a temporary register, MIPS software separates 18 of the registers into two groups:

- $t0–$t9 : ten temporary registers that are *not* preserved by the callee (called procedure) on a procedure call

- $s0–$s7 : eight saved registers that must be preserved on a procedure call (if used, the callee saves and restores them)

This simple convention reduces register spilling. In the example above, since the caller does not expect registers $t0 and $t1 to be preserved across a procedure call, we can drop two stores and two loads from the code. We still must save and restore $s0, since the callee must assume that the caller needs its value.

High address

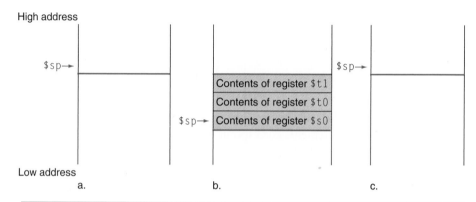

Low address
          a.   b.   c.

FIGURE 2.10   The values of the stack pointer and the stack (a) before, (b) during, and (c) after the procedure call. The stack pointer always points to the "top" of the stack, or the last word in the stack in this drawing.

Nested Procedures

Procedures that do not call others are called *leaf* procedures. Life would be simple if all procedures were leaf procedures, but they aren't. Just as a spy might employ other spies as part of a mission, who in turn might use even more spies, so do procedures invoke other procedures. Moreover, recursive procedures even invoke "clones" of themselves. Just as we need to be careful when using registers in procedures, more care must also be taken when invoking nonleaf procedures.

For example, suppose that the main program calls procedure A with an argument of 3, by placing the value 3 into register $a0 and then using jal A. Then suppose that procedure A calls procedure B via jal B with an argument of 7, also placed in $a0. Since A hasn't finished its task yet, there is a conflict over the use of register $a0. Similarly, there is a conflict over the return address in register $ra, since it now has the return address for B. Unless we take steps to prevent the problem, this conflict will eliminate procedure A's ability to return to its caller.

One solution is to push all the other registers that must be preserved onto the stack, just as we did with the saved registers. The caller pushes any argument registers ($a0–$a3) or temporary registers ($t0–$t9) that are needed after the call. The callee pushes the return address register $ra and any saved registers ($s0–$s7) used by the callee. The stack pointer $sp is adjusted to account for the number of registers placed on the stack. Upon the return, the registers are restored from memory and the stack pointer is readjusted.

Compiling a Recursive C Procedure, Showing Nested Procedure Linking

Let's tackle a recursive procedure that calculates factorial:

```
int fact (int n)
{
    if (n < 1) return (1);
        else return (n * fact(n - 1));
}
```

What is the MIPS assembly code?

EXAMPLE

The parameter variable n corresponds to the argument register $a0. The compiled program starts with the label of the procedure and then saves two registers on the stack, the return address and $a0:

ANSWER

```
fact:
    addi  $sp, $sp, -8  # adjust stack for 2 items
    sw    $ra, 4($sp)   # save the return address
    sw    $a0, 0($sp)   # save the argument n
```

The first time fact is called, sw saves an address in the program that called fact. The next two instructions test whether n is less than 1, going to L1 if n ≥ 1.

```
    slti  $t0,$a0,1     # test for n < 1
    beq   $t0,$zero,L1  # if n >= 1, go to L1
```

If n is less than 1, fact returns 1 by putting 1 into a value register: it adds 1 to 0 and places that sum in $v0. It then pops the two saved values off the stack and jumps to the return address:

```
    addi  $v0,$zero,1  # return 1
    addi  $sp,$sp,8    # pop 2 items off stack
    jr    $ra          # return to caller
```

Before popping two items off the stack, we could have loaded $a0 and $ra. Since $a0 and $ra don't change when n is less than 1, we skip those instructions.

If n is not less than 1, the argument n is decremented and then fact is called again with the decremented value:

```
L1: addi $a0,$a0,-1   # n >= 1: argument gets (n - 1)
    jal  fact         # call fact with (n - 1)
```

The next instruction is where `fact` returns. Now the old return address and old argument are restored, along with the stack pointer:

```
lw    $a0, 0($sp)     # return from jal: restore argument n
lw    $ra, 4($sp)     # restore the return address
addi  $sp, $sp, 8     # adjust stack pointer to pop 2 items
```

Next, the value register $v0 gets the product of old argument $a0 and the current value of the value register. We assume a multiply instruction is available, even though it is not covered until Chapter 3:

```
mul $v0,$a0,$v0   # return n * fact (n - 1)
```

Finally, `fact` jumps again to the return address:

```
jr    $ra              # return to the caller
```

Hardware/ Software Interface

A C variable is generally a location in storage, and its interpretation depends both on its *type* and *storage class*. Examples include integers and characters (see Section 2.9). C has two storage classes: *automatic* and *static*. Automatic variables are local to a procedure and are discarded when the procedure exits. Static variables exist across exits from and entries to procedures. C variables declared outside all procedures are considered static, as are any variables declared using the keyword *static*. The rest are automatic. To simplify access to static data, MIPS software reserves another register, called the **global pointer**, or $gp.

global pointer The register that is reserved to point to the static area.

Figure 2.11 summarizes what is preserved across a procedure call. Note that several schemes preserve the stack, guaranteeing that the caller will get the same data back on a load from the stack as it stored onto the stack. The stack above $sp is preserved simply by making sure the callee does not write above $sp; $sp is itself preserved by the callee adding exactly the same amount that was subtracted from it; and the other registers are preserved by saving them on the stack (if they are used) and restoring them from there.

Preserved	Not preserved
Saved registers: $s0–$s7	Temporary registers: $t0–$t9
Stack pointer register: $sp	Argument registers: $a0–$a3
Return address register: $ra	Return value registers: $v0–$v1
Stack above the stack pointer	Stack below the stack pointer

FIGURE 2.11   What is and what is not preserved across a procedure call. If the software relies on the frame pointer register or on the global pointer register, discussed in the following subsections, they are also preserved.

Allocating Space for New Data on the Stack

The final complexity is that the stack is also used to store variables that are local to the procedure but do not fit in registers, such as local arrays or structures. The segment of the stack containing a procedure's saved registers and local variables is called a **procedure frame** or **activation record**. Figure 2.12 shows the state of the stack before, during, and after the procedure call.

Some MIPS software uses a **frame pointer** ($fp) to point to the first word of the frame of a procedure. A stack pointer might change during the procedure, and so references to a local variable in memory might have different offsets depending on where they are in the procedure, making the procedure harder to understand. Alternatively, a frame pointer offers a stable base register within a procedure for local memory-references. Note that an activation record appears on the stack whether or not an explicit frame pointer is used. We've been avoiding using $fp by avoiding changes to $sp within a procedure: in our examples, the stack is adjusted only on entry and exit of the procedure.

procedure frame Also called activation record. The segment of the stack containing a procedure's saved registers and local variables.

frame pointer A value denoting the location of the saved registers and local variables for a given procedure.

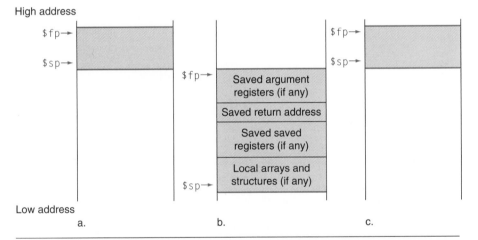

FIGURE 2.12 Illustration of the stack allocation (a) before, (b) during, and (c) after the procedure call. The frame pointer ($fp) points to the first word of the frame, often a saved argument register, and the stack pointer ($sp) points to the top of the stack. The stack is adjusted to make room for all the saved registers and any memory-resident local variables. Since the stack pointer may change during program execution, it's easier for programmers to reference variables via the stable frame pointer, although it could be done just with the stack pointer and a little address arithmetic. If there are no local variables on the stack within a procedure, the compiler will save time by *not* setting and restoring the frame pointer. When a frame pointer is used, it is initialized using the address in $sp on a call, and $sp is restored using $fp. This information is also found in Column 4 of the MIPS Reference Data Card at the front of this book.

Allocating Space for New Data on the Heap

In addition to automatic variables that are local to procedures, C programmers need
space in memory for static variables and for dynamic data structures. Figure 2.13
shows the MIPS convention for allocation of memory. The stack starts in the
high end of memory and grows down. The first part of the low end of memory is
reserved, followed by the home of the MIPS machine code, traditionally called the
text segment. Above the code is the *static data segment*, which is the place for constants and other static variables. Although arrays tend to be a fixed length and thus
are a good match to the static data segment, data structures like linked lists tend to
grow and shrink during their lifetimes. The segment for such data structures is traditionally called the *heap*, and it is placed next in memory. Note that this allocation
allows the stack and heap to grow toward each other, thereby allowing the efficient
use of memory as the two segments wax and wane.

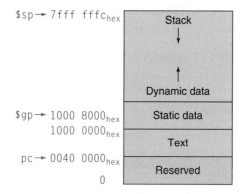

FIGURE 2.13 The MIPS memory allocation for program and data. These addresses are
only a software convention, and not part of the MIPS architecture. The stack pointer is initialized to
$7\text{fff fffc}_{\text{hex}}$ and grows down toward the data segment. At the other end, the program code ("text") starts
at $0040\ 0000_{\text{hex}}$. The static data starts at $1000\ 0000_{\text{hex}}$. Dynamic data, allocated by malloc in C and
by new in Java, is next. It grows up toward the stack in an area called the heap. The global pointer, $gp, is
set to an address to make it easy to access data. It is initialized to $1000\ 8000_{\text{hex}}$ so that it can access from
$1000\ 0000_{\text{hex}}$ to $1000\ \text{ffff}_{\text{hex}}$ using the positive and negative 16-bit offsets from $gp. This information
is also found in Column 4 of the MIPS Reference Data Card at the front of this book.

C allocates and frees space on the heap with explicit functions. malloc() allocates space on the heap and returns a pointer to it, and free() releases space on
the heap to which the pointer points. Memory allocation is controlled by programs
in C, and it is the source of many common and difficult bugs. Forgetting to free space
leads to a "memory leak," which eventually uses up so much memory that the operating system may crash. Freeing space too early leads to "dangling pointers," which
can cause pointers to point to things that the program never intended. Java uses
automatic memory allocation and garbage collection just to avoid such bugs.

Figure 2.14 summarizes the register conventions for the MIPS assembly language.

Name	Register number	Usage	Preserved on call?
$zero	0	The constant value 0	n.a.
$v0–$v1	2–3	Values for results and expression evaluation	no
$a0–$a3	4–7	Arguments	no
$t0–$t7	8–15	Temporaries	no
$s0–$s7	16–23	Saved	yes
$t8–$t9	24–25	More temporaries	no
$gp	28	Global pointer	yes
$sp	29	Stack pointer	yes
$fp	30	Frame pointer	yes
$ra	31	Return address	yes

FIGURE 2.14   MIPS register conventions. Register 1, called $at, is reserved for the assembler (see Section 2.12), and registers 26–27, called $k0–$k1, are reserved for the operating system. This information is also found in Column 2 of the MIPS Reference Data Card at the front of this book.

Elaboration: What if there are more than four parameters? The MIPS convention is to place the extra parameters on the stack just above the frame pointer. The procedure then expects the first four parameters to be in registers $a0 through $a3 and the rest in memory, addressable via the frame pointer.

As mentioned in the caption of Figure 2.12, the frame pointer is convenient because all references to variables in the stack within a procedure will have the same offset. The frame pointer is not necessary, however. The GNU MIPS C compiler uses a frame pointer, but the C compiler from MIPS does not; it treats register 30 as another save register ($s8).

Elaboration: Some recursive procedures can be implemented iteratively without using recursion. Iteration can significantly improve performance by removing the overhead associated with procedure calls. For example, consider a procedure used to accumulate a sum:

```
int sum (int n, int acc) {
  if (n > 0)
      return sum(n - 1, acc + n);
  else
      return acc;
}
```

Consider the procedure call sum(3,0). This will result in recursive calls to sum(2,3), sum(1,5), and sum(0,6), and then the result 6 will be returned four times. This recursive call of sum is referred to as a *tail call*, and this example use of tail recursion can be implemented very efficiently (assume $a0 = n and $a1 = acc):

```
sum: slti $t0, $a0, 1     # test if n <= 0
     bne $t0, $zero, sum_exit # go to sum_exit if n <= 0
     add$a1, $a1, $a0      # add n to acc
```

```
        addi$a0, $a0, -1        # subtract 1 from n
        j sum                   # go to sum
    sum_exit:
        add$v0, $a1, $zero      # return value acc
        jr $ra                  # return to caller
```

Check Yourself   Which of the following statements about C and Java are generally true?

1. C programmers manage data explicitly, while it's automatic in Java.

2. C leads to more pointer bugs and memory leak bugs than does Java.

!(@| = > (wow open tab at bar is great)

Fourth line of the keyboard poem "Hatless Atlas," 1991 (some give names to ASCII characters: "!" is "wow," "(" is open, "|" is bar, and so on).

2.9 Communicating with People

Computers were invented to crunch numbers, but as soon as they became commercially viable they were used to process text. Most computers today offer 8-bit bytes to represent characters, with the American Standard Code for Information Interchange (ASCII) being the representation that nearly everyone follows. Figure 2.15 summarizes ASCII.

ASCII value	Character	ASCII value	Character	ASCII value	Character	ASCII value	Character	ASCII value	Character	ASCII value	Character
32	space	48	0	64	@	80	P	96	`	112	p
33	!	49	1	65	A	81	Q	97	a	113	q
34	"	50	2	66	B	82	R	98	b	114	r
35	#	51	3	67	C	83	S	99	c	115	s
36	$	52	4	68	D	84	T	100	d	116	t
37	%	53	5	69	E	85	U	101	e	117	u
38	&	54	6	70	F	86	V	102	f	118	v
39	'	55	7	71	G	87	W	103	g	119	w
40	(	56	8	72	H	88	X	104	h	120	x
41	)	57	9	73	I	89	Y	105	i	121	y
42	*	58	:	74	J	90	Z	106	j	122	z
43	+	59	;	75	K	91	[	107	k	123	{
44	,	60	<	76	L	92	\	108	l	124		
45	-	61	=	77	M	93	]	109	m	125	}
46	.	62	>	78	N	94	^	110	n	126	~
47	/	63	?	79	O	95	_	111	o	127	DEL

FIGURE 2.15   ASCII representation of characters. Note that upper- and lowercase letters differ by exactly 32; this observation can lead to shortcuts in checking or changing upper- and lowercase. Values not shown include formatting characters. For example, 8 represents a backspace, 9 represents a tab character, and 13 a carriage return. Another useful value is 0 for null, the value the programming language C uses to mark the end of a string. This information is also found in Column 3 of the MIPS Reference Data Card at the front of this book.

Base 2 is not natural to human beings; we have 10 fingers and so find base 10 natural. Why didn't computers use decimal? In fact, the first commercial computer *did* offer decimal arithmetic. The problem was that the computer still used on and off signals, so a decimal digit was simply represented by several binary digits. Decimal proved so inefficient that subsequent computers reverted to all binary, converting to base 10 only for the relatively infrequent input/output events.

Hardware/ Software Interface

ASCII versus Binary Numbers

We could represent numbers as strings of ASCII digits instead of as integers. How much does storage increase if the number 1 billion is represented in ASCII versus a 32-bit integer?

EXAMPLE

One billion is 1,000,000,000, so it would take 10 ASCII digits, each 8 bits long. Thus the storage expansion would be $(10 \times 8)/32$ or 2.5. In addition to the expansion in storage, the hardware to add, subtract, multiply, and divide such decimal numbers is difficult. Such difficulties explain why computing professionals are raised to believe that binary is natural and that the occasional decimal computer is bizarre.

ANSWER

A series of instructions can extract a byte from a word, so load word and store word are sufficient for transferring bytes as well as words. Because of the popularity of text in some programs, however, MIPS provides instructions to move bytes. Load byte (lb) loads a byte from memory, placing it in the rightmost 8 bits of a register. Store byte (sb) takes a byte from the rightmost 8 bits of a register and writes it to memory. Thus, we copy a byte with the sequence

```
lb $t0,0($sp)      # Read byte from source
sb $t0,0($gp)      # Write byte to destination
```

Hardware/ Software Interface

Signed versus unsigned applies to loads as well as to arithmetic. The *function* of a signed load is to copy the sign repeatedly to fill the rest of the register—called *sign extension*—but its *purpose* is to place a correct representation of the number within that register. Unsigned loads simply fill with 0s to the left of the data, since the number represented by the bit pattern is unsigned.

When loading a 32-bit word into a 32-bit register, the point is moot; signed and unsigned loads are identical. MIPS does offer two flavors of byte loads: *load byte* (1b) treats the byte as a signed number and thus sign-extends to fill the 24 left-most bits of the register, while *load byte unsigned* (1bu) works with unsigned integers. Since C programs almost always use bytes to represent characters rather than consider bytes as very short signed integers, 1bu is used practically exclusively for byte loads.

Characters are normally combined into strings, which have a variable number of characters. There are three choices for representing a string: (1) the first position of the string is reserved to give the length of a string, (2) an accompanying variable has the length of the string (as in a structure), or (3) the last position of a string is indicated by a character used to mark the end of a string. C uses the third choice, terminating a string with a byte whose value is 0 (named null in ASCII). Thus, the string "Cal" is represented in C by the following 4 bytes, shown as decimal numbers: 67, 97, 108, 0. (As we shall see, Java uses the first option.)

Compiling a String Copy Procedure, Showing How to Use C Strings

EXAMPLE

The procedure strcpy copies string y to string x using the null byte termination convention of C:

```
void strcpy (char x[], char y[])
{
    int i;

    i = 0;
    while ((x[i] = y[i]) != '\0') /* copy & test byte */
        i += 1;
}
```

What is the MIPS assembly code?

Below is the basic MIPS assembly code segment. Assume that base addresses for arrays x and y are found in $a0 and $a1, while i is in $s0. strcpy adjusts the stack pointer and then saves the saved register $s0 on the stack:

ANSWER

```
strcpy:
    addi   $sp,$sp,-4    # adjust stack for 1 more item
    sw     $s0, 0($sp)   # save $s0
```

To initialize i to 0, the next instruction sets $s0 to 0 by adding 0 to 0 and placing that sum in $s0:

```
    add    $s0,$zero,$zero # i = 0 + 0
```

This is the beginning of the loop. The address of y[i] is first formed by adding i to y[]:

```
L1: add    $t1,$s0,$a1   # address of y[i] in $t1
```

Note that we don't have to multiply i by 4 since y is an array of *bytes* and not of words, as in prior examples.

To load the character in y[i], we use load byte unsigned, which puts the character into $t2:

```
    lbu    $t2, 0($t1)   # $t2 = y[i]
```

A similar address calculation puts the address of x[i] in $t3, and then the character in $t2 is stored at that address.

```
    add    $t3,$s0,$a0   # address of x[i] in $t3
    sb     $t2, 0($t3)   # x[i] = y[i]
```

Next, we exit the loop if the character was 0. That is, we exit if it is the last character of the string:

```
    beq    $t2,$zero,L2  # if y[i] == 0, go to L2
```

If not, we increment i and loop back:

```
    addi   $s0, $s0,1    # i = i + 1
    j      L1            # go to L1
```

If we don't loop back, it was the last character of the string; we restore $s0 and the stack pointer, and then return.

```
L2: lw    $s0, 0($sp) # y[i] == 0: end of string. Re-
store old $s0

    addi  $sp,$sp,4   # pop 1 word off stack
    jr    $ra         # return
```

String copies usually use pointers instead of arrays in C to avoid the operations on i in the code above. See Section 2.14 for an explanation of arrays versus pointers.

Since the procedure strcpy above is a leaf procedure, the compiler could allocate i to a temporary register and avoid saving and restoring $s0. Hence, instead of thinking of the $t registers as being just for temporaries, we can think of them as registers that the callee should use whenever convenient. When a compiler finds a leaf procedure, it exhausts all temporary registers before using registers it must save.

Characters and Strings in Java

Unicode is a universal encoding of the alphabets of most human languages. Figure 2.16 is a list of Unicode alphabets; there are almost as many *alphabets* in Unicode as there are useful *symbols* in ASCII. To be more inclusive, Java uses Unicode for characters. By default, it uses 16 bits to represent a character.

The MIPS instruction set has explicit instructions to load and store such 16-bit quantities, called *halfwords*. Load half (lh) loads a halfword from memory, placing it in the rightmost 16 bits of a register. Like load byte, *load half* (lh) treats the halfword as a signed number and thus sign-extends to fill the 16 leftmost bits of the register, while *load halfword unsigned* (lhu) works with unsigned integers. Thus, lhu is the more popular of the two. Store half (sh) takes a halfword from the rightmost 16 bits of a register and writes it to memory. We copy a halfword with the sequence

```
lhu $t0,0($sp) # Read halfword (16 bits) from source
sh $t0,0($gp)  # Write halfword (16 bits) to destination
```

Strings are a standard Java class with special built-in support and predefined methods for concatenation, comparison, and conversion. Unlike C, Java includes a word that gives the length of the string, similar to Java arrays.

Elaboration: MIPS software tries to keep the stack aligned to word addresses, allowing the program to always use lw and sw (which must be aligned) to access the stack. This convention means that a char variable allocated on the stack occupies 4 bytes, even though it needs less. However, a C string variable or an array of bytes *will* pack 4 bytes per word, and a Java string variable or array of shorts packs 2 halfwords per word.

Latin	Malayalam	Tagbanwa	General Punctuation
Greek	Sinhala	Khmer	Spacing Modifier Letters
Cyrillic	Thai	Mongolian	Currency Symbols
Armenian	Lao	Limbu	Combining Diacritical Marks
Hebrew	Tibetan	Tai Le	Combining Marks for Symbols
Arabic	Myanmar	Kangxi Radicals	Superscripts and Subscripts
Syriac	Georgian	Hiragana	Number Forms
Thaana	Hangul Jamo	Katakana	Mathematical Operators
Devanagari	Ethiopic	Bopomofo	Mathematical Alphanumeric Symbols
Bengali	Cherokee	Kanbun	Braille Patterns
Gurmukhi	Unified Canadian Aboriginal Syllabic	Shavian	Optical Character Recognition
Gujarati	Ogham	Osmanya	Byzantine Musical Symbols
Oriya	Runic	Cypriot Syllabary	Musical Symbols
Tamil	Tagalog	Tai Xuan Jing Symbols	Arrows
Telugu	Hanunoo	Yijing Hexagram Symbols	Box Drawing
Kannada	Buhid	Aegean Numbers	Geometric Shapes

FIGURE 2.16 Example alphabets in Unicode. Unicode version 4.0 has more than 160 "blocks," which is their name for a collection of symbols. Each block is a multiple of 16. For example, Greek starts at 0370_{hex}, and Cyrillic at 0400_{hex}. The first three columns show 48 blocks that correspond to human languages in roughly Unicode numerical order. The last column has 16 blocks that are multilingual and are not in order. A 16-bit encoding, called UTF-16, is the default. A variable-length encoding, called UTF-8, keeps the ASCII subset as eight bits and uses 16–32 bits for the other characters. UTF-32 uses 32 bits per character. To learn more, see *www.unicode.org*.

I. Which of the following statements about characters and strings in C and Java are true?

Check Yourself

1. A string in C takes about half the memory as the same string in Java.

2. Strings are just an informal name for single-dimension arrays of characters in C and Java.

3. Strings in C and Java use null (0) to mark the end of a string.

4. Operations on strings, like length, are faster in C than in Java.

II. Which type of variable that can contain $1,000,000,000_{ten}$ takes the most memory space?

1. `int` in C

2. `string` in C

3. `string` in Java

2.10 MIPS Addressing for 32-Bit Immediates and Addresses

Although keeping all MIPS instructions 32 bits long simplifies the hardware, there are times where it would be convenient to have a 32-bit constant or 32-bit address. This section starts with the general solution for large constants, and then shows the optimizations for instruction addresses used in branches and jumps.

32-Bit Immediate Operands

Although constants are frequently short and fit into the 16-bit field, sometimes they are bigger. The MIPS instruction set includes the instruction *load upper immediate* (lui) specifically to set the upper 16 bits of a constant in a register, allowing a subsequent instruction to specify the lower 16 bits of the constant. Figure 2.17 shows the operation of lui.

EXAMPLE

ANSWER

Loading a 32-Bit Constant

What is the MIPS assembly code to load this 32-bit constant into register $s0?

    0000 0000 0011 1101 0000 1001 0000 0000

First, we would load the upper 16 bits, which is 61 in decimal, using lui:

    lui $s0, 61   # 61 decimal = 0000 0000 0011 1101 binary

The value of register $s0 afterward is

    0000 0000 0011 1101 0000 0000 0000 0000

The next step is to insert the lower 16 bits, whose decimal value is 2304:

    ori $s0, $s0, 2304 # 2304 decimal = 0000 1001 0000 0000

The final value in register $s0 is the desired value:

    0000 0000 0011 1101 0000 1001 0000 0000

The machine language version of `lui $t0, 255` `# $t0 is register 8:`

001111	00000	01000	0000 0000 1111 1111

Contents of register $t0 after executing `lui $t0, 255:`

0000 0000 1111 1111	0000 0000 0000 0000

FIGURE 2.17 The effect of the `lui` instruction. The instruction `lui` transfers the 16-bit immediate constant field value into the leftmost 16 bits of the register, filling the lower 16 bits with 0s.

Either the compiler or the assembler must break large constants into pieces and then reassemble them into a register. As you might expect, the immediate field's size restriction may be a problem for memory addresses in loads and stores as well as for constants in immediate instructions. If this job falls to the assembler, as it does for MIPS software, then the assembler must have a temporary register available in which to create the long values. This is a reason for the register $at, which is reserved for the assembler.

Hence, the symbolic representation of the MIPS machine language is no longer limited by the hardware, but by whatever the creator of an assembler chooses to include (see Section 2.12). We stick close to the hardware to explain the architecture of the computer, noting when we use the enhanced language of the assembler that is not found in the processor.

Hardware/ Software Interface

Elaboration: Creating 32-bit constants needs care. The instruction `addi` copies the leftmost bit of the 16-bit immediate field of the instruction into the upper 16 bits of a word. *Logical or immediate* from Section 2.6 loads 0s into the upper 16 bits and hence is used by the assembler in conjunction with `lui` to create 32-bit constants.

Addressing in Branches and Jumps

The MIPS jump instructions have the simplest addressing. They use the final MIPS instruction format, called the *J-type*, which consists of 6 bits for the operation field and the rest of the bits for the address field. Thus,

    j   10000   # go to location 10000

could be assembled into this format (it's actually a bit more complicated, as we will see):

2	10000
6 bits	26 bits

where the value of the jump opcode is 2 and the jump address is 10000.

Unlike the jump instruction, the conditional branch instruction must specify two operands in addition to the branch address. Thus,

```
bne  $s0,$s1,Exit   # go to Exit if $s0 ≠ $s1
```

is assembled into this instruction, leaving only 16 bits for the branch address:

5	16	17	Exit
6 bits	5 bits	5 bits	16 bits

If addresses of the program had to fit in this 16-bit field, it would mean that no program could be bigger than 2^{16}, which is far too small to be a realistic option today. An alternative would be to specify a register that would always be added to the branch address, so that a branch instruction would calculate the following:

$$\text{Program counter} = \text{Register} + \text{Branch address}$$

This sum allows the program to be as large as 2^{32} and still be able to use conditional branches, solving the branch address size problem. Then the question is, which register?

The answer comes from seeing how conditional branches are used. Conditional branches are found in loops and in *if* statements, so they tend to branch to a nearby instruction. For example, about half of all conditional branches in SPEC benchmarks go to locations less than 16 instructions away. Since the program counter (PC) contains the address of the current instruction, we can branch within $\pm 2^{15}$ words of the current instruction if we use the PC as the register to be added to the address. Almost all loops and *if* statements are much smaller than 2^{16} words, so the PC is the ideal choice.

PC-relative addressing An addressing regime in which the address is the sum of the program counter (PC) and a constant in the instruction.

This form of branch addressing is called **PC-relative addressing**. As we shall see in Chapter 4, it is convenient for the hardware to increment the PC early to point to the next instruction. Hence, the MIPS address is actually relative to the address of the following instruction (PC + 4) as opposed to the current instruction (PC).

Like most recent computers, MIPS uses PC-relative addressing for all conditional branches, because the destination of these instructions is likely to be close to the branch. On the other hand, jump-and-link instructions invoke procedures that have no reason to be near the call, so they normally use other forms of addressing. Hence, the MIPS architecture offers long addresses for procedure calls by using the J-type format for both jump and jump-and-link instructions.

Since all MIPS instructions are 4 bytes long, MIPS stretches the distance of the branch by having PC-relative addressing refer to the number of *words* to the next instruction instead of the number of bytes. Thus, the 16-bit field can branch four times as far by interpreting the field as a relative word address rather than as a relative byte address. Similarly, the 26-bit field in jump instructions is also a word address, meaning that it represents a 28-bit byte address.

Elaboration: Since the PC is 32 bits, 4 bits must come from somewhere else for jumps. The MIPS jump instruction replaces only the lower 28 bits of the PC, leaving the upper 4 bits of the PC unchanged. The loader and linker (Section 2.12) must be careful to avoid placing a program across an address boundary of 256 MB (64 million instructions); otherwise, a jump must be replaced by a jump register instruction preceded by other instructions to load the full 32-bit address into a register.

Showing Branch Offset in Machine Language

The *while* loop on page 107–108 was compiled into this MIPS assembler code:

EXAMPLE

```
Loop:sll    $t1,$s3,2    # Temp reg $t1 = 4 * i
     add $t1,$t1,$s6      # $t1 = address of save[i]
     lw  $t0,0($t1)       # Temp reg $t0 = save[i]
     bne $t0,$s5, Exit     # go to Exit if save[i] ≠ k
     addi $s3,$s3,1        # i = i + 1
     j   Loop             # go to Loop
Exit:
```

If we assume we place the loop starting at location 80000 in memory, what is the MIPS machine code for this loop?

The assembled instructions and their addresses are:

ANSWER

80000	0	0	19	9	2	0
80004	0	9	22	9	0	32
80008	35	9	8		0	
80012	5	8	21		2	
80016	8	19	19		1	
80020	2		20000			
80024	...					

Remember that MIPS instructions have byte addresses, so addresses of sequential words differ by 4, the number of bytes in a word. The `bne` instruction on the fourth line adds 2 words or 8 bytes to the address of the *following* instruction (80016), specifying the branch destination relative to that following instruction (8 + 80016) instead of relative to the branch instruction (12 + 80012) or using the full destination address (80024). The jump instruction on the last line does use the full address (20000 × 4 = 80000), corresponding to the label `Loop`.

Hardware/ Software Interface

Most conditional branches are to a nearby location, but occasionally they branch far away, farther than can be represented in the 16 bits of the conditional branch instruction. The assembler comes to the rescue just as it did with large addresses or constants: it inserts an unconditional jump to the branch target, and inverts the condition so that the branch decides whether to skip the jump.

EXAMPLE

Branching Far Away

Given a branch on register $s0 being equal to register $s1,

```
beq    $s0, $s1, L1
```

replace it by a pair of instructions that offers a much greater branching distance.

ANSWER

These instructions replace the short-address conditional branch:

```
        bne    $s0, $s1, L2
        j      L1
L2:
```

MIPS Addressing Mode Summary

addressing mode One of several addressing regimes delimited by their varied use of operands and/or addresses.

Multiple forms of addressing are generically called **addressing modes**. Figure 2.18 shows how operands are identified for each addressing mode. The MIPS addressing modes are the following:

1. *Immediate addressing*, where the operand is a constant within the instruction itself

2. *Register addressing*, where the operand is a register

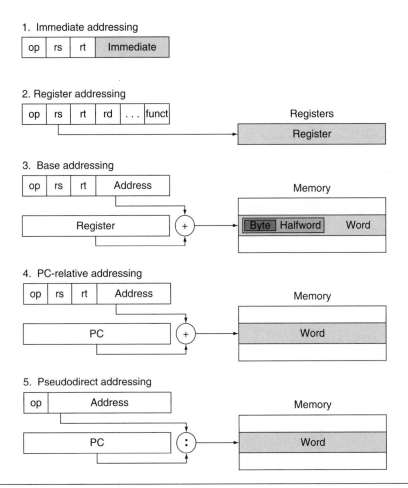

FIGURE 2.18   Illustration of the five MIPS addressing modes. The operands are shaded in color. The operand of mode 3 is in memory, whereas the operand for mode 2 is a register. Note that versions of load and store access bytes, halfwords, or words. For mode 1, the operand is 16 bits of the instruction itself. Modes 4 and 5 address instructions in memory, with mode 4 adding a 16-bit address shifted left 2 bits to the PC and mode 5 concatenating a 26-bit address shifted left 2 bits with the 4 upper bits of the PC.

3. *Base* or *displacement addressing,* where the operand is at the memory location whose address is the sum of a register and a constant in the instruction

4. *PC-relative addressing,* where the branch address is the sum of the PC and a constant in the instruction

5. *Pseudodirect addressing,* where the jump address is the 26 bits of the instruction concatenated with the upper bits of the PC

Hardware/ Software Interface

Although we show MIPS as having 32-bit addresses, nearly all microprocessors (including MIPS) have 64-bit address extensions (see ⊙ **Appendix E**). These extensions were in response to the needs of software for larger programs. The process of instruction set extension allows architectures to expand in such a way that is able to move software compatibly upward to the next generation of architecture.

Note that a single operation can use more than one addressing mode. Add, for example, uses both immediate (`addi`) and register (`add`) addressing.

Decoding Machine Language

Sometimes you are forced to reverse-engineer machine language to create the original assembly language. One example is when looking at "core dump." Figure 2.19 shows the MIPS encoding of the fields for the MIPS machine language. This figure helps when translating by hand between assembly language and machine language.

Decoding Machine Code

EXAMPLE

What is the assembly language statement corresponding to this machine instruction?

    00af8020hex

ANSWER

The first step in converting hexadecimal to binary is to find the op fields:

    (Bits:31 28 26   5   2 0)
         0000 0000 1010 1111 1000 0000 0010 0000

We look at the op field to determine the operation. Referring to Figure 2.19, when bits 31–29 are 000 and bits 28–26 are 000, it is an R-format instruction. Let's reformat the binary instruction into R-format fields, listed in Figure 2.20:

    op   rs   rt   rd   shamt   funct
    000000   00101   01111   10000   00000   100000

The bottom portion of Figure 2.19 determines the operation of an R-format instruction. In this case, bits 5–3 are 100 and bits 2–0 are 000, which means this binary pattern represents an `add` instruction.

We decode the rest of the instruction by looking at the field values. The decimal values are 5 for the rs field, 15 for rt, and 16 for rd (shamt is unused). Figure 2.14 shows that these numbers represent registers $a1, $t7, and $s0. Now we can reveal the assembly instruction:

    add $s0,$a1,$t7

op(31:26)							
28–26 / 31–29	0(000)	1(001)	2(010)	3(011)	4(100)	5(101)	6(110)	7(111)
0(000)	R-format	Bltz/gez	jump	jump & link	branch eq	branch ne	blez	bgtz
1(001)	add immediate	addiu	set less than imm.	set less than imm. unsigned	andi	ori	xori	load upper immediate
2(010)	TLB	FlPt						
3(011)								
4(100)	load byte	load half	lwl	load word	load byte unsigned	load half unsigned	lwr	
5(101)	store byte	store half	swl	store word			swr	
6(110)	load linked word	lwc1						
7(111)	store cond. word	swc1						

op(31:26)=010000 (TLB), rs(25:21)							
23–21 / 25–24	0(000)	1(001)	2(010)	3(011)	4(100)	5(101)	6(110)	7(111)
0(00)	mfc0		cfc0		mtc0		ctc0	
1(01)								
2(10)								
3(11)								

op(31:26)=000000 (R-format), funct(5:0)							
2–0 / 5–3	0(000)	1(001)	2(010)	3(011)	4(100)	5(101)	6(110)	7(111)
0(000)	shift left logical		shift right logical	sra	sllv		srlv	srav
1(001)	jump register	jalr			syscall	break		
2(010)	mfhi	mthi	mflo	mtlo				
3(011)	mult	multu	div	divu				
4(100)	add	addu	subtract	subu	and	or	xor	not or (nor)
5(101)			set l.t.	set l.t. unsigned				
6(110)								
7(111)								

FIGURE 2.19   MIPS instruction encoding. This notation gives the value of a field by row and by column. For example, the top portion of the figure shows load word in row number 4 (100_{two} for bits 31–29 of the instruction) and column number 3 (011_{two} for bits 28–26 of the instruction), so the corresponding value of the op field (bits 31–26) is 100011_{two}. Underscore means the field is used elsewhere. For example, R-format in row 0 and column 0 (op = 000000_{two}) is defined in the bottom part of the figure. Hence, subtract in row 4 and column 2 of the bottom section means that the funct field (bits 5–0) of the instruction is 100010_{two} and the op field (bits 31–26) is 000000_{two}. The floating point value in row 2, column 1 is defined in Figure 3.18 in Chapter 3. Bltz/gez is the opcode for four instructions found in Appendix B: bltz, bgez, bltzal, and bgezal. This chapter describes instructions given in full name using color, while Chapter 3 describes instructions given in mnemonics using color. Appendix B covers all instructions.

Name	Fields						Comments
Field size	6 bits	5 bits	5 bits	5 bits	5 bits	6 bits	All MIPS instructions are 32 bits long
R-format	op	rs	rt	rd	shamt	funct	Arithmetic instruction format
I-format	op	rs	rt	address/immediate			Transfer, branch, imm. format
J-format	op	target address					Jump instruction format

FIGURE 2.20   MIPS instruction formats.

Figure 2.20 shows all the MIPS instruction formats. Figure 2.1 on page 78 shows the MIPS assembly language revealed in this chapter. The remaining hidden portion of MIPS instructions deals mainly with arithmetic and real numbers, which are covered in the next chapter.

Check Yourself

I. What is the range of addresses for conditional branches in MIPS (K = 1024)?

1. Addresses between 0 and 64K − 1
2. Addresses between 0 and 256K − 1
3. Addresses up to about 32K before the branch to about 32K after
4. Addresses up to about 128K before the branch to about 128K after

II. What is the range of addresses for jump and jump and link in MIPS (M = 1024K)?

1. Addresses between 0 and 64M − 1
2. Addresses between 0 and 256M − 1
3. Addresses up to about 32M before the branch to about 32M after
4. Addresses up to about 128M before the branch to about 128M after
5. Anywhere within a block of 64M addresses where the PC supplies the upper 6 bits
6. Anywhere within a block of 256M addresses where the PC supplies the upper 4 bits

III. What is the MIPS assembly language instruction corresponding to the machine instruction with the value 0000 0000$_{hex}$?

1. j
2. R-format
3. addi
4. sll
5. mfc0
6. Undefined opcode: there is no legal instruction that corresponds to 0

2.11 Parallelism and Instructions: Synchronization

Parallel execution is easier when tasks are independent, but often they need to cooperate. Cooperation usually means some tasks are writing new values that others must read. To know when a task is finished writing so that it is safe for another to read, the tasks need to synchronize. If they don't synchronize, there is a danger of a **data race**, where the results of the program can change depending on how events happen to occur.

For example, recall the analogy of the eight reporters writing a story on page 43 of Chapter 1. Suppose one reporter needs to read all the prior sections before writing a conclusion. Hence, he must know when the other reporters have finished their sections, so that he or she need not worry about them being changed afterwards. That is, they had better synchronize the writing and reading of each section so that the conclusion will be consistent with what is printed in the prior sections.

In computing, synchronization mechanisms are typically built with user-level software routines that rely on hardware-supplied synchronization instructions. In this section, we focus on the implementation of *lock* and *unlock* synchronization operations. Lock and unlock can be used straightforwardly to create regions where only a single processor can operate, called *mutual exclusion*, as well as to implement more complex synchronization mechanisms.

The critical ability we require to implement synchronization in a multiprocessor is a set of hardware primitives with the ability to *atomically* read and modify a memory location. That is, nothing else can interpose itself between the read and the write of the memory location. Without such a capability, the cost of building basic synchronization primitives will be too high and will increase as the processor count increases.

There are a number of alternative formulations of the basic hardware primitives, all of which provide the ability to atomically read and modify a location, together with some way to tell if the read and write were performed atomically. In general, architects do not expect users to employ the basic hardware primitives, but instead expect that the primitives will be used by system programmers to build a synchronization library, a process that is often complex and tricky.

Let's start with one such hardware primitive and show how it can be used to build a basic synchronization primitive. One typical operation for building synchronization operations is the *atomic exchange* or *atomic swap*, which interchanges a value in a register for a value in memory.

To see how to use this to build a basic synchronization primitive, assume that we want to build a simple lock where the value 0 is used to indicate that the lock is free and 1 is used to indicate that the lock is unavailable. A processor tries to set the lock by doing an exchange of 1, which is in a register, with the memory address corresponding to the lock. The value returned from the exchange instruction is 1 if

data race Two memory accesses form a data race if they are from different threads to same location, at least one is a write, and they occur one after another.

some other processor had already claimed access and 0 otherwise. In the latter case, the value is also changed to 1, preventing any competing exchange in another processor from also retrieving a 0.

For example, consider two processors that each try to do the exchange simultaneously: this race is broken, since exactly one of the processors will perform the exchange first, returning 0, and the second processor will return 1 when it does the exchange. The key to using the exchange primitive to implement synchronization is that the operation is atomic: the exchange is indivisible, and two simultaneous exchanges will be ordered by the hardware. It is impossible for two processors trying to set the synchronization variable in this manner to both think they have simultaneously set the variable.

Implementing a single atomic memory operation introduces some challenges in the design of the processor, since it requires both a memory read and a write in a single, uninterruptible instruction.

An alternative is to have a pair of instructions in which the second instruction returns a value showing whether the pair of instructions was executed as if the pair were atomic. The pair of instructions is effectively atomic if it appears as if all other operations executed by any processor occurred before or after the pair. Thus, when an instruction pair is effectively atomic, no other processor can change the value between the instruction pair.

In MIPS this pair of instructions includes a special load called a *load linked* and a special store called a *store conditional*. These instructions are used in sequence: if the contents of the memory location specified by the load linked are changed before the store conditional to the same address occurs, then the store conditional fails. The store conditional is defined to both store the value of a register in memory *and* to change the value of that register to a 1 if it succeeds and to a 0 if it fails. Since the load linked returns the initial value, and the store conditional returns 1 only if it succeeds, the following sequence implements an atomic exchange on the memory location specified by the contents of $s1:

```
try: add $t0,$zero,$s4    ;copy exchange value
     ll  $t1,0($s1)       ;load linked
     sc  $t0,0($s1)       ;store conditional
     beq $t0,$zero,try    ;branch store fails
     add $s4,$zero,$t1    ;put load value in $s4
```

At the end of this sequence the contents of $s4 and the memory location specified by $s1 have been atomically exchanged. Any time a processor intervenes and modifies the value in memory between the ll and sc instructions, the sc returns 0 in $t0, causing the code sequence to try again.

Elaboration: Although it was presented for multiprocessor synchronization, atomic exchange is also useful for the operating system in dealing with multiple processes in a single processor. To make sure nothing interferes in a single processor, the store conditional also fails if the processor does a context switch between the two instructions (see Chapter 5).

Since the store conditional will fail after either another attempted store to the load linked address or any exception, care must be taken in choosing which instructions are inserted between the two instructions. In particular, only register-register instructions can safely be permitted; otherwise, it is possible to create deadlock situations where the processor can never complete the sc because of repeated page faults. In addition, the number of instructions between the load linked and the store conditional should be small to minimize the probability that either an unrelated event or a competing processor causes the store conditional to fail frequently.

An advantage of the load linked/store conditional mechanism is that it can be used to build other synchronization primitives, such as *atomic compare and swap* or *atomic fetch-and-increment*, which are used in some parallel programming models. These involve more instructions between the ll and the sc.

When do you use primitives like load linked and store conditional?

1. When cooperating threads of a parallel program need to synchronize to get proper behavior for reading and writing shared data

2. When cooperating processes on a uniprocessor need to synchronize for reading and writing shared data

Check Yourself

2.12   Translating and Starting a Program

This section describes the four steps in transforming a C program in a file on disk into a program running on a computer. Figure 2.21 shows the translation hierarchy. Some systems combine these steps to reduce translation time, but these are the logical four phases that programs go through. This section follows this translation hierarchy.

Compiler

The compiler transforms the C program into an *assembly language program,* a symbolic form of what the machine understands. High-level language programs take many fewer lines of code than assembly language, so programmer productivity is much higher.

In 1975, many operating systems and assemblers were written in **assembly language** because memories were small and compilers were inefficient. The 500,000-fold increase in memory capacity per single DRAM chip has reduced program size concerns, and optimizing compilers today can produce assembly language programs nearly as good as an assembly language expert, and sometimes even better for large programs.

assembly language
A symbolic language that can be translated into binary machine language.

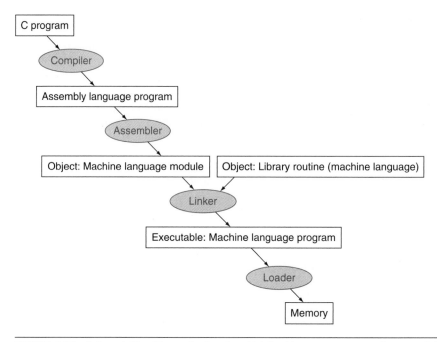

FIGURE 2.21 A translation hierarchy for C. A high-level language program is first compiled into an assembly language program and then assembled into an object module in machine language. The linker combines multiple modules with library routines to resolve all references. The loader then places the machine code into the proper memory locations for execution by the processor. To speed up the translation process, some steps are skipped or combined. Some compilers produce object modules directly, and some systems use linking loaders that perform the last two steps. To identify the type of file, UNIX follows a suffix convention for files: C source files are named x.c, assembly files are x.s, object files are named x.o, statically linked library routines are x.a, dynamically linked library routes are x.so, and executable files by default are called a.out. MS-DOS uses the suffixes .C, .ASM, .OBJ, .LIB, .DLL, and .EXE to the same effect.

Assembler

pseudoinstruction
A common variation of assembly language instructions often treated as if it were an instruction in its own right.

Since assembly language is an interface to higher-level software, the assembler can also treat common variations of machine language instructions as if they were instructions in their own right. The hardware need not implement these instructions; however, their appearance in assembly language simplifies translation and programming. Such instructions are called **pseudoinstructions**.

As mentioned above, the MIPS hardware makes sure that register $zero always has the value 0. That is, whenever register $zero is used, it supplies a 0, and the programmer cannot change the value of register $zero. Register $zero is used to create the assembly language instruction `move` that copies the contents of one register to another. Thus the MIPS assembler accepts this instruction even though it is not found in the MIPS architecture:

```
move $t0,$t1        # register $t0 gets register $t1
```

The assembler converts this assembly language instruction into the machine language equivalent of the following instruction:

```
add  $t0,$zero,$t1 # register $t0 gets 0 + register $t1
```

The MIPS assembler also converts `blt` (branch on less than) into the two instructions `slt` and `bne` mentioned in the example on page 128. Other examples include `bgt`, `bge`, and `ble`. It also converts branches to faraway locations into a branch and jump. As mentioned above, the MIPS assembler allows 32-bit constants to be loaded into a register despite the 16-bit limit of the immediate instructions.

In summary, pseudoinstructions give MIPS a richer set of assembly language instructions than those implemented by the hardware. The only cost is reserving one register, $at, for use by the assembler. If you are going to write assembly programs, use pseudoinstructions to simplify your task. To understand the MIPS architecture and be sure to get best performance, however, study the real MIPS instructions found in Figures 2.1 and 2.19.

Assemblers will also accept numbers in a variety of bases. In addition to binary and decimal, they usually accept a base that is more succinct than binary yet converts easily to a bit pattern. MIPS assemblers use hexadecimal.

Such features are convenient, but the primary task of an assembler is assembly into machine code. The assembler turns the assembly language program into an *object file*, which is a combination of machine language instructions, data, and information needed to place instructions properly in memory.

To produce the binary version of each instruction in the assembly language program, the assembler must determine the addresses corresponding to all labels. Assemblers keep track of labels used in branches and data transfer instructions in a **symbol table**. As you might expect, the table contains pairs of symbols and addresses.

The object file for UNIX systems typically contains six distinct pieces:

symbol table A table that matches names of labels to the addresses of the memory words that instructions occupy.

- The *object file header* describes the size and position of the other pieces of the object file.

- The *text segment* contains the machine language code.

- The *static data segment* contains data allocated for the life of the program. (UNIX allows programs to use both *static data*, which is allocated throughout the program, and *dynamic data*, which can grow or shrink as needed by the program. See Figure 2.13.)

- The *relocation information* identifies instructions and data words that depend on absolute addresses when the program is loaded into memory.

■ The *symbol table* contains the remaining labels that are not defined, such as external references.

■ The *debugging information* contains a concise description of how the modules were compiled so that a debugger can associate machine instructions with C source files and make data structures readable.

The next subsection shows how to attach such routines that have already been assembled, such as library routines.

Linker

linker Also called link editor. A systems program that combines independently assembled machine language programs and resolves all undefined labels into an executable file.

What we have presented so far suggests that a single change to one line of one procedure requires compiling and assembling the whole program. Complete retranslation is a terrible waste of computing resources. This repetition is particularly wasteful for standard library routines, because programmers would be compiling and assembling routines that by definition almost never change. An alternative is to compile and assemble each procedure independently, so that a change to one line would require compiling and assembling only one procedure. This alternative requires a new systems program, called a **link editor** or **linker**, which takes all the independently assembled machine language programs and "stitches" them together.

There are three steps for the linker:

1. Place code and data modules symbolically in memory.

2. Determine the addresses of data and instruction labels.

3. Patch both the internal and external references.

The linker uses the relocation information and symbol table in each object module to resolve all undefined labels. Such references occur in branch instructions, jump instructions, and data addresses, so the job of this program is much like that of an editor: it finds the old addresses and replaces them with the new addresses. Editing is the origin of the name "link editor," or linker for short. The reason a linker is useful is that it is much faster to patch code than it is to recompile and reassemble.

executable file A functional program in the format of an object file that contains no unresolved references. It can contain symbol tables and debugging information. A "stripped executable" does not contain that information. Relocation information may be included for the loader.

If all external references are resolved, the linker next determines the memory locations each module will occupy. Recall that Figure 2.13 on page 120 shows the MIPS convention for allocation of program and data to memory. Since the files were assembled in isolation, the assembler could not know where a module's instructions and data would be placed relative to other modules. When the linker places a module in memory, all *absolute* references, that is, memory addresses that are not relative to a register, must be *relocated* to reflect its true location.

The linker produces an **executable file** that can be run on a computer. Typically, this file has the same format as an object file, except that it contains no unresolved references. It is possible to have partially linked files, such as library routines, that still have unresolved addresses and hence result in object files.

Linking Object Files

Link the two object files below. Show updated addresses of the first few instructions of the completed executable file. We show the instructions in assembly language just to make the example understandable; in reality, the instructions would be numbers.

EXAMPLE

Note that in the object files we have highlighted the addresses and symbols that must be updated in the link process: the instructions that refer to the addresses of procedures A and B and the instructions that refer to the addresses of data words X and Y.

Object file header			
	Name	Procedure A	
	Text size	100_{hex}	
	Data size	20_{hex}	
Text segment	Address	Instruction	
	0	lw $a0, 0($gp)	
	4	jal 0	
	...	...	
Data segment	0	(X)	
	...	...	
Relocation information	Address	Instruction type	Dependency
	0	lw	X
	4	jal	B
Symbol table	Label	Address	
	X	–	
	B	–	
Object file header			
	Name	Procedure B	
	Text size	200_{hex}	
	Data size	30_{hex}	
Text segment	Address	Instruction	
	0	sw $a1, 0($gp)	
	4	jal 0	
	...	...	
Data segment	0	(Y)	
	...	...	
Relocation information	Address	Instruction type	Dependency
	0	sw	Y
	4	jal	A
Symbol table	Label	Address	
	Y	–	
	A	–	

ANSWER

Procedure A needs to find the address for the variable labeled X to put in the load instruction and to find the address of procedure B to place in the jal instruction. Procedure B needs the address of the variable labeled Y for the store instruction and the address of procedure A for its jal instruction.

From Figure 2.13 on page 120, we know that the text segment starts at address $40\ 0000_{hex}$ and the data segment at $1000\ 0000_{hex}$. The text of procedure A is placed at the first address and its data at the second. The object file header for procedure A says that its text is 100_{hex} bytes and its data is 20_{hex} bytes, so the starting address for procedure B text is $40\ 0100_{hex}$, and its data starts at $1000\ 0020_{hex}$.

Executable file header		
	Text size	300_{hex}
	Data size	50_{hex}
Text segment	Address	Instruction
	$0040\ 0000_{hex}$	lw $a0, 8000_{hex}($gp)
	$0040\ 0004_{hex}$	jal $40\ 0100_{hex}$
	...	...
	$0040\ 0100_{hex}$	sw $a1, 8020_{hex}($gp)
	$0040\ 0104_{hex}$	jal $40\ 0000_{hex}$
	...	...
Data segment	Address	
	$1000\ 0000_{hex}$	(X)
	...	...
	$1000\ 0020_{hex}$	(Y)
	...	...

Figure 2.13 also shows that the text segment starts at address $40\ 0000_{hex}$ and the data segment at $1000\ 0000_{hex}$. The text of procedure A is placed at the first address and its data at the second. The object file header for procedure A says that its text is 100_{hex} bytes and its data is 20_{hex} bytes, so the starting address for procedure B text is $40\ 0100_{hex}$, and its data starts at $1000\ 0020_{hex}$.

Now the linker updates the address fields of the instructions. It uses the instruction type field to know the format of the address to be edited. We have two types here:

1. The jals are easy because they use pseudodirect addressing. The jal at address $40\ 0004_{hex}$ gets $40\ 0100_{hex}$ (the address of procedure B) in its address field, and the jal at $40\ 0104_{hex}$ gets $40\ 0000_{hex}$ (the address of procedure A) in its address field.

2. The load and store addresses are harder because they are relative to a base register. This example uses the global pointer as the base register. Figure 2.13 shows that $gp is initialized to $1000\ 8000_{hex}$. To get the address $1000\ 0000_{hex}$ (the address of word X), we place -8000_{hex} in the address field of lw at address $40\ 0000_{hex}$. Similarly, we place -7980_{hex} in the address field of sw at address $40\ 0100_{hex}$ to get the address $1000\ 0020_{hex}$ (the address of word Y).

Elaboration: Recall that MIPS instructions are word aligned, so jal drops the right two bits to increase the instruction's address range. Thus, it use 26 bits to create a 28-bit byte address. Hence, the actual address in the lower 26 bits of the jal instruction in this example is $10\ 0040_{hex}$, rather than $40\ 0100_{hex}$.

Loader

Now that the executable file is on disk, the operating system reads it to memory and starts it. The **loader** follows these steps in UNIX systems:

1. Reads the executable file header to determine size of the text and data segments.

2. Creates an address space large enough for the text and data.

3. Copies the instructions and data from the executable file into memory.

4. Copies the parameters (if any) to the main program onto the stack.

5. Initializes the machine registers and sets the stack pointer to the first free location.

6. Jumps to a start-up routine that copies the parameters into the argument registers and calls the main routine of the program. When the main routine returns, the start-up routine terminates the program with an exit system call.

Sections B.3 and B.4 in Appendix B describe linkers and loaders in more detail.

loader A systems program that places an object program in main memory so that it is ready to execute.

Dynamically Linked Libraries

The first part of this section describes the traditional approach to linking libraries before the program is run. Although this static approach is the fastest way to call library routines, it has a few disadvantages:

■ The library routines become part of the executable code. If a new version of the library is released that fixes bugs or supports new hardware devices, the statically linked program keeps using the old version.

■ It loads all routines in the library that are called anywhere in the executable, even if those calls are not executed. The library can be large relative to the program; for example, the standard C library is 2.5 MB.

dynamically linked libraries (DLLs) Library routines that are linked to a program during execution.

These disadvantages lead to **dynamically linked libraries (DLLs)**, where the library routines are not linked and loaded until the program is run. Both the program and library routines keep extra information on the location of nonlocal procedures and their names. In the initial version of DLLs, the loader ran a dynamic linker, using the extra information in the file to find the appropriate libraries and to update all external references.

The downside of the initial version of DLLs was that it still linked all routines of the library that might be called, versus only those that are called during the running of the program. This observation led to the lazy procedure linkage version of DLLs, where each routine is linked only *after* it is called.

Like many innovations in our field, this trick relies on a level of indirection. Figure 2.22 shows the technique. It starts with the nonlocal routines calling a set of dummy routines at the end of the program, with one entry per nonlocal routine. These dummy entries each contain an indirect jump.

The first time the library routine is called, the program calls the dummy entry and follows the indirect jump. It points to code that puts a number in a register to identify the desired library routine and then jumps to the dynamic linker/loader. The linker/loader finds the desired routine, remaps it, and changes the address in the indirect jump location to point to that routine. It then jumps to it. When the routine completes, it returns to the original calling site. Thereafter, the call to the library routine jumps indirectly to the routine without the extra hops.

In summary, DLLs require extra space for the information needed for dynamic linking, but do not require that whole libraries be copied or linked. They pay a good deal of overhead the first time a routine is called, but only a single indirect jump thereafter. Note that the return from the library pays no extra overhead. Microsoft's Windows relies extensively on dynamically linked libraries, and it is also the default when executing programs on UNIX systems today.

Starting a Java Program

The discussion above captures the traditional model of executing a program, where the emphasis is on fast execution time for a program targeted to a specific instruction set architecture, or even a specific implementation of that architecture. Indeed, it is possible to execute Java programs just like C. Java was invented with a different set of goals, however. One was to run safely on any computer, even if it might slow execution time.

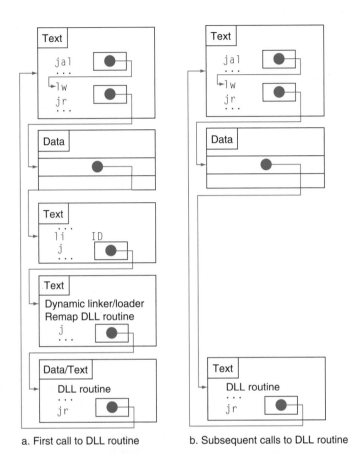

a. First call to DLL routine   b. Subsequent calls to DLL routine

FIGURE 2.22 Dynamically linked library via lazy procedure linkage. (a) Steps for the first time a call is made to the DLL routine. (b) The steps to find the routine, remap it, and link it are skipped on subsequent calls. As we will see in Chapter 5, the operating system may avoid copying the desired routine by remapping it using virtual memory management.

Figure 2.23 shows the typical translation and execution steps for Java. Rather than compile to the assembly language of a target computer, Java is compiled first to instructions that are easy to interpret: the **Java bytecode** instruction set (see ⊙ Section 2.15 on the CD). This instruction set is designed to be close to the Java language so that this compilation step is trivial. Virtually no optimizations are performed. Like the C compiler, the Java compiler checks the types of data and produces the proper operation for each type. Java programs are distributed in the binary version of these bytecodes.

A software interpreter, called a **Java Virtual Machine** (JVM), can execute Java bytecodes. An interpreter is a program that simulates an instruction set architecture. For example, the MIPS simulator used with this book is an interpreter. There is no need for a separate assembly step since either the translation is so simple that the compiler fills in the addresses or JVM finds them at runtime.

Java bytecode Instruction from an instruction set designed to interpret Java programs.

Java Virtual Machine (JVM) The program that interprets Java bytecodes.

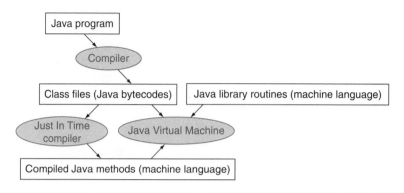

FIGURE 2.23   A translation hierarchy for Java. A Java program is first compiled into a binary version of Java bytecodes, with all addresses defined by the compiler. The Java program is now ready to run on the interpreter, called the Java Virtual Machine (JVM). The JVM links to desired methods in the Java library while the program is running. To achieve greater performance, the JVM can invoke the JIT compiler, which selectively compiles methods into the native machine language of the machine on which it is running.

The upside of interpretation is portability. The availability of software Java virtual machines meant that most people could write and run Java programs shortly after Java was announced. Today, Java virtual machines are found in hundreds of millions of devices, in everything from cell phones to Internet browsers.

The downside of interpretation is lower performance. The incredible advances in performance of the 1980s and 1990s made interpretation viable for many important applications, but the factor of 10 slowdown when compared to traditionally compiled C programs made Java unattractive for some applications.

To preserve portability and improve execution speed, the next phase of Java development was compilers that translated *while* the program was running. Such **Just In Time compilers** (JIT) typically profile the running program to find where the "hot" methods are and then compile them into the native instruction set on which the virtual machine is running. The compiled portion is saved for the next time the program is run, so that it can run faster each time it is run. This balance of interpretation and compilation evolves over time, so that frequently run Java programs suffer little of the overhead of interpretation.

As computers get faster so that compilers can do more, and as researchers invent betters ways to compile Java on the fly, the performance gap between Java and C or C++ is closing. 🔘 **Section 2.15** on the CD goes into much greater depth on the implementation of Java, Java bytecodes, JVM, and JIT compilers.

Just In Time compiler (JIT) The name commonly given to a compiler that operates at runtime, translating the interpreted code segments into the native code of the computer.

Check Yourself Which of the advantages of an interpreter over a translator do you think was most important for the designers of Java?

1. Ease of writing an interpreter

2. Better error messages

3. Smaller object code

4. Machine independence

2.13   A C Sort Example to Put It All Together

One danger of showing assembly language code in snippets is that you will have no idea what a full assembly language program looks like. In this section, we derive the MIPS code from two procedures written in C: one to swap array elements and one to sort them.

```
void swap(int v[], int k)
{
  int temp;
  temp = v[k];
  v[k] = v[k+1];
  v[k+1] = temp;
}
```

FIGURE 2.24   A C procedure that swaps two locations in memory. This subsection uses this procedure in a sorting example.

The Procedure swap

Let's start with the code for the procedure swap in Figure 2.24. This procedure simply swaps two locations in memory. When translating from C to assembly language by hand, we follow these general steps:

1. Allocate registers to program variables.

2. Produce code for the body of the procedure.

3. Preserve registers across the procedure invocation.

This section describes the swap procedure in these three pieces, concluding by putting all the pieces together.

Register Allocation for swap

As mentioned on pages 112–113, the MIPS convention on parameter passing is to use registers $a0, $a1, $a2, and $a3. Since swap has just two parameters, v and k, they will be found in registers $a0 and $a1. The only other variable is temp, which we associate with register $t0 since swap is a leaf procedure (see page 116).

This register allocation corresponds to the variable declarations in the first part of the swap procedure in Figure 2.24.

Code for the Body of the Procedure swap

The remaining lines of C code in swap are

```
temp = v[k];
v[k] = v[k+1];
v[k+1] = temp;
```

Recall that the memory address for MIPS refers to the *byte* address, and so words are really 4 bytes apart. Hence we need to multiply the index k by 4 before adding it to the address. *Forgetting that sequential word addresses differ by 4 instead of by 1 is a common mistake in assembly language programming.* Hence the first step is to get the address of v[k] by multiplying k by 4 via a shift left by 2:

```
sll    $t1, $a1,2      # reg $t1 = k * 4
add    $t1, $a0,$t1    # reg $t1 = v + (k * 4)
                       # reg $t1 has the address of v[k]
```

Now we load v[k] using $t1, and then v[k+1] by adding 4 to $t1:

```
lw     $t0, 0($t1)     # reg $t0 (temp) = v[k]
lw     $t2, 4($t1)     # reg $t2 = v[k + 1]
                       # refers to next element of v
```

Next we store $t0 and $t2 to the swapped addresses:

```
sw     $t2, 0($t1)     # v[k] = reg $t2
sw     $t0, 4($t1)     # v[k+1] = reg $t0 (temp)
```

Now we have allocated registers and written the code to perform the operations of the procedure. What is missing is the code for preserving the saved registers used within swap. Since we are not using saved registers in this leaf procedure, there is nothing to preserve.

The Full swap Procedure

We are now ready for the whole routine, which includes the procedure label and the return jump. To make it easier to follow, we identify in Figure 2.25 each block of code with its purpose in the procedure.

The Procedure sort

To ensure that you appreciate the rigor of programming in assembly language, we'll try a second, longer example. In this case, we'll build a routine that calls the swap procedure. This program sorts an array of integers, using bubble or exchange sort, which is one of the simplest if not the fastest sorts. Figure 2.26 shows the C

Procedure body		
swap: sll	$t1, $a1, 2	# reg $t1 = k * 4
add	$t1, $a0, $t1	# reg $t1 = v + (k * 4)
		# reg $t1 has the address of v[k]
lw	$t0, 0($t1)	# reg $t0 (temp) = v[k]
lw	$t2, 4($t1)	# reg $t2 = v[k + 1]
		# refers to next element of v
sw	$t2, 0($t1)	# v[k] = reg $t2
sw	$t0, 4($t1)	# v[k+1] = reg $t0 (temp)

Procedure return	
jr $ra	# return to calling routine

FIGURE 2.25   MIPS assembly code of the procedure *swap* in Figure 2.24.

version of the program. Once again, we present this procedure in several steps, concluding with the full procedure.

```
void sort (int v[], int n)
{
    int i, j;
    for (i = 0; i < n; i += 1) {
        for (j = i - 1; j >= 0 && v[j] > v[j + 1]; j -= 1) {
            swap(v,j);
        }
    }
}
```

FIGURE 2.26   A C procedure that performs a sort on the array v.

Register Allocation for sort

The two parameters of the procedure sort, v and n, are in the parameter registers $a0 and $a1, and we assign register $s0 to i and register $s1 to j.

Code for the Body of the Procedure sort

The procedure body consists of two nested *for* loops and a call to swap that includes parameters. Let's unwrap the code from the outside to the middle.

The first translation step is the first *for* loop:

```
for (i = 0; i < n; i += 1) {
```

Recall that the C *for* statement has three parts: initialization, loop test, and iteration increment. It takes just one instruction to initialize i to 0, the first part of the *for* statement:

```
move    $s0, $zero      # i = 0
```

(Remember that `move` is a pseudoinstruction provided by the assembler for the convenience of the assembly language programmer; see page 141.) It also takes just one instruction to increment i, the last part of the *for* statement:

```
addi    $s0, $s0, 1    # i += 1
```

The loop should be exited if i < n is *not* true or, said another way, should be exited if i ≥ n. The set on less than instruction sets register $t0 to 1 if $s0 < $a1 and to 0 otherwise. Since we want to test if $s0 ≥ $a1, we branch if register $t0 is 0. This test takes two instructions:

```
for1tst:slt $t0, $s0, $a1 # reg $t0 = 0 if $s0 ≥ $a1 (i≥n)
        beq $t0, $zero,exit1 # go to exit1 if $s0 ≥ $a1 (i≥n)
```

The bottom of the loop just jumps back to the loop test:

```
        j   for1tst             # jump to test of outer loop
exit1:
```

The skeleton code of the first *for* loop is then

```
        move   $s0, $zero       # i = 0
for1tst:slt $t0, $s0, $a1 # reg $t0 = 0 if $s0 ≥ $a1 (i≥n)
        beq    $t0, $zero,exit1 # go to exit1 if $s0 ≥ $a1 (i≥n)
        . . .
        (body of first for loop)
        . . .
        addi   $s0, $s0, 1      # i += 1
        j      for1tst          # jump to test of outer loop
exit1:
```

Voila! (The exercises explore writing faster code for similar loops.)

The second *for* loop looks like this in C:

```
for (j = i - 1; j >= 0 && v[j] > v[j + 1]; j -= 1) {
```

The initialization portion of this loop is again one instruction:

```
addi    $s1, $s0, -1 # j = i - 1
```

The decrement of j at the end of the loop is also one instruction:

```
addi    $s1, $s1, -1 # j -= 1
```

The loop test has two parts. We exit the loop if either condition fails, so the first test must exit the loop if it fails (j < 0):

```
for2tst: slti $t0, $s1, 0 # reg $t0 = 1 if $s1 < 0 (j < 0)
         bne $t0, $zero, exit2 # go to exit2 if $s1 < 0 (j < 0)
```

This branch will skip over the second condition test. If it doesn't skip, j ≥ 0.

The second test exits if v[j] > v[j + 1] is *not* true, or exits if v[j] ≤ v[j + 1]. First we create the address by multiplying j by 4 (since we need a byte address) and add it to the base address of v:

```
sll     $t1, $s1, 2    # reg $t1 = j * 4
add     $t2, $a0, $t1  # reg $t2 = v + (j * 4)
```

Now we load v[j]:

```
lw      $t3, 0($t2)    # reg $t3    = v[j]
```

Since we know that the second element is just the following word, we add 4 to the address in register $t2 to get v[j + 1]:

```
lw      $t4, 4($t2)    # reg $t4    = v[j + 1]
```

The test of v[j] ≤ v[j + 1] is the same as v[j + 1] ≥ v[j], so the two instructions of the exit test are

```
slt     $t0, $t4, $t3        # reg $t0 = 0 if $t4 ≥ $t3
beq     $t0, $zero, exit2    # go to exit2 if $t4 ≥ $t3
```

The bottom of the loop jumps back to the inner loop test:

```
j       for2tst    # jump to test of inner loop
```

Combining the pieces, the skeleton of the second *for* loop looks like this:

```
          addi $s1, $s0, -1      # j = i - 1
for2tst:slti $t0, $s1, 0         # reg $t0 = 1 if $s1 < 0 (j < 0)
          bne  $t0, $zero, exit2 # go to exit2 if $s1 < 0 (j < 0)
          sll  $t1, $s1, 2       # reg $t1 = j * 4
          add  $t2, $a0, $t1     # reg $t2 = v + (j * 4)
          lw   $t3, 0($t2)       # reg $t3    = v[j]
          lw   $t4, 4($t2)       # reg $t4    = v[j + 1]
          slt  $t0, $t4, $t3     # reg $t0 = 0 if $t4 ≥ $t3
          beq  $t0, $zero, exit2 # go to exit2 if $t4 ≥ $t3
          ...
          (body of second for loop)
          ...
          addi $s1, $s1, -1      # j -= 1
          j    for2tst           # jump to test of inner loop
exit2:
```

The Procedure Call in sort

The next step is the body of the second *for* loop:

```
swap(v,j);
```

Calling swap is easy enough:

```
jal       swap
```

Passing Parameters in sort

The problem comes when we want to pass parameters because the sort procedure needs the values in registers $a0 and $a1, yet the swap procedure needs to have its parameters placed in those same registers. One solution is to copy the parameters for sort into other registers earlier in the procedure, making registers $a0 and $a1 available for the call of swap. (This copy is faster than saving and restoring on the stack.) We first copy $a0 and $a1 into $s2 and $s3 during the procedure:

```
move   $s2, $a0     # copy parameter $a0 into $s2
move   $s3, $a1     # copy parameter $a1 into $s3
```

Then we pass the parameters to swap with these two instructions:

```
move   $a0, $s2     # first swap parameter is v
move   $a1, $s1     # second swap parameter is j
```

Preserving Registers in sort

The only remaining code is the saving and restoring of registers. Clearly, we must save the return address in register $ra, since sort is a procedure and is called itself. The sort procedure also uses the saved registers $s0, $s1, $s2, and $s3, so they must be saved. The prologue of the sort procedure is then

```
addi   $sp,$sp,-20   # make room on stack for 5 registers
sw     $ra,16($sp)   # save $ra on stack
sw     $s3,12($sp)   # save $s3 on stack
sw     $s2, 8($sp)   # save $s2 on stack
sw     $s1, 4($sp)   # save $s1 on stack
sw     $s0, 0($sp)   # save $s0 on stack
```

The tail of the procedure simply reverses all these instructions, then adds a jr to return.

The Full Procedure sort

Now we put all the pieces together in Figure 2.27, being careful to replace references to registers $a0 and $a1 in the *for* loops with references to registers $s2 and $s3. Once again, to make the code easier to follow, we identify each block of code with its purpose in the procedure. In this example, nine lines of the sort procedure in C became 35 lines in the MIPS assembly language.

Elaboration: One optimization that works with this example is *procedure inlining*. Instead of passing arguments in parameters and invoking the code with a jal instruction, the compiler would copy the code from the body of the swap procedure where the call to swap appears in the code. Inlining would avoid four instructions in this example. The downside of the inlining optimization is that the compiled code would be bigger if the inlined procedure is called from several locations. Such a code expansion might turn into *lower* performance if it increased the cache miss rate; see Chapter 5.

Saving registers				
sort:	addi	$sp,$sp, -20		# make room on stack for 5 registers
	sw	$ra, 16($sp)		# save $ra on stack
	sw	$s3,12($sp)		# save $s3 on stack
	sw	$s2, 8($sp)		# save $s2 on stack
	sw	$s1, 4($sp)		# save $s1 on stack
	sw	$s0, 0($sp)		# save $s0 on stack

Procedure body			
Move parameters	move	$s2, $a0	# copy parameter $a0 into $s2 (save $a0)
	move	$s3, $a1	# copy parameter $a1 into $s3 (save $a1)
Outer loop	move	$s0, $zero	# i = 0
	for1tst: slt	$t0, $s0, $s3	# reg $t0 = 0 if $s0 Š $s3 (i Š n)
	beq	$t0, $zero, exit1	# go to exit1 if $s0 Š $s3 (i Š n)
Inner loop	addi	$s1, $s0, -1	# j = i - 1
	for2tst: slti	$t0, $s1, 0	# reg $t0 = 1 if $s1 < 0 (j < 0)
	bne	$t0, $zero, exit2	# go to exit2 if $s1 < 0 (j < 0)
	sll	$t1, $s1, 2	# reg $t1 = j * 4
	add	$t2, $s2, $t1	# reg $t2 = v + (j * 4)
	lw	$t3, 0($t2)	# reg $t3 = v[j]
	lw	$t4, 4($t2)	# reg $t4 = v[j + 1]
	slt	$t0, $t4, $t3	# reg $t0 = 0 if $t4 Š $t3
	beq	$t0, $zero, exit2	# go to exit2 if $t4 Š $t3
Pass parameters and call	move	$a0, $s2	# 1st parameter of swap is v (old $a0)
	move	$a1, $s1	# 2nd parameter of swap is j
	jal	swap	# swap code shown in Figure 2.25
Inner loop	addi	$s1, $s1, -1	# j -= 1
	j	for2tst	# jump to test of inner loop
Outer loop	exit2: addi	$s0, $s0, 1	# i += 1
	j	for1tst	# jump to test of outer loop

Restoring registers				
exit1:	lw	$s0, 0($sp)		# restore $s0 from stack
	lw	$s1, 4($sp)		# restore $s1 from stack
	lw	$s2, 8($sp)		# restore $s2 from stack
	lw	$s3,12($sp)		# restore $s3 from stack
	lw	$ra,16($sp)		# restore $ra from stack
	addi	$sp,$sp, 20		# restore stack pointer

Procedure return		
	jr	$ra	# return to calling routine

FIGURE 2.27 MIPS assembly version of procedure sort in Figure 2.26.

Understanding Program Performance

Figure 2.28 shows the impact of compiler optimization on sort program performance, compile time, clock cycles, instruction count, and CPI. Note that unoptimized code has the best CPI, and O1 optimization has the lowest instruction count, but O3 is the fastest, reminding us that time is the only accurate measure of program performance.

Figure 2.29 compares the impact of programming languages, compilation versus interpretation, and algorithms on performance of sorts. The fourth column shows that the unoptimized C program is 8.3 times faster than the interpreted Java code for Bubble Sort. Using the JIT compiler makes Java 2.1 times *faster* than the unoptimized C and within a factor of 1.13 of the highest optimized C code. (Section 2.15 on the CD gives more details on interpretation versus compilation of Java and the Java and MIPS code for Bubble Sort.) The ratios aren't as close for Quicksort in Column 5, presumably because it is harder to amortize the cost of runtime compilation over the shorter execution time. The last column demonstrates the impact of a better algorithm, offering three orders of magnitude a performance increases by when sorting 100,000 items. Even comparing interpreted Java in Column 5 to the C compiler at highest optimization in Column 4, Quicksort beats Bubble Sort by a factor of 50 (0.05×2468, or 123 times faster than the unoptimized C code versus 2.41 times faster).

Elaboration: The MIPS compilers always save room on the stack for the arguments in case they need to be stored, so in reality they always decrement $sp by 16 to make room for all four argument registers (16 bytes). One reason is that C provides a `vararg` option that allows a pointer to pick, say, the third argument to a procedure. When the compiler encounters the rare `vararg`, it copies the four argument registers onto the stack into the four reserved locations.

gcc optimization	Relative performance	Clock cycles (millions)	Instruction count (millions)	CPI
None	1.00	158,615	114,938	1.38
O1 (medium)	2.37	66,990	37,470	1.79
O2 (full)	2.38	66,521	39,993	1.66
O3 (procedure integration)	2.41	65,747	44,993	1.46

FIGURE 2.28   Comparing performance, instruction count, and CPI using compiler optimization for Bubble Sort. The programs sorted 100,000 words with the array initialized to random values. These programs were run on a Pentium 4 with a clock rate of 3.06 GHz and a 533 MHz system bus with 2 GB of PC2100 DDR SDRAM. It used Linux version 2.4.20.

Language	Execution method	Optimization	Bubble Sort relative performance	Quicksort relative performance	Speedup Quicksort vs. Bubble Sort
C	Compiler	None	1.00	1.00	2468
	Compiler	O1	2.37	1.50	1562
	Compiler	O2	2.38	1.50	1555
	Compiler	O3	2.41	1.91	1955
Java	Interpreter	–	0.12	0.05	1050
	JIT compiler	–	2.13	0.29	338

FIGURE 2.29 Performance of two sort algorithms in C and Java using interpretation and optimizing compilers relative to unoptimized C version. The last column shows the advantage in performance of Quicksort over Bubble Sort for each language and execution option. These programs were run on the same system as Figure 2.28. The JVM is Sun version 1.3.1, and the JIT is Sun Hotspot version 1.3.1.

2.14 Arrays versus Pointers

A challenge for any new C programmer is understanding pointers. Comparing assembly code that uses arrays and array indices to the assembly code that uses pointers offers insights about pointers. This section shows C and MIPS assembly versions of two procedures to clear a sequence of words in memory: one using array indices and one using pointers. Figure 2.30 shows the two C procedures.

The purpose of this section is to show how pointers map into MIPS instructions, and not to endorse a dated programming style. We'll see the impact of modern compiler optimization on these two procedures at the end of the section.

Array Version of Clear

Let's start with the array version, clear1, focusing on the body of the loop and ignoring the procedure linkage code. We assume that the two parameters array and size are found in the registers $a0 and $a1, and that i is allocated to register $t0.

The initialization of i, the first part of the *for* loop, is straightforward:

```
        move    $t0,$zero       # i = 0 (register $t0 = 0)
```

To set array[i] to 0 we must first get its address. Start by multiplying i by 4 to get the byte address:

```
loop1:  sll     $t1,$t0,2       # $t1 = i * 4
```

Since the starting address of the array is in a register, we must add it to the index to get the address of array[i] using an add instruction:

```
        add     $t2,$a0,$t1     # $t2 = address of array[i]
```

Finally, we can store 0 in that address:

```
clear1(int array[], int size)
{
    int i;
    for (i = 0; i < size; i += 1)
        array[i] = 0;
}


clear2(int *array, int size)
{
    int *p;
    for (p = &array[0]; p <
&array[size]; p = p + 1)
        *p = 0;
}
```

FIGURE 2.30 Two C procedures for setting an array to all zeros. Clear1 uses indices, while clear2 uses pointers. The second procedure needs some explanation for those unfamiliar with C. The address of a variable is indicated by &, and the object pointed to by a pointer is indicated by *. The declarations declare that array and p are pointers to integers. The first part of the *for* loop in clear2 assigns the address of the first element of array to the pointer p. The second part of the *for* loop tests to see if the pointer is pointing beyond the last element of array. Incrementing a pointer by one, in the last part of the *for* loop, means moving the pointer to the next sequential object of its declared size. Since p is a pointer to integers, the compiler will generate MIPS instructions to increment p by four, the number of bytes in a MIPS integer. The assignment in the loop places 0 in the object pointed to by p.

```
sw      $zero, 0($t2)  # array[i] = 0
```

This instruction is the end of the body of the loop, so the next step is to increment i:

```
addi    $t0,$t0,1      # i = i + 1
```

The loop test checks if i is less than size:

```
slt     $t3,$t0,$a1       # $t3 = (i < size)
bne     $t3,$zero,loop1   # if (i < size) go to loop1
```

We have now seen all the pieces of the procedure. Here is the MIPS code for clearing an array using indices:

```
        move  $t0,$zero        # i = 0
loop1:  sll   $t1,$t0,2        # $t1 = i * 4
        add   $t2,$a0,$t1      # $t2 = address of array[i]
        sw    $zero, 0($t2)    # array[i] = 0
        addi  $t0,$t0,1        # i = i + 1
        slt   $t3,$t0,$a1      # $t3 = (i < size)
        bne   $t3,$zero,loop1  # if (i < size) go to loop1
```

(This code works as long as size is greater than 0; ANSI C requires a test of size before the loop, but we'll skip that legality here.)

Pointer Version of Clear

The second procedure that uses pointers allocates the two parameters array and size to the registers $a0 and $a1 and allocates p to register $t0. The code for the second procedure starts with assigning the pointer p to the address of the first element of the array:

```
       move   $t0,$a0          # p = address of array[0]
```

The next code is the body of the *for* loop, which simply stores 0 into p:

```
  loop2: sw     $zero,0($t0)     # Memory[p] = 0
```

This instruction implements the body of the loop, so the next code is the iteration increment, which changes p to point to the next word:

```
       addi   $t0,$t0,4        # p = p + 4
```

Incrementing a pointer by 1 means moving the pointer to the next sequential object in C. Since p is a pointer to integers, each of which uses 4 bytes, the compiler increments p by 4.

The loop test is next. The first step is calculating the address of the last element of array. Start with multiplying size by 4 to get its byte address:

```
       sll    $t1,$a1,2        # $t1 = size * 4
```

and then we add the product to the starting address of the array to get the address of the first word *after* the array:

```
     add   $t2,$a0,$t1        # $t2 = address of array[size]
```

The loop test is simply to see if p is less than the last element of array:

```
     slt   $t3,$t0,$t2     # $t3 = (p<&array[size])
     bne   $t3,$zero,loop2  # if (p<&array[size]) go to loop2
```

With all the pieces completed, we can show a pointer version of the code to zero an array:

```
     move $t0,$a0           # p = address of array[0]
     loop2:sw$zero,0($t0)   # Memory[p] = 0
     addi $t0,$t0,4         # p = p + 4
     sll  $t1,$a1,2         # $t1 = size * 4
     add  $t2,$a0,$t1       # $t2 = address of array[size]
     slt  $t3,$t0,$t2       # $t3 = (p<&array[size])
     bne  $t3,$zero,loop2   # if (p<&array[size]) go to loop2
```

As in the first example, this code assumes size is greater than 0.

Note that this program calculates the address of the end of the array in every iteration of the loop, even though it does not change. A faster version of the code moves this calculation outside the loop:

```
      move  $t0,$a0          # p = address of array[0]
      sll   $t1,$a1,2        # $t1 = size * 4
      add   $t2,$a0,$t1      # $t2 = address of array[size]
loop2:sw$zero,0($t0)        # Memory[p] = 0
      addi  $t0,$t0,4        # p = p + 4
      slt   $t3,$t0,$t2      # $t3 = (p<&array[size])
      bne   $t3,$zero,loop2  # if (p<&array[size]) go to loop2
```

Comparing the Two Versions of Clear

Comparing the two code sequences side by side illustrates the difference between array indices and pointers (the changes introduced by the pointer version are highlighted):

```
      move $t0,$zero      # i = 0              move  $t0,$a0         # p = & array[0]
loop1:sll  $t1,$t0,2      # $t1 = i * 4        sll   $t1,$a1,2       # $t1 = size * 4
      add  $t2,$a0,$t1    # $t2 = &array[i]    add   $t2,$a0,$t1     # $t2 = &array[size]
      sw   $zero, 0($t2)  # array[i] = 0  loop2:sw      $zero,0($t0)  # Memory[p] = 0
      addi $t0,$t0,1      # i = i + 1          addi  $t0,$t0,4       # p = p + 4
      slt  $t3,$t0,$a1    # $t3 = (i < size)   slt   $t3,$t0,$t2     # $t3=(p<&array[size])
      bne  $t3,$zero,loop1# if () go to loop1  bne   $t3,$zero,loop2# if () go to loop2
```

The version on the left must have the "multiply" and add inside the loop because i is incremented and each address must be recalculated from the new index. The memory pointer version on the right increments the pointer p directly. The pointer version moves them outside the loop, thereby reducing the instructions executed per iteration from 6 to 4. This manual optimization corresponds to the compiler optimization of strength reduction (shift instead of multiply) and induction variable elimination (eliminating array address calculations within loops). 🔘 Section 2.15 on the CD describes these two and many other optimizations.

Elaboration: As mentioned ealier, a C compiler would add a test to be sure that size is greater than 0. One way would be to add a jump just before the first instruction of the loop to the slt instruction.

People used to be taught to use pointers in C to get greater efficiency than that available with arrays: "Use pointers, even if you can't understand the code." Modern optimizing compilers can produce code for the array version that is just as good. Most programmers today prefer that the compiler do the heavy lifting.

Understanding Program Performance

2.15   Advanced Material: Compiling C and Interpreting Java

This section gives a brief overview of how the C compiler works and how Java is executed. Because the compiler will significantly affect the performance of a computer, understanding compiler technology today is critical to understanding performance. Keep in mind that the subject of compiler construction is usually taught in a one- or two-semester course, so our introduction will necessarily only touch on the basics.

The second part of this section is for readers interested in seeing how an **objected oriented language** like Java executes on a MIPS architecture. It shows the Java bytecodes used for interpretation and the MIPS code for the Java version of some of the C segments in prior sections, including Bubble Sort. It covers both the Java Virtual Machine and JIT compilers.

The rest of this section is on the CD.

object oriented language A programming language that is oriented around objects rather than actions, or data versus logic.

2.16   Real Stuff: ARM Instructions

ARM is the most popular instruction set architecture for embedded devices, with more than three billion devices per year using ARM. Standing originally for the Acorn RISC Machine, later changed to Advanced RISC Machine, ARM came out the same year as MIPS and followed similar philosophies. Figure 2.31 lists the similarities. The principle difference is that MIPS has more registers and ARM has more addressing modes.

There is a similar core of instruction sets for arithmetic-logical and data transfer instructions for MIPS and ARM, as Figure 2.32 shows.

Addressing Modes

Figure 2.33 shows the data addressing modes supported by ARM. Unlike MIPS, ARM does not reserve a register to contain 0. Although MIPS has just three simple data addressing modes (see Figure 2.18), ARM has nine, including fairly complex calculations. For example, ARM has an addressing mode that can shift one register

	ARM	MIPS
Date announced	1985	1985
Instruction size (bits)	32	32
Address space (size, model)	32 bits, flat	32 bits, flat
Data alignment	Aligned	Aligned
Data addressing modes	9	3
Integer registers (number, model, size)	15 GPR × 32 bits	31 GPR × 32 bits
I/O	Memory mapped	Memory mapped

FIGURE 2.31   Similarities in ARM and MIPS instruction sets.

	Instruction name	ARM	MIPS
Register-register	Add	add	addu, addiu
	Add (trap if overflow)	adds; swivs	add
	Subtract	sub	subu
	Subtract (trap if overflow)	subs; swivs	sub
	Multiply	mul	mult, multu
	Divide	—	div, divu
	And	and	and
	Or	orr	or
	Xor	eor	xor
	Load high part register	—	lui
	Shift left logical	lsl[1]	sllv, sll
	Shift right logical	lsr[1]	srlv, srl
	Shift right arithmetic	asr[1]	srav, sra
	Compare	cmp, cmn, tst, teq	slt/i, slt/iu
Data transfer	Load byte signed	ldrsb	lb
	Load byte unsigned	ldrb	lbu
	Load halfword signed	ldrsh	lh
	Load halfword unsigned	ldrh	lhu
	Load word	ldr	lw
	Store byte	strb	sb
	Store halfword	strh	sh
	Store word	str	sw
	Read, write special registers	mrs, msr	move
	Atomic Exchange	swp, swpb	ll;sc

FIGURE 2.32   ARM register-register and data transfer instructions equivalent to MIPS core. Dashes mean the operation is not available in that architecture or not synthesized in a few instructions. If there are several choices of instructions equivalent to the MIPS core, they are separated by commas. ARM includes shifts as part of every data operation instruction, so the shifts with superscript 1 are just a variation of a move instruction, such as lsr[1]. Note that ARM has no divide instruction.

by any amount, add it to the other registers to form the address, and then update one register with this new address.

Addressing mode	ARM v.4	MIPS
Register operand	X	X
Immediate operand	X	X
Register + offset (displacement or based)	X	X
Register + register (indexed)	X	—
Register + scaled register (scaled)	X	—
Register + offset and update register	X	—
Register + register and update register	X	—
Autoincrement, autodecrement	X	—
PC-relative data	X	—

FIGURE 2.33   Summary of data addressing modes. ARM has separate register indirect and register + offset addressing modes, rather than just putting 0 in the offset of the latter mode. To get greater addressing range, ARM shifts the offset left 1 or 2 bits if the data size is halfword or word.

Compare and Conditional Branch

MIPS uses the contents of registers to evaluate conditional branches. ARM uses the traditional four condition code bits stored in the program status word: *negative, zero, carry,* and *overflow.* They can be set on any arithmetic or logical instruction; unlike earlier architectures, this setting is optional on each instruction. An explicit option leads to fewer problems in a pipelined implementation. ARM uses conditional branches to test condition codes to determine all possible unsigned and signed relations.

CMP subtracts one operand from the other and the difference sets the condition codes. Compare negative (CMN) *adds* one operand to the other, and the sum sets the condition codes. TST performs logical AND on the two operands to set all condition codes but overflow, while TEQ uses exclusive OR to set the first three condition codes.

One unusual feature of ARM is that every instruction has the option of executing conditionally, depending on the condition codes. Every instruction starts with a 4-bit field that determines whether it will act as a no operation instruction (nop) or as a real instruction, depending on the condition codes. Hence, conditional branches are properly considered as conditionally executing the unconditional branch instruction. Conditional execution allows avoiding a branch to jump over a single instruction. It takes less code space and time to simply conditionally execute one instruction.

Figure 2.34 shows the instruction formats for ARM and MIPS. The principal differences are the 4-bit conditional execution field in every instruction and the smaller register field, because ARM has half the number of registers.

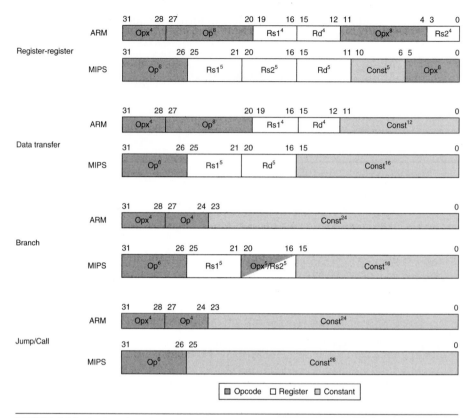

FIGURE 2.34   Instruction formats, ARM, and MIPS. The differences result from whether the architecture has 16 or 32 registers.

Unique Features of ARM

Figure 2.35 shows a few arithmetic-logical instructions not found in MIPS. Since it does not have a dedicated register for 0, it has separate opcodes to perform some operations that MIPS can do with $zero. In addition, ARM has support for multiword arithmetic.

ARM's 12-bit immediate field has a novel interpretation. The eight least-significant bits are zero-extended to a 32-bit value, then rotated right the number of bits specified in the first four bits of the field multiplied by two. One advantage is that this scheme can represent all powers of two in a 32-bit word. Whether this split actually catches more immediates than a simple 12-bit field would be an interesting study.

Operand shifting is not limited to immediates. The second register of all arithmetic and logical processing operations has the option of being shifted before being operated on. The shift options are shift left logical, shift right logical, shift right arithmetic, and rotate right.

Name	Definition	ARM v.4	MIPS
Load immediate	Rd = Imm	mov	addi, $0,
Not	Rd = ~(Rs1)	mvn	nor, $0,
Move	Rd = Rs1	mov	or, $0,
Rotate right	Rd = Rs i >> i $Rd_{0...i-1} = Rs_{31-i...31}$	ror	
And not	Rd = Rs1 & ~(Rs2)	bic	
Reverse subtract	Rd = Rs2 - Rs1	rsb, rsc	
Support for multiword integer add	CarryOut, Rd = Rd + Rs1 + OldCarryOut	adcs	—
Support for multiword integer sub	CarryOut, Rd = Rd – Rs1 + OldCarryOut	sbcs	—

FIGURE 2.35 ARM arithmetic/logical instructions not found in MIPS.

ARM also has instructions to save groups of registers, called *block loads and stores*. Under control of a 16-bit mask within the instructions, any of the 16 registers can be loaded or stored into memory in a single instruction. These instructions can save and restore registers on procedure entry and return. These instructions can also be used for block memory copy, and today block copies are the most important use of this instruction.

2.17 Real Stuff: x86 Instructions

Beauty is altogether in the eye of the beholder.

Margaret Wolfe Hungerford, *Molly Bawn*, 1877

Designers of instruction sets sometimes provide more powerful operations than those found in ARM and MIPS. The goal is generally to reduce the number of instructions executed by a program. The danger is that this reduction can occur at the cost of simplicity, increasing the time a program takes to execute because the instructions are slower. This slowness may be the result of a slower clock cycle time or of requiring more clock cycles than a simpler sequence.

The path toward operation complexity is thus fraught with peril. To avoid these problems, designers have moved toward simpler instructions. Section 2.18 demonstrates the pitfalls of complexity.

Evolution of the Intel x86

ARM and MIPS were the vision of single small groups in 1985; the pieces of these architectures fit nicely together, and the whole architecture can be described succinctly. Such is not the case for the x86; it is the product of several independent groups who evolved the architecture over 30 years, adding new features to the original instruction set as someone might add clothing to a packed bag. Here are important x86 milestones.

general-purpose register (GPR) A register that can be used for addresses or for data with virtually any instruction.

- **1978**: The Intel 8086 architecture was announced as an assembly language–compatible extension of the then successful Intel 8080, an 8-bit microprocessor. The 8086 is a 16-bit architecture, with all internal registers 16 bits wide. Unlike MIPS, the registers have dedicated uses, and hence the 8086 is not considered a **general-purpose register** architecture.

- **1980**: The Intel 8087 floating-point coprocessor is announced. This architecture extends the 8086 with about 60 floating-point instructions. Instead of using registers, it relies on a stack (see ⊙ **Section 2.20** and Section 3.7).

- **1982**: The 80286 extended the 8086 architecture by increasing the address space to 24 bits, by creating an elaborate memory-mapping and protection model (see Chapter 5), and by adding a few instructions to round out the instruction set and to manipulate the protection model.

- **1985**: The 80386 extended the 80286 architecture to 32 bits. In addition to a 32-bit architecture with 32-bit registers and a 32-bit address space, the 80386 added new addressing modes and additional operations. The added instructions make the 80386 nearly a general-purpose register machine. The 80386 also added paging support in addition to segmented addressing (see Chapter 5). Like the 80286, the 80386 has a mode to execute 8086 programs without change.

- **1989–95**: The subsequent 80486 in 1989, Pentium in 1992, and Pentium Pro in 1995 were aimed at higher performance, with only four instructions added to the user-visible instruction set: three to help with multiprocessing (Chapter 7) and a conditional move instruction.

- **1997**: After the Pentium and Pentium Pro were shipping, Intel announced that it would expand the Pentium and the Pentium Pro architectures with MMX (Multi Media Extensions). This new set of 57 instructions uses the floating-point stack to accelerate multimedia and communication applications. MMX instructions typically operate on multiple short data elements at a time, in the tradition of single instruction, multiple data (SIMD) architectures (see Chapter 7). Pentium II did not introduce any new instructions.

- **1999**: Intel added another 70 instructions, labeled SSE (Streaming SIMD Extensions) as part of Pentium III. The primary changes were to add eight separate registers, double their width to 128 bits, and add a single precision floating-point data type. Hence, four 32-bit floating-point operations can be performed in parallel. To improve memory performance, SSE includes cache prefetch instructions plus streaming store instructions that bypass the caches and write directly to memory.

- **2001**: Intel added yet another 144 instructions, this time labeled SSE2. The new data type is double precision arithmetic, which allows pairs of 64-bit floating-point operations in parallel. Almost all of these 144 instructions are versions of existing MMX and SSE instructions that operate on 64 bits of data in parallel. Not only does this change enable more multimedia operations, it gives the compiler a different target for floating-point operations than the unique stack architecture. Compilers can choose to use the eight SSE registers as floating-point registers like those found in other computers. This change boosted the floating-point performance of the Pentium 4, the first microprocessor to include SSE2 instructions.

■ **2003**: A company other than Intel enhanced the x86 architecture this time. AMD announced a set of architectural extensions to increase the address space from 32 to 64 bits. Similar to the transition from a 16- to 32-bit address space in 1985 with the 80386, AMD64 widens all registers to 64 bits. It also increases the number of registers to 16 and increases the number of 128-bit SSE registers to 16. The primary ISA change comes from adding a new mode called *long mode* that redefines the execution of all x86 instructions with 64-bit addresses and data. To address the larger number of registers, it adds a new prefix to instructions. Depending how you count, long mode also adds four to ten new instructions and drops 27 old ones. PC-relative data addressing is another extension. AMD64 still has a mode that is identical to x86 (*legacy mode*) plus a mode that restricts user programs to x86 but allows operating systems to use AMD64 (*compatibility mode*). These modes allow a more graceful transition to 64-bit addressing than the HP/Intel IA-64 architecture.

■ **2004**: Intel capitulates and embraces AMD64, relabeling it Extended Memory 64 Technology (EM64T). The major difference is that Intel added a 128-bit atomic compare and swap instruction, which probably should have been included in AMD64. At the same time, Intel announced another generation of media extensions. SSE3 adds 13 instructions to support complex arithmetic, graphics operations on arrays of structures, video encoding, floating-point conversion, and thread synchronization (see Section 2.11). AMD will offer SSE3 in subsequent chips and it will almost certainly add the missing atomic swap instruction to AMD64 to maintain binary compatibility with Intel.

■ **2006**: Intel announces 54 new instructions as part of the SSE4 instruction set extensions. These extensions perform tweaks like sum of absolute differences, dot products for arrays of structures, sign or zero extension of narrow data to wider sizes, population count, and so on. They also added support for virtual machines (see Chapter 5).

■ **2007**: AMD announces 170 instructions as part of SSE5, including 46 instructions of the base instruction set that adds three operand instructions like MIPS.

■ **2008**: Intel announces the Advanced Vector Extension that expands the SSE register width from 128 to 256 bits, thereby redefining about 250 instructions and adding 128 new instructions.

This history illustrates the impact of the "golden handcuffs" of compatibility on the x86, as the existing software base at each step was too important to jeopardize with significant architectural changes. If you looked over the life of the x86, on average the architecture has been extended by one instruction per month!

Whatever the artistic failures of the x86, keep in mind that there are more instances of this architectural family on desktop computers than of any other architecture, increasing by more than 250 million per year. Nevertheless, this checkered ancestry has led to an architecture that is difficult to explain and impossible to love.

Brace yourself for what you are about to see! Do *not* try to read this section with the care you would need to write x86 programs; the goal instead is to give you familiarity with the strengths and weaknesses of the world's most popular desktop architecture.

Rather than show the entire 16-bit and 32-bit instruction set, in this section we concentrate on the 32-bit subset that originated with the 80386, as this portion of the architecture is what is used today. We start our explanation with the registers and addressing modes, move on to the integer operations, and conclude with an examination of instruction encoding.

x86 Registers and Data Addressing Modes

The registers of the 80386 show the evolution of the instruction set (Figure 2.36). The 80386 extended all 16-bit registers (except the segment registers) to 32 bits, prefixing an *E* to their name to indicate the 32-bit version. We'll refer to them generically as GPRs (general-purpose registers). The 80386 contains only eight GPRs. This means MIPS programs can use four times as many and ARM twice as many.

Figure 2.37 shows the arithmetic, logical, and data transfer instructions are two-operand instructions. There are two important differences here. The x86 arithmetic and logical instructions must have one operand act as both a source and a destination; ARM and MIPS allow separate registers for source and destination. This restriction puts more pressure on the limited registers, since one source register must be modified. The second important difference is that one of the operands can be in memory. Thus, virtually any instruction may have one operand in memory, unlike ARM and MIPS.

Data memory-addressing modes, described in detail below, offer two sizes of addresses within the instruction. These so-called *displacements* can be 8 bits or 32 bits.

Although a memory operand can use any addressing mode, there are restrictions on which *registers* can be used in a mode. Figure 2.38 shows the x86 addressing modes and which GPRs cannot be used with each mode, as well as how to get the same effect using MIPS instructions.

x86 Integer Operations

The 8086 provides support for both 8-bit (*byte*) and 16-bit (*word*) data types. The 80386 adds 32-bit addresses and data (*double words*) in the x86. (AMD64 adds 64-bit addresses and data, called *quad words*; we'll stick to the 80386 in this section.) The data type distinctions apply to register operations as well as memory accesses.

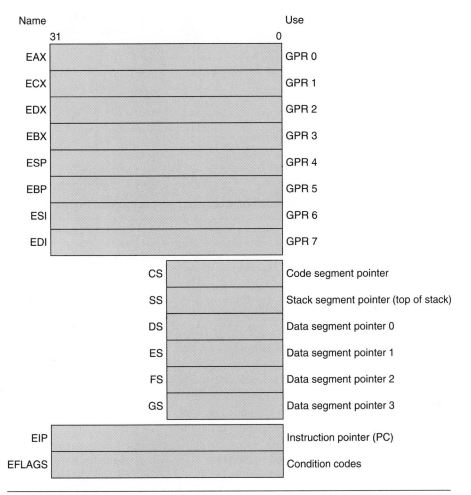

Name   Use

FIGURE 2.36   The 80386 register set. Starting with the 80386, the top eight registers were extended to 32 bits and could also be used as general-purpose registers.

Source/destination operand type	Second source operand
Register	Register
Register	Immediate
Register	Memory
Memory	Register
Memory	Immediate

FIGURE 2.37   Instruction types for the arithmetic, logical, and data transfer instructions. The x86 allows the combinations shown. The only restriction is the absence of a memory-memory mode. Immediates may be 8, 16, or 32 bits in length; a register is any one of the 14 major registers in Figure 2.36 (not EIP or EFLAGS).

Mode	Description	Register restrictions	MIPS equivalent
Register indirect	Address is in a register.	Not ESP or EBP	`lw $s0,0($s1)`
Based mode with 8- or 32-bit displacement	Address is contents of base register plus displacement.	Not ESP	`lw $s0,100($s1) # <= 16-bit` `                # displacement`

Base plus scaled index	The address is
	Base + (2^Scale x Index)
	where Scale has the value 0, 1, 2, or 3.
		Base: any GPR
		Index: not ESP
			`mul   $t0,$s2,4`
			`add   $t0,$t0,$s1`
			`lw    $s0,0($t0)`

Base plus scaled index with 8- or 32-bit displacement	The address is
	Base + (2^Scale x Index) + displacement
	where Scale has the value 0, 1, 2, or 3.
		Base: any GPR
		Index: not ESP
			`mul   $t0,$s2,4`
			`add   $t0,$t0,$s1`
			`lw    $s0,100($t0) # õ16-bit`
			`                   # displacement`

FIGURE 2.38   x86 32-bit addressing modes with register restrictions and the equivalent MIPS code. The Base plus Scaled Index addressing mode, not found in ARM or MIPS, is included to avoid the multiplies by 4 (scale factor of 2) to turn an index in a register into a byte address (see Figures 2.25 and 2.27). A scale factor of 1 is used for 16-bit data, and a scale factor of 3 for 64-bit data. A scale factor of 0 means the address is not scaled. If the displacement is longer than 16 bits in the second or fourth modes, then the MIPS equivalent mode would need two more instructions: a `lui` to load the upper 16 bits of the displacement and an `add` to sum the upper address with the base register `$s1`. (Intel gives two different names to what is called Based addressing mode—Based and Indexed—but they are essentially identical and we combine them here.)

Almost every operation works on both 8-bit data and on one longer data size. That size is determined by the mode and is either 16 bits or 32 bits.

Clearly, some programs want to operate on data of all three sizes, so the 80386 architects provided a convenient way to specify each version without expanding code size significantly. They decided that either 16-bit or 32-bit data dominates most programs, and so it made sense to be able to set a default large size. This default data size is set by a bit in the code segment register. To override the default data size, an 8-bit *prefix* is attached to the instruction to tell the machine to use the other large size for this instruction.

The prefix solution was borrowed from the 8086, which allows multiple prefixes to modify instruction behavior. The three original prefixes override the default segment register, lock the bus to support synchronization (see Section 2.11), or repeat the following instruction until the register ECX counts down to 0. This last prefix was intended to be paired with a byte move instruction to move a variable number of bytes. The 80386 also added a prefix to override the default address size.

The x86 integer operations can be divided into four major classes:

1. Data movement instructions, including move, push, and pop

2. Arithmetic and logic instructions, including test, integer, and decimal arithmetic operations

3. Control flow, including conditional branches, unconditional jumps, calls, and returns

4. String instructions, including string move and string compare

The first two categories are unremarkable, except that the arithmetic and logic instruction operations allow the destination to be either a register or a memory location. Figure 2.39 shows some typical x86 instructions and their functions.

Instruction	Function
`je name`	`if equal(condition code) {EIP=name};` `EIP-128 <= name < EIP+128`
`jmp name`	`EIP=name`
`call name`	`SP=SP-4; M[SP]=EIP+5; EIP=name;`
`movw EBX,[EDI+45]`	`EBX=M[EDI+45]`
`push ESI`	`SP=SP-4; M[SP]=ESI`
`pop EDI`	`EDI=M[SP]; SP=SP+4`
`add EAX,#6765`	`EAX= EAX+6765`
`test EDX,#42`	Set condition code (flags) with EDX and 42
`movsl`	`M[EDI]=M[ESI];` `EDI=EDI+4; ESI=ESI+4`

FIGURE 2.39 Some typical x86 instructions and their functions. A list of frequent operations appears in Figure 2.40. The CALL saves the EIP of the next instruction on the stack. (EIP is the Intel PC.)

Conditional branches on the x86 are based on *condition codes* or *flags*, like ARM. Condition codes are set as a side effect of an operation; most are used to compare the value of a result to 0. Branches then test the condition codes. PC-relative branch addresses must be specified in the number of bytes, since unlike ARM and MIPS, 80386 instructions are not all 4 bytes in length.

String instructions are part of the 8080 ancestry of the x86 and are not commonly executed in most programs. They are often slower than equivalent software routines (see the fallacy on page 174).

Figure 2.40 lists some of the integer x86 instructions. Many of the instructions are available in both byte and word formats.

x86 Instruction Encoding

Saving the worst for last, the encoding of instructions in the 80386 is complex, with many different instruction formats. Instructions for the 80386 may vary from 1 byte, when there are no operands, up to 15 bytes.

Figure 2.41 shows the instruction format for several of the example instructions in Figure 2.39. The opcode byte usually contains a bit saying whether the operand is 8 bits or 32 bits. For some instructions, the opcode may include the addressing mode and the register; this is true in many instructions that have the form "register = register op immediate." Other instructions use a "postbyte" or extra opcode byte, labeled "mod, reg, r/m," which contains the addressing mode information. This postbyte is used for many of the instructions that address memory. The base plus scaled index mode uses a second postbyte, labeled "sc, index, base."

Instruction	Meaning
Control	**Conditional and unconditional branches**
jnz, jz	Jump if condition to EIP + 8-bit offset; JNE (for JNZ), JE (for JZ) are alternative names
jmp	Unconditional jump—8-bit or 16-bit offset
call	Subroutine call—16-bit offset; return address pushed onto stack
ret	Pops return address from stack and jumps to it
loop	Loop branch—decrement ECX; jump to EIP + 8-bit displacement if ECX ≠ 0
Data transfer	**Move data between registers or between register and memory**
move	Move between two registers or between register and memory
push, pop	Push source operand on stack; pop operand from stack top to a register
les	Load ES and one of the GPRs from memory
Arithmetic, logical	**Arithmetic and logical operations using the data registers and memory**
add, sub	Add source to destination; subtract source from destination; register-memory format
cmp	Compare source and destination; register-memory format
shl, shr, rcr	Shift left; shift logical right; rotate right with carry condition code as fill
cbw	Convert byte in eight rightmost bits of EAX to 16-bit word in right of EAX
test	Logical AND of source and destination sets condition codes
inc, dec	Increment destination, decrement destination
or, xor	Logical OR; exclusive OR; register-memory format
String	**Move between string operands; length given by a repeat prefix**
movs	Copies from string source to destination by incrementing ESI and EDI; may be repeated
lods	Loads a byte, word, or doubleword of a string into the EAX register

FIGURE 2.40   Some typical operations on the x86. Many operations use register-memory format, where either the source or the destination may be memory and the other may be a register or immediate operand.

Figure 2.42 shows the encoding of the two postbyte address specifiers for both 16-bit and 32-bit mode. Unfortunately, to understand fully which registers and which addressing modes are available, you need to see the encoding of all addressing modes and sometimes even the encoding of the instructions.

x86 Conclusion

Intel had a 16-bit microprocessor two years before its competitors' more elegant architectures, such as the Motorola 68000, and this head start led to the selection of the 8086 as the CPU for the IBM PC. Intel engineers generally acknowledge that the x86 is more difficult to build than computers like ARM and MIPS, but the large

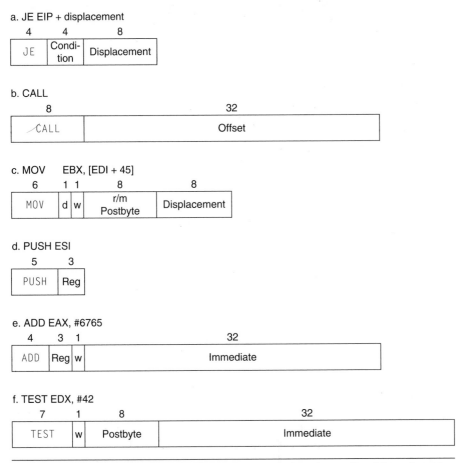

FIGURE 2.41 Typical x86 instruction formats. Figure 2.42 shows the encoding of the postbyte. Many instructions contain the 1-bit field w, which says whether the operation is a byte or a double word. The d field in MOV is used in instructions that may move to or from memory and shows the direction of the move. The ADD instruction requires 32 bits for the immediate field, because in 32-bit mode, the immediates are either 8 bits or 32 bits. The immediate field in the TEST is 32 bits long because there is no 8-bit immediate for test in 32-bit mode. Overall, instructions may vary from 1 to 17 bytes in length. The long length comes from extra 1-byte prefixes, having both a 4-byte immediate and a 4-byte displacement address, using an opcode of 2 bytes, and using the scaled index mode specifier, which adds another byte.

market means AMD and Intel can afford more resources to help overcome the added complexity. What the x86 lacks in style, it makes up for in quantity, making it beautiful from the right perspective.

Its saving grace is that the most frequently used x86 architectural components are not too difficult to implement, as AMD and Intel have demonstrated by rapidly improving performance of integer programs since 1978. To get that performance, compilers must avoid the portions of the architecture that are hard to implement fast.

reg	w = 0	w = 1		r/m	mod = 0		mod = 1		mod = 2		mod = 3
		16b	32b		16b	32b	16b	32b	16b	32b	
0	AL	AX	EAX	0	addr=BX+SI	=EAX	*same*	*same*	*same*	*same*	*same*
1	CL	CX	ECX	1	addr=BX+DI	=ECX	*addr as*	*addr as*	*addr as*	*addr as*	*as*
2	DL	DX	EDX	2	addr=BP+SI	=EDX	*mod=0*	*mod=0*	*mod=0*	*mod=0*	*reg*
3	BL	BX	EBX	3	addr=BP+SI	=EBX	*+ disp8*	*+ disp8*	*+ disp16*	*+ disp32*	*field*
4	AH	SP	ESP	4	addr=SI	=(sib)	SI+disp8	(sib)+disp8	SI+disp16	(sib)+disp32	"
5	CH	BP	EBP	5	addr=DI	=disp32	DI+disp8	EBP+disp8	DI+disp16	EBP+disp32	"
6	DH	SI	ESI	6	addr=disp16	=ESI	BP+disp8	ESI+disp8	BP+disp16	ESI+disp16	"
7	BH	DI	EDI	7	addr=BX	=EDI	BX+disp8	EDI+disp8	BX+disp16	EDI+disp32	"

FIGURE 2.42 The encoding of the first address specifier of the x86: mod, reg, r/m. The first four columns show the encoding of the 3-bit reg field, which depends on the w bit from the opcode and whether the machine is in 16-bit mode (8086) or 32-bit mode (80386). The remaining columns explain the mod and r/m fields. The meaning of the 3-bit r/m field depends on the value in the 2-bit mod field and the address size. Basically, the registers used in the address calculation are listed in the sixth and seventh columns, under mod = 0, with mod = 1 adding an 8-bit displacement and mod = 2 adding a 16-bit or 32-bit displacement, depending on the address mode. The exceptions are 1) r/m = 6 when mod = 1 or mod = 2 in 16-bit mode selects BP plus the displacement; 2) r/m = 5 when mod = 1 or mod = 2 in 32-bit mode selects EBP plus displacement; and 3) r/m = 4 in 32-bit mode when mod does not equal 3, where (sib) means use the scaled index mode shown in Figure 2.38. When mod = 3, the r/m field indicates a register, using the same encoding as the reg field combined with the w bit.

2.18 Fallacies and Pitfalls

Fallacy: More powerful instructions mean higher performance.

Part of the power of the Intel x86 is the prefixes that can modify the execution of the following instruction. One prefix can repeat the following instruction until a counter counts down to 0. Thus, to move data in memory, it would seem that the natural instruction sequence is to use move with the repeat prefix to perform 32-bit memory-to-memory moves.

An alternative method, which uses the standard instructions found in all computers, is to load the data into the registers and then store the registers back to memory. This second version of this program, with the code replicated to reduce loop overhead, copies at about 1.5 times faster. A third version, which uses the larger floating-point registers instead of the integer registers of the x86, copies at about 2.0 times faster than the complex move instruction.

Fallacy: Write in assembly language to obtain the highest performance.

At one time compilers for programming languages produced naïve instruction sequences; the increasing sophistication of compilers means the gap between compiled code and code produced by hand is closing fast. In fact, to compete with current compilers, the assembly language programmer needs to understand the concepts in Chapters 4 and 5 thoroughly (processor pipelining and memory hierarchy).

This battle between compilers and assembly language coders is one situation in which humans are losing ground. For example, C offers the programmer a chance to give a hint to the compiler about which variables to keep in registers versus spilled to memory. When compilers were poor at register allocation, such hints were vital to performance. In fact, some old C textbooks spent a fair amount of time giving examples that effectively use register hints. Today's C compilers generally ignore such hints, because the compiler does a better job at allocation than the programmer does.

Even *if* writing by hand resulted in faster code, the dangers of writing in assembly language are the longer time spent coding and debugging, the loss in portability, and the difficulty of maintaining such code. One of the few widely accepted axioms of software engineering is that coding takes longer if you write more lines, and it clearly takes many more lines to write a program in assembly language than in C or Java. Moreover, once it is coded, the next danger is that it will become a popular program. Such programs always live longer than expected, meaning that someone will have to update the code over several years and make it work with new releases of operating systems and new models of machines. Writing in higher-level language instead of assembly language not only allows future compilers to tailor the code to future machines, it also makes the software easier to maintain and allows the program to run on more brands of computers.

Fallacy: The importance of commercial binary compatibility means successful instruction sets don't change.

While backwards binary compatibility is sacrosanct, Figure 2.43 shows that the x86 architecture has grown dramatically. The average is more than one instruction per month over its 30-year lifetime!

Pitfall: Forgetting that sequential word addresses in machines with byte addressing do not differ by one.

Many an assembly language programmer has toiled over errors made by assuming that the address of the next word can be found by incrementing the address in a register by one instead of by the word size in bytes. Forewarned is forearmed!

Pitfall: Using a pointer to an automatic variable outside its defining procedure.

A common mistake in dealing with pointers is to pass a result from a procedure that includes a pointer to an array that is local to that procedure. Following the stack discipline in Figure 2.12, the memory that contains the local array will be reused as soon as the procedure returns. Pointers to automatic variables can lead to chaos.

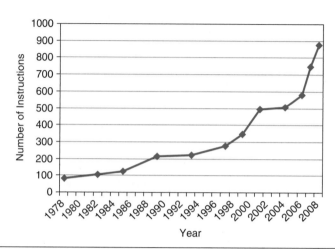

FIGURE 2.43   Growth of x86 instruction set over time. While there is clear technical value to some of these extensions, this rapid change also increases the difficulty for other companies to try to build compatible processors.

Less is more.

Robert Browning,
Andrea del Sarto, 1855

2.19   Concluding Remarks

The two principles of the *stored-program* computer are the use of instructions that are indistinguishable from numbers and the use of alterable memory for programs. These principles allow a single machine to aid environmental scientists, financial advisers, and novelists in their specialties. The selection of a set of instructions that the machine can understand demands a delicate balance among the number of instructions needed to execute a program, the number of clock cycles needed by an instruction, and the speed of the clock. As illustrated in this chapter, four design principles guide the authors of instruction sets in making that delicate balance:

1. *Simplicity favors regularity.* Regularity motivates many features of the MIPS instruction set: keeping all instructions a single size, always requiring three register operands in arithmetic instructions, and keeping the register fields in the same place in each instruction format.

2. *Smaller is faster.* The desire for speed is the reason that MIPS has 32 registers rather than many more.

3. *Make the common case fast.* Examples of making the common MIPS case fast include PC-relative addressing for conditional branches and immediate addressing for larger constant operands.

4. *Good design demands good compromises.* One MIPS example was the compromise between providing for larger addresses and constants in instructions and keeping all instructions the same length.

Above this machine level is assembly language, a language that humans can read. The assembler translates it into the binary numbers that machines can understand, and it even "extends" the instruction set by creating symbolic instructions that aren't in the hardware. For instance, constants or addresses that are too big are broken into properly sized pieces, common variations of instructions are given their own name, and so on. Figure 2.44 lists the MIPS instructions we have covered so far, both real and pseudoinstructions.

Each category of MIPS instructions is associated with constructs that appear in programming languages:

■ The arithmetic instructions correspond to the operations found in assignment statements.

■ Data transfer instructions are most likely to occur when dealing with data structures like arrays or structures.

■ The conditional branches are used in *if* statements and in loops.

■ The unconditional jumps are used in procedure calls and returns and for *case/switch* statements.

These instructions are not born equal; the popularity of the few dominates the many. For example, Figure 2.45 shows the popularity of each class of instructions for SPEC CPU2006. The varying popularity of instructions plays an important role in the chapters about datapath, control, and pipelining.

After we explain computer arithmetic in Chapter 3, we reveal the rest of the MIPS instruction set architecture.

MIPS instructions	Name	Format	Pseudo MIPS	Name	Format
add	add	R	move	move	R
subtract	sub	R	multiply	mult	R
add immediate	addi	I	multiply immediate	multi	I
load word	lw	I	load immediate	li	I
store word	sw	I	branch less than	blt	I
load half	lh	I	branch less than or equal	ble	I
load half unsigned	lhu	I			
store half	sh	I	branch greater than	bgt	I
load byte	lb	I	branch greater than or equal	bge	I
load byte unsigned	lbu	I			
store byte	sb	I			
load linked	ll	I			
store conditional	sc	I			
load upper immediate	lui	I			
and	and	R			
or	or	R			
nor	nor	R			
and immediate	andi	I			
or immediate	ori	I			
shift left logical	sll	R			
shift right logical	srl	R			
branch on equal	beq	I			
branch on not equal	bne	I			
set less than	slt	R			
set less than immediate	slti	I			
set less than immediate unsigned	sltiu	I			
jump	j	J			
jump register	jr	R			
jump and link	jal	J			

FIGURE 2.44 The MIPS instruction set covered so far, with the real MIPS instructions on the left and the pseudoinstructions on the right. Appendix B (Section B.10) describes the full MIPS architecture. Figure 2.1 shows more details of the MIPS architecture revealed in this chapter. The information given here is also found in Columns 1 and 2 of the MIPS Reference Data Card at the front of the book.

Instruction class	MIPS examples	HLL correspondence	Frequency	
			Integer	Ft. pt.
Arithmetic	add, sub, addi	Operations in assignment statements	16%	48%
Data transfer	lw, sw, lb, lbu, lh, lhu, sb, lui	References to data structures, such as arrays	35%	36%
Logical	and, or, nor, andi, ori, sll, srl	Operations in assignment statements	12%	4%
Conditional branch	beq, bne, slt, slti, sltiu	*If* statements and loops	34%	8%
Jump	j, jr, jal	Procedure calls, returns, and *case/switch* statements	2%	0%

FIGURE 2.45 MIPS instruction classes, examples, correspondence to high-level program language constructs, and percentage of MIPS instructions executed by category for the average SPEC CPU2006 benchmarks. Figure 3.26 in Chapter 3 shows average percentage of the individual MIPS instructions executed.

2.20 Historical Perspective and Further Reading

This section surveys the history of instruction set architectures (ISAs) over time, and we give a short history of programming languages and compilers. ISAs include accumulator architectures, general-purpose register architectures, stack architectures, and a brief history of ARM and the x86. We also review the controversial subjects of high-level-language computer architectures and reduced instruction set computer architectures. The history of programming languages includes Fortran, Lisp, Algol, C, Cobol, Pascal, Simula, Smalltalk, C++, and Java, and the history of compilers includes the key milestones and the pioneers who achieved them. The rest of this section is on the CD.

2.21 Exercises

Contributed by John Oliver of Cal Poly, San Luis Obispo, with contributions from Nicole Kaiyan (University of Adelaide) and Milos Prvulovic (Georgia Tech)

Appendix B describes the MIPS simulator, which is helpful for these exercises. Although the simulator accepts pseudoinstructions, try not to use pseudo-instructions for any exercises that ask you to produce MIPS code. Your goal should be to learn the real MIPS instruction set, and if you are asked to count instructions, your count should reflect the actual instructions that will be executed and not the pseudoinstructions.

There are some cases where pseudoinstructions must be used (for example, the la instruction when an actual value is not known at assembly time). In many cases, they are quite convenient and result in more readable code (for example, the `li` and `move` instructions). If you choose to use pseudoinstructions for these reasons, please add a sentence or two to your solution stating which pseudoinstructions you have used and why.

Exercise 2.1

The following problems explore translating from C to MIPS. Assume that the variables f, g, h, and i are given and could be considered 32-bit integers as declared in a C program.

a.	f = g - h;
b.	f = g + (h - 5);

2.1.1 [5] <2.2> For the C statements above, what is the corresponding MIPS assembly code? Use a minimal number of MIPS assembly instructions.

2.1.2 [5] <2.2> For the C statements above, how many MIPS assembly instructions are needed to perform the C statement?

2.1.3 [5] <2.2> If the variables f, g, h, and i have values 1, 2, 3, and 4, respectively, what is the end value of f?

The following problems deal with translating from MIPS to C. Assume that the variables g, h, i, and j are given and could be considered 32-bit integers as declared in a C program.

a.	addi f, f, 4
b.	add f, g, h add f, i, f

2.1.4 [5] <2.2> For the MIPS assembly instructions above, what is a corresponding C statement?

2.1.5 [5] <2.2> If the variables f, g, h, and i have values 1, 2, 3, and 4, respectively, what is the end value of f?

Exercise 2.2

The following problems deal with translating from C to MIPS. Assume that the variables g, h, i, and j are given and could be considered 32-bit integers as declared in a C program.

| a. | `f = g - f;` |
| b. | `f = i + (h - 2);` |

2.2.1 [5] <2.2> For the C statements above, what is the corresponding MIPS assembly code? Use a minimal number of MIPS assembly instructions.

2.2.2 [5] <2.2> For the C statements above, how many MIPS assembly instructions are needed to perform the C statement?

2.2.3 [5] <2.2> If the variables f, g, h, and i have values 1, 2, 3, and 4, respectively, what is the end value of f?

The following problems deal with translating from MIPS to C. For the following exercise, assume that the variables g, h, i, and j are given and could be considered 32-bit integers as declared in a C program.

| a. | `addi f, f, 4` |
| b. | `add  f, g, h`
`sub  f, i, f` |

2.2.4 [5] <2.2> For the MIPS assembly instructions above, what is a corresponding C statement?

2.2.5 [5] <2.2> If the variables f, g, h, and i have values 1, 2, 3, and 4, respectively, what is the end value of f?

Exercise 2.3

The following problems explore translating from C to MIPS. Assume that the variables f and g are given and could be considered 32-bit integers as declared in a C program.

| a. | `f = -g - f;` |
| b. | `f = g + (-f - 5);` |

2.3.1 [5] <2.2> For the C statements above, what is the corresponding MIPS assembly code? Use a minimal number of MIPS assembly instructions.

2.3.2 [5] <2.2> For the C statements above, how many MIPS assembly instructions are needed to perform the C statement?

2.3.3 [5] <2.2> If the variables f, g, h, i, and j have values 1, 2, 3, 4, and 5, respectively, what is the end value of f?

The following problems deal with translating from MIPS to C. Assume that the variables g, h, i, and j are given and could be considered 32-bit integers as declared in a C program.

a.	addi f, f, -4
b.	add i, g, h add f, i, f

2.3.4 [5] <2.2> For the MIPS statements above, what is a corresponding C statement?

2.3.5 [5] <2.2> If the variables f, g, h, and i have values 1, 2, 3, and 4, respectively, what is the end value of f?

Exercise 2.4

The following problems deal with translating from C to MIPS. Assume that the variables f, g, h, i, and j are assigned to registers $s0, $s1, $s2, $s3, and $s4, respectively. Assume that the base address of the arrays A and B are in registers $s6 and $s7, respectively.

a.	f = -g - A[4];
b.	B[8] = A[i-j];

2.4.1 [10] <2.2, 2.3> For the C statements above, what is the corresponding MIPS assembly code?

2.4.2 [5] <2.2, 2.3> For the C statements above, how many MIPS assembly instructions are needed to perform the C statement?

2.4.3 [5] <2.2, 2.3> For the C statements above, how many different registers are needed to carry out the C statement?

The following problems deal with translating from MIPS to C. Assume that the variables f, g, h, i, and j are assigned to registers $s0, $s1, $s2, $s3, and $s4, respectively. Assume that the base address of the arrays A and B are in registers $s6 and $s7, respectively.

a.	slli $s2, $s4, 1 add $s0, $s2, $s3 add $s0, $s0, $s1

b.	add $t0, $s6, $s0
	add $t1, $s7, $s1
	lw $s0, 0($t0)
	addi $t2, $t0, 4
	lw $t0, 0($t2)
	add $t0, $t0, $s0
	sw $t0, 0($t1)

2.4.4 [10] <2.2, 2.3> For the MIPS assembly instructions above, what is the corresponding C statement?

2.4.5 [5] <2.2, 2.3> For the MIPS assembly instructions above, rewrite the assembly code to minimize the number if MIPS instructions (if possible) needed to carry out the same function.

2.4.6 [5] <2.2, 2.3> How many registers are needed to carry out the MIPS assembly as written above? If you could rewrite the code above, what is the minimal number of registers needed?

Exercise 2.5

In the following problems, we will be investigating memory operations in the context of an MIPS processor. The table below shows the values of an array stored in memory. Assume the base address of the array is stored in register $s6 and offset it with respect to the base address of the array.

a.	Address	Data
	20	4
	24	5
	28	3
	32	2
	34	1

b.	Address	Data
	24	2
	38	4
	32	3
	36	6
	40	1

2.5.1 [10] <2.2, 2.3> For the memory locations in the table above, write C code to sort the data from lowest to highest, placing the lowest value in the smallest memory location shown in the figure. Assume that the data shown represents the C variable called Array, which is an array of type int, and that the first number in the array shown is the first element in the array. Assume that this particular machine is a byte-addressable machine and a word consists of four bytes.

2.5.2 [10] <2.2, 2.3> For the memory locations in the table above, write MIPS code to sort the data from lowest to highest, placing the lowest value in the smallest memory location. Use a minimum number of MIPS instructions. Assume the base address of Array is stored in register $s6.

2.5.3 [5] <2.2, 2.3> To sort the array above, how many instructions are required for the MIPS code? If you are not allowed to use the immediate field in lw and sw instructions, how many MIPS instructions do you need?

The following problems explore the translation of hexadecimal numbers to other number formats.

a.	0xabcdef12
b.	0x10203040

2.5.4 [5] <2.3> Translate the hexadecimal numbers above into decimal.

2.5.5 [5] <2.3> Show how the data in the table would be arranged in memory of a little-endian and a big-endian machine. Assume the data is stored starting at address 0.

Exercise 2.6

The following problems deal with translating from C to MIPS. Assume that the variables f, g, h, i, and j are assigned to registers $s0, $s1, $s2, $s3, and $s4, respectively. Assume that the base address of the arrays A and B are in registers $s6 and $s7, respectively. Assume that the elements of the arrays A and B are 4-byte words:

a.	f = f + A[2];
b.	B[8] = A[i] + A[j];

2.6.1 [10] <2.2, 2.3> For the C statements above, what is the corresponding MIPS assembly code?

2.6.2 [5] <2.2, 2.3> For the C statements above, how many MIPS assembly instructions are needed to perform the C statement?

2.6.3 [5] <2.2, 2.3> For the C statements above, how many registers are needed to carry out the C statement using MIPS assembly code?

The following problems deal with translating from MIPS to C. Assume that the variables f, g, h, i, and j are assigned to registers $s0, $s1, $s2, $s3, and $s4, respectively. Assume that the base address of the arrays A and B are in registers $s6 and $s7, respectively.

a.	`sub $s0, $s0, $s1`
	`sub $s0, $s0, $s3`
	`add $s0, $s0, $s1`

b.	`addi $t0, $s6, 4`
	`add  $t1, $s6, $0`
	`sw   $t1, 0($t0)`
	`lw   $t0, 0($t0)`
	`add  $s0, $t1, $t0`

2.6.4 [5] <2.2, 2.3> For the MIPS assembly instructions above, what is the corresponding C statement?

2.6.5 [5] <2.2, 2.3> For the MIPS assembly above, assume that the registers $s0, $s1, $s2, and $s3 contain the values 0x0000000a, 0x00000014, 0x0000001e, and 0x00000028, respectively. Also, assume that register $s6 contains the value 0x00000100, and that memory contains the following values:

Address	Value
0x00000100	0x00000064
0x00000104	0x000000c8
0x00000108	0x0000012c

Find the value of $s0 at the end of the assembly code.

2.6.6 [10] <2.3, 2.5> For each MIPS instruction, show the value of the opcode (OP), source register (RS), and target register (RT) fields. For the I-type instructions, show the value of the immediate field, and for the R-type instructions, show the value of the destination register (RD) field.

Exercise 2.7

The following problems explore number conversions from signed and unsigned binary numbers to decimal numbers.

a.	0010 0100 1001 0010 0100 1001 0010 0100$_{two}$
b.	0101 1111 1011 1110 0100 0000 0000 0000$_{two}$

2.7.1 [5] <2.4> For the patterns above, what base 10 number does the binary number represent, assuming that it is a two's complement integer?

2.7.2 [5] <2.4> For the patterns above, what base 10 number does the binary number represent, assuming that it is an unsigned integer?

2.7.3 [5] <2.4> For the patterns above, what hexadecimal number does it represent?

The following problems explore number conversions from decimal to signed and unsigned binary numbers.

a.	-1_{ten}
b.	1024_{ten}

2.7.4 [5] <2.4> For the base ten numbers above, convert to 2's complement binary.

2.7.5 [5] <2.4> For the base ten numbers above, convert to 2's complement hexadecimal.

2.7.6 [5] <2.4> For the base ten numbers above, convert the negated values from the table to 2's complement hexadecimal.

Exercise 2.8

The following problems deal with sign extension and overflow. Registers $s0 and $s1 hold the values as shown in the table below. You will be asked to perform an MIPS assembly language instruction on these registers and show the result.

a.	$s0 = 0x80000000$_sixteen_, $s1 = 0xD0000000$_sixteen_
b.	$s0 = 0x00000001$_sixteen_, $s1 = 0xFFFFFFFF$_sixteen_

2.8.1 [5] <2.4> For the contents of registers $s0 and $s1 as specified above, what is the value of $t0 for the following assembly code?

```
add $t0, $s0, $s1
```

Is the result in $t0 the desired result, or has there been overflow?

2.8.2 [5] <2.4> For the contents of registers $s0 and $s1 as specified above, what is the value of $t0 for the following assembly code?

```
sub $t0, $s0, $s1
```

Is the result in $t0 the desired result, or has there been overflow?

2.8.3 [5] <2.4> For the contents of registers $s0 and $s1 as specified above, what is the value of $t0 for the following assembly code?

```
add $t0, $s0, $s1
add $t0, $t0, $s0
```

Is the result in $t0 the desired result, or has there been overflow?

In the following problems, you will perform various MIPS operations on a pair of registers, $s0 and $s1. Given the values of $s0 and $s1 in each of the questions below, state if there will be overflow.

a.	add $s0, $s0, $s1 add $s0, $s0, $s1
b.	add $s0, $s0, $s1 add $s0, $s0, $s1 add $s0, $s0, $s1

2.8.4 [5] <2.4> Assume that register $s0 = 0x70000000 and $s1 = 0x10000000. For the table above, will there be overflow?

2.8.5 [5] <2.4> Assume that register $s0 = 0x40000000 and $s1 = 0x20000000. For the table above, will there be overflow?

2.8.6 [5] <2.4> Assume that register $s0 = 0x8FFFFFFF and $s1 = 0xD0000000. For the table above, will there be overflow?

Exercise 2.9

The table below contains various values for register $s1. You will be asked to evaluate if there would be overflow for a given operation.

a.	-1_{ten}
b.	1024_{ten}

2.9.1 [5] <2.4> Assume that register $s0 = 0x70000000 and $s1 has the value as given in the table. If the instruction: add $s0, $s0, $s1 is executed, will there be overflow?

2.9.2 [5] <2.4> Assume that register $s0 = 0x80000000 and $s1 has the value as given in the table. If the instruction: sub $s0, $s0, $s1 is executed, will there be overflow?

2.9.3 [5] <2.4> Assume that register $s0 = 0x7FFFFFFF and $s1 has the value as given in the table. If the instruction: sub $s0, $s0, $s1 is executed, will there be overflow?

The table below contains various values for register $s1. You will be asked to evaluate if there would be overflow for a given operation.

a.	$0010\ 0100\ 1001\ 0010\ 0100\ 1001\ 0010\ 0100_{two}$
b.	$0101\ 1111\ 1011\ 1110\ 0100\ 0000\ 0000\ 0000_{two}$

2.9.4 [5] <2.4> Assume that register $s0 = 0x70000000 and $s1 has the value as given in the table. If the instruction: add $s0, $s0, $s1 is executed, will there be overflow?

2.9.5 [5] <2.4> Assume that register $s0 = 0x70000000 and $s1 has the value as given in the table. If the instruction: add $s0, $s0, $s1 is executed, what is the result in hex?

2.9.6 [5] <2.4> Assume that register $s0 = 0x70000000 and $s1 has the value as given in the table. If the instruction: add $s0, $s0, $s1 is executed, what is the result in base ten?

Exercise 2.10

In the following problems, the data table contains bits that represent the opcode of an instruction. You will be asked to interpret the bits as MIPS instructions into assembly code and determine what format of MIPS instruction the bits represent.

a.	0000 0010 0001 0000 1000 0000 0010 0000$_{two}$
b.	0000 0001 0100 1011 0100 1000 0010 0010$_{two}$

2.10.1 [5] <2.5> For the binary entries above, what instruction do they represent?

2.10.2 [5] <2.5> What type (I-type, R-type, J-type) instruction do the binary entries above represent?

2.10.3 [5] <2.4, 2.5> If the binary entries above were data bits, what number would they represent in hexadecimal?

In the following problems, the data table contains MIPS instructions. You will be asked to translate the entries into the bits of the opcode and determine the MIPS instruction format.

a.	addi $t0, $t0, 0
b.	sw $t1, 32($t2)

2.10.4 [5] <2.4, 2.5> For the instructions above, show the binary then hexadecimal representation of these instructions.

2.10.5 [5] <2.5> What type (I-type, R-type, J-type) instruction do the instructions above represent?

2.10.6 [5] <2.5> What is the binary then hexadecimal representation of the opcode, Rs, and Rt fields in this instruction? For R-type instructions, what is the hexadecimal representation of the Rd and funct fields? For I-type instructions, what is the hexadecimal representation of the immediate field?

Exercise 2.11

In the following problems, the data table contains bits that represent the opcode of an instruction. You will be asked to translate the entries into assembly code and determine what format of MIPS instruction the bits represent.

a.	0x01084020
b.	0x02538822

2.11.1 [5] <2.4, 2.5> What binary number does the above hexadecimal number represent?

2.11.2 [5] <2.4, 2.5> What decimal number does the above hexadecimal number represent?

2.11.3 [5] <2.5> What instruction does the above hexadecimal number represent?

In the following problems, the data table contains the values of various fields of MIPS instructions. You will be asked to determine what the instruction is, and find the MIPS format for the instruction.

a.	op=0, rs=3, rt=2, rd=3, shamt=0, funct=34
b.	op=0x23, rs=1, rt=2, const=0x4

2.11.4 [5] <2.5> What type (I-type, R-type) instruction do the instructions above represent?

2.11.5 [5] <2.5> What is the MIPS assembly instruction described above?

2.11.6 [5] <2.4, 2.5> What is the binary representation of the instructions above?

Exercise 2.12

In the following problems, the data table contains various modifications that could be made to the MIPS instruction set architecture. You will investigate the impact of these changes on the instruction format of the MIPS architecture.

a.	128 registers
b.	Four times as many different instructions

2.12.1 [5] <2.5> If the instruction set of the MIPS processor is modified, the instruction format must also be changed. For each of the suggested changes above, show the size of the bit fields of an R-type format instruction. What is the total number of bits needed for each instruction?

2.12.2 [5] <2.5> If the instruction set of the MIPS processor is modified, the instruction format must also be changed. For each of the suggested changes above, show the size of the bit fields of an I-type format instruction. What is the total number of bits needed for each instruction?

2.12.3 [5] <2.5, 2.10> Why could the suggested change in the table above decrease the size of an MIPS assembly program? Why could the suggested change in the table above increase the size of an MIPS assembly program?

In the following problems, the data table contains hexadecimal values. You will be asked to determine what MIPS instruction the value represents, and find the MIPS instruction format.

a.	0x01090012
b.	0xAD090012

2.12.4 [5] <2.5> For the entries above, what is the value of the number in decimal?

2.12.5 [5] <2.5> For the hexadecimal entries above, what instruction do they represent?

2.12.6 [5] <2.4, 2.5> What type (I-type, R-type, J-type) instruction do the binary entries above represent? What is the value of the op field and the rt field?

Exercise 2.13

In the following problems, the data table contains the values for registers $t0 and $t1. You will be asked to perform several MIPS logical operations on these registers.

a.	$t0 = 0xAAAAAAAA, $t1 = 0x12345678
b.	$t0 = 0xF00DD00D, $t1 = 0x11111111

2.13.1 [5] <2.6> For the lines above, what is the value of $t2 for the following sequence of instructions?

```
sll $t2, $t0, 44
or $t2, $t2, $t1
```

2.13.2 [5] <2.6> For the values in the table above, what is the value of $t2 for the following sequence of instructions?

```
sll $t2, $t0, 4
andi $t2, $t2, -1
```

2.13.3 [5] <2.6> For the lines above, what is the value of $t2 for the following sequence of instructions?

```
srl $t2, $t0, 3
andi $t2, $t2, 0xFFEF
```

In the following exercise, the data table contains various MIPS logical operations. You will be asked to find the result of these operations given values for registers $t0 and $t1.

a.	`sll  $t2, $t0, 1` `andi $t2, $t2, -1`
b.	`andi $t2, $t1, 0x00F0` `srl  $t2, 2`

2.13.4 [5] <2.6> Assume that $t0 = 0x0000A5A5 and $t1 = 00005A5A. What is the value of $t2 after the two instructions in the table?

2.13.5 [5] <2.6> Assume that $t0 = 0xA5A50000 and $t1 = A5A50000. What is the value of $t2 after the two instructions in the table?

2.13.6 [5] <2.6> Assume that $t0 = 0xA5A5FFFF and $t1 = A5A5FFFF. What is the value of $t2 after the two instructions in the table?

Exercise 2.14

The following figure shows the placement of a bit field in register $t0.

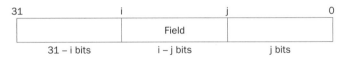

In the following problems, you will be asked to write MIPS instructions to extract the bits "Field" from register $t0 and place them into register $t1 at the location indicated in the following table.

a.	31 31 − (i − j) 0 Field 000 ... 000
b.	31 14 + i − j bits 14 0 1 1 1 ... 1 1 1 Field 1 1 1 ... 1 1 1

2.14.1 [20] <2.6> Find the shortest sequence of MIPS instructions that extracts a field from $t0 for the constant values i = 22 and j = 5 and places the field into $t1 in the format shown in the data table.

2.14.2 [5] <2.6> Find the shortest sequence of MIPS instructions that extracts a field from $t0 for the constant values i = 4 and j = 0 and places the field into $t1 in the format shown in the data table.

2.14.3 [5] <2.6> Find the shortest sequence of MIPS instructions that extracts a field from $t0 for the constant values i = 31 and j = 28 and places the field into $t1 in the format shown in the data table.

In the following problems, you will be asked to write MIPS instructions to extract the bits "Field" from register $t0 shown in the figure and place them into register $t1 at the location indicated in the following table. The bits shown as "XXX" are to remain unchanged.

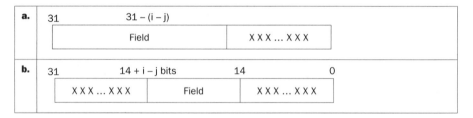

2.14.4 [20] <2.6> Find the shortest sequence of MIPS instructions that extracts a field from $t0 for the constant values i = 17 and j = 11 and places the field into $t1 in the format shown in the data table.

2.14.5 [5] <2.6> Find the shortest sequence of MIPS instructions that extracts a field from $t0 for the constant values i = 5 and j = 0 and places the field into $t1 in the format shown in the data table.

2.14.6 [5] <2.6> Find the shortest sequence of MIPS instructions that extracts a field from $t0 for the constant values i = 31 and j = 29 and places the field into $t1 in the format shown in the data table.

Exercise 2.15

For these problems, the table holds some logical operations that are not included in the MIPS instruction set. How can these instructions be implemented?

a.	`not $t1, $t2`	`// bit-wise invert`
b.	`orn $t1, $t2, $t3`	`// bit-wise OR of $t2, !$t3`

2.15.1 [5] <2.6> The logical instructions above are not included in the MIPS instruction set, but are described above. If the value of $t2 = 0x00FFA5A5$ and the value of $t3 = 0xFFFF003C$, what is the result in $t1$?

2.15.2 [10] <2.6> The logical instructions above are not included in the MIPS instruction set, but can be synthesized using one or more MIPS assembly instructions. Provide a minimal set of MIPS instructions that may be used in place of the instructions in the table above.

2.15.3 [5] <2.6> For your sequence of instructions in 2.15.2, show the bit-level representation of each instruction.

Various C-level logical statements are shown in the table below. In this exercise, you will be asked to evaluate the statements and implement these C statements using MIPS assembly instructions.

a.	A = B	!A;
b.	A = C[0] << 4;

2.15.4 [5] <2.6> The table above shows different C statements that use logical operators. If the memory location at C[0] contains the integer values 0x00001234, and the initial integer values of A and B are 0x00000000 and 0x00002222, what is the result value of A?

2.15.5 [5] <2.6> For the C statements in the table above, write a minimal sequence of MIPS assembly instructions that does the identical operation. Assume $t1 = A$, $t2 = B$, and $s1$ is the base address of C.

2.15.6 [5] <2.6> For your sequence of instructions in 2.15.5, show the bit-level representation of each instruction.

Exercise 2.16

For these problems, the table holds various binary values for register $t0$. Given the value of $t0$, you will be asked to evaluate the outcome of different branches.

a.	0010 0100 1001 0010 0100 1001 0010 0100$_{two}$
b.	0101 1111 1011 1110 0100 0000 0000 0000$_{two}$

2.16.1 [5] <2.7> Suppose that register $t0$ contains a value from above and $t1$ has the value

0011 1111 1111 1000 0000 0000 0000 0000$_{two}$

Note the result of executing these instructions on particular registers. What is the value of $t2 after the following instructions?

```
          slt   $t2, $t0, $t1
          beq   $t2, $0, ELSE
          j     DONE
ELSE: addi $t2, $0, 2
DONE:
```

2.16.2 [5] <2.7> Suppose that register $t0 contains a value from the table above and is compared against the value X, as used in the MIPS instruction below. Note the format of the slti instruction. For what values of X, if any, will $t2 be equal to 1?

```
     slti $t2, $t0, X
```

2.16.3 [5] <2.7> Suppose the program counter (PC) is set to 0x0000 0020. Is it possible to use the jump MIPS assembly instruction to get set the PC to the address as shown in the data table above? Is it possible to use the branch-on-equal MIPS assembly instruction to get set the PC to the address as shown in the data table above?

For these problems, the table holds various binary values for register $t0. Given the value of $t0, you will be asked to evaluate the outcome of different branches.

a.	0x00101000
b.	0x80001000

2.16.4 [5] <2.7> Suppose that register $t0 contains a value from above. What is the value of $t2 after the following instructions?

```
          slt   $t2, $0,  $t0
          bne   $t2, $0,  ELSE
          j     DONE
ELSE: addi $t2, $t2, 2
DONE:
```

2.16.5 [5] <2.6, 2.7> Suppose that register $t0 contains a value from above. What is the value of $t2 after the following instructions?

```
    sll $t0, $t0, 2
    slt $t2, $t0, $0
```

2.16.6 [5] <2.7> Suppose the program counter (PC) is set to 0x2000 0000. Is it possible to use the jump (j) MIPS assembly instruction to get set the PC to the address as shown in the data table above? Is it possible to use the branch-on-equal (beq) MIPS assembly instruction to set the PC to the address as shown in the data table above? Note the format of the J-type instruction.

Exercise 2.17

For these problems, there are several instructions that are not included in the MIPS instruction set are shown.

a.	`subi $t2, $t3, 5`	`# R[rt] = R[rs] - SignExtImm`
b.	`rpt $t2, loop`	`# if(R[rs]>0) R[rs]=R[rs]-1, PC=PC+4+BranchAddr`

2.17.1 [5] <2.7> The table above contains some instructions not included in the MIPS instruction set and the description of each instruction. Why are these instructions not included in the MIPS instruction set?

2.17.2 [5] <2.7> The table above contains some instructions not included in the MIPS instruction set and the description of each instruction. If these instructions were to be implemented in the MIPS instruction set, what is the most appropriate instruction format?

2.17.3 [5] <2.7> For each instruction in the table above, find the shortest sequence of MIPS instructions that performs the same operation.

For these problems, the table holds MIPS assembly code fragments. You will be asked to evaluate each of the code fragments, familiarizing you with the different MIPS branch instructions.

a.	```LOOP: addi $s2, $s2, 2` ` subi $t1, $t1, 1` ` bne $t1, $0, LOOP` `DONE:```
b.	```LOOP: slt $t2, $0, $t1` ` beq $t2, $0, DONE` ` subi $t1, $t1, 1` ` addi $s2, $s2, 2` ` j LOOP` `DONE:```

2.17.4 [5] <2.7> For the loops written in MIPS assembly above, assume that the register $t1 is initialized to the value 10. What is the value in register $s2 assuming the $s2 is initially zero?

2.17.5 [5] <2.7> For each of the loops above, write the equivalent C code routine. Assume that the registers $s1, $s2, $t1, and $t2 are integers A, B, i, and temp, respectively.

2.17.6 [5] <2.7> For the loops written in MIPS assembly above, assume that the register $t1 is initialized to the value N. How many MIPS instructions are executed?

Exercise 2.18

For these problems, the table holds some C code. You will be asked to evaluate these C code statements in MIPS assembly code.

a.	```for(i=0; i<a; i++)``` ``` a += b;```

b.	```for(i=0; i<a; i++)```
	``` for(j=0; j<b; j++)```
	``` D[4*j] = i + j;```

2.18.1 [5] <2.7> For the table above, draw a control-flow graph of the C code.

2.18.2 [5] <2.7> For the table above, translate the C code to MIPS assembly code. Use a minimum number of instructions. Assume that the values of a, b, i, and j are in registers $s0, $s1, $t0, and $t1, respectively. Also, assume that register $s2 holds the base address of the array D.

2.18.3 [5] <2.7> How many MIPS instructions does it take to implement the C code? If the variables a and b are initialized to 10 and 1 and all elements of D are initially 0, what is the total number of MIPS instructions that is executed to complete the loop?

For these problems, the table holds MIPS assembly code fragments. You will be asked to evaluate each of the code fragments, familiarizing you with the different MIPS branch instructions.

a.	``` addi $t1, $0, 50```
	```LOOP: lw $s1, 0($s0)```
	``` add $s2, $s2, $s1```
	``` lw $s1, 4($s0)```
	``` add $s2, $s2, $s1```
	``` addi $s0, $s0, 8```
	``` subi $t1, $t1, 1```
	``` bne $t1, $0, LOOP```

b.	``` addi $t1, $0, $0```
	```LOOP: lw $s1, 0($s0)```
	``` add $s2, $s2, $s1```
	``` addi $s0, $s0, 4```
	``` addi $t1, $t1, 1```
	``` slti $t2, $t1, 100```
	``` bne $t2, $s0, LOOP```

2.18.4 [5] <2.7> What is the total number of MIPS instructions executed?

2.18.5 [5] <2.7> Translate the loops above into C. Assume that the C-level integer i is held in register $t1, $s2 holds the C-level integer called result, and $s0 holds the base address of the integer MemArray.

2.18.6 [5] <2.7> Rewrite the loop to reduce the number of MIPS instructions executed.

Exercise 2.19

For the following problems, the table holds C code functions. Assume that the first function listed in the table is called first. You will be asked to translate these C code routines into MIPS assembly.

a.	```int fib(int n){```
	``` if (n==0)```
	``` return 0;```
	``` else if (n == 1)```
	``` return 1;```
	``` else```
	``` fib(n-1) + fib(n-2);```

b.	```int positive(int a, int b) {```
	``` if (addit(a, b) > 0)```
	``` return 1;```
	``` else```
	``` return 0;```
	``` }```
	```int addit(int a, int b) {```
	``` return a+b;```
	``` }```

2.19.1 [15] <2.8> Implement the C code in the table in MIPS assembly. What is the total number of MIPS instructions needed to execute the function?

2.19.2 [5] <2.8> Functions can often be implemented by compilers "in-line." An in-line function is when the body of the function is copied into the program space, allowing the overhead of the function call to be eliminated. Implement an "in-line" version of the the C code in the table in MIPS assembly. What is the reduction in the total number of MIPS assembly instructions needed to complete the function? Assume that the C variable n is initialized to 5.

2.19.3 [5] <2.8> For each function call, show the contents of the stack after the function call is made. Assume the stack pointer is originally at address 0x7ffffffc, and follow the register conventions as specified in Figure 2.11.

The following three problems in this Exercise refer to a function f that calls another function func. The code for C function func is already compiled in another module using the MIPS calling convention from Figure 2.14. The function declaration for func is "int func(int a, int b);". The code for function f is as follows:

a.	```int f(int a, int b, int c, int d){
return func(func(a,b),c+d);
}```
b.	```int f(int a, int b, int c, int d){
if(a+b>c+d)
return func(a+b,c+d);
return func(c+d,a+b);
}```

2.19.4 [10] <2.8> Translate function f into MIPS assembly language, also using the MIPS calling convention from Figure 2.14. If you need to use registers $t0 through $t7, use the lower-numbered registers first.

2.19.5 [5] <2.8> Can we use the tail-call optimization in this function? If no, explain why not. If yes, what is the difference in the number of executed instructions in f with and without the optimization?

2.19.6 [5] <2.8> Right before your function f from Problem 2.19.4 returns, what do we know about contents of registers $t5, $s3, $ra, and $sp? Keep in mind that we know what the entire function f looks like, but for function func we only know its declaration.

Exercise 2.20

This exercise deals with recursive procedure calls. For the following problems, the table has an assembly code fragment that computes the factorial of a number. However, the entries in the table have errors, and you will be asked to fix these errors. For number n, factorial of n = 1 x 2 x 3 x .. .. x n.

| **a.** | ```
FACT:   sw    $ra, 4($sp)
        sw    $a0, 0($sp)
        addi  $sp, $sp, -8
        slti  $t0, $a0, 1
        beq   $t0, $0, L1
        addi  $v0, $0, 1
        addi  $sp, $sp, 8
        jr    $ra

L1:     addi  $a0, $a0, -1
        jal   FACT
        addi  $sp, $sp, 8
        lw    $a0, 0($sp)
        lw    $ra, 4($sp)
        mul   $v0, $a0, $v0
        jr    $ra
``` |
```

```
b.  FACT:   addi $sp, $sp, 8
            sw   $ra, 4($sp)
            sw   $a0, 0($sp)
            add  $s0, $0, $a0
            slti $t0, $a0, 2
            beq  $t0, $0, L1
            mul  $v0, $s0, $v0
            addi $sp, $sp, -8
            jr   $ra

    L1:     addi $a0, $a0, -1
            jal  FACT
            addi $v0, $0, 1
            lw   $a0, 0($sp)
            lw   $ra, 4($sp)
            addi $sp, $sp, -8
            jr   $ra
```

2.20.1 [5] <2.8> The MIPS assembly program above computes the factorial of a given input. The integer input is passed through register $a0, and the result is returned in register $v0. In the assembly code, there are a few errors. Correct the MIPS errors.

2.20.2 [10] <2.8> For the recursive factorial MIPS program above, assume that the input is 4. Rewrite the factorial program to operate in a non-recursive manner. Restrict your register usage to registers $s0-$s7. What is the total number of instructions used to execute your solution from 2.20.2 versus the recursive version of the factorial program?

2.20.3 [5] <2.8> Show the contents of the stack after each function call, assuming that the input is 4.

For the following problems, the table has an assembly code fragment that computes a Fibonacci number. However, the entries in the table have errors, and you will be asked to fix these errors. For number n, the Fibonacci of n is calculated as follows:

n	fibonacci of n
1	1
2	1
3	2
4	3
5	5
6	8
7	13
8	21

a.	FIB:	addi	$sp, $sp, -12
		sw	$ra, 0($sp)
		sw	$s1, 4($sp)
		sw	$a0, 8($sp)
		slti	$t0, $a0, 1
		beq	$t0, $0, L1
		addi	$v0, $a0, $0
		j	EXIT
	L1:	addi	$a0, $a0, -1
		jal	FIB
		addi	$s1, $v0, $0
		addi	$a0, $a0, -1
		jal	FIB
		add	$v0, $v0, $s1
	EXIT:	lw	$ra, 0($sp)
		lw	$a0, 8($sp)
		lw	$s1, 4($sp)
		addi	$sp, $sp, 12
		jr	$ra
b.	FIB:	addi	$sp, $sp, -12
		sw	$ra, 8($sp)
		sw	$s1, 4($sp)
		sw	$a0, 0($sp)
		slti	$t0, $a0, 3
		beq	$t0, $0, L1
		addi	$v0, $0, 1
		j	EXIT
	L1:	addi	$a0, $a0, -1
		jal	FIB
		addi	$a0, $a0, -2
		jal	FIB
		add	$v0, $v0, $s1
	EXIT:	lw	$a0, 0($sp)
		lw	$s1, 4($sp)
		lw	$ra, 8($sp)
		addi	$sp, $sp, 12
		jr	$ra

2.20.4 [5] <2.8> The MIPS assembly program above computes the Fibonacci of a given input. The integer input is passed through register $a0, and the result is returned in register $v0. In the assembly code, there are a few errors. Correct the MIPS errors.

2.20.5 [10] <2.8> For the recursive Fibonacci MIPS program above, assume that the input is 4. Rewrite the Fibonacci program to operate in a non-recursive manner. Restrict your register usage to registers $s0-$s7. What is the total number of instructions used to execute your solution from 2.20.2 versus the recursive version of the factorial program?

2.20.6 [5] <2.8> Show the contents of the stack after each function call, assuming that the input is 4.

Exercise 2.21

Assume that the stack and the static data segments are empty and that the stack and global pointers start at address 0x7fff fffc and 0x1000 8000, respectively. Assume the calling conventions as specified in Figure 2.11 and that function inputs are passed using registers $a0-$a3 and returned in register $r0. Assume that leaf functions may only use saved registers.

a.	```int my_global = 100;
main()
{
int x = 10;
int y = 20;
int z;
z = my_function(x, y)
}
int my_function(int x, int y)
{
return x - y + my_global;
}```
b.	```int my_global = 100;
main()
{
int z;
my_global += 1;
z = leaf_function(my_global);
}
int leaf_function(int x)
{
return x + 1;
}```

2.21.1 [5] <2.8> Write MIPS assembly code for the code in the table above.

2.21.2 [5] <2.8> Show the contents of the stack and the static data segments after each function call.

2.21.3 [5] <2.8> If the leaf function could use temporary registers ($t0, $t1, etc.), write the MIPS code for the code in the table above.

The following three problems in this Exercise refer to this function, written in MIPS assembly following the calling conventions from Figure 2.14:

| a. | ```
f: add    $v0,$a1,$a0
   bnez   $a2,L
   sub    $v0,$a0,$a1
L: jr     $v0
``` |
|----|----|
| b. | ```
f: add    $a2,$a3,$a2
   slt    $a2,$a2,$a0
   move   $v0,$a1
   beqz   $a2, L
   jr     $ra
L: move   $a0,$a1
   jal    g          ; Tail call
``` |

2.21.4 [10] <2.8> This code contains a mistake that violates the MIPS calling convention. What is this mistake and how should it be fixed?

2.21.5 [10] <2.8> What is the C equivalent of this code? Assume that the function's arguments are named a, b, c, etc. in the C version of the function.

2.21.6 [10] <2.8> At the point where this function is called register $a0, $a1, $a2, and $a3 have values 1, 100, 1000, and 30, respectively. What is the value returned by this function? If another function g is called from f, assume that the value returned from g is always 500.

Exercise 2.22

This exercise explores ASCII and Unicode conversion.

The following table shows strings of characters.

a.	hello world
b.	0123456789

2.22.1 [5] <2.9> Translate the strings into hexadecimal ASCII byte values.

2.22.2 [5] <2.9> Translate the strings into 16-bit Unicode (using hex notation and the Basic Latin character set).

The following table shows hexadecimal ASCII character values.

a.	41 44 44
b.	4D 49 50 53

2.22.3 [5] <2.5, 2.9> Translate the hexadecimal ASCII values to text.

Exercise 2.23

In this exercise, you will be asked to write an MIPS assembly program that converts strings into the number format as specified in the table.

a.	positive and negative integer decimal strings
b.	positive hexadecimal integers

2.23.1 [10] <2.9> Write a program in MIPS assembly language to convert an ASCII number string with the conditions listed in the table above, to an integer. Your program should expect register $a0 to hold the address of a null-terminated string containing some combination of the digits 0 through 9. Your program should compute the integer value equivalent to this string of digits, then place the number in register $v0. If a non-digit character appears anywhere in the string, your program should stop with the value –1 in register $v0. For example, if register $a0 points to a sequence of three bytes 50_{ten}, 52_{ten}, 0_{ten} (the null-terminated string "24"), then when the program stops, register $v0 should contain the value 24_{ten}.

Exercise 2.24

Assume that the register $t1 contains the address 0x1000 0000 and the register $t2 contains the address 0x1000 0010. Note the MIPS architecture utilizes big-endian addressing.

a.	`lbu $t0, 0($t1)` `sw  $t0, 0($t2)`
b.	`lb  $t0, 0($t1)` `sh  $t0, 0($t2)`

2.24.1 [5] <2.9> Assume that the data (in hexadecimal) at address 0x1000 0000 is:

1000 0000	12	34	56	78

What value is stored at the address pointed to by register $t2? Assume that the memory location pointed to $t2 is initialized to 0xFFFF FFFF.

2.24.2 [5] <2.9> Assume that the data (in hexadecimal) at address 0x1000 0000 is:

1000 0000	80	80	80	80

What value is stored at the address pointed to by register $t2? Assume that the memory location pointed to $t2 is initialized to 0x0000 0000.

2.24.3 [5] <2.9> Assume that the data (in hexadecimal) at address 0x1000 0000 is:

1000 0000	11	00	00	FF

What value is stored at the address pointed to by register $t2? Assume that the memory location pointed to $t2 is initialized to 0x5555 5555.

Exercise 2.25

In this exercise, you will explore 32-bit constants in MIPS. For the following problems, you will be using the binary data in the table below.

a.	0010 0000 0000 0001 0100 1001 0010 0100$_{two}$
b.	0000 1111 1011 1110 0100 0000 0000 0000$_{two}$

2.25.1 [10] <2.10> Write the MIPS assembly code that creates the 32-bit constants listed above and stores that value to register $t1.

2.25.2 [5] <2.6, 2.10> If the current value of the PC is 0x00000000, can you use a single jump instruction to get to the PC address as shown in the table above?

2.25.3 [5] <2.6, 2.10> If the current value of the PC is 0x00000600, can you use a single branch instruction to get to the PC address as shown in the table above?

2.25.4 [5] <2.6, 2.10> If the current value of the PC is 0x1FFFf000, can you use a single branch instruction to get to the PC address as shown in the table above?

2.25.5 [10] <2.10> If the immediate field of an MIPS instruction was only 8 bits wide, write the MIPS code that creates the 32-bit constants listed above and stores that value to register $t1. Do not use the lui instruction.

For the following problems, you will be using the MIPS assembly code as listed in the table.

a.	```lui $t0, 0x1234``` ```addi $t0, $t0, 0x5678```
b.	```lui $t0, 0x1234``` ```andi $t0, $t0, 0x5678```

2.25.6 [5] <2.6, 2.10> What is the value of register $t0 after the sequence of code in the table above?

2.25.7 [5] <2.6, 2.10> Write C code that is equivalent to the assembly code in the table. Assume that the largest constant that you can load into a 32-bit integer is 16 bits.

Exercise 2.26

For this exercise, you will explore the range of branch and jump instructions in MIPS. For the following problems, use the hexadecimal data in the table below.

a.	0x00020000
b.	0xFFFFFF00

2.26.1 [10] <2.6, 2.10> If the PC is at address 0x00000000, how many branch (no jump instructions) do you need to get to the address in the table above?

2.26.2 [10] <2.6, 2.10> If the PC is at address 0x00000000, how many jump instructions (no jump register instructions or branch instructions) are required to get to the target address in the table above?

2.26.3 [10] <2.6, 2.10> In order to reduce the size of MIPS programs, MIPS designers have decided to cut the immediate field of I-type instructions from 16 bits to 8 bits. If the PC is at address 0x0000000, how many branch instructions are needed to set the PC to the address in the table above?

For the following problems, you will be using making modifications to the MIPS instruction set architecture.

a.	128 registers
b.	Four times as many different operations

2.26.4 [10] <2.6, 2.10> If the instruction set of the MIPS processor is modified, the instruction format must also be changed. For each of the suggested changes above, what is the impact on the range of addresses for a beq instruction? Assume that all instructions remain 32 bits long and any changes made to the instruction format of i-type instructions only increase/decrease the immediate field of the beq instruction.

2.26.5 [10] <2.6, 2.10> If the instruction set of the MIPS processor is modified, the instruction format must also be changed. For each of the suggested changes above, what is the impact on the range of addresses for a jump instruction? Assume that instructions remain 32 bits long and any changes made to the instruction format of J-type instructions only impact the address field of the jump instruction.

2.26.6 [10] <2.6, 2.10> If the instruction set of the MIPS processor is modified, the instruction format must also be changed. For each of the suggested changes above, what is the impact on the range of addresses for a jump register instruction, assuming that each instruction must be 32 bits.

Exercise 2.27

In the following problems, you will be exploring different addressing modes in the MIPS instruction set architecture. These different addressing modes are listed in the table below.

a.	Base or Displacement Addressing
b.	Pseudodirect Addressing

2.27.1 [5] <2.10> In the table above are different addressing modes of the MIPS instruction set. Give an example MIPS instructios that shows the MIPS addressing mode.

2.27.2 [5] <2.10> For the instructions in 2.27.1, what is the instruction format type used for the given instruction?

2.27.3 [5] <2.10> List the benefits and drawbacks of a particular MIPS addressing mode. Write MIPS code that shows these benefits and drawbacks.

In the following problems, you will be using the MIPS assembly code as listed below to explore the trade-offs of the immediate field in the MIPS I-type instructions.

a.	`0x00400000` `beq  $s0, $0, FAR`
	`...`
	`0x00403100 FAR:  addi $s0, $s0, 1`

b.	`0x00000100           j   AWAY`
	`...`
	`0x04000010 AWAY:  addi $s0, $s0, 1`

2.27.4 [15] <2.10> For the MIPS statements above, show the bit-level instruction representation of each of the instructions in hexadecimal.

2.27.5 [10] <2.10> By reducing the size of the immediate fields of the I-type and J-type instructions, we can save on the number of bits needed to represent these types of instructions. If the immediate field of I-type instructions were 8 bits and the immediate field of J-type instructions were 18 bits, rewrite the MIPS code above to reflect this change. Avoid using the `lui` instruction.

2.27.6 [5] <2.10> How many extra instructions are needed to do execute your code in 2.27.5 MIPS statements in the table versus the code shown in the table above?

Exercise 2.28

The following table contains MIPS assembly code for a lock. Refer to the definition of the ll and sc pairs of MIPS instructions.

| a. | ```
try: MOV   R3,R4
     LL    R2,0(R2)
     ADDI  R2,R2, 1
     SC    R3,0(R1)
     BEQZ  R3,try
     MOV   R4,R2
``` |
|----|---|

2.28.1 [5] <2.11> For each test and fail of the store conditional, how many instructions need to be executed?

2.28.2 [5] <2.11> For the load locked/store conditional code above, explain why this code may fail.

2.28.3 [15] <2.11> Rewrite the code above so that the code may operate correctly. Be sure to avoid any race conditions.

Each entry in the following table has code and also shows the contents of various registers. The notation "($s1)" shows the contents of a memory location pointed to by register $s1. The assembly code in each table is executed in the cycle shown on parallel processors with a shared memory space.

a.

Processor 1	Processor 2	Cycle	Processor 1		Mem	Processor 2	
			$t1	$t0	($s1)	$t1	$t0
		0	1	2	99	30	40
	ll $t1, 0($s1)	1					
ll $t1, 0($s1)		2					
	sc $t0, 0($s1)	3					
sc $t0, 0($s1)		4					
```

b.

Processor 1	Processor 2	Cycle	Processor 1 $t1	$t0	Mem ($s1)	Processor 2 $t1	$t0
		0	1	2	99	30	40
ll $t1,0($s1)		1					
	ll $t1,0($s1)	2					
	addi $t1,$t1,1	3					
	sc $t1,0($s1)	4					
sc $t0,0($s1)		5					

2.28.4 [5] <2.11> Fill out the table with the value of the registers for each given cycle.

Exercise 2.29

The first three problems in this Exercise refer to a critical section of the form

```
lock(lk);
operation
unlock(lk);
```

where the "operation" updates the shared variable shvar using the local (non-shared) variable x as follows:

	Operation
a.	shvar=max(shvar,x);
b.	if(shvar>0) shvar=max(shvar,x);

2.29.1 [10] <2.11> Write the MIPS assembly code for this critical section, assuming that the address of the lk variable is in $a0, the address of the shvar variable is in $a1, and the value of variable x is in $a2. Your critical section should not contain any function calls, i.e., you should include the MIPS instructions for lock(), unlock(), max(), and min() operations. Use ll/sc instructions to implement the lock() operation, and the unlock() operation is simply an ordinary store instruction.

2.29.2 [10] <2.11> Repeat problem 2.29.1, but this time use ll/sc to perform an atomic update of the shvar variable directly, without using lock() and unlock(). Note that in this problem there is no variable lk.

2.29.3 [10] <2.11> Compare the best-case performance of your code from 2.29.1 and 2.29.2, assuming that each instruction takes one cycle to execute. Note: best-case means that ll/sc always succeeds, the lock is always free when we want to lock(), and if there is a branch we take the path that completes the operation with fewer executed instructions.

2.29.4 [10] <2.11> Using your code from 2.29.2 as an example, explain what happens when two processors begin to execute this critical section at the same time, assuming that each processor executes exactly one instruction per cycle.

2.29.5 [10] <2.11> Explain why in your code from 2.29.2 register $a1 contains the address of variable shvar and not the value of that variable, and why register $a2 contains the value of variable x and not its address.

2.29.6 [10] <2.11> If we want to atomically perform the same operation on two shared variables (e.g., shvar1 and shvar2) in the same critical section, we can do this easily using the approach from 2.29.1 (simply put both updates between the lock operation and the corresponding unlock operation). Explain why we cannot do this using the approach from 2.29.2. i.e., why we cannot use ll/sc to access both shared variables in a way that guarantees that both updates are executed together as a single atomic operation.

Exercise 2.30

Assembler instructions are not a part of the MIPS instruction set, but often appear in MIPS programs. The table below contains some MIPS assembly instructions that get translated to actual MIPS instructions.

a.	clear $t0
b.	beq $t1, large, LOOP

2.30.1 [5] <2.12> For each assembly instruction in the table above, produce a minimal sequence of actual MIPS instructions to accomplish the same thing. You may need to use temporary registers in some cases. In the table large refers to a number that requires 32 bits to represent and small to a number that can fit into 16 bits.

The table below contains some MIPS assembly instructions that get translated to actual MIPS instructions.

a.	bltu $s0, $t1, Loop
b.	ulw $v0, v

2.30.2 [5] <2.12> Does the instruction in the table above need to be edited during the link phase? Why?

Exercise 2.31

The table below contains the link-level details of two different procedures. In this exercise, you will be taking the place of the linker.

a.	Procedure A				Procedure B			
Text Segment	Address	Instruction		Text Segment	Address	Instruction	
	0	lbu $a0, 0($gp)			0	sw $a1, 0($gp)	
	4	jal 0			4	jal 0	
Data Segment	0	(X)		Data Segment	0	(Y)	
	...	...			...	...	
Relocation Info	Address	Instruction Type	Dependency	Relocation Info	Address	Instruction Type	Dependency
	0	lbu	X		0	sw	Y
	4	jal	B		4	jal	A
Symbol Table	Address	Symbol		Symbol Table	Address	Symbol	
	—	X			—	Y	
	—	B			—	A	

b.	Procedure A				Procedure B			
Text Segment	Address	Instruction		Text Segment	Address	Instruction	
	0	lui $at, 0			0	sw $a0, 0($gp)	
	4	ori $a0, $at, 0			4	jmp 0	
	...	...			...	...	
	0x84	jr $ra			0x180	jal 0	
	...	...			...	...	
Data Segment	0	(X)		Data Segment	0	(Y)	
	...	...			...	...	
Relocation Info	Address	Instruction Type	Dependency	Relocation Info	Address	Instruction Type	Dependency
	0	lui	X		0	sw	Y
	4	ori	X		4	jmp	F00
					0x180	jal	A
Symbol Table	Address	Symbol		Symbol Table	Address	Symbol	
	—	X			—	Y	
					0x180	F00	
					—	A	

2.31.1 [5] <2.12> Link the object files above to form the executable file header. Assume that Procedure A has a text size of 0x140 and data size of 0x40 and Procedure B has a text size of 0x300 and data size of 0x50. Also assume the memory allocation strategy as shown in Figure 2.13.

2.31.2 [5] <2.12> What limitations, if any, are there on the size of an executable?

2.31.3 [5] <2.12> Given your understanding of the limitations of branch and jump instructions, why might an assembler have problems directly implementing branch and jump instructions an object file?

Exercise 2.32

The first three problems in this exercise assume that the function swap, instead of the code in Figure 2.24, is defined in C as follows:

| a. | ```c
void swap(int *p, int *q){
    int temp;
    temp=*p;
    *p=*q;
    *q=temp;
}
``` |
|----|----|
| b. | ```c
void swap(int *p, int *q){
    *p=*p+*q;
    *q=*p-*q;
    *p=*p-*q;
}
``` |

2.32.1 [10] <2.13> Translate this function into MIPS assembler code.

2.32.2 [5] <2.13> What needs to change in the sort function?

2.32.3 [5] <2.13> If we were sorting 8-bit bytes, not 32-bit words, how would your MIPS code for swap in 2.32.1 change?

For the remaining three problems in this Exercise, we assume that the sort function from Figure 2.27 is changed in the following way:

a.	Use the swap function from the beginning of this exercise.
b.	Sort an array of n bytes instead of n words.

2.32.4 [5] <2.13> Does this change affect the code for saving and restoring registers in Figure 2.27?

2.32.5 [10] <2.13> When sorting a 10-element array that was already sorted, how many more (or fewer) instructions are executed as a result of this change?

2.32.6 [10] <2.13> When sorting a 10-element array that was sorted in descending order (opposite of the order that sort() creates), how many more (or fewer) instructions are executed as a result of this change?

Exercise 2.33

The problems in this Exercise refer to the following function, given as array code:

a.	```void copy(int a[], int b[], int n){ int i; for(i=0;i!=n;i++) a[i]=b[i]; }```
b.	```void shift(int a[], int n){ int i; for(i=0;i!=n-1;i++) a[i]=a[i+1]; }```

2.33.1 [10] <2.14> Translate this function into MIPS assembly.

2.33.2 [10] <2.14> Convert this function into pointer-based code (in C).

2.33.3 [10] <2.14> Translate your pointer-based C code from 2.33.2 into MIPS assembly.

2.33.4 [5] <2.14> Compare the worst-case number of executed instructions per non-last loop iteration in your array-based code from 2.33.1 and your pointer-based code from 2.33.3. Note: the worst case occurs when branch conditions are such that the longest path through the code is taken, i.e., if there is an if statement, the result of the condition check is such that the path with more instructions is taken. However, if the result of the condition check would cause the loop to exit, then we assume that the path that keeps us in the loop is taken.

2.33.5 [5] <2.14> Compare the number of temporary registers (t-registers) needed for your array-based code from 2.33.1 and for your pointer-based code from 2.33.3.

2.33.6 [5] <2.14> What would change in your answer from 2.33.4 if registers $t0-$t7 and $a0-$a3 in the MIPS calling convention were all callee-saved, just like $s0-$s7?

Exercise 2.34

The table below contains ARM assembly code. In the following problems, you will translate ARM assembly code to MIPS.

a.	ADD r0, r1, r2 ADC r0, r1, r2	;r0 = r1 + r2 ;r0 = r1 + r2 + Carrybit
b.	CMP r0, #4 ADDNE r1, r1, r0	;if (r0 != 4) { ;r1 += r0 }

2.34.1 [5] <2.16> For the table above, translate this ARM assembly code to MIPS assembly code. Assume that ARM registers r0, r1, and r2 hold the same values as MIPS registers $s0, $s1, and $s2, respectively. Use MIPS temporary registers ($t0, etc.) where necessary.

2.34.2 [5] <2.16> For the ARM assembly instructions in the table above, show the bit fields that represent the ARM instructions.

The table below contains MIPS assembly code. In the following problems, you will translate MIPS assembly code to ARM.

a.	nor $t0, #s0, 0 and $s1, $s1, $t0
b.	sll $s1, $s2, 16 srl $s2, $s2, 16 or $s1, $s1, $s2

2.34.3 [5] <2.16> For the table above, find the ARM assembly code that corresponds to the sequence of MIPS assembly code.

2.34.4 [5] <2.16> Show the bit fields that represent the ARM assembly code.

Exercise 2.35

The ARM processor has a few different addressing modes that are not supported in MIPS. The following problems explore these new addressing modes.

a.	LDR r0, [r1, #4]	; r0 = memory[r1+4],	r1 += 4
b.	LDMIA r0!, {r1-r3}	; r1 = memory[r0], ; r3 = memory[r0+8],	r2 = memory[r0+4] r0 += 3*4

2.35.1 [5] <2.16> Identify the type of addressing mode of the ARM assembly instructions in the table above.

2.35.2 [5] <2.16> For the ARM assembly instructions above, write a sequence of MIPS assembly instructions to accomplish the same data transfer.

In the following problems, you will compare code written using the ARM and MIPS instruction sets. The following table shows code written in the ARM instruction set.

a.		`MOV   r0, #10`
		`LOOP:  ADD   r0, r1`
		`       SUBS  r0, 1`
		`       BNE   LOOP`
			`;init loop counter to 10`
			`;add r1 to r0`
			`;decrement counter`
			`;if Z=0 repeat loop`

b.		`ADD   r0, r1` `ADC   r2, r3`	`;r0 = r0 + r1` `;r2 = r2 + r3 + carry`

2.35.3 [10] <2.16> For the ARM assembly code above, write an equivalent MIPS assembly code routine.

2.35.4 [5] <2.16> What is the total number of ARM assembly instructions required to execute the code? What is the total number of MIPS assembly instructions required to execute the code?

2.35.5 [5] <2.16> Assuming that the average CPI of the MIPS assembly routine is the same as the average CPI of the ARM assembly routine, and the MIPS processor has an operation frequency that is 1.5 times that of the ARM processor, how much faster is the ARM processor than the MIPS processor?

Exercise 2.36

The ARM processor has an interesting way of supporting immediate constants. This exercise investigates those differences.

The following table contains ARM instructions.

a.	`ADD, r3, r2, r1, LSR #4   ;r3 = r2 + (r1 >> 4)`
b.	`ADD, r3, r2, r2           ;r3 = r2 + r1`

2.36.1 [5] <2.16> Write the equivalent MIPS code for the ARM assembly code above.

2.36.2 [5] <2.16> If the register R1 had the constant value of 8, rewrite your MIPS code to minimize the number of MIPS assembly instructions needed.

2.36.3 [5] <2.16> If the register R1 had the constant value of 0x06000000, rewrite your MIPS code to minimize the number of MIPS assembly instructions needed.

The following table contains MIPS instructions.

a.	`addi r3, r2, 0x2`
b.	`addi r3, r2, -1`

2.36.4 [5] <2.16> For the MIPS assembly code above, write the equivalent ARM assembly code.

Exercise 2.37

This exercise explores the differences between the MIP and x86 instruction sets. The following table contains x86 assembly code.

| a. | ```
START: mov   eax, 3
       push eax
       mov   eax, 4
       mov   ecx, 4
       add   eax, ecx
       pop   ecx
       add   eax, ecx
``` |
|----|----|
| b. | ```
START: mov   ecx, 100
       mov   eax, 0
LOOP:  add   eax, ecx
       dec   ecx
       cmp   ecx, 0
       jne   LOOP
DONE:
``` |

2.37.1 [10] <2.17> Write pseudo code for the given routine.

2.37.2 [10] <2.17> For the code in the table above, what is the equivalent MIPS for the given routine?

The following table contains x86 assembly instructions.

a.	`push eax`
b.	`test eax, 0x00200010`

2.37.3 [5] <2.17> For each assembly instruction, show the size of each of the bit fields that represent the instruction. Treat the label MY_FUNCTION as a 32-bit constant.

2.37.4 [10] <2.17> Write equivalent MIPS assembly statements.

Exercise 2.38

The x86 instruction set includes the REP prefix that causes the instruction to be repeated a given number of times or until a condition is satisfied. Note that x86 instructions refer to 8 bits as a byte, 16 bits as a word, and 32 bits as a double word. The first three problems in this Exercise refer to the following x86 instruction:

	Instruction	Interpretation
a.	REP MOVSW	Repeat until ECX is zero: Mem16[EDI]=Mem16[ESI], EDI=EDI+2, ESI=ESI+2, ECX=ECX-1
b.	REPNE SCASB	Repeat until ECX is zero: If Mem8[EDI] == AL then go to next instruction, otherwise EDI=EDI+1, ECX=ECI+1. Note: AL is the least-significant byte of the EAX register.

2.38.1 [5] <2.17> What would be a typical use for this instruction?

2.38.2 [5] <2.17> Write MIPS code that performs the same operation, assuming that $a0 corresponds to ECX, $a1 to EDI, $a2 to ESI, and $a3 to EAX.

2.38.3 [5] <2.17> If the x86 instruction takes one cycle to read memory, one cycle to write memory, and one cycle for each register update, and if MIPS takes one cycle per instruction, what is the speedup of using this x86 instruction instead of the equivalent MIPS code when ECX is very large? Assume that the clock cycle time for x86 and MIPS is the same.

The remaining three problems in this exercise refer to the following function, given in both C and x86 assembly. For each x86 instruction, we also show its length in the x86 variable-length instruction format and the interpretation (what the instruction does). Note that the x86 architecture has very few registers compared to MIPS, and as a result the x86 calling convention is to push all arguments onto the stack. The return value of an x86 function is passed back to the caller in the EAX register.

	C Code	x86 Code

a.	`int f(int a, int b, int c, int d){`
	`  if(a>b)`
	`    return c;`
	`  return d;`
	`}`
		`f: push %ebp        ; 1B, push %ebp to stack`
		`   mov  %esp,%ebp   ; 2B, move %esp to %ebp`
		`   mov  12(%ebp),%eax ; 3B, load 2`[nd]` arg into %eax`
		`   cmp  %eax,8(%ebp) ; 3B, compare %eax w/ 1`[st]` arg`
		`   mov  16(%ebp),%edx ; 3B, load 3`[rd]` arg into %edx`
		`   jle  S           ; 2B, jump if cmp result is <=`
		`   pop  %ebp        ; 1B, restore %ebp`
		`   mov  %edx,%eax   ; 2B, move %edx into %eax`
		`   ret              ; 1B, return`
		`S: mov  20(%ebp),%edx ; 3B, load 4`[th]` arg into %edx`
		`   pop  %ebp        ; 1B, restore %ebp`
		`   mov  %edx,%eax   ; 2B, move %edx into %eax`
		`   ret              ; 1B, return`

| **b.** | ``` void f(int a[], int n){ int i; for(i=0;i!=n;i++) a[i]=0; } ``` | ``` f: push %ebp mov %esp,%ebp mov 12(%ebp),%edx mov 8(%ebp),%ecx test %edx,%edx jz D xor %eax,%eax L: movl 0,(%ecx,%eax,4) add 1,%eax cmp %edx,%eax jne L D: pop %ebp ret ``` | ``` ; 1B, push %ebp to stack ; 2B, move %esp to %ebp ; 3B, move 2nd arg into %edx ; 3B, move 1st arg into %ecx ; 2B, set flags based on %edx ; 2B, jump if %edx was 0 ; 2B, zero into %eax ; 7B, Mem[%ecx+4*%eax]=0 ; 3B, add 1 to %eax ; 2B, compare %edx and %eax ; 2B, jump if cmp was != ; 1B, restore %ebp ; 1B, return ``` |

2.38.4 [5] <2.17> Translate this function into MIPS assembly. Compare the size (how many bytes of instruction memory are needed) for this x86 code and for your MIPS code.

2.38.5 [5] <2.17> If the processor can execute two instructions per cycle, it must at least be able to read two consecutive instructions in each cycle. Explain how it would be done in MIPS and how it would be done in x86.

2.38.6 [5] <2.17> If each MIPS instruction takes one cycle, and if each x86 instruction takes one cycle plus a cycle for each memory read or write it has to perform, what is the speedup of using x86 instead of MIPS? Assume that the clock cycle time is the same in both x86 and MIPS, and that the execution takes the shortest possible path through the function (i.e., every loop is exited immediately and every if statement takes the direction that leads toward the return from the function). Note that the x86 `ret` instruction reads the return address from the stack.

Exercise 2.39

The CPI of the different instruction types is given in the following table.

	Arithmetic	**Load/Store**	**Branch**
a.	1	10	3
b.	4	40	3

2.39.1 [5] <2.18> Assume the following instruction breakdown given for executing a given program:

	Instructions (in millions)
Arithmetic	500
Load/Store	300
Branch	100

What is the execution time for the processor if the operation frequency is 5 GHz?

2.39.2 [5] <2.18> Suppose that new, more powerful arithmetic instructions are added to the instruction set. On average, through the use of these more powerful arithmetic instructions, we can reduce the number of arithmetic instructions needed to execute a program by 25%, and the cost of increasing the clock cycle time by only 10%. Is this a good design choice? Why?

2.39.3 [5] <2.18> Suppose that we find a way to double the performance of arithmetic instructions. What is the overall speedup of our machine? What if we find a way to improve the performance of arithmetic instructions by 10 times?

The following table shows the proportions of instruction execution for the different instruction types.

	Arithmetic	Load/Store	Branch
a.	70%	10%	20%
b.	50%	40%	10%

2.39.4 [5] <2.18> Given the instruction mix above and the assumption that an arithmetic instruction requires 2 cycles, a load/store instruction takes 6 cycles, and a branch instruction takes 3 cycles, find the average CPI.

2.39.5 [5] <2.18> For a 25% improvement in performance, how many cycles, on average, may an arithmetic instruction take if load/store and branch instructions are not improved at all?

2.39.6 [5] <2.18> For a 50% improvement in performance, how many cycles, on average, may an arithmetic instruction take if load/store and branch instructions are not improved at all?

Exercise 2.40

The first three problems in this Exercise refer to the following function, given in MIPS assembly. Unfortunately, the programmer of this function has fallen prey to the pitfall of assuming that MIPS is a word-addressed machine, but in fact MIPS is byte-addressed.

```
a.   ; int f(int *a, int n, int x);
     f: move $v0,$0        ; ret=0
        move $t0,$a0       ; ptr=a
        add  $t1,$a1,$a0   ; &(a[n])
     L: lw   $t2,0($t0)    ; read *p
        bne  $t2,$a2,S     ; if(*p==x)
        addi $v0,$v0,1     ;   ret++;
     S: addi $t0,$t0,1     ; p=p+1
        bne  $t0,$t1,L     ; repeat if p!=&(a[n])
        jr   $ra           ; return ret
```

```
b.  ; void f(int a[], int n);
    f: move $t0,$0       ; i=0;
       addi $t1,$a1,-1    ; n-1
    L: add $t2,$t0,$a0   ; address of a[i]
       lw   $t3,1($t2)    ; read a[i+1]
       sw   $t3,0($t2)    ; a[i]=a[i+1]
       addi $t0,$t0,1     ; i=i+1
       bne  $t0,$t1,L     ; repeat if i!=n-1
       jr   $ra           ; return
```

Note that in MIPS assembly the ";" character denotes that the remainder of the line is a comment.

2.40.1 [5] <2.18> The MIPS architecture requires word-sized accesses (lw and sw) to be word-aligned, i.e., the lowermost 2 bits of the address must both be zero. If an address is not word-aligned, the processor raises a "bus error" exception. Explain how this alignment requirement affects the execution of this function.

2.40.2 [5] <2.18> If "a" was a pointer to the beginning of an array of 1-byte elements, and if we replaced lw and sw with lb (load byte) and sb (store byte), respectively, would this function be correct? Note: lb reads a byte from memory, sign-extends it, and places it into the destination register, while sb stores the least-significant byte of the register into memory.

2.40.3 [5] <2.18> Change this code to make it correct for 32-bit integers.

The remaining three problems in this exercise refer to a program that allocates memory for an array, fills the array with some numbers, calls the sort function from Figure 2.27, and then prints out the array. The main function of the program is as follows (given as both C and MIPS code):

Main Code in C	MIPS Version of the Main Code
| ```
main(){
  int *v;
  int n=5;
  v=my_alloc(5);
  my_init(v,n);
sort(v,n);
  .
  .
  .
``` | ```
main:
  li    $s0,5
  move  $a0,$s0
  jal   my_alloc
  move  $s1,$v0
  move  $a0,$s1
  move  $a1,$s0
  jal   my_init
  move  $a0,$s1
  move  $a1,$s0
  jal   sort
``` |

The my_alloc function is defined as follows (given as both C and MIPS code). Note that the programmer of this function has fallen prey to the pitfall of using a pointer to an automatic variable `arr` outside the function in which it is defined.

my_alloc **in C**	**MIPS Code for** my_alloc

```int *my_alloc(int n){```
 ``` int arr[n];```
 ``` return arr;```
 ```}```
	```my_alloc:```
	 ``` addu $sp,$sp,-4 ; Push```
	 ``` sw $fp,0($sp) ; $fp to stack```
	 ``` move $fp,$sp ; Save $sp in $fp```
	 ``` sll $t0,$a0,2 ; We need 4*n bytes```
	 ``` sub $sp,$sp,$t0 ; Make room for arr```
	 ``` move $v0,$sp ; Return address of arr```
	 ``` move $sp,$fp ; Restore $sp from $fp```
	 ``` lw $fp,0(sp) ; Pop $fp```
	 ``` addiu $sp,$sp,4 ; from stack```
	 ``` jr ra```

The `my_init` function is defined as follows (MIPS code):

a.	```my_init:```
	 ``` move $t0,$0 ; i=0```
	 ``` move $t1,$a0```
	 ```L: addi $t2,$t0,10```
	 ``` sw $t2,0($t1) ; v[i]=i+10```
	 ``` addiu $t1,$t1,4```
	 ``` addiu $t0,$t0,1 ; i=i+1```
	 ``` bne $t0,$a1,L ; until i==n```
	 ``` jr $ra```

b.	```my_init:```
	 ``` move $t0,$0 ; i=0```
	 ``` move $t1,$a0```
	 ```L: sll $t2,$t0,1```
	 ``` addi $t2,$t2,100```
	 ``` sw $t2,0($t1) ; a[i]=100+2*i;```
	 ``` addiu $t1,$t1,4```
	 ``` addiu $t0,$t0,1 ; i=i+1```
	 ``` bne $t0,$a1,L ; until i==n```
	 ``` jr $ra```

2.40.4 [5] <2.18> What are the contents (values of all five elements) of array v right before the "`jal sort`" instruction in the main code is executed?

2.40.5 [15] <2.18, 2.13> What are the contents of array v right before the sort function enters its outer loop for the first time? Assume that registers $sp, $s0, $s1, $s2, and $s3 have values of 0x1000, 20, 40, 7, and 1, respectively, at the beginning of the main code (right before "`li $s0, 5`" is executed).

2.40.6 [10] <2.18, 2.13> What are the contents of the 5-element array pointed by v right after "`jal sort`" returns to the main code?

§2.2, page 80: MIPS, C, Java

§2.3, page 87: 2) Very slow

§2.4, page 93: 3) -8_{ten}

§2.5, page 101: 4) `sub $s2, $s0, $s1`

§2.6, page 105: Both. AND with a mask pattern of 1s will leaves 0s everywhere but the desired field. Shifting left by the right amount removes the bits from the left of the field. Shifting right by the appropriate amount puts the field into the rightmost bits of the word, with 0s in the rest of the word. Note that AND leaves the field where it was originally, and the shift pair moves the field into the rightmost part of the word.

§2.7, page 111: I. All are true. II. 1).

§2.8, page 122: Both are true.

§2.9, page 127: I. 2) II. 3)

§2.10, page 136: I. 4) +-128K. II. 6) a block of 256M. III. 4) `sll`

§2.11, page 139: Both are true.

§2.12, page 148: 4) Machine independence.

Answers to Check Yourself

Arithmetic for Computers

*Numerical precision
is the very soul
of science.*

Sir D'arcy Wentworth Thompson
On Growth and Form, 1917

The Five Classic Components of a Computer

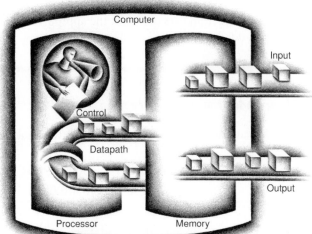

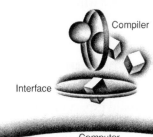

3.1   Introduction

Computer words are composed of bits; thus, words can be represented as binary numbers. Chapter 2 shows that integers can be represented either in decimal or binary form, but what about the other numbers that commonly occur? For example:

- What about fractions and other real numbers?

- What happens if an operation creates a number bigger than can be represented?

- And underlying these questions is a mystery: How does hardware really multiply or divide numbers?

The goal of this chapter is to unravel these mysteries including representation of real numbers, arithmetic algorithms, hardware that follows these algorithms, and the implications of all this for instruction sets. These insights may explain quirks that you have already encountered with computers.

Subtraction: Addition's Tricky Pal

No. 10, Top Ten Courses for Athletes at a Football Factory, David Letterman et al., *Book of Top Ten Lists*, 1990

3.2   Addition and Subtraction

Addition is just what you would expect in computers. Digits are added bit by bit from right to left, with carries passed to the next digit to the left, just as you would do by hand. Subtraction uses addition: the appropriate operand is simply negated before being added.

Binary Addition and Subtraction

EXAMPLE

Let's try adding 6_{ten} to 7_{ten} in binary and then subtracting 6_{ten} from 7_{ten} in binary.

$$
\begin{array}{rll}
 & 0000\ 0000\ 0000\ 0000\ 0000\ 0000\ 0000\ 0111_{two} & =\ 7_{ten} \\
+ & 0000\ 0000\ 0000\ 0000\ 0000\ 0000\ 0000\ 0110_{two} & =\ 6_{ten} \\
\hline
= & 0000\ 0000\ 0000\ 0000\ 0000\ 0000\ 0000\ 1101_{two} & =\ 13_{ten}
\end{array}
$$

The 4 bits to the right have all the action; Figure 3.1 shows the sums and carries. The carries are shown in parentheses, with the arrows showing how they are passed.

Subtracting 6_{ten} from 7_{ten} can be done directly:

$$
\begin{array}{rl}
& 0000\ 0000\ 0000\ 0000\ 0000\ 0000\ 0000\ 0111_{two} = 7_{ten} \\
- & 0000\ 0000\ 0000\ 0000\ 0000\ 0000\ 0000\ 0110_{two} = 6_{ten} \\
\hline
= & 0000\ 0000\ 0000\ 0000\ 0000\ 0000\ 0000\ 0001_{two} = 1_{ten}
\end{array}
$$

or via addition using the two's complement representation of −6:

$$
\begin{array}{rl}
& 0000\ 0000\ 0000\ 0000\ 0000\ 0000\ 0000\ 0111_{two} = 7_{ten} \\
+ & 1111\ 1111\ 1111\ 1111\ 1111\ 1111\ 1111\ 1010_{two} = -6_{ten} \\
\hline
= & 0000\ 0000\ 0000\ 0000\ 0000\ 0000\ 0000\ 0001_{two} = 1_{ten}
\end{array}
$$

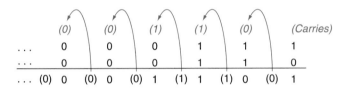

FIGURE 3.1 Binary addition, showing carries from right to left. The rightmost bit adds 1 to 0, resulting in the sum of this bit being 1 and the carry out from this bit being 0. Hence, the operation for the second digit to the right is 0 + 1 + 1. This generates a 0 for this sum bit and a carry out of 1. The third digit is the sum of 1 + 1 + 1, resulting in a carry out of 1 and a sum bit of 1. The fourth bit is 1 + 0 + 0, yielding a 1 sum and no carry.

Recall that overflow occurs when the result from an operation cannot be represented with the available hardware, in this case a 32-bit word. When can overflow occur in addition? When adding operands with different signs, overflow cannot occur. The reason is the sum must be no larger than one of the operands. For example, −10 + 4 = −6. Since the operands fit in 32 bits and the sum is no larger than an operand, the sum must fit in 32 bits as well. Therefore, no overflow can occur when adding positive and negative operands.

There are similar restrictions to the occurrence of overflow during subtract, but it's just the opposite principle: when the signs of the operands are the *same*, overflow cannot occur. To see this, remember that $x - y = x + (-y)$ because we subtract by negating the second operand and then add. Therefore, when we subtract operands of the same sign we end up by *adding* operands of *different* signs. From the prior paragraph, we know that overflow cannot occur in this case either.

Knowing when overflow cannot occur in addition and subtraction is all well and good, but how do we detect it when it *does* occur? Clearly, adding or subtracting two 32-bit numbers can yield a result that needs 33 bits to be fully expressed.

The lack of a 33rd bit means that when overflow occurs, the sign bit is set with the *value* of the result instead of the proper sign of the result. Since we need just one extra bit, only the sign bit can be wrong. Hence, overflow occurs when adding two positive numbers and the sum is negative, or vice versa. This means a carry out occurred into the sign bit.

Overflow occurs in subtraction when we subtract a negative number from a positive number and get a negative result, or when we subtract a positive number from a negative number and get a positive result. This means a borrow occurred from the sign bit. Figure 3.2 shows the combination of operations, operands, and results that indicate an overflow.

We have just seen how to detect overflow for two's complement numbers in a computer. What about overflow with unsigned integers? Unsigned integers are commonly used for memory addresses where overflows are ignored.

The computer designer must therefore provide a way to ignore overflow in some cases and to recognize it in others. The MIPS solution is to have two kinds of arithmetic instructions to recognize the two choices:

- Add (add), add immediate (addi), and subtract (sub) cause exceptions on overflow.

- Add unsigned (addu), add immediate unsigned (addiu), and subtract unsigned (subu) do *not* cause exceptions on overflow.

Because C ignores overflows, the MIPS C compilers will always generate the unsigned versions of the arithmetic instructions addu, addiu, and subu, no matter what the type of the variables. The MIPS Fortran compilers, however, pick the appropriate arithmetic instructions, depending on the type of the operands.

Operation	Operand A	Operand B	Result indicating overflow
$A + B$	≥ 0	≥ 0	< 0
$A + B$	< 0	< 0	≥ 0
$A - B$	≥ 0	< 0	< 0
$A - B$	< 0	≥ 0	≥ 0

FIGURE 3.2   Overflow conditions for addition and subtraction.

Arithmetic Logic Unit (ALU) Hardware that performs addition, subtraction, and usually logical operations such as AND and OR.

◉ Appendix C describes the hardware that performs addition and subtraction, which is called an **Arithmetic Logic Unit** or **ALU**.

The computer designer must decide how to handle arithmetic overflows. Although some languages like C and Java ignore integer overflow, languages like Ada and Fortran require that the program be notified. The programmer or the programming environment must then decide what to do when overflow occurs.

MIPS detects overflow with an **exception**, also called an **interrupt** on many computers. An exception or interrupt is essentially an unscheduled procedure call. The address of the instruction that overflowed is saved in a register, and the computer jumps to a predefined address to invoke the appropriate routine for that exception. The interrupted address is saved so that in some situations the program can continue after corrective code is executed. (Section 4.9 covers exceptions in more detail; Chapters 5 and 6 describe other situations where exceptions and interrupts occur.)

MIPS includes a register called the *exception program counter* (EPC) to contain the address of the instruction that caused the exception. The instruction *move from system control* (mfc0) is used to copy EPC into a general-purpose register so that MIPS software has the option of returning to the offending instruction via a jump register instruction.

Hardware/ Software Interface

exception Also called **interrupt**. An unscheduled event that disrupts program execution; used to detect overflow.

interrupt An exception that comes from outside of the processor. (Some architectures use the term *interrupt* for all exceptions.)

Arithmetic for Multimedia

Since every desktop microprocessor by definition has its own graphical displays, as transistor budgets increased it was inevitable that support would be added for graphics operations.

Many graphics systems originally used 8 bits to represent each of the three primary colors plus 8 bits for a location of a pixel. The addition of speakers and microphones for teleconferencing and video games suggested support of sound as well. Audio samples need more than 8 bits of precision, but 16 bits are sufficient.

Every microprocessor has special support so that bytes and halfwords take up less space when stored in memory (see Section 2.9), but due to the infrequency of arithmetic operations on these data sizes in typical integer programs, there is little support beyond data transfers. Architects recognized that many graphics and audio applications would perform the same operation on vectors of this data. By partitioning the carry chains within a 64-bit adder, a processor could perform simultaneous operations on short vectors of eight 8-bit operands, four 16-bit operands, or two 32-bit operands. The cost of such partitioned adders was small. These extensions have been called vector or SIMD, for single instruction, multiple data (see Section 2.17 and Chapter 7).

One feature not generally found in general-purpose microprocessors is *saturating* operations. Saturation means that when a calculation overflows, the result is set to the largest positive number or most negative number, rather than a modulo calculation as in two's complement arithmetic. Saturation is likely what you want for media operations. For example, the volume knob on a radio set would be frustrating if, as you turned, it would get continuously louder for a while and then immediately very soft. A knob with saturation would stop at the highest volume no matter how far you turned it. Figure 3.3 shows arithmetic and logical operations found in many multimedia extensions to modern instruction sets.

Instruction category	Operands
Unsigned add/subtract	Eight 8-bit or Four 16-bit
Saturating add/subtract	Eight 8-bit or Four 16-bit
Max/min/minimum	Eight 8-bit or Four 16-bit
Average	Eight 8-bit or Four 16-bit
Shift right/left	Eight 8-bit or Four 16-bit

FIGURE 3.3   Summary of multimedia support for desktop computers.

Elaboration: MIPS can trap on overflow, but unlike many other computers, there is no conditional branch to test overflow. A sequence of MIPS instructions can discover overflow. For signed addition, the sequence is the following (see the *Elaboration* on page 104 in Chapter 2 for a description of the xor instruction):

```
addu $t0, $t1, $t2 # $t0 = sum, but don't trap
xor  $t3, $t1, $t2 # Check if signs differ
slt  $t3, $t3, $zero # $t3 = 1 if signs differ
bne  $t3, $zero, No_overflow # $t1, $t2 signs ≠,
                             # so no overflow
xor  $t3, $t0, $t1 # signs =; sign of sum match too?
                   # $t3 negative if sum sign different
slt  $t3, $t3, $zero # $t3 = 1 if sum sign different
bne  $t3, $zero, Overflow # All 3 signs ≠; go to overflow
```

For unsigned addition ($t0 = $t1 + $t2), the test is

```
addu $t0, $t1, $t2    # $t0 = sum
nor  $t3, $t1, $zero  # $t3 = NOT $t1
                      # (2's comp - 1: 2^32 - $t1 - 1)
sltu $t3, $t3, $t2    # (2^32 - $t1 - 1) < $t2
                      # ⟹ 2^32 - 1 < $t1 + $t2
bne $t3,$zero,Overflow # if(2^32-1<$t1+$t2) goto overflow
```

Summary

A major point of this section is that, independent of the representation, the finite word size of computers means that arithmetic operations can create results that are too large to fit in this fixed word size. It's easy to detect overflow in unsigned numbers, although these are almost always ignored because programs don't want to detect overflow for address arithmetic, the most common use of natural numbers. Two's complement presents a greater challenge, yet some software systems require detection of overflow, so today all computers have a way to detect it.

The rising popularity of multimedia applications led to arithmetic instructions that support narrower operations that can easily operate in parallel.

Some programming languages allow two's complement integer arithmetic on variables declared byte and half. What MIPS instructions would be used?

Check Yourself

1. Load with `lbu`, `lhu`; arithmetic with `add`, `sub`, `mult`, `div`; then store using `sb`, `sh`.

2. Load with `lb`, `lh`; arithmetic with `add`, `sub`, `mult`, `div`; then store using `sb`, `sh`.

3. Load with `lb`, `lh`; arithmetic with `add`, `sub`, `mult`, `div`, using `AND` to mask result to 8 or 16 bits after each operation; then store using `sb`, `sh`.

Elaboration: In the preceding text, we said that you copy EPC into a register via `mfc0` and then return to the interrupted code via jump register. This leads to an interesting question: since you must first transfer EPC to a register to use with jump register, how can jump register return to the interrupted code *and* restore the original values of *all* registers? Either you restore the old registers first, thereby destroying your return address from EPC, which you placed in a register for use in jump register, or you restore all registers but the one with the return address so that you can jump—meaning an exception would result in changing that one register at any time during program execution! Neither option is satisfactory.

To rescue the hardware from this dilemma, MIPS programmers agreed to reserve registers $k0 and $k1 for the operating system; these registers are *not* restored on exceptions. Just as the MIPS compilers avoid using register $at so that the assembler can use it as a temporary register (see *Hardware/Software Interface* in Section 2.10), compilers also abstain from using registers $k0 and $k1 to make them available for the operating system. Exception routines place the return address in one of these registers and then use jump register to restore the instruction address.

Elaboration: The speed of addition is increased by determining the carry in to the high-order bits sooner. There are a variety of schemes to anticipate the carry so that the worst-case scenario is a function of the $\log_2$ of the number of bits in the adder. These anticipatory signals are faster because they go through fewer gates in sequence, but it takes many more gates to anticipate the proper carry. The most popular is *carry lookahead*, which Section C.6 in ◉ **Appendix C** on the CD describes.

Multiplication is vexation, Division is as bad; The rule of three doth puzzle me, And practice drives me mad.

Anonymous, Elizabethan manuscript, 1570

3.3 Multiplication

Now that we have completed the explanation of addition and subtraction, we are ready to build the more vexing operation of multiplication.

First, let's review the multiplication of decimal numbers in longhand to remind ourselves of the steps of multiplication and the names of the operands. For reasons that will become clear shortly, we limit this decimal example to using only the digits 0 and 1. Multiplying 1000_{ten} by 1001_{ten}:

$$
\begin{array}{lr}
\text{Multiplicand} & 1000_{ten} \\
\text{Multiplier} \quad \times & 1001_{ten} \\
\hline
& 1000 \\
& 0000 \\
& 0000 \\
& 1000 \\
\hline
\text{Product} & 1001000_{ten}
\end{array}
$$

The first operand is called the *multiplicand* and the second the *multiplier*. The final result is called the *product*. As you may recall, the algorithm learned in grammar school is to take the digits of the multiplier one at a time from right to left, multiplying the multiplicand by the single digit of the multiplier, and shifting the intermediate product one digit to the left of the earlier intermediate products.

The first observation is that the number of digits in the product is considerably larger than the number in either the multiplicand or the multiplier. In fact, if we ignore the sign bits, the length of the multiplication of an n-bit multiplicand and an m-bit multiplier is a product that is $n + m$ bits long. That is, $n + m$ bits are required to represent all possible products. Hence, like add, multiply must cope with overflow because we frequently want a 32-bit product as the result of multiplying two 32-bit numbers.

In this example, we restricted the decimal digits to 0 and 1. With only two choices, each step of the multiplication is simple:

1. Just place a copy of the multiplicand ($1 \times$ multiplicand) in the proper place if the multiplier digit is a 1, or

2. Place 0 ($0 \times$ multiplicand) in the proper place if the digit is 0.

Although the decimal example above happens to use only 0 and 1, multiplication of binary numbers must always use 0 and 1, and thus always offers only these two choices.

Now that we have reviewed the basics of multiplication, the traditional next step is to provide the highly optimized multiply hardware. We break with tradition in the belief that you will gain a better understanding by seeing the evolution of the multiply hardware and algorithm through multiple generations. For now, let's assume that we are multiplying only positive numbers.

Sequential Version of the Multiplication Algorithm and Hardware

This design mimics the algorithm we learned in grammar school; Figure 3.4 shows the hardware. We have drawn the hardware so that data flows from top to bottom to resemble more closely the paper-and-pencil method.

Let's assume that the multiplier is in the 32-bit Multiplier register and that the 64-bit Product register is initialized to 0. From the paper-and-pencil example above, it's clear that we will need to move the multiplicand left one digit each step, as it may be added to the intermediate products. Over 32 steps, a 32-bit multiplicand would move 32 bits to the left. Hence, we need a 64-bit Multiplicand register, initialized with the 32-bit multiplicand in the right half and zero in the left half. This register is then shifted left 1 bit each step to align the multiplicand with the sum being accumulated in the 64-bit Product register.

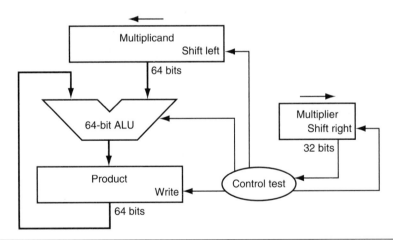

FIGURE 3.4 First version of the multiplication hardware. The Multiplicand register, ALU, and Product register are all 64 bits wide, with only the Multiplier register containing 32 bits. (⊙ Appendix C describes ALUs.) The 32-bit multiplicand starts in the right half of the Multiplicand register and is shifted left 1 bit on each step. The multiplier is shifted in the opposite direction at each step. The algorithm starts with the product initialized to 0. Control decides when to shift the Multiplicand and Multiplier registers and when to write new values into the Product register.

Figure 3.5 shows the three basic steps needed for each bit. The least significant bit of the multiplier (Multiplier0) determines whether the multiplicand is added to the Product register. The left shift in step 2 has the effect of moving the intermediate operands to the left, just as when multiplying with paper and pencil. The shift right in step 3 gives us the next bit of the multiplier to examine in the following iteration. These three steps are repeated 32 times to obtain the product. If each step took a clock cycle, this algorithm would require almost 100 clock cycles to multiply

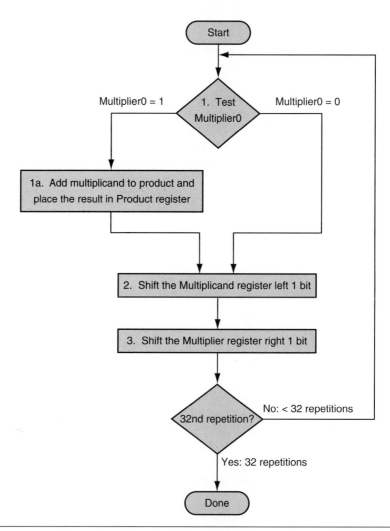

FIGURE 3.5 The first multiplication algorithm, using the hardware shown in Figure 3.4. If the least significant bit of the multiplier is 1, add the multiplicand to the product. If not, go to the next step. Shift the multiplicand left and the multiplier right in the next two steps. These three steps are repeated 32 times.

two 32-bit numbers. The relative importance of arithmetic operations like multiply varies with the program, but addition and subtraction may be anywhere from 5 to 100 times more popular than multiply. Accordingly, in many applications, multiply can take multiple clock cycles without significantly affecting performance. Yet Amdahl's law (see Section 1.8) reminds us that even a moderate frequency for a slow operation can limit performance.

This algorithm and hardware are easily refined to take 1 clock cycle per step. The speed-up comes from performing the operations in parallel: the multiplier and multiplicand are shifted while the multiplicand is added to the product if the multiplier bit is a 1. The hardware just has to ensure that it tests the right bit of the multiplier and gets the preshifted version of the multiplicand. The hardware is usually further optimized to halve the width of the adder and registers by noticing where there are unused portions of registers and adders. Figure 3.6 shows the revised hardware.

Replacing arithmetic by shifts can also occur when multiplying by constants. Some compilers replace multiplies by short constants with a series of shifts and adds. Because one bit to the left represents a number twice as large in base 2, shifting the bits left has the same effect as multiplying by a power of 2. As mentioned in Chapter 2, almost every compiler will perform the strength reduction optimization of substituting a left shift for a multiply by a power of 2.

**Hardware/
Software
Interface**

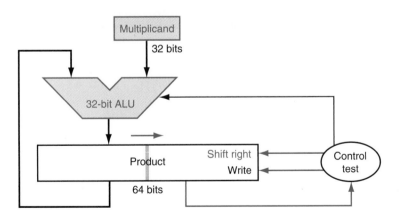

FIGURE 3.6 Refined version of the multiplication hardware. Compare with the first version in Figure 3.4. The Multiplicand register, ALU, and Multiplier register are all 32 bits wide, with only the Product register left at 64 bits. Now the product is shifted right. The separate Multiplier register also disappeared. The multiplier is placed instead in the right half of the Product register. These changes are highlighted in color. (The Product register should really be 65 bits to hold the carry out of the adder, but it's shown here as 64 bits to highlight the evolution from Figure 3.4.)

EXAMPLE

ANSWER

A Multiply Algorithm

Using 4-bit numbers to save space, multiply $2_{ten} \times 3_{ten}$, or $0010_{two} \times 0011_{two}$.

Figure 3.7 shows the value of each register for each of the steps labeled according to Figure 3.5, with the final value of $0000\ 0110_{two}$ or 6_{ten}. Color is used to indicate the register values that change on that step, and the bit circled is the one examined to determine the operation of the next step.

Signed Multiplication

So far, we have dealt with positive numbers. The easiest way to understand how to deal with signed numbers is to first convert the multiplier and multiplicand to positive numbers and then remember the original signs. The algorithms should then be run for 31 iterations, leaving the signs out of the calculation. As we learned in grammar school, we need negate the product only if the original signs disagree.

It turns out that the last algorithm will work for signed numbers, provided that we remember that we are dealing with numbers that have infinite digits, and we are only representing them with 32 bits. Hence, the shifting steps would need to extend the sign of the product for signed numbers. When the algorithm completes, the lower word would have the 32-bit product.

Iteration	Step	Multiplier	Multiplicand	Product
0	Initial values	001①	0000 0010	0000 0000
1	1a: 1 ⟹ Prod = Prod + Mcand	0011	0000 0010	0000 0010
	2: Shift left Multiplicand	0011	0000 0100	0000 0010
	3: Shift right Multiplier	000①	0000 0100	0000 0010
2	1a: 1 ⟹ Prod = Prod + Mcand	0001	0000 0100	0000 0110
	2: Shift left Multiplicand	0001	0000 1000	0000 0110
	3: Shift right Multiplier	000⓪	0000 1000	0000 0110
3	1: 0 ⟹ No operation	0000	0000 1000	0000 0110
	2: Shift left Multiplicand	0000	0001 0000	0000 0110
	3: Shift right Multiplier	000⓪	0001 0000	0000 0110
4	1: 0 ⟹ No operation	0000	0001 0000	0000 0110
	2: Shift left Multiplicand	0000	0010 0000	0000 0110
	3: Shift right Multiplier	0000	0010 0000	0000 0110

FIGURE 3.7   Multiply example using algorithm in Figure 3.5. The bit examined to determine the next step is circled in color.

Faster Multiplication

Moore's law has provided so much more in resources that hardware designers can now build much faster multiplication hardware. Whether the multiplicand is to be added or not is known at the beginning of the multiplication by looking at each of the 32 multiplier bits. Faster multiplications are possible by essentially providing one 32-bit adder for each bit of the multiplier: one input is the multiplicand ANDed with a multiplier bit, and the other is the output of a prior adder.

A straightforward approach would be to connect the outputs of adders on the right to the inputs of adders on the left, making a stack of adders 32 high. An alternative way to organize these 32 additions is in a parallel tree, as Figure 3.8 shows. Instead of waiting for 32 add times, we wait just the $\log_2 (32)$ or five 32-bit add times. Figure 3.8 shows how this is a faster way to connect them.

In fact, multiply can go even faster than five add times because of the use of *carry save adders* (see Section C.6 in ⊙ **Appendix C**) and because it is easy to pipeline such a design to be able to support many multiplies simultaneously (see Chapter 4).

Multiply in MIPS

MIPS provides a separate pair of 32-bit registers to contain the 64-bit product, called *Hi* and *Lo*. To produce a properly signed or unsigned product, MIPS has two instructions: multiply (mult) and multiply unsigned (multu). To fetch the integer 32-bit product, the programmer uses *move from lo* (mflo). The MIPS assembler generates a pseudoinstruction for multiply that specifies three general-purpose registers, generating mflo and mfhi instructions to place the product into registers.

Summary

Multiplication hardware is simply shifts and add, derived from the paper-and-pencil method learned in grammar school. Compilers even use shift instructions for multiplications by powers of 2.

Both MIPS multiply instructions ignore overflow, so it is up to the software to check to see if the product is too big to fit in 32 bits. There is no overflow if Hi is 0 for multu or the replicated sign of Lo for mult. The instruction *move from hi* (mfhi) can be used to transfer Hi to a general-purpose register to test for overflow.

Hardware/ Software Interface

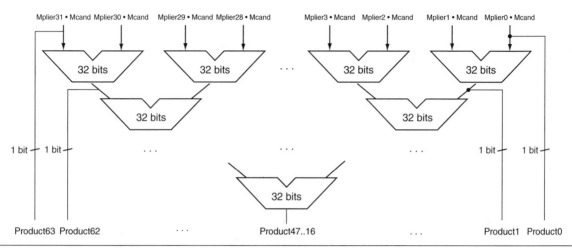

FIGURE 3.8   Fast multiplication hardware. Rather than use a single 32-bit adder 31 times, this hardware "unrolls the loop" to use 31 adders and then organizes them to minimize delay.

Divide et impera.

Latin for "Divide and rule," ancient political maxim cited by Machiavelli, 1532

 Division

The reciprocal operation of multiply is divide, an operation that is even less frequent and even more quirky. It even offers the opportunity to perform a mathematically invalid operation: dividing by 0.

Let's start with an example of long division using decimal numbers to recall the names of the operands and the grammar school division algorithm. For reasons similar to those in the previous section, we limit the decimal digits to just 0 or 1. The example is dividing $1,001,010_{ten}$ by 1000_{ten}:

$$
\begin{array}{r}
1001_{ten} \\
\text{Divisor } 1000_{ten} \overline{)\,1001010_{ten}} \\
-1000 \\
\hline
10 \\
101 \\
1010 \\
-1000 \\
\hline
10_{ten}
\end{array}
$$

Quotient

Dividend

Remainder

Divide's two operands, called the **dividend** and **divisor**, and the result, called the **quotient**, are accompanied by a second result, called the **remainder**. Here is another way to express the relationship between the components:

$$\text{Dividend} = \text{Quotient} \times \text{Divisor} + \text{Remainder}$$

where the remainder is smaller than the divisor. Infrequently, programs use the divide instruction just to get the remainder, ignoring the quotient.

The basic grammar school division algorithm tries to see how big a number can be subtracted, creating a digit of the quotient on each attempt. Our carefully selected decimal example uses only the numbers 0 and 1, so it's easy to figure out how many times the divisor goes into the portion of the dividend: it's either 0 times or 1 time. Binary numbers contain only 0 or 1, so binary division is restricted to these two choices, thereby simplifying binary division.

Let's assume that both the dividend and the divisor are positive and hence the quotient and the remainder are nonnegative. The division operands and both results are 32-bit values, and we will ignore the sign for now.

dividend A number being divided.

divisor A number that the dividend is divided by.

quotient The primary result of a division; a number that when multiplied by the divisor and added to the remainder produces the dividend.

remainder The secondary result of a division; a number that when added to the product of the quotient and the divisor produces the dividend.

A Division Algorithm and Hardware

Figure 3.9 shows hardware to mimic our grammar school algorithm. We start with the 32-bit Quotient register set to 0. Each iteration of the algorithm needs to move the divisor to the right one digit, so we start with the divisor placed in the left half of the 64-bit Divisor register and shift it right 1 bit each step to align it with the dividend. The Remainder register is initialized with the dividend.

FIGURE 3.9   First version of the division hardware. The Divisor register, ALU, and Remainder register are all 64 bits wide, with only the Quotient register being 32 bits. The 32-bit divisor starts in the left half of the Divisor register and is shifted right 1 bit each iteration. The remainder is initialized with the dividend. Control decides when to shift the Divisor and Quotient registers and when to write the new value into the Remainder register.

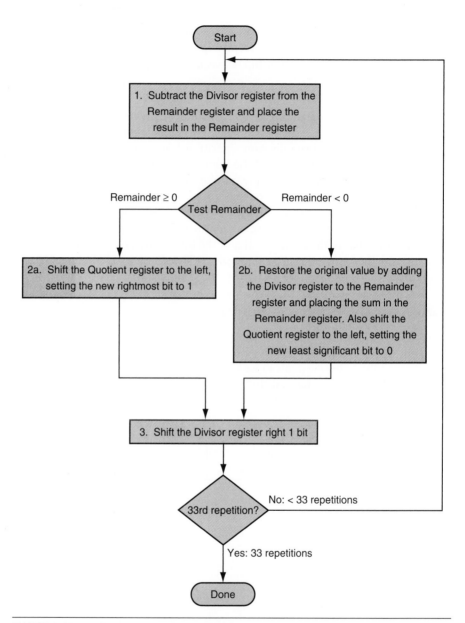

FIGURE 3.10 A division algorithm, using the hardware in Figure 3.9. If the remainder is positive, the divisor did go into the dividend, so step 2a generates a 1 in the quotient. A negative remainder after step 1 means that the divisor did not go into the dividend, so step 2b generates a 0 in the quotient and adds the divisor to the remainder, thereby reversing the subtraction of step 1. The final shift, in step 3, aligns the divisor properly, relative to the dividend for the next iteration. These steps are repeated 33 times.

Figure 3.10 shows three steps of the first division algorithm. Unlike a human, the computer isn't smart enough to know in advance whether the divisor is smaller than the dividend. It must first subtract the divisor in step 1; remember that this is how we performed the comparison in the set on less than instruction. If the result is positive, the divisor was smaller or equal to the dividend, so we generate a 1 in the quotient (step 2a). If the result is negative, the next step is to restore the original value by adding the divisor back to the remainder and generate a 0 in the quotient (step 2b). The divisor is shifted right and then we iterate again. The remainder and quotient will be found in their namesake registers after the iterations are complete.

A Divide Algorithm

Using a 4-bit version of the algorithm to save pages, let's try dividing 7_{ten} by 2_{ten}, or $0000\ 0111_{two}$ by 0010_{two}.

EXAMPLE

Figure 3.11 shows the value of each register for each of the steps, with the quotient being 3_{ten} and the remainder 1_{ten}. Notice that the test in step 2 of whether the remainder is positive or negative simply tests whether the sign bit of the Remainder register is a 0 or 1. The surprising requirement of this algorithm is that it takes $n + 1$ steps to get the proper quotient and remainder.

ANSWER

This algorithm and hardware can be refined to be faster and cheaper. The speed-up comes from shifting the operands and the quotient simultaneously with the subtraction. This refinement halves the width of the adder and registers by noticing where there are unused portions of registers and adders. Figure 3.12 shows the revised hardware.

Signed Division

So far, we have ignored signed numbers in division. The simplest solution is to remember the signs of the divisor and dividend and then negate the quotient if the signs disagree.

Elaboration: The one complication of signed division is that we must also set the sign of the remainder. Remember that the following equation must always hold:

Dividend = Quotient × Divisor + Remainder

To understand how to set the sign of the remainder, let's look at the example of dividing all the combinations of $\pm 7_{ten}$ by $\pm 2_{ten}$. The first case is easy:

+7 ÷ +2: Quotient = +3, Remainder = +1

Iteration	Step	Quotient	Divisor	Remainder
0	Initial values	0000	0010 0000	0000 0111
1	1: Rem = Rem – Div	0000	0010 0000	①110 0111
	2b: Rem < 0 ⟹ +Div, sll Q, Q0 = 0	0000	0010 0000	0000 0111
	3: Shift Div right	0000	0001 0000	0000 0111
2	1: Rem = Rem – Div	0000	0001 0000	①111 0111
	2b: Rem < 0 ⟹ +Div, sll Q, Q0 = 0	0000	0001 0000	0000 0111
	3: Shift Div right	0000	0000 1000	0000 0111
3	1: Rem = Rem – Div	0000	0000 1000	①111 1111
	2b: Rem < 0 ⟹ +Div, sll Q, Q0 = 0	0000	0000 1000	0000 0111
	3: Shift Div right	0000	0000 0100	0000 0111
4	1: Rem = Rem – Div	0000	0000 0100	⓪000 0011
	2a: Rem ≥ 0 ⟹ sll Q, Q0 = 1	0001	0000 0100	0000 0011
	3: Shift Div right	0001	0000 0010	0000 0011
5	1: Rem = Rem – Div	0001	0000 0010	⓪000 0001
	2a: Rem ≥ 0 ⟹ sll Q, Q0 = 1	0011	0000 0010	0000 0001
	3: Shift Div right	0011	0000 0001	0000 0001

FIGURE 3.11   Division example using the algorithm in Figure 3.10. The bit examined to determine the next step is circled in color.

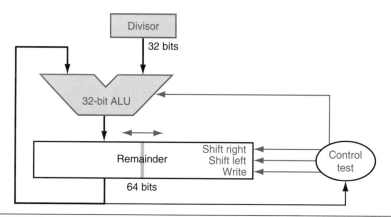

FIGURE 3.12   An improved version of the division hardware. The Divisor register, ALU, and Quotient register are all 32 bits wide, with only the Remainder register left at 64 bits. Compared to Figure 3.9, the ALU and Divisor registers are halved and the remainder is shifted left. This version also combines the Quotient register with the right half of the Remainder register. (As in Figure 3.6, the Remainder register should really be 65 bits to make sure the carry out of the adder is not lost.)

Checking the results:

$$7 = 3 \times 2 + (+1) = 6 + 1$$

If we change the sign of the dividend, the quotient must change as well:

$$-7 \div +2: \text{Quotient} = -3$$

Rewriting our basic formula to calculate the remainder:

Remainder = (Dividend − Quotient × Divisor) = −7 − (−3 × +2) = −7−(−6) = −1

So,

−7 ÷ +2: Quotient = −3, Remainder = −1

Checking the results again:

−7 = −3 × 2 + (−1) = − 6 − 1

The reason the answer isn't a quotient of −4 and a remainder of +1, which would also fit this formula, is that the absolute value of the quotient would then change depending on the sign of the dividend and the divisor! Clearly, if

$-(x \div y) \neq (-x) \div y$

programming would be an even greater challenge. This anomalous behavior is avoided by following the rule that the dividend and remainder must have the same signs, no matter what the signs of the divisor and quotient.

We calculate the other combinations by following the same rule:

+7 ÷ −2: Quotient = −3, Remainder = +1
−7 ÷ −2: Quotient = +3, Remainder = −1

Thus the correctly signed division algorithm negates the quotient if the signs of the operands are opposite and makes the sign of the nonzero remainder match the dividend.

Faster Division

We used many adders to speed up multiply, but we cannot do the same trick for divide. The reason is that we need to know the sign of the difference before we can perform the next step of the algorithm, whereas with multiply we could calculate the 32 partial products immediately.

There are techniques to produce more than one bit of the quotient per step. The *SRT division* technique tries to guess several quotient bits per step, using a table lookup based on the upper bits of the dividend and remainder. It relies on subsequent steps to correct wrong guesses. A typical value today is 4 bits. The key is guessing the value to subtract. With binary division, there is only a single choice. These algorithms use 6 bits from the remainder and 4 bits from the divisor to index a table that determines the guess for each step.

The accuracy of this fast method depends on having proper values in the lookup table. The fallacy on page 276 in Section 3.8 shows what can happen if the table is incorrect.

Divide in MIPS

You may have already observed that the same sequential hardware can be used for both multiply and divide in Figures 3.6 and 3.12. The only requirement is a 64-bit register that can shift left or right and a 32-bit ALU that adds or subtracts. Hence, MIPS uses the 32-bit Hi and 32-bit Lo registers for both multiply and divide.

As we might expect from the algorithm above, Hi contains the remainder, and Lo contains the quotient after the divide instruction completes.

To handle both signed integers and unsigned integers, MIPS has two instructions: *divide* (div) and *divide unsigned* (divu). The MIPS assembler allows divide instructions to specify three registers, generating the mflo or mfhi instructions to place the desired result into a general-purpose register.

Summary

The common hardware support for multiply and divide allows MIPS to provide a single pair of 32-bit registers that are used both for multiply and divide. Figure 3.13 summarizes the additions to the MIPS architecture for the last two sections.

**Hardware/
Software
Interface**

MIPS divide instructions ignore overflow, so software must determine whether the quotient is too large. In addition to overflow, division can also result in an improper calculation: division by 0. Some computers distinguish these two anomalous events. MIPS software must check the divisor to discover division by 0 as well as overflow.

Elaboration: An even faster algorithm does not immediately add the divisor back if the remainder is negative. It simply *adds* the dividend to the shifted remainder in the following step, since $(r + d) \times 2 - d = r \times 2 + d \times 2 - d = r \times 2 + d$. This *nonrestoring* division algorithm, which takes 1 clock cycle per step, is explored further in the exercises; the algorithm here is called *restoring* division. A third algorithm that doesn't save the result of the subtract if its negative is called a *nonperforming* division algorithm. It averages one-third fewer arithmetic operations.

*Speed gets you nowhere
if you're headed the
wrong way.*

American proverb

 3.5 **Floating Point**

Going beyond signed and unsigned integers, programming languages support numbers with fractions, which are called *reals* in mathematics. Here are some examples of reals:

$3.14159265 \ldots_{\text{ten}}$ (pi)

$2.71828 \ldots_{\text{ten}}$ (e)

0.000000001_{ten} or $1.0_{\text{ten}} \times 10^{-9}$ (seconds in a nanosecond)

$3{,}155{,}760{,}000_{\text{ten}}$ or $3.15576_{\text{ten}} \times 10^{9}$ (seconds in a typical century)

MIPS assembly language

Category	Instruction	Example	Meaning	Comments
Arithmetic	add	`add $s1,$s2,$s3`	$s1 = $s2 + $s3	Three operands; overflow detected
	subtract	`sub $s1,$s2,$s3`	$s1 = $s2 – $s3	Three operands; overflow detected
	add immediate	`addi $s1,$s2,100`	$s1 = $s2 + 100	+ constant; overflow detected
	add unsigned	`addu $s1,$s2,$s3`	$s1 = $s2 + $s3	Three operands; overflow undetected
	subtract unsigned	`subu $s1,$s2,$s3`	$s1 = $s2 – $s3	Three operands; overflow undetected
	add immediate unsigned	`addiu $s1,$s2,100`	$s1 = $s2 + 100	+ constant; overflow undetected
	move from coprocessor register	`mfc0 $s1,$epc`	$s1 = $epc	Copy Exception PC + special regs
	multiply	`mult $s2,$s3`	Hi, Lo = $s2 × $s3	64-bit signed product in Hi, Lo
	multiply unsigned	`multu $s2,$s3`	Hi, Lo = $s2 × $s3	64-bit unsigned product in Hi, Lo
	divide	`div $s2,$s3`	Lo = $s2 / $s3, Hi = $s2 mod $s3	Lo = quotient, Hi = remainder
	divide unsigned	`divu $s2,$s3`	Lo = $s2 / $s3, Hi = $s2 mod $s3	Unsigned quotient and remainder
	move from Hi	`mfhi $s1`	$s1 = Hi	Used to get copy of Hi
	move from Lo	`mflo $s1`	$s1 = Lo	Used to get copy of Lo
Data transfer	load word	`lw $s1,20($s2)`	$s1 = Memory[$s2 + 20]	Word from memory to register
	store word	`sw $s1,20($s2)`	Memory[$s2 + 20] = $s1	Word from register to memory
	load half unsigned	`lhu $s1,20($s2)`	$s1 = Memory[$s2 + 20]	Halfword memory to register
	store half	`sh $s1,20($s2)`	Memory[$s2 + 20] = $s1	Halfword register to memory
	load byte unsigned	`lbu $s1,20($s2)`	$s1 = Memory[$s2 + 20]	Byte from memory to register
	store byte	`sb $s1,20($s2)`	Memory[$s2 + 20] = $s1	Byte from register to memory
	load linked word	`ll $s1,20($s2)`	$s1 = Memory[$s2 + 20]	Load word as 1st half of atomic swap
	store conditional word	`sc $s1,20($s2)`	Memory[$s2+20]=$s1;$s1=0 or 1	Store word as 2nd half atomic swap
	load upper immediate	`lui $s1,100`	$s1 = 100 * 2^{16}	Loads constant in upper 16 bits
Logical	AND	`AND $s1,$s2,$s3`	$s1 = $s2 & $s3	Three reg. operands; bit-by-bit AND
	OR	`OR $s1,$s2,$s3`	$s1 = $s2 | $s3	Three reg. operands; bit-by-bit OR
	NOR	`NOR $s1,$s2,$s3`	$s1 = ~ ($s2 |$s3)	Three reg. operands; bit-by-bit NOR
	AND immediate	`ANDi $s1,$s2,100`	$s1 = $s2 & 100	Bit-by-bit AND with constant
	OR immediate	`ORi $s1,$s2,100`	$s1 = $s2 | 100	Bit-by-bit OR with constant
	shift left logical	`sll $s1,$s2,10`	$s1 = $s2 << 10	Shift left by constant
	shift right logical	`srl $s1,$s2,10`	$s1 = $s2 >> 10	Shift right by constant
Conditional branch	branch on equal	`beq $s1,$s2,25`	if ($s1 == $s2) go to PC + 4 + 100	Equal test; PC-relative branch
	branch on not equal	`bne $s1,$s2,25`	if ($s1 != $s2) go to PC + 4 + 100	Not equal test; PC-relative
	set on less than	`slt $s1,$s2,$s3`	if ($s2 < $s3) $s1 = 1; else $s1 = 0	Compare less than; two's complement
	set less than immediate	`slti $s1,$s2,100`	if ($s2 < 100) $s1 = 1; else $s1=0	Compare < constant; two's complement
	set less than unsigned	`sltu $s1,$s2,$s3`	if ($s2 < $s3) $s1 = 1; else $s1=0	Compare less than; natural numbers
	set less than immediate unsigned	`sltiu $s1,$s2,100`	if ($s2 < 100) $s1 = 1; else $s1 = 0	Compare < constant; natural numbers
Unconditional jump	jump	`j 2500`	go to 10000	Jump to target address
	jump register	`jr $ra`	go to $ra	For switch, procedure return
	jump and link	`jal 2500`	$ra = PC + 4; go to 10000	For procedure call

FIGURE 3.13 MIPS core architecture. The memory and registers of the MIPS architecture are not included for space reasons, but this section added the Hi and Lo registers to support multiply and divide. MIPS machine language is listed in the MIPS Reference Data Card at the front of this book.

scientific notation
A notation that renders
numbers with a single
digit to the left of the
decimal point.

Notice that in the last case, the number didn't represent a small fraction, but it was bigger than we could represent with a 32-bit signed integer. The alternative notation for the last two numbers is called **scientific notation**, which has a single digit to the left of the decimal point. A number in scientific notation that has no leading 0s is called a **normalized** number, which is the usual way to write it. For example, $1.0_{ten} \times 10^{-9}$ is in normalized scientific notation, but $0.1_{ten} \times 10^{-8}$ and $10.0_{ten} \times 10^{-10}$ are not.

normalized A number
in floating-point notation
that has no leading 0s.

Just as we can show decimal numbers in scientific notation, we can also show binary numbers in scientific notation:

$$1.0_{two} \times 2^{-1}$$

To keep a binary number in normalized form, we need a base that we can increase or decrease by exactly the number of bits the number must be shifted to have one nonzero digit to the left of the decimal point. Only a base of 2 fulfills our need. Since the base is not 10, we also need a new name for decimal point; *binary point* will do fine.

floating point Computer
arithmetic that represents
numbers in which the
binary point is not fixed.

Computer arithmetic that supports such numbers is called **floating point** because it represents numbers in which the binary point is not fixed, as it is for integers. The programming language C uses the name *float* for such numbers. Just as in scientific notation, numbers are represented as a single nonzero digit to the left of the binary point. In binary, the form is

$$1.xxxxxxxxx_{two} \times 2^{yyyy}$$

(Although the computer represents the exponent in base 2 as well as the rest of the number, to simplify the notation we show the exponent in decimal.)

A standard scientific notation for reals in normalized form offers three advantages. It simplifies exchange of data that includes floating-point numbers; it simplifies the floating-point arithmetic algorithms to know that numbers will always be in this form; and it increases the accuracy of the numbers that can be stored in a word, since the unnecessary leading 0s are replaced by real digits to the right of the binary point.

Floating-Point Representation

A designer of a floating-point representation must find a compromise between the size of the **fraction** and the size of the **exponent**, because a fixed word size means you must take a bit from one to add a bit to the other. This tradeoff is between precision and range: increasing the size of the fraction enhances the precision of the fraction, while increasing the size of the exponent increases the range of numbers that can be represented. As our design guideline from Chapter 2 reminds us, good design demands good compromise.

fraction The value,
generally between 0 and 1,
placed in the fraction
field.

exponent In the
numerical representation
system of floating-point
arithmetic, the value that
is placed in the exponent
field.

Floating-point numbers are usually a multiple of the size of a word. The representation of a MIPS floating-point number is shown below, where *s* is the sign of the floating-point number (1 meaning negative), *exponent* is the value of the 8-bit exponent field (including the sign of the exponent), and *fraction* is the

23-bit number. This representation is called *sign and magnitude*, since the sign is a separate bit from the rest of the number.

31	30	29	28	27	26	25	24	23	22	21	20	19	18	17	16	15	14	13	12	11	10	9	8	7	6	5	4	3	2	1	0
s	exponent								fraction																						

1 bit   8 bits   23 bits

In general, floating-point numbers are of the form

$$(-1)^S \times F \times 2^E$$

F involves the value in the fraction field and E involves the value in the exponent field; the exact relationship to these fields will be spelled out soon. (We will shortly see that MIPS does something slightly more sophisticated.)

These chosen sizes of exponent and fraction give MIPS computer arithmetic an extraordinary range. Fractions almost as small as $2.0_{ten} \times 10^{-38}$ and numbers almost as large as $2.0_{ten} \times 10^{38}$ can be represented in a computer. Alas, extraordinary differs from infinite, so it is still possible for numbers to be too large. Thus, overflow interrupts can occur in floating-point arithmetic as well as in integer arithmetic. Notice that **overflow** here means that the exponent is too large to be represented in the exponent field.

Floating point offers a new kind of exceptional event as well. Just as programmers will want to know when they have calculated a number that is too large to be represented, they will want to know if the nonzero fraction they are calculating has become so small that it cannot be represented; either event could result in a program giving incorrect answers. To distinguish it from overflow, we call this event **underflow**. This situation occurs when the negative exponent is too large to fit in the exponent field.

One way to reduce chances of underflow or overflow is to offer another format that has a larger exponent. In C this number is called *double*, and operations on doubles are called **double precision** floating-point arithmetic; **single precision** floating point is the name of the earlier format.

The representation of a double precision floating-point number takes two MIPS words, as shown below, where *s* is still the sign of the number, *exponent* is the value of the 11-bit exponent field, and *fraction* is the 52-bit number in the fraction field.

overflow (floating-point) A situation in which a positive exponent becomes too large to fit in the exponent field.

underflow (floating-point) A situation in which a negative exponent becomes too large to fit in the exponent field.

double precision A floating-point value represented in two 32-bit words.

single precision A floating-point value represented in a single 32-bit word.

31	30	29	28	27	26	25	24	23	22	21	20	19	18	17	16	15	14	13	12	11	10	9	8	7	6	5	4	3	2	1	0
s	exponent											fraction																		

1 bit   11 bits   20 bits

fraction (continued)

32 bits

MIPS double precision allows numbers almost as small as $2.0_{ten} \times 10^{-308}$ and almost as large as $2.0_{ten} \times 10^{308}$. Although double precision does increase the exponent range, its primary advantage is its greater precision because of the much larger significand.

These formats go beyond MIPS. They are part of the *IEEE 754 floating-point standard*, found in virtually every computer invented since 1980. This standard has greatly improved both the ease of porting floating-point programs and the quality of computer arithmetic.

To pack even more bits into the significand, IEEE 754 makes the leading 1-bit of normalized binary numbers implicit. Hence, the number is actually 24 bits long in single precision (implied 1 and a 23-bit fraction), and 53 bits long in double precision $(1 + 52)$. To be precise, we use the term *significand* to represent the 24- or 53-bit number that is 1 plus the fraction, and *fraction* when we mean the 23- or 52-bit number. Since 0 has no leading 1, it is given the reserved exponent value 0 so that the hardware won't attach a leading 1 to it.

Thus $00 \ldots 00_{\text{two}}$ represents 0; the representation of the rest of the numbers uses the form from before with the hidden 1 added:

$$(-1)^S \times (1 + \text{Fraction}) \times 2^E$$

where the bits of the fraction represent a number between 0 and 1 and E specifies the value in the exponent field, to be given in detail shortly. If we number the bits of the fraction from *left to right* s1, s2, s3, . . . , then the value is

$$(-1)^S \times (1 + (s1 \times 2^{-1}) + (s2 \times 2^{-2}) + (s3 \times 2^{-3}) + (s4 \times 2^{-4}) + \ldots) \times 2^E$$

Figure 3.14 shows the encodings of IEEE 754 floating-point numbers. Other features of IEEE 754 are special symbols to represent unusual events. For example, instead of interrupting on a divide by 0, software can set the result to a bit pattern representing $+\infty$ or $-\infty$; the largest exponent is reserved for these special symbols. When the programmer prints the results, the program will print an infinity symbol. (For the mathematically trained, the purpose of infinity is to form topological closure of the reals.)

Single precision		Double precision		Object represented
Exponent	Fraction	Exponent	Fraction	
0	0	0	0	0
0	Nonzero	0	Nonzero	± denormalized number
1–254	Anything	1–2046	Anything	± floating-point number
255	0	2047	0	± infinity
255	Nonzero	2047	Nonzero	NaN (Not a Number)

FIGURE 3.14 IEEE 754 encoding of floating-point numbers. A separate sign bit determines the sign. Denormalized numbers are described in the *Elaboration* on page 270. This information is also found in Column 4 of the MIPS Reference Data Card at the front of this book.

IEEE 754 even has a symbol for the result of invalid operations, such as 0/0 or subtracting infinity from infinity. This symbol is *NaN*, for *Not a Number*. The purpose of NaNs is to allow programmers to postpone some tests and decisions to a later time in the program when they are convenient.

The designers of IEEE 754 also wanted a floating-point representation that could be easily processed by integer comparisons, especially for sorting. This desire is why the sign is in the most significant bit, allowing a quick test of less than, greater than, or equal to 0. (It's a little more complicated than a simple integer sort, since this notation is essentially sign and magnitude rather than two's complement.)

Placing the exponent before the significand also simplifies the sorting of floating-point numbers using integer comparison instructions, since numbers with bigger exponents look larger than numbers with smaller exponents, as long as both exponents have the same sign.

Negative exponents pose a challenge to simplified sorting. If we use two's complement or any other notation in which negative exponents have a 1 in the most significant bit of the exponent field, a negative exponent will look like a big number. For example, $1.0_{two} \times 2^{-1}$ would be represented as

31	30	29	28	27	26	25	24	23	22	21	20	19	18	17	16	15	14	13	12	11	10	9	8	7	6	5	4	3	2	1	0
0	1	1	1	1	1	1	1	1	0	0	0	0	0	0	0	0	0	0	0	0	0	0	0	0	0	0	0	.	.	.	

(Remember that the leading 1 is implicit in the significand.) The value $1.0_{two} \times 2^{+1}$ would look like the smaller binary number

31	30	29	28	27	26	25	24	23	22	21	20	19	18	17	16	15	14	13	12	11	10	9	8	7	6	5	4	3	2	1	0
0	0	0	0	0	0	0	0	1	0	0	0	0	0	0	0	0	0	0	0	0	0	0	0	0	0	0	0	.	.	.	

The desirable notation must therefore represent the most negative exponent as $00 \ldots 00_{two}$ and the most positive as $11 \ldots 11_{two}$. This convention is called *biased notation*, with the bias being the number subtracted from the normal, unsigned representation to determine the real value.

IEEE 754 uses a bias of 127 for single precision, so an exponent of −1 is represented by the bit pattern of the value $-1 + 127_{ten}$, or $126_{ten} = 0111\ 1110_{two}$, and +1 is represented by $1 + 127$, or $128_{ten} = 1000\ 0000_{two}$. The exponent bias for double precision is 1023. Biased exponent means that the value represented by a floating-point number is really

$$(-1)^S \times (1 + \text{Fraction}) \times 2^{(\text{Exponent} - \text{Bias})}$$

The range of single precision numbers is then from as small as

$\pm 1.0000\ 0000\ 0000\ 0000\ 0000\ 000_{two} \times 2^{-126}$

to as large as

$\pm 1.1111\ 1111\ 1111\ 1111\ 1111\ 111_{two} \times 2^{+127}$.

Let's show the representation.

Floating-Point Representation

Show the IEEE 754 binary representation of the number -0.75_{ten} in single and double precision.

The number -0.75_{ten} is also

$$-3/4_{ten} \text{ or } -3/2^2{}_{ten}$$

It is also represented by the binary fraction

$$-11_{two}/2^2{}_{ten} \text{ or } -0.11_{two}$$

In scientific notation, the value is

$$-0.11_{two} \times 2^0$$

and in normalized scientific notation, it is

$$-1.1_{two} \times 2^{-1}$$

The general representation for a single precision number is

$$(-1)^S \times (1 + \text{Fraction}) \times 2^{(\text{Exponent} - 127)}$$

Subtracting the bias 127 from the exponent of $-1.1_{two} \times 2^{-1}$ yields

$$(-1)^1 \times (1 + .1000\ 0000\ 0000\ 0000\ 0000\ 000_{two}) \times 2^{(126-127)}$$

The single precision binary representation of -0.75_{ten} is then

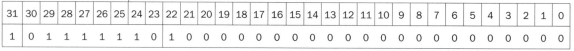

31	30	29	28	27	26	25	24	23	22	21	20	19	18	17	16	15	14	13	12	11	10	9	8	7	6	5	4	3	2	1	0
1	0	1	1	1	1	1	1	0	1	0	0	0	0	0	0	0	0	0	0	0	0	0	0	0	0	0	0	0	0	0	0

1 bit   8 bits   23 bits

The double precision representation is

$$(-1)^1 \times (1 + .1000\ 0000\ 0000\ 0000\ 0000\ 0000\ 0000\ 0000\ 0000\ 0000\ 0000\ 0000\ 0000_{two}) \times 2^{(1022-1023)}$$

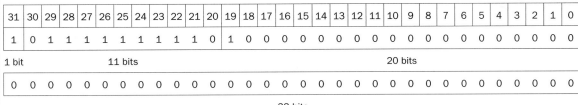

31	30	29	28	27	26	25	24	23	22	21	20	19	18	17	16	15	14	13	12	11	10	9	8	7	6	5	4	3	2	1	0
1	0	1	1	1	1	1	1	1	1	1	0	1	0	0	0	0	0	0	0	0	0	0	0	0	0	0	0	0	0	0	0

1 bit · 11 bits · 20 bits

0	0	0	0	0	0	0	0	0	0	0	0	0	0	0	0	0	0	0	0	0	0	0	0	0	0	0	0	0	0	0	0

32 bits

Now let's try going the other direction.

Converting Binary to Decimal Floating Point

What decimal number is represented by this single precision float?

EXAMPLE

31	30	29	28	27	26	25	24	23	22	21	20	19	18	17	16	15	14	13	12	11	10	9	8	7	6	5	4	3	2	1	0
1	1	0	0	0	0	0	0	1	0	1	0	0	0	0	0	0	0	0	0	0	0	0	0	0	0	0	0	0	.	.	.

The sign bit is 1, the exponent field contains 129, and the fraction field contains $1 \times 2^{-2} = 1/4$, or 0.25. Using the basic equation,

ANSWER

$$(-1)^S \times (1 + \text{Fraction}) \times 2^{(\text{Exponent} - \text{Bias})} = (-1)^1 \times (1 + 0.25) \times 2^{(129-127)}$$
$$= -1 \times 1.25 \times 2^2$$
$$= -1.25 \times 4$$
$$= -5.0$$

In the next subsections, we will give the algorithms for floating-point addition and multiplication. At their core, they use the corresponding integer operations on the significands, but extra bookkeeping is necessary to handle the exponents and normalize the result. We first give an intuitive derivation of the algorithms in decimal and then give a more detailed, binary version in the figures.

Elaboration: In an attempt to increase range without removing bits from the significand, some computers before the IEEE 754 standard used a base other than 2. For example, the IBM 360 and 370 mainframe computers use base 16. Since changing the IBM exponent by one means shifting the significand by 4 bits, "normalized" base 16 numbers can have up to 3 leading bits of 0s! Hence, hexadecimal digits mean that up to 3 bits must be dropped from the significand, which leads to surprising problems in the accuracy of floating-point arithmetic. Recent IBM mainframes support IEEE 754 as well as the hex format.

Floating-Point Addition

Let's add numbers in scientific notation by hand to illustrate the problems in floating-point addition: $9.999_{ten} \times 10^1 + 1.610_{ten} \times 10^{-1}$. Assume that we can store only four decimal digits of the significand and two decimal digits of the exponent.

Step 1.   To be able to add these numbers properly, we must align the decimal point of the number that has the smaller exponent. Hence, we need a form of the smaller number, $1.610_{ten} \times 10^{-1}$, that matches the larger exponent. We obtain this by observing that there are multiple representations of an unnormalized floating-point number in scientific notation:

$$1.610_{ten} \times 10^{-1} = 0.1610_{ten} \times 10^0 = 0.01610_{ten} \times 10^1$$

The number on the right is the version we desire, since its exponent matches the exponent of the larger number, $9.999_{ten} \times 10^1$. Thus, the first step shifts the significand of the smaller number to the right until its corrected exponent matches that of the larger number. But we can represent only four decimal digits so, after shifting, the number is really

$$0.016_{ten} \times 10^1$$

Step 2.   Next comes the addition of the significands:

$$
\begin{array}{r}
9.999_{ten} \\
+ \quad 0.016_{ten} \\
\hline
10.015_{ten}
\end{array}
$$

The sum is $10.015_{ten} \times 10^1$.

Step 3. This sum is not in normalized scientific notation, so we need to adjust it:

$$10.015_{ten} \times 10^1 = 1.0015_{ten} \times 10^2$$

Thus, after the addition we may have to shift the sum to put it into normalized form, adjusting the exponent appropriately. This example shows shifting to the right, but if one number were positive and the other were negative, it would be possible for the sum to have many leading 0s, requiring left shifts. Whenever the exponent is increased or decreased, we must check for overflow or underflow—that is, we must make sure that the exponent still fits in its field.

Step 4. Since we assumed that the significand can be only four digits long (excluding the sign), we must round the number. In our grammar school algorithm, the rules truncate the number if the digit to the right of the desired point is between 0 and 4 and add 1 to the digit if the number to the right is between 5 and 9. The number

$$1.0015_{ten} \times 10^2$$

is rounded to four digits in the significand to

$$1.002_{ten} \times 10^2$$

since the fourth digit to the right of the decimal point was between 5 and 9. Notice that if we have bad luck on rounding, such as adding 1 to a string of 9s, the sum may no longer be normalized and we would need to perform step 3 again.

Figure 3.15 shows the algorithm for binary floating-point addition that follows this decimal example. Steps 1 and 2 are similar to the example just discussed: adjust the significand of the number with the smaller exponent and then add the two significands. Step 3 normalizes the results, forcing a check for overflow or underflow. The test for overflow and underflow in step 3 depends on the precision of the operands. Recall that the pattern of all 0 bits in the exponent is reserved and used for the floating-point representation of zero. Moreover, the pattern of all 1 bits in the exponent is reserved for indicating values and situations outside the scope of normal floating-point numbers (see the *Elaboration* on page 270). Thus, for single precision, the maximum exponent is 127, and the minimum exponent is −126. The limits for double precision are 1023 and −1022.

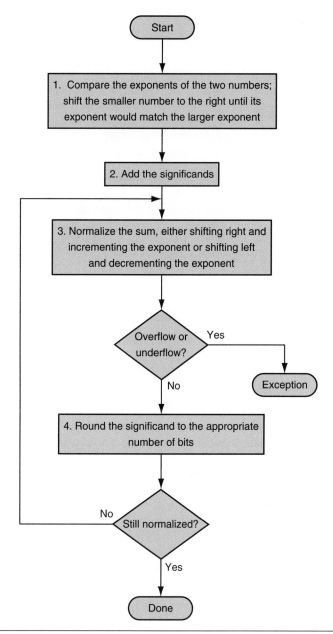

FIGURE 3.15 Floating-point addition. The normal path is to execute steps 3 and 4 once, but if rounding causes the sum to be unnormalized, we must repeat step 3.

Binary Floating-Point Addition

Try adding the numbers 0.5_{ten} and -0.4375_{ten} in binary using the algorithm in Figure 3.15.

Let's first look at the binary version of the two numbers in normalized scientific notation, assuming that we keep 4 bits of precision:

$$0.5_{ten} = 1/2_{ten} \quad\quad = 1/2^1_{ten}$$
$$= 0.1_{two} \quad\quad = 0.1_{two} \times 2^0 \quad\quad = 1.000_{two} \times 2^{-1}$$
$$-0.4375_{ten} = -7/16_{ten} \quad = -7/2^4_{ten}$$
$$= -0.0111_{two} = -0.0111_{two} \times 2^0 = -1.110_{two} \times 2^{-2}$$

Now we follow the algorithm:

Step 1.   The significand of the number with the lesser exponent ($-1.11_{two} \times 2^{-2}$) is shifted right until its exponent matches the larger number:

$$-1.110_{two} \times 2^{-2} = -0.111_{two} \times 2^{-1}$$

Step 2.   Add the significands:

$$1.000_{two} \times 2^{-1} + (-0.111_{two} \times 2^{-1}) = 0.001_{two} \times 2^{-1}$$

Step 3.   Normalize the sum, checking for overflow or underflow:

$$0.001_{two} \times 2^{-1} = 0.010_{two} \times 2^{-2} = 0.100_{two} \times 2^{-3}$$
$$= 1.000_{two} \times 2^{-4}$$

Since $127 \geq -4 \geq -126$, there is no overflow or underflow. (The biased exponent would be $-4 + 127$, or 123, which is between 1 and 254, the smallest and largest unreserved biased exponents.)

Step 4.   Round the sum:

$$1.000_{two} \times 2^{-4}$$

The sum already fits exactly in 4 bits, so there is no change to the bits due to rounding.

This sum is then

$$1.000_{two} \times 2^{-4} = 0.0001000_{two} = 0.0001_{two}$$
$$= 1/2^4_{ten} \quad\quad = 1/16_{ten} \quad\quad = 0.0625_{ten}$$

This sum is what we would expect from adding 0.5_{ten} to -0.4375_{ten}.

Many computers dedicate hardware to run floating-point operations as fast as possible. Figure 3.16 sketches the basic organization of hardware for floating-point addition.

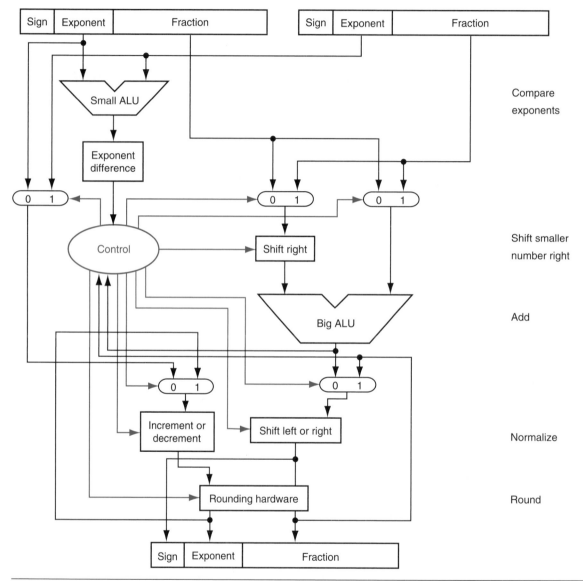

FIGURE 3.16 Block diagram of an arithmetic unit dedicated to floating-point addition. The steps of Figure 3.15 correspond to each block, from top to bottom. First, the exponent of one operand is subtracted from the other using the small ALU to determine which is larger and by how much. This difference controls the three multiplexors; from left to right, they select the larger exponent, the significand of the smaller number, and the significand of the larger number. The smaller significand is shifted right, and then the significands are added together using the big ALU. The normalization step then shifts the sum left or right and increments or decrements the exponent. Rounding then creates the final result, which may require normalizing again to produce the final result.

Floating-Point Multiplication

Now that we have explained floating-point addition, let's try floating-point multiplication. We start by multiplying decimal numbers in scientific notation by hand: $1.110_{ten} \times 10^{10} \times 9.200_{ten} \times 10^{-5}$. Assume that we can store only four digits of the significand and two digits of the exponent.

Step 1. Unlike addition, we calculate the exponent of the product by simply adding the exponents of the operands together:

$$\text{New exponent} = 10 + (-5) = 5$$

Let's do this with the biased exponents as well to make sure we obtain the same result: $10 + 127 = 137$, and $-5 + 127 = 122$, so

$$\text{New exponent} = 137 + 122 = 259$$

This result is too large for the 8-bit exponent field, so something is amiss! The problem is with the bias because we are adding the biases as well as the exponents:

$$\text{New exponent} = (10 + 127) + (-5 + 127) = (5 + 2 \times 127) = 259$$

Accordingly, to get the correct biased sum when we add biased numbers, we must subtract the bias from the sum:

$$\text{New exponent} = 137 + 122 - 127 = 259 - 127 = 132 = (5 + 127)$$

and 5 is indeed the exponent we calculated initially.

Step 2. Next comes the multiplication of the significands:

$$
\begin{array}{r}
1.110_{ten} \\
\times\ 9.200_{ten} \\
\hline
0000 \\
0000 \\
2220 \\
9990 \\
\hline
10212000_{ten}
\end{array}
$$

There are three digits to the right of the decimal point for each operand, so the decimal point is placed six digits from the right in the product significand:

$$10.212000_{ten}$$

Assuming that we can keep only three digits to the right of the decimal point, the product is 10.212×10^5.

Step 3. This product is unnormalized, so we need to normalize it:

$$10.212_{ten} \times 10^5 = 1.0212_{ten} \times 10^6$$

Thus, after the multiplication, the product can be shifted right one digit to put it in normalized form, adding 1 to the exponent. At this point, we can check for overflow and underflow. Underflow may occur if both operands are small—that is, if both have large negative exponents.

Step 4. We assumed that the significand is only four digits long (excluding the sign), so we must round the number. The number

$$1.0212_{ten} \times 10^6$$

is rounded to four digits in the significand to

$$1.021_{ten} \times 10^6$$

Step 5. The sign of the product depends on the signs of the original operands. If they are both the same, the sign is positive; otherwise, it's negative. Hence, the product is

$$+1.021_{ten} \times 10^6$$

The sign of the sum in the addition algorithm was determined by addition of the significands, but in multiplication, the sign of the product is determined by the signs of the operands.

Once again, as Figure 3.17 shows, multiplication of binary floating-point numbers is quite similar to the steps we have just completed. We start with calculating the new exponent of the product by adding the biased exponents, being sure to subtract one bias to get the proper result. Next is multiplication of significands, followed by an optional normalization step. The size of the exponent is checked for overflow or underflow, and then the product is rounded. If rounding leads to further normalization, we once again check for exponent size. Finally, set the sign bit to 1 if the signs of the operands were different (negative product) or to 0 if they were the same (positive product).

Binary Floating-Point Multiplication

EXAMPLE

Let's try multiplying the numbers 0.5_{ten} and -0.4375_{ten}, using the steps in Figure 3.17.

In binary, the task is multiplying $1.000_{two} \times 2^{-1}$ by $-1.110_{two} \times 2^{-2}$.

Step 1.   Adding the exponents without bias:

$$-1 + (-2) = -3$$

or, using the biased representation:

$$(-1 + 127) + (-2 + 127) - 127 = (-1 - 2) + (127 + 127 - 127)$$
$$= -3 + 127 = 124$$

Step 2.   Multiplying the significands:

$$
\begin{array}{r}
1.000_{two} \\
\times \quad 1.110_{two} \\
\hline
0000 \\
1000 \\
1000 \\
1000 \\
\hline
1110000_{two}
\end{array}
$$

The product is $1.110000_{two} \times 2^{-3}$, but we need to keep it to 4 bits, so it is $1.110_{two} \times 2^{-3}$.

Step 3.   Now we check the product to make sure it is normalized, and then check the exponent for overflow or underflow. The product is already normalized and, since $127 \geq -3 \geq -126$, there is no overflow or underflow. (Using the biased representation, $254 \geq 124 \geq 1$, so the exponent fits.)

Step 4.   Rounding the product makes no change:

$$1.110_{two} \times 2^{-3}$$

Step 5.   Since the signs of the original operands differ, make the sign of the product negative. Hence, the product is

$$-1.110_{two} \times 2^{-3}$$

Converting to decimal to check our results:

$$-1.110_{two} \times 2^{-3} = -0.001110_{two} = -0.00111_{two}$$
$$= -7/2^5{}_{ten} = -7/32_{ten} = -0.21875_{ten}$$

The product of 0.5_{ten} and -0.4375_{ten} is indeed -0.21875_{ten}.

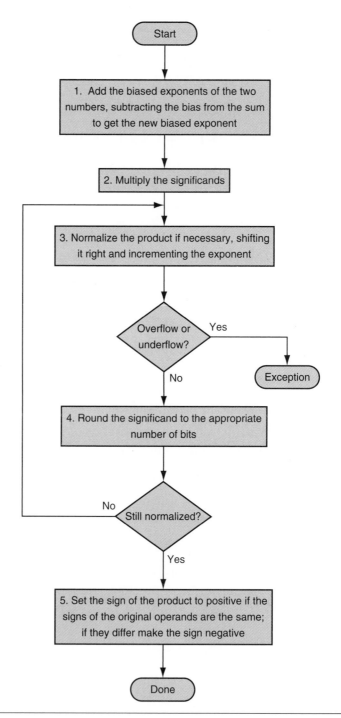

FIGURE 3.17 Floating-point multiplication. The normal path is to execute steps 3 and 4 once, but if rounding causes the sum to be unnormalized, we must repeat step 3.

Floating-Point Instructions in MIPS

MIPS supports the IEEE 754 single precision and double precision formats with these instructions:

- Floating-point *addition, single* (add.s) and *addition, double* (add.d)

- Floating-point *subtraction, single* (sub.s) and *subtraction, double* (sub.d)

- Floating-point *multiplication, single* (mul.s) and *multiplication, double* (mul.d)

- Floating-point *division, single* (div.s) and *division, double* (div.d)

- Floating-point *comparison, single* (c.x.s) and *comparison, double* (c.x.d), where x may be *equal* (eq), *not equal* (neq), *less than* (lt), *less than or equal* (le), *greater than* (gt), or *greater than or equal* (ge)

- Floating-point *branch, true* (bc1t) and *branch, false* (bc1f)

Floating-point comparison sets a bit to true or false, depending on the comparison condition, and a floating-point branch then decides whether or not to branch, depending on the condition.

The MIPS designers decided to add separate floating-point registers—called $f0, $f1, $f2, ...—used either for single precision or double precision. Hence, they included separate loads and stores for floating-point registers: lwc1 and swc1. The base registers for floating-point data transfers remain integer registers. The MIPS code to load two single precision numbers from memory, add them, and then store the sum might look like this:

```
lwc1    $f4,x($sp)    # Load 32-bit F.P. number into F4
lwc1    $f6,y($sp)    # Load 32-bit F.P. number into F6
add.s   $f2,$f4,$f6   # F2 = F4 + F6 single precision
swc1    $f2,z($sp)    # Store 32-bit F.P. number from F2
```

A double precision register is really an even-odd pair of single precision registers, using the even register number as its name. Thus, the pair of single precision registers $f2 and $f3 also form the double precision register named $f2.

Figure 3.18 summarizes the floating-point portion of the MIPS architecture revealed in this chapter, with the additions to support floating point shown in color. Similar to Figure 2.19 in Chapter 2, Figure 3.19 shows the encoding of these instructions.

MIPS floating-point **operands**

Name	Example	Comments
32 floating-point registers	`$f0, $f1, $f2, . . . , $f31`	MIPS floating-point registers are used in pairs for double precision numbers.
2^{30} memory words	Memory[0], Memory[4], . . . , Memory[4294967292]	Accessed only by data transfer instructions. MIPS uses byte addresses, so sequential word addresses differ by 4. Memory holds data structures, such as arrays, and spilled registers, such as those saved on procedure calls.

MIPS floating-point **assembly language**

Category	Instruction	Example	Meaning	Comments
Arithmetic	FP add single	`add.s  $f2,$f4,$f6`	$f2 = $f4 + $f6	FP add (single precision)
	FP subtract single	`sub.s  $f2,$f4,$f6`	$f2 = $f4 − $f6	FP sub (single precision)
	FP multiply single	`mul.s  $f2,$f4,$f6`	$f2 = $f4 × $f6	FP multiply (single precision)
	FP divide single	`div.s  $f2,$f4,$f6`	$f2 = $f4 / $f6	FP divide (single precision)
	FP add double	`add.d  $f2,$f4,$f6`	$f2 = $f4 + $f6	FP add (double precision)
	FP subtract double	`sub.d  $f2,$f4,$f6`	$f2 = $f4 − $f6	FP sub (double precision)
	FP multiply double	`mul.d  $f2,$f4,$f6`	$f2 = $f4 × $f6	FP multiply (double precision)
	FP divide double	`div.d  $f2,$f4,$f6`	$f2 = $f4 / $f6	FP divide (double precision)
Data transfer	load word copr. 1	`lwc1   $f1,100($s2)`	$f1 = Memory[$s2 + 100]	32-bit data to FP register
	store word copr. 1	`swc1   $f1,100($s2)`	Memory[$s2 + 100] = $f1	32-bit data to memory
Conditional branch	branch on FP true	`bc1t   25`	if (cond == 1) go to PC + 4 + 100	PC-relative branch if FP cond.
	branch on FP false	`bc1f   25`	if (cond == 0) go to PC + 4 + 100	PC-relative branch if not cond.
	FP compare single (eq,ne,lt,le,gt,ge)	`c.lt.s $f2,$f4`	if ($f2 < $f4) cond = 1; else cond = 0	FP compare less than single precision
	FP compare double (eq,ne,lt,le,gt,ge)	`c.lt.d $f2,$f4`	if ($f2 < $f4) cond = 1; else cond = 0	FP compare less than double precision

MIPS floating-point **machine language**

Name	Format	Example						Comments
`add.s`	R	17	16	6	4	2	0	`add.s  $f2,$f4,$f6`
`sub.s`	R	17	16	6	4	2	1	`sub.s  $f2,$f4,$f6`
`mul.s`	R	17	16	6	4	2	2	`mul.s  $f2,$f4,$f6`
`div.s`	R	17	16	6	4	2	3	`div.s  $f2,$f4,$f6`
`add.d`	R	17	17	6	4	2	0	`add.d  $f2,$f4,$f6`
`sub.d`	R	17	17	6	4	2	1	`sub.d  $f2,$f4,$f6`
`mul.d`	R	17	17	6	4	2	2	`mul.d  $f2,$f4,$f6`
`div.d`	R	17	17	6	4	2	3	`div.d  $f2,$f4,$f6`
`lwc1`	I	49	20	2	100			`lwc1   $f2,100($s4)`
`swc1`	I	57	20	2	100			`swc1   $f2,100($s4)`
`bc1t`	I	17	8	1	25			`bc1t   25`
`bc1f`	I	17	8	0	25			`bc1f   25`
`c.lt.s`	R	17	16	4	2	0	60	`c.lt.s $f2,$f4`
`c.lt.d`	R	17	17	4	2	0	60	`c.lt.d $f2,$f4`
Field size		6 bits	5 bits	5 bits	5 bits	5 bits	6 bits	All MIPS instructions 32 bits

FIGURE 3.18   MIPS floating-point architecture revealed thus far. See Appendix B, Section B.10, for more detail. This information is also found in column 2 of the MIPS Reference Data Card at the front of this book.

op(31:26):								
28–26 31–29	0(000)	1(001)	2(010)	3(011)	4(100)	5(101)	6(110)	7(111)
0(000)	Rfmt	Bltz/gez	j	jal	beq	bne	blez	bgtz
1(001)	addi	addiu	slti	sltiu	ANDi	ORi	xORi	lui
2(010)	TLB	FlPt						
3(011)								
4(100)	lb	lh	lwl	lw	lbu	lhu	lwr	
5(101)	sb	sh	swl	sw			swr	
6(110)	lwc0	lwc1						
7(111)	swc0	swc1						

op(31:26) = 010001 (FlPt), (rt(16:16) = 0 => c = f, rt(16:16) = 1 => c = t), rs(25:21):								
23–21 25–24	0(000)	1(001)	2(010)	3(011)	4(100)	5(101)	6(110)	7(111)
0(00)	mfc1		cfc1		mtc1		ctc1	
1(01)	bc1.c							
2(10)	f = single	f = double						
3(11)								

op(31:26) = 010001 (FlPt), (f above: 10000 => f = s, 10001 => f = d), funct(5:0):								
2–0 5–3	0(000)	1(001)	2(010)	3(011)	4(100)	5(101)	6(110)	7(111)
0(000)	add.f	sub.f	mul.f	div.f		abs.f	mov.f	neg.f
1(001)								
2(010)								
3(011)								
4(100)	cvt.s.f	cvt.d.f			cvt.w.f			
5(101)								
6(110)	c.f.f	c.un.f	c.eq.f	c.ueq.f	c.olt.f	c.ult.f	c.ole.f	c.ule.f
7(111)	c.sf.f	c.ngle.f	c.seq.f	c.ngl.f	c.lt.f	c.nge.f	c.le.f	c.ngt.f

FIGURE 3.19 MIPS floating-point instruction encoding. This notation gives the value of a field by row and by column. For example, in the top portion of the figure, lw is found in row number 4 (100_{two} for bits 31–29 of the instruction) and column number 3 (011_{two} for bits 28–26 of the instruction), so the corresponding value of the op field (bits 31–26) is 100011_{two}. Underscore means the field is used elsewhere. For example, FlPt in row 2 and column 1 (op = 010001_{two}) is defined in the bottom part of the figure. Hence sub.f in row 0 and column 1 of the bottom section means that the funct field (bits 5–0) of the instruction is 000001_{two} and the op field (bits 31–26) is 010001_{two}. Note that the 5-bit rs field, specified in the middle portion of the figure, determines whether the operation is single precision ($f = s$, so rs = 10000) or double precision ($f = d$, so rs = 10001). Similarly, bit 16 of the instruction determines if the bc1.c instruction tests for true (bit 16 = 1 =>bc1.t) or false (bit 16 = 0 =>bc1.f). Instructions in color are described in Chapter 2 or this chapter, with Appendix B covering all instructions. This information is also found in column 2 of the MIPS Reference Data Card at the front of this book.

Hardware/ Software Interface

One issue that architects face in supporting floating-point arithmetic is whether to use the same registers used by the integer instructions or to add a special set for floating point. Because programs normally perform integer operations and floating-point operations on different data, separating the registers will only slightly increase the number of instructions needed to execute a program. The major impact is to create a separate set of data transfer instructions to move data between floating-point registers and memory.

The benefits of separate floating-point registers are having twice as many registers without using up more bits in the instruction format, having twice the register bandwidth by having separate integer and floating-point register sets, and being able to customize registers to floating point; for example, some computers convert all sized operands in registers into a single internal format.

Compiling a Floating-Point C Program into MIPS Assembly Code

EXAMPLE

Let's convert a temperature in Fahrenheit to Celsius:

```
float f2c (float fahr)
        {
                return ((5.0/9.0) * (fahr - 32.0));
        }
```

Assume that the floating-point argument fahr is passed in $f12 and the result should go in $f0. (Unlike integer registers, floating-point register 0 can contain a number.) What is the MIPS assembly code?

ANSWER

We assume that the compiler places the three floating-point constants in memory within easy reach of the global pointer $gp. The first two instructions load the constants 5.0 and 9.0 into floating-point registers:

```
f2c:

        lwc1 $f16,const5($gp)  # $f16 = 5.0 (5.0 in memory)
        lwc1 $f18,const9($gp)  # $f18 = 9.0 (9.0 in memory)
```

They are then divided to get the fraction 5.0/9.0:

```
        div.s $f16, $f16, $f18 # $f16 = 5.0 / 9.0
```

(Many compilers would divide 5.0 by 9.0 at compile time and save the single constant 5.0/9.0 in memory, thereby avoiding the divide at runtime.) Next, we load the constant 32.0 and then subtract it from fahr ($f12):

```
lwc1 $f18, const32($gp)# $f18 = 32.0
sub.s $f18, $f12, $f18 # $f18 = fahr - 32.0
```

Finally, we multiply the two intermediate results, placing the product in $f0 as the return result, and then return

```
mul.s $f0,  $f16, $f18 # $f0 = (5/9)*(fahr - 32.0)
jr  $ra                # return
```

Now let's perform floating-point operations on matrices, code commonly found in scientific programs.

Compiling Floating-Point C Procedure with Two-Dimensional Matrices into MIPS

Most floating-point calculations are performed in double precision. Let's perform matrix multiply of X = X + Y * Z. Let's assume X, Y, and Z are all square matrices with 32 elements in each dimension.

EXAMPLE

```
void mm (double x[][], double y[][], double z[][])
{
        int i, j, k;

        for (i = 0; i != 32; i = i + 1)
        for (j = 0; j != 32; j = j + 1)
        for (k = 0; k != 32; k = k + 1)
          x[i][j] = x[i][j] + y[i][k] * z[k][j];
}
```

The array starting addresses are parameters, so they are in $a0, $a1, and $a2. Assume that the integer variables are in $s0, $s1, and $s2, respectively. What is the MIPS assembly code for the body of the procedure?

Note that x[i][j] is used in the innermost loop above. Since the loop index is k, the index does not affect x[i][j], so we can avoid loading and storing x[i][j] each iteration. Instead, the compiler loads x[i][j] into a register outside the loop, accumulates the sum of the products of y[i][k] and z[k][j] in that same register, and then stores the sum into x[i][j] upon termination of the innermost loop.

ANSWER

We keep the code simpler by using the assembly language pseudoinstructions li (which loads a constant into a register), and l.d and s.d (which the assembler turns into a pair of data transfer instructions, lwc1 or swc1, to a pair of floating-point registers).

The body of the procedure starts with saving the loop termination value of 32 in a temporary register and then initializing the three *for* loop variables:

```
mm: ...
          li      $t1, 32   # $t1 = 32 (row size/loop end)
          li      $s0, 0    # i = 0; initialize 1st for loop
L1:       li      $s1, 0    # j = 0; restart 2nd for loop
L2:       li      $s2, 0    # k = 0; restart 3rd for loop
```

To calculate the address of x[i][j], we need to know how a 32 × 32, two-dimensional array is stored in memory. As you might expect, its layout is the same as if there were 32 single-dimension arrays, each with 32 elements. So the first step is to skip over the i "single-dimensional arrays," or rows, to get the one we want. Thus, we multiply the index in the first dimension by the size of the row, 32. Since 32 is a power of 2, we can use a shift instead:

```
sll   $t2, $s0, 5        # $t2 = i * 2^5 (size of row of x)
```

Now we add the second index to select the jth element of the desired row:

```
addu  $t2, $t2, $s1      # $t2 = i * size(row) + j
```

To turn this sum into a byte index, we multiply it by the size of a matrix element in bytes. Since each element is 8 bytes for double precision, we can instead shift left by 3:

```
sll   $t2, $t2, 3        # $t2 = byte offset of [i][j]
```

Next we add this sum to the base address of x, giving the address of x[i][j], and then load the double precision number x[i][j] into $f4:

```
addu  $t2, $a0, $t2      # $t2 = byte address of x[i][j]
l.d   $f4, 0($t2)        # $f4 = 8 bytes of x[i][j]
```

The following five instructions are virtually identical to the last five: calculate the address and then load the double precision number z[k][j].

```
L3:    sll $t0, $s2, 5       # $t0 = k * 2^5 (size of row of z)
       addu $t0, $t0, $s1    # $t0 = k * size(row) + j
       sll $t0, $t0, 3       # $t0 = byte offset of [k][j]
       addu $t0, $a2, $t0    # $t0 = byte address of z[k][j]
       l.d $f16, 0($t0)      # $f16 = 8 bytes of z[k][j]
```

Similarly, the next five instructions are like the last five: calculate the address and then load the double precision number y[i][k].

```
sll     $t0, $s0, 5     # $t0 = i * 2^5 (size of row of y)
addu    $t0, $t0, $s2   # $t0 = i * size(row) + k
sll     $t0, $t0, 3     # $t0 = byte offset of [i][k]
addu    $t0, $a1, $t0   # $t0 = byte address of y[i][k]
l.d     $f18, 0($t0)    # $f18 = 8 bytes of y[i][k]
```

Now that we have loaded all the data, we are finally ready to do some floating-point operations! We multiply elements of y and z located in registers $f18 and $f16, and then accumulate the sum in $f4.

```
mul.d $f16, $f18, $f16  # $f16 = y[i][k] * z[k][j]
add.d $f4, $f4, $f16    # f4 = x[i][j]+ y[i][k] * z[k][j]
```

The final block increments the index k and loops back if the index is not 32. If it is 32, and thus the end of the innermost loop, we need to store the sum accumulated in $f4 into x[i][j].

```
addiu   $s2, $s2, 1     # $k k + 1
bne     $s2, $t1, L3    # if (k != 32) go to L3
s.d     $f4, 0($t2)     # x[i][j] = $f4
```

Similarly, these final four instructions increment the index variable of the middle and outermost loops, looping back if the index is not 32 and exiting if the index is 32.

```
addiu   $s1, $s1, 1     # $j = j + 1
bne     $s1, $t1, L2    # if (j != 32) go to L2
addiu   $s0, $s0, 1     # $i = i + 1
bne     $s0, $t1, L1    # if (i != 32) go to L1
. . .
```

Elaboration: The array layout discussed in the example, called *row-major order,* is used by C and many other programming languages. Fortran instead uses *column-major order,* whereby the array is stored column by column.

Elaboration: Only 16 of the 32 MIPS floating-point registers could originally be used for double precision operations: $f0, $f2, $f4, ..., $f30. Double precision is computed using pairs of these single precision registers. The odd-numbered floating-point registers were used only to load and store the right half of 64-bit floating-point numbers. MIPS-32 added l.d and s.d to the instruction set. MIPS-32 also added "paired single" versions of all floating-point instructions, where a single instruction results in two parallel floating-point operations on two 32-bit operands inside 64-bit registers. For example, add.ps $f0, $f2, $f4 is equivalent to add.s $f0, $f2, $f4 followed by add.s $f1, $f3, $f5.

Elaboration: Another reason for separate integers and floating-point registers is that microprocessors in the 1980s didn't have enough transistors to put the floating-point unit on the same chip as the integer unit. Hence, the floating-point unit, including the floating-point registers, was optionally available as a second chip. Such optional accelerator chips are called *coprocessors,* and explain the acronym for floating-point loads in MIPS: `lwc1` means load word to coprocessor 1, the floating-point unit. (Coprocessor 0 deals with virtual memory, described in Chapter 5.) Since the early 1990s, microprocessors have integrated floating point (and just about everything else) on chip, and hence the term *coprocessor* joins *accumulator* and *core memory* as quaint terms that date the speaker.

Elaboration: As mentioned in Section 3.4, accelerating division is more challenging than multiplication. In addition to SRT, another technique to leverage a fast multiplier is *Newton's iteration*, where division is recast as finding the zero of a function to find the reciprocal $1/x$, which is then multiplied by the other operand. Iteration techniques *cannot* be rounded properly without calculating many extra bits. A TI chip solves this problem by calculating an extra-precise reciprocal.

Elaboration: Java embraces IEEE 754 by name in its definition of Java floating-point data types and operations. Thus, the code in the first example could have well been generated for a class method that converted Fahrenheit to Celsius.

The second example uses multiple dimensional arrays, which are not explicitly supported in Java. Java allows arrays of arrays, but each array may have its own length, unlike multiple dimensional arrays in C. Like the examples in Chapter 2, a Java version of this second example would require a good deal of checking code for array bounds, including a new length calculation at the end of row access. It would also need to check that the object reference is not null.

Accurate Arithmetic

guard The first of two extra bits kept on the right during intermediate calculations of floating-point numbers; used to improve rounding accuracy.

round Method to make the intermediate floating-point result fit the floating-point format; the goal is typically to find the nearest number that can be represented in the format.

Unlike integers, which can represent exactly every number between the smallest and largest number, floating-point numbers are normally approximations for a number they can't really represent. The reason is that an infinite variety of real numbers exists between, say, 0 and 1, but no more than 2^{53} can be represented exactly in double precision floating point. The best we can do is getting the floating-point representation close to the actual number. Thus, IEEE 754 offers several modes of rounding to let the programmer pick the desired approximation.

Rounding sounds simple enough, but to round accurately requires the hardware to include extra bits in the calculation. In the preceding examples, we were vague on the number of bits that an intermediate representation can occupy, but clearly, if every intermediate result had to be truncated to the exact number of digits, there would be no opportunity to round. IEEE 754, therefore, always keeps two extra bits on the right during intermediate additions, called **guard** and **round**, respectively. Let's do a decimal example to illustrate their value.

Rounding with Guard Digits

Add $2.56_{ten} \times 10^0$ to $2.34_{ten} \times 10^2$, assuming that we have three significant decimal digits. Round to the nearest decimal number with three significant decimal digits, first with guard and round digits, and then without them.

First we must shift the smaller number to the right to align the exponents, so $2.56_{ten} \times 10^0$ becomes $0.0256_{ten} \times 10^2$. Since we have guard and round digits, we are able to represent the two least significant digits when we align exponents. The guard digit holds 5 and the round digit holds 6. The sum is

$$
\begin{array}{r}
2.3400_{ten} \\
+ \ 0.0256_{ten} \\
\hline
2.3656_{ten}
\end{array}
$$

Thus the sum is $2.3656_{ten} \times 10^2$. Since we have two digits to round, we want values 0 to 49 to round down and 51 to 99 to round up, with 50 being the tiebreaker. Rounding the sum up with three significant digits yields $2.37_{ten} \times 10^2$.

Doing this *without* guard and round digits drops two digits from the calculation. The new sum is then

$$
\begin{array}{r}
2.34_{ten} \\
+ \ 0.02_{ten} \\
\hline
2.36_{ten}
\end{array}
$$

The answer is $2.36_{ten} \times 10^2$, off by 1 in the last digit from the sum above.

Since the worst case for rounding would be when the actual number is halfway between two floating-point representations, accuracy in floating point is normally measured in terms of the number of bits in error in the least significant bits of the significand; the measure is called the number of **units in the last place**, or **ulp**. If a number were off by 2 in the least significant bits, it would be called off by 2 ulps. Provided there is no overflow, underflow, or invalid operation exceptions, IEEE 754 guarantees that the computer uses the number that is within one-half ulp.

units in the last place (ulp) The number of bits in error in the least significant bits of the significand between the actual number and the number that can be represented.

Elaboration: Although the example above really needed just one extra digit, multiply can need two. A binary product may have one leading 0 bit; hence, the normalizing step must shift the product one bit left. This shifts the guard digit into the least significant bit of the product, leaving the round bit to help accurately round the product.

IEEE 754 has four rounding modes: always round up (toward $+\infty$), always round down (toward $-\infty$), truncate, and round to nearest even. The final mode determines what to do if the number is exactly halfway in between. The U.S. Internal Revenue Service (IRS) always rounds 0.50 dollars up, possibly to the benefit of the IRS. A more equitable way would be to round up this case half the time and round down the other half. IEEE 754 says that if the least significant bit retained in a halfway case would be odd, add one; if it's even, truncate. This method always creates a 0 in the least significant bit in the tie-breaking case, giving the rounding mode its name. This mode is the most commonly used, and the only one that Java supports.

The goal of the extra rounding bits is to allow the computer to get the same results as if the intermediate results were calculated to infinite precision and then rounded. To support this goal and round to the nearest even, the standard has a third bit in addition to guard and round; it is set whenever there are nonzero bits to the right of the round bit. This sticky bit allows the computer to see the difference between $0.50\ldots00_{ten}$ and $0.50\ldots01_{ten}$ when rounding.

sticky bit A bit used in rounding in addition to guard and round that is set whenever there are nonzero bits to the right of the round bit.

The sticky bit may be set, for example, during addition, when the smaller number is shifted to the right. Suppose we added $5.01_{ten} \times 10^{-1}$ to $2.34_{ten} \times 10^2$ in the example above. Even with guard and round, we would be adding 0.0050 to 2.34, with a sum of 2.3450. The sticky bit would be set, since there are nonzero bits to the right. Without the sticky bit to remember whether any 1s were shifted off, we would assume the number is equal to $2.345000\ldots00$ and round to the nearest even of 2.34. With the sticky bit to remember that the number is larger than $2.345000\ldots00$, we round instead to 2.35.

Elaboration: PowerPC, SPARC64, and AMD SSE5 architectures provide a single instruction that does a multiply and add on three registers: $a = a + (b \times c)$. Obviously, this instruction allows potentially higher floating-point performance for this common operation. Equally important is that instead of performing two roundings—after the multiply and then after the add—which would happen with separate instructions, the multiply add instruction can perform a single rounding after the add. A single rounding step increases the precision of multiply add. Such operations with a single rounding are called fused multiply add. It was added to the revised IEEE 754 standard (see ⊚ **Section 3.10** on the CD).

fused multiply add A floating-point instruction that performs both a multiply and an add, but rounds only once after the add.

Summary

The *Big Picture* that follows reinforces the stored-program concept from Chapter 2; the meaning of the information cannot be determined just by looking at the bits, for the same bits can represent a variety of objects. This section shows that computer arithmetic is finite and thus can disagree with natural arithmetic. For example, the IEEE 754 standard floating-point representation

$$(-1)^S \times (1 + \text{Fraction}) \times 2^{(\text{Exponent} - \text{Bias})}$$

is almost always an approximation of the real number. Computer systems must take care to minimize this gap between computer arithmetic and arithmetic in the real world, and programmers at times need to be aware of the implications of this approximation.

Bit patterns have no inherent meaning. They may represent signed integers, unsigned integers, floating-point numbers, instructions, and so on. What is represented depends on the instruction that operates on the bits in the word.

The major difference between computer numbers and numbers in the real world is that computer numbers have limited size and hence limited precision; it's possible to calculate a number too big or too small to be represented in a word. Programmers must remember these limits and write programs accordingly.

The **BIG**
Picture

C type	Java type	Data transfers	Operations
int	int	lw, sw, lui	addu, addiu, subu, mult, div, AND, ANDi, OR, ORi, NOR, slt, slti
unsigned int	—	lw, sw, lui	addu, addiu, subu, multu, divu, AND, ANDi, OR, ORi, NOR, sltu, sltiu
char	—	lb, sb, lui	add, addi, sub, mult, div AND, ANDi, OR, ORi, NOR, slt, slti
—	char	lh, sh, lui	addu, addiu, subu, multu, divu, AND, ANDi, OR, ORi, NOR, sltu, sltiu
float	float	lwc1, swc1	add.s, sub.s, mult.s, div.s, c.eq.s, c.lt.s, c.le.s
double	double	l.d, s.d	add.d, sub.d, mult.d, div.d, c.eq.d, c.lt.d, c.le.d

In the last chapter, we presented the storage classes of the programming language C (see the *Hardware/Software Interface* section in Section 2.7). The table above shows some of the C and Java data types, the MIPS data transfer instructions, and instructions that operate on those types that appear in Chapter 2 and this chapter. Note that Java omits unsigned integers.

Hardware/ Software Interface

Suppose there was a 16-bit IEEE 754 floating-point format with five exponent bits. What would be the likely range of numbers it could represent?

Check Yourself

1. $1.0000\ 0000\ 00 \times 2^0$ to $1.1111\ 1111\ 11 \times 2^{31}, 0$

2. $\pm 1.0000\ 0000\ 0 \times 2^{-14}$ to $\pm 1.1111\ 1111\ 1 \times 2^{15}, \pm 0, \pm \infty, \text{NaN}$

3. $\pm 1.0000\ 0000\ 00 \times 2^{-14}$ to $\pm 1.1111\ 1111\ 11 \times 2^{15}, \pm 0, \pm \infty, \text{NaN}$

4. $\pm 1.0000\ 0000\ 00 \times 2^{-15}$ to $\pm 1.1111\ 1111\ 11 \times 2^{14}, \pm 0, \pm \infty, \text{NaN}$

Elaboration: To accommodate comparisons that may include NaNs, the standard includes *ordered* and *unordered* as options for compares. Hence, the full MIPS instruction set has many flavors of compares to support NaNs. (Java does not support unordered compares.)

In an attempt to squeeze every last bit of precision from a floating-point operation, the standard allows some numbers to be represented in unnormalized form. Rather than having a gap between 0 and the smallest normalized number, IEEE allows *denormalized numbers* (also known as *denorms* or *subnormals*). They have the same exponent as zero but a nonzero fraction. They allow a number to degrade in significance until it becomes 0, called *gradual underflow*. For example, the smallest positive single precision normalized number is

$$1.0000\ 0000\ 0000\ 0000\ 0000\ 000_{two} \times 2^{-126}$$

but the smallest single precision denormalized number is

$$0.0000\ 0000\ 0000\ 0000\ 0000\ 001_{two} \times 2^{-126}, \text{ or } 1.0_{two} \times 2^{-149}$$

For double precision, the denorm gap goes from 1.0×2^{-1022} to 1.0×2^{-1074}.

The possibility of an occasional unnormalized operand has given headaches to floating-point designers who are trying to build fast floating-point units. Hence, many computers cause an exception if an operand is denormalized, letting software complete the operation. Although software implementations are perfectly valid, their lower performance has lessened the popularity of denorms in portable floating-point software. Moreover, if programmers do not expect denorms, their programs may surprise them.

3.6   Parallelism and Computer Arithmetic: Associativity

Programs have typically been written first to run sequentially before being rewritten to run concurrently, so a natural question is, "do the two versions get the same answer?" If the answer is no, you presume there is a bug in the parallel version that you need to track down.

This approach assumes that computer arithmetic does not affect the results when going from sequential to parallel. That is, if you were to add a million numbers together, you would get the same results whether you used 1 processor or 1000 processors. This assumption holds for two's complement integers, even if the computation overflows. Another way to say this is that integer addition is associative.

Alas, because floating-point numbers are approximations of real numbers and because computer arithmetic has limited precision, it does not hold for floating-point numbers. That is, floating-point addition is not associative.

Testing Associativity of Floating-Point Addition

EXAMPLE

See if $x + (y + z) = (x + y) + z$. For example, suppose $x = -1.5_{ten} \times 10^{38}$, $y = 1.5_{ten} \times 10^{38}$, and $z = 1.0$, and that these are all single precision numbers.

Given the great range of numbers that can be represented in floating point, problems occur when adding two large numbers of opposite signs plus a small number, as we shall see:

$$x + (y + z) = -1.5_{ten} \times 10^{38} + (1.5_{ten} \times 10^{38} + 1.0)$$
$$= -1.5_{ten} \times 10^{38} + (1.5_{ten} \times 10^{38}) = 0.0$$
$$(x + y) + z = (-1.5_{ten} \times 10^{38} + 1.5_{ten} \times 10^{38}) + 1.0$$
$$= (0.0_{ten}) + 1.0$$
$$= 1.0$$

Therefore $x + (y + z) \neq (x + y) + z$, so floating-point addition is not associative.

Since floating-point numbers have limited precision and result in approximations of real results, $1.5_{ten} \times 10^{38}$ is so much larger than 1.0_{ten} that $1.5_{ten} \times 10^{38} + 1.0$ is still $1.5_{ten} \times 10^{38}$. That is why the sum of x, y, and z is 0.0 or 1.0, depending on the order of the floating-point additions, and hence floating-point add is *not* associative.

A more vexing version of this pitfall occurs on a parallel computer where the operating system scheduler may use a different number of processors depending on what other programs are running on a parallel computer. The unaware parallel programmer may be flummoxed by his or her program getting slightly different answers each time it is run for the same identical code and the same identical input, as the varying number of processors from each run would cause the floating-point sums to be calculated in different orders.

Given this quandary, programmers who write parallel code with floating-point numbers need to verify whether the results are credible even if they don't give the same exact answer as the sequential code. The field that deals with such issues is called numerical analysis, which is the subject of textbooks in its own right. Such concerns are one reason for the popularity of numerical libraries such as LAPACK and SCALAPAK, which have been validated in both their sequential and parallel forms.

Elaboration: A subtle version of the associativity issue occurs when two processors perform a redundant computation that is executed in different order so they get slightly different answers, although both answers are considered accurate. The bug occurs if a conditional branch compares to a floating-point number and the two processors take different branches when common sense reasoning suggests they should take the same branch.

3.7   Real Stuff: Floating Point in the x86

The x86 has regular multiply and divide instructions that operate entirely on its normal registers, unlike the reliance on separate Hi and Lo registers in MIPS. (In fact, later versions of the MIPS instruction set have added similar instructions.)

The main differences are found in floating-point instructions. The x86 floating-point architecture is different from all other computers in the world.

The x86 Floating-Point Architecture

The Intel 8087 floating-point coprocessor was announced in 1980. This architecture extended the 8086 with about 60 floating-point instructions.

Intel provided a stack architecture with its floating-point instructions: *loads* push numbers onto the stack, *operations* find operands in the two top elements of the stacks, and *stores* can pop elements off the stack. Intel supplemented this stack architecture with instructions and addressing modes that allow the architecture to have some of the benefits of a register-memory model. In addition to finding operands in the top two elements of the stack, one operand can be in memory or in one of the seven registers on-chip below the top of the stack. Thus, a complete stack instruction set is supplemented by a limited set of register-memory instructions.

This hybrid is still a restricted register-memory model, however, since loads always move data to the top of the stack while incrementing the top-of-stack pointer, and stores can only move the top of stack to memory. Intel uses the notation ST to indicate the top of stack, and ST(i) to represent the ith register below the top of stack.

Another novel feature of this architecture is that the operands are wider in the register stack than they are stored in memory, and all operations are performed at this wide internal precision. Unlike the maximum of 64 bits on MIPS, the x86 floating-point operands on the stack are 80 bits wide. Numbers are automatically converted to the internal 80-bit format on a load and converted back to the appropriate size on a store. This *double extended precision* is not supported by programming languages, although it has been useful to programmers of mathematical software.

Memory data can be 32-bit (single precision) or 64-bit (double precision) floating-point numbers. The register-memory version of these instructions will then convert the memory operand to this Intel 80-bit format before performing the operation. The data transfer instructions also will automatically convert 16- and 32-bit integers to floating point, and vice versa, for integer loads and stores.

The x86 floating-point operations can be divided into four major classes:

1. Data movement instructions, including load, load constant, and store

2. Arithmetic instructions, including add, subtract, multiply, divide, square root, and absolute value

3. Comparison, including instructions to send the result to the integer processor so that it can branch

4. Transcendental instructions, including sine, cosine, log, and exponentiation

Figure 3.20 shows some of the 60 floating-point operations. Note that we get even more combinations when we include the operand modes for these operations. Figure 3.21 shows the many options for floating-point add.

Data transfer	Arithmetic	Compare	Transcendental
F{I}LD mem/ST(i)	F{I}ADD{P} mem/ST(i)	F{I}COM{P}	FPATAN
F{I}ST{P} mem/ST(i)	F{I}SUB{R}{P} mem/ST(i)	F{I}UCOM{P}{P}	F2XM1
FLDPI	F{I}MUL{P} mem/ST(i)	FSTSW AX/mem	FCOS
FLD1	F{I}DIV{R}{P} mem/ST(i)		FPTAN
FLDZ	FSQRT		FPREM
	FABS		FSIN
	FRNDINT		FYL2X

FIGURE 3.20 The floating-point instructions of the x86. We use the curly brackets {} to show optional variations of the basic operations: {I} means there is an integer version of the instruction, {P} means this variation will pop one operand off the stack after the operation, and {R} means reverse the order of the operands in this operation. The first column shows the data transfer instructions, which move data to memory or to one of the registers below the top of the stack. The last three operations in the first column push constants on the stack: pi, 1.0, and 0.0. The second column contains the arithmetic operations described above. Note that the last three operate only on the top of stack. The third column is the compare instructions. Since there are no special floating-point branch instructions, the result of the compare must be transferred to the integer CPU via the FSTSW instruction, either into the AX register or into memory, followed by an SAHF instruction to set the condition codes. The floating-point comparison can then be tested using integer branch instructions. The final column gives the higher-level floating-point operations. Not all combinations suggested by the notation are provided. Hence, F{I}SUB{R}{P} operations represent these instructions found in the x86: FSUB, FISUB, FSUBR, FISUBR, FSUBP, FSUBRP. For the integer subtract instructions, there is no pop (FISUBP) or reverse pop (FISUBRP).

The floating-point instructions are encoded using the ESC opcode of the 8086 and the postbyte address specifier (see Figure 2.47). The memory operations reserve 2 bits to decide whether the operand is a 32- or 64-bit floating point or a 16- or 32-bit integer. Those same 2 bits are used in versions that do not access memory to decide whether the stack should be popped after the operation and whether the top of stack or a lower register should get the result.

Instruction	Operands	Comment
FADD		Both operands in stack; result replaces top of stack.
FADD	ST(i)	One source operand is *i*th register below the top of stack; result replaces the top of stack.
FADD	ST(i), ST	One source operand is the top of stack; result replaces *i*th register below the top of stack.
FADD	mem32	One source operand is a 32-bit location in memory; result replaces the top of stack.
FADD	mem64	One source operand is a 64-bit location in memory; result replaces the top of stack.

FIGURE 3.21   The variations of operands for floating-point add in the x86.

In the past, floating-point performance of the x86 family lagged far behind other computers. As a result, Intel created a more traditional floating-point architecture as part of SSE2.

The Intel Streaming SIMD Extension 2 (SSE2) Floating-Point Architecture

Chapter 2 notes that in 2001 Intel added 144 instructions to its architecture, including double precision floating-point registers and operations. It includes eight 64-bit registers that can be used for floating-point operands, giving the compiler a different target for floating-point operations than the unique stack architecture. Compilers can choose to use the eight SSE2 registers as floating-point registers like those found in other computers. AMD expanded the number to 16 registers as part of AMD64, which Intel relabeled EM64T for its use. Figure 3.22 summarizes the SSE and SSE2 instructions.

In addition to holding a single precision or double precision number in a register, Intel allows multiple floating-point operands to be packed into a single 128-bit SSE2 register: four single precision or two double precision. Thus, the 16 floating-point registers for SSE2 are actually 128 bits wide. If the operands can be arranged in memory as 128-bit aligned data, then 128-bit data transfers can load and store multiple operands per instruction. This packed floating-point format is supported by arithmetic operations that can operate simultaneously on four singles (PS) or two doubles (PD). This architecture more than doubles performance over the stack architecture.

Data transfer	Arithmetic	Compare
`MOV{A/U}{SS/PS/SD/` `PD} xmm, mem/xmm`	`ADD{SS/PS/SD/PD} xmm,` `mem/xmm`	`CMP{SS/PS/SD/` `PD}`
	`SUB{SS/PS/SD/PD} xmm,` `mem/xmm`	
`MOV {H/L} {PS/PD}` `xmm, mem/xmm`	`MUL{SS/PS/SD/PD} xmm,` `mem/xmm`	
	`DIV{SS/PS/SD/PD} xmm,` `mem/xmm`	
	`SQRT{SS/PS/SD/PD} mem/xmm`	
	`MAX {SS/PS/SD/PD} mem/xmm`	
	`MIN{SS/PS/SD/PD} mem/xmm`	

FIGURE 3.22   The SSE/SSE2 floating-point instructions of the x86. xmm means one operand is a 128-bit SSE2 register, and mem/xmm means the other operand is either in memory or it is an SSE2 register. We use the curly brackets {} to show optional variations of the basic operations: {SS} stands for Scalar Single precision floating point, or one 32-bit operand in a 128-bit register; {PS} stands for Packed Single precision floating point, or four 32-bit operands in a 128-bit register; {SD} stands for Scalar Double precision floating point, or one 64-bit operand in a 128-bit register; {PD} stands for Packed Double precision floating point, or two 64-bit operands in a 128-bit register; {A} means the 128-bit operand is aligned in memory; {U} means the 128-bit operand is unaligned in memory; {H} means move the high half of the 128-bit operand; and {L} means move the low half of the 128-bit operand.

3.8   Fallacies and Pitfalls

Thus mathematics may be defined as the subject in which we never know what we are talking about, nor whether what we are saying is true.

Bertrand Russell, *Recent Words on the Principles of Mathematics,* 1901

Arithmetic fallacies and pitfalls generally stem from the difference between the limited precision of computer arithmetic and the unlimited precision of natural arithmetic.

Fallacy: Just as a left shift instruction can replace an integer multiply by a power of 2, a right shift is the same as an integer division by a power of 2.

Recall that a binary number x, where xi means the ith bit, represents the number

$$\ldots + (x3 \times 2^3) + (x2 \times 2^2) + (x1 \times 2^1) + (x0 \times 2^0)$$

Shifting the bits of x right by n bits would seem to be the same as dividing by 2^n. And this *is* true for unsigned integers. The problem is with signed integers. For example, suppose we want to divide -5_{ten} by 4_{ten}; the quotient should be -1_{ten}. The two's complement representation of -5_{ten} is

$$1111\ 1111\ 1111\ 1111\ 1111\ 1111\ 1111\ 1011_{two}$$

According to this fallacy, shifting right by two should divide by 4_{ten} (2^2):

$$0011\ 1111\ 1111\ 1111\ 1111\ 1111\ 1111\ 1110_{two}$$

With a 0 in the sign bit, this result is clearly wrong. The value created by the shift right is actually $1{,}073{,}741{,}822_{ten}$ instead of -1_{ten}.

A solution would be to have an arithmetic right shift that extends the sign bit instead of shifting in 0s. A 2-bit arithmetic shift right of -5_{ten} produces

$$1111\ 1111\ 1111\ 1111\ 1111\ 1111\ 1111\ 1110_{two}$$

The result is -2_{ten} instead of -1_{ten}; close, but no cigar.

*Pitfall: The MIPS instruction add immediate unsigned (*addiu*) sign-extends its 16-bit immediate field.*

Despite its name, add immediate unsigned (addiu) is used to add constants to signed integers when we don't care about overflow. MIPS has no subtract immediate instruction, and negative numbers need sign extension, so the MIPS architects decided to sign-extend the immediate field.

Fallacy: Only theoretical mathematicians care about floating-point accuracy.

Newspaper headlines of November 1994 prove this statement is a fallacy (see Figure 3.23). The following is the inside story behind the headlines.

The Pentium uses a standard floating-point divide algorithm that generates multiple quotient bits per step, using the most significant bits of divisor and dividend to guess the next 2 bits of the quotient. The guess is taken from a lookup table containing -2, -1, 0, $+1$, or $+2$. The guess is multiplied by the divisor and subtracted from the remainder to generate a new remainder. Like nonrestoring division, if a previous guess gets too large a remainder, the partial remainder is adjusted in a subsequent pass.

Evidently, there were five elements of the table from the 80486 that Intel thought could never be accessed, and they optimized the PLA to return 0 instead of 2 in these situations on the Pentium. Intel was wrong: while the first 11 bits were always correct, errors would show up occasionally in bits 12 to 52, or the 4th to 15th decimal digits.

The following is a timeline of the Pentium bug morality play.

■ *July 1994:* Intel discovers the bug in the Pentium. The actual cost to fix the bug was several hundred thousand dollars. Following normal bug fix procedures, it will take months to make the change, reverify, and put the corrected chip into production. Intel planned to put good chips into production in January 1995, estimating that 3 to 5 million Pentiums would be produced with the bug.

FIGURE 3.23   A sampling of newspaper and magazine articles from November 1994, **including the** *New York Times, San Jose Mercury News, San Francisco Chronicle*, **and** *Infoworld*. The Pentium floating-point divide bug even made the "Top 10 List" of the *David Letterman Late Show* on television. Intel eventually took a $300 million write-off to replace the buggy chips.

- *September 1994:* A math professor at Lynchburg College in Virginia, Thomas Nicely, discovers the bug. After calling Intel technical support and getting no official reaction, he posts his discovery on the Internet. It quickly gained a following, and some pointed out that even small errors become big when multiplied by big numbers: the fraction of people with a rare disease times the population of Europe, for example, might lead to the wrong estimate of the number of sick people.

- *November 7, 1994: Electronic Engineering Times* puts the story on its front page, which is soon picked up by other newspapers.

- *November 22, 1994:* Intel issues a press release, calling it a "glitch." The Pentium "can make errors in the ninth digit. … Even most engineers and financial analysts require accuracy only to the fourth or fifth decimal point. Spreadsheet and word processor users need not worry. . . . There are maybe several dozen people that this would affect. So far, we've only heard from one. . . . [Only] theoretical mathematicians (with Pentium computers purchased before the summer) should be concerned." What irked many was that customers were told to describe their application to Intel, and then *Intel* would decide whether or not their application merited a new Pentium without the divide bug.

- *December 5, 1994:* Intel claims the flaw happens once in 27,000 years for the typical spreadsheet user. Intel assumes a user does 1000 divides per day and multiplies the error rate assuming floating-point numbers are random, which is one in 9 billion, and then gets 9 million days, or 27,000 years. Things begin to calm down, despite Intel neglecting to explain why a typical customer would access floating-point numbers randomly.

- *December 12, 1994:* IBM Research Division disputes Intel's calculation of the rate of errors (you can access this article by visiting *www.mkp.com/books_ catalog/cod/links.htm*). IBM claims that common spreadsheet programs, recalculating for 15 minutes a day, could produce Pentium-related errors as often as once every 24 days. IBM assumes 5000 divides per second, for 15 minutes, yielding 4.2 million divides per day, and does not assume random distribution of numbers, instead calculating the chances as one in 100 million. As a result, IBM immediately stops shipment of all IBM personal computers based on the Pentium. Things heat up again for Intel.

- *December 21, 1994:* Intel releases the following, signed by Intel's president, chief executive officer, chief operating officer, and chairman of the board:

> "We at Intel wish to sincerely apologize for our handling of the recently publicized Pentium processor flaw. The Intel Inside symbol means that your computer has a microprocessor second to none in quality and performance. Thousands of Intel employees work very hard to ensure that this is true. But no microprocessor is ever perfect. What Intel continues to believe is technically an extremely minor problem has taken on a life of its own. Although Intel firmly stands behind the quality of the current version of the Pentium processor, we recognize that many users have concerns. We want to resolve these concerns. Intel will exchange the current version of the Pentium processor for an updated version, in which this floating-point divide flaw is corrected, for any owner who requests it, free of charge anytime during the life of their computer."

Analysts estimate that this recall cost Intel $500 million, and Intel engineers did not get a Christmas bonus that year.

This story brings up a few points for everyone to ponder. How much cheaper would it have been to fix the bug in July 1994? What was the cost to repair the damage to Intel's reputation? And what is the corporate responsibility in disclosing bugs in a product so widely used and relied upon as a microprocessor?

MIPS core instructions	Name	Format	MIPS arithmetic core	Name	Format
add	add	R	multiply	mult	R
add immediate	addi	I	multiply unsigned	multu	R
add unsigned	addu	R	divide	div	R
add immediate unsigned	addiu	I	divide unsigned	divu	R
subtract	sub	R	move from Hi	mfhi	R
subtract unsigned	subu	R	move from Lo	mflo	R
AND	AND	R	move from system control (EPC)	mfc0	R
AND immediate	ANDi	I	floating-point add single	add.s	R
OR	OR	R	floating-point add double	add.d	R
OR immediate	ORi	I	floating-point subtract single	sub.s	R
NOR	NOR	R	floating-point subtract double	sub.d	R
shift left logical	sll	R	floating-point multiply single	mul.s	R
shift right logical	srl	R	floating-point multiply double	mul.d	R
load upper immediate	lui	I	floating-point divide single	div.s	R
load word	lw	I	floating-point divide double	div.d	R
store word	sw	I	load word to floating-point single	lwc1	I
load halfword unsigned	lhu	I	store word to floating-point single	swc1	I
store halfword	sh	I	load word to floating-point double	ldc1	I
load byte unsigned	lbu	I	store word to floating-point double	sdc1	I
store byte	sb	I	branch on floating-point true	bc1t	I
load linked (*atomic update*)	ll	I	branch on floating-point false	bc1f	I
store cond. (*atomic update*)	sc	I	floating-point compare single	c.x.s	R
branch on equal	beq	I	(x = eq, neq, lt, le, gt, ge)		
branch on not equal	bne	I	floating-point compare double	c.x.d	R
jump	j	J	(x = eq, neq, lt, le, gt, ge)		
jump and link	jal	J			
jump register	jr	R			
set less than	slt	R			
set less than immediate	slti	I			
set less than unsigned	sltu	R			
set less than immediate unsigned	sltiu	I			

FIGURE 3.24   The MIPS instruction set. This book concentrates on the instructions in the left column. This information is also found in columns 1 and 2 of the MIPS Reference Data Card at the front of this book.

In April 1997, another floating-point bug was revealed in the Pentium Pro and Pentium II microprocessors. When the floating-point-to-integer store instructions (fist, fistp) encounter a negative floating-point number that is too large to fit in a 16- or 32-bit word after being converted to integer, they set the wrong bit in the FPO status word (precision exception instead of invalid operation exception). To Intel's credit, this time they publicly acknowledged the bug and offered a software patch to get around it—quite a different reaction from what they did in 1994.

3.9   Concluding Remarks

A side effect of the stored-program computer is that bit patterns have no inherent meaning. The same bit pattern may represent a signed integer, unsigned integer, floating-point number, instruction, and so on. It is the instruction that operates on the word that determines its meaning.

Computer arithmetic is distinguished from paper-and-pencil arithmetic by the constraints of limited precision. This limit may result in invalid operations through calculating numbers larger or smaller than the predefined limits. Such anomalies, called "overflow" or "underflow," may result in exceptions or interrupts, emergency events similar to unplanned subroutine calls. Chapter 4 discusses exceptions in more detail.

Floating-point arithmetic has the added challenge of being an approximation of real numbers, and care needs to be taken to ensure that the computer number selected is the representation closest to the actual number. The challenges of imprecision and limited representation are part of the inspiration for the field of numerical analysis. The recent switch to parallelism will shine the searchlight on numerical analysis again, as solutions that were long considered safe on sequential computers must be reconsidered when trying to find the fastest algorithm for parallel computers that still achieves a correct result.

Over the years, computer arithmetic has become largely standardized, greatly enhancing the portability of programs. Two's complement binary integer arithmetic and IEEE 754 binary floating-point arithmetic are found in the vast majority of computers sold today. For example, every desktop computer sold since this book was first printed follows these conventions.

With the explanation of computer arithmetic in this chapter comes a description of much more of the MIPS instruction set. One point of confusion is the instructions covered in these chapters versus instructions executed by MIPS chips versus the instructions accepted by MIPS assemblers. Two figures try to make this clear.

Figure 3.24 lists the MIPS instructions covered in this chapter and Chapter 2. We call the set of instructions on the left-hand side of the figure the *MIPS core*. The instructions on the right we call the *MIPS arithmetic core*. On the left of Figure 3.25 are the instructions the MIPS processor executes that are not found in Figure 3.24. We call the full set of hardware instructions *MIPS-32*. On the right of Figure 3.25 are the instructions accepted by the assembler that are not part of MIPS-32. We call this set of instructions *Pseudo MIPS*.

Figure 3.26 gives the popularity of the MIPS instructions for SPEC CPU2006 integer and floating-point benchmarks. All instructions are listed that were responsible for at least 0.2% of the instructions executed.

Note that although programmers and compiler writers may use MIPS-32 to have a richer menu of options, MIPS core instructions dominate integer SPEC

Remaining MIPS-32	Name	Format	Pseudo MIPS	Name	Format
exclusive or (*rs* ⊕ *rt*)	xor	R	absolute value	abs	rd,rs
exclusive or immediate	xori	I	negate (*signed or underline{u}nsigned*)	neg*s*	rd,rs
shift right arithmetic	sra	R	rotate left	rol	rd,rs,rt
shift left logical variable	sllv	R	rotate right	ror	rd,rs,rt
shift right logical variable	srlv	R	multiply and don't check oflw (*signed or underline{u}ns.*)	mul*s*	rd,rs,rt
shift right arithmetic variable	srav	R	multiply and check oflw (*signed or underline{u}ns.*)	mulo*s*	rd,rs,rt
move to Hi	mthi	R	divide and check overflow	div	rd,rs,rt
move to Lo	mtlo	R	divide and don't check overflow	divu	rd,rs,rt
load halfword	lh	I	remainder (*signed or underline{u}nsigned*)	rem*s*	rd,rs,rt
load byte	lb	I	load immediate	li	rd,imm
load word left (*unaligned*)	lwl	I	load address	la	rd,addr
load word right (*unaligned*)	lwr	I	load double	ld	rd,addr
store word left (*unaligned*)	swl	I	store double	sd	rd,addr
store word right (*unaligned*)	swr	I	unaligned load word	ulw	rd,addr
load linked (*atomic update*)	ll	I	unaligned store word	usw	rd,addr
store cond. (*atomic update*)	sc	I	unaligned load halfword (*signed or underline{u}ns.*)	ulh*s*	rd,addr
move if zero	movz	R	unaligned store halfword	ush	rd,addr
move if not zero	movn	R	branch	b	Label
multiply and add (S or underline{u}ns.)	madd*s*	R	branch on equal zero	beqz	rs,L
multiply and subtract (S or underline{u}ns.)	msub*s*	I	branch on compare (*signed or underline{u}nsigned*)	bx*s*	rs,rt,L
branch on ≥ zero and link	bgezal	I	(x = lt, le, gt, ge)		
branch on < zero and link	bltzal	I	set equal	seq	rd,rs,rt
jump and link register	jalr	R	set not equal	sne	rd,rs,rt
branch compare to zero	bxz	I	set on compare (*signed or underline{u}nsigned*)	sx*s*	rd,rs,rt
branch compare to zero likely	bxzl	I	(x = lt, le, gt, ge)		
(x = lt, le, gt, ge)			load to floating point (*underline{s} or underline{d}*)	l.*f*	rd,addr
branch compare reg likely	bxl	I	store from floating point (*underline{s} or underline{d}*)	s.*f*	rd,addr
trap if compare reg	tx	R			
trap if compare immediate	txi	I			
(x = eq, neq, lt, le, gt, ge)					
return from exception	rfe	R			
system call	syscall	I			
break (*cause exception*)	break	I			
move from FP to integer	mfc1	R			
move to FP from integer	mtc1	R			
FP move (*underline{s} or underline{d}*)	mov.*f*	R			
FP move if zero (*underline{s} or underline{d}*)	movz.*f*	R			
FP move if not zero (*underline{s} or underline{d}*)	movn.*f*	R			
FP square root (*underline{s} or underline{d}*)	sqrt.*f*	R			
FP absolute value (*underline{s} or underline{d}*)	abs.*f*	R			
FP negate (*underline{s} or underline{d}*)	neg.*f*	R			
FP convert (*underline{w}, underline{s}, or underline{d}*)	cvt.*f.f*	R			
FP compare un (*underline{s} or underline{d}*)	c.xn.*f*	R			

FIGURE 3.25 Remaining MIPS-32 and Pseudo MIPS instruction sets. *f* means single (s) or double (d) precision floating-point instructions, and *s* means signed and unsigned (u) versions. MIPS-32 also has FP instructions for multiply and add/sub (madd.*f*/msub.*f*), ceiling (ceil.*f*), truncate (trunc.*f*), round (round.*f*), and reciprocal (recip.*f*). The underscore represents the letter to include to represent that datatype.

Core MIPS	Name	Integer	Fl. pt.	Arithmetic core + MIPS-32	Name	Integer	Fl. pt.
add	add	0.0%	0.0%	FP add double	add.d	0.0%	10.6%
add immediate	addi	0.0%	0.0%	FP subtract double	sub.d	0.0%	4.9%
add unsigned	addu	5.2%	3.5%	FP multiply double	mul.d	0.0%	15.0%
add immediate unsigned	addiu	9.0%	7.2%	FP divide double	div.d	0.0%	0.2%
subtract unsigned	subu	2.2%	0.6%	FP add single	add.s	0.0%	1.5%
AND	AND	0.2%	0.1%	FP subtract single	sub.s	0.0%	1.8%
AND immediate	ANDi	0.7%	0.2%	FP multiply single	mul.s	0.0%	2.4%
OR	OR	4.0%	1.2%	FP divide single	div.s	0.0%	0.2%
OR immediate	ORi	1.0%	0.2%	load word to FP double	l.d	0.0%	17.5%
NOR	NOR	0.4%	0.2%	store word to FP double	s.d	0.0%	4.9%
shift left logical	sll	4.4%	1.9%	load word to FP single	l.s	0.0%	4.2%
shift right logical	srl	1.1%	0.5%	store word to FP single	s.s	0.0%	1.1%
load upper immediate	lui	3.3%	0.5%	branch on floating-point true	bc1t	0.0%	0.2%
load word	lw	18.6%	5.8%	branch on floating-point false	bc1f	0.0%	0.2%
store word	sw	7.6%	2.0%	floating-point compare double	c.x.d	0.0%	0.6%
load byte	lbu	3.7%	0.1%	multiply	mul	0.0%	0.2%
store byte	sb	0.6%	0.0%	shift right arithmetic	sra	0.5%	0.3%
branch on equal (zero)	beq	8.6%	2.2%	load half	lhu	1.3%	0.0%
branch on not equal (zero)	bne	8.4%	1.4%	store half	sh	0.1%	0.0%
jump and link	jal	0.7%	0.2%				
jump register	jr	1.1%	0.2%				
set less than	slt	9.9%	2.3%				
set less than immediate	slti	3.1%	0.3%				
set less than unsigned	sltu	3.4%	0.8%				
set less than imm. uns.	sltiu	1.1%	0.1%				

FIGURE 3.26   The frequency of the MIPS instructions for SPEC CPU2006 integer and floating point. All instructions that accounted for at least 0.2% of the instructions are included in the table. Pseudoinstructions are converted into MIPS-32 before execution, and hence do not appear here.

CPU2006 execution, and the integer core plus arithmetic core dominate SPEC CPU2006 floating point, as the table below shows.

Instruction subset	Integer	Fl. pt.
MIPS core	98%	31%
MIPS arithmetic core	2%	66%
Remaining MIPS-32	0%	3%

For the rest of the book, we concentrate on the MIPS core instructions—the integer instruction set excluding multiply and divide—to make the explanation of computer design easier. As you can see, the MIPS core includes the most popular MIPS instructions; be assured that understanding a computer that runs the MIPS core will give you sufficient background to understand even more ambitious computers.

Historical Perspective and Further Reading

This section surveys the history of the floating point going back to von Neumann, including the surprisingly controversial IEEE standards effort, plus the rationale for the 80-bit stack architecture for floating point in the x86. See ⊙ Section 3.10.

3.11 Exercises

Contributed by Matthew Farrens, UC Davis

Gresham's Law ("Bad money drives out Good") for computers would say, "The Fast drives out the Slow even if the Fast is wrong."

W. Kahan, 1992

Never give in, never give in, never, never, never—in nothing, great or small, large or petty—never give in.

Winston Churchill, address at Harrow School, 1941

Exercise 3.1

The book shows how to add and subtract binary and decimal numbers. However, other numbering systems are also very popular when dealing with computers. The octal (base 8) numbering system is one of these. The following table shows pairs of octal numbers.

	A	B
a.	3174	0522
b.	4165	1654

3.1.1 [5] <3.2> What is the sum of A and B if they represent unsigned 12-bit octal numbers? The result should be written in octal. Show your work.

3.1.2 [5] <3.2> What is the sum of A and B if they represent signed 12-bit octal numbers stored in sign-magnitude format? The result should be written in octal. Show your work.

3.1.3 [10] <3.2> Convert A into a decimal number, assuming it is unsigned. Repeat assuming it stored in sign-magnitude format. Show your work.

The following table also shows pairs of octal numbers.

	A	B
a.	7040	0444
b.	4365	3412

3.1.4 [5] <3.2> What is A – B if they represent unsigned 12-bit octal numbers? The result should be written in octal. Show your work.

3.1.5 [5] <3.2> What is A – B if they represent signed 12-bit octal numbers stored in sign-magnitude format? The result should be written in octal. Show your work.

3.1.6 [10] <3.2> Convert A into a binary number. What makes base 8 (octal) an attractive numbering system for representing values in computers?

Exercise 3.2

Hexadecimal (base 16) is also a commonly used numbering system for representing values in computers. In fact, it has become much more popular than octal. The following table shows pairs of hexadecimal numbers.

	A	B
a.	1446	672F
b.	2460	4935

3.2.1 [5] <3.2> What is the sum of A and B if they represent unsigned 16-bit hexadecimal numbers? The result should be written in hexadecimal. Show your work.

3.2.2 [5] <3.2> What is the sum of A and B if they represent signed 16-bit hexadecimal numbers stored in sign-magnitude format? The result should be written in hexadecimal. Show your work.

3.2.3 [10] <3.2> Convert A into a decimal number, assuming it is unsigned. Repeat assuming it stored in sign-magnitude format. Show your work.

The following table also shows pairs of hexadecimal numbers.

	A	B
a.	C352	36AE
b.	5ED4	07A4

3.2.4 [5] <3.2> What is A – B if they represent unsigned 16-bit hexadecimal numbers? The result should be written in hexadecimal. Show your work.

3.2.5 [5] <3.2> What is A − B if they represent signed 16-bit hexadecimal numbers stored in sign-magnitude format? The result should be written in hexadecimal. Show your work.

3.2.6 [10] <3.2> Convert A into a binary number. What makes base 16 (hexadecimal) an attractive numbering system for representing values in computers?

Exercise 3.3

Overflow occurs when a result is too large to be represented accurately given a finite word size. Underflow occurs when a number is too small to be represented correctly—a negative result when doing unsigned arithmetic, for example. (The case when a positive result is generated by the addition of two negative integers is also referred to as underflow by many, but in this textbook, that is considered an overflow.) The following table shows pairs of decimal numbers.

	A	B
a.	216	255
b.	185	122

3.3.1 [5] <3.2> Assume A and B are unsigned 8-bit decimal integers. Calculate A − B. Is there overflow, underflow, or neither?

3.3.2 [5] <3.2> Assume A and B are signed 8-bit decimal integers stored in sign-magnitude format. Calculate A + B. Is there overflow, underflow, or neither?

3.3.3 [5] <3.2> Assume A and B are signed 8-bit decimal integers stored in sign-magnitude format. Calculate A − B. Is there overflow, underflow, or neither?

The following table also shows pairs of decimal numbers.

	A	B
a.	15	139
b.	151	214

3.3.4 [10] <3.2> Assume A and B are signed 8-bit decimal integers stored in two's complement format. Calculate A + B using saturating arithmetic. The result should be written in decimal. Show your work.

3.3.5 [10] <3.2> Assume A and B are signed 8-bit decimal integers stored in two's complement format. Calculate A − B using saturating arithmetic. The result should be written in decimal. Show your work.

3.3.6 [10] <3.2> Assume A and B are unsigned 8-bit integers. Calculate A + B using saturating arithmetic. The result should be written in decimal. Show your work.

Exercise 3.4

Let's look in more detail at multiplication. We will use the numbers in the following table.

	A	B
a.	62	12
b.	35	26

3.4.1 [20] <3.3> Using a table similar to that shown in Figure 3.7, calculate the product of the octal unsigned 6-bit integers A and B using the hardware described in Figure 3.4. You should show the contents of each register on each step.

3.4.2 [20] <3.3> Using a table similar to that shown in Figure 3.7, calculate the product of the hexadecimal unsigned 8-bit integers A and B using the hardware described in Figure 3.6. You should show the contents of each register on each step.

3.4.3 [60] <3.3> Write an MIPS assembly language program to calculate the product of unsigned integers A and B, using the approach described in Figure 3.4.

The following table shows pairs of octal numbers.

	A	B
a.	41	33
b.	60	26

3.4.4 [30] <3.3> When multiplying signed numbers, one way to get the correct answer is to convert the multiplier and multiplicand to positive numbers, save the original signs, and then adjust the final value accordingly. Using a table similar to that shown in Figure 3.7, calculate the product of A and B using the hardware described in Figure 3.4. You should show the contents of each register on each step, and include the step necessary to produce the correctly signed result. Assume A and B are stored in 6-bit sign-magnitude format.

3.4.5 [30] <3.3> When shifting a register one bit to the right, there are several ways to decide what the new entering bit should be. It can always be a zero, or always a one, or the incoming bit could be the one that is being pushed out of the right side (turning a shift into a rotate), or the value that is already in the leftmost bit can simply be retained (called an arithmetic shift right, because it preserves the sign of the number that is being shift). Using a table similar to that shown in Figure 3.7, calculate the product of the 6-bit two's complement numbers A and B using the hardware described in Figure 3.6. The right shifts should be done using an arithmetic shift right. Note that the algorithm described in the text will need to be modified slightly to make this work—in particular, things must be done differently if the multiplier is negative. You can find details by searching the web. Show the contents of each register on each step.

3.4.6 [60] <3.3> Write an MIPS assembly language program to calculate the product of the signed integers A and B. State if you are using the approach given in 3.4.4 or 3.4.5.

Exercise 3.5

For many reasons, we would like to design multipliers that require less time. Many different approaches have been taken to accomplish this goal. In the following table, A represents the bit width of an integer, and B represents the number of time units (tu) taken to perform a step of an operation.

	A (bit width)	B (time units)
a.	8	4tu
b.	64	8tu

3.5.1 [10] <3.3> Calculate the time necessary to perform a multiply using the approach given in Figures 3.4 and 3.5 if an integer is A bits wide and each step of the operation takes B time units. Assume that in step 1a an addition is always performed—either the multiplicand will be added, or a zero will be. Also assume that the registers have already been initialized (you are just counting how long it takes to do the multiplication loop itself). If this is being done in hardware, the shifts of the multiplicand and multiplier can be done simultaneously. If this is being done in software, they will have to be done one after the other. Solve for each case.

3.5.2 [10] <3.3> Calculate the time necessary to perform a multiply using the approach described in the text (31 adders stacked vertically) if an integer is A bits wide and an adder takes B time units.

3.5.3 [20] <3.3> Calculate the time necessary to perform a multiply using the approach given in Figure 3.8 if an integer is A bits wide and an adder takes B time units.

Exercise 3.6

In this exercise we will look at a couple of other ways to improve the performance of multiplication, based primarily on doing more shifts and fewer arithmetic operations. The following table shows pairs of hexadecimal numbers.

	A	B
a.	33	55
b.	8a	6d

3.6.1 [20] <3.3> As discussed in the text, one possible performance enhancement is to do a shift and add instead of an actual multiplication. Since 9×6, for example, can be written $(2 \times 2 \times 2 + 1) \times 6$, we can calculate 9×6 by shifting 6 to the left 3 times and then adding 6 to that result. Show the best way to calculate $A \times B$ using shifts and adds/subtracts. Assume that A and B are 8-bit unsigned integers.

3.6.2 [20] <3.3> Show the best way to calculate $A \times B$ using shifts and add, if A and B are 8-bit signed integers stored in sign-magnitude format.

3.6.3 [60] <3.3> Write an MIPS assembly language program that performs a multiplication on signed integers using shifts and adds, using the approach described in 3.6.1.

The following table shows further pairs of hexadecimal numbers.

	A	B
a.	F6	7F
b.	08	55

3.6.4 [30] <3.3> Booth's algorithm is another approach to reducing the number of arithmetic operations necessary to perform a multiplication. This algorithm has been around for years and involves identifying runs of ones and zeros and performing only shifts instead of shifts and adds during the runs. Find a description of the algorithm on the web and explain in detail how it works.

3.6.5 [30] <3.3> Show the step-by-step result of multiplying A and B, using Booth's algorithm. Assume A and B are 8-bit two's complement integers, stored in hexadecimal format.

3.6.6 [60] <3.3> Write an MIPS assembly language program to perform the multiplication of A and B using Booth's algorithm.

Exercise 3.7

Let's look in more detail at division. We will use the octal numbers in the following table.

	A	B
a.	74	21
b.	76	52

3.7.1 [20] <3.4> Using a table similar to that shown in Figure 3.11, calculate A divided by B using the hardware described in Figure 3.9. You should show the contents of each register on each step. Assume A and B are unsigned 6-bit integers.

3.7.2 [30] <3.4> Using a table similar to that shown in Figure 3.11, calculate A divided by B using the hardware described in Figure 3.12. You should show the contents of each register on each step. Assume A and B are unsigned 6-bit integers. This algorithm requires a slightly different approach than that shown in Figure 3.10. You will want to think hard about this, do an experiment or two, or else go to the web to figure out how to make this work correctly. (Hint: one possible solution involves using the fact that Figure 3.12 implies the remainder register can be shifted either direction.)

3.7.3 [60] <3.4> Write an MIPS assembly language program to calculate A divided by B, using the approach described in Figure 3.9. Assume A and B are unsigned 6-bit integers.

The following table shows further pairs of octal numbers.

	A	B
a.	72	07
b.	75	47

3.7.4 [30] <3.4> Using a table similar to that shown in Figure 3.11, calculate A divided by B using the hardware described in Figure 3.9. You should show the contents of each register on each step. Assume A and B are 6-bit signed integers in sign-magnitude format. Be sure to include how you are calculating the signs of the quotient and remainder.

3.7.5 [30] <3.4> Using a table similar to that shown in Figure 3.11, calculate A divided by B using the hardware described in Figure 3.12. You should show the contents of each register on each step. Assume A and B are 6-bit signed integers in sign-magnitude format. Be sure to include how you are calculating the signs of the quotient and remainder.

3.7.6 [60] <3.4> Write an MIPS assembly language program to calculate A divided by B, using the approach described in Figure 3.12. Assume A and B are signed integers.

Exercise 3.8

Figure 3.10 describes a restoring division algorithm, because when subtracting the divisor from the remainder produces a negative result, the divisor is added back to the remainder (thus restoring the value). However, there are other algorithms that have been developed that eliminate the extra addition. Many references to these algorithms are easily found on the web. We will explore these algorithms using the pairs of octal numbers in the following table.

	A	B
a.	26	05
b.	37	15

3.8.1 [30] <3.4> Using a table similar to that shown in Figure 3.11, calculate A divided by B using non-restoring division. You should show the contents of each register on each step. Assume A and B are 6-bit unsigned integers.

3.8.2 [60] <3.4> Write an MIPS assembly language program to calculate A divided by B using non-restoring division. Assume A and B are 6-bit signed (two's complement) integers.

3.8.3 [60] <3.4> How does the performance of restoring and non-restoring division compare? Demonstrate by showing the number of steps necessary to calculate A divided by B using each method. Assume A and B are 6-bit signed (sign-magnitude) integers. Writing a program to perform the restoring and non-restoring divisions is acceptable.

The following table shows further pairs of octal numbers.

	A	B
a.	27	06
b.	54	12

3.8.4 [30] <3.4> Using a table similar to that shown in Figure 3.11, calculate A divided by B using non-performing division. You should show the contents of each register on each step. Assume A and B are 6-bit unsigned integers.

3.8.5 [60] <3.4> Write an MIPS assembly language program to calculate A divided by B using nonperforming division. Assume A and B are 6-bit two's complement signed integers.

3.8.6 [60] <3.4> How does the performance of non-restoring and nonperforming division compare? Demonstrate by showing the number of steps necessary to calculate A divided by B using each method. Assume A and B are signed 6-bit integers, stored in sign-magnitude format. Writing a program to perform the nonperforming and non-restoring divisions is acceptable.

Exercise 3.9

Division is so time-consuming and difficult that the CRAY T3E Fortran Optimization guide states, "The best strategy for division is to avoid it whenever possible." This exercise looks at the following different strategies for performing divisions.

a.	non-restoring division
b.	division by reciprocal multiplication

3.9.1 [30] <3.4> Describe the algorithm in detail.

3.9.2 [60] <3.4> Use a flow chart (or a high-level code snippet) to describe how the algorithm works.

3.9.3 [60] <3.4> Write an MIPS assembly language program to perform division using the algorithm.

Exercise 3.10

In a Von Neumann architecture, groups of bits have no intrinsic meanings by themselves. What a bit pattern represents depends entirely on how it is used. The following table shows bit patterns expressed in hexademical notation.

a.	0x0C000000
b.	0xC4630000

3.10.1 [5] <3.5> What decimal number does the bit pattern represent if it is a two's complement integer? An unsigned integer?

3.10.2 [10] <3.5> If this bit pattern is placed into the Instruction Register, what MIPS instruction will be executed?

3.10.3 [10] <3.5> What decimal number does the bit pattern represent if it is a floating point number? Use the IEEE 754 standard.

The following table shows decimal numbers.

a.	63.25
b.	146987.40625

3.10.4 [10] <3.5> Write down the binary representation of the decimal number, assuming the IEEE 754 single precision format.

3.10.5 [10] <3.5> Write down the binary representation of the decimal number, assuming the IEEE 754 double precision format.

3.10.6 [10] <3.5> Write down the binary representation of the decimal number assuming it was stored using the single precision IBM format (base 16, instead of base 2, with 7 bits of exponent).

Exercise 3.11

In the IEEE 754 floating point standard the exponent is stored in "bias" (also known as "Excess-N") format. This approach was selected because we want an all-zero pattern to be as close to zero as possible. Because of the use of a hidden 1, if we were to represent the exponent in two's complement format an all-zero pattern would actually be the number 1! (Remember, anything raised to the zeroth power is 1, so $1.0^0 = 1$.) There are many other aspects of the IEEE 754 standard that exist in order to help hardware floating point units work more quickly. However, in many older machines floating point calculations were handled in software, and therefore other formats were used. The following table shows decimal numbers.

a.	-1.5625×10^{-1}
b.	9.356875×10^{2}

3.11.1 [20] <3.5> Write down the binary bit pattern assuming a format similar to that employed by the DEC PDP-8 (the leftmost 12 bits are the exponent stored as a two's complement number, and the rightmost 24 bits are the mantissa stored as a two's complement number). No hidden 1 is used. Comment on how the range and accuracy of this 36-bit pattern compares to the single and double precision IEEE 754 standards.

3.11.2 [20] <3.5> NVIDIA has a "half" format, which is similar to IEEE 754 except that it is only 16 bits wide. The leftmost bit is still the sign bit, the exponent is 5 bits wide and stored in excess-56 format, and the mantissa is 10 bits long.

A hidden 1 is assumed. Write down the bit pattern assuming a modified version of this format, which uses an excess-16 format to store the exponent. Comment on how the range and accuracy of this 16-bit floating point format compares to the single precision IEEE 754 standard.

3.11.3 [20] <3.5> The Hewlett-Packard 2114, 2115, and 2116 used a format with the leftmost 16 bits being the mantissa stored in two's complement format, followed by another 16-bit field which had the leftmost 8 bits as an extension of the mantissa (making the mantissa 24 bits long), and the rightmost 8 bits representing the exponent. However, in an interesting twist, the exponent was stored in sign-magnitude format with the sign bit on the far right! Write down the bit pattern assuming this format. No hidden 1 is used. Comment on how the range and accuracy of this 32-bit pattern compares to the single precision IEEE 754 standard.

The following table shows pairs of decimal numbers.

	A	B
a.	2.6125×10^1	$4.150390625 \times 10^{-1}$
b.	-4.484375×10^1	1.3953125×10^1

3.11.4 [20] <3.5> Calculate the sum of A and B by hand, assuming A and B are stored in the modified 16-bit NVIDIA format described in 3.11.2. Assume 1 guard, 1 round bit, and 1 sticky bit, and round to the nearest even. Show all the steps.

3.11.5 [60] <3.5> Write an MIPS assembly language program to calculate the sum of A and B, assuming they are stored in the modified 16-bit NVIDIA format described in 3.11.2. Assume 1 guard, 1 round bit, and 1 sticky bit, and round to the nearest even.

3.11.6 [60] <3.5> Write an MIPS assembly language program to calculate the sum of A and B, assuming they are stored using the format described in 3.11.1. Now modify the program to calculate the sum assuming the format described in 3.11.3. Which format is easier for a programmer to deal with? How do they each compare to the IEEE 754 format? (Do not worry about sticky bits for this question.)

Exercise 3.12

Floating point multiplication is even more complicated and challenging than floating point addition, and both pale in comparison to floating point division. The following table shows pairs of decimal numbers.

	A	B
a.	-8.0546875×10^0	$-1.79931640625 \times 10^{-1}$
b.	8.59375×10^{-2}	8.125×10^{-1}

3.12.1 [30] <3.5> Calculate the product of A and B by hand, assuming A and B are stored in the modified 16-bit NVIDIA format described in 3.11.2. Assume 1 guard, 1 round bit, and 1 sticky bit, and round to the nearest even. Show all the steps; however, as is done in the example in the text, you can do the multiplication in human-readable format instead of using the techniques described in Exercises 3.4 through 3.6. Indicate if there is overflow or underflow. Write your answer as a 16-bit pattern, and also as a decimal number. How accurate is your result? How does it compare to the number you get if you do the multiplication on a calculator?

3.12.2 [60] <3.5> Write an MIPS assembly language program to calculate the product of A and B, assuming they are stored in IEEE 754 format. Indicate if there is overflow or underflow. (Remember, IEEE 754 assumes 1 guard, 1 round bit, and 1 sticky bit, and rounds to the nearest even.)

3.12.3 [60] <3.5> Write an MIPS assembly language program to calculate the product of A and B, assuming they are stored using the format described in 3.11.1. Now modify the program to calculate the sum assuming the format described in 3.11.3. Which format is easier for a programmer to deal with? How do they each compare to the IEEE 754 format? (Do not worry about sticky bits for this question.)

The following table shows further pairs of decimal numbers.

	A	B
a.	8.625×10^1	-4.875×10^0
b.	1.84375×10^0	1.3203125×10^0

3.12.4 [30] <3.5> Calculate by hand A divided by B. Show all the steps necessary to achieve your answer. Assume there is a guard, a round bit, and a sticky bit, and use them if necessary. Write the final answer in both the 16-bit floating point format described in 3.11.2 and in decimal and compare the decimal result to that which you get if you use a calculator.

The Livermore Loops are a set of floating point–intensive kernels taken from scientific programs run at Lawrence Livermore Laboratory. The following table identifies individual kernels from the set.

a.	Livermore Loop 3
b.	Livermore Loop 9

3.12.5 [60] <3.5> Write the loop in MIPS assembly language.

3.12.6 [60] <3.5> Describe in detail one technique for performing floating point division in a digital computer. Be sure to include references to the sources you used.

Exercise 3.13

Operations performed on fixed-point integers behave the way one expects—the commutative, associative, and distributive laws all hold. This is not always the case when working with floating point numbers, however. Let's first look at the associative law. The following table shows sets of decimal numbers.

	A	B	C
a.	3.984375×10^{-1}	3.4375×10^{-1}	1.771×10^3
b.	3.96875×10^0	8.46875×10^0	2.1921875×10^1

3.13.1 [20] <3.2, 3.5, 3.6> Calculate (A + B) + C by hand, assuming A, B, and C are stored in the modified 16-bit NVIDIA format described in 3.11.2 (and also described in the text). Assume 1 guard, 1 round bit, and 1 sticky bit, and round to the nearest even. Show all the steps, and write your answer in both the 16-bit floating point format and in decimal.

3.13.2 [20] <3.2, 3.5, 3.6> Calculate A + (B + C) by hand, assuming A, B, and C are stored in the modified 16-bit NVIDIA format described in 3.11.2 (and also described in the text). Assume 1 guard, 1 round bit, and 1 sticky bit, and round to the nearest even. Show all the steps, and write your answer in both the 16-bit floating point format and in decimal.

3.13.3 [10] <3.2, 3.5, 3.6> Based on your answers to 3.13.1 and 3.13.2, does (A + B) + C = A + (B + C)?

The following table shows further sets of decimal numbers.

	A	B	C
a.	$3.41796875 \ 10^{-3}$	$6.34765625 \times 10^{-3}$	1.05625×10^2
b.	1.140625×10^2	-9.135×10^2	9.84375×10^{-1}

3.13.4 [30] <3.3, 3.5, 3.6> Calculate (A × B) × C by hand, assuming A, B, and C are stored in the modified 16-bit NVIDIA format described in 3.11.2 (and also described in the text). Assume 1 guard, 1 round bit, and 1 sticky bit, and round to the nearest even. Show all the steps, and write your answer in both the 16-bit floating point format and in decimal.

3.13.5 [30] <3.3, 3.5, 3.6> Calculate A × (B × C) by hand, assuming A, B, and C are stored in the modified 16-bit NVIDIA format described in 3.11.2 (and also described in the text). Assume 1 guard, 1 round bit, and 1 sticky bit, and round to the nearest even. Show all the steps, and write your answer in both the 16-bit floating point format and in decimal.

3.13.6 [10] <3.3, 3.5, 3.6> Based on your answers to 3.13.4 and 3.13.5, does (A × B) × C = A × (B × C)?

Exercise 3.14

The Associative law is not the only one that does not always hold in dealing with floating point numbers. There are other oddities that occur as well. The following table shows sets of decimal numbers.

	A	B	C
a.	1.666015625×10^0	1.9760×10^4	-1.9744×10^4
b.	3.48×10^2	$6.34765625 \times 10^{-2}$	$-4.052734375 \times 10^{-2}$

3.14.1 [30] <3.2, 3.3, 3.5, 3.6> Calculate A × (B + C) by hand, assuming A, B, and C are stored in the modified 16-bit NVIDIA format described in 3.11.2 (and also described in the text). Assume 1 guard, 1 round bit, and 1 sticky bit, and round to the nearest even. Show all the steps, and write your answer in both the 16-bit floating point format and in decimal.

3.14.2 [30] <3.2, 3.3, 3.5, 3.6> Calculate (A × B) + (A × C) by hand, assuming A, B, and C are stored in the modified 16-bit NVIDIA format described in 3.11.2 (and also described in the text). Assume 1 guard, 1 round bit, and 1 sticky bit, and round to the nearest even. Show all the steps, and write your answer in both the 16-bit floating point format and in decimal.

3.14.3 [10] <3.2, 3.3, 3.5, 3.6> Based on your answers to 3.14.1. and 3.14.2, does (A × B) + (A × C) = A × (B + C)?

The following table shows pairs, each consisting of a fraction and an integer.

	A	B
a.	−1/4	4
b.	1/10	10

3.14.4 [10] <3.5> Using the IEEE 754 floating point format, write down the bit pattern that would represent A. Can you represent A exactly?

3.14.5 [10] <3.2, 3.3, 3.5, 3.6> What do you get if you add A to itself B times? What is A × B? Are they the same? What should they be?

3.14.6 [60] <3.2, 3.3, 3.4, 3.5, 3.6> What do you get if you take the square root of B and then multiply that value by itself? What should you get? Do for both single and double precision floating point numbers. (Write a program to do these calculations.)

Exercise 3.15

Binary numbers are used in the mantissa field, but they do not have to be. IBM used base 16 numbers, for example, in some of their floating point formats. There are other approaches that are possible as well, each with their own particular advantages and disadvantages. The following table shows fractions to be represented in various floating point formats.

a.	1/3
b.	1/10

3.15.1 [10] <3.5, 3.6> Write down the bit pattern in the mantissa assuming a floating point format that uses binary numbers in the mantissa (essentially what you have been doing in this chapter). Assume there are 24 bits, and you do not need to normalize. Is this representation exact?

3.15.2 [10] <3.5, 3.6> Write down the bit pattern in the mantissa assuming a floating point format that uses Binary Coded Decimal (base 10) numbers in the mantissa instead of base 2. Assume there are 24 bits, and you do not need to normalize. Is this representation exact?

3.15.3 [10] <3.5, 3.6> Write down the bit pattern assuming that we are using base 15 numbers in the mantissa instead of base 2. (Base 16 numbers use the symbols 0–9 and A–F. Base 15 numbers would use 0–9 and A–E.) Assume there are 24 bits, and you do not need to normalize. Is this representation exact?

3.15.4 [20] <3.5, 3.6> Write down the bit pattern assuming that we are using base 30 numbers in the mantissa instead of base 2. (Base 16 numbers use the symbols 0–9 and A–F. Base 30 numbers would use 0–9 and A–T.) Assume there are 20 bits, and you do not need to normalize. Is this representation exact? Do you see any advantage to using this approach?

§3.2, page 229: 2.
§3.5, page 269: 3.

**Answers to
Check Yourself**

The Processor

*In a major matter,
no details are small.*

French Proverb

The Five Classic Components of a Computer

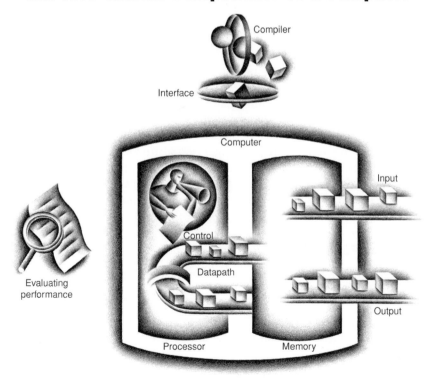

4.1   Introduction

Chapter 1 explains that the performance of a computer is determined by three key factors: instruction count, clock cycle time, and clock cycles per instruction (CPI). Chapter 2 explains that the compiler and the instruction set architecture determine the instruction count required for a given program. However, the implementation of the processor determines both the clock cycle time and the number of clock cycles per instruction. In this chapter, we construct the datapath and control unit for two different implementations of the MIPS instruction set.

This chapter contains an explanation of the principles and techniques used in implementing a processor, starting with a highly abstract and simplified overview in this section. It is followed by a section that builds up a datapath and constructs a simple version of a processor sufficient to implement an instruction set like MIPS. The bulk of the chapter covers a more realistic pipelined MIPS implementation, followed by a section that develops the concepts necessary to implement more complex instruction sets, like the x86.

For the reader interested in understanding the high-level interpretation of instructions and its impact on program performance, this initial section and Section 4.5 present the basic concepts of pipelining. Recent trends are covered in Section 4.10, and Section 4.11 describes the recent AMD Opteron X4 (Barcelona) microprocessor. These sections provide enough background to understand the pipeline concepts at a high level.

For the reader interested in understanding the processor and its performance in more depth, Sections 4.3, 4.4, and 4.6 will be useful. Those interested in learning how to build a processor should also cover 4.2, 4.7, 4.8, and 4.9. For readers with an interest in modern hardware design, ⊙ Section 4.12 on the CD describes how hardware design languages and CAD tools are used to implement hardware, and then how to use a hardware design language to describe a pipelined implementation. It also gives several more illustrations of how pipelining hardware executes.

A Basic MIPS Implementation

We will be examining an implementation that includes a subset of the core MIPS instruction set:

- The memory-reference instructions load word (lw) and store word (sw)
- The arithmetic-logical instructions add, sub, AND, OR, and slt
- The instructions branch equal (beq) and jump (j), which we add last

This subset does not include all the integer instructions (for example, shift, multiply, and divide are missing), nor does it include any floating-point instructions. However, the key principles used in creating a datapath and designing the control are illustrated. The implementation of the remaining instructions is similar.

In examining the implementation, we will have the opportunity to see how the instruction set architecture determines many aspects of the implementation, and how the choice of various implementation strategies affects the clock rate and CPI for the computer. Many of the key design principles introduced in Chapter 1 can be illustrated by looking at the implementation, such as the guidelines *Make the common case fast* and *Simplicity favors regularity*. In addition, most concepts used to implement the MIPS subset in this chapter are the same basic ideas that are used to construct a broad spectrum of computers, from high-performance servers to general-purpose microprocessors to embedded processors.

An Overview of the Implementation

In Chapter 2, we looked at the core MIPS instructions, including the integer arithmetic-logical instructions, the memory-reference instructions, and the branch instructions. Much of what needs to be done to implement these instructions is the same, independent of the exact class of instruction. For every instruction, the first two steps are identical:

1. Send the program counter (PC) to the memory that contains the code and fetch the instruction from that memory.

2. Read one or two registers, using fields of the instruction to select the registers to read. For the load word instruction, we need to read only one register, but most other instructions require that we read two registers.

After these two steps, the actions required to complete the instruction depend on the instruction class. Fortunately, for each of the three instruction classes (memory-reference, arithmetic-logical, and branches), the actions are largely the same, independent of the exact instruction. The simplicity and regularity of the MIPS instruction set simplifies the implementation by making the execution of many of the instruction classes similar.

For example, all instruction classes, except jump, use the arithmetic-logical unit (ALU) after reading the registers. The memory-reference instructions use the ALU for an address calculation, the arithmetic-logical instructions for the operation execution, and branches for comparison. After using the ALU, the actions required to complete various instruction classes differ. A memory-reference instruction will need to access the memory either to read data for a load or write data for a store. An arithmetic-logical or load instruction must write the data from the ALU or memory back into a register. Lastly, for a branch instruction, we may need to change the next instruction address based on the comparison; otherwise, the PC should be incremented by 4 to get the address of the next instruction.

Figure 4.1 shows the high-level view of a MIPS implementation, focusing on the various functional units and their interconnection. Although this figure shows most of the flow of data through the processor, it omits two important aspects of instruction execution.

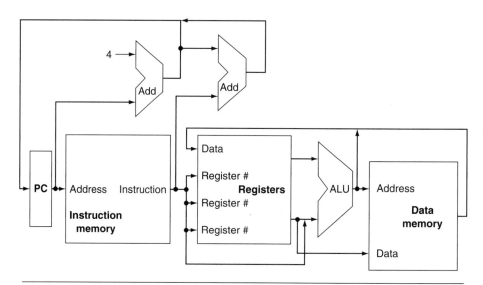

FIGURE 4.1 An abstract view of the implementation of the MIPS subset showing the major functional units and the major connections between them. All instructions start by using the program counter to supply the instruction address to the instruction memory. After the instruction is fetched, the register operands used by an instruction are specified by fields of that instruction. Once the register operands have been fetched, they can be operated on to compute a memory address (for a load or store), to compute an arithmetic result (for an integer arithmetic-logical instruction), or a compare (for a branch). If the instruction is an arithmetic-logical instruction, the result from the ALU must be written to a register. If the operation is a load or store, the ALU result is used as an address to either store a value from the registers or load a value from memory into the registers. The result from the ALU or memory is written back into the register file. Branches require the use of the ALU output to determine the next instruction address, which comes either from the ALU (where the PC and branch offset are summed) or from an adder that increments the current PC by 4. The thick lines interconnecting the functional units represent buses, which consist of multiple signals. The arrows are used to guide the reader in knowing how information flows. Since signal lines may cross, we explicitly show when crossing lines are connected by the presence of a dot where the lines cross.

First, in several places, Figure 4.1 shows data going to a particular unit as coming from two different sources. For example, the value written into the PC can come from one of two adders, the data written into the register file can come from either the ALU or the data memory, and the second input to the ALU can come from a register or the immediate field of the instruction. In practice, these data lines cannot simply be wired together; we must add a logic element that chooses from among the multiple sources and steers one of those sources to its destination. This selection is commonly done with a device called a *multiplexor*, although this device might better be called a *data selector*. **Appendix C** describes the multiplexor, which selects from among several inputs based on the setting of its control lines. The control lines are set based primarily on information taken from the instruction being executed.

The second omission in Figure 4.1 is that several of the units must be controlled depending on the type of instruction. For example, the data memory must read on a load and write on a store. The register file must be written on a load and an arithmetic-logical instruction. And, of course, the ALU must perform one of several operations, as we saw in Chapter 2. (**Appendix C** describes the detailed design of the ALU.) Like the multiplexors, these operations are directed by control lines that are set on the basis of various fields in the instruction.

Figure 4.2 shows the datapath of Figure 4.1 with the three required multiplexors added, as well as control lines for the major functional units. A *control unit*, which has the instruction as an input, is used to determine how to set the control lines for the functional units and two of the multiplexors. The third multiplexor, which determines whether PC + 4 or the branch destination address is written into the PC, is set based on the Zero output of the ALU, which is used to perform the comparison of a beq instruction. The regularity and simplicity of the MIPS instruction set means that a simple decoding process can be used to determine how to set the control lines.

In the remainder of the chapter, we refine this view to fill in the details, which requires that we add further functional units, increase the number of connections between units, and, of course, enhance a control unit to control what actions are taken for different instruction classes. Sections 4.3 and 4.4 describe a simple implementation that uses a single long clock cycle for every instruction and follows the general form of Figures 4.1 and 4.2. In this first design, every instruction begins execution on one clock edge and completes execution on the next clock edge.

While easier to understand, this approach is not practical, since the clock cycle must be stretched to accommodate the longest instruction. After designing the control for this simple computer, we will look at pipelined implementation with all its complexities, including exceptions.

How many of the five classic components of a computer—shown on page 299—do Figures 4.1 and 4.2 include?   **Check Yourself**

4.2 Logic Design Conventions

To discuss the design of a computer, we must decide how the logic implementing the computer will operate and how the computer is clocked. This section reviews a few key ideas in digital logic that we will use extensively in this chapter. If

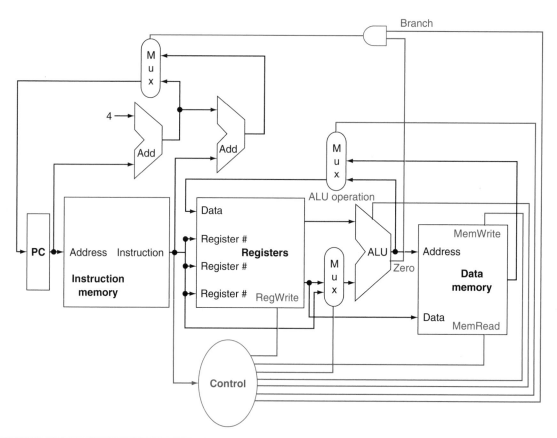

FIGURE 4.2   The basic implementation of the MIPS subset, including the necessary multiplexors and control lines.
The top multiplexor ("Mux") controls what value replaces the PC (PC + 4 or the branch destination address); the multiplexor is controlled
by the gate that "ANDs" together the Zero output of the ALU and a control signal that indicates that the instruction is a branch. The middle
multiplexor, whose output returns to the register file, is used to steer the output of the ALU (in the case of an arithmetic-logical instruction)
or the output of the data memory (in the case of a load) for writing into the register file. Finally, the bottommost multiplexor is used to
determine whether the second ALU input is from the registers (for an arithmetic-logical instruction OR a branch) or from the offset field of
the instruction (for a load or store). The added control lines are straightforward and determine the operation performed at the ALU, whether
the data memory should read or write, and whether the registers should perform a write operation. The control lines are shown in color to
make them easier to see.

combinational element
An operational element,
such as an AND gate or
an ALU.

you have little or no background in digital logic, you will find it helpful to read
⊙ **Appendix C** before continuing.

The datapath elements in the MIPS implementation consist of two different
types of logic elements: elements that operate on data values and elements that
contain state. The elements that operate on data values are all **combinational**,
which means that their outputs depend only on the current inputs. Given the same
input, a combinational element always produces the same output. The ALU shown
in Figure 4.1 and discussed in ⊙ **Appendix C** is an example of a combinational

element. Given a set of inputs, it always produces the same output because it has no internal storage.

Other elements in the design are not combinational, but instead contain *state*. An element contains state if it has some internal storage. We call these elements **state elements** because, if we pulled the power plug on the computer, we could restart it by loading the state elements with the values they contained before we pulled the plug. Furthermore, if we saved and restored the state elements, it would be as if the computer had never lost power. Thus, these state elements completely characterize the computer. In Figure 4.1, the instruction and data memories, as well as the registers, are all examples of state elements.

state element A memory element, such as a register or a memory.

A state element has at least two inputs and one output. The required inputs are the data value to be written into the element and the clock, which determines when the data value is written. The output from a state element provides the value that was written in an earlier clock cycle. For example, one of the logically simplest state elements is a D-type flip-flop (see ⊙ **Appendix C**), which has exactly these two inputs (a value and a clock) and one output. In addition to flip-flops, our MIPS implementation also uses two other types of state elements: memories and registers, both of which appear in Figure 4.1. The clock is used to determine when the state element should be written; a state element can be read at any time.

Logic components that contain state are also called *sequential*, because their outputs depend on both their inputs and the contents of the internal state. For example, the output from the functional unit representing the registers depends both on the register numbers supplied and on what was written into the registers previously. The operation of both the combinational and sequential elements and their construction are discussed in more detail in ⊙ **Appendix C**.

We will use the word **asserted** to indicate a signal that is logically high and *assert* to specify that a signal should be driven logically high, and *deassert* or **deasserted** to represent logically low.

asserted The signal is logically high or true.

deasserted The signal is logically low or false.

Clocking Methodology

A **clocking methodology** defines when signals can be read and when they can be written. It is important to specify the timing of reads and writes, because if a signal is written at the same time it is read, the value of the read could correspond to the old value, the newly written value, or even some mix of the two! Computer designs cannot tolerate such unpredictability. A clocking methodology is designed to ensure predictability.

clocking methodology The approach used to determine when data is valid and stable relative to the clock.

For simplicity, we will assume an **edge-triggered clocking** methodology. An edge-triggered clocking methodology means that any values stored in a sequential logic element are updated only on a clock edge. Because only state elements can store a data value, any collection of combinational logic must have its inputs come from a set of state elements and its outputs written into a set of state elements.

edge-triggered clocking A clocking scheme in which all state changes occur on a clock edge.

The inputs are values that were written in a previous clock cycle, while the outputs are values that can be used in a following clock cycle.

Figure 4.3 shows the two state elements surrounding a block of combinational logic, which operates in a single clock cycle: all signals must propagate from state element 1, through the combinational logic, and to state element 2 in the time of one clock cycle. The time necessary for the signals to reach state element 2 defines the length of the clock cycle.

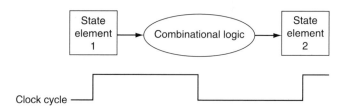

FIGURE 4.3   Combinational logic, state elements, and the clock are closely related. In a synchronous digital system, the clock determines when elements with state will write values into internal storage. Any inputs to a state element must reach a stable value (that is, have reached a value from which they will not change until after the clock edge) before the active clock edge causes the state to be updated. All state elements in this chapter, including memory, are assumed to be edge-triggered.

control signal A signal used for multiplexor selection or for directing the operation of a functional unit; contrasts with a **data signal**, which contains information that is operated on by a functional unit.

For simplicity, we do not show a write **control signal** when a state element is written on every active clock edge. In contrast, if a state element is not updated on every clock, then an explicit write control signal is required. Both the clock signal and the write control signal are inputs, and the state element is changed only when the write control signal is asserted and a clock edge occurs.

An edge-triggered methodology allows us to read the contents of a register, send the value through some combinational logic, and write that register in the same clock cycle. Figure 4.4 gives a generic example. It doesn't matter whether we assume that all writes take place on the rising clock edge or on the falling clock edge, since the inputs to the combinational logic block cannot change except on

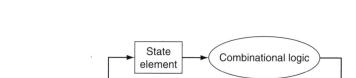

FIGURE 4.4   An edge-triggered methodology allows a state element to be read and written in the same clock cycle without creating a race that could lead to indeterminate data values. Of course, the clock cycle still must be long enough so that the input values are stable when the active clock edge occurs. Feedback cannot occur within one clock cycle because of the edge-triggered update of the state element. If feedback were possible, this design could not work properly. Our designs in this chapter and the next rely on the edge-triggered timing methodology and on structures like the one shown in this figure.

the chosen clock edge. With an edge-triggered timing methodology, there is *no* feedback within a single clock cycle, and the logic in Figure 4.4 works correctly. In ◉ Appendix C, we briefly discuss additional timing constraints (such as setup and hold times) as well as other timing methodologies.

For the 32-bit MIPS architecture, nearly all of these state and logic elements will have inputs and outputs that are 32 bits wide, since that is the width of most of the data handled by the processor. We will make it clear whenever a unit has an input or output that is other than 32 bits in width. The figures will indicate *buses*, which are signals wider than 1 bit, with thicker lines. At times, we will want to combine several buses to form a wider bus; for example, we may want to obtain a 32-bit bus by combining two 16-bit buses. In such cases, labels on the bus lines will make it clear that we are concatenating buses to form a wider bus. Arrows are also added to help clarify the direction of the flow of data between elements. Finally, color indicates a control signal as opposed to a signal that carries data; this distinction will become clearer as we proceed through this chapter.

True or false: Because the register file is both read and written on the same clock cycle, any MIPS datapath using edge-triggered writes must have more than one copy of the register file.

Check Yourself

Elaboration: There is also a 64-bit version of the MIPS architecture, and, naturally enough, most paths in its implementation would be 64 bits wide. Also, we use the terms assert and deassert because at times 1 represents logically high and at times it can represent logically low.

4.3   Building a Datapath

A reasonable way to start a datapath design is to examine the major components required to execute each class of MIPS instructions. Let's start by looking at which **datapath elements** each instruction needs. When we show the datapath elements, we will also show their control signals.

Figure 4.5a shows the first element we need: a memory unit to store the instructions of a program and supply instructions given an address. Figure 4.5b also shows the **program counter (PC)**, which as we saw in Chapter 2 is a register that holds the address of the current instruction. Lastly, we will need an adder to increment the PC to the address of the next instruction. This adder, which is combinational, can be built from the ALU described in detail in ◉ Appendix C simply by wiring the control lines so that the control always specifies an add

datapath element A unit used to operate on or hold data within a processor. In the MIPS implementation, the datapath elements include the instruction and data memories, the register file, the ALU, and adders.

program counter (PC) The register containing the address of the instruction in the program being executed.

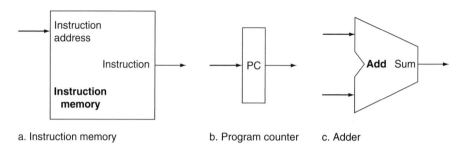

a. Instruction memory   b. Program counter   c. Adder

FIGURE 4.5 Two state elements are needed to store and access instructions, and an adder is needed to compute the next instruction address. The state elements are the instruction memory and the program counter. The instruction memory need only provide read access because the datapath does not write instructions. Since the instruction memory only reads, we treat it as combinational logic: the output at any time reflects the contents of the location specified by the address input, and no read control signal is needed. (We will need to write the instruction memory when we load the program; this is not hard to add, and we ignore it for simplicity.) The program counter is a 32-bit register that is written at the end of every clock cycle and thus does not need a write control signal. The adder is an ALU wired to always add its two 32-bit inputs and place the sum on its output.

operation. We will draw such an ALU with the label *Add*, as in Figure 4.5, to indicate that it has been permanently made an adder and cannot perform the other ALU functions.

To execute any instruction, we must start by fetching the instruction from memory. To prepare for executing the next instruction, we must also increment the program counter so that it points at the next instruction, 4 bytes later. Figure 4.6 shows how to combine the three elements from Figure 4.5 to form a datapath that fetches instructions and increments the PC to obtain the address of the next sequential instruction.

Now let's consider the R-format instructions (see Figure 2.20 on page 136). They all read two registers, perform an ALU operation on the contents of the registers, and write the result to a register. We call these instructions either *R-type instructions* or *arithmetic-logical instructions* (since they perform arithmetic or logical operations). This instruction class includes add, sub, AND, OR, and slt, which were introduced in Chapter 2. Recall that a typical instance of such an instruction is add $t1,$t2,$t3, which reads $t2 and $t3 and writes $t1.

The processor's 32 general-purpose registers are stored in a structure called a **register file**. A register file is a collection of registers in which any register can be read or written by specifying the number of the register in the file. The register file contains the register state of the computer. In addition, we will need an ALU to operate on the values read from the registers.

R-format instructions have three register operands, so we will need to read two data words from the register file and write one data word into the register file for each instruction. For each data word to be read from the registers, we need an

register file A state element that consists of a set of registers that can be read and written by supplying a register number to be accessed.

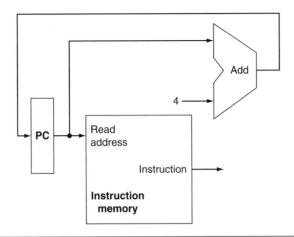

FIGURE 4.6 A portion of the datapath used for fetching instructions and incrementing the program counter. The fetched instruction is used by other parts of the datapath.

input to the register file that specifies the register number to be read and an output from the register file that will carry the value that has been read from the registers. To write a data word, we will need two inputs: one to specify the *register number* to be written and one to supply the *data* to be written into the register. The register file always outputs the contents of whatever register numbers are on the Read register inputs. Writes, however, are controlled by the write control signal, which must be asserted for a write to occur at the clock edge. Figure 4.7a shows the result; we need a total of four inputs (three for register numbers and one for data) and two outputs (both for data). The register number inputs are 5 bits wide to specify one of 32 registers ($32 = 2^5$), whereas the data input and two data output buses are each 32 bits wide.

Figure 4.7b shows the ALU, which takes two 32-bit inputs and produces a 32-bit result, as well as a 1-bit signal if the result is 0. The 4-bit control signal of the ALU is described in detail in ⊙ Appendix C; we will review the ALU control shortly when we need to know how to set it.

Next, consider the MIPS load word and store word instructions, which have the general form `lw $t1,offset_value($t2)` or `sw $t1,offset_value($t2)`. These instructions compute a memory address by adding the base register, which is `$t2`, to the 16-bit signed offset field contained in the instruction. If the instruction is a store, the value to be stored must also be read from the register file where it resides in `$t1`. If the instruction is a load, the value read from memory must be written into the register file in the specified register, which is `$t1`. Thus, we will need both the register file and the ALU from Figure 4.7.

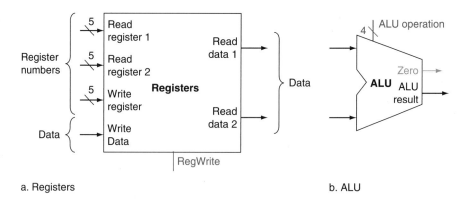

a. Registers

b. ALU

FIGURE 4.7 The two elements needed to implement R-format ALU operations are the register file and the ALU. The register file contains all the registers and has two read ports and one write port. The design of multiported register files is discussed in Section C.8 of ⊙ **Appendix C**. The register file always outputs the contents of the registers corresponding to the Read register inputs on the outputs; no other control inputs are needed. In contrast, a register write must be explicitly indicated by asserting the write control signal. Remember that writes are edge-triggered, so that all the write inputs (i.e., the value to be written, the register number, and the write control signal) must be valid at the clock edge. Since writes to the register file are edge-triggered, our design can legally read and write the same register within a clock cycle: the read will get the value written in an earlier clock cycle, while the value written will be available to a read in a subsequent clock cycle. The inputs carrying the register number to the register file are all 5 bits wide, whereas the lines carrying data values are 32 bits wide. The operation to be performed by the ALU is controlled with the ALU operation signal, which will be 4 bits wide, using the ALU designed in ⊙ **Appendix C**. We will use the Zero detection output of the ALU shortly to implement branches. The overflow output will not be needed until Section 4.9, when we discuss exceptions; we omit it until then.

sign-extend To increase the size of a data item by replicating the high-order sign bit of the original data item in the high-order bits of the larger, destination data item.

branch target address The address specified in a branch, which becomes the new program counter (PC) if the branch is taken. In the MIPS architecture the branch target is given by the sum of the offset field of the instruction and the address of the instruction following the branch.

In addition, we will need a unit to **sign-extend** the 16-bit offset field in the instruction to a 32-bit signed value, and a data memory unit to read from or write to. The data memory must be written on store instructions; hence, data memory has read and write control signals, an address input, and an input for the data to be written into memory. Figure 4.8 shows these two elements.

The beq instruction has three operands, two registers that are compared for equality, and a 16-bit offset used to compute the **branch target address** relative to the branch instruction address. Its form is beq $t1,$t2,offset. To implement this instruction, we must compute the branch target address by adding the sign-extended offset field of the instruction to the PC. There are two details in the definition of branch instructions (see Chapter 2) to which we must pay attention:

■ The instruction set architecture specifies that the base for the branch address calculation is the address of the instruction following the branch. Since we compute PC + 4 (the address of the next instruction) in the instruction fetch datapath, it is easy to use this value as the base for computing the branch target address.

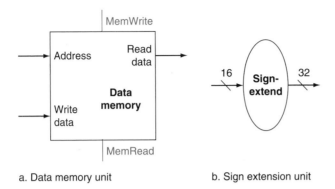

a. Data memory unit   b. Sign extension unit

FIGURE 4.8 The two units needed to implement loads and stores, in addition to the register file and ALU of Figure 4.7, are the data memory unit and the sign extension unit. The memory unit is a state element with inputs for the address and the write data, and a single output for the read result. There are separate read and write controls, although only one of these may be asserted on any given clock. The memory unit needs a read signal, since, unlike the register file, reading the value of an invalid address can cause problems, as we will see in Chapter 5. The sign extension unit has a 16-bit input that is sign-extended into a 32-bit result appearing on the output (see Chapter 2). We assume the data memory is edge-triggered for writes. Standard memory chips actually have a write enable signal that is used for writes. Although the write enable is not edge-triggered, our edge-triggered design could easily be adapted to work with real memory chips. See Section C.8 of ⊙ Appendix C for further discussion of how real memory chips work.

■ The architecture also states that the offset field is shifted left 2 bits so that it is a word offset; this shift increases the effective range of the offset field by a factor of 4.

To deal with the latter complication, we will need to shift the offset field by 2.

As well as computing the branch target address, we must also determine whether the next instruction is the instruction that follows sequentially or the instruction at the branch target address. When the condition is true (i.e., the operands are equal), the branch target address becomes the new PC, and we say that the **branch** is **taken**. If the operands are not equal, the incremented PC should replace the current PC (just as for any other normal instruction); in this case, we say that the **branch** is **not taken**.

Thus, the branch datapath must do two operations: compute the branch target address and compare the register contents. (Branches also affect the instruction fetch portion of the datapath, as we will deal with shortly.) Figure 4.9 shows the structure of the datapath segment that handles branches. To compute the branch target address, the branch datapath includes a sign extension unit, from Figure 4.8 and an adder. To perform the compare, we need to use the register file shown in Figure 4.7a to supply the two register operands (although we will not need to write into the register file). In addition, the comparison can be done using the ALU we designed in ⊙ Appendix C. Since that ALU provides an output signal that indicates whether the result was 0, we can send the two register operands to the ALU with the

branch taken A branch where the branch condition is satisfied and the program counter (PC) becomes the branch target. All unconditional branches are taken branches.

branch not taken or **(untaken branch)** A branch where the branch condition is false and the program counter (PC) becomes the address of the instruction that sequentially follows the branch.

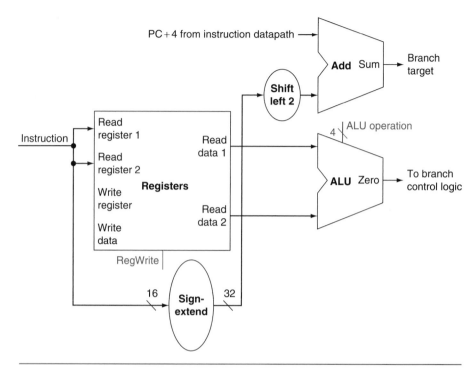

FIGURE 4.9   The datapath for a branch uses the ALU to evaluate the branch condition and a separate adder to compute the branch target as the sum of the incremented PC and the sign-extended, lower 16 bits of the instruction (the branch displacement), shifted left 2 bits. The unit labeled *Shift left 2* is simply a routing of the signals between input and output that adds 00_{two} to the low-order end of the sign-extended offset field; no actual shift hardware is needed, since the amount of the "shift" is constant. Since we know that the offset was sign-extended from 16 bits, the shift will throw away only "sign bits." Control logic is used to decide whether the incremented PC or branch target should replace the PC, based on the Zero output of the ALU.

control set to do a subtract. If the Zero signal out of the ALU unit is asserted, we know that the two values are equal. Although the Zero output always signals if the result is 0, we will be using it only to implement the equal test of branches. Later, we will show exactly how to connect the control signals of the ALU for use in the datapath.

The jump instruction operates by replacing the lower 28 bits of the PC with the lower 26 bits of the instruction shifted left by 2 bits. This shift is accomplished simply by concatenating 00 to the jump offset, as described in Chapter 2.

Elaboration: In the MIPS instruction set, branches are delayed, meaning that the instruction immediately following the branch is always executed, *independent* of whether the branch condition is true or false. When the condition is false, the execution looks like a normal branch. When the condition is true, a delayed branch first executes the instruction immediately following the branch in sequential instruction order before jumping to the specified branch target address. The motivation for delayed branches arises from how pipelining affects branches (see Section 4.8). For simplicity, we generally ignore delayed branches in this chapter and implement a nondelayed beq instruction.

delayed branch A type of branch where the instruction immediately following the branch is always executed, independent of whether the branch condition is true or false.

Creating a Single Datapath

Now that we have examined the datapath components needed for the individual instruction classes, we can combine them into a single datapath and add the control to complete the implementation. This simplest datapath will attempt to execute all instructions in one clock cycle. This means that no datapath resource can be used more than once per instruction, so any element needed more than once must be duplicated. We therefore need a memory for instructions separate from one for data. Although some of the functional units will need to be duplicated, many of the elements can be shared by different instruction flows.

To share a datapath element between two different instruction classes, we may need to allow multiple connections to the input of an element, using a multiplexor and control signal to select among the multiple inputs.

Building a Datapath

The operations of arithmetic-logical (or R-type) instructions and the memory instructions datapath are quite similar. The key differences are the following:

EXAMPLE

- The arithmetic-logical instructions use the ALU, with the inputs coming from the two registers. The memory instructions can also use the ALU to do the address calculation, although the second input is the sign-extended 16-bit offset field from the instruction.

- The value stored into a destination register comes from the ALU (for an R-type instruction) or the memory (for a load).

Show how to build a datapath for the operational portion of the memory-reference and arithmetic-logical instructions that uses a single register file and a single ALU to handle both types of instructions, adding any necessary multiplexors.

ANSWER

To create a datapath with only a single register file and a single ALU, we must support two different sources for the second ALU input, as well as two different sources for the data stored into the register file. Thus, one multiplexor is placed at the ALU input and another at the data input to the register file. Figure 4.10 shows the operational portion of the combined datapath.

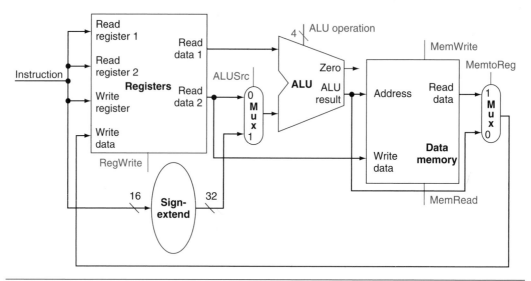

FIGURE 4.10   The datapath for the memory instructions and the R-type instructions. This example shows how a single datapath can be assembled from the pieces in Figures 4.7 and 4.8 by adding multiplexors. Two multiplexors are needed, as described in the example.

Now we can combine all the pieces to make a simple datapath for the MIPS architecture by adding the datapath for instruction fetch (Figure 4.6), the datapath from R-type and memory instructions (Figure 4.10), and the datapath for branches (Figure 4.9). Figure 4.11 shows the datapath we obtain by composing the separate pieces. The branch instruction uses the main ALU for comparison of the register operands, so we must keep the adder from Figure 4.9 for computing the branch target address. An additional multiplexor is required to select either the sequentially following instruction address (PC + 4) or the branch target address to be written into the PC.

Now that we have completed this simple datapath, we can add the control unit. The control unit must be able to take inputs and generate a write signal for each state element, the selector control for each multiplexor, and the ALU control. The

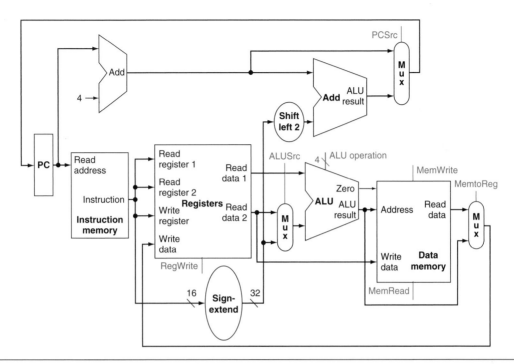

FIGURE 4.11   The simple datapath for the MIPS architecture combines the elements required by different instruction classes. The components come from Figures 4.6, 4.9, and 4.10. This datapath can execute the basic instructions (load-store word, ALU operations, and branches) in a single clock cycle. An additional multiplexor is needed to integrate branches. The support for jumps will be added later.

ALU control is different in a number of ways, and it will be useful to design it first before we design the rest of the control unit.

Check Yourself

I. Which of the following is correct for a load instruction? Refer to Figure 4.10.

    a. MemtoReg should be set to cause the data from memory to be sent to the register file.

    b. MemtoReg should be set to cause the correct register destination to be sent to the register file.

    c. We do not care about the setting of MemtoReg for loads.

II. The single-cycle datapath conceptually described in this section *must* have separate instruction and data memories, because

    a. the formats of data and instructions are different in MIPS, and hence different memories are needed.

b. having separate memories is less expensive.

c. the processor operates in one cycle and cannot use a single-ported memory for two different accesses within that cycle

4.4   A Simple Implementation Scheme

In this section, we look at what might be thought of as the simplest possible implementation of our MIPS subset. We build this simple implementation using the datapath of the last section and adding a simple control function. This simple implementation covers load word (`lw`), store word (`sw`), branch equal (`beq`), and the arithmetic-logical instructions `add`, `sub`, `AND`, `OR`, and `set on less than`. We will later enhance the design to include a jump instruction (`j`).

The ALU Control

The MIPS ALU in **Appendix C** defines the 6 following combinations of four control inputs:

ALU control lines	Function
0000	AND
0001	OR
0010	add
0110	subtract
0111	set on less than
1100	NOR

Depending on the instruction class, the ALU will need to perform one of these first five functions. (NOR is needed for other parts of the MIPS instruction set not found in the subset we are implementing.) For load word and store word instructions, we use the ALU to compute the memory address by addition. For the R-type instructions, the ALU needs to perform one of the five actions (AND, OR, subtract, add, or set on less than), depending on the value of the 6-bit funct (or function) field in the low-order bits of the instruction (see Chapter 2). For branch equal, the ALU must perform a subtraction.

We can generate the 4-bit ALU control input using a small control unit that has as inputs the function field of the instruction and a 2-bit control field, which we call ALUOp. ALUOp indicates whether the operation to be performed should be add (00) for loads and stores, subtract (01) for `beq`, or determined by the operation encoded in the funct field (10). The output of the ALU control unit is a 4-bit signal that directly controls the ALU by generating one of the 4-bit combinations shown previously.

In Figure 4.12, we show how to set the ALU control inputs based on the 2-bit ALUOp control and the 6-bit function code. Later in this chapter we will see how the ALUOp bits are generated from the main control unit.

Instruction opcode	ALUOp	Instruction operation	Funct field	Desired ALU action	ALU control input
LW	00	load word	XXXXXX	add	0010
SW	00	store word	XXXXXX	add	0010
Branch equal	01	branch equal	XXXXXX	subtract	0110
R-type	10	add	100000	add	0010
R-type	10	subtract	100010	subtract	0110
R-type	10	AND	100100	AND	0000
R-type	10	OR	100101	OR	0001
R-type	10	set on less than	101010	set on less than	0111

FIGURE 4.12 How the ALU control bits are set depends on the ALUOp control bits and the different function codes for the R-type instruction. The opcode, listed in the first column, determines the setting of the ALUOp bits. All the encodings are shown in binary. Notice that when the ALUOp code is 00 or 01, the desired ALU action does not depend on the function code field; in this case, we say that we "don't care" about the value of the function code, and the funct field is shown as XXXXXX. When the ALUOp value is 10, then the function code is used to set the ALU control input. See ⊙ Appendix C.

This style of using multiple levels of decoding—that is, the main control unit generates the ALUOp bits, which then are used as input to the ALU control that generates the actual signals to control the ALU unit—is a common implementation technique. Using multiple levels of control can reduce the size of the main control unit. Using several smaller control units may also potentially increase the speed of the control unit. Such optimizations are important, since the speed of the control unit is often critical to clock cycle time.

There are several different ways to implement the mapping from the 2-bit ALUOp field and the 6-bit funct field to the four ALU operation control bits. Because only a small number of the 64 possible values of the function field are of interest and the function field is used only when the ALUOp bits equal 10, we can use a small piece of logic that recognizes the subset of possible values and causes the correct setting of the ALU control bits.

As a step in designing this logic, it is useful to create a truth table for the interesting combinations of the function code field and the ALUOp bits, as we've done in Figure 4.13; this **truth table** shows how the 4-bit ALU control is set depending on these two input fields. Since the full truth table is very large ($2^8 = 256$ entries) and we don't care about the value of the ALU control for many of these input

truth table From logic, a representation of a logical operation by listing all the values of the inputs and then in each case showing what the resulting outputs should be.

ALUOp		Funct field						Operation
ALUOp1	ALUOp0	F5	F4	F3	F2	F1	F0	
0	0	X	X	X	X	X	X	0010
0	1	X	X	X	X	X	X	0110
1	0	X	X	0	0	0	0	0010
1	X	X	X	0	0	1	0	0110
1	0	X	X	0	1	0	0	0000
1	0	X	X	0	1	0	1	0001
1	X	X	X	1	0	1	0	0111

FIGURE 4.13 The truth table for the 4 ALU control bits (called Operation). The inputs are the ALUOp and function code field. Only the entries for which the ALU control is asserted are shown. Some don't-care entries have been added. For example, the ALUOp does not use the encoding 11, so the truth table can contain entries 1X and X1, rather than 10 and 01. Note that when the function field is used, the first 2 bits (F5 and F4) of these instructions are always 10, so they are don't-care terms and are replaced with XX in the truth table.

combinations, we show only the truth table entries for which the ALU control must have a specific value. Throughout this chapter, we will use this practice of showing only the truth table entries for outputs that must be asserted and not showing those that are all deasserted or don't care. (This practice has a disadvantage, which we discuss in Section D.2 of ⊙ **Appendix D**.)

don't-care term An element of a logical function in which the output does not depend on the values of all the inputs. Don't-care terms may be specified in different ways.

Because in many instances we do not care about the values of some of the **inputs**, and because we wish to keep the tables compact, we also include **don't-care terms**. A don't-care term in this truth table (represented by an X in an input column) indicates that the output does not depend on the value of the input corresponding to that column. For example, when the ALUOp bits are 00, as in the first row of Figure 4.13, we always set the ALU control to 0010, independent of the function code. In this case, then, the function code inputs will be don't cares in this line of the truth table. Later, we will see examples of another type of don't-care term. If you are unfamiliar with the concept of don't-care terms, see ⊙ **Appendix C** for more information.

Once the truth table has been constructed, it can be optimized and then turned into gates. This process is completely mechanical. Thus, rather than show the final steps here, we describe the process and the result in Section D.2 of ⊙ **Appendix D**.

Designing the Main Control Unit

Now that we have described how to design an ALU that uses the function code and a 2-bit signal as its control inputs, we can return to looking at the rest of the control. To start this process, let's identify the fields of an instruction and the control lines that are needed for the datapath we constructed in Figure 4.11. To understand how to connect the fields of an instruction to the datapath, it is useful to review the formats of the three instruction classes: the R-type, branch, and load-store instructions. Figure 4.14 shows these formats.

Field	0	rs	rt	rd	shamt	funct
Bit positions	31:26	25:21	20:16	15:11	10:6	5:0

a. R-type instruction

Field	35 or 43	rs	rt	address
Bit positions	31:26	25:21	20:16	15:0

b. Load or store instruction

Field	4	rs	rt	address
Bit positions	31:26	25:21	20:16	15:0

c. Branch instruction

FIGURE 4.14 The three instruction classes (R-type, load and store, and branch) use two different instruction formats. The jump instructions use another format, which we will discuss shortly. (a) Instruction format for R-format instructions, which all have an opcode of 0. These instructions have three register operands: rs, rt, and rd. Fields rs and rt are sources, and rd is the destination. The ALU function is in the funct field and is decoded by the ALU control design in the previous section. The R-type instructions that we implement are add, sub, AND, OR, and slt. The shamt field is used only for shifts; we will ignore it in this chapter. (b) Instruction format for load (opcode = 35_{ten}) and store (opcode = 43_{ten}) instructions. The register rs is the base register that is added to the 16-bit address field to form the memory address. For loads, rt is the destination register for the loaded value. For stores, rt is the source register whose value should be stored into memory. (c) Instruction format for branch equal (opcode = 4). The registers rs and rt are the source registers that are compared for equality. The 16-bit address field is sign-extended, shifted, and added to the PC+4 to compute the branch target address.

There are several major observations about this instruction format that we will rely on:

- The op field, also called the **opcode**, is always contained in bits 31:26. We will refer to this field as Op[5:0].

  > **opcode** The field that denotes the operation and format of an instruction.

- The two registers to be read are always specified by the rs and rt fields, at positions 25:21 and 20:16. This is true for the R-type instructions, branch equal, and store.

- The base register for load and store instructions is always in bit positions 25:21 (rs).

- The 16-bit offset for branch equal, load, and store is always in positions 15:0.

- The destination register is in one of two places. For a load it is in bit positions 20:16 (rt), while for an R-type instruction it is in bit positions 15:11 (rd). Thus, we will need to add a multiplexor to select which field of the instruction is used to indicate the register number to be written.

The first design principle from Chapter 2—*simplicity favors regularity*—pays off here in specifying control.

Using this information, we can add the instruction labels and extra multiplexor (for the Write register number input of the register file) to the simple datapath. Figure 4.15 shows these additions plus the ALU control block, the write signals for state elements, the read signal for the data memory, and the control signals for the multiplexors. Since all the multiplexors have two inputs, they each require a single control line.

Figure 4.15 shows seven single-bit control lines plus the 2-bit ALUOp control signal. We have already defined how the ALUOp control signal works, and it is useful to define what the seven other control signals do informally before we determine how to set these control signals during instruction execution. Figure 4.16 describes the function of these seven control lines.

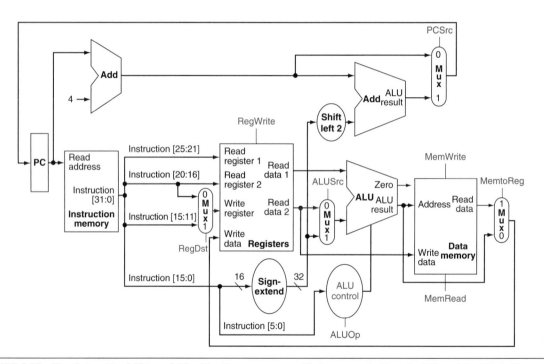

FIGURE 4.15   The datapath of Figure 4.11 with all necessary multiplexors and all control lines identified. The control lines are shown in color. The ALU control block has also been added. The PC does not require a write control, since it is written once at the end of every clock cycle; the branch control logic determines whether it is written with the incremented PC or the branch target address.

Signal name	Effect when deasserted	Effect when asserted
RegDst	The register destination number for the Write register comes from the rt field (bits 20:16).	The register destination number for the Write register comes from the rd field (bits 15:11).
RegWrite	None.	The register on the Write register input is written with the value on the Write data input.
ALUSrc	The second ALU operand comes from the second register file output (Read data 2).	The second ALU operand is the sign-extended, lower 16 bits of the instruction.
PCSrc	The PC is replaced by the output of the adder that computes the value of PC + 4.	The PC is replaced by the output of the adder that computes the branch target.
MemRead	None.	Data memory contents designated by the address input are put on the Read data output.
MemWrite	None.	Data memory contents designated by the address input are replaced by the value on the Write data input.
MemtoReg	The value fed to the register Write data input comes from the ALU.	The value fed to the register Write data input comes from the data memory.

FIGURE 4.16   The effect of each of the seven control signals. When the 1-bit control to a two-way multiplexor is asserted, the multiplexor selects the input corresponding to 1. Otherwise, if the control is deasserted, the multiplexor selects the 0 input. Remember that the state elements all have the clock as an implicit input and that the clock is used in controlling writes. Gating the clock externally to a state element can create timing problems. (See ⊙ Appendix C for further discussion of this problem.)

Now that we have looked at the function of each of the control signals, we can look at how to set them. The control unit can set all but one of the control signals based solely on the opcode field of the instruction. The PCSrc control line is the exception. That control line should be asserted if the instruction is branch on equal (a decision that the control unit can make) *and* the Zero output of the ALU, which is used for equality comparison, is asserted. To generate the PCSrc signal, we will need to AND together a signal from the control unit, which we call *Branch*, with the Zero signal out of the ALU.

These nine control signals (seven from Figure 4.16 and two for ALUOp) can now be set on the basis of six input signals to the control unit, which are the opcode bits 31 to 26. Figure 4.17 shows the datapath with the control unit and the control signals.

Before we try to write a set of equations or a truth table for the control unit, it will be useful to try to define the control function informally. Because the setting of the control lines depends only on the opcode, we define whether each control signal should be 0, 1, or don't care (X) for each of the opcode values. Figure 4.18 defines how the control signals should be set for each opcode; this information follows directly from Figures 4.12, 4.16, and 4.17.

Operation of the Datapath

With the information contained in Figures 4.16 and 4.18, we can design the control unit logic, but before we do that, let's look at how each instruction uses the

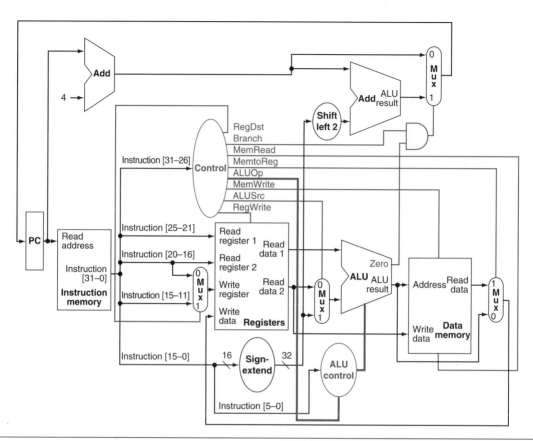

FIGURE 4.17   The simple datapath with the control unit. The input to the control unit is the 6-bit opcode field from the instruction. The outputs of the control unit consist of three 1-bit signals that are used to control multiplexors (RegDst, ALUSrc, and MemtoReg), three signals for controlling reads and writes in the register file and data memory (RegWrite, MemRead, and MemWrite), a 1-bit signal used in determining whether to possibly branch (Branch), and a 2-bit control signal for the ALU (ALUOp). An AND gate is used to combine the branch control signal and the Zero output from the ALU; the AND gate output controls the selection of the next PC. Notice that PCSrc is now a derived signal, rather than one coming directly from the control unit. Thus, we drop the signal name in subsequent figures.

datapath. In the next few figures, we show the flow of three different instruction classes through the datapath. The asserted control signals and active datapath elements are highlighted in each of these. Note that a multiplexor whose control is 0 has a definite action, even if its control line is not highlighted. Multiple-bit control signals are highlighted if any constituent signal is asserted.

Instruction	RegDst	ALUSrc	Memto-Reg	Reg-Write	Mem-Read	Mem-Write	Branch	ALUOp1	ALUOp0
R-format	1	0	0	1	0	0	0	1	0
lw	0	1	1	1	1	0	0	0	0
sw	X	1	X	0	0	1	0	0	0
beq	X	0	X	0	0	0	1	0	1

FIGURE 4.18 The setting of the control lines is completely determined by the opcode fields of the instruction. The first row of the table corresponds to the R-format instructions (add, sub, AND, OR, and slt). For all these instructions, the source register fields are rs and rt, and the destination register field is rd; this defines how the signals ALUSrc and RegDst are set. Furthermore, an R-type instruction writes a register (RegWrite = 1), but neither reads nor writes data memory. When the Branch control signal is 0, the PC is unconditionally replaced with PC + 4; otherwise, the PC is replaced by the branch target if the Zero output of the ALU is also high. The ALUOp field for R-type instructions is set to 10 to indicate that the ALU control should be generated from the funct field. The second and third rows of this table give the control signal settings for lw and sw. These ALUSrc and ALUOp fields are set to perform the address calculation. The MemRead and MemWrite are set to perform the memory access. Finally, RegDst and RegWrite are set for a load to cause the result to be stored into the rt register. The branch instruction is similar to an R-format operation, since it sends the rs and rt registers to the ALU. The ALUOp field for branch is set for a subtract (ALU control = 01), which is used to test for equality. Notice that the MemtoReg field is irrelevant when the RegWrite signal is 0: since the register is not being written, the value of the data on the register data write port is not used. Thus, the entry MemtoReg in the last two rows of the table is replaced with X for don't care. Don't cares can also be added to RegDst when RegWrite is 0. This type of don't care must be added by the designer, since it depends on knowledge of how the datapath works.

Figure 4.19 shows the operation of the datapath for an R-type instruction, such as add $t1,$t2,$t3. Although everything occurs in one clock cycle, we can think of four steps to execute the instruction; these steps are ordered by the flow of information:

1. The instruction is fetched, and the PC is incremented.

2. Two registers, $t2 and $t3, are read from the register file; also, the main control unit computes the setting of the control lines during this step.

3. The ALU operates on the data read from the register file, using the function code (bits 5:0, which is the funct field, of the instruction) to generate the ALU function.

4. The result from the ALU is written into the register file using bits 15:11 of the instruction to select the destination register ($t1).

Similarly, we can illustrate the execution of a load word, such as

    lw $t1, offset($t2)

in a style similar to Figure 4.19. Figure 4.20 shows the active functional units and asserted control lines for a load. We can think of a load instruction as operating in five steps (similar to the R-type executed in four):

1. An instruction is fetched from the instruction memory, and the PC is incremented.

2. A register ($t2) value is read from the register file.

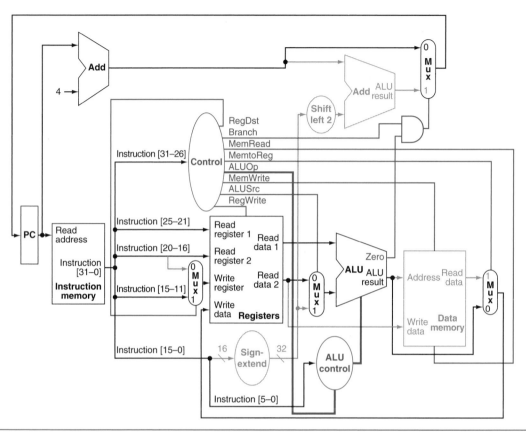

FIGURE 4.19 The datapath in operation for an R-type instruction, such as add $t1,$t2,$t3**.** The control lines, datapath units, and connections that are active are highlighted.

3. The ALU computes the sum of the value read from the register file and the sign-extended, lower 16 bits of the instruction (offset).

4. The sum from the ALU is used as the address for the data memory.

5. The data from the memory unit is written into the register file; the register destination is given by bits 20:16 of the instruction ($t1).

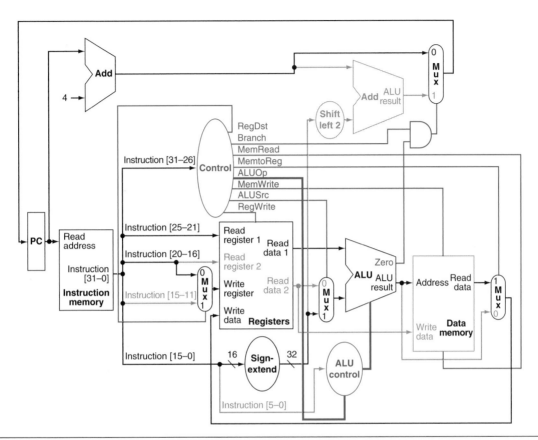

FIGURE 4.20   The datapath in operation for a load instruction. The control lines, datapath units, and connections that are active are highlighted. A store instruction would operate very similarly. The main difference would be that the memory control would indicate a write rather than a read, the second register value read would be used for the data to store, and the operation of writing the data memory value to the register file would not occur.

Finally, we can show the operation of the branch-on-equal instruction, such as beq $t1,$t2,offset, in the same fashion. It operates much like an R-format instruction, but the ALU output is used to determine whether the PC is written with PC + 4 or the branch target address. Figure 4.21 shows the four steps in execution:

1. An instruction is fetched from the instruction memory, and the PC is incremented.

2. Two registers, $t1 and $t2, are read from the register file.

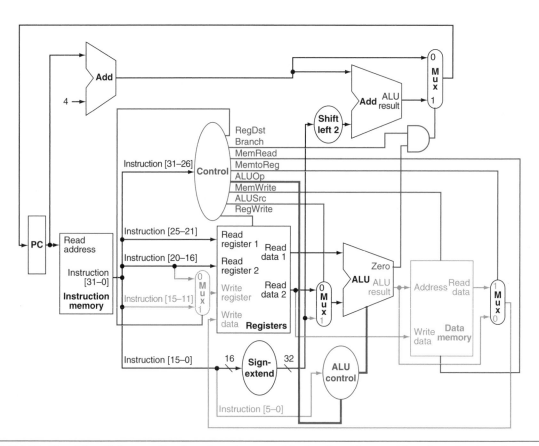

FIGURE 4.21 The datapath in operation for a branch-on-equal instruction. The control lines, datapath units, and connections that are active are highlighted. After using the register file and ALU to perform the compare, the Zero output is used to select the next program counter from between the two candidates.

3. The ALU performs a subtract on the data values read from the register file. The value of PC + 4 is added to the sign-extended, lower 16 bits of the instruction (offset) shifted left by two; the result is the branch target address.

4. The Zero result from the ALU is used to decide which adder result to store into the PC.

Finalizing Control

Now that we have seen how the instructions operate in steps, let's continue with the control implementation. The control function can be precisely defined using the contents of Figure 4.18. The outputs are the control lines, and the input is the 6-bit opcode field, Op [5:0]. Thus, we can create a truth table for each of the outputs based on the binary encoding of the opcodes.

Figure 4.22 shows the logic in the control unit as one large truth table that combines all the outputs and that uses the opcode bits as inputs. It completely specifies the control function, and we can implement it directly in gates in an automated fashion. We show this final step in Section D.2 in ◉ **Appendix D**.

Now that we have a **single-cycle implementation** of most of the MIPS core instruction set, let's add the jump instruction to show how the basic datapath and control can be extended to handle other instructions in the instruction set.

single-cycle implementation Also called single clock cycle implementation. An implementation in which an instruction is executed in one clock cycle.

Input or output	Signal name	R-format	lw	sw	beq
Inputs	Op5	0	1	1	0
	Op4	0	0	0	0
	Op3	0	0	1	0
	Op2	0	0	0	1
	Op1	0	1	1	0
	Op0	0	1	1	0
Outputs	RegDst	1	0	X	X
	ALUSrc	0	1	1	0
	MemtoReg	0	1	X	X
	RegWrite	1	1	0	0
	MemRead	0	1	0	0
	MemWrite	0	0	1	0
	Branch	0	0	0	1
	ALUOp1	1	0	0	0
	ALUOp0	0	0	0	1

FIGURE 4.22   The control function for the simple single-cycle implementation is completely specified by this truth table. The top half of the table gives the combinations of input signals that correspond to the four opcodes, one per column, that determine the control output settings. (Remember that Op [5:0] corresponds to bits 31:26 of the instruction, which is the op field.) The bottom portion of the table gives the outputs for each of the four opcodes. Thus, the output RegWrite is asserted for two different combinations of the inputs. If we consider only the four opcodes shown in this table, then we can simplify the truth table by using don't cares in the input portion. For example, we can detect an R-format instruction with the expression $\overline{Op5} \cdot \overline{Op2}$, since this is sufficient to distinguish the R-format instructions from lw, sw, and beq. We do not take advantage of this simplification, since the rest of the MIPS opcodes are used in a full implementation.

EXAMPLE

Implementing Jumps

Figure 4.17 shows the implementation of many of the instructions we looked at in Chapter 2. One class of instructions missing is that of the jump instruction. Extend the datapath and control of Figure 4.17 to include the jump instruction. Describe how to set any new control lines.

ANSWER

The jump instruction, shown in Figure 4.23, looks somewhat like a branch instruction but computes the target PC differently and is not conditional. Like a branch, the low-order 2 bits of a jump address are always 00_{two}. The next lower 26 bits of this 32-bit address come from the 26-bit immediate field in the instruction. The upper 4 bits of the address that should replace the PC come from the PC of the jump instruction plus 4. Thus, we can implement a jump by storing into the PC the concatenation of

- the upper 4 bits of the current PC + 4 (these are bits 31:28 of the sequentially following instruction address)
- the 26-bit immediate field of the jump instruction
- the bits 00_{two}

Figure 4.24 shows the addition of the control for jump added to Figure 4.17. An additional multiplexor is used to select the source for the new PC value, which is either the incremented PC (PC + 4), the branch target PC, or the jump target PC. One additional control signal is needed for the additional multiplexor. This control signal, called *Jump*, is asserted only when the instruction is a jump—that is, when the opcode is 2.

Field	000010	address
Bit positions	31:26	25:0

FIGURE 4.23 Instruction format for the jump instruction (opcode = 2). The destination address for a jump instruction is formed by concatenating the upper 4 bits of the current PC + 4 to the 26-bit address field in the jump instruction and adding 00 as the 2 low-order bits.

Why a Single-Cycle Implementation Is Not Used Today

Although the single-cycle design will work correctly, it would not be used in modern designs because it is inefficient. To see why this is so, notice that the clock cycle must have the same length for every instruction in this single-cycle design. Of course,

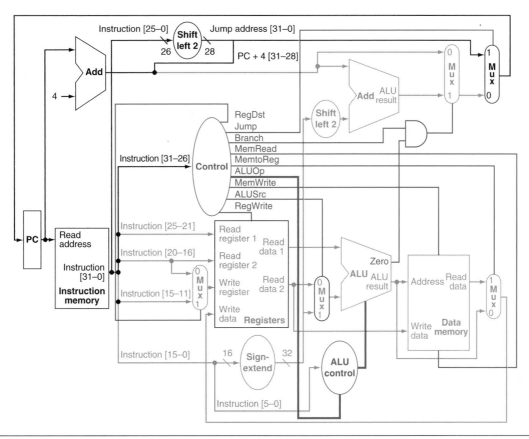

FIGURE 4.24 The simple control and datapath are extended to handle the jump instruction. An additional multiplexor (at the upper right) is used to choose between the jump target and either the branch target or the sequential instruction following this one. This multiplexor is controlled by the jump control signal. The jump target address is obtained by shifting the lower 26 bits of the jump instruction left 2 bits, effectively adding 00 as the low-order bits, and then concatenating the upper 4 bits of PC + 4 as the high-order bits, thus yielding a 32-bit address.

the clock cycle is determined by the longest possible path in the processor. This path is almost certainly a load instruction, which uses five functional units in series: the instruction memory, the register file, the ALU, the data memory, and the register file. Although the CPI is 1 (see Chapter 1), the overall performance of a single-cycle implementation is likely to be poor, since the clock cycle is too long.

The penalty for using the single-cycle design with a fixed clock cycle is significant, but might be considered acceptable for this small instruction set. Historically, early computers with very simple instruction sets did use this implementation technique. However, if we tried to implement the floating-point unit or an instruction set with more complex instructions, this single-cycle design wouldn't work well at all.

Because we must assume that the clock cycle is equal to the worst-case delay for all instructions, it's useless to try implementation techniques that reduce the delay of the common case but do not improve the worst-case cycle time. A single-cycle implementation thus violates our key design principle from Chapter 2 of making the common case fast.

In next section, we'll look at another implementation technique, called pipelining, that uses a datapath very similar to the single-cycle datapath but is much more efficient by having a much higher throughput. Pipelining improves efficiency by executing multiple instructions simultaneously.

Check Yourself

Look at the control signals in Figure 4.22. Can you combine any together? Can any control signal output in the figure be replaced by the inverse of another? (Hint: take into account the don't cares.) If so, can you use one signal for the other without adding an inverter?

Never waste time.

American proverb

4.5 An Overview of Pipelining

pipelining An implementation technique in which multiple instructions are overlapped in execution, much like an assembly line.

Pipelining is an implementation technique in which multiple instructions are overlapped in execution. Today, pipelining is nearly universal.

This section relies heavily on one analogy to give an overview of the pipelining terms and issues. If you are interested in just the big picture, you should concentrate on this section and then skip to Sections 4.10 and 4.11 to see an introduction to the advanced pipelining techniques used in recent processors such as the AMD Opteron X4 (Barcelona) or Intel Core. If you are interested in exploring the anatomy of a pipelined computer, this section is a good introduction to Sections 4.6 through 4.9.

Anyone who has done a lot of laundry has intuitively used pipelining. The *non-pipelined* approach to laundry would be

1. Place one dirty load of clothes in the washer.

2. When the washer is finished, place the wet load in the dryer.

3. When the dryer is finished, place the dry load on a table and fold.

4. When folding is finished, ask your roommate to put the clothes away.

When your roommate is done, then start over with the next dirty load.

The *pipelined* approach takes much less time, as Figure 4.25 shows. As soon as the washer is finished with the first load and placed in the dryer, you load the washer with the second dirty load. When the first load is dry, you place it on the table to start folding, move the wet load to the dryer, and the next dirty load into the washer. Next you have your roommate put the first load away, you start folding the second load, the dryer has the third load, and you put the fourth load into the washer. At this point all steps—called *stages* in pipelining—are operating concurrently. As long as we have separate resources for each stage, we can pipeline the tasks.

The pipelining paradox is that the time from placing a single dirty sock in the washer until it is dried, folded, and put away is not shorter for pipelining; the reason pipelining is faster for many loads is that everything is working in parallel, so more loads are finished per hour. Pipelining improves throughput of our laundry system. Hence, pipelining would not decrease the time to complete one load of laundry, but when we have many loads of laundry to do, the improvement in throughput decreases the total time to complete the work.

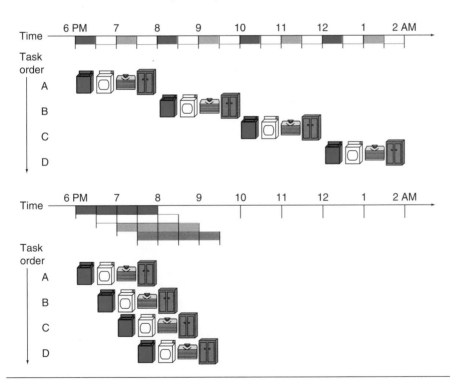

FIGURE 4.25 The laundry analogy for pipelining. Ann, Brian, Cathy, and Don each have dirty clothes to be washed, dried, folded, and put away. The washer, dryer, "folder," and "storer" each take 30 minutes for their task. Sequential laundry takes 8 hours for 4 loads of wash, while pipelined laundry takes just 3.5 hours. We show the pipeline stage of different loads over time by showing copies of the four resources on this two-dimensional time line, but we really have just one of each resource.

If all the stages take about the same amount of time and there is enough work to do, then the speed-up due to pipelining is equal to the number of stages in the pipeline, in this case four: washing, drying, folding, and putting away. Therefore, pipelined laundry is potentially four times faster than nonpipelined: 20 loads would take about 5 times as long as 1 load, while 20 loads of sequential laundry takes 20 times as long as 1 load. It's only 2.3 times faster in Figure 4.25, because we only show 4 loads. Notice that at the beginning and end of the workload in the pipelined version in Figure 4.25, the pipeline is not completely full; this start-up and wind-down affects performance when the number of tasks is not large compared to the number of stages in the pipeline. If the number of loads is much larger than 4, then the stages will be full most of the time and the increase in throughput will be very close to 4.

The same principles apply to processors where we pipeline instruction execution. MIPS instructions classically take five steps:

1. Fetch instruction from memory.

2. Read registers while decoding the instruction. The regular format of MIPS instructions allows reading and decoding to occur simultaneously.

3. Execute the operation or calculate an address.

4. Access an operand in data memory.

5. Write the result into a register.

Hence, the MIPS pipeline we explore in this chapter has five stages. The following example shows that pipelining speeds up instruction execution just as it speeds up the laundry.

EXAMPLE

Single-Cycle versus Pipelined Performance

To make this discussion concrete, let's create a pipeline. In this example, and in the rest of this chapter, we limit our attention to eight instructions: load word (lw), store word (sw), add (add), subtract (sub), AND (and), OR (or), set less than (slt), and branch on equal (beq).

Compare the average time between instructions of a single-cycle implementation, in which all instructions take one clock cycle, to a pipelined implementation. The operation times for the major functional units in this example are 200 ps for memory access, 200 ps for ALU operation, and 100 ps for register file read or write. In the single-cycle model, every instruction takes exactly one clock cycle, so the clock cycle must be stretched to accommodate the slowest instruction.

Figure 4.26 shows the time required for each of the eight instructions. The single-cycle design must allow for the slowest instruction—in Figure 4.26 it is `lw`—so the time required for every instruction is 800 ps. Similarly to Figure 4.25, Figure 4.27 compares nonpipelined and pipelined execution of three load word instructions. Thus, the time between the first and fourth instructions in the nonpipelined design is 3×800 ns or 2400 ps.

All the pipeline stages take a single clock cycle, so the clock cycle must be long enough to accommodate the slowest operation. Just as the single-cycle design must take the worst-case clock cycle of 800 ps, even though some instructions can be as fast as 500 ps, the pipelined execution clock cycle must have the worst-case clock cycle of 200 ps, even though some stages take only 100 ps. Pipelining still offers a fourfold performance improvement: the time between the first and fourth instructions is 3×200 ps or 600 ps.

ANSWER

Instruction class	Instruction fetch	Register read	ALU operation	Data access	Register write	Total time
Load word (`lw`)	200 ps	100 ps	200 ps	200 ps	100 ps	800 ps
Store word (`sw`)	200 ps	100 ps	200 ps	200 ps		700 ps
R-format (`add`, `sub`, `AND`, `OR`, `slt`)	200 ps	100 ps	200 ps		100 ps	600 ps
Branch (`beq`)	200 ps	100 ps	200 ps			500 ps

FIGURE 4.26 Total time for each instruction calculated from the time for each component. This calculation assumes that the multiplexors, control unit, PC accesses, and sign extension unit have no delay.

We can turn the pipelining speed-up discussion above into a formula. If the stages are perfectly balanced, then the time between instructions on the pipelined processor—assuming ideal conditions—is equal to

$$\text{Time between instructions}_{\text{pipelined}} = \frac{\text{Time between instructions}_{\text{nonpipelined}}}{\text{Number of pipe stages}}$$

Under ideal conditions and with a large number of instructions, the speed-up from pipelining is approximately equal to the number of pipe stages; a five-stage pipeline is nearly five times faster.

The formula suggests that a five-stage pipeline should offer nearly a fivefold improvement over the 800 ps nonpipelined time, or a 160 ps clock cycle. The example shows, however, that the stages may be imperfectly balanced. In addition, pipelining involves some overhead, the source of which will be more clear shortly. Thus, the time per instruction in the pipelined processor will exceed the minimum possible, and speed-up will be less than the number of pipeline stages.

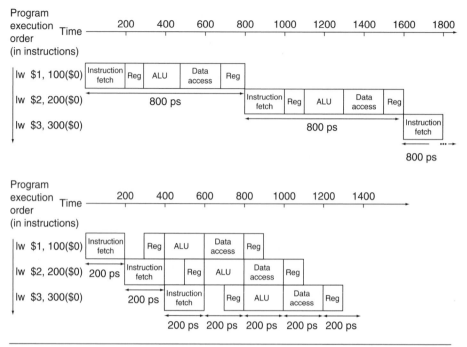

FIGURE 4.27   Single-cycle, nonpipelined execution in top versus pipelined execution in bottom. Both use the same hardware components, whose time is listed in Figure 4.26. In this case, we see a fourfold speed-up on average time between instructions, from 800 ps down to 200 ps. Compare this figure to Figure 4.25. For the laundry, we assumed all stages were equal. If the dryer were slowest, then the dryer stage would set the stage time. The pipeline stage times of a computer are also limited by the slowest resource, either the ALU operation or the memory access. We assume the write to the register file occurs in the first half of the clock cycle and the read from the register file occurs in the second half. We use this assumption throughout this chapter.

Moreover, even our claim of fourfold improvement for our example is not reflected in the total execution time for the three instructions: it's 1400 ps versus 2400 ps. Of course, this is because the number of instructions is not large. What would happen if we increased the number of instructions? We could extend the previous figures to 1,000,003 instructions. We would add 1,000,000 instructions in the pipelined example; each instruction adds 200 ps to the total execution time. The total execution time would be 1,000,000 × 200 ps + 1400 ps, or 200,001,400 ps. In the nonpipelined example, we would add 1,000,000 instructions, each taking 800 ps, so total execution time would be 1,000,000 × 800 ps + 2400 ps, or 800,002,400 ps. Under these conditions, the ratio of total execution times for real programs on nonpipelined to pipelined processors is close to the ratio of times between instructions:

$$\frac{800,002,400 \text{ ps}}{200,001,400 \text{ ps}} \approx \frac{800 \text{ ps}}{200 \text{ ps}} \approx 4.00$$

Pipelining improves performance by *increasing instruction throughput, as opposed to decreasing the execution time of an individual instruction*, but instruction throughput is the important metric because real programs execute billions of instructions.

Designing Instruction Sets for Pipelining

Even with this simple explanation of pipelining, we can get insight into the design of the MIPS instruction set, which was designed for pipelined execution.

First, all MIPS instructions are the same length. This restriction makes it much easier to fetch instructions in the first pipeline stage and to decode them in the second stage. In an instruction set like the x86, where instructions vary from 1 byte to 17 bytes, pipelining is considerably more challenging. Recent implementations of the x86 architecture actually translate x86 instructions into simple operations that look like MIPS instructions and then pipeline the simple operations rather than the native x86 instructions! (See Section 4.10.)

Second, MIPS has only a few instruction formats, with the source register fields being located in the same place in each instruction. This symmetry means that the second stage can begin reading the register file at the same time that the hardware is determining what type of instruction was fetched. If MIPS instruction formats were not symmetric, we would need to split stage 2, resulting in six pipeline stages. We will shortly see the downside of longer pipelines.

Third, memory operands only appear in loads or stores in MIPS. This restriction means we can use the execute stage to calculate the memory address and then access memory in the following stage. If we could operate on the operands in memory, as in the x86, stages 3 and 4 would expand to an address stage, memory stage, and then execute stage.

Fourth, as discussed in Chapter 2, operands must be aligned in memory. Hence, we need not worry about a single data transfer instruction requiring two data memory accesses; the requested data can be transferred between processor and memory in a single pipeline stage.

Pipeline Hazards

There are situations in pipelining when the next instruction cannot execute in the following clock cycle. These events are called *hazards*, and there are three different types.

Structural Hazards

The first hazard is called a **structural hazard**. It means that the hardware cannot support the combination of instructions that we want to execute in the same clock cycle. A structural hazard in the laundry room would occur if we used a washer-dryer combination instead of a separate washer and dryer, or if our roommate was busy doing something else and wouldn't put clothes away. Our carefully scheduled pipeline plans would then be foiled.

structural hazard When a planned instruction cannot execute in the proper clock cycle because the hardware does not support the combination of instructions that are set to execute.

As we said above, the MIPS instruction set was designed to be pipelined, making it fairly easy for designers to avoid structural hazards when designing a pipeline. Suppose, however, that we had a single memory instead of two memories. If the pipeline in Figure 4.27 had a fourth instruction, we would see that in the same clock cycle the first instruction is accessing data from memory while the fourth instruction is fetching an instruction from that same memory. Without two memories, our pipeline could have a structural hazard.

Data Hazards

data hazard Also called a pipeline data hazard. When a planned instruction cannot execute in the proper clock cycle because data that is needed to execute the instruction is not yet available.

Data hazards occur when the pipeline must be stalled because one step must wait for another to complete. Suppose you found a sock at the folding station for which no match existed. One possible strategy is to run down to your room and search through your clothes bureau to see if you can find the match. Obviously, while you are doing the search, loads that have completed drying and are ready to fold and those that have finished washing and are ready to dry must wait.

In a computer pipeline, data hazards arise from the dependence of one instruction on an earlier one that is still in the pipeline (a relationship that does not really exist when doing laundry). For example, suppose we have an add instruction followed immediately by a subtract instruction that uses the sum ($s0):

```
add    $s0, $t0, $t1
sub    $t2, $s0, $t3
```

Without intervention, a data hazard could severely stall the pipeline. The add instruction doesn't write its result until the fifth stage, meaning that we would have to waste three clock cycles in the pipeline.

Although we could try to rely on compilers to remove all such hazards, the results would not be satisfactory. These dependences happen just too often and the delay is just too long to expect the compiler to rescue us from this dilemma.

forwarding Also called **bypassing**. A method of resolving a data hazard by retrieving the missing data element from internal buffers rather than waiting for it to arrive from programmer-visible registers or memory.

The primary solution is based on the observation that we don't need to wait for the instruction to complete before trying to resolve the data hazard. For the code sequence above, as soon as the ALU creates the sum for the add, we can supply it as an input for the subtract. Adding extra hardware to retrieve the missing item early from the internal resources is called **forwarding** or **bypassing**.

EXAMPLE

Forwarding with Two Instructions

For the two instructions above, show what pipeline stages would be connected by forwarding. Use the drawing in Figure 4.28 to represent the datapath during the five stages of the pipeline. Align a copy of the datapath for each instruction, similar to the laundry pipeline in Figure 4.25.

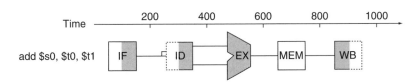

FIGURE 4.28 Graphical representation of the instruction pipeline, similar in spirit to the laundry pipeline in Figure 4.25. Here we use symbols representing the physical resources with the abbreviations for pipeline stages used throughout the chapter. The symbols for the five stages: *IF* for the instruction fetch stage, with the box representing instruction memory; *ID* for the instruction decode/register file read stage, with the drawing showing the register file being read; *EX* for the execution stage, with the drawing representing the ALU; *MEM* for the memory access stage, with the box representing data memory; and *WB* for the write-back stage, with the drawing showing the register file being written. The shading indicates the element is used by the instruction. Hence, MEM has a white background because add does not access the data memory. Shading on the right half of the register file or memory means the element is read in that stage, and shading of the left half means it is written in that stage. Hence the right half of ID is shaded in the second stage because the register file is read, and the left half of WB is shaded in the fifth stage because the register file is written.

Figure 4.29 shows the connection to forward the value in $s0 after the execution stage of the add instruction as input to the execution stage of the sub instruction.

ANSWER

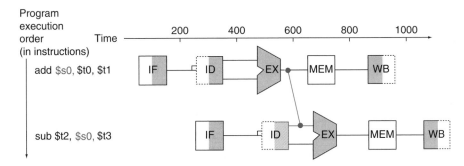

FIGURE 4.29 Graphical representation of forwarding. The connection shows the forwarding path from the output of the EX stage of add to the input of the EX stage for sub, replacing the value from register $s0 read in the second stage of sub.

In this graphical representation of events, forwarding paths are valid only if the destination stage is later in time than the source stage. For example, there cannot be a valid forwarding path from the output of the memory access stage in the first instruction to the input of the execution stage of the following, since that would mean going backward in time.

Forwarding works very well and is described in detail in Section 4.7. It cannot prevent all pipeline stalls, however. For example, suppose the first instruction was a

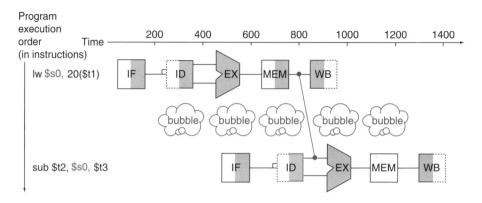

FIGURE 4.30 We need a stall even with forwarding when an R-format instruction following a load tries to use the data. Without the stall, the path from memory access stage output to execution stage input would be going backward in time, which is impossible. This figure is actually a simplification, since we cannot know until after the subtract instruction is fetched and decoded whether or not a stall will be necessary. Section 4.7 shows the details of what really happens in the case of a hazard.

load-use data hazard A specific form of data hazard in which the data being loaded by a load instruction has not yet become available when it is needed by another instruction.

pipeline stall Also called **bubble**. A stall initiated in order to resolve a hazard.

load of $s0 instead of an add. As we can imagine from looking at Figure 4.29, the desired data would be available only *after* the fourth stage of the first instruction in the dependence, which is too late for the *input* of the third stage of sub. Hence, even with forwarding, we would have to stall one stage for a **load-use data hazard**, as Figure 4.30 shows. This figure shows an important pipeline concept, officially called a **pipeline stall**, but often given the nickname **bubble**. We shall see stalls elsewhere in the pipeline. Section 4.7 shows how we can handle hard cases like these, using either hardware detection and stalls or software that reorders code to try to avoid load-use pipeline stalls, as this example illustrates.

EXAMPLE

Reordering Code to Avoid Pipeline Stalls

Consider the following code segment in C:

```
a = b + e;
c = b + f;
```

Here is the generated MIPS code for this segment, assuming all variables are in memory and are addressable as offsets from $t0:

```
lw    $t1, 0($t0)
lw    $t2, 4($t0)
add   $t3, $t1,$t2
sw    $t3, 12($t0)
lw    $t4, 8($t0)
add   $t5, $t1,$t4
sw    $t5, 16($t0)
```

Find the hazards in the preceding code segment and reorder the instructions to avoid any pipeline stalls.

Both add instructions have a hazard because of their respective dependence on the immediately preceding lw instruction. Notice that bypassing eliminates several other potential hazards, including the dependence of the first add on the first lw and any hazards for store instructions. Moving up the third lw instruction to become the third instruction eliminates both hazards:

ANSWER

```
lw    $t1, 0($t0)
lw    $t2, 4($t0)
lw    $t4, 8($t0)
add   $t3, $t1,$t2
sw    $t3, 12($t0)
add   $t5, $t1,$t4
sw    $t5, 16($t0)
```

On a pipelined processor with forwarding, the reordered sequence will complete in two fewer cycles than the original version.

Forwarding yields another insight into the MIPS architecture, in addition to the four mentioned on page 335. Each MIPS instruction writes at most one result and does this in the last stage of the pipeline. Forwarding is harder if there are multiple results to forward per instruction or they need to write a result early on in instruction execution.

Elaboration: The name "forwarding" comes from the idea that the result is passed forward from an earlier instruction to a later instruction. "Bypassing" comes from passing the result around the register file to the desired unit.

Control Hazards

The third type of hazard is called a **control hazard**, arising from the need to make a decision based on the results of one instruction while others are executing.

Suppose our laundry crew was given the happy task of cleaning the uniforms of a football team. Given how filthy the laundry is, we need to determine whether the detergent and water temperature setting we select is strong enough to get the uniforms clean but not so strong that the uniforms wear out sooner. In our laundry

control hazard Also called **branch hazard**. When the proper instruction cannot execute in the proper pipeline clock cycle because the instruction that was fetched is not the one that is needed; that is, the flow of instruction addresses is not what the pipeline expected.

pipeline, we have to wait until the second stage to examine the dry uniform to see if we need to change the washer setup or not. What to do?

Here is the first of two solutions to control hazards in the laundry room and its computer equivalent.

Stall: Just operate sequentially until the first batch is dry and then repeat until you have the right formula.

This conservative option certainly works, but it is slow.

The equivalent decision task in a computer is the branch instruction. Notice that we must begin fetching the instruction following the branch on the very next clock cycle. Nevertheless, the pipeline cannot possibly know what the next instruction should be, since it *only just received* the branch instruction from memory! Just as with laundry, one possible solution is to stall immediately after we fetch a branch, waiting until the pipeline determines the outcome of the branch and knows what instruction address to fetch from.

Let's assume that we put in enough extra hardware so that we can test registers, calculate the branch address, and update the PC during the second stage of the pipeline (see Section 4.8 for details). Even with this extra hardware, the pipeline involving conditional branches would look like Figure 4.31. The `lw` instruction, executed if the branch fails, is stalled one extra 200 ps clock cycle before starting.

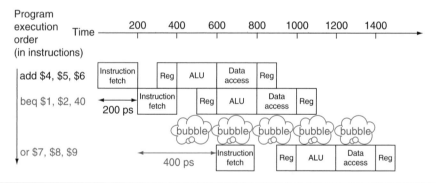

FIGURE 4.31   Pipeline showing stalling on every conditional branch as solution to control hazards. This example assumes the conditional branch is taken, and the instruction at the destination of the branch is the OR instruction. There is a one-stage pipeline stall, or bubble, after the branch. In reality, the process of creating a stall is slightly more complicated, as we will see in Section 4.8. The effect on performance, however, is the same as would occur if a bubble were inserted.

Performance of "Stall on Branch"

Estimate the impact on the clock cycles per instruction (CPI) of stalling on branches. Assume all other instructions have a CPI of 1.

Figure 3.27 in Chapter 3 shows that branches are 17% of the instructions executed in SPECint2006. Since the other instructions run have a CPI of 1, and branches took one extra clock cycle for the stall, then we would see a CPI of 1.17 and hence a slowdown of 1.17 versus the ideal case.

If we cannot resolve the branch in the second stage, as is often the case for longer pipelines, then we'd see an even larger slowdown if we stall on branches. The cost of this option is too high for most computers to use and motivates a second solution to the control hazard:

Predict: If you're pretty sure you have the right formula to wash uniforms, then just predict that it will work and wash the second load while waiting for the first load to dry.

This option does not slow down the pipeline when you are correct. When you are wrong, however, you need to redo the load that was washed while guessing the decision.

Computers do indeed use *prediction* to handle branches. One simple approach is to predict always that branches will be untaken. When you're right, the pipeline proceeds at full speed. Only when branches are taken does the pipeline stall. Figure 4.32 shows such an example.

A more sophisticated version of **branch prediction** would have some branches predicted as taken and some as untaken. In our analogy, the dark or home uniforms might take one formula while the light or road uniforms might take another. In the case of programming, at the bottom of loops are branches that jump back to the top of the loop. Since they are likely to be taken and they branch backward, we could always predict taken for branches that jump to an earlier address.

Such rigid approaches to branch prediction rely on stereotypical behavior and don't account for the individuality of a specific branch instruction. *Dynamic* hardware predictors, in stark contrast, make their guesses depending on the behavior of each branch and may change predictions for a branch over the life of a program. Following our analogy, in dynamic prediction a person would look at how dirty the uniform was and guess at the formula, adjusting the next guess depending on the success of recent guesses.

branch prediction A method of resolving a branch hazard that assumes a given outcome for the branch and proceeds from that assumption rather than waiting to ascertain the actual outcome.

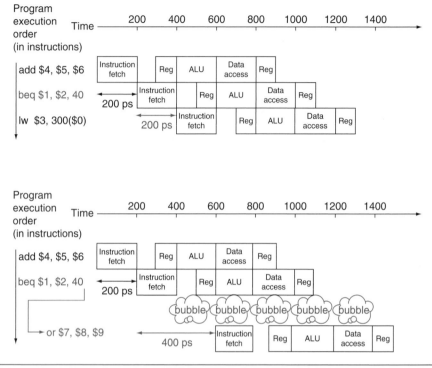

FIGURE 4.32 Predicting that branches are not taken as a solution to control hazard. The top drawing shows the pipeline when the branch is not taken. The bottom drawing shows the pipeline when the branch is taken. As we noted in Figure 4.31, the insertion of a bubble in this fashion simplifies what actually happens, at least during the first clock cycle immediately following the branch. Section 4.8 will reveal the details.

One popular approach to dynamic prediction of branches is keeping a history for each branch as taken or untaken, and then using the recent past behavior to predict the future. As we will see later, the amount and type of history kept have become extensive, with the result being that dynamic branch predictors can correctly predict branches with more than 90% accuracy (see Section 4.8). When the guess is wrong, the pipeline control must ensure that the instructions following the wrongly guessed branch have no effect and must restart the pipeline from the proper branch address. In our laundry analogy, we must stop taking new loads so that we can restart the load that we incorrectly predicted.

As in the case of all other solutions to control hazards, longer pipelines exacerbate the problem, in this case by raising the cost of misprediction. Solutions to control hazards are described in more detail in Section 4.8.

Elaboration: There is a third approach to the control hazard, called *delayed decision* mentioned above. In our analogy, whenever you are going to make such a decision about laundry, just place a load of nonfootball clothes in the washer while waiting for football uniforms to dry. As long as you have enough dirty clothes that are not affected by the test, this solution works fine.

Called the *delayed branch* in computers, this is the solution actually used by the MIPS architecture. The delayed branch always executes the next sequential instruction, with the branch taking place *after* that one instruction delay. It is hidden from the MIPS assembly language programmer because the assembler can automatically arrange the instructions to get the branch behavior desired by the programmer. MIPS software will place an instruction immediately after the delayed branch instruction that is not affected by the branch, and a taken branch changes the address of the instruction that *follows* this safe instruction. In our example, the add instruction before the branch in Figure 4.31 does not affect the branch and can be moved after the branch to fully hide the branch delay. Since delayed branches are useful when the branches are short, no processor uses a delayed branch of more than one cycle. For longer branch delays, hardware-based branch prediction is usually used.

Pipeline Overview Summary

Pipelining is a technique that exploits parallelism among the instructions in a sequential instruction stream. It has the substantial advantage that, unlike programming a multiprocessor, it is fundamentally invisible to the programmer.

In the next sections of this chapter, we cover the concept of pipelining using the MIPS instruction subset from the single-cycle implementation in Section 4.4 and show a simplified version of its pipeline. We then look at the problems that pipelining introduces and the performance attainable under typical situations.

If you wish to focus more on the software and the performance implications of pipelining, you now have sufficient background to skip to Section 4.10. Section 4.10 introduces advanced pipelining concepts, such as superscalar and dynamic scheduling, and Section 4.11 examines the pipelines of recent microprocessors.

Alternatively, if you are interested in understanding how pipelining is implemented and the challenges of dealing with hazards, you can proceed to examine the design of a pipelined datapath and the basic control, explained in Section 4.6. You can then use this understanding to explore the implementation of forwarding and stalls in Section 4.7. You can then read Section 4.8 to learn more about solutions to branch hazards, and then see how exceptions are handled in Section 4.9.

For each code sequence below, state whether it must stall, can avoid stalls using only forwarding, or can execute without stalling or forwarding.

Check Yourself

Sequence 1	Sequence 2	Sequence 3

lw $t0,0($t0)
 add $t1,$t0,$t0
	add $t1,$t0,$t0
	 addi $t2,$t0,#5
	 addi $t4,$t1,#5
		addi $t1,$t0,#1
		 addi $t2,$t0,#2
		 addi $t3,$t0,#2
		 addi $t3,$t0,#4
		 addi $t5,$t0,#5

**Understanding
Program
Performance**

Outside the memory system, the effective operation of the pipeline is usually the most important factor in determining the CPI of the processor and hence its performance. As we will see in Section 4.10, understanding the performance of a modern multiple-issue pipelined processor is complex and requires understanding more than just the issues that arise in a simple pipelined processor. Nonetheless, structural, data, and control hazards remain important in both simple pipelines and more sophisticated ones.

For modern pipelines, structural hazards usually revolve around the floating-point unit, which may not be fully pipelined, while control hazards are usually more of a problem in integer programs, which tend to have higher branch frequencies as well as less predictable branches. Data hazards can be performance bottlenecks in both integer and floating-point programs. Often it is easier to deal with data hazards in floating-point programs because the lower branch frequency and more regular memory access patterns allow the compiler to try to schedule instructions to avoid hazards. It is more difficult to perform such optimizations in integer programs that have less regular memory access, involving more use of pointers. As we will see in Section 4.10, there are more ambitious compiler and hardware techniques for reducing data dependences through scheduling.

**The BIG
Picture**

latency (pipeline) The number of stages in a pipeline or the number of stages between two instructions during execution.

Pipelining increases the number of simultaneously executing instructions and the rate at which instructions are started and completed. Pipelining does not reduce the time it takes to complete an individual instruction, also called the **latency**. For example, the five-stage pipeline still takes 5 clock cycles for the instruction to complete. In the terms used in Chapter 1, pipelining improves instruction *throughput* rather than individual instruction *execution time* or *latency*.

Instruction sets can either simplify or make life harder for pipeline designers, who must already cope with structural, control, and data hazards. Branch prediction and forwarding help make a computer fast while still getting the right answers.

*There is less in this
than meets the eye.*

Tallulah Bankhead,
remark to Alexander
Woollcott, 1922

4.6   Pipelined Datapath and Control

Figure 4.33 shows the single-cycle datapath from Section 4.4 with the pipeline stages identified. The division of an instruction into five stages means a five-stage

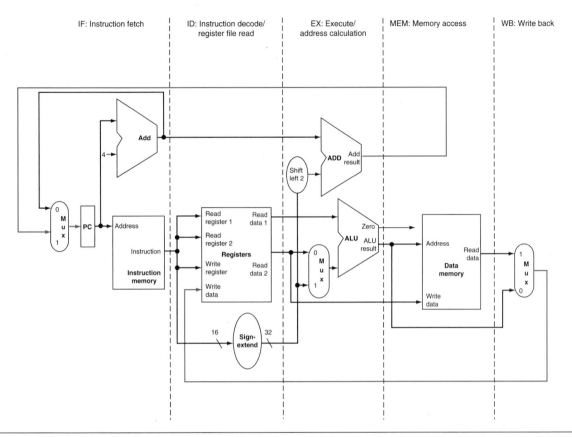

FIGURE 4.33 **The single-cycle datapath from Section 4.4 (similar to Figure 4.17).** Each step of the instruction can be mapped onto the datapath from left to right. The only exceptions are the update of the PC and the write-back step, shown in color, which sends either the ALU result or the data from memory to the left to be written into the register file. (Normally we use color lines for control, but these are data lines.)

pipeline, which in turn means that up to five instructions will be in execution during any single clock cycle. Thus, we must separate the datapath into five pieces, with each piece named corresponding to a stage of instruction execution:

1. IF: Instruction fetch

2. ID: Instruction decode and register file read

3. EX: Execution or address calculation

4. MEM: Data memory access

5. WB: Write back

In Figure 4.33, these five components correspond roughly to the way the datapath is drawn; instructions and data move generally from left to right through the five stages as they complete execution. Returning to our laundry analogy, clothes get cleaner, drier, and more organized as they move through the line, and they never move backward.

There are, however, two exceptions to this left-to-right flow of instructions:

- The write-back stage, which places the result back into the register file in the middle of the datapath

- The selection of the next value of the PC, choosing between the incremented PC and the branch address from the MEM stage

Data flowing from right to left does not affect the current instruction; only later instructions in the pipeline are influenced by these reverse data movements. Note that the first right-to-left flow of data can lead to data hazards and the second leads to control hazards.

One way to show what happens in pipelined execution is to pretend that each instruction has its own datapath, and then to place these datapaths on a timeline to show their relationship. Figure 4.34 shows the execution of the instructions in Figure 4.27 by displaying their private datapaths on a common timeline. We use a stylized version of the datapath in Figure 4.33 to show the relationships in Figure 4.34.

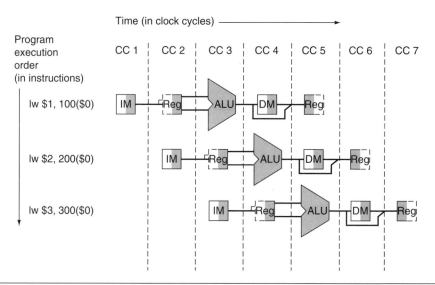

FIGURE 4.34 Instructions being executed using the single-cycle datapath in Figure 4.33, assuming pipelined execution. Similar to Figures 4.28 through 4.30, this figure pretends that each instruction has its own datapath, and shades each portion according to use. Unlike those figures, each stage is labeled by the physical resource used in that stage, corresponding to the portions of the datapath in Figure 4.33. *IM* represents the instruction memory and the PC in the instruction fetch stage, *Reg* stands for the register file and sign extender in the instruction decode/register file read stage (ID), and so on. To maintain proper time order, this stylized datapath breaks the register file into two logical parts: registers read during register fetch (ID) and registers written during write back (WB). This dual use is represented by drawing the unshaded left half of the register file using dashed lines in the ID stage, when it is not being written, and the unshaded right half in dashed lines in the WB stage, when it is not being read. As before, we assume the register file is written in the first half of the clock cycle and the register file is read during the second half.

Figure 4.34 seems to suggest that three instructions need three datapaths. Instead, we add registers to hold data so that portions of a single datapath can be shared during instruction execution.

For example, as Figure 4.34 shows, the instruction memory is used during only one of the five stages of an instruction, allowing it to be shared by following instructions during the other four stages. To retain the value of an individual instruction for its other four stages, the value read from instruction memory must be saved in a register. Similar arguments apply to every pipeline stage, so we must place registers wherever there are dividing lines between stages in Figure 4.33. Returning to our laundry analogy, we might have a basket between each pair of stages to hold the clothes for the next step.

Figure 4.35 shows the pipelined datapath with the pipeline registers highlighted. All instructions advance during each clock cycle from one pipeline register to the next. The registers are named for the two stages separated by that register. For example, the pipeline register between the IF and ID stages is called IF/ID.

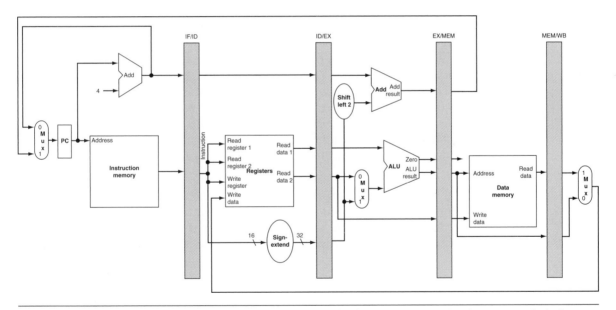

FIGURE 4.35 The pipelined version of the datapath in Figure 4.33. The pipeline registers, in color, separate each pipeline stage. They are labeled by the stages that they separate; for example, the first is labeled *IF/ID* because it separates the instruction fetch and instruction decode stages. The registers must be wide enough to store all the data corresponding to the lines that go through them. For example, the IF/ID register must be 64 bits wide, because it must hold both the 32-bit instruction fetched from memory and the incremented 32-bit PC address. We will expand these registers over the course of this chapter, but for now the other three pipeline registers contain 128, 97, and 64 bits, respectively.

Notice that there is no pipeline register at the end of the write-back stage. All instructions must update some state in the processor—the register file, memory, or the PC—so a separate pipeline register is redundant to the state that is updated. For example, a load instruction will place its result in 1 of the 32 registers, and any later instruction that needs that data will simply read the appropriate register.

Of course, every instruction updates the PC, whether by incrementing it or by setting it to a branch destination address. The PC can be thought of as a pipeline register: one that feeds the IF stage of the pipeline. Unlike the shaded pipeline registers in Figure 4.35, however, the PC is part of the visible architectural state; its contents must be saved when an exception occurs, while the contents of the pipeline registers can be discarded. In the laundry analogy, you could think of the PC as corresponding to the basket that holds the load of dirty clothes before the wash step.

To show how the pipelining works, throughout this chapter we show sequences of figures to demonstrate operation over time. These extra pages would seem to require much more time for you to understand. Fear not; the sequences take much less time than it might appear, because you can compare them to see what changes occur in each clock cycle. Section 4.7 describes what happens when there are data hazards between pipelined instructions; ignore them for now.

Figures 4.36 through 4.38, our first sequence, show the active portions of the datapath highlighted as a load instruction goes through the five stages of pipelined execution. We show a load first because it is active in all five stages. As in Figures 4.28 through 4.30, we highlight the *right half* of registers or memory when they are being *read* and highlight the *left half* when they are being *written*.

We show the instruction abbreviation lw with the name of the pipe stage that is active in each figure. The five stages are the following:

1. *Instruction fetch:* The top portion of Figure 4.36 shows the instruction being read from memory using the address in the PC and then being placed in the IF/ID pipeline register. The PC address is incremented by 4 and then written back into the PC to be ready for the next clock cycle. This incremented address is also saved in the IF/ID pipeline register in case it is needed later for an instruction, such as beq. The computer cannot know which type of instruction is being fetched, so it must prepare for any instruction, passing potentially needed information down the pipeline.

2. *Instruction decode and register file read:* The bottom portion of Figure 4.36 shows the instruction portion of the IF/ID pipeline register supplying the 16-bit immediate field, which is sign-extended to 32 bits, and the register numbers to read the two registers. All three values are stored in the ID/EX pipeline register, along with the incremented PC address. We again transfer everything that might be needed by any instruction during a later clock cycle.

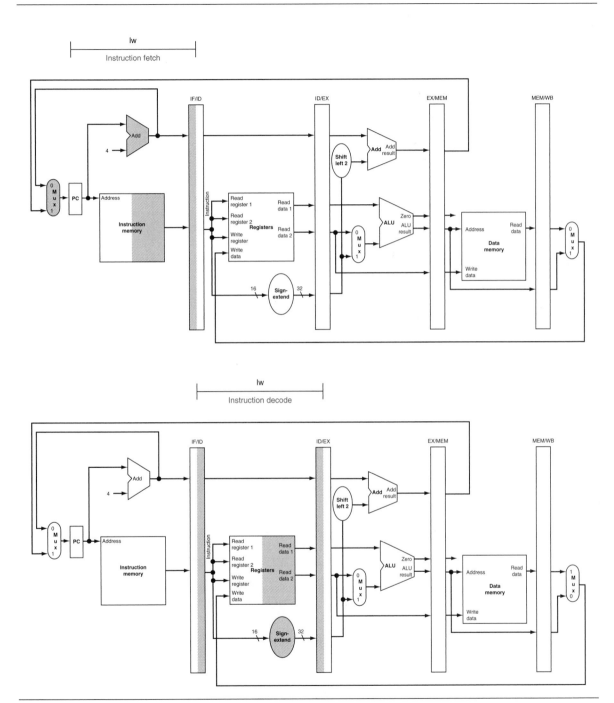

FIGURE 4.36 IF and ID: First and second pipe stages of an instruction, with the active portions of the datapath in Figure 4.35 highlighted. The highlighting convention is the same as that used in Figure 4.28. As in Section 4.2, there is no confusion when reading and writing registers, because the contents change only on the clock edge. Although the load needs only the top register in stage 2, the processor doesn't know what instruction is being decoded, so it sign-extends the 16-bit constant and reads both registers into the ID/EX pipeline register. We don't need all three operands, but it simplifies control to keep all three.

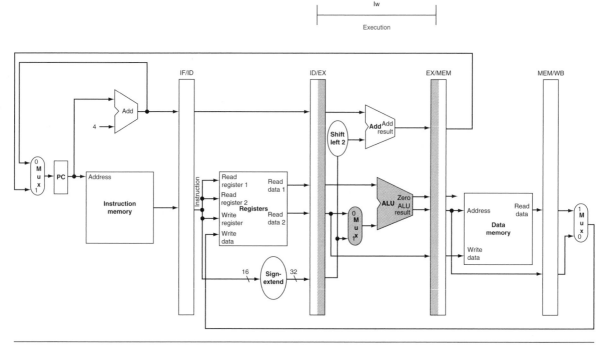

FIGURE 4.37   EX: The third pipe stage of a load instruction, highlighting the portions of the datapath in Figure 4.35 used in this pipe stage. The register is added to the sign-extended immediate, and the sum is placed in the EX/MEM pipeline register.

3. *Execute or address calculation:* Figure 4.37 shows that the load instruction reads the contents of register 1 and the sign-extended immediate from the ID/EX pipeline register and adds them using the ALU. That sum is placed in the EX/MEM pipeline register.

4. *Memory access:* The top portion of Figure 4.38 shows the load instruction reading the data memory using the address from the EX/MEM pipeline register and loading the data into the MEM/WB pipeline register.

5. *Write-back:* The bottom portion of Figure 4.38 shows the final step: reading the data from the MEM/WB pipeline register and writing it into the register file in the middle of the figure.

This walk-through of the load instruction shows that any information needed in a later pipe stage must be passed to that stage via a pipeline register. Walking through a store instruction shows the similarity of instruction execution, as well as passing the information for later stages. Here are the five pipe stages of the store instruction:

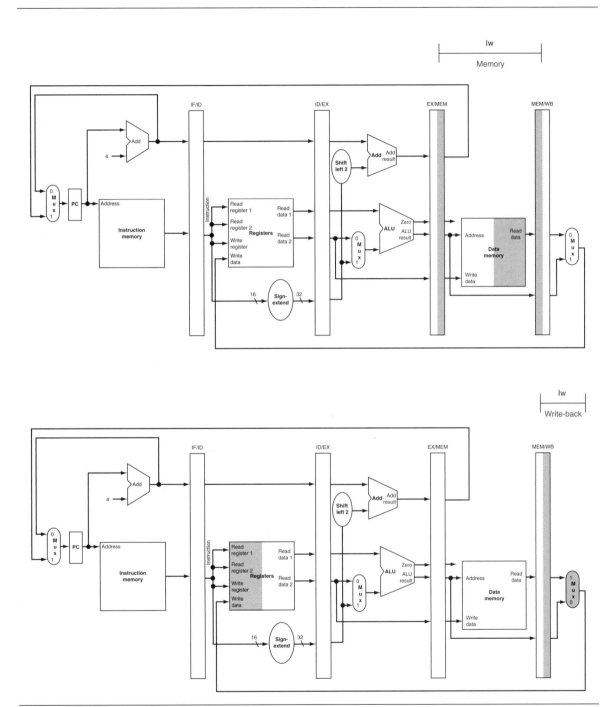

FIGURE 4.38 MEM and WB: The fourth and fifth pipe stages of a load instruction, highlighting the portions of the datapath in Figure 4.35 used in this pipe stage. Data memory is read using the address in the EX/MEM pipeline registers, and the data is placed in the MEM/WB pipeline register. Next, data is read from the MEM/WB pipeline register and written into the register file in the middle of the datapath. Note: there is a bug in this design that is repaired in Figure 4.41.

1. *Instruction fetch:* The instruction is read from memory using the address in the PC and then is placed in the IF/ID pipeline register. This stage occurs before the instruction is identified, so the top portion of Figure 4.36 works for store as well as load.

2. *Instruction decode and register file read:* The instruction in the IF/ID pipeline register supplies the register numbers for reading two registers and extends the sign of the 16-bit immediate. These three 32-bit values are all stored in the ID/EX pipeline register. The bottom portion of Figure 4.36 for load instructions also shows the operations of the second stage for stores. These first two stages are executed by all instructions, since it is too early to know the type of the instruction.

3. *Execute and address calculation:* Figure 4.39 shows the third step; the effective address is placed in the EX/MEM pipeline register.

4. *Memory access:* The top portion of Figure 4.40 shows the data being written to memory. Note that the register containing the data to be stored was read in an earlier stage and stored in ID/EX. The only way to make the data available during the MEM stage is to place the data into the EX/MEM pipeline register in the EX stage, just as we stored the effective address into EX/MEM.

5. *Write-back:* The bottom portion of Figure 4.40 shows the final step of the store. For this instruction, nothing happens in the write-back stage. Since every instruction behind the store is already in progress, we have no way to accelerate those instructions. Hence, an instruction passes through a stage even if there is nothing to do, because later instructions are already progressing at the maximum rate.

The store instruction again illustrates that to pass something from an early pipe stage to a later pipe stage, the information must be placed in a pipeline register; otherwise, the information is lost when the next instruction enters that pipeline stage. For the store instruction we needed to pass one of the registers read in the ID stage to the MEM stage, where it is stored in memory. The data was first placed in the ID/EX pipeline register and then passed to the EX/MEM pipeline register.

Load and store illustrate a second key point: each logical component of the datapath—such as instruction memory, register read ports, ALU, data memory, and register write port—can be used only within a *single* pipeline stage. Otherwise, we would have a *structural hazard* (see page 335). Hence these components, and their control, can be associated with a single pipeline stage.

Now we can uncover a bug in the design of the load instruction. Did you see it? Which register is changed in the final stage of the load? More specifically, which instruction supplies the write register number? The instruction in the IF/ID pipeline register supplies the write register number, yet this instruction occurs considerably *after* the load instruction!

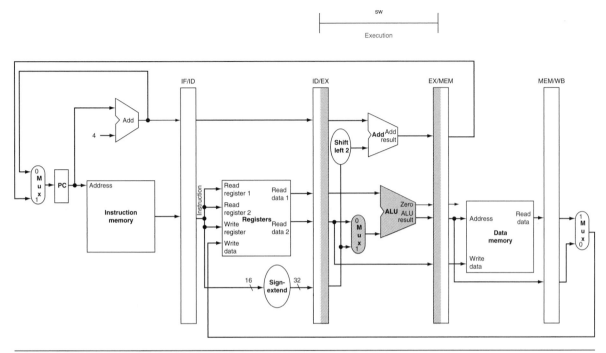

FIGURE 4.39 EX: The third pipe stage of a store instruction. Unlike the third stage of the load instruction in Figure 4.37, the second register value is loaded into the EX/MEM pipeline register to be used in the next stage. Although it wouldn't hurt to always write this second register into the EX/MEM pipeline register, we write the second register only on a store instruction to make the pipeline easier to understand.

Hence, we need to preserve the destination register number in the load instruction. Just as store passed the register *contents* from the ID/EX to the EX/MEM pipeline registers for use in the MEM stage, load must pass the register *number* from the ID/EX through EX/MEM to the MEM/WB pipeline register for use in the WB stage. Another way to think about the passing of the register number is that to share the pipelined datapath, we need to preserve the instruction read during the IF stage, so each pipeline register contains a portion of the instruction needed for that stage and later stages.

Figure 4.41 shows the correct version of the datapath, passing the write register number first to the ID/EX register, then to the EX/MEM register, and finally to the MEM/WB register. The register number is used during the WB stage to specify the register to be written. Figure 4.42 is a single drawing of the corrected datapath, highlighting the hardware used in all five stages of the load word instruction in Figures 4.36 through 4.38. See Section 4.8 for an explanation of how to make the branch instruction work as expected.

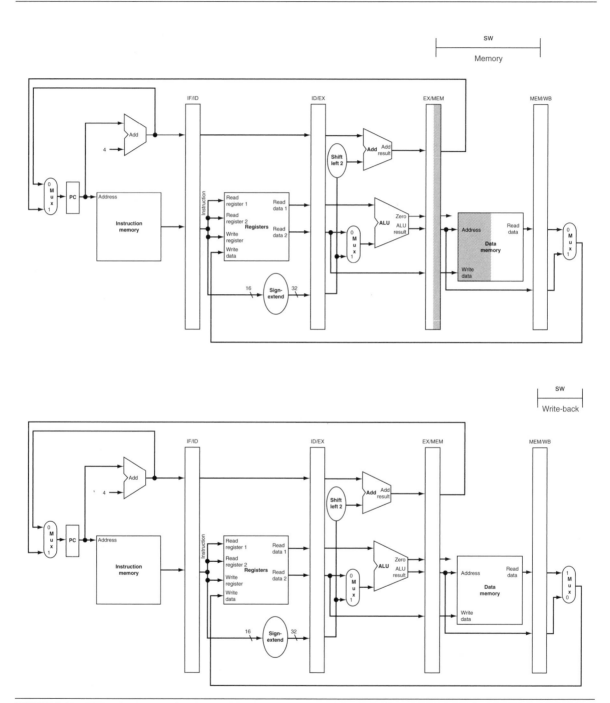

FIGURE 4.40 MEM and WB: The fourth and fifth pipe stages of a store instruction. In the fourth stage, the data is written into data memory for the store. Note that the data comes from the EX/MEM pipeline register and that nothing is changed in the MEM/WB pipeline register. Once the data is written in memory, there is nothing left for the store instruction to do, so nothing happens in stage 5.

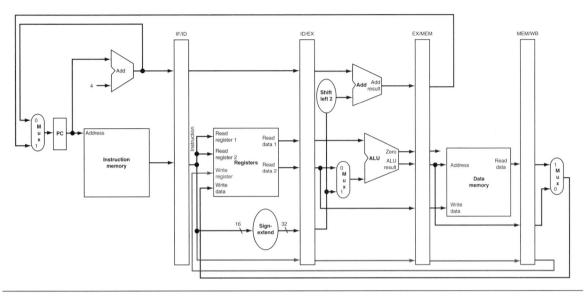

FIGURE 4.41 The corrected pipelined datapath to handle the load instruction properly. The write register number now comes from the MEM/WB pipeline register along with the data. The register number is passed from the ID pipe stage until it reaches the MEM/WB pipeline register, adding five more bits to the last three pipeline registers. This new path is shown in color.

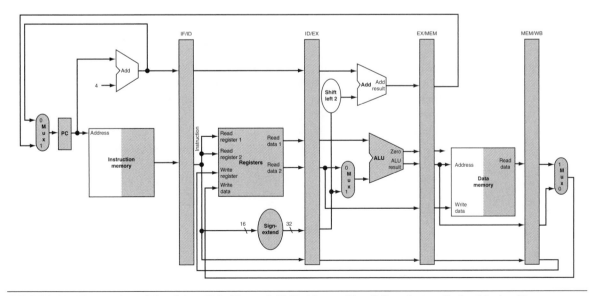

FIGURE 4.42 The portion of the datapath in Figure 4.41 that is used in all five stages of a load instruction.

Graphically Representing Pipelines

Pipelining can be difficult to understand, since many instructions are simultaneously executing in a single datapath in every clock cycle. To aid understanding, there are two basic styles of pipeline figures: *multiple-clock-cycle pipeline diagrams*, such as Figure 4.34 on page 346, and *single-clock-cycle pipeline diagrams*, such as Figures 4.36 through 4.40. The multiple-clock-cycle diagrams are simpler but do not contain all the details. For example, consider the following five-instruction sequence:

```
lw    $10, 20($1)
sub   $11, $2, $3
add   $12, $3, $4
lw    $13, 24($1)
add   $14, $5, $6
```

Figure 4.43 shows the multiple-clock-cycle pipeline diagram for these instructions. Time advances from left to right across the page in these diagrams, and instructions advance from the top to the bottom of the page, similar to the laundry pipeline in Figure 4.25. A representation of the pipeline stages is placed in each portion along the instruction axis, occupying the proper clock cycles. These stylized datapaths represent the five stages of our pipeline graphically, but a rectangle naming each pipe stage works just as well. Figure 4.44 shows the more traditional version of the multiple-clock-cycle pipeline diagram. Note that Figure 4.43 shows the physical resources used at each stage, while Figure 4.44 uses the *name* of each stage.

Single-clock-cycle pipeline diagrams show the state of the entire datapath during a single clock cycle, and usually all five instructions in the pipeline are identified by labels above their respective pipeline stages. We use this type of figure to show the details of what is happening within the pipeline during each clock cycle; typically, the drawings appear in groups to show pipeline operation over a sequence of clock cycles. We use multiple-clock-cycle diagrams to give overviews of pipelining situations. (Section 4.12 gives more illustrations of single-clock diagrams if you would like to see more details about Figure 4.43.) A single-clock-cycle diagram represents a vertical slice through a set of multiple-clock-cycle diagrams, showing the usage of the datapath by each of the instructions in the pipeline at the designated clock cycle. For example, Figure 4.45 shows the single-clock-cycle diagram corresponding to clock cycle 5 of Figures 4.43 and 4.44. Obviously, the single-clock-cycle diagrams have more detail and take significantly more space to show the same number of clock cycles. The exercises ask you to create such diagrams for other code sequences.

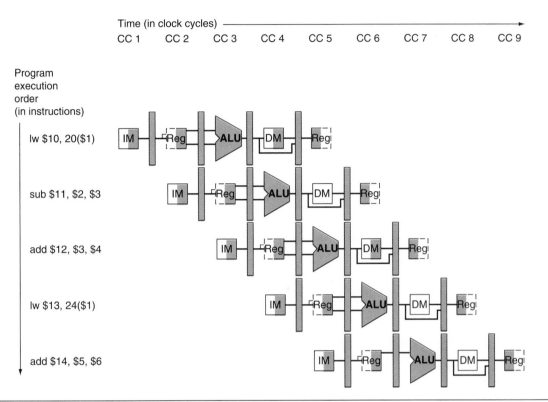

FIGURE 4.43 Multiple-clock-cycle pipeline diagram of five instructions. This style of pipeline representation shows the complete execution of instructions in a single figure. Instructions are listed in instruction execution order from top to bottom, and clock cycles move from left to right. Unlike Figure 4.28, here we show the pipeline registers between each stage. Figure 4.44 shows the traditional way to draw this diagram.

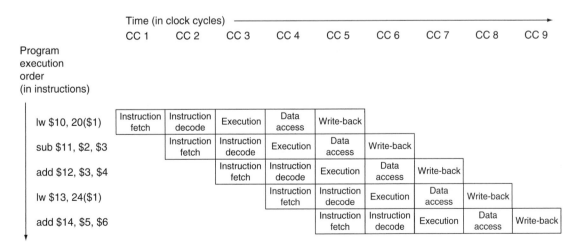

FIGURE 4.44 Traditional multiple-clock-cycle pipeline diagram of five instructions in Figure 4.43.

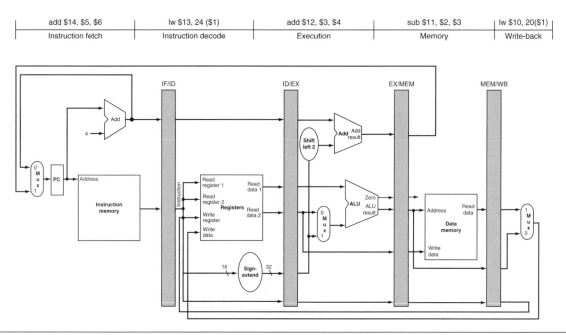

FIGURE 4.45   The single-clock-cycle diagram corresponding to clock cycle 5 of the pipeline in Figures 4.43 and 4.44. As you can see, a single-clock-cycle figure is a vertical slice through a multiple-clock-cycle diagram.

Check Yourself

A group of students were debating the efficiency of the five-stage pipeline when one student pointed out that not all instructions are active in every stage of the pipeline. After deciding to ignore the effects of hazards, they made the following five statements. Which ones are correct?

1. Allowing jumps, branches, and ALU instructions to take fewer stages than the five required by the load instruction will increase pipeline performance under all circumstances.

2. Trying to allow some instructions to take fewer cycles does not help, since the throughput is determined by the clock cycle; the number of pipe stages per instruction affects latency, not throughput.

3. You cannot make ALU instructions take fewer cycles because of the write-back of the result, but branches and jumps can take fewer cycles, so there is some opportunity for improvement.

4. Instead of trying to make instructions take fewer cycles, we should explore making the pipeline longer, so that instructions take more cycles, but the cycles are shorter. This could improve performance.

Pipelined Control

In the 6600 Computer, perhaps even more than in any previous computer, the control system is the difference.

James Thornton, *Design of a Computer: The Control Data 6600,* 1970

Just as we added control to the single-cycle datapath in Section 4.3, we now add control to the pipelined datapath. We start with a simple design that views the problem through rose-colored glasses; in Sections 4.7 through 4.9, we remove these glasses to reveal the pipeline hazards of the real world.

The first step is to label the control lines on the existing datapath. Figure 4.46 shows those lines. We borrow as much as we can from the control for the simple datapath in Figure 4.17. In particular, we use the same ALU control logic, branch logic, destination-register-number multiplexor, and control lines. These functions are defined in Figures 4.12, 4.16, and 4.18. We reproduce the key information in Figures 4.47 through 4.49 on a single page to make the following discussion easier to follow.

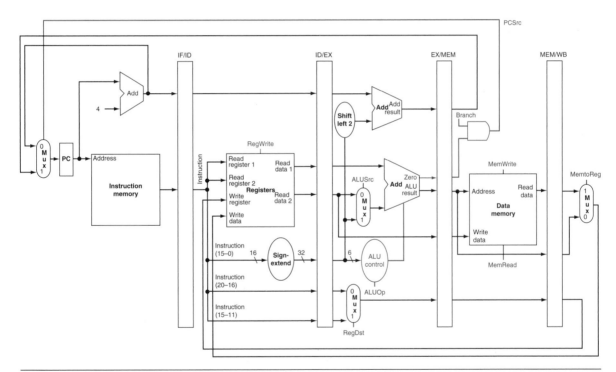

FIGURE 4.46 The pipelined datapath of Figure 4.41 with the control signals identified. This datapath borrows the control logic for PC source, register destination number, and ALU control from Section 4.4. Note that we now need the 6-bit funct field (function code) of the instruction in the EX stage as input to ALU control, so these bits must also be included in the ID/EX pipeline register. Recall that these 6 bits are also the 6 least significant bits of the immediate field in the instruction, so the ID/EX pipeline register can supply them from the immediate field since sign extension leaves these bits unchanged.

Instruction opcode	ALUOp	Instruction operation	Function code	Desired ALU action	ALU control input
LW	00	load word	XXXXXX	add	0010
SW	00	store word	XXXXXX	add	0010
Branch equal	01	branch equal	XXXXXX	subtract	0110
R-type	10	add	100000	add	0010
R-type	10	subtract	100010	subtract	0110
R-type	10	AND	100100	AND	0000
R-type	10	OR	100101	OR	0001
R-type	10	set on less than	101010	set on less than	0111

FIGURE 4.47 A copy of Figure 4.12. This figure shows how the ALU control bits are set depending on the ALUOp control bits and the different function codes for the R-type instruction.

Signal name	Effect when deasserted (0)	Effect when asserted (1)
RegDst	The register destination number for the Write register comes from the rt field (bits 20:16).	The register destination number for the Write register comes from the rd field (bits 15:11).
RegWrite	None.	The register on the Write register input is written with the value on the Write data input.
ALUSrc	The second ALU operand comes from the second register file output (Read data 2).	The second ALU operand is the sign-extended, lower 16 bits of the instruction.
PCSrc	The PC is replaced by the output of the adder that computes the value of PC + 4.	The PC is replaced by the output of the adder that computes the branch target.
MemRead	None.	Data memory contents designated by the address input are put on the Read data output.
MemWrite	None.	Data memory contents designated by the address input are replaced by the value on the Write data input.
MemtoReg	The value fed to the register Write data input comes from the ALU.	The value fed to the register Write data input comes from the data memory.

FIGURE 4.48 A copy of Figure 4.16. The function of each of seven control signals is defined. The ALU control lines (ALUOp) are defined in the second column of Figure 4.47. When a 1-bit control to a 2-way multiplexor is asserted, the multiplexor selects the input corresponding to 1. Otherwise, if the control is deasserted, the multiplexor selects the 0 input. Note that PCSrc is controlled by an AND gate in Figure 4.46. If the Branch signal and the ALU Zero signal are both set, then PCSrc is 1; otherwise, it is 0. Control sets the Branch signal only during a beq instruction; otherwise, PCSrc is set to 0.

Instruction	Execution/address calculation stage control lines				Memory access stage control lines			Write-back stage control lines	
	RegDst	ALUOp1	ALUOp0	ALUSrc	Branch	Mem-Read	Mem-Write	Reg-Write	Memto-Reg
R-format	1	1	0	0	0	0	0	1	0
lw	0	0	0	1	0	1	0	1	1
sw	X	0	0	1	0	0	1	0	X
beq	X	0	1	0	1	0	0	0	X

FIGURE 4.49 The values of the control lines are the same as in Figure 4.18, but they have been shuffled into three groups corresponding to the last three pipeline stages.

As was the case for the single-cycle implementation, we assume that the PC is written on each clock cycle, so there is no separate write signal for the PC. By the same argument, there are no separate write signals for the pipeline registers (IF/ID, ID/EX, EX/MEM, and MEM/WB), since the pipeline registers are also written during each clock cycle.

To specify control for the pipeline, we need only set the control values during each pipeline stage. Because each control line is associated with a component active in only a single pipeline stage, we can divide the control lines into five groups according to the pipeline stage.

1. *Instruction fetch:* The control signals to read instruction memory and to write the PC are always asserted, so there is nothing special to control in this pipeline stage.

2. *Instruction decode/register file read:* As in the previous stage, the same thing happens at every clock cycle, so there are no optional control lines to set.

3. *Execution/address calculation:* The signals to be set are RegDst, ALUOp, and ALUSrc (see Figures 4.47 and 4.48). The signals select the Result register, the ALU operation, and either Read data 2 or a sign-extended immediate for the ALU.

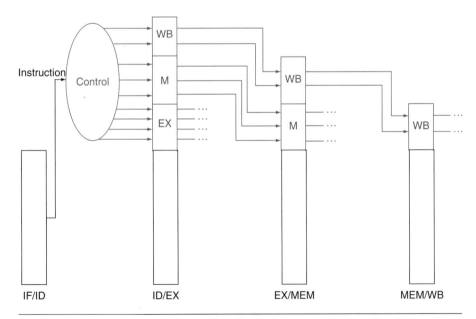

FIGURE 4.50 The control lines for the final three stages. Note that four of the nine control lines are used in the EX phase, with the remaining five control lines passed on to the EX/MEM pipeline register extended to hold the control lines; three are used during the MEM stage, and the last two are passed to MEM/WB for use in the WB stage.

4. *Memory access:* The control lines set in this stage are Branch, MemRead, and MemWrite. These signals are set by the branch equal, load, and store instructions, respectively. Recall that PCSrc in Figure 4.48 selects the next sequential address unless control asserts Branch and the ALU result was 0.

5. *Write-back:* The two control lines are MemtoReg, which decides between sending the ALU result or the memory value to the register file, and Reg-Write, which writes the chosen value.

Since pipelining the datapath leaves the meaning of the control lines unchanged, we can use the same control values. Figure 4.49 has the same values as in Section 4.4, but now the nine control lines are grouped by pipeline stage.

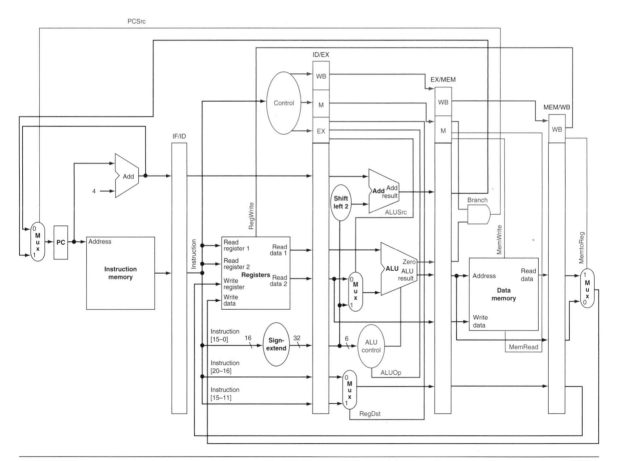

FIGURE 4.51 The pipelined datapath of Figure 4.46, with the control signals connected to the control portions of the pipeline registers. The control values for the last three stages are created during the instruction decode stage and then placed in the ID/EX pipeline register. The control lines for each pipe stage are used, and remaining control lines are then passed to the next pipeline stage.

Implementing control means setting the nine control lines to these values in each stage for each instruction. The simplest way to do this is to extend the pipeline registers to include control information.

Since the control lines start with the EX stage, we can create the control information during instruction decode. Figure 4.50 above shows that these control signals are then used in the appropriate pipeline stage as the instruction moves down the pipeline, just as the destination register number for loads moves down the pipeline in Figure 4.41. Figure 4.51 above shows the full datapath with the extended pipeline registers and with the control lines connected to the proper stage. (◉ **Section 4.12** gives more examples of MIPS code executing on pipelined hardware using single-clock diagrams, if you would like to see more details.)

4.7   Data Hazards: Forwarding versus Stalling

What do you mean, why's it got to be built? It's a bypass. You've got to build bypasses.

Douglas Adams, *The Hitchhiker's Guide to the Galaxy,* 1979

The examples in the previous section show the power of pipelined execution and how the hardware performs the task. It's now time to take off the rose-colored glasses and look at what happens with real programs. The instructions in Figures 4.43 through 4.45 were independent; none of them used the results calculated by any of the others. Yet in Section 4.5, we saw that data hazards are obstacles to pipelined execution.

Let's look at a sequence with many dependences, shown in color:

```
sub   $2, $1,$3     # Register $2 written by sub
and   $12,$2,$5     # 1st operand($2) depends on sub
or    $13,$6,$2     # 2nd operand($2) depends on sub
add   $14,$2,$2     # 1st($2) & 2nd($2) depend on sub
sw    $15,100($2)   # Base ($2) depends on sub
```

The last four instructions are all dependent on the result in register $2 of the first instruction. If register $2 had the value 10 before the subtract instruction and −20 afterwards, the programmer intends that −20 will be used in the following instructions that refer to register $2.

How would this sequence perform with our pipeline? Figure 4.52 illustrates the execution of these instructions using a multiple-clock-cycle pipeline representation. To demonstrate the execution of this instruction sequence in our current pipeline, the top of Figure 4.52 shows the value of register $2, which changes during the middle of clock cycle 5, when the sub instruction writes its result.

The last potential hazard can be resolved by the design of the register file hardware: What happens when a register is read and written in the same clock cycle? We assume that the write is in the first half of the clock cycle and the read is in the second half, so the read delivers what is written. As is the case for many implementations of register files, we have no data hazard in this case.

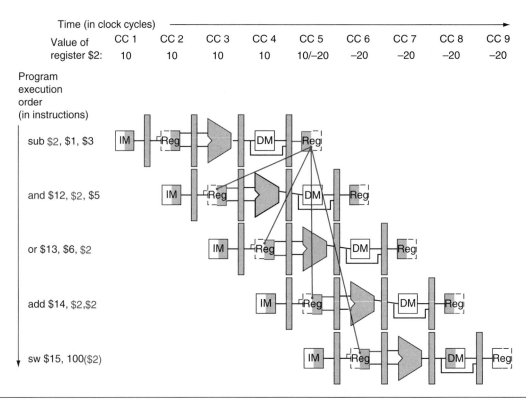

FIGURE 4.52 Pipelined dependences in a five-instruction sequence using simplified datapaths to show the dependences.
All the dependent actions are shown in color, and "CC 1" at the top of the figure means clock cycle 1. The first instruction writes into $2, and all the following instructions read $2. This register is written in clock cycle 5, so the proper value is unavailable before clock cycle 5. (A read of a register during a clock cycle returns the value written at the end of the first half of the cycle, when such a write occurs.) The colored lines from the top datapath to the lower ones show the dependences. Those that must go backward in time are *pipeline data hazards*.

Figure 4.52 shows that the values read for register $2 would *not* be the result of the sub instruction unless the read occurred during clock cycle 5 or later. Thus, the instructions that would get the correct value of −20 are add and sw; the AND and OR instructions would get the incorrect value 10! Using this style of drawing, such problems become apparent when a dependence line goes backward in time.

As mentioned in Section 4.5, the desired result is available at the end of the EX stage or clock cycle 3. When is the data actually needed by the AND and OR instructions? At the beginning of the EX stage, or clock cycles 4 and 5, respectively. Thus, we can execute this segment without stalls if we simply *forward* the data as soon as it is available to any units that need it before it is available to read from the register file.

How does forwarding work? For simplicity in the rest of this section, we consider only the challenge of forwarding to an operation in the EX stage, which may be either an ALU operation or an effective address calculation. This means that when an instruction tries to use a register in its EX stage that an earlier instruction intends to write in its WB stage, we actually need the values as inputs to the ALU.

A notation that names the fields of the pipeline registers allows for a more precise notation of dependences. For example, "ID/EX.RegisterRs" refers to the number of one register whose value is found in the pipeline register ID/EX; that is, the one from the first read port of the register file. The first part of the name, to the left of the period, is the name of the pipeline register; the second part is the name of the field in that register. Using this notation, the two pairs of hazard conditions are

1a. EX/MEM.RegisterRd = ID/EX.RegisterRs

1b. EX/MEM.RegisterRd = ID/EX.RegisterRt

2a. MEM/WB.RegisterRd = ID/EX.RegisterRs

2b. MEM/WB.RegisterRd = ID/EX.RegisterRt

The first hazard in the sequence on page 363 is on register $2, between the result of sub $2, $1, $3 and the first read operand of and $12, $2, $5. This hazard can be detected when the and instruction is in the EX stage and the prior instruction is in the MEM stage, so this is hazard 1a:

$$EX/MEM.RegisterRd = ID/EX.RegisterRs = \$2$$

Dependence Detection

Classify the dependences in this sequence from page 363:

EXAMPLE

```
sub   $2,   $1, $3   # Register $2 set by sub
and   $12,  $2, $5   # 1st operand($2) set by sub
or    $13,  $6, $2   # 2nd operand($2) set by sub
add   $14,  $2, $2   # 1st($2) & 2nd($2) set by sub
sw    $15,  100($2)  # Index($2) set by sub
```

As mentioned above, the sub-and is a type 1a hazard. The remaining hazards are as follows:

ANSWER

- The sub-or is a type 2b hazard:

  MEM/WB.RegisterRd = ID/EX.RegisterRt = $2

- The two dependences on sub-add are not hazards because the register file supplies the proper data during the ID stage of add.

- There is no data hazard between sub and sw because sw reads $2 the clock cycle *after* sub writes $2.

Because some instructions do not write registers, this policy is inaccurate; sometimes it would forward when it shouldn't. One solution is simply to check to see if the RegWrite signal will be active: examining the WB control field of the pipeline register during the EX and MEM stages determines whether RegWrite is asserted. Recall that MIPS requires that every use of $0 as an operand must yield an operand value of 0. In the event that an instruction in the pipeline has $0 as its destination (for example, sll $0, $1, 2), we want to avoid forwarding its possibly nonzero result value. Not forwarding results destined for $0 frees the assembly programmer and the compiler of any requirement to avoid using $0 as a destination. The conditions above thus work properly as long we add EX/MEM.RegisterRd ≠ 0 to the first hazard condition and MEM/WB.RegisterRd ≠ 0 to the second.

Now that we can detect hazards, half of the problem is resolved—but we must still forward the proper data.

Figure 4.53 shows the dependences between the pipeline registers and the inputs to the ALU for the same code sequence as in Figure 4.52. The change is that the dependence begins from a *pipeline* register, rather than waiting for the WB stage to write the register file. Thus, the required data exists in time for later instructions, with the pipeline registers holding the data to be forwarded.

If we can take the inputs to the ALU from *any* pipeline register rather than just ID/EX, then we can forward the proper data. By adding multiplexors to the input of the ALU, and with the proper controls, we can run the pipeline at full speed in the presence of these data dependences.

For now, we will assume the only instructions we need to forward are the four R-format instructions: add, sub, AND, and OR. Figure 4.54 shows a close-up of the ALU and pipeline register before and after adding forwarding. Figure 4.55 shows the values of the control lines for the ALU multiplexors that select either the register file values or one of the forwarded values.

This forwarding control will be in the EX stage, because the ALU forwarding multiplexors are found in that stage. Thus, we must pass the operand register numbers from the ID stage via the ID/EX pipeline register to determine whether to forward values. We already have the rt field (bits 20–16). Before forwarding, the ID/EX register had no need to include space to hold the rs field. Hence, rs (bits 25–21) is added to ID/EX.

Let's now write both the conditions for detecting hazards and the control signals to resolve them:

1. *EX hazard:*

```
if (EX/MEM.RegWrite
and (EX/MEM.RegisterRd ≠ 0)
and (EX/MEM.RegisterRd = ID/EX.RegisterRs)) ForwardA = 10

if (EX/MEM.RegWrite
and (EX/MEM.RegisterRd ≠ 0)
and (EX/MEM.RegisterRd = ID/EX.RegisterRt)) ForwardB = 10
```

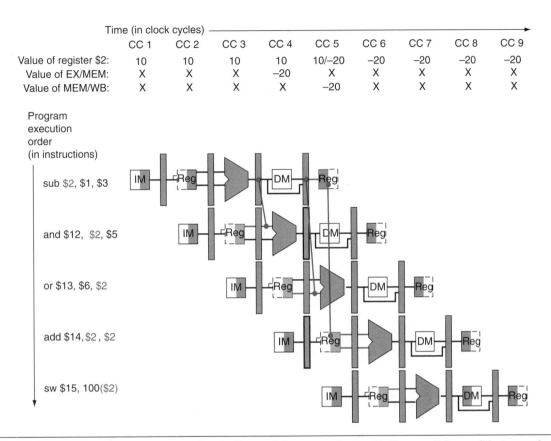

Time (in clock cycles)

	CC 1	CC 2	CC 3	CC 4	CC 5	CC 6	CC 7	CC 8	CC 9
Value of register $2:	10	10	10	10	10/–20	–20	–20	–20	–20
Value of EX/MEM:	X	X	X	–20	X	X	X	X	X
Value of MEM/WB:	X	X	X	X	–20	X	X	X	X

Program
execution
order
(in instructions)

sub $2, $1, $3

and $12, $2, $5

or $13, $6, $2

add $14, $2 , $2

sw $15, 100($2)

FIGURE 4.53 The dependences between the pipeline registers move forward in time, so it is possible to supply the inputs to the ALU needed by the AND **instruction and** OR **instruction by forwarding the results found in the pipeline registers.** The values in the pipeline registers show that the desired value is available before it is written into the register file. We assume that the register file forwards values that are read and written during the same clock cycle, so the add does not stall, but the values come from the register file instead of a pipeline register. Register file "forwarding"—that is, the read gets the value of the write in that clock cycle—is why clock cycle 5 shows register $2 having the value 10 at the beginning and –20 at the end of the clock cycle. As in the rest of this section, we handle all forwarding except for the value to be stored by a store instruction.

Note that the EX/MEM.RegisterRd field is the register destination for either an ALU instruction (which comes from the Rd field of the instruction) or a load (which comes from the Rt field).

This case forwards the result from the previous instruction to either input of the ALU. If the previous instruction is going to write to the register file, and the write register number matches the read register number of ALU inputs A or B, provided

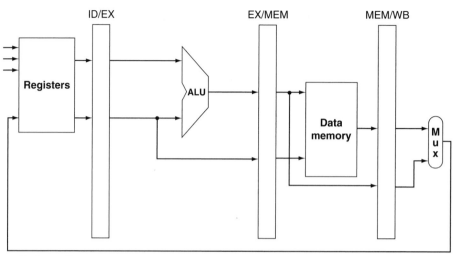

a. No forwarding

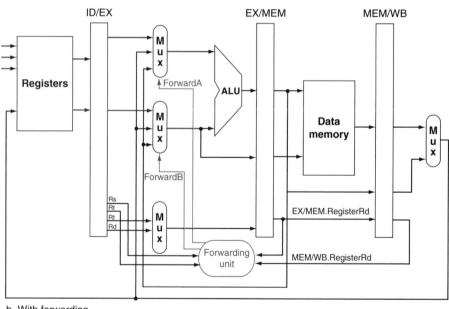

b. With forwarding

FIGURE 4.54   On the top are the ALU and pipeline registers before adding forwarding. On the bottom, the multiplexors have been expanded to add the forwarding paths, and we show the forwarding unit. The new hardware is shown in color. This figure is a stylized drawing, however, leaving out details from the full datapath such as the sign extension hardware. Note that the ID/EX.RegisterRt field is shown twice, once to connect to the mux and once to the forwarding unit, but it is a single signal. As in the earlier discussion, this ignores forwarding of a store value to a store instruction. Also note that this mechanism works for slt instructions as well.

it is not register 0, then steer the multiplexor to pick the value instead from the pipeline register EX/MEM.

2. *MEM hazard:*

```
if (MEM/WB.RegWrite
and (MEM/WB.RegisterRd ≠ 0)
and (MEM/WB.RegisterRd = ID/EX.RegisterRs)) ForwardA = 01

if (MEM/WB.RegWrite
and (MEM/WB.RegisterRd ≠ 0)
and (MEM/WB.RegisterRd = ID/EX.RegisterRt)) ForwardB = 01
```

As mentioned above, there is no hazard in the WB stage, because we assume that the register file supplies the correct result if the instruction in the ID stage reads the same register written by the instruction in the WB stage. Such a register file performs another form of forwarding, but it occurs within the register file.

One complication is potential data hazards between the result of the instruction in the WB stage, the result of the instruction in the MEM stage, and the source operand of the instruction in the ALU stage. For example, when summing a vector of numbers in a single register, a sequence of instructions will all read and write to the same register:

```
add $1,$1,$2
add $1,$1,$3
add $1,$1,$4
. . .
```

In this case, the result is forwarded from the MEM stage because the result in the MEM stage is the more recent result. Thus, the control for the MEM hazard would be (with the additions highlighted):

```
if (MEM/WB.RegWrite
and (MEM/WB.RegisterRd ≠ 0)
and not(EX/MEM.RegWrite and (EX/MEM.RegisterRd ≠ 0))
        and (EX/MEM.RegisterRd ≠ ID/EX.RegisterRs)
and (MEM/WB.RegisterRd = ID/EX.RegisterRs)) ForwardA = 01

if (MEM/WB.RegWrite
and (MEM/WB.RegisterRd ≠ 0)
and not(EX/MEM.RegWrite and (EX/MEM.RegisterRd ≠ 0))
        and (EX/MEM.RegisterRd ≠ ID/EX.RegisterRt)
and (MEM/WB.RegisterRd = ID/EX.RegisterRt)) ForwardB = 01
```

Figure 4.56 shows the hardware necessary to support forwarding for operations that use results during the EX stage. Note that the EX/MEM.RegisterRd field is the

Mux control	Source	Explanation
ForwardA = 00	ID/EX	The first ALU operand comes from the register file.
ForwardA = 10	EX/MEM	The first ALU operand is forwarded from the prior ALU result.
ForwardA = 01	MEM/WB	The first ALU operand is forwarded from data memory or an earlier ALU result.
ForwardB = 00	ID/EX	The second ALU operand comes from the register file.
ForwardB = 10	EX/MEM	The second ALU operand is forwarded from the prior ALU result.
ForwardB = 01	MEM/WB	The second ALU operand is forwarded from data memory or an earlier ALU result.

FIGURE 4.55 The control values for the forwarding multiplexors in Figure 4.54. The signed immediate that is another input to the ALU is described in the *Elaboration* at the end of this section.

register destination for either an ALU instruction (which comes from the Rd field of the instruction) or a load (which comes from the Rt field).

⊚ **Section 4.12** on the CD shows two pieces of MIPS code with hazards that cause forwarding, if you would like to see more illustrated examples using single-cycle pipeline drawings.

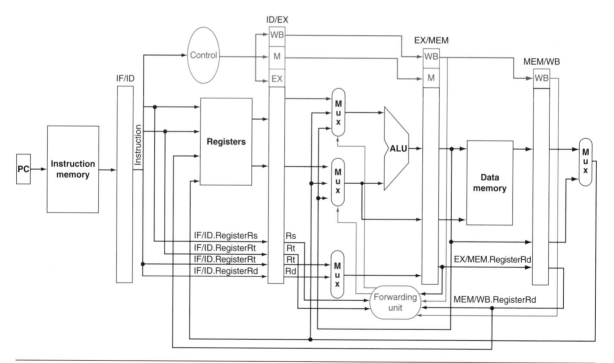

FIGURE 4.56 The datapath modified to resolve hazards via forwarding. Compared with the datapath in Figure 4.51, the additions are the multiplexors to the inputs to the ALU. This figure is a more stylized drawing, however, leaving out details from the full datapath, such as the branch hardware and the sign extension hardware.

Elaboration: Forwarding can also help with hazards when store instructions are dependent on other instructions. Since they use just one data value during the MEM stage, forwarding is easy. However, consider loads immediately followed by stores, useful when performing memory-to-memory copies in the MIPS architecture. Since copies are frequent, we need to add more forwarding hardware to make them run faster. If we were to redraw Figure 4.53, replacing the sub and AND instructions with lw and sw, we would see that it is possible to avoid a stall, since the data exists in the MEM/WB register of a load instruction in time for its use in the MEM stage of a store instruction. We would need to add forwarding into the memory access stage for this option. We leave this modification as an exercise to the reader.

In addition, the signed-immediate input to the ALU, needed by loads and stores, is missing from the datapath in Figure 4.56. Since central control decides between register and immediate, and since the forwarding unit chooses the pipeline register for a register input to the ALU, the easiest solution is to add a 2:1 multiplexor that chooses between the ForwardB multiplexor output and the signed immediate. Figure 4.57 shows this addition.

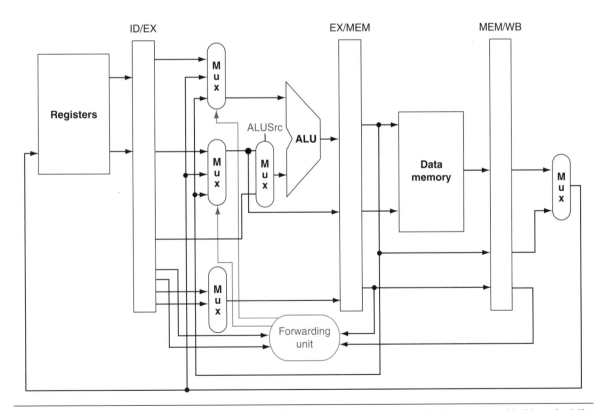

FIGURE 4.57   A close-up of the datapath in Figure 4.54 shows a 2:1 multiplexor, which has been added to select the signed immediate as an ALU input.

If at first you don't succeed, redefine success.

Anonymous

Data Hazards and Stalls

As we said in Section 4.5, one case where forwarding cannot save the day is when an instruction tries to read a register following a load instruction that writes the same register. Figure 4.58 illustrates the problem. The data is still being read from memory in clock cycle 4 while the ALU is performing the operation for the following instruction. Something must stall the pipeline for the combination of load followed by an instruction that reads its result.

Hence, in addition to a forwarding unit, we need a *hazard detection unit*. It operates during the ID stage so that it can insert the stall between the load and its use. Checking for load instructions, the control for the hazard detection unit is this single condition:

```
if (ID/EX.MemRead and
    ((ID/EX.RegisterRt = IF/ID.RegisterRs) or
     (ID/EX.RegisterRt = IF/ID.RegisterRt)))
       stall the pipeline
```

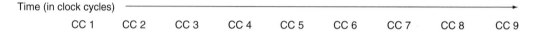

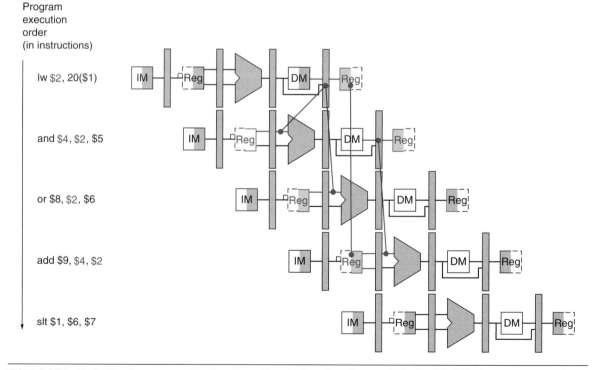

FIGURE 4.58   A pipelined sequence of instructions. Since the dependence between the load and the following instruction (and) goes backward in time, this hazard cannot be solved by forwarding. Hence, this combination must result in a stall by the hazard detection unit.

The first line tests to see if the instruction is a load: the only instruction that reads data memory is a load. The next two lines check to see if the destination register field of the load in the EX stage matches either source register of the instruction in the ID stage. If the condition holds, the instruction stalls one clock cycle. After this 1-cycle stall, the forwarding logic can handle the dependence and execution proceeds. (If there were no forwarding, then the instructions in Figure 4.58 would need another stall cycle.)

If the instruction in the ID stage is stalled, then the instruction in the IF stage must also be stalled; otherwise, we would lose the fetched instruction. Preventing these two instructions from making progress is accomplished simply by preventing the PC register and the IF/ID pipeline register from changing. Provided these registers are preserved, the instruction in the IF stage will continue to be read using the same PC, and the registers in the ID stage will continue to be read using the same instruction fields in the IF/ID pipeline register. Returning to our favorite analogy, it's as if you restart the washer with the same clothes and let the dryer continue tumbling empty. Of course, like the dryer, the back half of the pipeline starting with the EX stage must be doing something; what it is doing is executing instructions that have no effect: **nops**.

nop An instruction that does no operation to change state.

How can we insert these nops, which act like bubbles, into the pipeline? In Figure 4.49, we see that deasserting all nine control signals (setting them to 0) in the EX, MEM, and WB stages will create a "do nothing" or nop instruction. By identifying the hazard in the ID stage, we can insert a bubble into the pipeline by changing the EX, MEM, and WB control fields of the ID/EX pipeline register to 0. These benign control values are percolated forward at each clock cycle with the proper effect: no registers or memories are written if the control values are all 0.

Figure 4.59 shows what really happens in the hardware: the pipeline execution slot associated with the AND instruction is turned into a nop and all instructions beginning with the AND instruction are delayed one cycle. Like an air bubble in a water pipe, a stall bubble delays everything behind it and proceeds down the instruction pipe one stage each cycle until it exits at the end. In this example, the hazard forces the AND and OR instructions to repeat in clock cycle 4 what they did in clock cycle 3: AND reads registers and decodes, and OR is refetched from instruction memory. Such repeated work is what a stall looks like, but its effect is to stretch the time of the AND and OR instructions and delay the fetch of the add instruction.

Figure 4.60 highlights the pipeline connections for both the hazard detection unit and the forwarding unit. As before, the forwarding unit controls the ALU multiplexors to replace the value from a general-purpose register with the value from the proper pipeline register. The hazard detection unit controls the writing of the PC and IF/ID registers plus the multiplexor that chooses between the real control values and all 0s. The hazard detection unit stalls and deasserts the control fields if the load-use hazard test above is true. ⊙ Section 4.12 on the CD gives an example of MIPS code with hazards that causes stalling, illustrated using single-clock pipeline diagrams, if you would like to see more details.

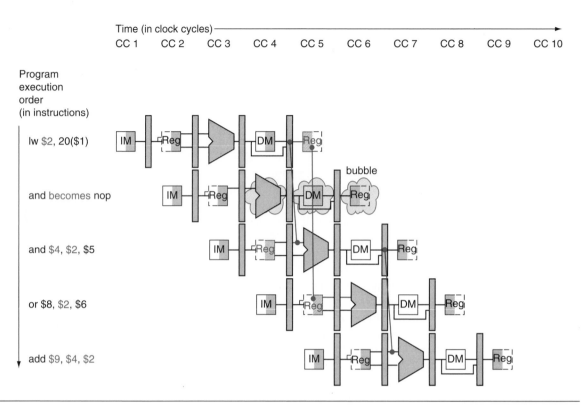

FIGURE 4.59   The way stalls are really inserted into the pipeline. A bubble is inserted beginning in clock cycle 4, by changing the and instruction to a nop. Note that the and instruction is really fetched and decoded in clock cycles 2 and 3, but its EX stage is delayed until clock cycle 5 (versus the unstalled position in clock cycle 4). Likewise the OR instruction is fetched in clock cycle 3, but its ID stage is delayed until clock cycle 5 (versus the unstalled clock cycle 4 position). After insertion of the bubble, all the dependences go forward in time and no further hazards occur.

The **BIG** Picture

Although the compiler generally relies upon the hardware to resolve hazards and thereby ensure correct execution, the compiler must understand the pipeline to achieve the best performance. Otherwise, unexpected stalls will reduce the performance of the compiled code.

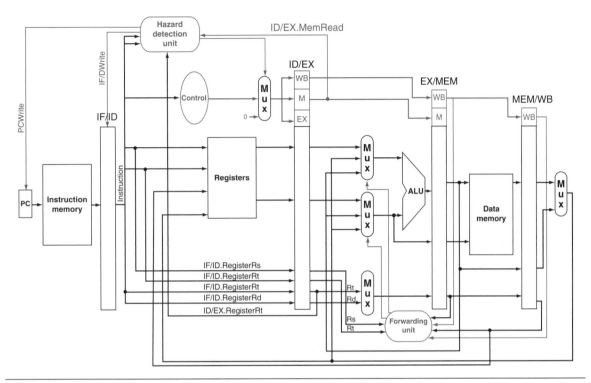

FIGURE 4.60 Pipelined control overview, showing the two multiplexors for forwarding, the hazard detection unit, and the forwarding unit. Although the ID and EX stages have been simplified—the sign-extended immediate and branch logic are missing—this drawing gives the essence of the forwarding hardware requirements.

Elaboration: Regarding the remark earlier about setting control lines to 0 to avoid writing registers or memory: only the signals RegWrite and MemWrite need be 0, while the other control signals can be don't cares.

4.8 Control Hazards

There are a thousand hacking at the branches of evil to one who is striking at the root.

Henry David Thoreau, *Walden*, 1854

Thus far, we have limited our concern to hazards involving arithmetic operations and data transfers. However, as we saw in Section 4.5, there are also pipeline hazards involving branches. Figure 4.61 shows a sequence of instructions and indicates when the branch would occur in this pipeline. An instruction must be fetched

Time (in clock cycles)

CC 1   CC 2   CC 3   CC 4   CC 5   CC 6   CC 7   CC 8   CC 9

Program
execution
order
(in instructions)

40 beq $1, $3, 28

44 and $12, $2, $5

48 or $13, $6, $2

52 add $14, $2, $2

72 lw $4, 50($7)

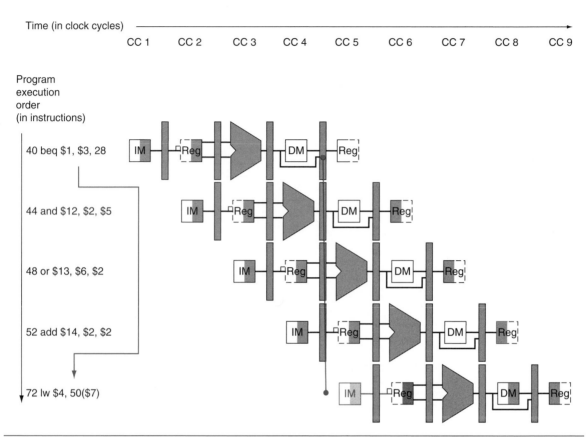

FIGURE 4.61 The impact of the pipeline on the branch instruction. The numbers to the left of the instruction (40, 44, . . .) are the addresses of the instructions. Since the branch instruction decides whether to branch in the MEM stage—clock cycle 4 for the beq instruction above—the three sequential instructions that follow the branch will be fetched and begin execution. Without intervention, those three following instructions will begin execution before beq branches to lw at location 72. (Figure 4.31 assumed extra hardware to reduce the control hazard to one clock cycle; this figure uses the nonoptimized datapath.)

at every clock cycle to sustain the pipeline, yet in our design the decision about whether to branch doesn't occur until the MEM pipeline stage. As mentioned in Section 4.5, this delay in determining the proper instruction to fetch is called a *control hazard* or *branch hazard*, in contrast to the *data hazards* we have just examined.

This section on control hazards is shorter than the previous sections on data hazards. The reasons are that control hazards are relatively simple to understand, they occur less frequently than data hazards, and there is nothing as effective against control hazards as forwarding is against data hazards. Hence, we use simpler schemes. We look at two schemes for resolving control hazards and one optimization to improve these schemes.

Assume Branch Not Taken

As we saw in Section 4.5, stalling until the branch is complete is too slow. A common improvement over branch stalling is to assume that the branch will not be taken and thus continue execution down the sequential instruction stream. If the branch is taken, the instructions that are being fetched and decoded must be discarded. Execution continues at the branch target. If branches are untaken half the time, and if it costs little to discard the instructions, this optimization halves the cost of control hazards.

To discard instructions, we merely change the original control values to 0s, much as we did to stall for a load-use data hazard. The difference is that we must also change the three instructions in the IF, ID, and EX stages when the branch reaches the MEM stage; for load-use stalls, we just changed control to 0 in the ID stage and let them percolate through the pipeline. Discarding instructions, then, means we must be able to **flush** instructions in the IF, ID, and EX stages of the pipeline.

flush To discard instructions in a pipeline, usually due to an unexpected event.

Reducing the Delay of Branches

One way to improve branch performance is to reduce the cost of the taken branch. Thus far, we have assumed the next PC for a branch is selected in the MEM stage, but if we move the branch execution earlier in the pipeline, then fewer instructions need be flushed. The MIPS architecture was designed to support fast single-cycle branches that could be pipelined with a small branch penalty. The designers observed that many branches rely only on simple tests (equality or sign, for example) and that such tests do not require a full ALU operation but can be done with at most a few gates. When a more complex branch decision is required, a separate instruction that uses an ALU to perform a comparison is required—a situation that is similar to the use of condition codes for branches (see Chapter 2).

Moving the branch decision up requires two actions to occur earlier: computing the branch target address and evaluating the branch decision. The easy part of this change is to move up the branch address calculation. We already have the PC value and the immediate field in the IF/ID pipeline register, so we just move the branch adder from the EX stage to the ID stage; of course, the branch target address calculation will be performed for all instructions, but only used when needed.

The harder part is the branch decision itself. For branch equal, we would compare the two registers read during the ID stage to see if they are equal. Equality can be tested by first exclusive ORing their respective bits and then ORing all the results. Moving the branch test to the ID stage implies additional forwarding and hazard detection hardware, since a branch dependent on a result still in the pipeline must still work properly with this optimization. For example, to implement branch on equal (and its inverse), we will need to forward results to the equality test logic that operates during ID. There are two complicating factors:

1. During ID, we must decode the instruction, decide whether a bypass to the equality unit is needed, and complete the equality comparison so that if the instruction is a branch, we can set the PC to the branch target address. Forwarding for the operands of branches was formerly handled by the ALU forwarding logic, but the introduction of the equality test unit in ID will require new forwarding logic. Note that the bypassed source operands of a branch can come from either the ALU/MEM or MEM/WB pipeline latches.

2. Because the values in a branch comparison are needed during ID but may be produced later in time, it is possible that a data hazard can occur and a stall will be needed. For example, if an ALU instruction immediately preceding a branch produces one of the operands for the comparison in the branch, a stall will be required, since the EX stage for the ALU instruction will occur after the ID cycle of the branch. By extension, if a load is immediately followed by a conditional branch that is on the load result, two stall cycles will be needed, as the result from the load appears at the end of the MEM cycle but is needed at the beginning of ID for the branch.

Despite these difficulties, moving the branch execution to the ID stage is an improvement, because it reduces the penalty of a branch to only one instruction if the branch is taken, namely, the one currently being fetched. The exercises explore the details of implementing the forwarding path and detecting the hazard.

To flush instructions in the IF stage, we add a control line, called IF.Flush, that zeros the instruction field of the IF/ID pipeline register. Clearing the register transforms the fetched instruction into a nop, an instruction that has no action and changes no state.

Pipelined Branch

EXAMPLE

Show what happens when the branch is taken in this instruction sequence, assuming the pipeline is optimized for branches that are not taken and that we moved the branch execution to the ID stage:

```
36 sub $10, $4, $8
40 beq  $1, $3, 7 # PC-relative branch to 40+4+7*4=72
44 and $12, $2, $5
48 or  $13, $2, $6
52 add $14, $4, $2
56 slt $15, $6, $7
   . . .
72 lw  $4,  50($7)
```

ANSWER

Figure 4.62 shows what happens when a branch is taken. Unlike Figure 4.61, there is only one pipeline bubble on a taken branch.

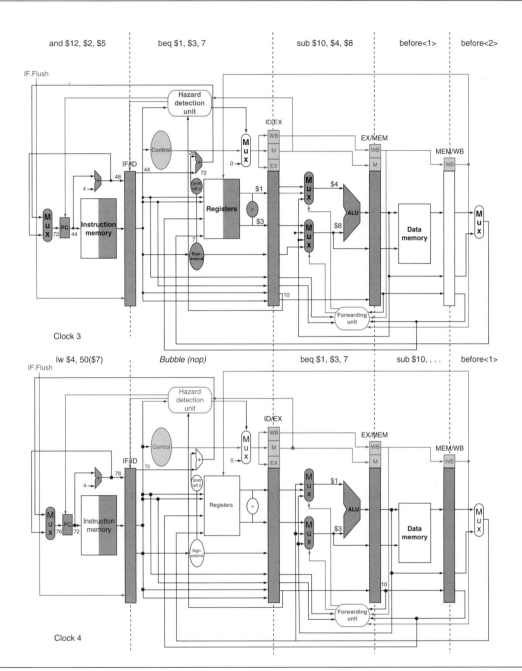

FIGURE 4.62 The ID stage of clock cycle 3 determines that a branch must be taken, so it selects 72 as the next PC address and zeros the instruction fetched for the next clock cycle. Clock cycle 4 shows the instruction at location 72 being fetched and the single bubble or nop instruction in the pipeline as a result of the taken branch. (Since the nop is really s11 $0, $0, 0, it's arguable whether or not the ID stage in clock 4 should be highlighted.)

Dynamic Branch Prediction

Assuming a branch is not taken is one simple form of *branch prediction*. In that case, we predict that branches are untaken, flushing the pipeline when we are wrong. For the simple five-stage pipeline, such an approach, possibly coupled with compiler-based prediction, is probably adequate. With deeper pipelines, the branch penalty increases when measured in clock cycles. Similarly, with multiple issue (see Section 4.10), the branch penalty increases in terms of instructions lost. This combination means that in an aggressive pipeline, a simple static prediction scheme will probably waste too much performance. As we mentioned in Section 4.5, with more hardware it is possible to try to predict branch behavior during program execution.

One approach is to look up the address of the instruction to see if a branch was taken the last time this instruction was executed, and, if so, to begin fetching new instructions from the same place as the last time. This technique is called **dynamic branch prediction**.

One implementation of that approach is a **branch prediction buffer** or **branch history table**. A branch prediction buffer is a small memory indexed by the lower portion of the address of the branch instruction. The memory contains a bit that says whether the branch was recently taken or not.

This is the simplest sort of buffer; we don't know, in fact, if the prediction is the right one—it may have been put there by another branch that has the same low-order address bits. However, this doesn't affect correctness. Prediction is just a hint that we hope is correct, so fetching begins in the predicted direction. If the hint turns out to be wrong, the incorrectly predicted instructions are deleted, the prediction bit is inverted and stored back, and the proper sequence is fetched and executed.

This simple 1-bit prediction scheme has a performance shortcoming: even if a branch is almost always taken, we can predict incorrectly twice, rather than once, when it is not taken. The following example shows this dilemma.

dynamic branch prediction Prediction of branches at runtime using runtime information.

branch prediction buffer Also called **branch history table**. A small memory that is indexed by the lower portion of the address of the branch instruction and that contains one or more bits indicating whether the branch was recently taken or not.

EXAMPLE

ANSWER

Loops and Prediction

Consider a loop branch that branches nine times in a row, then is not taken once. What is the prediction accuracy for this branch, assuming the prediction bit for this branch remains in the prediction buffer?

The steady-state prediction behavior will mispredict on the first and last loop iterations. Mispredicting the last iteration is inevitable since the prediction bit will indicate taken, as the branch has been taken nine times in a row at that point. The misprediction on the first iteration happens because the bit is flipped on prior execution of the last iteration of the loop, since the branch was not taken on that exiting iteration. Thus, the prediction accuracy for this branch that is taken 90% of the time is only 80% (two incorrect predictions and eight correct ones).

Ideally, the accuracy of the predictor would match the taken branch frequency for these highly regular branches. To remedy this weakness, 2-bit prediction schemes are often used. In a 2-bit scheme, a prediction must be wrong twice before it is changed. Figure 4.63 shows the finite-state machine for a 2-bit prediction scheme.

A branch prediction buffer can be implemented as a small, special buffer accessed with the instruction address during the IF pipe stage. If the instruction is predicted as taken, fetching begins from the target as soon as the PC is known; as mentioned on page 377, it can be as early as the ID stage. Otherwise, sequential fetching and executing continue. If the prediction turns out to be wrong, the prediction bits are changed as shown in Figure 4.63.

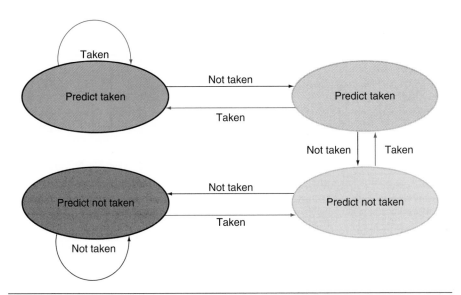

FIGURE 4.63 The states in a 2-bit prediction scheme. By using 2 bits rather than 1, a branch that strongly favors taken or not taken—as many branches do—will be mispredicted only once. The 2 bits are used to encode the four states in the system. The 2-bit scheme is a general instance of a counter-based predictor, which is incremented when the prediction is accurate and decremented otherwise, and uses the midpoint of its range as the division between taken and not taken.

Elaboration: As we described in Section 4.5, in a five-stage pipeline we can make the control hazard a feature by redefining the branch. A delayed branch always executes the following instruction, but the second instruction following the branch will be affected by the branch.

Compilers and assemblers try to place an instruction that always executes after the branch in the **branch delay slot**. The job of the software is to make the successor instructions valid and useful. Figure 4.64 shows the three ways in which the branch delay slot can be scheduled.

The limitations on delayed branch scheduling arise from (1) the restrictions on the instructions that are scheduled into the delay slots and (2) our ability to predict at compile time whether a branch is likely to be taken or not.

branch delay slot The slot directly after a delayed branch instruction, which in the MIPS architecture is filled by an instruction that does not affect the branch.

Delayed branching was a simple and effective solution for a five-stage pipeline issuing one instruction each clock cycle. As processors go to both longer pipelines and issuing multiple instructions per clock cycle (see Section 4.10), the branch delay becomes longer, and a single delay slot is insufficient. Hence, delayed branching has lost popularity compared to more expensive but more flexible dynamic approaches. Simultaneously, the growth in available transistors per chip has made dynamic prediction relatively cheaper.

Elaboration: A branch predictor tells us whether or not a branch is taken, but still requires the calculation of the branch target. In the five-stage pipeline, this calculation takes one cycle, meaning that taken branches will have a 1-cycle penalty. Delayed branches are

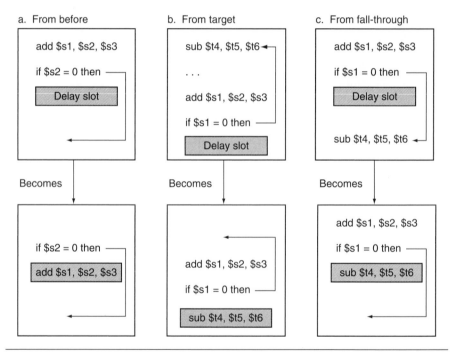

FIGURE 4.64 Scheduling the branch delay slot. The top box in each pair shows the code before scheduling; the bottom box shows the scheduled code. In (a), the delay slot is scheduled with an independent instruction from before the branch. This is the best choice. Strategies (b) and (c) are used when (a) is not possible. In the code sequences for (b) and (c), the use of $s1 in the branch condition prevents the add instruction (whose destination is $s1) from being moved into the branch delay slot. In (b) the branch delay slot is scheduled from the target of the branch; usually the target instruction will need to be copied because it can be reached by another path. Strategy (b) is preferred when the branch is taken with high probability, such as a loop branch. Finally, the branch may be scheduled from the not-taken fall-through as in (c). To make this optimization legal for (b) or (c), it must be OK to execute the sub instruction when the branch goes in the unexpected direction. By "OK" we mean that the work is wasted, but the program will still execute correctly. This is the case, for example, if $t4 were an unused temporary register when the branch goes in the unexpected direction.

one approach to eliminate that penalty. Another approach is to use a cache to hold the destination program counter or destination instruction using a **branch target buffer**.

The 2-bit dynamic prediction scheme uses only information about a particular branch. Researchers noticed that using information about both a local branch, and the global behavior of recently executed branches together yields greater prediction accuracy for the same number of prediction bits. Such predictors are called **correlating predictors**. A typical correlating predictor might have two 2-bit predictors for each branch, with the choice between predictors made based on whether the last executed branch was taken or not taken. Thus, the global branch behavior can be thought of as adding additional index bits for the prediction lookup.

A more recent innovation in branch prediction is the use of tournament predictors. A **tournament predictor** uses multiple predictors, tracking, for each branch, which predictor yields the best results. A typical tournament predictor might contain two predictions for each branch index: one based on local information and one based on global branch behavior. A selector would choose which predictor to use for any given prediction. The selector can operate similarly to a 1- or 2-bit predictor, favoring whichever of the two predictors has been more accurate. Some recent microprocessors use such elaborate predictors.

Elaboration: One way to reduce the number of conditional branches is to add *conditional move* instructions. Instead of changing the PC with a conditional branch, the instruction conditionally changes the destination register of the move. If the condition fails, the move acts as a nop. For example, one version of the MIPS instruction set architecture has two new instructions called movn (move if not zero) and movz (move if zero). Thus, movn $8, $11, $4 copies the contents of register 11 into register 8, provided that the value in register 4 is nonzero; otherwise, it does nothing.

The ARM instruction set has a condition field in most instructions. Hence, ARM programs could have fewer conditional branches than in MIPS programs.

branch target buffer
A structure that caches the destination PC or destination instruction for a branch. It is usually organized as a cache with tags, making it more costly than a simple prediction buffer.

correlating predictor
A branch predictor that combines local behavior of a particular branch and global information about the behavior of some recent number of executed branches.

tournament branch predictor A branch predictor with multiple predictions for each branch and a selection mechanism that chooses which predictor to enable for a given branch.

Pipeline Summary

We started in the laundry room, showing principles of pipelining in an everyday setting. Using that analogy as a guide, we explained instruction pipelining step-by-step, starting with the single-cycle datapath and then adding pipeline registers, forwarding paths, data hazard detection, branch prediction, and flushing instructions on exceptions. Figure 4.65 shows the final evolved datapath and control. We now are ready for yet another control hazard: the sticky issue of exceptions.

Consider three branch prediction schemes: branch not taken, predict taken, and dynamic prediction. Assume that they all have zero penalty when they predict correctly and two cycles when they are wrong. Assume that the average predict accuracy of the dynamic predictor is 90%. Which predictor is the best choice for the following branches?

1. A branch that is taken with 5% frequency

2. A branch that is taken with 95% frequency

3. A branch that is taken with 70% frequency

Check Yourself

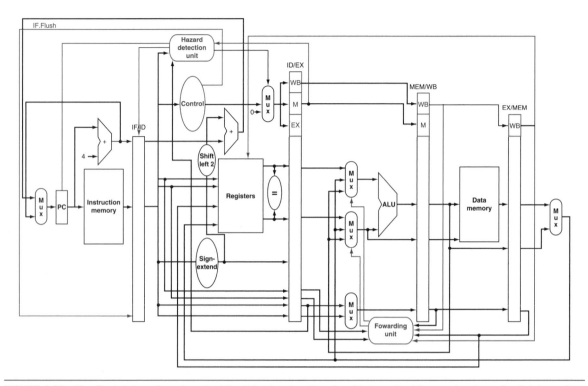

FIGURE 4.65   The final datapath and control for this chapter. Note that this is a stylized figure rather than a detailed datapath, so it's missing the ALUsrc mux from Figure 4.57 and the multiplexor controls from Figure 4.51.

> To make a computer
> with automatic
> program-interruption
> facilities behave
> [sequentially] was
> not an easy matter,
> because the number of
> instructions in various
> stages of processing
> when an interrupt
> signal occurs may be
> large.
>
> Fred Brooks, Jr.,
> *Planning a Computer
> System: Project Stretch*,
> 1962

4.9   Exceptions

Control is the most challenging aspect of processor design: it is both the hardest part to get right and the hardest part to make fast. One of the hardest parts of control is implementing **exceptions** and **interrupts**—events other than branches or jumps that change the normal flow of instruction execution. They were initially created to handle unexpected events from within the processor, like arithmetic overflow. The same basic mechanism was extended for I/O devices to communicate with the processor, as we will see in Chapter 6.

Many architectures and authors do not distinguish between interrupts and exceptions, often using the older name *interrupt* to refer to both types of events. For example, the Intel x86 uses interrupt. We follow the MIPS convention, using the term *exception* to refer to *any* unexpected change in control flow without distinguishing whether the cause is internal or external; we use the term *interrupt* only when the event is externally caused. Here are five examples showing whether the situation is internally generated by the processor or externally generated:

exception Also called **interrupt**. An unscheduled event that disrupts program execution; used to detect overflow.

Type of event	From where?	MIPS terminology
I/O device request	External	Interrupt
Invoke the operating system from user program	Internal	Exception
Arithmetic overflow	Internal	Exception
Using an undefined instruction	Internal	Exception
Hardware malfunctions	Either	Exception or interrupt

interrupt An exception that comes from outside of the processor. (Some architectures use the term *interrupt* for all exceptions.)

Many of the requirements to support exceptions come from the specific situation that causes an exception to occur. Accordingly, we will return to this topic in Chapter 5, when we discuss memory hierarchies, and in Chapter 6, when we discuss I/O, and we will better understand the motivation for additional capabilities in the exception mechanism. In this section, we deal with the control implementation for detecting two types of exceptions that arise from the portions of the instruction set and implementation that we have already discussed.

Detecting exceptional conditions and taking the appropriate action is often on the critical timing path of a processor, which determines the clock cycle time and thus performance. Without proper attention to exceptions during design of the control unit, attempts to add exceptions to a complicated implementation can significantly reduce performance, as well as complicate the task of getting the design correct.

How Exceptions Are Handled in the MIPS Architecture

The two types of exceptions that our current implementation can generate are execution of an undefined instruction and an arithmetic overflow. We'll use arithmetic overflow in the instruction add $1, $2, $1 as the example exception in the next few pages. The basic action that the processor must perform when an exception occurs is to save the address of the offending instruction in the *exception program counter* (*EPC*) and then transfer control to the operating system at some specified address.

The operating system can then take the appropriate action, which may involve providing some service to the user program, taking some predefined action in response to an overflow, or stopping the execution of the program and reporting an error. After performing whatever action is required because of the exception, the operating system can terminate the program or may continue its execution, using the EPC to determine where to restart the execution of the program. In Chapter 5, we will look more closely at the issue of restarting the execution.

For the operating system to handle the exception, it must know the reason for the exception, in addition to the instruction that caused it. There are two main methods used to communicate the reason for an exception. The method used in the MIPS architecture is to include a status register (called the *Cause register*), which holds a field that indicates the reason for the exception.

A second method, is to use **vectored interrupts**. In a vectored interrupt, the address to which control is transferred is determined by the cause of the exception. For example, to accommodate the two exception types listed above, we might define the following two exception vector addresses:

vectored interrupt An interrupt for which the address to which control is transferred is determined by the cause of the exception.

Exception type	Exception vector address (in hex)
Undefined instruction	$8000\ 0000_{hex}$
Arithmetic overflow	$8000\ 0180_{hex}$

The operating system knows the reason for the exception by the address at which it is initiated. The addresses are separated by 32 bytes or eight instructions, and the operating system must record the reason for the exception and may perform some limited processing in this sequence. When the exception is not vectored, a single entry point for all exceptions can be used, and the operating system decodes the status register to find the cause.

We can perform the processing required for exceptions by adding a few extra registers and control signals to our basic implementation and by slightly extending control. Let's assume that we are implementing the exception system used in the MIPS architecture, with the single entry point being the address $8000\ 0180_{hex}$. (Implementing vectored exceptions is no more difficult.) We will need to add two additional registers to the MIPS implementation:

- *EPC:* A 32-bit register used to hold the address of the affected instruction. (Such a register is needed even when exceptions are vectored.)

- *Cause:* A register used to record the cause of the exception. In the MIPS architecture, this register is 32 bits, although some bits are currently unused. Assume there is a five-bit field that encodes the two possible exception sources mentioned above, with 10 representing an undefined instruction and 12 representing arithmetic overflow.

Exceptions in a Pipelined Implementation

A pipelined implementation treats exceptions as another form of control hazard. For example, suppose there is an arithmetic overflow in an add instruction. Just as we did for the taken branch in the previous section, we must flush the instructions that follow the add instruction from the pipeline and begin fetching instructions from the new address. We will use the same mechanism we used for taken branches, but this time the exception causes the deasserting of control lines.

When we dealt with branch mispredict, we saw how to flush the instruction in the IF stage by turning it into a nop. To flush instructions in the ID stage, we use the multiplexor already in the ID stage that zeros control signals for stalls.

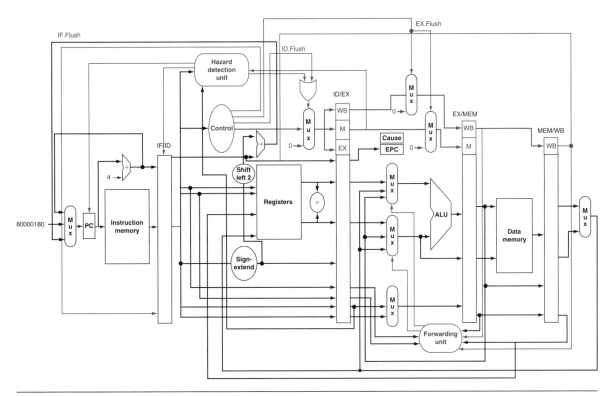

FIGURE 4.66 The datapath with controls to handle exceptions. The key additions include a new input with the value 8000 0180$_{hex}$ in the multiplexor that supplies the new PC value; a Cause register to record the cause of the exception; and an Exception PC register to save the address of the instruction that caused the exception. The 8000 0180$_{hex}$ input to the multiplexor is the initial address to begin fetching instructions in the event of an exception. Although not shown, the ALU overflow signal is an input to the control unit.

A new control signal, called ID.Flush, is ORed with the stall signal from the hazard detection unit to flush during ID. To flush the instruction in the EX phase, we use a new signal called EX.Flush to cause new multiplexors to zero the control lines. To start fetching instructions from location 8000 0180$_{hex}$, which is the MIPS exception address, we simply add an additional input to the PC multiplexor that sends 8000 0180$_{hex}$ to the PC. Figure 4.66 shows these changes.

This example points out a problem with exceptions: if we do not stop execution in the middle of the instruction, the programmer will not be able to see the original value of register $1 that helped cause the overflow because it will be clobbered as the Destination register of the add instruction. Because of careful planning, the overflow exception is detected during the EX stage; hence, we can use the EX.Flush signal to prevent the instruction in the EX stage from writing its result in the WB stage. Many exceptions require that we eventually complete the instruction that caused the exception as if it executed normally. The easiest way to do this is to flush the instruction and restart it from the beginning after the exception is handled.

The final step is to save the address of the offending instruction in the exception program counter (EPC). In reality, we save the address + 4, so the exception handling routine must first subtract 4 from the saved value. Figure 4.66 shows a stylized version of the datapath, including the branch hardware and necessary accommodations to handle exceptions.

EXAMPLE

Exception in a Pipelined Computer

Given this instruction sequence,

```
40hex   sub    $11, $2, $4
44hex   and    $12, $2, $5
48hex   or     $13, $2, $6
4Chex   add     $1, $2, $1
50hex   slt    $15, $6, $7
54hex   lw     $16, 50($7)
. . .
```

assume the instructions to be invoked on an exception begin like this:

```
80000180hex   sw     $26, 1000($0)
80000184hex   sw     $27, 1004($0)
. . .
```

Show what happens in the pipeline if an overflow exception occurs in the `add` instruction.

ANSWER

Figure 4.67 shows the events, starting with the `add` instruction in the EX stage. The overflow is detected during that phase, and $8000\ 0180_{hex}$ is forced into the PC. Clock cycle 7 shows that the `add` and following instructions are flushed, and the first instruction of the exception code is fetched. Note that the address of the instruction *following* the `add` is saved: $4C_{hex} + 4 = 50_{hex}$.

We mentioned five examples of exceptions on page 385, and we will see others in Chapters 5 and 6. With five instructions active in any clock cycle, the challenge is to associate an exception with the appropriate instruction. Moreover, multiple exceptions can occur simultaneously in a single clock cycle. The solution is to prioritize the exceptions so that it is easy to determine which is serviced first. In most MIPS implementations, the hardware sorts exceptions so that the earliest instruction is interrupted.

I/O device requests and hardware malfunctions are not associated with a specific instruction, so the implementation has some flexibility as to when to interrupt the pipeline. Hence, the mechanism used for other exceptions works just fine.

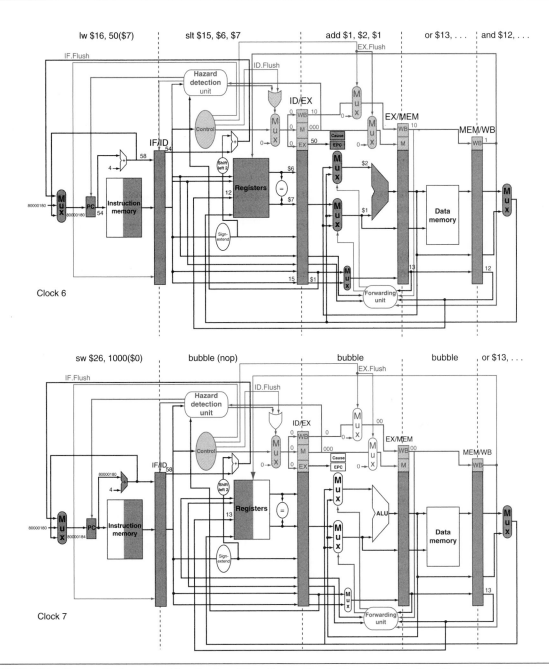

FIGURE 4.67 The result of an exception due to arithmetic overflow in the add instruction. The overflow is detected during the EX stage of clock 6, saving the address following the add in the EPC register (4C + 4 = 50$_{hex}$). Overflow causes all the Flush signals to be set near the end of this clock cycle, deasserting control values (setting them to 0) for the add. Clock cycle 7 shows the instructions converted to bubbles in the pipeline plus the fetching of the first instruction of the exception routine—sw $25, 1000($0)—from instruction location 8000 0180$_{hex}$. Note that the AND and OR instructions, which are prior to the add, still complete. Although not shown, the ALU overflow signal is an input to the control unit.

The EPC captures the address of the interrupted instructions, and the MIPS Cause register records all possible exceptions in a clock cycle, so the exception software must match the exception to the instruction. An important clue is knowing in which pipeline stage a type of exception can occur. For example, an undefined instruction is discovered in the ID stage, and invoking the operating system occurs in the EX stage. Exceptions are collected in the Cause register in a pending exception field so that the hardware can interrupt based on later exceptions, once the earliest one has been serviced.

Hardware/ Software Interface

The hardware and the operating system must work in conjunction so that exceptions behave as you would expect. The hardware contract is normally to stop the offending instruction in midstream, let all prior instructions complete, flush all following instructions, set a register to show the cause of the exception, save the address of the offending instruction, and then jump to a prearranged address. The operating system contract is to look at the cause of the exception and act appropriately. For an undefined instruction, hardware failure, or arithmetic overflow exception, the operating system normally kills the program and returns an indicator of the reason. For an I/O device request or an operating system service call, the operating system saves the state of the program, performs the desired task, and, at some point in the future, restores the program to continue execution. In the case of I/O device requests, we may often choose to run another task before resuming the task that requested the I/O, since that task may often not be able to proceed until the I/O is complete. This is why the ability to save and restore the state of any task is critical. One of the most important and frequent uses of exceptions is handling page faults and TLB exceptions; Chapter 5 describes these exceptions and their handling in more detail.

---

imprecise interrupt Also called **imprecise exception**. Interrupts or exceptions in pipelined computers that are not associated with the exact instruction that was the cause of the interrupt or exception.

precise interrupt Also called **precise exception**. An interrupt or exception that is always associated with the correct instrucion in pipelined computers.

Elaboration: The difficulty of always associating the correct exception with the correct instruction in pipelined computers has led some computer designers to relax this requirement in noncritical cases. Such processors are said to have **imprecise interrupts** or **imprecise exceptions**. In the example above, PC would normally have 58_{hex} at the start of the clock cycle after the exception is detected, even though the offending instruction is at address $4C_{hex}$. A processor with imprecise exceptions might put 58_{hex} into EPC and leave it up to the operating system to determine which instruction caused the problem. MIPS and the vast majority of computers today support **precise interrupts** or **precise exceptions**. (One reason is to support virtual memory, which we shall see in Chapter 5.)

Elaboration: Although MIPS uses the exception entry address 8000 0180$_{hex}$ for almost all exceptions, it uses the address 8000 0000$_{hex}$ to improve performance of the exception handler for TLB-miss exceptions (see Chapter 5).

Which exception should be recognized first in this sequence?

1. `add $1, $2, $1`   # arithmetic overflow

2. `XXX $1, $2, $1`   # undefined instruction

3. `sub $1, $2, $1`   # hardware error

4.10   Parallelism and Advanced Instruction-Level Parallelism

Be forewarned: this section is a brief overview of fascinating but advanced topics. If you want to learn more details, you should consult our more advanced book, *Computer Architecture: A Quantitative Approach*, fourth edition, where the material covered in the next 13 pages is expanded to almost 200 pages (including Appendices)!

Pipelining exploits the potential parallelism among instructions. This parallelism is called **instruction-level parallelism** (ILP). There are two primary methods for increasing the potential amount of instruction-level parallelism. The first is increasing the depth of the pipeline to overlap more instructions. Using our laundry analogy and assuming that the washer cycle was longer than the others were, we could divide our washer into three machines that perform the wash, rinse, and spin steps of a traditional washer. We would then move from a four-stage to a six-stage pipeline. To get the full speed-up, we need to rebalance the remaining steps so they are the same length, in processors or in laundry. The amount of parallelism being exploited is higher, since there are more operations being overlapped. Performance is potentially greater since the clock cycle can be shorter.

Another approach is to replicate the internal components of the computer so that it can launch multiple instructions in every pipeline stage. The general name for this technique is **multiple issue**. A multiple-issue laundry would replace our household washer and dryer with, say, three washers and three dryers. You would also have to recruit more assistants to fold and put away three times as much laundry in the same amount of time. The downside is the extra work to keep all the machines busy and transferring the loads to the next pipeline stage.

Launching multiple instructions per stage allows the instruction execution rate to exceed the clock rate or, stated alternatively, the CPI to be less than 1. It is sometimes useful to flip the metric and use *IPC*, or *instructions per clock cycle*. Hence, a 4 GHz four-way multiple-issue microprocessor can execute a peak rate of 16 billion instructions per second and have a best-case CPI of 0.25, or an IPC of 4. Assuming a five-stage pipeline, such a processor would have 20 instructions in execution at any given time. Today's high-end microprocessors attempt to issue from three to six instructions in every clock cycle. There are typically, however, many constraints on what types of instructions may be executed simultaneously and what happens when dependences arise.

instruction-level parallelism The parallelism among instructions.

multiple issue A scheme whereby multiple instructions are launched in one clock cycle.

static multiple issue
An approach to implementing a multiple-issue processor where many decisions are made by the compiler before execution.

dynamic multiple issue An approach to implementing a multiple-issue processor where many decisions are made during execution by the processor.

issue slots The positions from which instructions could issue in a given clock cycle; by analogy, these correspond to positions at the starting blocks for a sprint.

There are two major ways to implement a multiple-issue processor, with the major difference being the division of work between the compiler and the hardware. Because the division of work dictates whether decisions are being made statically (that is, at compile time) or dynamically (that is, during execution), the approaches are sometimes called **static multiple issue** and **dynamic multiple issue**. As we will see, both approaches have other, more commonly used names, which may be less precise or more restrictive.

There are two primary and distinct responsibilities that must be dealt with in a multiple-issue pipeline:

1. Packaging instructions into **issue slots**: how does the processor determine how many instructions and which instructions can be issued in a given clock cycle? In most static issue processors, this process is at least partially handled by the compiler; in dynamic issue designs, it is normally dealt with at runtime by the processor, although the compiler will often have already tried to help improve the issue rate by placing the instructions in a beneficial order.

2. Dealing with data and control hazards: in static issue processors, some or all of the consequences of data and control hazards are handled statically by the compiler. In contrast, most dynamic issue processors attempt to alleviate at least some classes of hazards using hardware techniques operating at execution time.

Although we describe these as distinct approaches, in reality techniques from one approach are often borrowed by the other, and neither approach can claim to be perfectly pure.

The Concept of Speculation

speculation An approach whereby the compiler or processor guesses the outcome of an instruction to remove it as a dependence in executing other instructions.

One of the most important methods for finding and exploiting more ILP is speculation. **Speculation** is an approach that allows the compiler or the processor to "guess" about the properties of an instruction, so as to enable execution to begin for other instructions that may depend on the speculated instruction. For example, we might speculate on the outcome of a branch, so that instructions after the branch could be executed earlier. Another example is that we might speculate that a store that precedes a load does not refer to the same address, which would allow the load to be executed before the store. The difficulty with speculation is that it may be wrong. So, any speculation mechanism must include both a method to check if the guess was right and a method to unroll or back out the effects of the instructions that were executed speculatively. The implementation of this back-out capability adds complexity.

Speculation may be done in the compiler or by the hardware. For example, the compiler can use speculation to reorder instructions, moving an instruction across

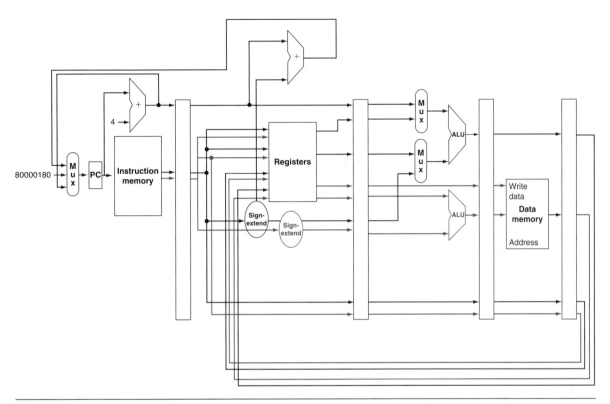

FIGURE 4.69 A static two-issue datapath. The additions needed for double issue are highlighted: another 32 bits from instruction memory, two more read ports and one more write port on the register file, and another ALU. Assume the bottom ALU handles address calculations for data transfers and the top ALU handles everything else.

two registers for the ALU operation and two more for a store, and also one write port for an ALU operation and one write port for a load. Since the ALU is tied up for the ALU operation, we also need a separate adder to calculate the effective address for data transfers. Without these extra resources, our two-issue pipeline would be hindered by structural hazards.

Clearly, this two-issue processor can improve performance by up to a factor of 2. Doing so, however, requires that twice as many instructions be overlapped in execution, and this additional overlap increases the relative performance loss from data and control hazards. For example, in our simple five-stage pipeline, loads have a **use latency** of one clock cycle, which prevents one instruction from using the result without stalling. In the two-issue, five-stage pipeline the result of a load instruction cannot be used on the next *clock cycle*. This means that the next *two* instructions cannot use the load result without stalling. Furthermore, ALU instructions that had no use latency in the simple five-stage pipeline now have a

use latency Number of clock cycles between a load instruction and an instruction that can use the result of the load without stalling the pipeline.

one-instruction use latency, since the results cannot be used in the paired load or store. To effectively exploit the parallelism available in a multiple-issue processor, more ambitious compiler or hardware scheduling techniques are needed, and static multiple issue requires that the compiler take on this role.

EXAMPLE

Simple Multiple-Issue Code Scheduling

How would this loop be scheduled on a static two-issue pipeline for MIPS?

```
Loop: lw      $t0, 0($s1)      # $t0=array element
      addu    $t0,$t0,$s2# add scalar in $s2
      sw      $t0, 0($s1)# store result
      addi    $s1,$s1,-4# decrement pointer
      bne     $s1,$zero,Loop# branch $s1!=0
```

Reorder the instructions to avoid as many pipeline stalls as possible. Assume branches are predicted, so that control hazards are handled by the hardware.

ANSWER

The first three instructions have data dependences, and so do the last two. Figure 4.70 shows the best schedule for these instructions. Notice that just one pair of instructions has both issue slots used. It takes four clocks per loop iteration; at four clocks to execute five instructions, we get the disappointing CPI of 0.8 versus the best case of 0.5., or an IPC of 1.25 versus 2.0. Notice that in computing CPI or IPC, we do not count any nops executed as useful instructions. Doing so would improve CPI, but not performance!

	ALU or branch instruction	Data transfer instruction	Clock cycle
Loop:		lw $t0, 0($s1)	1
	addi $s1,$s1,-4		2
	addu $t0,$t0,$s2		3
	bne $s1,$zero,Loop	sw $t0, 4($s1)	4

FIGURE 4.70   The scheduled code as it would look on a two-issue MIPS pipeline. The empty slots are nops.

An important compiler technique to get more performance from loops is **loop unrolling**, where multiple copies of the loop body are made. After unrolling, there is more ILP available by overlapping instructions from different iterations.

loop unrolling
A technique to get more performance from loops that access arrays, in which multiple copies of the loop body are made and instructions from different iterations are scheduled together.

Loop Unrolling for Multiple-Issue Pipelines

See how well loop unrolling and scheduling work in the example above. For simplicity assume that the loop index is a multiple of four.

EXAMPLE

To schedule the loop without any delays, it turns out that we need to make four copies of the loop body. After unrolling and eliminating the unnecessary loop overhead instructions, the loop will contain four copies each of `lw`, `add`, and `sw`, plus one `addi` and one `bne`. Figure 4.71 shows the unrolled and scheduled code.

ANSWER

During the unrolling process, the compiler introduced additional registers ($t1, $t2, $t3). The goal of this process, called **register renaming**, is to eliminate dependences that are not true data dependences, but could either lead to potential hazards or prevent the compiler from flexibly scheduling the code. Consider how the unrolled code would look using only $t0. There would be repeated instances of `lw $t0,0($$s1),addu $t0,$t0,$s2` followed by `sw t0,4($s1)`, but these sequences, despite using $t0, are actually completely independent—no data values flow between one pair of these instructions and the next pair. This is what is called an **antidependence** or **name dependence**, which is an ordering forced purely by the reuse of a name, rather than a real data dependence which is also called a true dependence.

register renaming The renaming of registers by the compiler or hardware to remove antidependences.

Renaming the registers during the unrolling process allows the compiler to move these independent instructions subsequently so as to better schedule the code. The renaming process eliminates the name dependences, while preserving the true dependences.

antidependence Also called name dependence. An ordering forced by the reuse of a name, typically a register, rather than by a true dependence that carries a value between two instructions.

Notice now that 12 of the 14 instructions in the loop execute as pairs. It takes 8 clocks for 4 loop iterations, or 2 clocks per iteration, which yields a CPI of $8/14 = 0.57$. Loop unrolling and scheduling with dual issue gave us an improvement factor of almost 2, partly from reducing the loop control instructions and partly from dual issue execution. The cost of this performance improvement is using four temporary registers rather than one, as well as a significant increase in code size.

Dynamic Multiple-Issue Processors

Dynamic multiple-issue processors are also known as **superscalar** processors, or simply superscalars. In the simplest superscalar processors, instructions issue in order, and the processor decides whether zero, one, or more instructions can issue

superscalar An advanced pipelining technique that enables the processor to execute more than one instruction per clock cycle by selecting them during execution.

	ALU or branch instruction		Data transfer instruction		Clock cycle
Loop:	addi	$s1,$s1,-16	lw	$t0, 0($s1)	1
			lw	$t1,12($s1)	2
	addu	$t0,$t0,$s2	lw	$t2, 8($s1)	3
	addu	$t1,$t1,$s2	lw	$t3, 4($s1)	4
	addu	$t2,$t2,$s2	sw	$t0, 16($s1)	5
	addu	$t3,$t3,$s2	sw	$t1,12($s1)	6
			sw	$t2, 8($s1)	7
	bne	$s1,$zero,Loop	sw	$t3, 4($s1)	8

FIGURE 4.71   The unrolled and scheduled code of Figure 4.70 as it would look on a static two-issue MIPS pipeline. The empty slots are nops. Since the first instruction in the loop decrements $s1 by 16, the addresses loaded are the original value of $s1, then that address minus 4, minus 8, and minus 12.

in a given clock cycle. Obviously, achieving good performance on such a processor still requires the compiler to try to schedule instructions to move dependences apart and thereby improve the instruction issue rate. Even with such compiler scheduling, there is an important difference between this simple superscalar and a VLIW processor: the code, whether scheduled or not, is guaranteed by the hardware to execute correctly. Furthermore, compiled code will always run correctly independent of the issue rate or pipeline structure of the processor. In some VLIW designs, this has not been the case, and recompilation was required when moving across different processor models; in other static issue processors, code would run correctly across different implementations, but often so poorly as to make compilation effectively required.

dynamic pipeline scheduling Hardware support for reordering the order of instruction execution so as to avoid stalls.

Many superscalars extend the basic framework of dynamic issue decisions to include **dynamic pipeline scheduling**. Dynamic pipeline scheduling chooses which instructions to execute in a given clock cycle while trying to avoid hazards and stalls. Let's start with a simple example of avoiding a data hazard. Consider the following code sequence:

```
lw      $t0, 20($s2)
addu    $t1, $t0, $t2
sub     $s4, $s4, $t3
slti    $t5, $s4, 20
```

Even though the sub instruction is ready to execute, it must wait for the lw and addu to complete first, which might take many clock cycles if memory is slow. (Chapter 5 explains cache misses, the reason that memory accesses are sometimes very slow.) Dynamic pipeline scheduling allows such hazards to be avoided either fully or partially.

Dynamic Pipeline Scheduling

Dynamic pipeline scheduling chooses which instructions to execute next, possibly reordering them to avoid stalls. In such processors, the pipeline is divided into three major units: an instruction fetch and issue unit, multiple functional units (a dozen or more in high-end designs in 2008), and a **commit unit.** Figure 4.72 shows the model. The first unit fetches instructions, decodes them, and sends each instruction to a corresponding functional unit for execution. Each functional unit has buffers, called **reservation stations**, which hold the operands and the operation. (In the next section, we will discuss an alternative to reservation stations used by many recent processors.) As soon as the buffer contains all its operands and the functional unit is ready to execute, the result is calculated. When the result is completed, it is sent to any reservation stations waiting for this particular result as well as to the commit unit, which buffers the result until it is safe to put the result into the register file or, for a store, into memory. The buffer in the commit unit, often called the **reorder buffer**, is also used to supply operands, in much the same way as forwarding logic does in a statically scheduled pipeline. Once a result is committed to the register file, it can be fetched directly from there, just as in a normal pipeline.

commit unit The unit in a dynamic or out-of-order execution pipeline that decides when it is safe to release the result of an operation to programmer-visible registers and memory.

reservation station A buffer within a functional unit that holds the operands and the operation.

reorder buffer The buffer that holds results in a dynamically scheduled processor until it is safe to store the results to memory or a register.

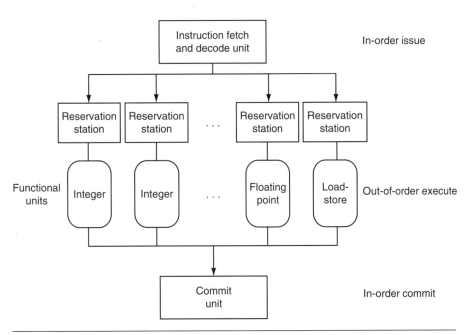

FIGURE 4.72 The three primary units of a dynamically scheduled pipeline. The final step of updating the state is also called retirement or graduation.

The combination of buffering operands in the reservation stations and results in the reorder buffer provides a form of register renaming, just like that used by the compiler in our earlier loop-unrolling example on page 397. To see how this conceptually works, consider the following steps:

1. When an instruction issues, it is copied to a reservation station for the appropriate functional unit. Any operands that are available in the register file or reorder buffer are also immediately copied into the reservation station. The instruction is buffered in the reservation station until all the operands and the functional unit are available. For the issuing instruction, the register copy of the operand is no longer required, and if a write to that register occurred, the value could be overwritten.

2. If an operand is not in the register file or reorder buffer, it must be waiting to be produced by a functional unit. The name of the functional unit that will produce the result is tracked. When that unit eventually produces the result, it is copied directly into the waiting reservation station from the functional unit bypassing the registers.

These steps effectively use the reorder buffer and the reservation stations to implement register renaming.

Conceptually, you can think of a dynamically scheduled pipeline as analyzing the data flow structure of a program. The processor then executes the instructions in some order that preserves the data flow order of the program. This style of execution is called an **out-of-order execution**, since the instructions can be executed in a different order than they were fetched.

To make programs behave as if they were running on a simple in-order pipeline, the instruction fetch and decode unit is required to issue instructions in order, which allows dependences to be tracked, and the commit unit is required to write results to registers and memory in program fetch order. This conservative mode is called **in-order commit**. Hence, if an exception occurs, the computer can point to the last instruction executed, and the only registers updated will be those written by instructions before the instruction causing the exception. Although, the front end (fetch and issue) and the back end (commit) of the pipeline run in order, the functional units are free to initiate execution whenever the data they need is available. Today, all dynamically scheduled pipelines use in-order commit.

Dynamic scheduling is often extended by including hardware-based speculation, especially for branch outcomes. By predicting the direction of a branch, a dynamically scheduled processor can continue to fetch and execute instructions along the predicted path. Because the instructions are committed in order, we know whether or not the branch was correctly predicted before any instructions from the predicted path are committed. A speculative, dynamically scheduled pipeline can also support speculation on load addresses, allowing load-store reordering, and using the commit unit to avoid incorrect speculation. In the next section, we will look at the use of dynamic scheduling with speculation in the AMD Opteron X4 (Barcelona) design.

out-of-order execution
A situation in pipelined execution when an instruction blocked from executing does not cause the following instructions to wait.

in-order commit
A commit in which the results of pipelined execution are written to the programmer-visible state in the same order that instructions are fetched.

Given that compilers can also schedule code around data dependences, you might ask why a superscalar processor would use dynamic scheduling. There are three major reasons. First, not all stalls are predictable. In particular, cache misses (see Chapter 5) cause unpredictable stalls. Dynamic scheduling allows the processor to hide some of those stalls by continuing to execute instructions while waiting for the stall to end.

Second, if the processor speculates on branch outcomes using dynamic branch prediction, it cannot know the exact order of instructions at compile time, since it depends on the predicted and actual behavior of branches. Incorporating dynamic speculation to exploit more instruction-level parallelism (ILP) without incorporating dynamic scheduling would significantly restrict the benefits of speculation.

Third, as the pipeline latency and issue width change from one implementation to another, the best way to compile a code sequence also changes. For example, how to schedule a sequence of dependent instructions is affected by both issue width and latency. The pipeline structure affects both the number of times a loop must be unrolled to avoid stalls as well as the process of compiler-based register renaming. Dynamic scheduling allows the hardware to hide most of these details. Thus, users and software distributors do not need to worry about having multiple versions of a program for different implementations of the same instruction set. Similarly, old legacy code will get much of the benefit of a new implementation without the need for recompilation.

Understanding Program Performance

Both pipelining and multiple-issue execution increase peak instruction throughput and attempt to exploit instruction-level parallelism (ILP). Data and control dependences in programs, however, offer an upper limit on sustained performance because the processor must sometimes wait for a dependence to be resolved. Software-centric approaches to exploiting ILP rely on the ability of the compiler to find and reduce the effects of such dependences, while hardware-centric approaches rely on extensions to the pipeline and issue mechanisms. Speculation, performed by the compiler or the hardware, can increase the amount of ILP that can be exploited, although care must be taken since speculating incorrectly is likely to reduce performance.

The BIG Picture

Hardware/
Software
Interface

Modern, high-performance microprocessors are capable of issuing several instructions per clock; unfortunately, sustaining that issue rate is very difficult. For example, despite the existence of processors with four to six issues per clock, very few applications can sustain more than two instructions per clock. There are two primary reasons for this.

First, within the pipeline, the major performance bottlenecks arise from dependences that cannot be alleviated, thus reducing the parallelism among instructions and the sustained issue rate. Although little can be done about true data dependences, often the compiler or hardware does not know precisely whether a dependence exists or not, and so must conservatively assume the dependence exists. For example, code that makes use of pointers, particularly in ways that may lead to aliasing, will lead to more implied potential dependences. In contrast, the greater regularity of array accesses often allows a compiler to deduce that no dependences exist. Similarly, branches that cannot be accurately predicted whether at runtime or compile time will limit the ability to exploit ILP. Often, additional ILP is available, but the ability of the compiler or the hardware to find ILP that may be widely separated (sometimes by the execution of thousands of instructions) is limited.

Second, losses in the memory system (the topic of Chapter 5) also limit the ability to keep the pipeline full. Some memory system stalls can be hidden, but limited amounts of ILP also limit the extent to which such stalls can be hidden.

Power Efficiency and Advanced Pipelining

The downside to the increasing exploitation of instruction-level parallelism via dynamic multiple issue and speculation is power efficiency. Each innovation was able to turn more transistors into performance, but they often did so very inefficiently. Now that we have hit the power wall, we are seeing designs with multiple processors per chip where the processors are not as deeply pipelined or as aggressively speculative as the predecessors.

The belief is that while the simpler processors are not as fast as their sophisticated brethren, they deliver better performance per watt, so that they can deliver more performance per chip when designs are constrained more by power than they are by number of transistors.

Figure 4.73 shows the number of pipeline stages, the issue width, speculation level, clock rate, cores per chip, and power of several past and recent microprocessors. Note the drop in pipeline stages and power as companies switch to multicore designs.

Elaboration: A commit unit controls updates to the register file *and* memory. Some dynamically scheduled processors update the register file immediately during execution, using extra registers to implement the renaming function and preserving the older copy

Microprocessor	Year	Clock Rate	Pipeline Stages	Issue Width	Out-of-Order/ Speculation	Cores/ Chip	Power	
Intel 486	1989	25 MHz	5	1	No	1	5	W
Intel Pentium	1993	66 MHz	5	2	No	1	10	W
Intel Pentium Pro	1997	200 MHz	10	3	Yes	1	29	W
Intel Pentium 4 Willamette	2001	2000 MHz	22	3	Yes	1	75	W
Intel Pentium 4 Prescott	2004	3600 MHz	31	3	Yes	1	103	W
Intel Core	2006	2930 MHz	14	4	Yes	2	75	W
UltraSPARC IV+	2005	2100 MHz	14	4	No	1	90	W
Sun UltraSPARC T1 (Niagara)	2005	1200 MHz	6	1	No	8	70	W

FIGURE 4.73 Record of Intel and Sun Microprocessors in terms of pipeline complexity, number of cores, and power.
The Pentium 4 pipeline stages do not include the commit stages. If we included them, the Pentium 4 pipelines would be even deeper.

of a register until the instruction updating the register is no longer speculative. Other processors buffer the result, typically in a structure called a reorder buffer, and the actual update to the register file occurs later as part of the commit. Stores to memory must be buffered until commit time either in a *store buffer* (see Chapter 5) or in the reorder buffer. The commit unit allows the store to write to memory from the buffer when the buffer has a valid address and valid data, and when the store is no longer dependent on predicted branches.

Elaboration: Memory accesses benefit from *nonblocking caches,* which continue servicing cache accesses during a cache miss (see Chapter 5). Out-of-order execution processors need the cache design to allow instructions to execute during a miss.

State whether the following techniques or components are associated primarily with a software- or hardware-based approach to exploiting ILP. In some cases, the answer may be both.

Check Yourself

1. Branch prediction

2. Multiple issue

3. VLIW

4. Superscalar

5. Dynamic scheduling

6. Out-of-order execution

7. Speculation

8. Reorder buffer

9. Register renaming

Real Stuff: the AMD Opteron X4 (Barcelona) Pipeline

4.11

Like most modern computers, x86 microprocessors employ sophisticated pipelining approaches. These processors, however, are still faced with the challenge of implementing the complex x86 instruction set, described in Chapter 2. Both AMD and Intel fetch x86 instructions and translate them internal to MIPS-like instructions, which AMD calls *RISC operations (Rops)* and Intel calls *micro-operations.* The RISC operations are then executed by a sophisticated, dynamically scheduled, speculative pipeline capable of sustaining an execution rate of three RISC operations per clock cycle in the AMD Opteron X4 (Barcelona). This section focuses on that RISC operation pipeline.

When we consider the design of sophisticated, dynamically scheduled processors, the design of the functional units, the cache and register file, instruction issue, and overall pipeline control become intermingled, making it difficult to separate the datapath from the pipeline. Because of this, many engineers and researchers have adopted the term **microarchitecture** to refer to the detailed internal architecture of a processor. Figure 4.74 shows the microarchitecture of the X4, focusing on the structures for executing the RISC operations.

Another way to look at the X4 is to see the pipeline stages that a typical instruction goes through. Figure 4.75 shows the pipeline structure and the typical number of clock cycles spent in each; of course, the number of clock cycles varies due to the nature of dynamic scheduling as well as the requirements of individual RISC operations.

microarchitecture The organization of the processor, including the major functional units, their interconnection, and control.

Elaboration: Opteron X4 uses a scheme for resolving antidependences and incorrect speculation that uses a reorder buffer together with register renaming. Register renaming explicitly renames the **architectural registers** in a processor (16 in the case of the 64-bit version of the x86 architecture) to a larger set of physical registers (72 in the X4). X4 uses register renaming to remove antidependences. Register renaming requires the processor to maintain a map between the architectural registers and the physical registers, indicating which physical register is the most current copy of an architectural register. By keeping track of the renamings that have occurred, register renaming offers another approach to recovery in the event of incorrect speculation: simply undo the mappings that have occurred since the first incorrectly speculated instruction. This will cause the state of the processor to return to the last correctly executed instruction, keeping the correct mapping between the architectural and physical registers.

architectural registers The instruction set of visible registers of a processor; for example, in MIPS, these are the 32 integer and 16 floating-point registers.

Check Yourself

Are the following statements true or false?

1. The Opteron X4 multiple-issue pipeline directly executes x86 instructions.

2. X4 uses dynamic scheduling but no speculation.

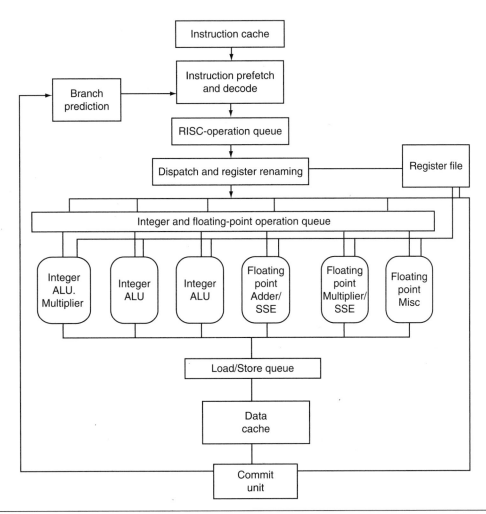

FIGURE 4.74 The microarchitecture of AMD Opteron X4. The extensive queues allow up to 106 RISC operations to be outstanding, including 24 integer operations, 36 floating point/SSE operations, and 44 loads and stores. The load and store units are actually separated into two parts, with the first part handling address calculation in the Integer ALU units and the second part responsible for the actual memory reference. There is an extensive bypass network among the functional units; since the pipeline is dynamic rather than static, bypassing is done by tagging results and tracking source operands, so as to allow a match when a result is produced for an instruction in one of the queues that needs the result.

3. The X4 microarchitecture has many more registers than x86 requires.

4. X4 uses less than half the pipeline stages of the earlier Pentium 4 Prescott (see Figure 4.73).

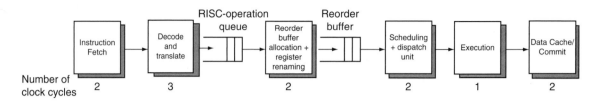

FIGURE 4.75   The Opteron X4 pipeline showing the pipeline flow for a typical instruction and the number of clock cycles for the major steps in the 12-stage pipeline for integer RISC-operations. The floating point execution queue is 17 stages long. The major buffers where RISC-operations wait are also shown.

Understanding Program Performance

The Opteron X4 combines a 12-stage pipeline and aggressive multiple issue to achieve high performance. By keeping the latencies for back-to-back operations low, the impact of data dependences is reduced. What are the most serious potential performance bottlenecks for programs running on this processor? The following list includes some potential performance problems, the last three of which can apply in some form to any high-performance pipelined processor.

- The use of x86 instructions that do not map to a few simple RISC operations

- Branches that are difficult to predict, causing misprediction stalls and restarts when speculation fails

- Long dependences—typically caused by long-running instructions or data cache misses—that lead to stalls

- Performance delays arising in accessing memory (see Chapter 5) that cause the processor to stall

4.12   Advanced Topic: an Introduction to Digital Design Using a Hardware Design Language to Describe and Model a Pipeline and More Pipelining Illustrations

Modern digital design is done using hardware description languages and modern computer-aided synthesis tools that can create detailed hardware designs from the descriptions using both libraries and logic synthesis. Entire books are written on such languages and their use in digital design. This section, which appears on the CD, gives a brief introduction and shows how a hardware design language, Verilog in this case, can be used to describe the MIPS control both behaviorally and in a form suitable for hardware synthesis. It then provides a series of behavioral models in Verilog of the MIPS five-stage pipeline. The initial model ignores hazards, and additions to the model highlight the changes for forwarding, data hazards, and branch hazards.

We then provide about a dozen illustrations using the single-cycle graphical pipeline representation for readers who want to see more detail on how pipelines work for a few sequences of MIPS instructions.

4.13 Fallacies and Pitfalls

Fallacy: Pipelining is easy.

Our books testify to the subtlety of correct pipeline execution. Our advanced book had a pipeline bug in its first edition, despite its being reviewed by more than 100 people and being class-tested at 18 universities. The bug was uncovered only when someone tried to build the computer in that book. The fact that the Verilog to describe a pipeline like that in Opteron X4 will be thousands of lines is an indication of the complexity. Beware!

Fallacy: Pipelining ideas can be implemented independent of technology.

When the number of transistors on-chip and the speed of transistors made a five-stage pipeline the best solution, then the delayed branch (see the first *Elaboration* on page 381) was a simple solution to control hazards. With longer pipelines, superscalar execution, and dynamic branch prediction, it is now redundant. In the early 1990s, dynamic pipeline scheduling took too many resources and was not required for high performance, but as transistor budgets continued to double and logic became much faster than memory, then multiple functional units and dynamic pipelining made more sense. Today, concerns about power are leading to less aggressive designs.

Pitfall: Failure to consider instruction set design can adversely impact pipelining.

Many of the difficulties of pipelining arise because of instruction set complications. Here are some examples:

- Widely variable instruction lengths and running times can lead to imbalance among pipeline stages and severely complicate hazard detection in a design pipelined at the instruction set level. This problem was overcome, initially in the DEC VAX 8500 in the late 1980s, using the micropipelined scheme that the Opteron X4 employs today. Of course, the overhead of translation and maintaining correspondence between the micro-operations and the actual instructions remains.

- Sophisticated addressing modes can lead to different sorts of problems. Addressing modes that update registers complicate hazard detection. Other addressing modes that require multiple memory accesses substantially complicate pipeline control and make it difficult to keep the pipeline flowing smoothly.

Perhaps the best example is the DEC Alpha and the DEC NVAX. In comparable technology, the newer instruction set architecture of the Alpha allowed an implementation whose performance is more than twice as fast as NVAX. In another example, Bhandarkar and Clark [1991] compared the MIPS M/2000 and the DEC VAX 8700 by counting clock cycles of the SPEC benchmarks; they concluded that although the MIPS M/2000 executes more instructions, the VAX on average executes 2.7 times as many clock cycles, so the MIPS is faster.

Nine-tenths of wisdom consists of being wise in time.

American proverb

4.14   Concluding Remarks

As we have seen in this chapter, both the datapath and control for a processor can be designed starting with the instruction set architecture and an understanding of the basic characteristics of the technology. In Section 4.3, we saw how the datapath for a MIPS processor could be constructed based on the architecture and the decision to build a single-cycle implementation. Of course, the underlying technology also affects many design decisions by dictating what components can be used in the datapath, as well as whether a single-cycle implementation even makes sense.

instruction latency The inherent execution time for an instruction.

Pipelining improves throughput but not the inherent execution time, or **instruction latency**, of instructions; for some instructions, the latency is similar in length to the single-cycle approach. Multiple instruction issue adds additional datapath hardware to allow multiple instructions to begin every clock cycle, but at an increase in effective latency. Pipelining was presented as reducing the clock cycle time of the simple single-cycle datapath. Multiple instruction issue, in comparison, clearly focuses on reducing clock cycles per instruction (CPI).

Pipelining and multiple issue both attempt to exploit instruction-level parallelism. The presence of data and control dependences, which can become hazards, are the primary limitations on how much parallelism can be exploited. Scheduling and speculation, both in hardware and in software, are the primary techniques used to reduce the performance impact of dependences.

The switch to longer pipelines, multiple instruction issue, and dynamic scheduling in the mid-1990s has helped sustain the 60% per year processor performance increase that started in the early 1980s. As mentioned in Chapter 1, these microprocessors preserved the sequential programming model, but they eventually ran into the power wall. Thus, the industry has been forced to try multiprocessors, which exploit parallelism at much coarser levels (the subject of Chapter 7). This trend has also caused designers to reassess the power-performance implications of some of the inventions since the mid-1990s, resulting in a simplification of pipelines in the more recent versions of microarchitectures.

To sustain the advances in processing performance via parallel processors, Amdahl's law suggests that another part of the system will become the bottleneck. That bottleneck is the topic of the next chapter: the memory system.

Historical Perspective and Further Reading

This section, which appears on the CD, discusses the history of the first pipelined processors, the earliest superscalars, and the development of out-of-order and speculative techniques, as well as important developments in the accompanying compiler technology.

Exercises

Contributed by Milos Prvulovic of Georgia Tech

Exercise 4.1

Different instructions utilize different hardware blocks in the basic single-cycle implementation. The next three problems in this exercise refer to the following instruction:

	Instruction	Interpretation
a.	AND Rd,Rs,Rt	Reg[Rd]=Reg[Rs] AND Reg[Rt]
b.	SW Rt,Offs(Rs)	Mem[Reg[Rs]+Offs]=Reg[Rt]

4.1.1 [5] <4.1> What are the values of control signals generated by the control in Figure 4.2 for this instruction?

4.1.2 [5] <4.1> Which resources (blocks) perform a useful function for this instruction?

4.1.3 [10] <4.1> Which resources (blocks) produce outputs, but their outputs are not used for this instruction? Which resources produce no outputs for this instruction?

Different execution units and blocks of digital logic have different latencies (time needed to do their work). In Figure 4.2 there are seven kinds of major blocks. Latencies of blocks along the critical (longest-latency) path for an instruction determine the minimum latency of that instruction. For the remaining three problems in this exercise, assume the following resource latencies:

	I-Mem	Add	Mux	ALU	Regs	D-Mem	Control
a.	200ps	70ps	20ps	90ps	90ps	250ps	40ps
b.	750ps	200ps	50ps	250ps	300ps	500ps	300ps

4.1.4 [5] <4.1> What is the critical path for an MIPS AND instruction?

4.1.5 [5] <4.1> What is the critical path for an MIPS load (LD) instruction?

4.1.6 [10] <4.1> What is the critical path for an MIPS BEQ instruction?

Exercise 4.2

The basic single-cycle MIPS implementation in Figure 4.2 can only implement some instructions. New instructions can be added to an existing ISA, but the decision whether or not to do that depends, among other things, on the cost and complexity such an addition introduces into the processor datapath and control. The first three problems in this exercise refer to this new instruction:

	Instruction	Interpretation
a.	SEQ Rd,Rs,Rt	Reg[Rd] = Boolean value (0 or 1) of (Reg[Rs] == Reg[Rs])
b.	LWI Rt,Rd(Rs)	Reg[Rt] = Mem[Reg[Rd]+Reg[Rs]]

4.2.1 [10] <4.1> Which existing blocks (if any) can be used for this instruction?

4.2.2 [10] <4.1> Which new functional blocks (if any) do we need for this instruction?

4.2.3 [10] <4.1> What new signals do we need (if any) from the control unit to support this instruction?

When processor designers consider a possible improvement to the processor datapath, the decision usually depends on the cost/performance trade-off. In the following three problems, assume that we are starting with a datapath from Figure 4.2, where I-Mem, Add, Mux, ALU, Regs, D-Mem, and Control blocks have latencies of 400ps, 100ps, 30ps, 120ps, 200ps, 350ps, and 100ps, respectively, and costs of 1000, 30, 10, 100, 200, 2000, and 500, respectively. The remaining three problems in this exercise refer to the following processor improvement:

	Improvement	Latency	Cost	Benefit
a.	Add Multiplier to ALU	+300ps for ALU	+600 for ALU	Lets us add MUL instruction. Allows us to execute 5% fewer instructions (MUL no longer emulated).
b.	Simpler Control	+100ps for Control	−400 for Control	Control becomes slower but cheaper logic.

4.2.4 [10] <4.1> What is the clock cycle time with and without this improvement?

4.2.5 [10] <4.1> What is the speedup achieved by adding this improvement?

4.2.6 [10] <4.1> Compare the cost/performance ratio with and without this improvement.

Exercise 4.3

Problems in this exercise refer to the following logic block:

	Logic Block
a.	Small Multiplexor (Mux) with four 8-bit data inputs
b.	Small 8-bit ALU that can do either AND, OR, or NOT

4.3.1 [5] <4.1, 4.2> Does this block contain logic only, flip-flops only, or both?

4.3.2 [20] <4.1, 4.2> Show how this block can be implemented. Use only AND, OR, NOT, and D Flip-Flops.

4.3.3 [10] <4.1, 4.2> Repeat Problem 4.3.2, but the AND and OR gates you use must all be 2-input gates.

Cost and latency of digital logic depends on the kinds of basic logic elements (gates) that are available and on the properties of these gates. The remaining three problems in this exercise refer to these gates, latencies, and costs:

	NOT		2-Input AND or OR		Each Additional Input for AND/OR		D-Element	
	Latency	Cost	Latency	Cost	Latency	Cost	Latency	Cost
a.	10ps	2	12ps	4	+2ps	+1	30ps	10
b.	20ps	2	40ps	3	+30ps	+1	80ps	9

4.3.4 [5] <4.1, 4.2> What is the latency of your implementation from 4.3.2?

4.3.5 [5] <4.1, 4.2> What is the cost of your implementation from 4.3.2?

4.3.6 [20] <4.1, 4.2> Change your design to minimize the latency, then to minimize the cost. Compare the cost and latency of these two optimized designs.

Exercise 4.4

When implementing a logic expression in digital logic, one must use the available logic gates to implement an operator for which a gate is not available. Problems in this exercise refer to the following logic expressions:

	Control Signal 1	**Control Signal 2**
a.	(((A AND B) XOR C) OR (A XOR C)) OR (A XOR B)	(A XOR B) OR (A XOR C)
b.	(((A OR B) AND C) OR ((A OR C) OR (A OR B))	(A AND C) OR (B AND C)

4.4.1 [5] <4.2> Implement the logic for the Control signal 1. Your circuit should directly implement the given expression (do not reorganize the expression to "optimize" it), using NOT gates and 2-input AND, OR, and XOR gates.

4.4.2 [10] Assuming that all gates have equal latencies, what is the length (in gates) of the critical path in your circuit from 4.4.1?

4.4.3 [10] <4.2> When multiple logic expressions are implemented, it is possible to reduce implementation cost by using the same signals in more than one expression. Repeat 4.4.1, but implement both Control signal 1 and Control signal 2, and try to "share" circuitry between expressions whenever possible.

For the remaining three problems in this exercise, we assume that the following basic digital logic elements are available, and that their latency and cost are as follows:

	NOT		**2-Input AND**		**2-Input OR**		**2-Input XOR**	
	Latency	**Cost**	**Latency**	**Cost**	**Latency**	**Cost**	**Latency**	**Cost**
a.	10ps	2	12ps	4	20ps	5	30ps	10
b.	20ps	2	40ps	3	50ps	3	50ps	8

4.4.4 [10] <4.2> What is the length of the critical path in your circuit from 4.4.3?

4.4.5 [10] <4.2> What is the cost of your circuit from 4.4.3?

4.4.6 [10] <4.2> What fraction of the cost was saved in your circuit from 4.4.3 by implementing these two control signals together instead of separately?

Exercise 4.5

The goal of this exercise is to help you familiarize yourself with the design and operation of sequential logical circuits. Problems in this exercise refer to this ALU operation:

	ALU Operation
a.	Add (X+Y)
b.	Subtract-one (X–1) in 2's complement

4.5.1 [20] <4.2> Design a circuit with 1-bit data inputs and a 1-bit data output that accomplishes this operation serially, starting with the least-significant bit. In a serial implementation, the circuit is processing input operands bit by bit, generating output bits one by one. For example, a serial AND circuit is simply an AND gate; in cycle N we give it the Nth bit from each of the operands and we get the Nth bit of the result. In addition to data inputs, the circuit has a Clk (clock) input and a "Start" input that is set to 1 only in the very first cycle of the operation. In your design, you can use D Flip-Flops and NOT, AND, OR, and XOR gates.

4.5.2 [20] <4.2> Repeat 4.5.1, but now design a circuit that accomplishes this operation 2 bits at a time.

In the rest of this exercise, we assume that the following basic digital logic elements are available, and that their latency and cost are as follows:

	NOT		AND		OR		XOR		D-Element	
	Latency	Cost	Latency	Cost	Latency	Cost	Latency	Cost	Latency	Cost
a.	10ps	2	12ps	4	12ps	4	14ps	6	30ps	10
b.	50ps	1	100ps	2	90ps	2	120ps	3	160ps	2

The time given for a D-element is its setup time. The data input of a flip-flop must have the correct value one setup-time before the clock edge (end of clock cycle) that stores that value into the flip-flop.

4.5.3 [10] <4.2> What is the cycle time for the circuit you designed in 4.5.1? How long does it take to perform the 32-bit operation?

4.5.4 [10] <4.2> What is the cycle time for the circuit you designed in 4.5.2? What is the speedup achieved by using this circuit instead of the one from 4.5.1 for a 32-bit operation?

4.5.5 [10] <4.2> Compute the cost for the circuit you designed in 4.5.1, and then for the circuit you designed in 4.5.2.

4.5.6 [5] <4.2> Compare cost/performance ratios for the two circuits you designed in 4.5.1 and 4.5.2. For this problem, performance of a circuit is the inverse of the time needed to perform a 32-bit operation.

Exercise 4.6

Problems in this exercise assume that logic blocks needed to implement a processor's datapath have the following latencies:

	I-Mem	Add	Mux	ALU	Regs	D-Mem	Sign-Extend	Shift-Left-2
a.	200ps	70ps	20ps	90ps	90ps	250ps	15ps	10ps
b.	750ps	200ps	50ps	250ps	300ps	500ps	100ps	0ps

4.6.1 [10] <4.3> If the only thing we need to do in a processor is fetch consecutive instructions (Figure 4.6), what would the cycle time be?

4.6.2 [10] <4.3> Consider a datapath similar to the one in Figure 4.11, but for a processor that only has one type of instruction: unconditional PC-relative branch. What would the cycle time be for this datapath?

4.6.3 [10] <4.3> Repeat 4.6.2, but this time we need to support only *conditional* PC-relative branches.

The remaining three problems in this exercise refer to the following logic block (resource) in the datapath:

	Resource
a.	Shift-left-2
b.	Registers

4.6.4 [10] <4.3> Which kinds of instructions require this resource?

4.6.5 [20] <4.3> For which kinds of instructions (if any) is this resource on the critical path?

4.6.6 [10] <4.3> Assuming that we only support BEQ and ADD instructions, discuss how changes in the given latency of this resource affect the cycle time of the processor. Assume that the latencies of other resources do not change.

Exercise 4.7

In this exercise we examine how latencies of individual components of the data-path affect the clock cycle time of the entire datapath, and how these components are utilized by instructions. For problems in this exercise, assume the following latencies for logic blocks in the datapath:

	I-Mem	Add	Mux	ALU	Regs	D-Mem	Sign-Extend	Shift-Left-2
a.	200ps	70ps	20ps	90ps	90ps	250ps	15ps	10ps
b.	750ps	200ps	50ps	250ps	300ps	500ps	100ps	5ps

4.7.1 [10] <4.3> What is the clock cycle time if the only types of instructions we need to support are ALU instructions (ADD, AND, etc.)?

4.7.2 [10] <4.3> What is the clock cycle time if we only have to support LW instructions?

4.7.3 [20] <4.3> What is the clock cycle time if we must support ADD, BEQ, LW, and SW instructions?

For the remaining problems in this exercise, assume that there are no pipeline stalls and that the breakdown of executed instructions is as follows:

	ADD	ADDI	NOT	BEQ	LW	SW
a.	20%	20%	0%	25%	25%	10%
b.	30%	10%	0%	10%	30%	20%

4.7.4 [10] <4.3> In what fraction of all cycles is the data memory used?

4.7.5 [10] <4.3> In what fraction of all cycles is the input of the sign-extend circuit needed? What is this circuit doing in cycles in which its input is not needed?

4.7.6 [10] <4.3> If we can improve the latency of one of the given datapath components by 10%, which component should it be? What is the speedup from this improvement?

Exercise 4.8

When silicon chips are fabricated, defects in materials (e.g., silicon) and manufac-turing errors can result in defective circuits. A very common defect is for one wire to affect the signal in another. This is called a cross-talk fault. A special class of cross-talk faults is when a signal is connected to a wire that has a constant logical value (e.g., a power supply wire). In this case we have a stuck-at-0 or a stuck-at-1 fault, and the affected signal always has a logical value of 0 or 1, respectively.

The following problems refer to the following signal from Figure 4.24:

	Signal
a.	Registers, input Write Register, bit 0
b.	Add unit in upper right corner, ALU result, bit 0

4.8.1 [10] <4.3, 4.4> Let us assume that processor testing is done by filling the PC, registers, and data and instruction memories with some values (you can choose which values), letting a single instruction execute, then reading the PC, memories, and registers. These values are then examined to determine if a particular fault is present. Can you design a test (values for PC, memories, and registers) that would determine if there is a stuck-at-0 fault on this signal?

4.8.2 [10] <4.3, 4.4> Repeat 4.8.1 for a stuck-at-1 fault. Can you use a single test for both stuck-at-0 and stuck-at-1? If yes, explain how; if no, explain why not.

4.8.3 [60] <4.3, 4.4> If we know that the processor has a stuck-at-1 fault on this signal, is the processor still usable? To be usable, we must be able to convert any program that executes on a normal MIPS processor into a program that works on this processor. You can assume that there is enough free instruction memory and data memory to let you make the program longer and store additional data. Hint: the processor is usable if every instruction "broken" by this fault can be replaced with a sequence of "working" instructions that achieve the same effect.

The following problems refer to the following fault:

	Fault
a.	Stuck-at-0
b.	Becomes 0 if RegDst control signal is 0, no fault otherwise

4.8.4 [10] <4.3, 4.4> Repeat 4.8.1, but now the fault to test for is whether the "MemRead" control signal has this fault.

4.8.5 [10] <4.3, 4.4> Repeat 4.8.1, but now the fault to test for is whether the "Jump" control signal has this fault.

4.8.6 [40] <4.3, 4.4> Using a single test described in 4.8.1, we can test for faults in several different signals, but typically not all of them. Describe a series of tests to look for this fault in all Mux outputs (every output bit from each of the five Muxes). Try to do this with as few single-instruction tests as possible.

Exercise 4.9

In this exercise we examine the operation of the single-cycle datapath for a particular instruction. Problems in this exercise refer to the following MIPS instruction:

	Instruction
a.	SW R4,-100(R16)
b.	SLT R1,R2,R3

4.9.1 [10] <4.4> What is the value of the instruction word?

4.9.2 [10] <4.4> What is the register number supplied to the register file's "Read register 1" input? Is this register actually read? How about "Read register 2"?

4.9.3 [10] <4.4> What is the register number supplied to the register file's "Write register" input? Is this register actually written?

Different instructions require different control signals to be asserted in the datapath. The remaining problems in this exercise refer to the following two control signals from Figure 4.24:

	Control Signal 1	Control Signal 2
a.	ALUSrc	Branch
b.	Jump	RegDst

4.9.4 [20] <4.4> What is the value of these two signals for this instruction?

4.9.5 [20] <4.4> For the datapath from Figure 4.24, draw the logic diagram for the part of the control unit that implements just the first signal. Assume that we only need to support LW, SW, BEQ, ADD, and J (jump) instructions.

4.9.6 [20] <4.4> Repeat 4.9.5, but now implement both of these signals.

Exercise 4.10

In this exercise we examine how the clock cycle time of the processor affects the design of the control unit, and vice versa. Problems in this exercise assume that the logic blocks used to implement the datapath have the following latencies:

	I-Mem	Add	Mux	ALU	Regs	D-Mem	Sign-Extend	Shift-Left-2	ALU Ctrl
a.	200ps	70ps	20ps	90ps	90ps	250ps	15ps	10ps	30ps
b.	750ps	200ps	50ps	250ps	300ps	500ps	100ps	5ps	70ps

4.10.1 [10] <4.2, 4.4> To avoid lengthening the critical path of the datapath shown in Figure 4.24, how much time can the control unit take to generate the MemWrite signal?

4.10.2 [20] <4.2, 4.4> Which control signal in Figure 4.24 has the most slack and how much time does the control unit have to generate it if it wants to avoid being on the critical path?

4.10.3 [20] <4.2, 4.4> Which control signal in Figure 4.24 is the most critical to generate quickly and how much time does the control unit have to generate it if it wants to avoid being on the critical path?

The remaining problems in this exercise assume that the time needed by the control unit to generate individual control signals is as follows

	RegDst	Jump	Branch	MemRead	MemtoReg	ALUOp	MemWrite	ALUSrc	RegWrite
a.	500ps	500ps	450ps	200ps	450ps	200ps	500ps	100ps	500ps
b.	1100ps	1000ps	1100ps	800ps	1200ps	300ps	1300ps	400ps	1200ps

4.10.4 [20] <4.4> What is the clock cycle time of the processor?

4.10.5 [20] <4.4> If you can speed up the generation of control signals, but the cost of the entire processor increases by $1 for each 5ps improvement of a single control signal, which control signals would you speed up and by how much to maximize performance? What is the cost (per processor) of this performance improvement?

4.10.6 [30] <4.4> If the processor is already too expensive, instead of paying to speed it up as we did in 4.10.5, we want to minimize its cost without further slowing it down. If you can use slower logic to implement control signals, saving $1 of the processor cost for each 5ps you add to the latency of a single control signal, which control signals would you slow down and by how much to reduce the processor's cost without slowing it down?

Exercise 4.11

In this exercise we examine in detail how an instruction is executed in a single-cycle datapath. Problems in this exercise refer to a clock cycle in which the processor fetches the following instruction word:

	Instruction word
a.	10101100011000100000000000010100
b.	00000000100000100000100000101010

4.11.1 [5] <4.4> What are the outputs of the sign-extend and the jump "Shift left 2" unit (near the top of Figure 4.24) for this instruction word?

4.11.2 [10] <4.4> What are the values of the ALU control unit's inputs for this instruction?

4.11.3 [10] <4.4> What is the new PC address after this instruction is executed? Highlight the path through which this value is determined.

The remaining problems in this exercise assume that data memory is all zeros and that the processor's registers have the following values at the beginning of the cycle in which the above instruction word is fetched:

	R0	R1	R2	R3	R4	R5	R6	R8	R12	R31
a.	0	−1	2	−3	−4	10	6	8	2	−16
b.	0	256	−128	19	−32	13	−6	−1	16	−2

4.11.4 [10] <4.4> For each Mux, show the values of its data output during the execution of this instruction and these register values.

4.11.5 [10] <4.4> For the ALU and the two add units, what are their data input values?

4.11.6 [10] <4.4> What are the values of all inputs for the "Registers" unit?

Exercise 4.12

In this exercise, we examine how pipelining affects the clock cycle time of the processor. Problems in this exercise assume that individual stages of the datapath have the following latencies:

	IF	ID	EX	MEM	WB
a.	250ps	350ps	150ps	300ps	200ps
b.	200ps	170ps	220ps	210ps	150ps

4.12.1 [5] <4.5> What is the clock cycle time in a pipelined and non-pipelined processor?

4.12.2 [10] <4.5> What is the total latency of an LW instruction in a pipelined and non-pipelined processor?

4.12.3 [10] <4.5> If we can split one stage of the pipelined datapath into two new stages, each with half the latency of the original stage, which stage would you split and what is the new clock cycle time of the processor?

The remaining problems in this exercise assume that instructions executed by the processor are broken down as follows:

	ALU	BEQ	LW	SW
a.	45%	20%	20%	15%
b.	55%	15%	15%	15%

4.12.4 [10] <4.5> Assuming there are no stalls or hazards, what is the utilization of the data memory?

4.12.5 [10] <4.5> Assuming there are no stalls or hazards, what is the utilization of the write-register port of the "Registers" unit?

4.12.6 [30] <4.5> Instead of a single-cycle organization, we can use a multi-cycle organization where each instruction takes multiple cycles but one instruction finishes before another is fetched. In this organization, an instruction only goes through stages it actually needs (e.g., ST only takes 4 cycles because it does not need the WB stage). Compare clock cycle times and execution times with single-cycle, multi-cycle, and pipelined organization.

Exercise 4.13

In this exercise, we examine how data dependences affect execution in the basic 5-stage pipeline described in Section 4.5. Problems in this exercise refer to the following sequence of instructions:

	Instruction Sequence

a.	SW R16,-100(R6)
	LW R4,8(R16)
	ADD R5,R4,R4

b.	OR R1,R2,R3 OR R2,R1,R4 OR R1,R1,R2

4.13.1 [10] <4.5> Indicate dependences and their type.

4.13.2 [10] <4.5> Assume there is no forwarding in this pipelined processor. Indicate hazards and add `NOP` instructions to eliminate them.

4.13.3 [10] <4.5> Assume there is full forwarding. Indicate hazards and add `NOP` instructions to eliminate them.

	Without Forwarding	With Full Forwarding	With ALU-ALU Forwarding Only
a.	250ps	300ps	290ps
b.	180ps	240ps	210ps

4.13.4 [10] <4.5> What is the total execution time of this instruction sequence without forwarding and with full forwarding? What is the speedup achieved by adding full forwarding to a pipeline that had no forwarding?

4.13.5 [10] <4.5> Add `NOP` instructions to this code to eliminate hazards if there is ALU-ALU forwarding only (no forwarding from the MEM to the EX stage).

4.13.6 [10] <4.5> What is the total execution time of this instruction sequence with only ALU-ALU forwarding? What is the speedup over a no-forwarding pipeline?

Exercise 4.14

In this exercise, we examine how resource hazards, control hazards, and ISA design can affect pipelined execution. Problems in this exercise refer to the following fragment of MIPS code:

	Instruction sequence

a.	`SW   R16,12(R6)`
	`LW   R16,8(R6)`
	`BEQ  R5,R4,Label ; Assume R5 != R4`
	`ADD  R5,R1,R4`
	`SLT  R5,R15,R4`

b.	`        SW   R2,0(R3)`
	`        OR   R1,R2,R3`
	`        BEQ  R2,R0,Label ; Assume R2 == R0`
	`        OR   R2,R2,R0`
	`Label:  ADD  R1,R4,R3`

4.14.1 [10] <4.5> For this problem, assume that all branches are perfectly predicted (this eliminates all control hazards) and that no delay slots are used. If we only have one memory (for both instructions and data), there is a structural hazard every time we need to fetch an instruction in the same cycle in which another instruction accesses data. To guarantee forward progress, this hazard must always be resolved in favor of the instruction that accesses data. What is the total execution time of this instruction sequence in the 5-stage pipeline that only has one memory? We have seen that data hazards can be eliminated by adding NOPs to the code. Can you do the same with this structural hazard? Why?

4.14.2 [20] <4.5> For this problem, assume that all branches are perfectly predicted (this eliminates all control hazards) and that no delay slots are used. If we change load/store instructions to use a register (without an offset) as the address, these instructions no longer need to use the ALU. As a result, MEM and EX stages can be overlapped and the pipeline has only 4 stages. Change this code to accommodate this changed ISA. Assuming this change does not affect clock cycle time, what speedup is achieved in this instruction sequence?

4.14.3 [10] <4.5> Assuming stall-on-branch and no delay slots, what speedup is achieved on this code if branch outcomes are determined in the ID stage, relative to the execution where branch outcomes are determined in the EX stage?

The remaining problems in this exercise assume that individual pipeline stages have the following latencies:

	IF	ID	EX	MEM	WB
a.	200ps	120ps	150ps	190ps	100ps
b.	150ps	200ps	200ps	200ps	100ps

4.14.4 [10] <4.5> Given these pipeline stage latencies, repeat the speedup calculation from 4.14.2, but take into account the (possible) change in clock cycle time. When EX and MEM are done in a single stage, most of their work can be done in parallel. As a result, the resulting EX/MEM stage has a latency that is the larger of the original two, plus 20ps needed for the work that could not be done in parallel.

4.14.5 [10] <4.5> Given these pipeline stage latencies, repeat the speedup calculation from 4.14.3, taking into account the (possible) change in clock cycle time. Assume that the latency ID stage increases by 50% and the latency of the EX stage decreases by 10ps when branch outcome resolution is moved from EX to ID.

4.14.6 [10] <4.5> Assuming stall-on-branch and no delay slots, what is the new clock cycle time and execution time of this instruction sequence if BEQ address computation is moved to the MEM stage? What is the speedup from this change? Assume that the latency of the EX stage is reduced by 20ps and the latency of the MEM stage is unchanged when branch outcome resolution is moved from EX to MEM.

Exercise 4.15

In this exercise, we examine how the ISA affects pipeline design. Problems in this exercise refer to the following new instruction:

a.	ADDM Rd,Rt+Offs(Rs)	Rd=Rt+Mem[Offs+Rs]
b.	BEQM Rd,Rt,Offs(Rs)	if Rt=Mem[Offs+Rs] then PC = Rd

4.15.1 [20] <4.5> What must be changed in the pipelined datapath to add this instruction to the MIPS ISA?

4.15.2 [10] <4.5> Which new control signals must be added to your pipeline from 4.15.1?

4.15.3 [20] <4.5, 4.13> Does support for this instruction introduce any new hazards? Are stalls due to existing hazards made worse?

4.15.4 [10] <4.5, 4.13> Give an example of where this instruction might be useful and a sequence of existing MIPS instructions that are replaced by this instruction.

4.15.5 [10] <4.5, 4.11, 4.13> If this instruction already exists in a legacy ISA, explain how it would be executed in a modern processor like AMD Barcelona.

The last problem in this exercise assumes that each use of the new instruction replaces the given number of original instructions, that the replacement can be made once in the given number of original instructions, and that each time the new instruction is executed the given number of extra stall cycles is added to the program's execution time:

	Replaces	**Once in every**	**Extra Stall Cycles**
a.	2	30	2
b.	3	40	1

4.15.6 [10] <4.5> What is the speedup achieved by adding this new instruction? In your calculation, assume that the CPI of the original program (without the new instruction) is 1.

Exercise 4.16

The first three problems in this exercise refer to the following MIPS instruction:

	Instruction
a.	SW R16,-100(R6)
b.	OR R2,R1,R0

4.16.1 [5] <4.6> As this instruction executes, what is kept in each register located between two pipeline stages?

4.16.2 [5] <4.6> Which registers need to be read, and which registers are actually read?

4.16.3 [5] <4.6> What does this instruction do in the EX and MEM stages?

The remaining three problems in this exercise refer to the following loop. Assume that perfect branch prediction is used (no stalls due to control hazards), that there are no delay slots, and that the pipeline has full forwarding support. Also assume that many iterations of this loop are executed before the loop exits.

	Loop		
a.	Loop:	ADD R1,R2,R1	
		LW R2,0(R1)	
		LW R2,16(R2)	
		SLT R1,R2,R4	
		BEQ R1,R9,Loop	
b.	Loop:	LW R1,0(R1)	
		AND R1,R1,R2	
		LW R1,0(R1)	
		LW R1,0(R1)	
		BEQ R1,R0,Loop	

4.16.4 [10] <4.6> Show a pipeline execution diagram for the third iteration of this loop, from the cycle in which we fetch the first instruction of that iteration up to (but not including) the cycle in which we can fetch the first instruction of the next iteration. Show all instructions that are in the pipeline during these cycles (not just those from the third iteration).

4.16.5 [10] <4.6> How often (as a percentage of all cycles) do we have a cycle in which all five pipeline stages are doing useful work?

4.16.6 [10] <4.6> At the start of the cycle in which we fetch the first instruction of the third iteration of this loop, what is stored in the IF/ID register?

Exercise 4.17

Problems in this exercise assume that instructions executed by a pipelined processor are broken down as follows:

	ADD	BEQ	LW	SW
a.	40%	30%	25%	5%
b.	60%	10%	20%	10%

4.17.1 [5] <4.6> Assuming there are no stalls and that 60% of all conditional branches are taken, in what percentage of clock cycles does the branch adder in the EX stage generate a value that is actually used?

4.17.2 [5] <4.6> Assuming there are no stalls, how often (percentage of all cycles) do we actually need to use all three register ports (two reads and a write) in the same cycle?

4.17.3 [5] <4.6> Assuming there are no stalls, how often (percentage of all cycles) do we use the data memory?

Each pipeline stage in Figure 4.33 has some latency. Additionally, pipelining introduces registers between stages (Figure 4.35), and each of these adds an additional latency. The remaining problems in this exercise assume the following latencies for logic within each pipeline stage and for each register between two stages:

	IF	ID	EX	MEM	WB	Pipeline Register
a.	200ps	120ps	150ps	190ps	100ps	15ps
b.	150ps	200ps	200ps	200ps	100ps	15ps

4.17.4 [5] <4.6> Assuming there are no stalls, what is the speedup achieved by pipelining a single-cycle datapath?

4.17.5 [10] <4.6> We can convert all load/store instructions into register-based (no offset) and put the memory access in parallel with the ALU. What is the clock cycle time if this is done in the single-cycle and in the pipelined datapath? Assume that the latency of the new EX/MEM stage is equal to the longer of their latencies.

4.17.6 [10] <4.6> The change in 4.17.5 requires many existing LW/SW instructions to be converted into two-instruction sequences. If this is needed for 50% of these instructions, what is the overall speedup achieved by changing from the 5-stage pipeline to the 4-stage pipeline where EX and MEM are done in parallel?

Exercise 4.18

The first three problems in this exercise refer to the execution of the following instruction in the pipelined datapath from Figure 4.51, and assume the following clock cycle time, ALU latency, and Mux latency:

	Instruction	Clock Cycle Time	ALU Latency	Mux Latency
a.	LW R1,32(R2)	50ps	30ps	15ps
b.	OR R1,R5,R6	200ps	170ps	25ps

4.18.1 [10] <4.6> For each stage of the pipeline, what are the values of the control signals asserted by this instruction in that pipeline stage?

4.18.2 [10] <4.6, 4.7> How much time does the control unit have to generate the ALUSrc control signal? Compare this to a single-cycle organization.

4.18.3 What is the value of the PCSrc signal for this instruction? This signal is generated early in the MEM stage (only a single AND gate). What would be a reason in favor of doing this in the EX stage? What is the reason against doing it in the EX stage?

The remaining problems in this exercise refer to the following signals from Figure 4.48:

	Signal 1	Signal 2
a.	ALUSrc	PCSrc
b.	Branch	RegWrite

4.18.4 [5] <4.6> For each of these signals, identify the pipeline stage in which it is generated and the stage in which it is used.

4.18.5 [5] <4.6> For which MIPS instruction(s) are both of these signals set to 1?

4.18.6 [10] <4.6> One of these signals goes back through the pipeline. Which signal is it? Is this a time-travel paradox? Explain.

Exercise 4.19

This exercise is intended to help you understand the cost/complexity/performance trade-offs of forwarding in a pipelined processor. Problems in this exercise refer to pipelined datapaths from Figure 4.45. These problems assume that, of all the instructions executed in a processor, the following fraction of these instructions have a particular type of RAW data dependence. The type of RAW data dependence is identified by the stage that produces the result (EX or MEM) and the instruction that consumes the result (1st instruction that follows the one that produces the result, 2nd instruction that follows, or both). We assume that the register write is done in the first half of the clock cycle and that register reads are done in the second half of the cycle, so "EX to 3rd" and "MEM to 3rd" dependences are not counted because they cannot result in data hazards. Also, assume that the CPI of the processor is 1 if there are no data hazards.

	EX to 1st Only	MEM to 1st Only	EX to 2nd only	MEM to 2nd Only	EX to 1st and MEM to 2nd	Other RAW Dependences
a.	5%	20%	5%	10%	10%	10%
b.	20%	10%	15%	10%	5%	0%

4.19.1 [10] <4.7> If we use no forwarding, what fraction of cycles are we stalling due to data hazards?

4.19.2 [5] <4.7> If we use full forwarding (forward all results that can be forwarded), what fraction of cycles are we staling due to data hazards?

4.19.3 [10] <4.7> Let us assume that we cannot afford to have three-input Muxes that are needed for full forwarding. We have to decide if it is better to forward only from the EX/MEM pipeline register (next-cycle forwarding) or only from the MEM/WB pipeline register (two-cycle forwarding). Which of the two options results in fewer data stall cycles?

The remaining three problems in this exercise refer to the following latencies for individual pipeline stages. For the EX stage, latencies are given separately for a processor without forwarding and for a processor with different kinds of forwarding.

	IF	ID	EX (no FW)	EX (full FW)	EX (FW from EX/MEM only)	EX (FW from MEM/WB only)	MEM	WB
a.	150ps	100ps	120ps	150ps	140ps	130ps	120ps	100ps
b.	300ps	200ps	300ps	350ps	330ps	320ps	290ps	100ps

4.19.4 [10] <4.7> For the given hazard probabilities and pipeline stage latencies, what is the speedup achieved by adding full forwarding to a pipeline that had no forwarding?

4.19.5 [10] <4.7> What would be the additional speedup (relative to a processor with forwarding) if we added time-travel forwarding that eliminates all data hazards? Assume that the yet-to-be-invented time-travel circuitry adds 100ps to the latency of the full-forwarding EX stage.

4.19.6 [20] <4.7> Repeat 4.19.3 but this time determine which of the two options results in shorter time per instruction.

Exercise 4.20

Problems in this exercise refer to the following instruction sequences:

	Instruction Sequence

a.	ADD R1,R2,R1
	LW R2,0(R1)
	LW R1,4(R1)
	OR R3,R1,R2

b.	LW R1,0(R1)
	AND R1,R1,R2
	LW R2,0(R1)
	LW R1,0(R3)

4.20.1 [5] <4.7> Find all data dependences in this instruction sequence.

4.20.2 [10] <4.7> Find all hazards in this instruction sequence for a 5-stage pipeline with and then without forwarding.

4.20.3 [10] <4.7> To reduce clock cycle time, we are considering a split of the MEM stage into two stages. Repeat 4.20.2 for this 6-stage pipeline.

The remaining three problems in this exercise assume that, before any of the above is executed, all values in data memory are zeroes and that registers R0 through R3 have the following initial values:

	R0	R1	R2	R3
a.	0	−1	31	1500
b.	0	4	63	3000

4.20.4 [5] <4.7> Which value is the first one to be forwarded and what is the value it overrides?

4.20.5 [10] <4.7> If we assume forwarding will be implemented when we design the hazard detection unit, but then we forget to actually implement forwarding, what are the final register values after this instruction sequence?

4.20.6 [10] <4.7> For the design described in 4.20.5, add NOPs to this instruction sequence to ensure correct execution in spite of missing support for forwarding.

Exercise 4.21

This exercise is intended to help you understand the relationship between forwarding, hazard detection, and ISA design. Problems in this exercise refer to the following sequences of instructions, and assume that it is executed on a 5-stage pipelined datapath:

	Instruction sequence

a.	ADD R5,R2,R1
	LW R3,4(R5)
	LW R2,0(R2)
	OR R3,R5,R3
	SW R3,0(R5)

b.	LW R2,0(R1)
	AND R1,R2,R1
	LW R3,0(R2)
	LW R1,0(R1)
	SW R1,0(R2)

4.21.1 [5] <4.7> If there is no forwarding or hazard detection, insert NOPs to ensure correct execution.

4.21.2 [10] <4.7> Repeat 4.21.1 but now use NOPs only when a hazard cannot be avoided by changing or rearranging these instructions. You can assume register R7 can be used to hold temporary values in your modified code.

4.21.3 [10] <4.7> If the processor has forwarding, but we forgot to implement the hazard detection unit, what happens when this code executes?

4.21.4 [20] <4.7> If there is forwarding, for the first five cycles during the execution of this code, specify which signals are asserted in each cycle by hazard detection and forwarding units in Figure 4.60.

4.21.5 [10] <4.7> If there is no forwarding, what new inputs and output signals do we need for the hazard detection unit in Figure 4.60? Using this instruction sequence as an example, explain why each signal is needed.

4.21.6 [20] <4.7> For the new hazard detection unit from 4.21.5, specify which output signals it asserts in each of the first five cycles during the execution of this code.

Exercise 4.22

This exercise is intended to help you understand the relationship between delay slots, control hazards, and branch execution in a pipelined processor. In this exercise, we assume that the following MIPS code is executed on a pipelined processor with a 5-stage pipeline, full forwarding, and a predict-taken branch predictor:

a.	```Label1: LW R2,0(R2)` ` BEQ R2,R0,Label ; Taken once, then not taken` ` OR R2,R2,R3` ` SW R2,0(R5)```

a.	`Label1: LW   R2,0(R2)`
	`        BEQ R2,R0,Label ; Taken once, then not taken`
	`        OR  R2,R2,R3`
	`        SW  R2,0(R5)`

b.	`        LW   R2,0(R1)`
	`Label1: BEQ R2,R0,Label2 ; Not taken once, then taken`
	`        LW  R3,0(R2)`
	`        BEQ R3,R0,Label1 ; Taken`
	`        ADD R1,R3,R1`
	`Label2: SW  R1,0(R2)`

4.22.1 [10] <4.8> Draw the pipeline execution diagram for this code, assuming there are no delay slots and that branches execute in the EX stage.

4.22.2 [10] <4.8> Repeat 4.22.1, but assume that delay slots are used. In the given code, the instruction that follows the branch is now the delay slot instruction for that branch.

4.22.3 [20] <4.8> One way to move the branch resolution one stage earlier is to not need an ALU operation in conditional branches. The branch instructions would be "BEZ Rd,Label" and "BNEZ Rd,Label", and it would branch if the register has and does not have a zero value, respectively. Change this code to use these branch instructions instead of BEQ. You can assume that register R8 is available for you to use as a temporary register, and that an SEQ (set if equal) R-type instruction can be used.

Section 4.8 describes how the severity of control hazards can be reduced by moving branch execution into the ID stage. This approach involves a dedicated comparator in the ID stage, as shown in Figure 4.62. However, this approach potentially adds to the latency of the ID stage, and requires additional forwarding logic and hazard detection.

4.22.4 [10] <4.8> Using the first branch instruction in the given code as an example, describe the hazard detection logic needed to support branch execution in the ID stage as in Figure 4.62. Which type of hazard is this new logic supposed to detect?

4.22.5 [10] <4.8> For the given code, what is the speedup achieved by moving branch execution into the ID stage? Explain your answer. In your speedup calculation, assume that the additional comparison in the ID stage does not affect clock cycle time.

4.22.6 [10] <4.8> Using the first branch instruction in the given code as an example, describe the forwarding support that must be added to support branch execution in the ID stage. Compare the complexity of this new forwarding unit to the complexity of the existing forwarding unit in Figure 4.62.

Exercise 4.23

The importance of having a good branch predictor depends on how often conditional branches are executed. Together with branch predictor accuracy, this will determine how much time is spent stalling due to mispredicted branches. In this exercise, assume that the breakdown of dynamic instructions into various instruction categories is as follows:

	R-Type	BEQ	JMP	LW	SW
a.	40%	25%	5%	25%	5%
b.	60%	8%	2%	20%	10%

Also, assume the following branch predictor accuracies:

	Always-Taken	Always-Not-Taken	2-Bit
a.	45%	55%	85%
b.	65%	35%	98%

4.23.1 [10] <4.8> Stall cycles due to mispredicted branches increase the CPI. What is the extra CPI due to mispredicted branches with the always-taken predictor? Assume that branch outcomes are determined in the EX stage, that there are no data hazards, and that no delay slots are used.

4.23.2 [10] <4.8> Repeat 4.23.1 for the "always-not-taken" predictor.

4.23.3 [10] <4.8> Repeat 4.23.1 for the 2-bit predictor.

4.23.4 [10] <4.8> With the 2-bit predictor, what speedup would be achieved if we could convert half of the branch instructions in a way that replaces a branch instruction with an ALU instruction? Assume that correctly and incorrectly predicted instructions have the same chance of being replaced.

4.23.5 [10] <4.8> With the 2-bit predictor, what speedup would be achieved if we could convert half of the branch instructions in a way that replaced each branch instruction with two ALU instructions? Assume that correctly and incorrectly predicted instructions have the same chance of being replaced.

4.23.6 [10] <4.8> Some branch instructions are much more predictable than others. If we know that 80% of all executed branch instructions are easy-to-predict loop-back branches that are always predicted correctly, what is the accuracy of the 2-bit predictor on the remaining 20% of the branch instructions?

Exercise 4.24

This exercise examines the accuracy of various branch predictors for the following repeating pattern (e.g., in a loop) of branch outcomes:

	Branch Outcomes
a.	T, T, NT, NT
b.	T, NT, T, T, NT

4.24.1 [5] <4.8> What is the accuracy of always-taken and always-not-taken predictors for this sequence of branch outcomes?

4.24.2 [5] <4.8> What is the accuracy of the two-bit predictor for the first 4 branches in this pattern, assuming that the predictor starts off in the bottom left state from Figure 4.63 (predict not taken)?

4.24.3 [10] <4.8> What is the accuracy of the two-bit predictor if this pattern is repeated forever?

4.24.4 [30] <4.8> Design a predictor that would achieve a perfect accuracy if this pattern is repeated forever. You predictor should be a sequential circuit with one output that provides a prediction (1 for taken, 0 for not taken) and no inputs other than the clock and the control signal that indicates that the instruction is a conditional branch.

4.24.5 [10] <4.8> What is the accuracy of your predictor from 4.24.4 if it is given a repeating pattern that is the exact opposite of this one?

4.24.6 [20] <4.8> Repeat 4.24.4, but now your predictor should be able to eventually (after a warm-up period during which it can make wrong predictions) start perfectly predicting both this pattern and its opposite. Your predictor should have an input that tells it what the real outcome was. Hint: this input lets your predictor determine which of the two repeating patterns it is given.

Exercise 4.25

This exercise explores how exception handling affects pipeline design. The first three problems in this exercise refer to the following two instructions:

	Instruction 1	Instruction 2
a.	BNE R1,R2,Label	LW R1,0(R1)
b.	JUMP Label	SW R5,0(R1)

4.25.1 [5] <4.9> Which exceptions can each of these instructions trigger? For each of these exceptions, specify the pipeline stage in which it is detected.

4.25.2 [10] <4.9> If there is a separate handler address for each exception, show how the pipeline organization must be changed to be able to handle this exception. You can assume that the addresses of these handlers are known when the processor is designed.

4.25.3 [10] <4.9> If the second instruction from this table is fetched right after the instruction from the first table, describe what happens in the pipeline when the first instruction causes the first exception you listed in 4.25.1. Show the pipeline execution diagram from the time the first instruction is fetched until the time the first instruction of the exception handler is completed.

The remaining three problems in this exercise assume that exception handlers are located at the following addresses:

	Overflow	Invalid Data Address	Undefined Instruction	Invalid Instruction Address	Hardware Malfunction
a.	0x1000CB05	0x1000D230	0x1000D780	0x1000E230	00x1000F254
b.	0x450064E8	0xC8203E20	0xC8203E20	0x678A0000	0x00000010

4.25.4 [5] <4.9> What is the address of the exception handler in 4.25.3? What happens if there is an invalid instruction at that address in instruction memory?

4.25.5 [20] <4.9> In vectored exception handling, the table of exception handler addresses is in data memory at a known (fixed) address. Change the pipeline to implement this exception handling mechanism. Repeat 4.25.3 using this modified pipeline and vectored exception handling.

4.25.6 [15] <4.9> We want to emulate vectored exception handling (described in 4.25.5) on a machine that has only one fixed handler address. Write the code that should be at that fixed address. Hint: this code should identify the exception, get the right address from the exception vector table, and transfer execution to that handler.

Exercise 4.26

This exercise explores how exception handling affects control unit design and processor clock cycle time. The first three problems in this exercise refer to the following MIPS instruction that triggers an exception:

	Instruction	Exception
a.	BNE R1,R2,Label	Invalid target address
b.	SUB R2,R4,R5	Arithmetic overflow

4.26.1 [10] <4.9> For each stage of the pipeline, determine the values of exception-related control signals from Figure 4.66 as this instruction passes through that pipeline stage.

4.26.2 [5] <4.9> Some of the control signals generated in the ID stage are stored into the ID/EX pipeline register, and some go directly into the EX stage. Explain why, using this instruction as an example.

4.26.3 [10] <4.9> We can make the EX stage faster if we check for exceptions in the stage after the one in which the exceptional condition occurs. Using this instruction as an example, describe the main disadvantage of this approach.

The remaining three problems in this exercise assume that pipeline stages have the following latencies:

	IF	ID	EX	MEM	WB
a.	220ps	150ps	250ps	200ps	200ps
b.	175ps	150ps	200ps	175ps	140ps

4.26.4 [10] <4.9> If an overflow exception occurs once for every 100,000 instructions executed, what is the overall speedup if we move overflow checking into the MEM stage? Assume that this change reduces EX latency by 30ns and that the IPC achieved by the pipelined processor is 1 when there are no exceptions.

4.26.5 [20] <4.9> Can we generate exception control signals in EX instead of in ID? Explain how this will work or why it will not work, using the "BNE R4,R5,Label" instruction and these pipeline stage latencies as an example.

4.26.6 [10] <4.9> Assuming that each Mux has a latency of 40ps, determine how much time does the control unit have to generate the flush signals? Which signal is the most critical?

Exercise 4.27

This exercise examines how exception handling interacts with branch and load/store instructions. Problems in this exercise refer to the following branch instruction and the corresponding delay slot instruction:

	Branch and Delay Slot
a.	BEQ R5,R4,Label SLT R5,R15,R4
b.	BEQ R1,R0,Label LW R1,0(R1)

4.27.1 [20] <4.9> Assume that this branch is correctly predicted as taken, but then the instruction at "Label" is an undefined instruction. Describe what is done in each pipeline stage for each cycle, starting with the cycle in which the branch is decoded up to the cycle in which the first instruction of the exception handler is fetched.

4.27.2 [10] <4.9> Repeat 4.27.1, but this time assume that the instruction in the delay slot also causes a hardware error exception when it is in MEM stage.

4.27.3 [10] <4.9> What is the value in the EPC if the branch is taken but the delay slot causes an exception? What happens after the execution of the exception handler is completed?

The remaining three problems in this exercise also refer to the following store instruction:

	Store Instruction
a.	SW R5,-40(R15)
b.	SW R1,0(R1)

4.27.4 [10] <4.9> What happens if the branch is taken, the instruction at "Label" is an invalid instruction, the first instruction of the exception handler is the SW instruction given above, and this store accesses an invalid data address?

4.27.5 [10] <4.9> If LD/ST address computation can overflow, can we delay overflow exception detection into the MEM stage? Use the given store instruction to explain what happens.

4.27.6 [10] <4.9> For debugging, it is useful to be able to detect when a particular value is written to a particular memory address. We want to add two new registers, WADDR and WVAL. The processor should trigger an exception when the value equal to WVAL is about to be written to address WADDR. How would you change the pipeline to implement this? How would this SW instruction be handled by your modified datapath?

Exercise 4.28

In this exercise we compare the performance of 1-issue and 2-issue processors, taking into account program transformations that can be made to optimize for 2-issue execution. Problems in this exercise refer to the following loop (written in C):

	C Code
a.	`for(i=0;i!=j;i+=2)` `    a[i+1]=a[i];`
b.	`for(i=0;i!=j;i+=2)` `    b[i]=a[i]-a[i+1];`

When writing MIPS code, assume that variables are kept in registers as follows, and that all registers except those indicated as Free are used to keep various variables, so they cannot be used for anything else.

	i	j	a	b	c	Free
a.	R2	R8	R9	R10	R11	R3,R4,R5
b.	R5	R6	R1	R2	R3	R10,R11,R12

4.28.1 [10] <4.10> Translate this C code into MIPS instructions. Your translation should be direct, without rearranging instructions to achieve better performance.

4.28.2 [10] <4.10> If the loop exits after executing only two iterations, draw a pipeline diagram for your MIPS code from 4.28.1 executed on a 2-issue processor shown in Figure 4.69. Assume the processor has perfect branch prediction and can fetch any two instructions (not just consecutive instructions) in the same cycle.

4.28.3 [10] <4.10> Rearrange your code from 4.28.1 to achieve better performance on a 2-issue statically scheduled processor from Figure 4.69.

4.28.4 [10] <4.10> Repeat 4.28.2, but this time use your MIPS code from 4.28.3.

4.28.5 [10] <4.10> What is the speedup of going from a 1-issue processor to a 2-issue processor from Figure 4.69? Use your code from 4.28.1 for both 1-issue and 2-issue, and assume that 1,000,000 iterations of the loop are executed. As in

4.28.2, assume that the processor has perfect branch predictions, and that a 2-issue processor can fetch any two instructions in the same cycle.

4.28.6 [10] <4.10> Repeat 4.28.5, but this time assume that in the 2-issue processor one of the instructions to be executed in a cycle can be of any kind, and the other must be a non-memory instruction.

Exercise 4.29

In this exercise, we consider the execution of a loop in a statically scheduled superscalar processor. To simplify the exercise, assume that any combination of instruction types can execute in the same cycle, e.g., in a 3-issue superscalar, the three instructions can be 3 ALU operations, 3 branches, 3 load/store instructions, or any combination of these instructions. Note that this only removes a resource constraint, but data and control dependences must still be handled correctly. Problems in this exercise refer to the following loop:

		Loop

a.	Loop:	ADDI R1,R1,4
		LW R2,0(R1)
		LW R3,16(R1)
		ADD R2,R2,R1
		ADD R2,R2,R3
		BEQ R2,zero,Loop

b.	Loop:	LW R1,0(R1)
		AND R1,R1,R2
		LW R2,0(R2)
		BEQ R1,zero,Loop

4.29.1 [10] <4.10> If many (e.g., 1,000,000) iterations of this loop are executed, determine the fraction of all register reads that are useful in a 2-issue static superscalar processor.

4.29.2 [10] <4.10> If many (e.g., 1,000,000) iterations of this loop are executed, determine the fraction of all register reads that are useful in a 3-issue static superscalar processor. Compare this to your result for a 2-issue processor from 4.29.1.

4.29.3 [10] <4.10> If many (e.g., 1,000,000) iterations of this loop are executed, determine the fraction of cycles in which two or three register write ports are used in a 3-issue static superscalar processor.

4.29.4 [20] <4.10> Unroll this loop once and schedule it for a 2-issue static superscalar processor. Assume that the loop always executes an even number of iterations. You can use registers R10 through R20 when changing the code to eliminate dependences.

4.29.5 [20] <4.10> What is the speedup of using your code from 4.29.4 instead of the original code with a 2-issue static superscalar processor? Assume that the loop has many (e.g., 1,000,000) iterations.

4.29.6 [10] <4.10> What is the speedup of using your code from 4.29.4 instead of the original code with a pipelined (1-issue) processor? Assume that the loop has many (e.g., 1,000,000) iterations.

Exercise 4.30

In this exercise, we make several assumptions. First, we assume that an N-issue superscalar processor can execute any N instructions in the same cycle, regardless of their types. Second, we assume that every instruction is independently chosen, without regard for the instruction that precedes or follows it. Third, we assume that there are no stalls due to data dependences, that no delay slots are used, and that branches execute in the EX stage of the pipeline. Finally, we assume that instructions executed in the program are distributed as follows:

	ALU	Correctly Predicted BEQ	Incorrectly Predicted BEQ	LW	SW
a.	40%	20%	5%	25%	10%
b.	45%	4%	1%	30%	20%

4.30.1 [5] <4.10> What is the CPI achieved by a 2-issue static superscalar processor on this program?

4.30.2 [10] <4.10> In a 2-issue static superscalar whose predictor can only handle one branch per cycle, what speedup is achieved by adding the ability to predict two branches per cycle? Assume a stall-on-branch policy for branches that the predictor cannot handle.

4.30.3 [10] <4.10> In a 2-issue static superscalar processor that only has one register write port, what speedup is achieved by adding a second register write port?

4.30.4 [5] <4.10> For a 2-issue static superscalar processor with a classic 5-stage pipeline, what speedup is achieved by making the branch prediction perfect?

4.30.5 [10] <4.10> Repeat 4.30.4, but for a 4-issue processor. What conclusion can you draw about the importance of good branch prediction when the issue width of the processor is increased?

4.30.6 <4.10> Repeat 4.30.5, but now assume that the 4-issue processor has 50 pipeline stages. Assume that each of the original 5 stages is broken into 10 new stages, and that branches are executed in the first of ten new EX stages. What conclusion can you draw about the importance of good branch prediction when the pipeline depth of the processor is increased?

Exercise 4.31

Problems in this exercise refer to the following loop, which is given as x86 code and also as an MIPS translation of that code. You can assume that this loop executes many iterations before it exits. When determining performance, this means that you only need to determine what the performance would be in the "steady state," not for the first few and the last few iterations of the loop. Also, you can assume full forwarding support and perfect branch prediction without delay slots, so the only hazards you have to worry about are resource hazards and data hazards. Note that most x86 instructions in this problem have two operands each. The last (usually second) operand of the instruction indicates both the first source data value and the destination. If the operation needs a second source data value, it is indicated by the other operand of the instruction. For example, "sub (edx),eax" reads the memory location pointed by register edx, subtracts that value from register eax, and puts the result back in register eax.

	x86 Instructions		MIPS-like Translation	

a.	Label:	mov -4(esp), eax
		mov -4(esp), edx
		add (edi,eax,4),edx
			Label:	lw r2,-4(sp)
				lw r3,-4(sp)
				sll r2,r2,2
				add r2,r2,r4
				lw r2,0(r2)
				add r3,r3,r2

		mov edx, -4(esp)
		mov -4(esp),eax
		cmp 0, (edi,eax,4)
		
		jne Label
				sw r3,-4(sp)
				lw r2,-4(sp)
				sll r2,r2,2
				add r2,r2,r4
				lw r2,0(r2)
				bne r2,zero,Label

b.	Label:	add 4, edx
		mov (edx), eax
		add 4(edx), eax
			Label:	addi r4,r4,4
				lw r3,0(r4)
				lw r2,4(r4)
				add r2,r2,r3

		add 8(edx), eax
		
		mov eax, -4(edx)
		test edx, edx
		jl Label
				lw r3,8(r4)
				add r2,r2,r3
				sw r2,-4(r4)
				slt r1,r4,zero
				bne r1,zero,Label

4.31.1 [20] <4.11> What CPI would be achieved if the MIPS version of this loop is executed on a 1-issue processor with static scheduling and a 5-stage pipeline?

4.31.2 [20] <4.11> What CPI would be achieved if the X86 version of this loop is executed on a 1-issue processor with static scheduling and a 7-stage pipeline? The stages of the pipeline are IF, ID, ARD, MRD, EXE, and WB. Stages IF and ID are similar to those in the 5-stage MIPS pipeline. ARD computes the address of the memory location to be read, MRD performs the memory read, EXE executes the operation, and WB writes the result to register or memory. The data memory has a read port (for instructions in the MRD stage) and a separate write port (for instructions in the WB stage).

4.31.3 [20] <4.11> What CPI would be achieved if the X86 version of this loop is executed on a processor that internally translates these instructions into MIPS-like micro-operations, then executes these micro-operations on a 1-issue 5-stage pipeline with static scheduling. Note that the instruction count used in CPI computation for this processor is the X86 instruction count.

4.31.4 [20] <4.11> What CPI would be achieved if the MIPS version of this loop is executed on a 1-issue processor with dynamic scheduling? Assume that our processor is not doing register renaming, so you can only reorder instructions that have no data dependences.

4.31.5 [30] <4.10, 4.11> Assuming that there are many free registers available, rename the MIPS version of this loop to eliminate as many data dependences as possible between instructions in the same iteration of the loop. Now repeat 4.31.4, using your new renamed code.

4.31.6 [20] <4.10, 4.11> Repeat 4.31.4, but this time assume that the processor assigns a new name to the result of each instruction as that instruction is decoded, and then renames registers used by subsequent instructions to use correct register values.

Exercise 4.32

Problems in this exercise assume that branches represent the following fraction of all executed instructions, and the following branch predictor accuracy. Assume that the processor is never stalled by data and resource dependences, i.e., the processor always fetches and executes the maximum number of instructions per cycle if there are no control hazards. For control dependences, the processor uses branch prediction and continues fetching from the predicted path. If the branch has been mispredicted, when the branch outcome is resolved the instructions fetched after the mispredicted branch are discarded, and in the next cycle the processor starts fetching from the correct path.

	Branches as a % of All Executed Instructions	Branch Prediction Accuracy
a.	25	95%
b.	25	99%

4.32.1 [5] <4.11> How many instructions are expected to be executed between the time one branch misprediction is detected and the time the next branch misprediction is detected?

The remaining problems in this exercise assume the following pipeline depth and that the branch outcome is determined in the following pipeline stage (counting from stage 1):

	Pipeline Depth	Branch Outcome Known in Stage
a.	15	12
b.	30	20

4.32.2 [5] <4.11> In a 4-issue processor with these pipeline parameters, how many branch instructions can be expected to be "in progress" (already fetched but not yet committed) at any given time?

4.32.3 [5] <4.11> How many instructions are fetched from the wrong path for each branch misprediction in a 4-issue processor?

4.32.4 [10] <4.11> What is the speedup achieved by changing the processor from 4-issue to 8-issue? Assume that the 8-issue and the 4-issue processor differ only in the number of instructions per cycle, and are otherwise identical (pipeline depth, branch resolution stage, etc.).

4.32.5 [10] <4.11> What is the speedup of executing branches 1 stage earlier in a 4-issue processor?

4.32.6 [10] <4.11> What is the speedup of executing branches 1 stage earlier in an 8-issue processor? Discuss the difference between this result and the result from 4.32.5.

Exercise 4.33

This exercise explores how branch prediction affects performance of a deeply pipelined multiple-issue processor. Problems in this exercise refer to a processor with the following number of pipeline stages and instructions issued per cycle:

	Pipeline Depth	Issue Width
a.	15	2
b.	30	8

4.33.1 [10] <4.11> How many register read ports should the processor have to avoid any resource hazards due to register reads?

4.33.2 [10] <4.11> If there are no branch mispredictions and no data dependences, what is the expected performance improvement over a 1-issue processor with the classical 5-stage pipeline? Assume that the clock cycle time decreases in proportion to the number of pipeline stages.

4.33.3 [10] <4.11> Repeat 4.33.2, but this time every executed instruction has a RAW data dependence to the instruction that executes right after it. You can assume that no stall cycles are needed, i.e., forwarding allows consecutive instructions to execute in back-to-back cycles.

For the remaining three problems in this exercise, unless the problem specifies otherwise, assume the following statistics about what percentage of instructions are branches, predictor accuracy, and performance loss due to branch mispredictions:

	Branches as a Fraction of All Executed Instructions	Branches Execute in Stage	Predictor Accuracy	Performance Loss
a.	10%	9	96%	5%
b.	10%	5	98%	1%

4.33.4 [10] <4.11> If we have the given fraction of branch instructions and branch prediction accuracy, what percentage of all cycles are entirely spent fetching wrong-path instructions? Ignore the performance loss number.

4.33.5 [20] <4.11> If we want to limit stalls due to mispredicted branches to no more than the given percentage of the ideal (no stalls) execution time, what should be our branch prediction accuracy? Ignore the given predictor accuracy number.

4.33.6 [10] <4.11> What should the branch prediction accuracy be if we are willing to have a speedup of 0.5 (one half) relative to the same processor with an ideal branch predictor?

Exercise 4.34

This exercise is designed to help you understand the discussion of the "Pipelining is easy" fallacy from Section 4.13. The first four problems in this exercise refer to the following MIPS instruction:

	Instruction	Interpretation
a.	`AND Rd,Rs,Rt`	`Reg[Rd]=Reg[Rs] AND Reg[Rt]`
b.	`SW Rt,Offs(Rs)`	`Mem[Reg[Rs]+Offs] = Reg[Rt]`

4.34.1 [10] <4.13> Describe a pipelined datapath needed to support only this instruction. Your datapath should be designed with the assumption that the only instructions that will ever be executed are instances of this instruction.

4.34.2 [10] <4.13> Describe the requirements of forwarding and hazard detection units for your datapath from 4.34.1.

4.34.3 [10] <4.13> What needs to be done to support undefined instruction exceptions in your datapath from 4.34.1? Note that the undefined instruction exception should be triggered whenever the processor encounters any other kind of instruction.

The remaining two problems in this exercise also refer to this MIPS instruction:

	Instruction	Interpretation
a.	ADD Rd,Rs,Rt	Reg[Rd]=Reg[Rs]+Reg[Rt]
b.	ADDI Rt,Rs,Imm	Reg[Rt]=Reg[Rs]+Imm

4.34.4 [10] <4.13> Describe how to extend your datapath from 4.34.1 so it can also support this instruction. Your extended datapath should be designed to only support instances of these two instructions.

4.34.5 [10] <4.13> Repeat 4.34.2 for your extended datapath from 4.34.4.

4.34.6 [10] <4.13> Repeat 4.34.3 for your extended datapath from 4.34.4.

Exercise 4.35

This exercise is intended to help you better understand the relationship between ISA design and pipelining. Problems in this exercise assume that we have a multiple-issue pipelined processor with the following number of pipeline stages, instructions issued per cycle, stage in which branch outcomes are resolved, and branch predictor accuracy:

	Pipeline Depth	Issue Width	Branches Execute in Stage	Branch Predictor Accuracy	Branches as a % of Instructions
a.	15	2	10	90%	25%
b.	25	4	15	96%	15%

4.35.1 [5] <4.8, 4.13> Control hazards can be eliminated by adding branch delay slots. How many delay slots must follow each branch if we want to eliminate all control hazards in this processor?

4.35.2 [10] <4.8, 4.13> What is the speedup that would be achieved by using four branch delay slots to reduce control hazards in this processor? Assume that there are no data dependences between instructions and that all four delay slots can be filled with useful instructions without increasing the number of executed instructions. To make your computations easier, you can also assume that the mispredicted branch instruction is always the last instruction to be fetched in a cycle, i.e., no instructions that are in the same pipeline stage as the branch are fetched from the wrong path.

4.35.3 [10] <4.8, 4.13> Repeat 4.35.2, but now assume that 10% of executed branches have all four delay slots filled with useful instruction, 20% have only three useful instructions in delay slots (the fourth delay slot is an NOP), 30% have only two useful instructions in delay slots, and 40% have no useful instructions in their delay slots.

The remaining four problems in this exercise refer to the following C loop:

a.	`for(i=0;i!=j;i++){`
	`    c+=a[i];`
	`}`

b.	`for(i=0;i!=j;i+=2){`
	`    c+=a[i]-a[i+1];`
	`}`

4.35.4 [10] <4.8, 4.13> Translate this C loop into MIPS instructions, assuming that our ISA requires one delay slot for every branch. Try to fill delay slots with non-NOP instructions when possible. You can assume that variables a, b, c, i, and j are kept in registers r1, r2, r3, r4, and r5.

4.35.5 [10] <4.7, 4.13> Repeat 4.35.4 for a processor that has two delay slots for every branch.

4.35.6 [10] <4.10, 4.13> How many iterations of your loop from 4.35.4 can be "in flight" within this processor's pipeline? We say that an iteration is "in flight" when at least one of its instructions has been fetched and has not yet been committed.

Exercise 4.36

This exercise is intended to help you better understand the last pitfall from Section 4.13—failure to consider pipelining in instruction set design. The first four problems in this exercise refer to the following new MIPS instruction:

	Instruction	Interpretation
a.	`SWINC Rt,Offset(Rs)`	`Mem[Reg[Rs]+Offset]=Reg[Rt]` `Reg[Rs]=Reg[Rs]+4`
b.	`SWI    Rt,Rd(Rs)`	`Mem[Reg[Rd]+Reg[Rs]]= Reg[Rt]`

4.36.1 [10] <4.11, 4.13> Translate this instruction into MIPS micro-operations.

4.36.2 [10] <4.11, 4.13> How would you change the 5-stage MIPS pipeline to add support for micro-op translation needed to support this new instruction?

4.36.3 [20] <4.13> If we want to add this instruction to the MIPS ISA, discuss the changes to the pipeline (which stages, which structures in which stage) that are needed to directly (without micro-ops) support this instruction.

4.36.4 [10] <4.13> How often do you expect this instruction can be used? Do you think that we would be justified if we added this instruction to the MIPS ISA?

The remaining two problems in this exercise are about adding a new ADDM instruction to the ISA. In a processor to which ADDM has been added, these problems assume the following breakdown of clock cycles according to which instruction is completed in that cycle (or which stall is preventing an instruction from completing):

	ADD	BEQ	LW	SW	ADDM	Control Stalls	Data Stalls
a.	25%	20%	20%	10%	3%	10%	12%
b.	25%	10%	25%	20%	5%	10%	5%

4.36.5 [10] <4.13> Given this breakdown of execution cycles in the processor with direct support for the ADDM instruction, what speedup is achieved by replacing this instruction with a 3-instruction sequence (LW, ADD, and then SW)? Assume that the ADDM instruction is somehow (magically) supported with a classical 5-stage pipeline without creating resource hazards.

4.36.6 [10] <4.13> Repeat 4.36.5, but now assume that ADDM was supported by adding a pipeline stage. When ADDM is translated, this extra stage can be removed and, as a result, half of the existing data stalls are eliminated. Note that the data stall elimination applies only to stalls that existed before ADDM translation, not to stalls added by the ADDM translation itself.

Exercise 4.37

This exercise explores some of the tradeoffs involved in pipelining, such as clock cycle time and utilization of hardware resources. The first three problems in this exercise refer to the following MIPS code. The code is written with an assumption that the processor does not use delay slots.

a.	
| | ```
SW   R16,-100(R6)
LW   R16,8(R6)
BEQ  R5,R4,Label ; Assume R5 != R4
ADD  R5,R16,R4
SLT  R5,R15,R4
``` |
| **b.** | |
| | ```
       OR  R1,R2,R3
       SW  R1,0(R2)
       BEQ R1,R0,Label ; Assume R1 == R0
       OR  R2,R1,R0
Label: ADD R1,R1,R3
``` |

4.37.1 [5] <4.3, 4.14> Which parts of the basic single-cycle datapath are used by all of these instructions? Which parts are the least utilized?

4.37.2 [10] <4.6, 4.14> What is the utilization for the read and for the write port of the data memory unit?

4.37.3 [10] <4.6, 4.14> Assume that we already have a single-cycle design. How many bits in total do we need for pipeline registers to implement the pipelined design?

The remaining three problems in this exercise assume that components of the datapath have the following latencies:

	I-Mem	Add	Mux	ALU	Regs	D-Mem	Sign-Extend	Shift-Left-2
a.	200ps	70ps	20ps	90ps	90ps	250ps	15ps	10ps
b.	750ps	200ps	50ps	250ps	300ps	500ps	100ps	5ps

4.37.4 [10] <4.3, 4.5, 4.14> Given these latencies for individual elements of the datapath, compare clock cycle times of the single-cycle and the 5-stage pipelined datapath.

4.37.5 [10] <4.3, 4.5, 4.14> Repeat 4.37.4, but now assume that we only want to support ADD instructions.

4.37.6 [20] <4.3, 4.5, 4.14> If it costs $1 to reduce the latency of a single component of the datapath by 1ps, what would it cost to reduce the clock cycle time by 20% in the single-cycle and in the pipelined design?

Exercise 4.38

This exercise explores energy efficiency and its relationship with performance. Problems in this exercise assume the following energy consumption for activity in Instruction memory, Registers, and Data memory. You can assume that the other components of the datapath spend a negligible amount of energy.

	I-Mem	1 Register Read	Register Write	D-Mem Read	D-Mem Write
a.	140pJ	70pJ	60pJ	140pJ	120pJ
b.	70pJ	40pJ	40pJ	90pJ	100pJ

4.38.1 [10] <4.3, 4.6, 4.14> How much energy is spent to execute an ADD instruction in a single-cycle design and in the 5-stage pipelined design?

4.38.2 [10] <4.6, 4.14> What is the worst-case MIPS instruction in terms of energy consumption, and what is the energy spent to execute it?

4.38.3 [10] <4.6, 4.14> If energy reduction is paramount, how would you change the pipelined design? What is the percentage reduction in the energy spent by an LW instruction after this change?

The remaining three problems in this exercise assume that components in the datapath have the following latencies. You can assume that the other components of the datapath have negligible latencies.

	I-Mem	Control	Register Read or Write	ALU	D-Mem Read or Write
a.	200ps	150ps	90ps	90ps	250ps
b.	750ps	500ps	300ps	250ps	500ps

4.38.4 [10] <4.6, 4.14> What is the performance impact of your changes from 4.38.3?

4.38.5 [10] <4.6, 4.14> We can eliminate the MemRead control signal and have the data memory be read in every cycle, i.e., we can permanently have MemRead=1. Explain why the processor still functions correctly after this change. What is the effect of this change on clock frequency and energy consumption?

4.38.6 [10] <4.6, 4.14> If an idle unit spends 10% of the power it would spend if it were active, what is the energy spent by the instruction memory in each cycle? What percentage of the overall energy spent by the instruction memory does this idle energy represent?

Exercise 4.39

Problems in this exercise assume that, during an execution of the program, processor cycles are spent in the following way. A cycle is "spent" on an instruction if the processor completes that type of instruction in that cycle; a cycle is "spent" on a stall if the processor could not complete an instruction in that cycle because of a stall.

	ADD	BEQ	LW	SW	Control Stalls	Data Stalls
a.	25%	20%	20%	10%	10%	15%
b.	25%	10%	25%	20%	10%	10%

Problems in this exercise also assume that individual pipeline stages have the following latency and energy consumption. The stage expends this energy in order to do its work within the given latency. Note that no energy is spent in the MEM stage during a cycle in which there is no memory access. Similarly, no energy is spent in the WB stage in a cycle in which there is no register write. In several of the following problems, we make assumptions about how energy consumption changes if a stage performs its work slower or faster than this.

	IF	ID	EX	MEM	WB
a.	250ps/100pJ	350ps/45pJ	150ps/50pJ	300ps/150pJ	200ps/50pJ
b.	200ps/75pJ	170ps/45pJ	220ps/100pJ	210ps/100pJ	150ps/35pJ

4.39.1 [10] <4.14> What is the performance (in instructions per second)?

4.39.2 [10] <4.14> What is the power dissipated in watts (joules per second)?

4.39.3 [10] <4.6, 4.14> Which pipeline stages can you slow down and by how much, without affecting the clock cycle time?

4.39.4 [20] <4.6, 4.14> It is often possible to sacrifice some speed in a circuit in order to reduce its energy consumption. Assume that we can reduce energy consumption by a factor of X (new energy is 1/X times the old energy) when we increase the latency by a factor of X (new latency is X times the old latency). Using this tradeoff, we can adjust latencies of pipeline stages to minimize energy consumption without sacrificing any performance. Repeat 4.39.2 for this adjusted processor.

4.39.5 [10] <4.6, 4.14> Repeat 4.39.4, but this time the goal is to minimize energy spent per instruction while increasing the clock cycle time by no more than 10%.

4.39.6 [10] <4.6, 4.14> Repeat 4.39.5, but now assume that energy consumption is reduced by a factor of X^2 when latency is made X times longer. What are the power savings compared to what you computed for 4.39.2?

Answers to Check Yourself

§4.1, page 303: 3 of 5: Control, Datapath, Memory. Input and Output are missing.
§4.2, page 307: false. Edge-triggered state elements make simultaneous reading and writing both possible and unambiguous.
§4.3, page 315: I. A. II. C.
§4.4, page 330: Yes, Branch and ALUOp0 are identical. In addition, MemtoReg and RegDst are inverses of one another. You don't need an inverter; simply use the other signal and flip the order of the inputs to the multiplexor!
§4.5, page 343: 1. Stall on the LW result. 2. Bypass the first ADD result written into $t1. 3. No stall or bypass required.
§4.6, page 358: Statements 2 and 4 are correct; the rest are incorrect.
§4.8, page 383: 1. Predict not taken. 2. Predict taken. 3. Dynamic prediction.
§4.9, page 391: The first instruction, since it is logically executed before the others.

§4.10, page 403: 1. Both. 2. Both. 3. Software. 4. Hardware. 5. Hardware. 6. Hardware. 7. Both. 8. Hardware. 9. Both.

§4.11, page 404: First two are false and last two are true.

§4.12, ◉ page 4.12-3: Statements 1 and 3 are both true.

§4.12, ◉ page 4.12-5: The best answer is 2 (see the Elaboration on page 371)

Large and Fast: Exploiting Memory Hierarchy

Ideally one would desire an indefinitely large memory capacity such that any particular . . . word would be immediately available. . . . We are . . . forced to recognize the possibility of constructing a hierarchy of memories, each of which has greater capacity than the preceding but which is less quickly accessible.

A. W. Burks, H. H. Goldstine, and J. von Neumann
Preliminary Discussion of the Logical Design of an Electronic Computing Instrument, 1946

The Five Classic Components of a Computer

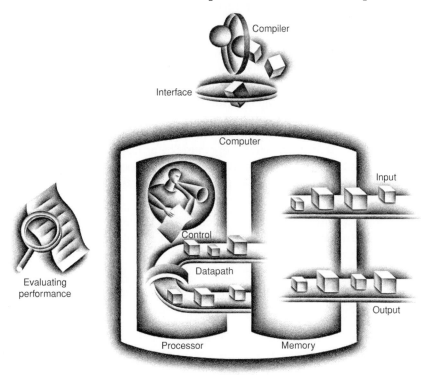

5.1   Introduction

From the earliest days of computing, programmers have wanted unlimited amounts of fast memory. The topics in this chapter aid programmers by creating that illusion. Before we look at creating the illusion, let's consider a simple analogy that illustrates the key principles and mechanisms that we use.

Suppose you were a student writing a term paper on important historical developments in computer hardware. You are sitting at a desk in a library with a collection of books that you have pulled from the shelves and are examining. You find that several of the important computers that you need to write about are described in the books you have, but there is nothing about the EDSAC. Therefore, you go back to the shelves and look for an additional book. You find a book on early British computers that covers the EDSAC. Once you have a good selection of books on the desk in front of you, there is a good probability that many of the topics you need can be found in them, and you may spend most of your time just using the books on the desk without going back to the shelves. Having several books on the desk in front of you saves time compared to having only one book there and constantly having to go back to the shelves to return it and take out another.

The same principle allows us to create the illusion of a large memory that we can access as fast as a very small memory. Just as you did not need to access all the books in the library at once with equal probability, a program does not access all of its code or data at once with equal probability. Otherwise, it would be impossible to make most memory accesses fast and still have large memory in computers, just as it would be impossible for you to fit all the library books on your desk and still find what you wanted quickly.

This *principle of locality* underlies both the way in which you did your work in the library and the way that programs operate. The principle of locality states that programs access a relatively small portion of their address space at any instant of time, just as you accessed a very small portion of the library's collection. There are two different types of locality:

temporal locality The principle stating that if a data location is referenced then it will tend to be referenced again soon.

spatial locality The locality principle stating that if a data location is referenced, data locations with nearby addresses will tend to be referenced soon.

- **Temporal locality** (locality in time): if an item is referenced, it will tend to be referenced again soon. If you recently brought a book to your desk to look at, you will probably need to look at it again soon.

- **Spatial locality** (locality in space): if an item is referenced, items whose addresses are close by will tend to be referenced soon. For example, when you brought out the book on early English computers to find out about the EDSAC, you also noticed that there was another book shelved next to it about early mechanical computers, so you also brought back that book and, later on, found something useful in that book. Libraries put books on the same topic together on the same shelves to increase spatial locality. We'll see how memory hierarchies use spatial locality in a little later in this chapter.

Just as accesses to books on the desk naturally exhibit locality, locality in programs arises from simple and natural program structures. For example, most programs contain loops, so instructions and data are likely to be accessed repeatedly, showing high amounts of temporal locality. Since instructions are normally accessed sequentially, programs also show high spatial locality. Accesses to data also exhibit a natural spatial locality. For example, sequential accesses to elements of an array or a record will naturally have high degrees of spatial locality.

We take advantage of the principle of locality by implementing the memory of a computer as a **memory hierarchy**. A memory hierarchy consists of multiple levels of memory with different speeds and sizes. The faster memories are more expensive per bit than the slower memories and thus are smaller.

Today, there are three primary technologies used in building memory hierarchies. Main memory is implemented from DRAM (dynamic random access memory), while levels closer to the processor (caches) use SRAM (static random access memory). DRAM is less costly per bit than SRAM, although it is substantially slower. The price difference arises because DRAM uses significantly less area per bit of memory, and DRAMs thus have larger capacity for the same amount of silicon; the speed difference arises from several factors described in Section C.9 of Appendix C. The third technology, used to implement the largest and slowest level in the hierarchy, is usually magnetic disk. (Flash memory is used instead of disks in many embedded devices; see Section 6.4.) The access time and price per bit vary widely among these technologies, as the table below shows, using typical values for 2008:

memory hierarchy A structure that uses multiple levels of memories; as the distance from the processor increases, the size of the memories and the access time both increase.

Memory technology	Typical access time	$ per GB in 2008
SRAM	0.5–2.5 ns	$2000–$5000
DRAM	50–70 ns	$20–$75
Magnetic disk	5,000,000–20,000,000 ns	$0.20–$2

Because of these differences in cost and access time, it is advantageous to build memory as a hierarchy of levels. Figure 5.1 shows the faster memory is close to the processor and the slower, less expensive memory is below it. The goal is to present the user with as much memory as is available in the cheapest technology, while providing access at the speed offered by the fastest memory.

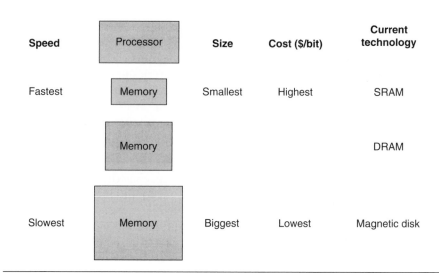

FIGURE 5.1   The basic structure of a memory hierarchy. By implementing the memory system as a hierarchy, the user has the illusion of a memory that is as large as the largest level of the hierarchy, but can be accessed as if it were all built from the fastest memory. Flash memory has replaced disks in many embedded devices, and may lead to a new level in the storage hierarchy for desktop and server computers; see Section 6.4.

The data is similarly hierarchical: a level closer to the processor is generally a subset of any level further away, and all the data is stored at the lowest level. By analogy, the books on your desk form a subset of the library you are working in, which is in turn a subset of all the libraries on campus. Furthermore, as we move away from the processor, the levels take progressively longer to access, just as we might encounter in a hierarchy of campus libraries.

A memory hierarchy can consist of multiple levels, but data is copied between only two adjacent levels at a time, so we can focus our attention on just two levels. The upper level—the one closer to the processor—is smaller and faster than the lower level, since the upper level uses technology that is more expensive. Figure 5.2 shows that the minimum unit of information that can be either present or not present in the two-level hierarchy is called a **block** or a **line**; in our library analogy, a block of information is one book.

If the data requested by the processor appears in some block in the upper level, this is called a *hit* (analogous to your finding the information in one of the books on your desk). If the data is not found in the upper level, the request is called a *miss*. The lower level in the hierarchy is then accessed to retrieve the block containing the requested data. (Continuing our analogy, you go from your desk to the shelves to find the desired book.) The **hit rate**, or *hit ratio*, is the fraction of memory accesses found in the upper level; it is often used as a measure of the performance of the memory hierarchy. The **miss rate** (1 − hit rate) is the fraction of memory accesses not found in the upper level.

block (or line) The minimum unit of information that can be either present or not present in a cache.

hit rate The fraction of memory accesses found in a level of the memory hierarchy.

miss rate The fraction of memory accesses not found in a level of the memory hierarchy.

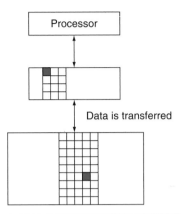

FIGURE 5.2 Every pair of levels in the memory hierarchy can be thought of as having an upper and lower level. Within each level, the unit of information that is present or not is called a *block* or a *line*. Usually we transfer an entire block when we copy something between levels.

Since performance is the major reason for having a memory hierarchy, the time to service hits and misses is important. **Hit time** is the time to access the upper level of the memory hierarchy, which includes the time needed to determine whether the access is a hit or a miss (that is, the time needed to look through the books on the desk). The **miss penalty** is the time to replace a block in the upper level with the corresponding block from the lower level, plus the time to deliver this block to the processor (or the time to get another book from the shelves and place it on the desk). Because the upper level is smaller and built using faster memory parts, the hit time will be much smaller than the time to access the next level in the hierarchy, which is the major component of the miss penalty. (The time to examine the books on the desk is much smaller than the time to get up and get a new book from the shelves.)

As we will see in this chapter, the concepts used to build memory systems affect many other aspects of a computer, including how the operating system manages memory and I/O, how compilers generate code, and even how applications use the computer. Of course, because all programs spend much of their time accessing memory, the memory system is necessarily a major factor in determining performance. The reliance on memory hierarchies to achieve performance has meant that programmers, who used to be able to think of memory as a flat, random access storage device, now need to understand that memory is a hierarchy to get good performance. We show how important this understanding is in later examples, such as Figure 5.18 on page 490.

Since memory systems are critical to performance, computer designers devote a great deal of attention to these systems and develop sophisticated mechanisms for improving the performance of the memory system. In this chapter, we discuss the major conceptual ideas, although we use many simplifications and abstractions to keep the material manageable in length and complexity.

hit time The time required to access a level of the memory hierarchy, including the time needed to determine whether the access is a hit or a miss.

miss penalty The time required to fetch a block into a level of the memory hierarchy from the lower level, including the time to access the block, transmit it from one level to the other, insert it in the level that experienced the miss, and then pass the block to the requestor.

The BIG Picture

Programs exhibit both temporal locality, the tendency to reuse recently accessed data items, and spatial locality, the tendency to reference data items that are close to other recently accessed items. Memory hierarchies take advantage of temporal locality by keeping more recently accessed data items closer to the processor. Memory hierarchies take advantage of spatial locality by moving blocks consisting of multiple contiguous words in memory to upper levels of the hierarchy.

Figure 5.3 shows that a memory hierarchy uses smaller and faster memory technologies close to the processor. Thus, accesses that hit in the highest level of the hierarchy can be processed quickly. Accesses that miss go to lower levels of the hierarchy, which are larger but slower. If the hit rate is high enough, the memory hierarchy has an effective access time close to that of the highest (and fastest) level and a size equal to that of the lowest (and largest) level.

In most systems, the memory is a true hierarchy, meaning that data cannot be present in level i unless it is also present in level $i + 1$.

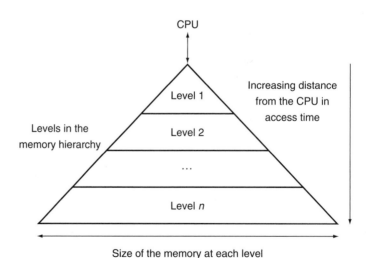

FIGURE 5.3   This diagram shows the structure of a memory hierarchy: as the distance from the processor increases, so does the size. This structure, with the appropriate operating mechanisms, allows the processor to have an access time that is determined primarily by level 1 of the hierarchy and yet have a memory as large as level n. Maintaining this illusion is the subject of this chapter. Although the local disk is normally the bottom of the hierarchy, some systems use tape or a file server over a local area network as the next levels of the hierarchy.

Which of the following statements are generally true?

1. Caches take advantage of temporal locality.

2. On a read, the value returned depends on which blocks are in the cache.

3. Most of the cost of the memory hierarchy is at the highest level.

4. Most of the capacity of the memory hierarchy is at the lowest level.

*Cache: a safe place
for hiding or storing
things.*

Webster's New World
Dictionary of the
American Language,
Third College Edition,
1988

5.2 The Basics of Caches

In our library example, the desk acted as a cache—a safe place to store things (books) that we needed to examine. *Cache* was the name chosen to represent the level of the memory hierarchy between the processor and main memory in the first commercial computer to have this extra level. The memories in the datapath in Chapter 4 are simply replaced by caches. Today, although this remains the dominant use of the word *cache*, the term is also used to refer to any storage managed to take advantage of locality of access. Caches first appeared in research computers in the early 1960s and in production computers later in that same decade; every general-purpose computer built today, from servers to low-power embedded processors, includes caches.

In this section, we begin by looking at a very simple cache in which the processor requests are each one word and the blocks also consist of a single word. (Readers already familiar with cache basics may want to skip to Section 5.3.) Figure 5.4 shows such a simple cache, before and after requesting a data item that is not initially in the cache. Before the request, the cache contains a collection of recent references $X_1, X_2, \ldots, X_{n-1}$, and the processor requests a word X_n that is not in the cache. This request results in a miss, and the word X_n is brought from memory into the cache.

In looking at the scenario in Figure 5.4, there are two questions to answer: How do we know if a data item is in the cache? Moreover, if it is, how do we find it? The answers are related. If each word can go in exactly one place in the cache, then it is straightforward to find the word if it is in the cache. The simplest way to assign a location in the cache for each word in memory is to assign the cache location based on the *address* of the word in memory. This cache structure is called **direct mapped**, since each memory location is mapped directly to exactly one location in the cache. The typical mapping between addresses and cache locations for a direct-mapped cache is usually simple. For example, almost all direct-mapped caches use this mapping to find a block:

direct-mapped cache A cache structure in which each memory location is mapped to exactly one location in the cache.

(Block address) modulo (Number of blocks in the cache)

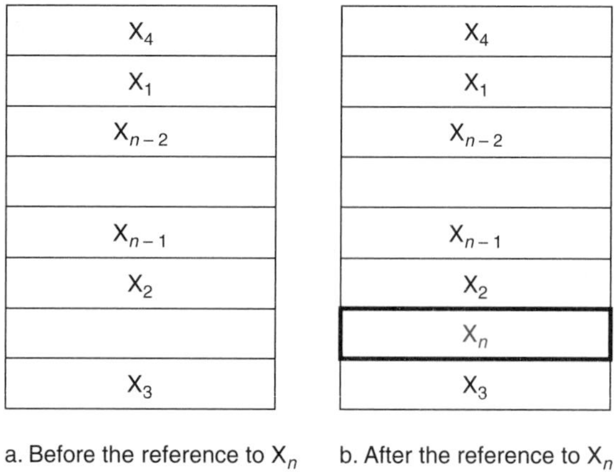

a. Before the reference to X_n b. After the reference to X_n

FIGURE 5.4   The cache just before and just after a reference to a word X_n that is not initially in the cache. This reference causes a miss that forces the cache to fetch X_n from memory and insert it into the cache.

If the number of entries in the cache is a power of 2, then modulo can be computed simply by using the low-order $\log_2$ (cache size in blocks) bits of the address. Thus, an 8-block cache uses the three lowest bits ($8 = 2^3$) of the block address. For example, Figure 5.5 shows how the memory addresses between 1_{ten} (00001_{two}) and 29_{ten} (11101_{two}) map to locations 1_{ten} (001_{two}) and 5_{ten} (101_{two}) in a direct-mapped cache of eight words.

Because each cache location can contain the contents of a number of different memory locations, how do we know whether the data in the cache corresponds to a requested word? That is, how do we know whether a requested word is in the cache or not? We answer this question by adding a set of **tags** to the cache. The tags contain the address information required to identify whether a word in the cache corresponds to the requested word. The tag needs only to contain the upper portion of the address, corresponding to the bits that are not used as an index into the cache. For example, in Figure 5.5 we need only have the upper 2 of the 5 address bits in the tag, since the lower 3-bit index field of the address selects the block. Architects omit the index bits because they are redundant, since by definition the index field of any address of a cache block must be that block number.

We also need a way to recognize that a cache block does not have valid information. For instance, when a processor starts up, the cache does not have good data, and the tag fields will be meaningless. Even after executing many instructions, some of the cache entries may still be empty, as in Figure 5.4. Thus, we need to know that the tag should be ignored for such entries. The most common method is to add a **valid bit** to indicate whether an entry contains a valid address. If the bit is not set, there cannot be a match for this block.

tag A field in a table used for a memory hierarchy that contains the address information required to identify whether the associated block in the hierarchy corresponds to a requested word.

valid bit A field in the tables of a memory hierarchy that indicates that the associated block in the hierarchy contains valid data.

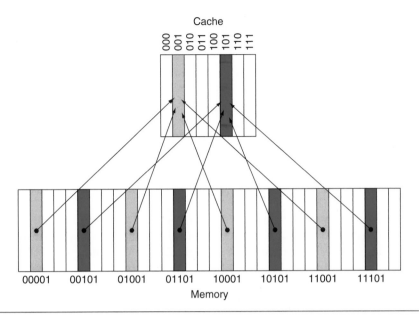

Cache

FIGURE 5.5   A direct-mapped cache with eight entries showing the addresses of memory words between 0 and 31 that map to the same cache locations. Because there are eight words in the cache, an address X maps to the direct-mapped cache word X modulo 8. That is, the low-order $\log_2(8) =$ 3 bits are used as the cache index. Thus, addresses 00001_{two}, 01001_{two}, 10001_{two}, and 11001_{two} all map to entry 001_{two} of the cache, while addresses 00101_{two}, 01101_{two}, 10101_{two}, and 11101_{two} all map to entry 101_{two} of the cache.

For the rest of this section, we will focus on explaining how a cache deals with reads. In general, handling reads is a little simpler than handling writes, since reads do not have to change the contents of the cache. After seeing the basics of how reads work and how cache misses can be handled, we'll examine the cache designs for real computers and detail how these caches handle writes.

Accessing a Cache

Below is a sequence of nine memory references to an empty eight-block cache, including the action for each reference. Figure 5.6 shows how the contents of the cache change on each miss. Since there are eight blocks in the cache, the low-order three bits of an address give the block number:

Decimal address of reference	Binary address of reference	Hit or miss in cache	Assigned cache block (where found or placed)
22	10110_{two}	miss (5.6b)	$(10110_{two}$ mod 8$) = 110_{two}$
26	11010_{two}	miss (5.6c)	$(11010_{two}$ mod 8$) = 010_{two}$
22	10110_{two}	hit	$(10110_{two}$ mod 8$) = 110_{two}$
26	11010_{two}	hit	$(11010_{two}$ mod 8$) = 010_{two}$
16	10000_{two}	miss (5.6d)	$(10000_{two}$ mod 8$) = 000_{two}$
3	00011_{two}	miss (5.6e)	$(00011_{two}$ mod 8$) = 011_{two}$
16	10000_{two}	hit	$(10000_{two}$ mod 8$) = 000_{two}$
18	10010_{two}	miss (5.6f)	$(10010_{two}$ mod 8$) = 010_{two}$
16	10000_{two}	hit	$(10000_{two}$ mod 8$) = 000_{two}$

Since the cache is empty, several of the first references are misses; the caption of Figure 5.6 describes the actions for each memory reference. On the eighth reference we have conflicting demands for a block. The word at address 18 (10010_{two}) should be brought into cache block 2 (010_{two}). Hence, it must replace the word at address 26 (11010_{two}), which is already in cache block 2 (010_{two}). This behavior allows a cache to take advantage of temporal locality: recently referenced words replace less recently referenced words.

This situation is directly analogous to needing a book from the shelves and having no more space on your desk—some book already on your desk must be returned to the shelves. In a direct-mapped cache, there is only one place to put the newly requested item and hence only one choice of what to replace.

We know where to look in the cache for each possible address: the low-order bits of an address can be used to find the unique cache entry to which the address could map. Figure 5.7 shows how a referenced address is divided into

- A *tag field*, which is used to compare with the value of the tag field of the cache

- A *cache index*, which is used to select the block

The index of a cache block, together with the tag contents of that block, uniquely specifies the memory address of the word contained in the cache block. Because the index field is used as an address to reference the cache, and because an *n*-bit field has 2^n values, the total number of entries in a direct-mapped cache must be a power of 2. In the MIPS architecture, since words are aligned to multiples of four bytes, the least significant two bits of every address specify a byte within a word. Hence, the least significant two bits are ignored when selecting a word in the block.

The total number of bits needed for a cache is a function of the cache size and the address size, because the cache includes both the storage for the data and the tags. The size of the block above was one word, but normally it is several. For the following situation:

Index	V	Tag	Data
000	N		
001	N		
010	N		
011	N		
100	N		
101	N		
110	N		
111	N		

a. The initial state of the cache after power-on

Index	V	Tag	Data
000	N		
001	N		
010	N		
011	N		
100	N		
101	N		
110	Y	10_{two}	Memory (10110_{two})
111	N		

b. After handling a miss of address (10110_{two})

Index	V	Tag	Data
000	N		
001	N		
010	Y	11_{two}	Memory (11010_{two})
011	N		
100	N		
101	N		
110	Y	10_{two}	Memory (10110_{two})
111	N		

c. After handling a miss of address (11010_{two})

Index	V	Tag	Data
000	Y	10_{two}	Memory (10000_{two})
001	N		
010	Y	11_{two}	Memory (11010_{two})
011	N		
100	N		
101	N		
110	Y	10_{two}	Memory (10110_{two})
111	N		

d. After handling a miss of address (10000_{two})

Index	V	Tag	Data
000	Y	10_{two}	Memory (10000_{two})
001	N		
010	Y	11_{two}	Memory (11010_{two})
011	Y	00_{two}	Memory (00011_{two})
100	N		
101	N		
110	Y	10_{two}	Memory (10110_{two})
111	N		

e. After handling a miss of address (00011_{two})

Index	V	Tag	Data
000	Y	10_{two}	Memory (10000_{two})
001	N		
010	Y	10_{two}	Memory (10010_{two})
011	Y	00_{two}	Memory (00011_{two})
100	N		
101	N		
110	Y	10_{two}	Memory (10110_{two})
111	N		

f. After handling a miss of address (10010_{two})

FIGURE 5.6 The cache contents are shown after each reference request that *misses*, with the index and tag fields shown in binary for the sequence of addresses on page 460. The cache is initially empty, with all valid bits (V entry in cache) turned off (N). The processor requests the following addresses: 10110_{two} (miss), 11010_{two} (miss), 10110_{two} (hit), 11010_{two} (hit), 10000_{two} (miss), 00011_{two} (miss), 10000_{two} (hit), 10010_{two} (miss), and 10000_{two} (hit). The figures show the cache contents after each miss in the sequence has been handled. When address 10010_{two} (18) is referenced, the entry for address 11010_{two} (26) must be replaced, and a reference to 11010_{two} will cause a subsequent miss. The tag field will contain only the upper portion of the address. The full address of a word contained in cache block i with tag field j for this cache is $j \times 8 + i$, or equivalently the concatenation of the tag field j and the index i. For example, in cache f above, index 010_{two} has tag 10_{two} and corresponds to address 10010_{two}.

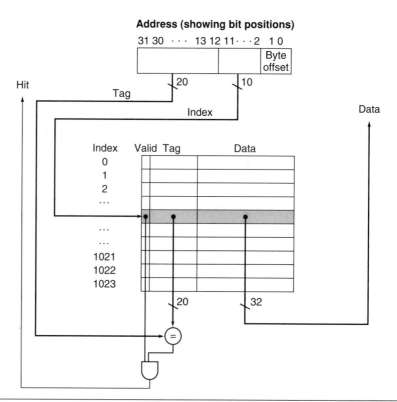

Address (showing bit positions)

FIGURE 5.7   For this cache, the lower portion of the address is used to select a cache entry consisting of a data word and a tag. This cache holds 1024 words or 4 KB. We assume 32-bit addresses in this chapter. The tag from the cache is compared against the upper portion of the address to determine whether the entry in the cache corresponds to the requested address. Because the cache has 2^{10} (or 1024) words and a block size of one word, 10 bits are used to index the cache, leaving $32 - 10 - 2 = 20$ bits to be compared against the tag. If the tag and upper 20 bits of the address are equal and the valid bit is on, then the request hits in the cache, and the word is supplied to the processor. Otherwise, a miss occurs.

- 32-bit byte addresses

- A direct-mapped cache

- The cache size is 2^n blocks, so n bits are used for the index

- The block size is 2^m words (2^{m+2} bytes), so m bits are used for the word within the block, and two bits are used for the byte part of the address

the size of the tag field is

$$32 - (n + m + 2).$$

The total number of bits in a direct-mapped cache is

$$2^n \times (\text{block size} + \text{tag size} + \text{valid field size}).$$

Since the block size is 2^m words (2^{m+5} bits), and we need 1 bit for the valid field, the number of bits in such a cache is

$$2^n \times (2^m \times 32 + (32 - n - m - 2) + 1) = 2^n \times (2^m \times 32 + 31 - n - m).$$

Although this is the actual size in bits, the naming convention is to exclude the size of the tag and valid field and to count only the size of the data. Thus, the cache in Figure 5.7 is called a 4 KB cache.

Bits in a Cache

How many total bits are required for a direct-mapped cache with 16 KB of data and 4-word blocks, assuming a 32-bit address?

EXAMPLE

We know that 16 KB is 4K (2^{12}) words. With a block size of 4 words (2^2), there are 1024 (2^{10}) blocks. Each block has 4×32 or 128 bits of data plus a tag, which is $32 - 10 - 2 - 2$ bits, plus a valid bit. Thus, the total cache size is

ANSWER

$$2^{10} \times (4 \times 32 + (32 - 10 - 2 - 2) + 1) = 2^{10} \times 147 = 147 \text{ Kbits}$$

or 18.4 KB for a 16 KB cache. For this cache, the total number of bits in the cache is about 1.15 times as many as needed just for the storage of the data.

Mapping an Address to a Multiword Cache Block

Consider a cache with 64 blocks and a block size of 16 bytes. To what block number does byte address 1200 map?

EXAMPLE

We saw the formula on page 457. The block is given by

ANSWER

(Block address) modulo (Number of blocks in the cache)

where the address of the block is

$$\frac{\text{Byte address}}{\text{Bytes per block}}$$

Notice that this block address is the block containing all addresses between

$$\left\lfloor \frac{\text{Byte address}}{\text{Bytes per block}} \right\rfloor \times \text{Bytes per block}$$

and

$$\left\lfloor \frac{\text{Byte address}}{\text{Bytes per block}} \right\rfloor \times \text{Bytes per block} + (\text{Bytes per block} - 1)$$

Thus, with 16 bytes per block, byte address 1200 is block address

$$\left\lfloor \frac{1200}{6} \right\rfloor = 75$$

which maps to cache block number (75 modulo 64) = 11. In fact, this block maps all addresses between 1200 and 1215.

Larger blocks exploit spatial locality to lower miss rates. As Figure 5.8 shows, increasing the block size usually decreases the miss rate. The miss rate may go up eventually if the block size becomes a significant fraction of the cache size, because the number of blocks that can be held in the cache will become small, and there will be a great deal of competition for those blocks. As a result, a block will be bumped out of the cache before many of its words are accessed. Stated alternatively, spatial locality among the words in a block decreases with a very large block; consequently, the benefits in the miss rate become smaller.

A more serious problem associated with just increasing the block size is that the cost of a miss increases. The miss penalty is determined by the time required to fetch the block from the next lower level of the hierarchy and load it into the cache. The time to fetch the block has two parts: the latency to the first word and the transfer time for the rest of the block. Clearly, unless we change the memory system, the transfer time—and hence the miss penalty—will likely increase as the block size increases. Furthermore, the improvement in the miss rate starts to decrease as the blocks become larger. The result is that the increase in the miss penalty overwhelms the decrease in the miss rate for blocks that are too large, and cache performance thus decreases. Of course, if we design the memory to transfer larger blocks more efficiently, we can increase the block size and obtain further improvements in cache performance. We discuss this topic in the next section.

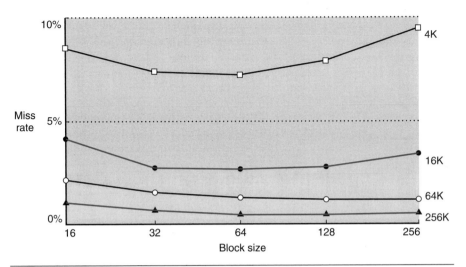

FIGURE 5.8   Miss rate versus block size. Note that the miss rate actually goes up if the block size is too large relative to the cache size. Each line represents a cache of different size. (This figure is independent of associativity, discussed soon.) Unfortunately, SPEC CPU2000 traces would take too long if block size were included, so this data is based on SPEC92.

Elaboration: Although it is hard to do anything about the longer latency component of the miss penalty for large blocks, we may be able to hide some of the transfer time so that the miss penalty is effectively smaller. The simplest method for doing this, called *early restart*, is simply to resume execution as soon as the requested word of the block is returned, rather than wait for the entire block. Many processors use this technique for instruction access, where it works best. Instruction accesses are largely sequential, so if the memory system can deliver a word every clock cycle, the processor may be able to restart operation when the requested word is returned, with the memory system delivering new instruction words just in time. This technique is usually less effective for data caches because it is likely that the words will be requested from the block in a less predictable way, and the probability that the processor will need another word from a different cache block before the transfer completes is high. If the processor cannot access the data cache because a transfer is ongoing, then it must stall.

An even more sophisticated scheme is to organize the memory so that the requested word is transferred from the memory to the cache first. The remainder of the block is then transferred, starting with the address after the requested word and wrapping around to the beginning of the block. This technique, called *requested word first* or *critical word first*, can be slightly faster than early restart, but it is limited by the same properties that limit early restart.

Handling Cache Misses

Before we look at the cache of a real system, let's see how the control unit deals with **cache misses**. (We describe a cache controller in detail in Section 5.7). The control unit must detect a miss and process the miss by fetching the requested data

cache miss A request for data from the cache that cannot be filled because the data is not present in the cache.

from memory (or, as we shall see, a lower-level cache). If the cache reports a hit, the computer continues using the data as if nothing happened.

Modifying the control of a processor to handle a hit is trivial; misses, however, require some extra work. The cache miss handling is done in collaboration with the processor control unit and with a separate controller that initiates the memory access and refills the cache. The processing of a cache miss creates a pipeline stall (Chapter 4) as opposed to an interrupt, which would require saving the state of all registers. For a cache miss, we can stall the entire processor, essentially freezing the contents of the temporary and programmer-visible registers, while we wait for memory. More sophisticated out-of-order processors can allow execution of instructions while waiting for a cache miss, but we'll assume in-order processors that stall on cache misses in this section.

Let's look a little more closely at how instruction misses are handled; the same approach can be easily extended to handle data misses. If an instruction access results in a miss, then the content of the Instruction register is invalid. To get the proper instruction into the cache, we must be able to instruct the lower level in the memory hierarchy to perform a read. Since the program counter is incremented in the first clock cycle of execution, the address of the instruction that generates an instruction cache miss is equal to the value of the program counter minus 4. Once we have the address, we need to instruct the main memory to perform a read. We wait for the memory to respond (since the access will take multiple clock cycles), and then write the words containing the desired instruction into the cache.

We can now define the steps to be taken on an instruction cache miss:

1. Send the original PC value (current PC – 4) to the memory.

2. Instruct main memory to perform a read and wait for the memory to complete its access.

3. Write the cache entry, putting the data from memory in the data portion of the entry, writing the upper bits of the address (from the ALU) into the tag field, and turning the valid bit on.

4. Restart the instruction execution at the first step, which will refetch the instruction, this time finding it in the cache.

The control of the cache on a data access is essentially identical: on a miss, we simply stall the processor until the memory responds with the data.

Handling Writes

Writes work somewhat differently. Suppose on a store instruction, we wrote the data into only the data cache (without changing main memory); then, after the write into the cache, memory would have a different value from that in the cache. In such a case, the cache and memory are said to be *inconsistent*. The simplest way to keep the main memory and the cache consistent is always to write the data into both the memory and the cache. This scheme is called **write-through**.

The other key aspect of writes is what occurs on a write miss. We first fetch the words of the block from memory. After the block is fetched and placed into the cache, we can overwrite the word that caused the miss into the cache block. We also write the word to main memory using the full address.

Although this design handles writes very simply, it would not provide very good performance. With a write-through scheme, every write causes the data to be written to main memory. These writes will take a long time, likely at least 100 processor clock cycles, and could slow down the processor considerably. For example, suppose 10% of the instructions are stores. If the CPI without cache misses was 1.0, spending 100 extra cycles on every write would lead to a CPI of $1.0 + 100 \times 10\% = 11$, reducing performance by more than a factor of 10.

One solution to this problem is to use a **write buffer**. A write buffer stores the data while it is waiting to be written to memory. After writing the data into the cache and into the write buffer, the processor can continue execution. When a write to main memory completes, the entry in the write buffer is freed. If the write buffer is full when the processor reaches a write, the processor must stall until there is an empty position in the write buffer. Of course, if the rate at which the memory can complete writes is less than the rate at which the processor is generating writes, no amount of buffering can help, because writes are being generated faster than the memory system can accept them.

The rate at which writes are generated may also be *less* than the rate at which memory can accept them, and yet stalls may still occur. This can happen when the writes occur in bursts. To reduce the occurrence of such stalls, processors usually increase the depth of the write buffer beyond a single entry.

The alternative to a write-through scheme is a scheme called **write-back** or *copy back*. In a write-back scheme, when a write occurs, the new value is written only to the block in the cache. The modified block is written to the lower level of the hierarchy when it is replaced. Write-back schemes can improve performance, especially when processors can generate writes as fast or faster than the writes can be handled by main memory; a write-back scheme is, however, more complex to implement than write-through.

In the rest of this section, we describe caches from real processors, and we examine how they handle both reads and writes. In Section 5.5, we will describe the handling of writes in more detail.

write-through A scheme in which writes always update both the cache and the next lower level of the memory hierarchy, ensuring that data is always consistent between the two.

write buffer A queue that holds data while the data is waiting to be written to memory.

write-back A scheme that handles writes by updating values only to the block in the cache, then writing the modified block to the lower level of the hierarchy when the block is replaced.

Elaboration: Writes introduce several complications into caches that are not present for reads. Here we discuss two of them: the policy on write misses and efficient implementation of writes in write-back caches.

Consider a miss in a write-through cache. The most common strategy is to allocate a block in the cache, called *write allocate*. The block is fetched from memory and then the appropriate portion of the block is overwritten. An alternative strategy is to update the portion of the block in memory but not put it in the cache, called *no write allocate*. The motivation is that sometimes programs write entire blocks of data, such as when the operating system zeros a page of memory. In such cases, the fetch associated with the initial write miss may be unnecessary. Some computers allow the write allocation policy to be changed on a per page basis.

Actually implementing stores efficiently in a cache that uses a write-back strategy is more complex than in a write-through cache. A write-through cache can write the data into the cache and read the tag; if the tag mismatches, then a miss occurs. Because the cache is write-through, the overwriting of the block in the cache is not catastrophic, since memory has the correct value. In a write-back cache, we must first write the block back to memory if the data in the cache is modified and we have a cache miss. If we simply overwrote the block on a store instruction before we knew whether the store had hit in the cache (as we could for a write-through cache), we would destroy the contents of the block, which is not backed up in the next lower level of the memory hierarchy.

In a write-back cache, because we cannot overwrite the block, stores either require two cycles (a cycle to check for a hit followed by a cycle to actually perform the write) or require a write buffer to hold that data—effectively allowing the store to take only one cycle by pipelining it. When a store buffer is used, the processor does the cache lookup and places the data in the store buffer during the normal cache access cycle. Assuming a cache hit, the new data is written from the store buffer into the cache on the next unused cache access cycle.

By comparison, in a write-through cache, writes can always be done in one cycle. We read the tag and write the data portion of the selected block. If the tag matches the address of the block being written, the processor can continue normally, since the correct block has been updated. If the tag does not match, the processor generates a write miss to fetch the rest of the block corresponding to that address.

Many write-back caches also include write buffers that are used to reduce the miss penalty when a miss replaces a modified block. In such a case, the modified block is moved to a write-back buffer associated with the cache while the requested block is read from memory. The write-back buffer is later written back to memory. Assuming another miss does not occur immediately, this technique halves the miss penalty when a dirty block must be replaced.

An Example Cache: The Intrinsity FastMATH Processor

The Intrinsity FastMATH is a fast embedded microprocessor that uses the MIPS architecture and a simple cache implementation. Near the end of the chapter, we will examine the more complex cache design of the AMD Opteron X4 (Barcelona), but we start with this simple, yet real, example for pedagogical reasons. Figure 5.9 shows the organization of the Intrinsity FastMATH data cache.

This processor has a 12-stage pipeline, similar to that discussed late in Chapter 4. When operating at peak speed, the processor can request both an instruction word and a data word on every clock. To satisfy the demands of the pipeline without stalling, separate instruction and data caches are used. Each cache is 16 KB, or 4K words, with 16-word blocks.

Read requests for the cache are straightforward. Because there are separate data and instruction caches, we need separate control signals to read and write

Address (showing bit positions)

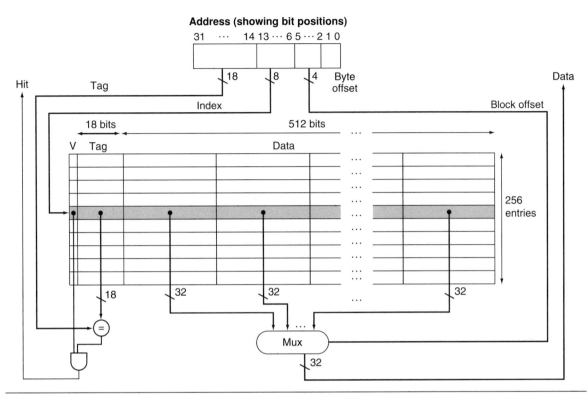

FIGURE 5.9 The 16 KB caches in the Intrinsity FastMATH each contain 256 blocks with 16 words per block. The tag field is 18 bits wide and the index field is 8 bits wide, while a 4-bit field (bits 5–2) is used to index the block and select the word from the block using a 16-to-1 multiplexor. In practice, to eliminate the multiplexor, caches use a separate large RAM for the data and a smaller RAM for the tags, with the block offset supplying the extra address bits for the large data RAM. In this case, the large RAM is 32 bits wide and must have 16 times as many words as blocks in the cache.

each cache. (Remember that we need to update the instruction cache when a miss occurs.) Thus, the steps for a read request to either cache are as follows:

1. Send the address to the appropriate cache. The address comes either from the PC (for an instruction) or from the ALU (for data).

2. If the cache signals hit, the requested word is available on the data lines. Since there are 16 words in the desired block, we need to select the right one. A block index field is used to control the multiplexor (shown at the bottom of the figure), which selects the requested word from the 16 words in the indexed block.

3. If the cache signals miss, we send the address to the main memory. When the memory returns with the data, we write it into the cache and then read it to fulfill the request.

For writes, the Intrinsity FastMATH offers both write-through and write-back, leaving it up to the operating system to decide which strategy to use for an application. It has a one-entry write buffer.

Instruction miss rate	Data miss rate	Effective combined miss rate
0.4%	11.4%	3.2%

FIGURE 5.10 Approximate instruction and data miss rates for the Intrinsity FastMATH processor for SPEC CPU2000 benchmarks. The combined miss rate is the effective miss rate seen for the combination of the 16 KB instruction cache and 16 KB data cache. It is obtained by weighting the instruction and data individual miss rates by the frequency of instruction and data references.

What cache miss rates are attained with a cache structure like that used by the Intrinsity FastMATH? Figure 5.10 shows the miss rates for the instruction and data caches. The combined miss rate is the effective miss rate per reference for each program after accounting for the differing frequency of instruction and data accesses.

Although miss rate is an important characteristic of cache designs, the ultimate measure will be the effect of the memory system on program execution time; we'll see how miss rate and execution time are related shortly.

split cache A scheme in which a level of the memory hierarchy is composed of two independent caches that operate in parallel with each other, with one handling instructions and one handling data.

Elaboration: A combined cache with a total size equal to the sum of the two **split caches** will usually have a better hit rate. This higher rate occurs because the combined cache does not rigidly divide the number of entries that may be used by instructions from those that may be used by data. Nonetheless, many processors use a split instruction and data cache to increase cache *bandwidth*. (There may also be fewer conflict misses; see Section 5.5.)

Here are miss rates for caches the size of those found in the Intrinsity FastMATH processor, and for a combined cache whose size is equal to the sum of the two caches:

- Total cache size: 32 KB
- Split cache effective miss rate: 3.24%
- Combined cache miss rate: 3.18%

The miss rate of the split cache is only slightly worse.

The advantage of doubling the cache bandwidth, by supporting both an instruction and data access simultaneously, easily overcomes the disadvantage of a slightly increased miss rate. This observation cautions us that we cannot use miss rate as the sole measure of cache performance, as Section 5.3 shows.

Designing the Memory System to Support Caches

Cache misses are satisfied from main memory, which is constructed from DRAMs. In Section 5.1, we saw that the primary emphasis with DRAMs is on cost and density. Although it is difficult to reduce the latency to fetch the first word from memory, we can reduce the miss penalty if we increase the bandwidth from the memory to the cache. This reduction allows larger block sizes to be used while still maintaining a low miss penalty, similar to that for a smaller block.

The processor is traditionally connected to memory over a bus. (As we'll see in Chapter 6, that tradition is changing, but the actual interconnect technology doesn't matter in this chapter, so we'll use the term bus.) The clock rate of the bus is usually much slower than the processor. The speed of this bus affects the miss penalty.

To understand the impact of different organizations of memory, let's define a set of hypothetical memory access times. Assume

- 1 memory bus clock cycle to send the address

- 15 memory bus clock cycles for each DRAM access initiated

- 1 memory bus clock cycle to send a word of data

If we have a cache block of four words and a one-word-wide bank of DRAMs, the miss penalty would be $1 + 4 \times 15 + 4 \times 1 = 65$ memory bus clock cycles. Thus, the number of bytes transferred per bus clock cycle for a single miss would be

$$\frac{4 \times 4}{65} = 0.25$$

Figure 5.11 shows three options for designing the memory system. The first option follows what we have been assuming: memory is one word wide, and all accesses are made sequentially. The second option increases the bandwidth to memory by widening the memory and the buses between the processor and memory; this allows parallel access to multiple words of the block. The third option increases the bandwidth by widening the memory but not the interconnection bus. Thus, we still pay a cost to transmit each word, but we can avoid paying the cost of the access latency more than once. Let's look at how much these other two options improve the 65-cycle miss penalty that we would see for the first option in Figure 5.11(a).

Increasing the width of the memory and the bus will increase the memory bandwidth proportionally, decreasing both the access time and transfer time portions of the miss penalty. With a main memory width of two words, the miss penalty drops from 65 memory bus clock cycles to $1 + (2 \times 15) + 2 \times 1 = 33$ memory bus clock cycles. The bandwidth for a single miss is then 0.48 (almost twice as high) bytes per bus clock cycle for a memory that is two words wide. The major costs of this enhancement are the wider bus and the potential increase in cache access time due to the multiplexor and control logic between the processor and cache.

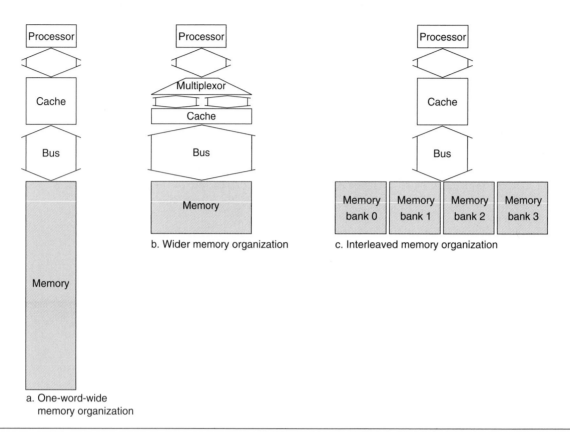

FIGURE 5.11 The primary method of achieving higher memory bandwidth is to increase the physical or logical width of the memory system. In this figure, memory bandwidth is improved two ways. The simplest design, (a), uses a memory where all components are one word wide; (b) shows a wider memory, bus, and cache; while (c) shows a narrow bus and cache with an interleaved memory. In (b), the logic between the cache and processor consists of a multiplexor used on reads and control logic to update the appropriate words of the cache on writes.

Instead of making the entire path between the memory and cache wider, the memory chips can be organized in banks to read or write multiple words in one access time rather than reading or writing a single word each time. Each bank could be one word wide so that the width of the bus and the cache need not change, but sending an address to several banks permits them all to read simultaneously. This scheme, which is called *interleaving*, retains the advantage of incurring the full memory latency only once. For example, with four banks, the time to get a four-word block would consist of 1 cycle to transmit the address and read request to the banks, 15 cycles for all four banks to access memory, and 4 cycles to send the four words back to the cache. This yields a miss penalty of $1 + (1 \times 15) + 4 \times 1 = 20$ memory bus clock cycles. This is an effective bandwidth per miss of 0.80 bytes per clock, or about three times the bandwidth for the one-word-wide memory and bus.

Banks are also valuable on writes. Each bank can write independently, quadrupling the write bandwidth and leading to fewer stalls in a write-through cache. As we will see, an alternative strategy for writes makes interleaving even more attractive.

Because of the ubiquity of caches and the desire for larger block sizes, DRAM manufacturers provide for a burst access to data from a series of sequential locations in the DRAM. The newest development is *Double Data Rate* (DDR) DRAMs. The name means data transfers on both the leading and falling edge of the clock, thereby getting twice as much bandwidth as you might expect based on the clock rate and the data width. To deliver such high bandwidth, the internal DRAM is organized as interleaved memory banks.

The advantage of such optimizations is that they use the circuitry already largely on the DRAMs, adding little cost to the system while achieving a significant improvement in bandwidth. Section C.9 of ⊙ **Appendix C** describes the internal architecture of DRAMs and how these optimizations are implemented.

Elaboration: Memory chips are organized to produce a number of output bits, usually 4 to 32, with 16 being the most popular in 2008. We describe the organization of a RAM as $d \times w$, where d is the number of addressable locations (the depth) and w is the output (or width of each location). DRAMs are logically organized as rectangular arrays, and access time is divided into row access and column access. DRAMs buffer a row. Burst transfers allow repeated accesses to the buffer without a row access time. The buffer acts like an SRAM; by changing column address, random bits can be accessed in the buffer until the next row access. This capability changes the access time significantly, since the access time to bits in the row is much lower. Figure 5.12 shows how the density, cost, and access time of DRAMs have changed over the years.

To improve the interface to processors, DRAMs added clocks and are properly called Synchronous DRAMs or SDRAMs. The advantage of SDRAMs is that the use of a clock eliminates the time for the memory and processor to synchronize.

Elaboration: One way to measure the performance of the memory system behind the caches is the Stream benchmark [McCalpin, 1995]. It measures the performance of long vector operations. They have no temporal locality and they access arrays that are larger than the cache of the computer being tested.

Elaboration: The burst mode for DDR memory is also found on memory buses, such as the Intel Duo Core Front Side Bus.

Year introduced	Chip size	$ per GB	Total access time to a new row/column	Column access time to existing row
1980	64 Kbit	$1,500,000	250 ns	150 ns
1983	256 Kbit	$500,000	185 ns	100 ns
1985	1 Mbit	$200,000	135 ns	40 ns
1989	4 Mbit	$50,000	110 ns	40 ns
1992	16 Mbit	$15,000	90 ns	30 ns
1996	64 Mbit	$10,000	60 ns	12 ns
1998	128 Mbit	$4,000	60 ns	10 ns
2000	256 Mbit	$1,000	55 ns	7 ns
2004	512 Mbit	$250	50 ns	5 ns
2007	1 Gbit	$50	40 ns	1.25 ns

FIGURE 5.12 DRAM size increased by multiples of four approximately once every three years until 1996, and thereafter considerably slower. The improvements in access time have been slower but continuous, and cost roughly tracks density improvements, although cost is often affected by other issues, such as availability and demand. The cost per gigabyte is not adjusted for inflation.

Summary

We began the previous section by examining the simplest of caches: a direct-mapped cache with a one-word block. In such a cache, both hits and misses are simple, since a word can go in exactly one location and there is a separate tag for every word. To keep the cache and memory consistent, a write-through scheme can be used, so that every write into the cache also causes memory to be updated. The alternative to write-through is a write-back scheme that copies a block back to memory when it is replaced; we'll discuss this scheme further in upcoming sections.

To take advantage of spatial locality, a cache must have a block size larger than one word. The use of a larger block decreases the miss rate and improves the efficiency of the cache by reducing the amount of tag storage relative to the amount of data storage in the cache. Although a larger block size decreases the miss rate, it can also increase the miss penalty. If the miss penalty increased linearly with the block size, larger blocks could easily lead to lower performance.

To avoid performance loss, the bandwidth of main memory is increased to transfer cache blocks more efficiently. Common methods for increasing bandwidth external to the DRAM are making the memory wider and interleaving. DRAM designers have steadily improved the interface between the processor and memory to increase the bandwidth of burst mode transfers to reduce the cost of larger cache block sizes.

The speed of the memory system affects the designer's decision on the size of the cache block. Which of the following cache designer guidelines are generally valid?

1. The shorter the memory latency, the smaller the cache block

2. The shorter the memory latency, the larger the cache block

3. The higher the memory bandwidth, the smaller the cache block

4. The higher the memory bandwidth, the larger the cache block

5.3   Measuring and Improving Cache Performance

In this section, we begin by examining ways to measure and analyze cache performance. We then explore two different techniques for improving cache performance. One focuses on reducing the miss rate by reducing the probability that two different memory blocks will contend for the same cache location. The second technique reduces the miss penalty by adding an additional level to the hierarchy. This technique, called *multilevel caching*, first appeared in high-end computers selling for more than $100,000 in 1990; since then it has become common on desktop computers selling for less than $500!

CPU time can be divided into the clock cycles that the CPU spends executing the program and the clock cycles that the CPU spends waiting for the memory system. Normally, we assume that the costs of cache accesses that are hits are part of the normal CPU execution cycles. Thus,

$$\text{CPU time} = (\text{CPU execution clock cycles} + \text{Memory-stall clock cycles}) \times \text{Clock cycle time}$$

The memory-stall clock cycles come primarily from cache misses, and we make that assumption here. We also restrict the discussion to a simplified model of the memory system. In real processors, the stalls generated by reads and writes can be quite complex, and accurate performance prediction usually requires very detailed simulations of the processor and memory system.

Memory-stall clock cycles can be defined as the sum of the stall cycles coming from reads plus those coming from writes:

$$\text{Memory-stall clock cycles} = \text{Read-stall cycles} + \text{Write-stall cycles}$$

The read-stall cycles can be defined in terms of the number of read accesses per program, the miss penalty in clock cycles for a read, and the read miss rate:

$$\text{Read-stall cycles} = \frac{\text{Reads}}{\text{Program}} \times \text{Read miss rate} \times \text{Read miss penalty}$$

Writes are more complicated. For a write-through scheme, we have two sources of stalls: write misses, which usually require that we fetch the block before continuing the write (see the *Elaboration* on page 467 for more details on dealing with writes), and write buffer stalls, which occur when the write buffer is full when a write occurs. Thus, the cycles stalled for writes equals the sum of these two:

$$\text{Write-stall cycles} = \left(\frac{\text{Writes}}{\text{Program}} \times \text{Write miss rate} \times \text{Write miss penalty} \right)$$
$$+ \text{Write buffer stalls}$$

Because the write buffer stalls depend on the proximity of writes, and not just the frequency, it is not possible to give a simple equation to compute such stalls. Fortunately, in systems with a reasonable write buffer depth (e.g., four or more words) and a memory capable of accepting writes at a rate that significantly exceeds the average write frequency in programs (e.g., by a factor of 2), the write buffer stalls will be small, and we can safely ignore them. If a system did not meet these criteria, it would not be well designed; instead, the designer should have used either a deeper write buffer or a write-back organization.

Write-back schemes also have potential additional stalls arising from the need to write a cache block back to memory when the block is replaced. We will discuss this more in Section 5.5.

In most write-through cache organizations, the read and write miss penalties are the same (the time to fetch the block from memory). If we assume that the write buffer stalls are negligible, we can combine the reads and writes by using a single miss rate and the miss penalty:

$$\text{Memory-stall clock cycles} = \frac{\text{Memory accesses}}{\text{Program}} \times \text{Miss rate} \times \text{Miss penalty}$$

We can also factor this as

$$\text{Memory-stall clock cycles} = \frac{\text{Instructions}}{\text{Program}} \times \frac{\text{Misses}}{\text{Instruction}} \times \text{Miss penalty}$$

Let's consider a simple example to help us understand the impact of cache performance on processor performance.

Calculating Cache Performance

Assume the miss rate of an instruction cache is 2% and the miss rate of the data cache is 4%. If a processor has a CPI of 2 without any memory stalls and the miss penalty is 100 cycles for all misses, determine how much faster a processor would run with a perfect cache that never missed. Assume the frequency of all loads and stores is 36%.

EXAMPLE

The number of memory miss cycles for instructions in terms of the Instruction count (I) is

ANSWER

$$\text{Instruction miss cycles} = I \times 2\% \times 100 = 2.00 \times I$$

As the frequency of all loads and stores is 36%, we can find the number of memory miss cycles for data references:

$$\text{Data miss cycles} = I \times 36\% \times 4\% \times 100 = 1.44 \times I$$

The total number of memory-stall cycles is $2.00\,I + 1.44\,I = 3.44\,I$. This is more than three cycles of memory stall per instruction. Accordingly, the total CPI including memory stalls is $2 + 3.44 = 5.44$. Since there is no change in instruction count or clock rate, the ratio of the CPU execution times is

$$\frac{\text{CPU time with stalls}}{\text{CPU time with perfect cache}} = \frac{I \times \text{CPI}_{\text{stall}} \times \text{Clock cycle}}{I \times \text{CPI}_{\text{perfect}} \times \text{Clock cycle}}$$

$$= \frac{\text{CPI}_{\text{stall}}}{\text{CPI}_{\text{perfect}}} = \frac{5.44}{2}$$

The performance with the perfect cache is better by $\frac{5.44}{2} = 2.72$.

What happens if the processor is made faster, but the memory system is not? The amount of time spent on memory stalls will take up an increasing fraction of the execution time; Amdahl's law, which we examined in Chapter 1, reminds us of this fact. A few simple examples show how serious this problem can be. Suppose we speed-up the computer in the previous example by reducing its CPI from 2 to 1 without changing the clock rate, which might be done with an improved pipeline. The system with cache misses would then have a CPI of $1 + 3.44 = 4.44$, and the system with the perfect cache would be

$$\frac{4.44}{1} = 4.44 \text{ times faster.}$$

The amount of execution time spent on memory stalls would have risen from

$$\frac{3.44}{5.44} = 63\%$$

to

$$\frac{3.44}{4.44} = 77\%.$$

Similarly, increasing the clock rate without changing the memory system also increases the performance lost due to cache misses.

The previous examples and equations assume that the hit time is not a factor in determining cache performance. Clearly, if the hit time increases, the total time to access a word from the memory system will increase, possibly causing an increase in the processor cycle time. Although we will see additional examples of what can increase hit time shortly, one example is increasing the cache size. A larger cache could clearly have a longer access time, just as, if your desk in the library was very large (say, 3 square meters), it would take longer to locate a book on the desk. An increase in hit time likely adds another stage to the pipeline, since it may take multiple cycles for a cache hit. Although it is more complex to calculate the performance impact of a deeper pipeline, at some point the increase in hit time for a larger cache could dominate the improvement in hit rate, leading to a decrease in processor performance.

To capture the fact that the time to access data for both hits and misses affects performance, designers sometime use *average memory access time* (AMAT) as a way to examine alternative cache designs. Average memory access time is the average time to access memory considering both hits and misses and the frequency of different accesses; it is equal to the following:

$$\text{AMAT} = \text{Time for a hit} + \text{Miss rate} \times \text{Miss penalty}$$

Calculating Average Memory Access Time

EXAMPLE

Find the AMAT for a processor with a 1 ns clock cycle time, a miss penalty of 20 clock cycles, a miss rate of 0.05 misses per instruction, and a cache access time (including hit detection) of 1 clock cycle. Assume that the read and write miss penalties are the same and ignore other write stalls.

The average memory access time per instruction is

$$\text{AMAT} = \text{Time for a hit} + \text{Miss rate} \times \text{Miss penalty}$$
$$= 1 + 0.05 \times 20$$
$$= 2 \text{ clock cycles}$$

or 2 ns.

The next subsection discusses alternative cache organizations that decrease miss rate but may sometimes increase hit time; additional examples appear in Section 5.11, Fallacies and Pitfalls.

Reducing Cache Misses by More Flexible Placement of Blocks

So far, when we place a block in the cache, we have used a simple placement scheme: A block can go in exactly one place in the cache. As mentioned earlier, it is called *direct mapped* because there is a direct mapping from any block address in memory to a single location in the upper level of the hierarchy. However, there is actually a whole range of schemes for placing blocks. Direct mapped, where a block can be placed in exactly one location, is at one extreme.

At the other extreme is a scheme where a block can be placed in *any* location in the cache. Such a scheme is called **fully associative**, because a block in memory may be associated with any entry in the cache. To find a given block in a fully associative cache, all the entries in the cache must be searched because a block can be placed in any one. To make the search practical, it is done in parallel with a comparator associated with each cache entry. These comparators significantly increase the hardware cost, effectively making fully associative placement practical only for caches with small numbers of blocks.

The middle range of designs between direct mapped and fully associative is called **set associative**. In a set-associative cache, there are a fixed number of locations where each block can be placed. A set-associative cache with *n* locations for a block is called an *n*-way set-associative cache. An *n*-way set-associative cache consists of a number of sets, each of which consists of *n* blocks. Each block in the memory maps to a unique *set* in the cache given by the index field, and a block can be placed in *any* element of that set. Thus, a set-associative placement combines direct-mapped

fully associative cache A cache structure in which a block can be placed in any location in the cache.

set-associative cache A cache that has a fixed number of locations (at least two) where each block can be placed.

placement and fully associative placement: a block is directly mapped into a set, and then all the blocks in the set are searched for a match. For example, Figure 5.13 shows where block 12 may be placed in a cache with eight blocks total, according to the three block placement policies.

FIGURE 5.13   The location of a memory block whose address is 12 in a cache with eight blocks varies for direct-mapped, set-associative, and fully associative placement. In direct-mapped placement, there is only one cache block where memory block 12 can be found, and that block is given by (12 modulo 8) = 4. In a two-way set-associative cache, there would be four sets, and memory block 12 must be in set (12 mod 4) = 0; the memory block could be in either element of the set. In a fully associative placement, the memory block for block address 12 can appear in any of the eight cache blocks.

Remember that in a direct-mapped cache, the position of a memory block is given by

(Block number) modulo (Number of *blocks* in the cache)

In a set-associative cache, the set containing a memory block is given by

(Block number) modulo (Number of *sets* in the cache)

Since the block may be placed in any element of the set, *all the tags of all the elements of the set* must be searched. In a fully associative cache, the block can go anywhere, and *all tags of all the blocks in the cache* must be searched.

We can also think of all block placement strategies as a variation on set associativity. Figure 5.14 shows the possible associativity structures for an eight-block cache. A direct-mapped cache is simply a one-way set-associative cache: each cache entry holds one block and each set has one element. A fully associative cache with m entries is simply an m-way set-associative cache; it has one set with m blocks, and an entry can reside in any block within that set.

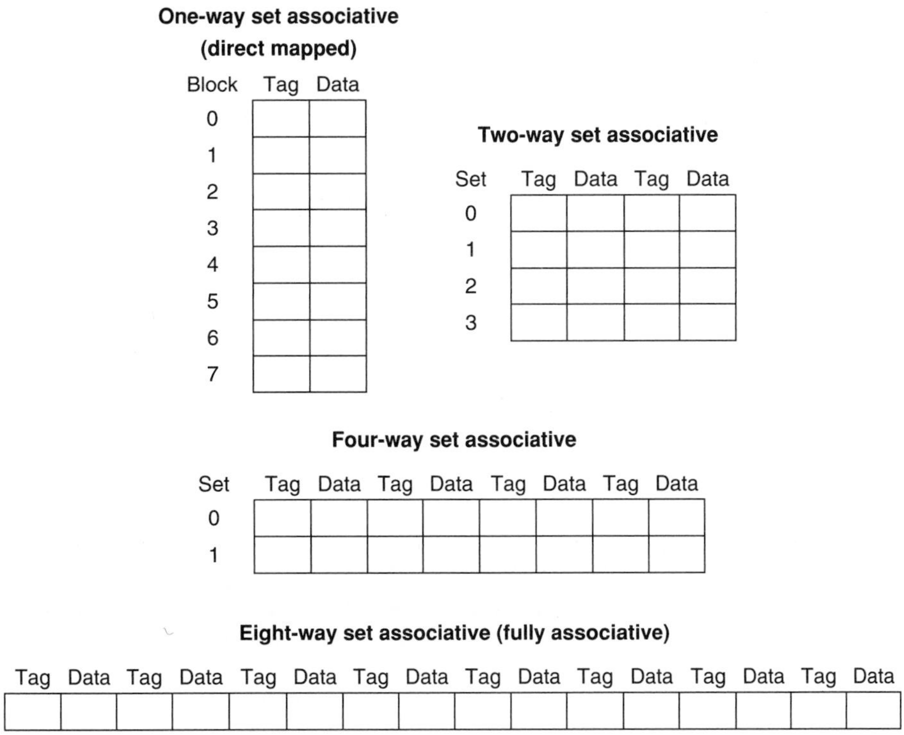

FIGURE 5.14 An eight-block cache configured as direct mapped, two-way set associative, four-way set associative, and fully associative. The total size of the cache in blocks is equal to the number of sets times the associativity. Thus, for a fixed cache size, increasing the associativity decreases the number of sets while increasing the number of elements per set. With eight blocks, an eight-way set-associative cache is the same as a fully associative cache.

The advantage of increasing the degree of associativity is that it usually decreases the miss rate, as the next example shows. The main disadvantage, which we discuss in more detail shortly, is a potential increase in the hit time.

EXAMPLE

ANSWER

Misses and Associativity in Caches

Assume there are three small caches, each consisting of four one-word blocks. One cache is fully associative, a second is two-way set-associative, and the third is direct-mapped. Find the number of misses for each cache organization given the following sequence of block addresses: 0, 8, 0, 6, and 8.

The direct-mapped case is easiest. First, let's determine to which cache block each block address maps:

Block address	Cache block
0	(0 modulo 4) = 0
6	(6 modulo 4) = 2
8	(8 modulo 4) = 0

Now we can fill in the cache contents after each reference, using a blank entry to mean that the block is invalid, colored text to show a new entry added to the cache for the associated reference, and plain text to show an old entry in the cache:

Address of memory block accessed	Hit or miss	Contents of cache blocks after reference			
		0	1	2	3
0	miss	Memory[0]			
8	miss	Memory[8]			
0	miss	Memory[0]			
6	miss	Memory[0]		Memory[6]	
8	miss	Memory[8]		Memory[6]	

The direct-mapped cache generates five misses for the five accesses.

The set-associative cache has two sets (with indices 0 and 1) with two elements per set. Let's first determine to which set each block address maps:

Block address	Cache set
0	(0 modulo 2) = 0
6	(6 modulo 2) = 0
8	(8 modulo 2) = 0

Because we have a choice of which entry in a set to replace on a miss, we need a replacement rule. Set-associative caches usually replace the least recently used block within a set; that is, the block that was used furthest in the past is replaced. (We will discuss other replacement rules in more detail shortly.) Using this replacement rule, the contents of the set-associative cache after each reference looks like this:

Address of memory block accessed	Hit or miss	Contents of cache blocks after reference			
		Set 0	Set 0	Set 1	Set 1
0	miss	Memory[0]			
8	miss	Memory[0]	Memory[8]		
0	hit	Memory[0]	Memory[8]		
6	miss	Memory[0]	Memory[6]		
8	miss	Memory[8]	Memory[6]		

Notice that when block 6 is referenced, it replaces block 8, since block 8 has been less recently referenced than block 0. The two-way set-associative cache has four misses, one less than the direct-mapped cache.

The fully associative cache has four cache blocks (in a single set); any memory block can be stored in any cache block. The fully associative cache has the best performance, with only three misses:

Address of memory block accessed	Hit or miss	Contents of cache blocks after reference			
		Block 0	Block 1	Block 2	Block 3
0	miss	Memory[0]			
8	miss	Memory[0]	Memory[8]		
0	hit	Memory[0]	Memory[8]		
6	miss	Memory[0]	Memory[8]	Memory[6]	
8	hit	Memory[0]	Memory[8]	Memory[6]	

For this series of references, three misses is the best we can do, because three unique block addresses are accessed. Notice that if we had eight blocks in the cache, there would be no replacements in the two-way set-associative cache (check this for yourself), and it would have the same number of misses as the fully associative cache. Similarly, if we had 16 blocks, all 3 caches would have the same number of misses. Even this trivial example shows that cache size and associativity are not independent in determining cache performance.

How much of a reduction in the miss rate is achieved by associativity? Figure 5.15 shows the improvement for a 64 KB data cache with a 16-word block, and associativity ranging from direct mapped to eight-way. Going from one-way to two-way associativity decreases the miss rate by about 15%, but there is little further improvement in going to higher associativity.

Associativity	Data miss rate
1	10.3%
2	8.6%
4	8.3%
8	8.1%

FIGURE 5.15   The data cache miss rates for an organization like the Intrinsity FastMATH processor for SPEC CPU2000 benchmarks with associativity varying from one-way to eight-way. These results for 10 SPEC CPU2000 programs are from Hennessy and Patterson [2003].

Locating a Block in the Cache

Now, let's consider the task of finding a block in a cache that is set associative. Just as in a direct-mapped cache, each block in a set-associative cache includes an address tag that gives the block address. The tag of every cache block within the appropriate set is checked to see if it matches the block address from the processor. Figure 5.16 decomposes the address. The index value is used to select the set containing the address of interest, and the tags of all the blocks in the set must be searched. Because speed is of the essence, all the tags in the selected set are searched in parallel. As in a fully associative cache, a sequential search would make the hit time of a set-associative cache too slow.

Tag	Index	Block offset

FIGURE 5.16   The three portions of an address in a set-associative or direct-mapped cache. The index is used to select the set, then the tag is used to choose the block by comparison with the blocks in the selected set. The block offset is the address of the desired data within the block.

If the total cache size is kept the same, increasing the associativity increases the number of blocks per set, which is the number of simultaneous compares needed to perform the search in parallel: each increase by a factor of 2 in associativity doubles the number of blocks per set and halves the number of sets. Accordingly, each factor-of-2 increase in associativity decreases the size of the index by 1 bit and increases the size of the tag by 1 bit. In a fully associative cache, there is effectively only one set, and all the blocks must be checked in parallel. Thus, there is no index, and the entire address, excluding the block offset, is compared against the tag of every block. In other words, we search the entire cache without any indexing.

In a direct-mapped cache, only a single comparator is needed, because the entry can be in only one block, and we access the cache simply by indexing. Figure 5.17 shows that in a four-way set-associative cache, four comparators are needed, together with a 4-to-1 multiplexor to choose among the four potential members of the selected set. The cache access consists of indexing the appropriate set and then searching the tags of the set. The costs of an associative cache are the extra comparators and any delay imposed by having to do the compare and select from among the elements of the set.

The choice among direct-mapped, set-associative, or fully associative mapping in any memory hierarchy will depend on the cost of a miss versus the cost of implementing associativity, both in time and in extra hardware.

Elaboration: A *Content Addressable Memory* (*CAM*) is a circuit that combines comparison and storage in a single device. Instead of supplying an address and reading a word like a RAM, you supply the data and the CAM looks to see if it has a copy and returns the index of the matching row. CAMs mean that cache designers can afford to implement much higher set associativity than if they needed to build the hardware out of SRAMs and comparators. In 2008, the greater size and power of CAM generally leads to 2-way and 4-way set associativity being built from standard SRAMs and comparators, with 8-way and above built using CAMs.

Choosing Which Block to Replace

When a miss occurs in a direct-mapped cache, the requested block can go in exactly one position, and the block occupying that position must be replaced. In an associative cache, we have a choice of where to place the requested block, and hence a choice of which block to replace. In a fully associative cache, all blocks are candidates for replacement. In a set-associative cache, we must choose among the blocks in the selected set.

The most commonly used scheme is **least recently used** (LRU), which we used in the previous example. In an LRU scheme, the block replaced is the one that has been unused for the longest time. The set associative example on page 482 uses LRU, which is why we replaced Memory(0) instead of Memory(6).

LRU replacement is implemented by keeping track of when each element in a set was used relative to the other elements in the set. For a two-way set-associative cache, tracking when the two elements were used can be implemented by keeping a single bit in each set and setting the bit to indicate an element whenever that element is referenced. As associativity increases, implementing LRU gets harder; in Section 5.5, we will see an alternative scheme for replacement.

least recently used (LRU) A replacement scheme in which the block replaced is the one that has been unused for the longest time.

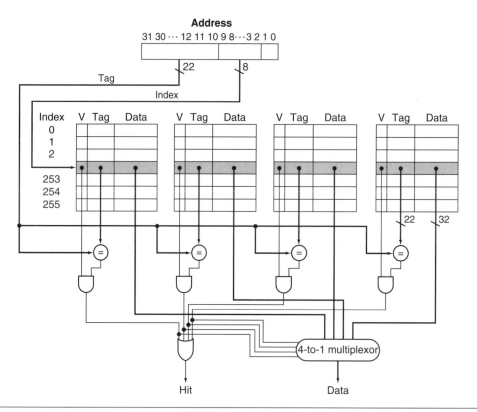

FIGURE 5.17   The implementation of a four-way set-associative cache requires four comparators and a 4-to-1 multiplexor. The comparators determine which element of the selected set (if any) matches the tag. The output of the comparators is used to select the data from one of the four blocks of the indexed set, using a multiplexor with a decoded select signal. In some implementations, the Output enable signals on the data portions of the cache RAMs can be used to select the entry in the set that drives the output. The Output enable signal comes from the comparators, causing the element that matches to drive the data outputs. This organization eliminates the need for the multiplexor.

Size of Tags versus Set Associativity

EXAMPLE

Increasing associativity requires more comparators and more tag bits per cache block. Assuming a cache of 4K blocks, a 4-word block size, and a 32-bit address, find the total number of sets and the total number of tag bits for caches that are direct mapped, two-way and four-way set associative, and fully associative.

Since there are 16 (= 2^4) bytes per block, a 32-bit address yields 32 − 4 = 28 bits to be used for index and tag. The direct-mapped cache has the same number of sets as blocks, and hence 12 bits of index, since $\log_2(4K) = 12$; hence, the total number is (28 − 12) × 4K = 16 × 4K = 64 K tag bits.

Each degree of associativity decreases the number of sets by a factor of 2 and thus decreases the number of bits used to index the cache by 1 and increases the number of bits in the tag by 1. Thus, for a two-way set-associative cache, there are 2K sets, and the total number of tag bits is (28 −11) × 2 × 2K = 34 × 2K = 68 Kbits. For a four-way set-associative cache, the total number of sets is 1K, and the total number is (28 − 10) × 4 × 1K = 72 × 1K = 72 K tag bits.

For a fully associative cache, there is only one set with 4K blocks, and the tag is 28 bits, leading to 28 × 4K × 1 = 112K tag bits.

Reducing the Miss Penalty Using Multilevel Caches

All modern computers make use of caches. To close the gap further between the fast clock rates of modern processors and the increasingly long time required to access DRAMs, most microprocessors support an additional level of caching. This second-level cache is usually on the same chip and is accessed whenever a miss occurs in the primary cache. If the second-level cache contains the desired data, the miss penalty for the first-level cache will be essentially the access time of the second-level cache, which will be much less than the access time of main memory. If neither the primary nor the secondary cache contains the data, a main memory access is required, and a larger miss penalty is incurred.

How significant is the performance improvement from the use of a secondary cache? The next example shows us.

Performance of Multilevel Caches

Suppose we have a processor with a base CPI of 1.0, assuming all references hit in the primary cache, and a clock rate of 4 GHz. Assume a main memory access time of 100 ns, including all the miss handling. Suppose the miss rate per instruction at the primary cache is 2%. How much faster will the processor be if we add a secondary cache that has a 5 ns access time for either a hit or a miss and is large enough to reduce the miss rate to main memory to 0.5%?

EXAMPLE

The miss penalty to main memory is

ANSWER

$$\frac{100 \text{ ns}}{0.25 \frac{\text{ns}}{\text{clock cycle}}} = 400 \text{ clock cycles}$$

The effective CPI with one level of caching is given by

Total CPI = Base CPI + Memory-stall cycles per instruction

For the processor with one level of caching,

Total CPI = 1.0 + Memory-stall cycles per instruction = $1.0 + 2\% \times 400 = 9$

With two levels of caching, a miss in the primary (or first-level) cache can be satisfied either by the secondary cache or by main memory. The miss penalty for an access to the second-level cache is

$$\frac{5 \text{ ns}}{0.25 \dfrac{\text{ns}}{\text{clock cycle}}} = 20 \text{ clock cycles}$$

If the miss is satisfied in the secondary cache, then this is the entire miss penalty. If the miss needs to go to main memory, then the total miss penalty is the sum of the secondary cache access time and the main memory access time.

Thus, for a two-level cache, total CPI is the sum of the stall cycles from both levels of cache and the base CPI:

$$
\begin{aligned}
\text{Total CPI} &= 1 + \text{Primary stalls per instruction} \\
&\quad + \text{Secondary stalls per instruction} \\
&= 1 + 2\% \times 20 + 0.5\% \times 400 = 1 + 0.4 + 2.0 = 3.4
\end{aligned}
$$

Thus, the processor with the secondary cache is faster by

$$\frac{9.0}{3.4} = 2.6$$

Alternatively, we could have computed the stall cycles by summing the stall cycles of those references that hit in the secondary cache $((2\% - 0.5\%) \times 20 = 0.3)$. Those references that go to main memory, which must include the cost to access the secondary cache as well as the main memory access time, is $(0.5\% \times (20 + 400) = 2.1)$. The sum, $1.0 + 0.3 + 2.1$, is again 3.4.

The design considerations for a primary and secondary cache are significantly different, because the presence of the other cache changes the best choice versus a single-level cache. In particular, a two-level cache structure allows the primary cache to focus on minimizing hit time to yield a shorter clock cycle or fewer pipeline stages, while allowing the secondary cache to focus on miss rate to reduce the penalty of long memory access times.

The effect of these changes on the two caches can be seen by comparing each cache to the optimal design for a single level of cache. In comparison to a single-level cache, the primary cache of a **multilevel cache** is often smaller. Furthermore, the primary cache may use a smaller block size, to go with the smaller cache size and also to reduce the miss penalty. In comparison, the secondary cache will be much larger than in a single-level cache, since the access time of the secondary cache is less critical. With a larger total size, the secondary cache may use a larger block size than appropriate with a single-level cache. It often uses higher associativity than the primary cache given the focus of reducing miss rates.

multilevel cache A memory hierarchy with multiple levels of caches, rather than just a cache and main memory.

Understanding Program Performance

Sorting has been exhaustively analyzed to find better algorithms: Bubble Sort, Quicksort, Radix Sort, and so on. Figure 5.18(a) shows instructions executed by item searched for Radix Sort versus Quicksort. As expected, for large arrays, Radix Sort has an algorithmic advantage over Quicksort in terms of number of operations. Figure 5.18(b) shows time per key instead of instructions executed. We see that the lines start on the same trajectory as Figure 5.18(a), but then the Radix Sort line diverges as the data to sort increases. What is going on? Figure 5.18(c) answers by looking at the cache misses per item sorted: Quicksort consistently has many fewer misses per item to be sorted.

Alas, standard algorithmic analysis often ignores the impact of the memory hierarchy. As faster clock rates and Moore's law allow architects to squeeze all of the performance out of a stream of instructions, using the memory hierarchy well is critical to high performance. As we said in the introduction, understanding the behavior of the memory hierarchy is critical to understanding the performance of programs on today's computers.

Elaboration: Multilevel caches create several complications. First, there are now several different types of misses and corresponding miss rates. In the example on pages 487–488. we saw the primary cache miss rate and the **global miss rate**—the fraction of references that missed in all cache levels. There is also a miss rate for the secondary cache, which is the ratio of all misses in the secondary cache divided by the number of accesses to it. This miss rate is called the **local miss rate** of the secondary cache. Because the primary cache filters accesses, especially those with good spatial and temporal locality, the local miss rate of the secondary cache is much higher than the global miss rate. For the example on pages 487–488. we can compute the local miss rate of the secondary cache as 0.5%/2% = 25%! Luckily, the global miss rate dictates how often we must access the main memory.

global miss rate The fraction of references that miss in all levels of a multilevel cache.

local miss rate The fraction of references to one level of a cache that miss; used in multilevel hierarchies.

Elaboration: With out-of-order processors (see Chapter 4), performance is more complex, since they execute instructions during the miss penalty. Instead of instruction miss rates and data miss rates, we use misses per instruction, and this formula:

$$\frac{\text{Memory-stall cycles}}{\text{Instruction}} = \frac{\text{Misses}}{\text{Instruction}} \times (\text{Total miss latency} - \text{Overlapped miss latency})$$

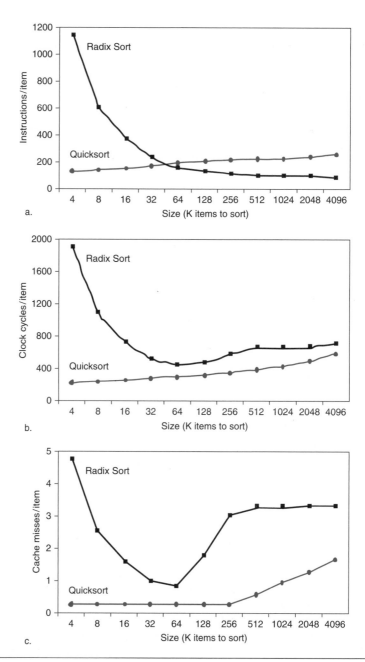

FIGURE 5.18   Comparing Quicksort and Radix Sort by (a) instructions executed per item sorted, (b) time per item sorted, and (c) cache misses per item sorted. This data is from a paper by LaMarca and Ladner [1996]. Although the numbers would change for newer computers, the idea still holds. Due to such results, new versions of Radix Sort have been invented that take memory hierarchy into account, to regain its algorithmic advantages (see Section 5.11). The basic idea of cache optimizations is to use all the data in a block repeatedly before it is replaced on a miss.

There is no general way to calculate overlapped miss latency, so evaluations of memory hierarchies for out-of-order processors inevitably require simulation of the processor and memory hierarchy. Only by seeing the execution of the processor during each miss can we see if the processor stalls waiting for data or simply finds other work to do. A guideline is that the processor often hides the miss penalty for an L1 cache miss that hits in the L2 cache, but it rarely hides a miss to the L2 cache.

Elaboration: The performance challenge for algorithms is that the memory hierarchy varies between different implementations of the same architecture in cache size, associativity, block size, and number of caches. To cope with such variability, some recent numerical libraries parameterize their algorithms and then search the parameter space at runtime to find the best combination for a particular computer. This approach is called *autotuning*.

Which of the following is generally true about a design with multiple levels of caches?

Check Yourself

1. First-level caches are more concerned about hit time, and second-level caches are more concerned about miss rate.

2. First-level caches are more concerned about miss rate, and second-level caches are more concerned about hit time.

Summary

In this section, we focused on three topics: cache performance, using associativity to reduce miss rates, and the use of multilevel cache hierarchies to reduce miss penalties.

The memory system has a significant effect on program execution time. The number of memory-stall cycles depends on both the miss rate and the miss penalty. The challenge, as we will see in Section 5.5, is to reduce one of these factors without significantly affecting other critical factors in the memory hierarchy.

To reduce the miss rate, we examined the use of associative placement schemes. Such schemes can reduce the miss rate of a cache by allowing more flexible placement of blocks within the cache. Fully associative schemes allow blocks to be placed anywhere, but also require that every block in the cache be searched to satisfy a request. The higher costs make large fully associative caches impractical. Set-associative caches are a practical alternative, since we need only search among the elements of a unique set that is chosen by indexing. Set-associative caches have higher miss rates but are faster to access. The amount of associativity that yields the best performance depends on both the technology and the details of the implementation.

Finally, we looked at multilevel caches as a technique to reduce the miss penalty by allowing a larger secondary cache to handle misses to the primary cache. Second-level caches have become commonplace as designers find that limited silicon and the goals of high clock rates prevent primary caches from becoming large. The secondary cache, which is often ten or more times larger than the primary cache, handles many accesses that miss in the primary cache. In such cases, the miss penalty is that of the access time to the secondary cache (typically < 10 processor cycles) versus the access time to memory (typically > 100 processor cycles). As with associativity, the design tradeoffs between the size of the secondary cache and its access time depend on a number of aspects of the implementation.

... a system has been devised to make the core drum combination appear to the programmer as a single level store, the requisite transfers taking place automatically.

Kilburn et al., *One-level storage system*, 1962

virtual memory
A technique that uses main memory as a "cache" for secondary storage.

 ## 5.4   Virtual Memory

In the previous section, we saw how caches provided fast access to recently used portions of a program's code and data. Similarly, the main memory can act as a "cache" for the secondary storage, usually implemented with magnetic disks. This technique is called **virtual memory**. Historically, there were two major motivations for virtual memory: to allow efficient and safe sharing of memory among multiple programs, and to remove the programming burdens of a small, limited amount of main memory. Four decades after its invention, it's the former reason that reigns today.

Consider a collection of programs running all at once on a computer. Of course, to allow multiple programs to share the same memory, we must be able to protect the programs from each other, ensuring that a program can only read and write the portions of main memory that have been assigned to it. Main memory need contain only the active portions of the many programs, just as a cache contains only the active portion of one program. Thus, the principle of locality enables virtual memory as well as caches, and virtual memory allows us to efficiently share the processor as well as the main memory.

physical address An address in main memory.

protection A set of mechanisms for ensuring that multiple processes sharing the processor, memory, or I/O devices cannot interfere, intentionally or unintentionally, with one another by reading or writing each other's data. These mechanisms also isolate the operating system from a user process.

We cannot know which programs will share the memory with other programs when we compile them. In fact, the programs sharing the memory change dynamically while the programs are running. Because of this dynamic interaction, we would like to compile each program into its own *address space*—a separate range of memory locations accessible only to this program. Virtual memory implements the translation of a program's address space to **physical addresses**. This translation process enforces **protection** of a program's address space from other programs.

The second motivation for virtual memory is to allow a single user program to exceed the size of primary memory. Formerly, if a program became too large for memory, it was up to the programmer to make it fit. Programmers divided programs into pieces and then identified the pieces that were mutually exclusive. These *overlays* were loaded or unloaded under user program control during execution, with the programmer ensuring that the program never tried to access an overlay that was not loaded and that the overlays loaded never exceeded the total size of the memory. Overlays were traditionally organized as modules, each containing both code and data. Calls between procedures in different modules would lead to overlaying of one module with another.

As you can well imagine, this responsibility was a substantial burden on programmers. Virtual memory, which was invented to relieve programmers of this difficulty, automatically manages the two levels of the memory hierarchy represented by main memory (sometimes called *physical memory* to distinguish it from virtual memory) and secondary storage.

Although the concepts at work in virtual memory and in caches are the same, their differing historical roots have led to the use of different terminology. A virtual memory block is called a *page*, and a virtual memory miss is called a **page fault**. With virtual memory, the processor produces a **virtual address**, which is translated by a combination of hardware and software to a *physical address*, which in turn can be used to access main memory. Figure 5.19 shows the virtually addressed memory with pages mapped to main memory. This process is called *address mapping* or **address translation**. Today, the two memory hierarchy levels controlled by virtual memory are usually DRAMs and magnetic disks (see Chapter 1, pages 22–23). If we return to our library analogy, we can think of a virtual address as the title of a book and a physical address as the location of that book in the library, such as might be given by the Library of Congress call number.

page fault An event that occurs when an accessed page is not present in main memory.

virtual address An address that corresponds to a location in virtual space and is translated by address mapping to a physical address when memory is accessed.

address translation Also called address mapping. The process by which a virtual address is mapped to an address used to access memory.

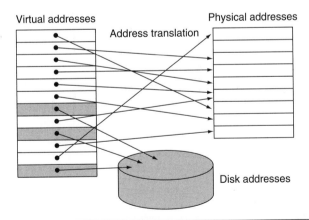

FIGURE 5.19 In virtual memory, blocks of memory (called *pages*) are mapped from one set of addresses (called *virtual addresses*) to another set (called *physical addresses*). The processor generates virtual addresses while the memory is accessed using physical addresses. Both the virtual memory and the physical memory are broken into pages, so that a virtual page is mapped to a physical page. Of course, it is also possible for a virtual page to be absent from main memory and not be mapped to a physical address; in that case, the page resides on disk. Physical pages can be shared by having two virtual addresses point to the same physical address. This capability is used to allow two different programs to share data or code.

Virtual memory also simplifies loading the program for execution by providing *relocation*. Relocation maps the virtual addresses used by a program to different physical addresses before the addresses are used to access memory. This relocation allows us to load the program anywhere in main memory. Furthermore, all virtual memory systems in use today relocate the program as a set of fixed-size blocks (pages), thereby eliminating the need to find a contiguous block of memory to allocate to a program; instead, the operating system need only find a sufficient number of pages in main memory.

In virtual memory, the address is broken into a *virtual page number* and a *page offset*. Figure 5.20 shows the translation of the virtual page number to a *physical page number*. The physical page number constitutes the upper portion of the physical address, while the page offset, which is not changed, constitutes the lower portion. The number of bits in the page offset field determines the page size. The number of pages addressable with the virtual address need not match the number of pages addressable with the physical address. Having a larger number of virtual pages than physical pages is the basis for the illusion of an essentially unbounded amount of virtual memory.

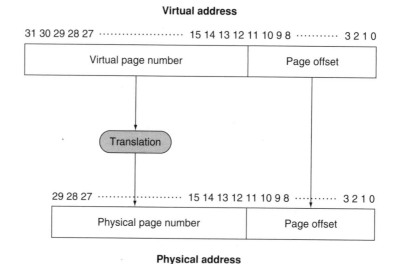

FIGURE 5.20 Mapping from a virtual to a physical address. The page size is $2^{12} = 4$ KB. The number of physical pages allowed in memory is 2^{18}, since the physical page number has 18 bits in it. Thus, main memory can have at most 1 GB, while the virtual address space is 4 GB.

Many design choices in virtual memory systems are motivated by the high cost of a miss, which in virtual memory is traditionally called a page fault. A page fault will take millions of clock cycles to process. (The table on page 453 shows that main memory latency is about 100,000 times quicker than disk.) This enormous miss penalty, dominated by the time to get the first word for typical page sizes, leads to several key decisions in designing virtual memory systems:

- Pages should be large enough to try to amortize the high access time. Sizes from 4 KB to 16 KB are typical today. New desktop and server systems are being developed to support 32 KB and 64 KB pages, but new embedded systems are going in the other direction, to 1 KB pages.

- Organizations that reduce the page fault rate are attractive. The primary technique used here is to allow fully associative placement of pages in memory.

- Page faults can be handled in software because the overhead will be small compared to the disk access time. In addition, software can afford to use clever algorithms for choosing how to place pages because even small reductions in the miss rate will pay for the cost of such algorithms.

- Write-through will not work for virtual memory, since writes take too long. Instead, virtual memory systems use write-back.

The next few subsections address these factors in virtual memory design.

Elaboration: Although we normally think of virtual addresses as much larger than physical addresses, the opposite can occur when the processor address size is small relative to the state of the memory technology. No single program can benefit, but a collection of programs running at the same time can benefit from not having to be swapped to memory or by running on parallel processors. For servers and desktop computers, 32-bit address processors are problematic.

Elaboration: The discussion of virtual memory in this book focuses on paging, which uses fixed-size blocks. There is also a variable-size block scheme called **segmentation**. In segmentation, an address consists of two parts: a segment number and a segment offset. The segment register is mapped to a physical address, and the offset is *added* to find the actual physical address. Because the segment can vary in size, a bounds check is also needed to make sure that the offset is within the segment. The major use of segmentation is to support more powerful methods of protection and sharing in an address space. Most operating system textbooks contain extensive discussions of segmentation compared to paging and of the use of segmentation to logically share the address space. The major disadvantage of segmentation is that it splits the address space into logically separate pieces that must be manipulated as a two-part address: the segment number and the offset. Paging, in contrast, makes the boundary between page number and offset invisible to programmers and compilers.

segmentation
A variable-size address mapping scheme in which an address consists of two parts: a segment number, which is mapped to a physical address, and a segment offset.

Segments have also been used as a method to extend the address space without changing the word size of the computer. Such attempts have been unsuccessful because of the awkwardness and performance penalties inherent in a two-part address, of which programmers and compilers must be aware.

Many architectures divide the address space into large fixed-size blocks that simplify protection between the operating system and user programs and increase the efficiency of implementing paging. Although these divisions are often called "segments," this mechanism is much simpler than variable block size segmentation and is not visible to user programs; we discuss it in more detail shortly.

Placing a Page and Finding It Again

Because of the incredibly high penalty for a page fault, designers reduce page fault frequency by optimizing page placement. If we allow a virtual page to be mapped to any physical page, the operating system can then choose to replace any page it wants when a page fault occurs. For example, the operating system can use a sophisticated algorithm and complex data structures that track page usage to try to choose a page that will not be needed for a long time. The ability to use a clever and flexible replacement scheme reduces the page fault rate and simplifies the use of fully associative placement of pages.

As mentioned in Section 5.3, the difficulty in using fully associative placement is in locating an entry, since it can be anywhere in the upper level of the hierarchy. A full search is impractical. In virtual memory systems, we locate pages by using a table that indexes the memory; this structure is called a **page table**, and it resides in memory. A page table is indexed with the page number from the virtual address to discover the corresponding physical page number. Each program has its own page table, which maps the virtual address space of that program to main memory. In our library analogy, the page table corresponds to a mapping between book titles and library locations. Just as the card catalog may contain entries for books in another library on campus rather than the local branch library, we will see that the page table may contain entries for pages not present in memory. To indicate the location of the page table in memory, the hardware includes a register that points to the start of the page table; we call this the *page table register*. Assume for now that the page table is in a fixed and contiguous area of memory.

page table The table containing the virtual to physical address translations in a virtual memory system. The table, which is stored in memory, is typically indexed by the virtual page number; each entry in the table contains the physical page number for that virtual page if the page is currently in memory.

Hardware/ Software Interface

The page table, together with the program counter and the registers, specifies the *state* of a program. If we want to allow another program to use the processor, we must save this state. Later, after restoring this state, the program can continue execution. We often refer to this state as a *process*. The process is considered *active* when it is in possession of the processor; otherwise, it is considered *inactive*. The operating system can make a process active by loading the process's state, including the program counter, which will initiate execution at the value of the saved program counter.

The process's address space, and hence all the data it can access in memory, is defined by its page table, which resides in memory. Rather than save the entire page table, the operating system simply loads the page table register to point to the page table of the process it wants to make active. Each process has its own page table, since different processes use the same virtual addresses. The operating system is responsible for allocating the physical memory and updating the page tables, so that the virtual address spaces of different processes do not collide. As we will see shortly, the use of separate page tables also provides protection of one process from another.

Figure 5.21 uses the page table register, the virtual address, and the indicated page table to show how the hardware can form a physical address. A valid bit is used in each page table entry, just as we did in a cache. If the bit is off, the page is not present in main memory and a page fault occurs. If the bit is on, the page is in memory and the entry contains the physical page number.

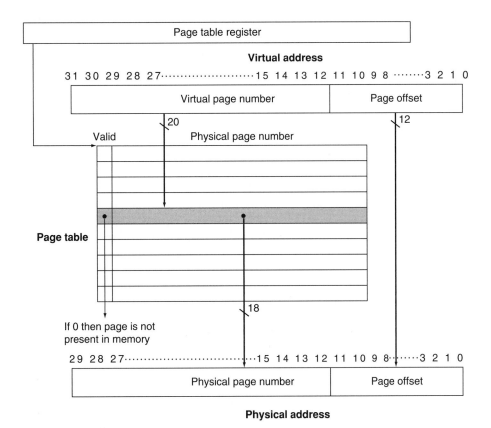

FIGURE 5.21 The page table is indexed with the virtual page number to obtain the corresponding portion of the physical address. We assume a 32-bit address. The starting address of the page table is given by the page table pointer. In this figure, the page size is 2^{12} bytes, or 4 KB. The virtual address space is 2^{32} bytes, or 4 GB, and the physical address space is 2^{30} bytes, which allows main memory of up to 1 GB. The number of entries in the page table is 2^{20}, or 1 million entries. The valid bit for each entry indicates whether the mapping is legal. If it is off, then the page is not present in memory. Although the page table entry shown here need only be 19 bits wide, it would typically be rounded up to 32 bits for ease of indexing. The extra bits would be used to store additional information that needs to be kept on a per-page basis, such as protection.

Because the page table contains a mapping for every possible virtual page, no tags are required. In cache terminology, the index that is used to access the page table consists of the full block address, which is the virtual page number.

Page Faults

If the valid bit for a virtual page is off, a page fault occurs. The operating system must be given control. This transfer is done with the exception mechanism, which we discuss later in this section. Once the operating system gets control, it must find the page in the next level of the hierarchy (usually magnetic disk) and decide where to place the requested page in main memory.

The virtual address alone does not immediately tell us where the page is on disk. Returning to our library analogy, we cannot find the location of a library book on the shelves just by knowing its title. Instead, we go to the catalog and look up the book, obtaining an address for the location on the shelves, such as the Library of Congress call number. Likewise, in a virtual memory system, we must keep track of the location on disk of each page in virtual address space.

swap space The space on the disk reserved for the full virtual memory space of a process.

Because we do not know ahead of time when a page in memory will be replaced, the operating system usually creates the space on disk for all the pages of a process when it creates the process. This disk space is called the **swap space**. At that time, it also creates a data structure to record where each virtual page is stored on disk. This data structure may be part of the page table or may be an auxiliary data structure indexed in the same way as the page table. Figure 5.22 shows the organization when a single table holds either the physical page number or the disk address.

The operating system also creates a data structure that tracks which processes and which virtual addresses use each physical page. When a page fault occurs, if all the pages in main memory are in use, the operating system must choose a page to replace. Because we want to minimize the number of page faults, most operating systems try to choose a page that they hypothesize will not be needed in the near future. Using the past to predict the future, operating systems follow the least recently used (LRU) replacement scheme, which we mentioned in Section 5.3. The operating system searches for the least recently used page, assuming that a page that has not been used in a long time is less likely to be needed than a more recently accessed page. The replaced pages are written to swap space on the disk. In case you are wondering, the operating system is just another process, and these tables controlling memory are in memory; the details of this seeming contradiction will be explained shortly.

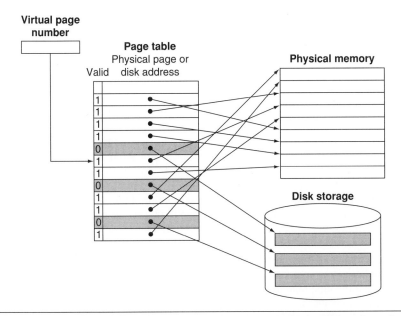

FIGURE 5.22 The page table maps each page in virtual memory to either a page in main memory or a page stored on disk, which is the next level in the hierarchy. The virtual page number is used to index the page table. If the valid bit is on, the page table supplies the physical page number (i.e., the starting address of the page in memory) corresponding to the virtual page. If the valid bit is off, the page currently resides only on disk, at a specified disk address. In many systems, the table of physical page addresses and disk page addresses, while logically one table, is stored in two separate data structures. Dual tables are justified in part because we must keep the disk addresses of all the pages, even if they are currently in main memory. Remember that the pages in main memory and the pages on disk are the same size.

Implementing a completely accurate LRU scheme is too expensive, since it requires updating a data structure on *every* memory reference. Instead, most operating systems approximate LRU by keeping track of which pages have and which pages have not been recently used. To help the operating system estimate the LRU pages, some computers provide a **reference bit** or **use bit**, which is set whenever a page is accessed. The operating system periodically clears the reference bits and later records them so it can determine which pages were touched during a particular time period. With this usage information, the operating system can select a page that is among the least recently referenced (detected by having its reference bit off). If this bit is not provided by the hardware, the operating system must find another way to estimate which pages have been accessed.

Hardware/ Software Interface

reference bit Also called **use bit**. A field that is set whenever a page is accessed and that is used to implement LRU or other replacement schemes.

Elaboration: With a 32-bit virtual address, 4 KB pages, and 4 bytes per page table entry, we can compute the total page table size:

$$\text{Number of page table entries} = \frac{2^{32}}{2^{12}} = 2^{20}$$

$$\text{Size of page table} = 2^{20} \text{ page table entries} \times 2^2 \frac{\text{bytes}}{\text{page table entry}} = 4 \text{ MB}$$

That is, we would need to use 4 MB of memory for each program in execution at any time. This amount is not so bad for a single program. What if there are hundreds of programs running, each with their own page table? And how should we handle 64-bit addresses, which by this calculation would need 2^{52} words?

A range of techniques is used to reduce the amount of storage required for the page table. The five techniques below aim at reducing the total maximum storage required as well as minimizing the main memory dedicated to page tables:

1. The simplest technique is to keep a limit register that restricts the size of the page table for a given process. If the virtual page number becomes larger than the contents of the limit register, entries must be added to the page table. This technique allows the page table to grow as a process consumes more space. Thus, the page table will only be large if the process is using many pages of virtual address space. This technique requires that the address space expand in only one direction.

2. Allowing growth in only one direction is not sufficient, since most languages require two areas whose size is expandable: one area holds the stack and the other area holds the heap. Because of this duality, it is convenient to divide the page table and let it grow from the highest address down, as well as from the lowest address up. This means that there will be two separate page tables and two separate limits. The use of two page tables breaks the address space into two segments. The high-order bit of an address usually determines which segment and thus which page table to use for that address. Since the segment is specified by the high-order address bit, each segment can be as large as one-half of the address space. A limit register for each segment specifies the current size of the segment, which grows in units of pages. This type of segmentation is used by many architectures, including MIPS. Unlike the type of segmentation discussed in the second elaboration on page 495, this form of segmentation is invisible to the application program, although not to the operating system. The major disadvantage of this scheme is that it does not work well when the address space is used in a sparse fashion rather than as a contiguous set of virtual addresses.

3. Another approach to reducing the page table size is to apply a hashing function to the virtual address so that the page table need be only the size of the number of *physical* pages in main memory. Such a structure is called an *inverted page table*. Of course, the lookup process is slightly more complex with an inverted page table, because we can no longer just index the page table.

4. Multiple levels of page tables can also be used to reduce the total amount of page table storage. The first level maps large fixed-size blocks of virtual address space, perhaps 64 to 256 pages in total. These large blocks are sometimes called segments, and this first-level mapping table is sometimes called a segment table, though the

segments are again invisible to the user. Each entry in the segment table indicates whether any pages in that segment are allocated and, if so, points to a page table for that segment. Address translation happens by first looking in the segment table, using the highest-order bits of the address. If the segment address is valid, the next set of high-order bits is used to index the page table indicated by the segment table entry. This scheme allows the address space to be used in a sparse fashion (multiple noncontiguous segments can be active) without having to allocate the entire page table. Such schemes are particularly useful with very large address spaces and in software systems that require noncontiguous allocation. The primary disadvantage of this two-level mapping is the more complex process for address translation.

5. To reduce the actual main memory tied up in page tables, most modern systems also allow the page tables to be paged. Although this sounds tricky, it works by using the same basic ideas of virtual memory and simply allowing the page tables to reside in the virtual address space. In addition, there are some small but critical problems, such as a never-ending series of page faults, which must be avoided. How these problems are overcome is both very detailed and typically highly processor specific. In brief, these problems are avoided by placing all the page tables in the address space of the operating system and placing at least some of the page tables for the operating system in a portion of main memory that is physically addressed and is always present and thus never on disk.

What about Writes?

The difference between the access time to the cache and main memory is tens to hundreds of cycles, and write-through schemes can be used, although we need a write buffer to hide the latency of the write from the processor. In a virtual memory system, writes to the next level of the hierarchy (disk) take millions of processor clock cycles; therefore, building a write buffer to allow the system to write-through to disk would be completely impractical. Instead, virtual memory systems must use write-back, performing the individual writes into the page in memory, and copying the page back to disk when it is replaced in the memory.

Hardware/ Software Interface

A write-back scheme has another major advantage in a virtual memory system. Because the disk transfer time is small compared with its access time, copying back an entire page is much more efficient than writing individual words back to the disk. A write-back operation, although more efficient than transferring individual words, is still costly. Thus, we would like to know whether a page *needs* to be copied back when we choose to replace it. To track whether a page has been written since it was read into the memory, a *dirty bit* is added to the page table. The dirty bit is set when any word in a page is written. If the operating system chooses to replace the page, the dirty bit indicates whether the page needs to be written out before its location in memory can be given to another page. Hence, a modified page is often called a **dirty** page.

Making Address Translation Fast: the TLB

Since the page tables are stored in main memory, every memory access by a program can take at least twice as long: one memory access to obtain the physical address and a second access to get the data. The key to improving access performance is to rely on locality of reference to the page table. When a translation for a virtual page number is used, it will probably be needed again in the near future, because the references to the words on that page have both temporal and spatial locality.

Accordingly, modern processors include a special cache that keeps track of recently used translations. This special address translation cache is traditionally referred to as a **translation-lookaside buffer** (TLB), although it would be more accurate to call it a translation cache. The TLB corresponds to that little piece of paper we typically use to record the location of a set of books we look up in the card catalog; rather than continually searching the entire catalog, we record the location of several books and use the scrap of paper as a cache of Library of Congress call numbers.

Figure 5.23 shows that each tag entry in the TLB holds a portion of the virtual page number, and each data entry of the TLB holds a physical page number. Because

translation-lookaside buffer (TLB) A cache that keeps track of recently used address mappings to try to avoid an access to the page table.

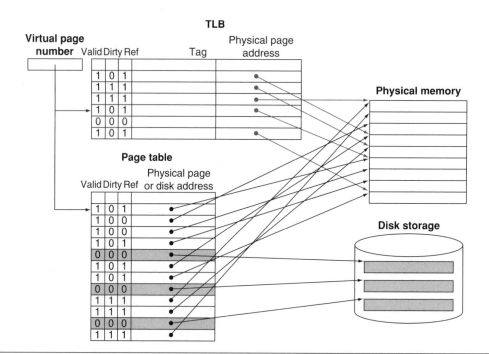

FIGURE 5.23   The TLB acts as a cache of the page table for the entries that map to physical pages only. The TLB contains a subset of the virtual-to-physical page mappings that are in the page table. The TLB mappings are shown in color. Because the TLB is a cache, it must have a tag field. If there is no matching entry in the TLB for a page, the page table must be examined. The page table either supplies a physical page number for the page (which can then be used to build a TLB entry) or indicates that the page resides on disk, in which case a page fault occurs. Since the page table has an entry for every virtual page, no tag field is needed; in other words, unlike a TLB, a page table is *not* a cache.

we access the TLB instead of the page table on every reference, the TLB will need to include other status bits, such as the dirty and the reference bits.

On every reference, we look up the virtual page number in the TLB. If we get a hit, the physical page number is used to form the address, and the corresponding reference bit is turned on. If the processor is performing a write, the dirty bit is also turned on. If a miss in the TLB occurs, we must determine whether it is a page fault or merely a TLB miss. If the page exists in memory, then the TLB miss indicates only that the translation is missing. In such cases, the processor can handle the TLB miss by loading the translation from the page table into the TLB and then trying the reference again. If the page is not present in memory, then the TLB miss indicates a true page fault. In this case, the processor invokes the operating system using an exception. Because the TLB has many fewer entries than the number of pages in main memory, TLB misses will be much more frequent than true page faults.

TLB misses can be handled either in hardware or in software. In practice, with care there can be little performance difference between the two approaches, because the basic operations are the same in either case.

After a TLB miss occurs and the missing translation has been retrieved from the page table, we will need to select a TLB entry to replace. Because the reference and dirty bits are contained in the TLB entry, we need to copy these bits back to the page table entry when we replace an entry. These bits are the only portion of the TLB entry that can be changed. Using write-back—that is, copying these entries back at miss time rather than when they are written—is very efficient, since we expect the TLB miss rate to be small. Some systems use other techniques to approximate the reference and dirty bits, eliminating the need to write into the TLB except to load a new table entry on a miss.

Some typical values for a TLB might be

- TLB size: 16–512 entries

- Block size: 1–2 page table entries (typically 4–8 bytes each)

- Hit time: 0.5–1 clock cycle

- Miss penalty: 10–100 clock cycles

- Miss rate: 0.01%–1%

Designers have used a wide variety of associativities in TLBs. Some systems use small, fully associative TLBs because a fully associative mapping has a lower miss rate; furthermore, since the TLB is small, the cost of a fully associative mapping is not too high. Other systems use large TLBs, often with small associativity. With a fully associative mapping, choosing the entry to replace becomes tricky since implementing a hardware LRU scheme is too expensive. Furthermore, since TLB misses are much more frequent than page faults and thus must be handled more cheaply, we cannot afford an expensive software algorithm, as we can for page faults. As a result, many systems provide some support for randomly choosing an entry to replace. We'll examine replacement schemes in a little more detail in Section 5.5.

The Intrinsity FastMATH TLB

To see these ideas in a real processor, let's take a closer look at the TLB of the Intrinsity FastMATH. The memory system uses 4 KB pages and a 32-bit address space; thus, the virtual page number is 20 bits long, as in the top of Figure 5.24. The physical address is the same size as the virtual address. The TLB contains 16 entries, it is fully associative, and it is shared between the instruction and data references. Each entry is 64 bits wide and contains a 20-bit tag (which is the virtual page number for that TLB entry), the corresponding physical page number (also 20 bits), a valid bit, a dirty bit, and other bookkeeping bits.

Figure 5.24 shows the TLB and one of the caches, while Figure 5.25 shows the steps in processing a read or write request. When a TLB miss occurs, the MIPS hardware saves the page number of the reference in a special register and generates an exception. The exception invokes the operating system, which handles the miss in software. To find the physical address for the missing page, the TLB miss routine indexes the page table using the page number of the virtual address and the page table register, which indicates the starting address of the active process page table. Using a special set of system instructions that can update the TLB, the operating system places the physical address from the page table into the TLB. A TLB miss takes about 13 clock cycles, assuming the code and the page table entry are in the instruction cache and data cache, respectively. (We will see the MIPS TLB code on page 513.) A true page fault occurs if the page table entry does not have a valid physical address. The hardware maintains an index that indicates the recommended entry to replace; the recommended entry is chosen randomly.

There is an extra complication for write requests: namely, the write access bit in the TLB must be checked. This bit prevents the program from writing into pages for which it has only read access. If the program attempts a write and the write access bit is off, an exception is generated. The write access bit forms part of the protection mechanism, which we will discuss shortly.

Integrating Virtual Memory, TLBs, and Caches

Our virtual memory and cache systems work together as a hierarchy, so that data cannot be in the cache unless it is present in main memory. The operating system helps maintain this hierarchy by flushing the contents of any page from the cache when it decides to migrate that page to disk. At the same time, the OS modifies the page tables and TLB, so that an attempt to access any data on the migrated page will generate a page fault.

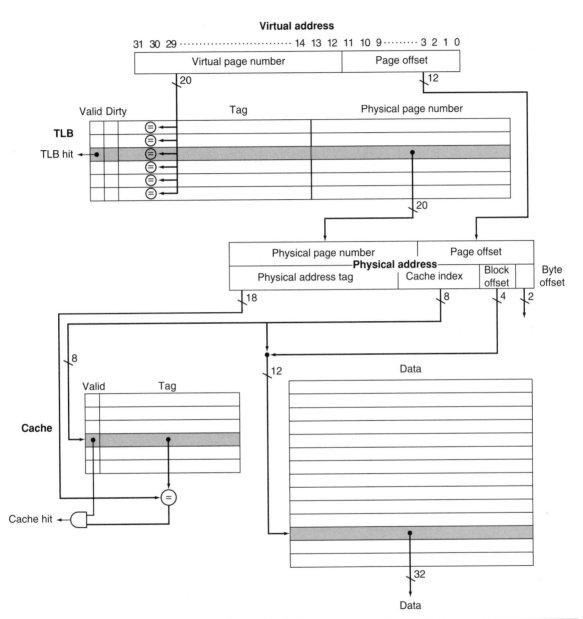

FIGURE 5.24 The TLB and cache implement the process of going from a virtual address to a data item in the Intrinsity FastMATH. This figure shows the organization of the TLB and the data cache, assuming a 4 KB page size. This diagram focuses on a read; Figure 5.25 describes how to handle writes. Note that unlike Figure 5.9, the tag and data RAMs are split. By addressing the long but narrow data RAM with the cache index concatenated with the block offset, we select the desired word in the block without a 16:1 multiplexor. While the cache is direct mapped, the TLB is fully associative. Implementing a fully associative TLB requires that every TLB tag be compared against the virtual page number, since the entry of interest can be anywhere in the TLB. (See content addressable memories in the *Elaboration* on page 485.) If the valid bit of the matching entry is on, the access is a TLB hit, and bits from the physical page number together with bits from the page offset form the index that is used to access the cache.

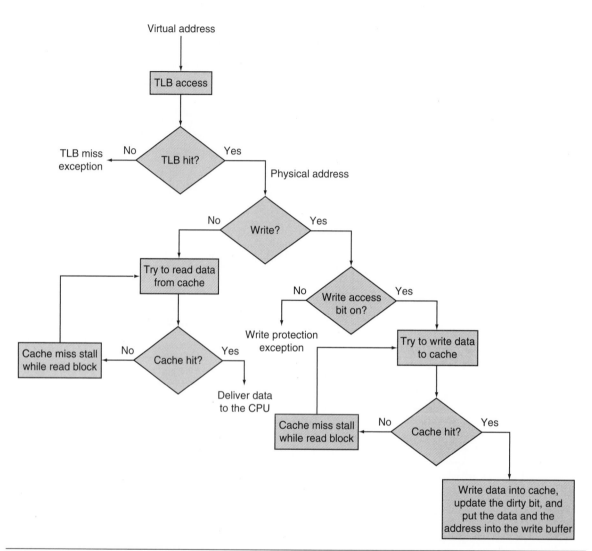

FIGURE 5.25   Processing a read or a write-through in the Intrinsity FastMATH TLB and cache. If the TLB generates a hit, the cache can be accessed with the resulting physical address. For a read, the cache generates a hit or miss and supplies the data or causes a stall while the data is brought from memory. If the operation is a write, a portion of the cache entry is overwritten for a hit and the data is sent to the write buffer if we assume write-through. A write miss is just like a read miss except that the block is modified after it is read from memory. Write-back requires writes to set a dirty bit for the cache block, and a write buffer is loaded with the whole block only on a read miss or write miss if the block to be replaced is dirty. Notice that a TLB hit and a cache hit are independent events, but a cache hit can only occur after a TLB hit occurs, which means that the data must be present in memory. The relationship between TLB misses and cache misses is examined further in the following example and the exercises at the end of this chapter.

Under the best of circumstances, a virtual address is translated by the TLB and sent to the cache where the appropriate data is found, retrieved, and sent back to the processor. In the worst case, a reference can miss in all three components of the memory hierarchy: the TLB, the page table, and the cache. The following example illustrates these interactions in more detail.

Overall Operation of a Memory Hierarchy

In a memory hierarchy like that of Figure 5.24, which includes a TLB and a cache organized as shown, a memory reference can encounter three different types of misses: a TLB miss, a page fault, and a cache miss. Consider all the combinations of these three events with one or more occurring (seven possibilities). For each possibility, state whether this event can actually occur and under what circumstances.

EXAMPLE

Figure 5.26 shows all combinations and whether each is possible in practice.

ANSWER

TLB	Page table	Cache	Possible? If so, under what circumstance?
Hit	Hit	Miss	Possible, although the page table is never really checked if TLB hits.
Miss	Hit	Hit	TLB misses, but entry found in page table; after retry, data is found in cache.
Miss	Hit	Miss	TLB misses, but entry found in page table; after retry, data misses in cache.
Miss	Miss	Miss	TLB misses and is followed by a page fault; after retry, data must miss in cache.
Hit	Miss	Miss	Impossible: cannot have a translation in TLB if page is not present in memory.
Hit	Miss	Hit	Impossible: cannot have a translation in TLB if page is not present in memory.
Miss	Miss	Hit	Impossible: data cannot be allowed in cache if the page is not in memory.

FIGURE 5.26 The possible combinations of events in the TLB, virtual memory system, and cache. Three of these combinations are impossible, and one is possible (TLB hit, virtual memory hit, cache miss) but never detected.

Elaboration: Figure 5.26 assumes that all memory addresses are translated to physical addresses before the cache is accessed. In this organization, the cache is *physically indexed* and *physically tagged* (both the cache index and tag are physical, rather than virtual, addresses). In such a system, the amount of time to access memory,

virtually addressed cache A cache that is accessed with a virtual address rather than a physical address.

assuming a cache hit, must accommodate both a TLB access and a cache access; of course, these accesses can be pipelined.

Alternatively, the processor can index the cache with an address that is completely or partially virtual. This is called a **virtually addressed cache**, and it uses tags that are virtual addresses; hence, such a cache is *virtually indexed* and *virtually tagged*. In such caches, the address translation hardware (TLB) is unused during the normal cache access, since the cache is accessed with a virtual address that has not been translated to a physical address. This takes the TLB out of the critical path, reducing cache latency. When a cache miss occurs, however, the processor needs to translate the address to a physical address so that it can fetch the cache block from main memory.

aliasing A situation in which the same object is accessed by two addresses; can occur in virtual memory when there are two virtual addresses for the same physical page.

When the cache is accessed with a virtual address and pages are shared between programs (which may access them with different virtual addresses), there is the possibility of **aliasing**. Aliasing occurs when the same object has two names—in this case, two virtual addresses for the same page. This ambiguity creates a problem, because a word on such a page may be cached in two different locations, each corresponding to different virtual addresses. This ambiguity would allow one program to write the data without the other program being aware that the data had changed. Completely virtually addressed caches either introduce design limitations on the cache and TLB to reduce aliases or require the operating system, and possibly the user, to take steps to ensure that aliases do not occur.

physically addressed cache A cache that is addressed by a physical address.

A common compromise between these two design points is caches that are virtually indexed—sometimes using just the page offset portion of the address, which is really a physical address since it is not translated—but use physical tags. These designs, which are *virtually indexed but physically tagged*, attempt to achieve the performance advantages of virtually indexed caches with the architecturally simpler advantages of a **physically addressed cache**. For example, there is no alias problem in this case. Figure 5.24 assumed a 4 KB page size, but it's really 16 KB, so the Intrinsity FastMATH can use this trick. To pull it off, there must be careful coordination between the minimum page size, the cache size, and associativity.

Implementing Protection with Virtual Memory

Perhaps the most important function of virtual memory is to allow sharing of a single main memory by multiple processes, while providing memory protection among these processes and the operating system. The protection mechanism must ensure that although multiple processes are sharing the same main memory, one renegade process cannot write into the address space of another user process or into the operating system either intentionally or unintentionally. The write access bit in the TLB can protect a page from being written. Without this level of protection, computer viruses would be even more widespread.

To enable the operating system to implement protection in the virtual memory system, the hardware must provide at least the three basic capabilities summarized below.

Hardware/
Software
Interface

1. Support at least two modes that indicate whether the running process is a user process or an operating system process, variously called a **supervisor** process, a **kernel** process, or an *executive* process.

2. Provide a portion of the processor state that a user process can read but not write. This includes the user/supervisor mode bit, which dictates whether the processor is in user or supervisor mode, the page table pointer, and the TLB. To write these elements, the operating system uses special instructions that are only available in supervisor mode.

3. Provide mechanisms whereby the processor can go from user mode to supervisor mode and vice versa. The first direction is typically accomplished by a **system call** exception, implemented as a special instruction (*syscall* in the MIPS instruction set) that transfers control to a dedicated location in supervisor code space. As with any other exception, the program counter from the point of the system call is saved in the exception PC (EPC), and the processor is placed in supervisor mode. To return to user mode from the exception, use the *return from exception* (ERET) instruction, which resets to user mode and jumps to the address in EPC.

supervisor mode Also called kernel mode. A mode indicating that a running process is an operating system process.

system call A special instruction that transfers control from user mode to a dedicated location in supervisor code space, invoking the exception mechanism in the process.

By using these mechanisms and storing the page tables in the operating system's address space, the operating system can change the page tables while preventing a user process from changing them, ensuring that a user process can access only the storage provided to it by the operating system.

We also want to prevent a process from reading the data of another process. For example, we wouldn't want a student program to read the grades while they were in the processor's memory. Once we begin sharing main memory, we must provide the ability for a process to protect its data from both reading and writing by another process; otherwise, sharing the main memory will be a mixed blessing!

Remember that each process has its own virtual address space. Thus, if the operating system keeps the page tables organized so that the independent virtual pages map to disjoint physical pages, one process will not be able to access another's data. Of course, this also requires that a user process be unable to change the page table mapping. The operating system can assure safety if it prevents the user process from modifying its own page tables. However, the operating system must be able to modify the page tables. Placing the page tables in the protected address space of the operating system satisfies both requirements.

When processes want to share information in a limited way, the operating system must assist them, since accessing the information of another process requires changing the page table of the accessing process. The write access bit can be used to restrict the sharing to just read sharing, and, like the rest of the page table, this bit can be changed only by the operating system. To allow another process, say, P1, to read a page owned by process P2, P2 would ask the operating system to create a page table entry for a virtual page in P1's address space that points to the same physical page that P2 wants to share. The operating system could use the write protection bit to prevent P1 from writing the data, if that was P2's wish. Any bits that determine the access rights for a page must be included in both the page table and the TLB, because the page table is accessed only on a TLB *miss*.

context switch A changing of the internal state of the processor to allow a different process to use the processor that includes saving the state needed to return to the currently executing process.

Elaboration: When the operating system decides to change from running process P1 to running process P2 (called a **context switch** or *process switch*), it must ensure that P2 cannot get access to the page tables of P1 because that would compromise protection. If there is no TLB, it suffices to change the page table register to point to P2's page table (rather than to P1's); with a TLB, we must clear the TLB entries that belong to P1—both to protect the data of P1 and to force the TLB to load the entries for P2. If the process switch rate were high, this could be quite inefficient. For example, P2 might load only a few TLB entries before the operating system switched back to P1. Unfortunately, P1 would then find that all its TLB entries were gone and would have to pay TLB misses to reload them. This problem arises because the virtual addresses used by P1 and P2 are the same, and we must clear out the TLB to avoid confusing these addresses.

A common alternative is to extend the virtual address space by adding a *process identifier* or *task identifier*. The Intrinsity FastMATH has an 8-bit address space ID (ASID) field for this purpose. This small field identifies the currently running process; it is kept in a register loaded by the operating system when it switches processes. The process identifier is concatenated to the tag portion of the TLB, so that a TLB hit occurs only if both the page number *and* the process identifier match. This combination eliminates the need to clear the TLB, except on rare occasions.

Similar problems can occur for a cache, since on a process switch the cache will contain data from the running process. These problems arise in different ways for physically addressed and virtually addressed caches, and a variety of different solutions, such as process identifiers, are used to ensure that a process gets its own data.

Handling TLB Misses and Page Faults

Although the translation of virtual to physical addresses with a TLB is straightforward when we get a TLB hit, handling TLB misses and page faults is more complex. A TLB miss occurs when no entry in the TLB matches a virtual address. A TLB miss can indicate one of two possibilities:

1. The page is present in memory, and we need only create the missing TLB entry.

2. The page is not present in memory, and we need to transfer control to the operating system to deal with a page fault.

How do we know which of these two circumstances has occurred? When we process the TLB miss, we will look for a page table entry to bring into the TLB. If the matching page table entry has a valid bit that is turned off, then the corresponding page is not in memory and we have a page fault, rather than just a TLB miss. If the valid bit is on, we can simply retrieve the desired entry.

A TLB miss can be handled in software or hardware because it will require only a short sequence of operations to copy a valid page table entry from memory into the TLB. MIPS traditionally handles a TLB miss in software. It brings in the page table entry from memory and then re-executes the instruction that caused the TLB miss. Upon re-executing, it will get a TLB hit. If the page table entry indicates the page is not in memory, this time it will get a page fault exception.

Handling a TLB miss or a page fault requires using the exception mechanism to interrupt the active process, transferring control to the operating system, and later resuming execution of the interrupted process. A page fault will be recognized sometime during the clock cycle used to access memory. To restart the instruction after the page fault is handled, the program counter of the instruction that caused the page fault must be saved. Just as in Chapter 4, the exception program counter (EPC) is used to hold this value.

In addition, a TLB miss or page fault exception must be asserted by the end of the same clock cycle that the memory access occurs, so that the next clock cycle will begin exception processing rather than continue normal instruction execution. If the page fault was not recognized in this clock cycle, a load instruction could overwrite a register, and this could be disastrous when we try to restart the instruction. For example, consider the instruction `lw $1,0($1)`: the computer must be able to prevent the write pipeline stage from occurring; otherwise, it could not properly restart the instruction, since the contents of $1 would have been destroyed. A similar complication arises on stores. We must prevent the write into memory from actually completing when there is a page fault; this is usually done by deasserting the write control line to the memory.

Register	CP0 register number	Description
EPC	14	Where to restart after exception
Cause	13	Cause of exception
BadVAddr	8	Address that caused exception
Index	0	Location in TLB to be read or written
Random	1	Pseudorandom location in TLB
EntryLo	2	Physical page address and flags
EntryHi	10	Virtual page address
Context	4	Page table address and page number

FIGURE 5.27 MIPS control registers. These are considered to be in coprocessor 0, and hence are read using `mfc0` and written using `mtc0`.

**Hardware/
Software
Interface**

exception enable Also
called interrupt enable.
A signal or action that
controls whether the
process responds to
an exception or not;
necessary for preventing
the occurrence of
exceptions during
intervals before the
processor has safely saved
the state needed to restart.

Between the time we begin executing the exception handler in the operating system and the time that the operating system has saved all the state of the process, the operating system is particularly vulnerable. For example, if another exception occurred when we were processing the first exception in the operating system, the control unit would overwrite the exception program counter, making it impossible to return to the instruction that caused the page fault! We can avoid this disaster by providing the ability to disable and **enable exceptions**. When an exception first occurs, the processor sets a bit that disables all other exceptions; this could happen at the same time the processor sets the supervisor mode bit. The operating system will then save just enough state to allow it to recover if another exception occurs—namely, the exception program counter (EPC) and Cause registers. EPC and Cause are two of the special control registers that help with exceptions, TLB misses, and page faults; Figure 5.27 shows the rest. The operating system can then re-enable exceptions. These steps make sure that exceptions will not cause the processor to lose any state and thereby be unable to restart execution of the interrupting instruction.

Once the operating system knows the virtual address that caused the page fault, it must complete three steps:

1. Look up the page table entry using the virtual address and find the location of the referenced page on disk.

2. Choose a physical page to replace; if the chosen page is dirty, it must be written out to disk before we can bring a new virtual page into this physical page.

3. Start a read to bring the referenced page from disk into the chosen physical page.

Of course, this last step will take millions of processor clock cycles (so will the second if the replaced page is dirty); accordingly, the operating system will usually select another process to execute in the processor until the disk access completes. Because the operating system has saved the state of the process, it can freely give control of the processor to another process.

When the read of the page from disk is complete, the operating system can restore the state of the process that originally caused the page fault and execute the instruction that returns from the exception. This instruction will reset the processor from kernel to user mode, as well as restore the program counter. The user process then re-executes the instruction that faulted, accesses the requested page successfully, and continues execution.

Page fault exceptions for data accesses are difficult to implement properly in a processor because of a combination of three characteristics:

1. They occur in the middle of instructions, unlike instruction page faults.

2. The instruction cannot be completed before handling the exception.

3. After handling the exception, the instruction must be restarted as if nothing had occurred.

Making instructions **restartable**, so that the exception can be handled and the instruction later continued, is relatively easy in an architecture like the MIPS. Because each instruction writes only one data item and this write occurs at the end of the instruction cycle, we can simply prevent the instruction from completing (by not writing) and restart the instruction at the beginning.

restartable instruction An instruction that can resume execution after an exception is resolved without the exception's affecting the result of the instruction.

Let's look in more detail at MIPS. When a TLB miss occurs, the MIPS hardware saves the page number of the reference in a special register called BadVAddr and generates an exception.

The exception invokes the operating system, which handles the miss in software. Control is transferred to address 8000 0000$_{hex}$, the location of the TLB miss **handler**. To find the physical address for the missing page, the TLB miss routine indexes the page table using the page number of the virtual address and the page table register, which indicates the starting address of the active process page table. To make this indexing fast, MIPS hardware places everything you need in the special Context register: the upper 12 bits have the address of the base of the page table, and the next 18 bits have the virtual address of the missing page. Each page table entry is one word, so the last 2 bits are 0. Thus, the first two instructions copy the Context register into the kernel temporary register $k1 and then load the page table entry from that address into $k1. Recall that $k0 and $k1 are reserved for the operating system to use without saving; a major reason for this convention is to make the TLB miss handler fast. Below is the MIPS code for a typical TLB miss handler:

handler Name of a software routine invoked to "handle" an exception or interrupt.

```
TLBmiss:
  mfc0  $k1,Context    # copy address of PTE into temp $k1
  lw    $k1, 0($k1)    # put PTE into temp $k1
  mtc0  $k1,EntryLo    # put PTE into special register EntryLo
  tlbwr                # put EntryLo into TLB entry at Random
  eret                 # return from TLB miss exception
```

As shown above, MIPS has a special set of system instructions to update the TLB. The instruction tlbwr copies from control register EntryLo into the TLB entry selected by the control register Random. Random implements random replacement, so it is basically a free-running counter. A TLB miss takes about a dozen clock cycles.

Note that the TLB miss handler does not check to see if the page table entry is valid. Because the exception for TLB entry missing is much more frequent than a page fault, the operating system loads the TLB from the page table without examining the entry and restarts the instruction. If the entry is invalid, another and different exception occurs, and the operating system recognizes the page fault. This method makes the frequent case of a TLB miss fast, at a slight performance penalty for the infrequent case of a page fault.

Once the process that generated the page fault has been interrupted, it transfers control to $8000\ 0180_{hex}$, a different address than the TLB miss handler. This is the general address for exception; TLB miss has a special entry point to lower the penalty for a TLB miss. The operating system uses the exception Cause register to diagnose the cause of the exception. Because the exception is a page fault, the operating system knows that extensive processing will be required. Thus, unlike a TLB miss, it saves the entire state of the active process. This state includes all the general-purpose and floating-point registers, the page table address register, the EPC, and the exception Cause register. Since exception handlers do not usually use the floating-point registers, the general entry point does not save them, leaving that to the few handlers that need them.

Figure 5.28 sketches the MIPS code of an exception handler. Note that we save and restore the state in MIPS code, taking care when we enable and disable exceptions, but we invoke C code to handle the particular exception.

The virtual address that caused the fault depends on whether the fault was an instruction or data fault. The address of the instruction that generated the fault is in the EPC. If it was an instruction page fault, the EPC contains the virtual address of the faulting page; otherwise, the faulting virtual address can be computed by examining the instruction (whose address is in the EPC) to find the base register and offset field.

unmapped A portion of the address space that cannot have page faults.

Elaboration: This simplified version assumes that the stack pointer (sp) is valid. To avoid the problem of a page fault during this low-level exception code, MIPS sets aside a portion of its address space that cannot have page faults, called **unmapped**. The operating system places the exception entry point code and the exception stack in unmapped memory. MIPS hardware translates virtual addresses $8000\ 0000_{hex}$ to $BFFF\ FFFF_{hex}$ to physical addresses simply by ignoring the upper bits of the virtual address, thereby placing these addresses in the low part of physical memory. Thus, the operating system places exception entry points and exception stacks in unmapped memory.

Elaboration: The code in Figure 5.28 shows the MIPS-32 exception return sequence. The older MIPS-I architecture uses `rfe` and `jr` instead of `eret`.

Save state				
Save GPR	addi	$k1,$sp, -XCPSIZE	# save space on stack for state	
	sw	$sp, XCT_SP($k1)	# save $sp on stack	
	sw	$v0, XCT_V0($k1)	# save $v0 on stack	
	...		# save $v1, $ai, $si, $ti,... on stack	
	sw	$ra, XCT_RA($k1)	# save $ra on stack	
Save hi, lo	mfhi	$v0	# copy Hi	
	mflo	$v1	# copy Lo	
	sw	$v0, XCT_HI($k1)	# save Hi value on stack	
	sw	$v1, XCT_LO($k1)	# save Lo value on stack	
Save exception registers	mfc0	$a0, $cr	# copy cause register	
	sw	$a0, XCT_CR($k1)	# save $cr value on stack	
	...		# save $v1,....	
	mfc0	$a3, $sr	# copy status register	
	sw	$a3, XCT_SR($k1)	# save $sr on stack	
Set sp	move	$sp, $k1	# sp = sp - XCPSIZE	
Enable nested exceptions				
	andi	$v0, $a3, MASK1	# $v0 = $sr & MASK1, enable exceptions	
	mtc0	$v0, $sr	# $sr = value that enables exceptions	
Call C exception handler				
Set $gp	move	$gp, GPINIT	# set $gp to point to heap area	
Call C code	move	$a0, $sp	# arg1 = pointer to exception stack	
	jal	xcpt_deliver	# call C code to handle exception	
Restoring state				
Restore most GPR, hi, lo	move	$at, $sp	# temporary value of $sp	
	lw	$ra, XCT_RA($at)	# restore $ra from stack	
	...		# restore $t0,....., $a1	
	lw	$a0, XCT_A0($k1)	# restore $a0 from stack	
Restore status register	lw	$v0, XCT_SR($at)	# load old $sr from stack	
	li	$v1, MASK2	# mask to disable exceptions	
	and	$v0, $v0, $v1	# $v0 = $sr & MASK2, disable exceptions	
	mtc0	$v0, $sr	# set status register	
Exception return				
Restore $sp and rest of GPR used as temporary registers	lw	$sp, XCT_SP($at)	# restore $sp from stack	
	lw	$v0, XCT_V0($at)	# restore $v0 from stack	
	lw	$v1, XCT_V1($at)	# restore $v1 from stack	
	lw	$k1, XCT_EPC($at)	# copy old $epc from stack	
	lw	$at, XCT_AT($at)	# restore $at from stack	
Restore ERC and return	mtc0	$k1, $epc	# restore $epc	
	eret	$ra	# return to interrupted instruction	

FIGURE 5.28 MIPS code to save and restore state on an exception.

Elaboration: For processors with more complex instructions that can touch many memory locations and write many data items, making instructions restartable is much harder. Processing one instruction may generate a number of page faults in the middle of the instruction. For example, x86 processors have block move instructions that touch thousands of data words. In such processors, instructions often cannot be restarted from the beginning, as we do for MIPS instructions. Instead, the instruction must be interrupted and later continued midstream in its execution. Resuming an instruction in the middle of its execution usually requires saving some special state, processing the exception, and restoring that special state. Making this work properly requires careful and detailed coordination between the exception-handling code in the operating system and the hardware.

Summary

Virtual memory is the name for the level of memory hierarchy that manages caching between the main memory and disk. Virtual memory allows a single program to expand its address space beyond the limits of main memory. More importantly, virtual memory supports sharing of the main memory among multiple, simultaneously active processes, in a protected manner.

Managing the memory hierarchy between main memory and disk is challenging because of the high cost of page faults. Several techniques are used to reduce the miss rate:

1. Pages are made large to take advantage of spatial locality and to reduce the miss rate.

2. The mapping between virtual addresses and physical addresses, which is implemented with a page table, is made fully associative so that a virtual page can be placed anywhere in main memory.

3. The operating system uses techniques, such as LRU and a reference bit, to choose which pages to replace.

Writes to disk are expensive, so virtual memory uses a write-back scheme and also tracks whether a page is unchanged (using a dirty bit) to avoid writing unchanged pages back to disk.

The virtual memory mechanism provides address translation from a virtual address used by the program to the physical address space used for accessing memory. This address translation allows protected sharing of the main memory and provides several additional benefits, such as simplifying memory allocation. Ensuring that processes are protected from each other requires that only the operating system can change the address translations, which is implemented by preventing user programs from changing the page tables. Controlled sharing of pages among processes can be implemented with the help of the operating system and access bits in the page table that indicate whether the user program has read or write access to a page.

If a processor had to access a page table resident in memory to translate every access, virtual memory would be too expensive, as caches would be pointless! Instead, a TLB acts as a cache for translations from the page table. Addresses are then translated from virtual to physical using the translations in the TLB.

Caches, virtual memory, and TLBs all rely on a common set of principles and policies. The next section discusses this common framework.

Although virtual memory was invented to enable a small memory to act as a large one, the performance difference between disk and memory means that if a program routinely accesses more virtual memory than it has physical memory, it will run very slowly. Such a program would be continuously swapping pages between memory and disk, called *thrashing*. Thrashing is a disaster if it occurs, but it is rare. If your program thrashes, the easiest solution is to run it on a computer with more memory or buy more memory for your computer. A more complex choice is to re-examine your algorithm and data structures to see if you can change the locality and thereby reduce the number of pages that your program uses simultaneously. This set of popular pages is informally called the *working set*.

A more common performance problem is TLB misses. Since a TLB might handle only 32–64 page entries at a time, a program could easily see a high TLB miss rate, as the processor may access less than a quarter megabyte directly: $64 \times 4\,\text{KB} = 0.25\,\text{MB}$. For example, TLB misses are often a challenge for Radix Sort. To try to alleviate this problem, most computer architectures now support variable page sizes. For example, in addition to the standard 4 KB page, MIPS hardware supports 16 KB, 64 KB, 256 KB, 1 MB, 4 MB, 16 MB, 64 MB, and 256 MB pages. Hence, if a program uses large page sizes, it can access more memory directly without TLB misses.

The practical challenge is getting the operating system to allow programs to select these larger page sizes. Once again, the more complex solution to reducing TLB misses is to re-examine the algorithm and data structures to reduce the working set of pages; given the importance of memory accesses to performance and the frequency of TLB misses, some programs with large working sets have been redesigned with that goal.

Understanding Program Performance

Match the memory hierarchy element on the left with the closest phrase on the right:

Check Yourself

1. L1 cache	a. A cache for a cache
2. L2 cache	b. A cache for disks
3. Main memory	c. A cache for a main memory
4. TLB	d. A cache for page table entries

<table>
<tr><td></td></tr>
</table>

5.5	A Common Framework for Memory Hierarchies

By now, you've recognized that the different types of memory hierarchies share a great deal in common. Although many of the aspects of memory hierarchies differ quantitatively, many of the policies and features that determine how a hierarchy functions are similar qualitatively. Figure 5.29 shows how some of the quantitative characteristics of memory hierarchies can differ. In the rest of this section, we will discuss the common operational alternatives for memory hierarchies, and how these determine their behavior. We will examine these policies as a series of four questions that apply between any two levels of a memory hierarchy, although for simplicity we will primarily use terminology for caches.

Feature	Typical values for L1 caches	Typical values for L2 caches	Typical values for paged memory	Typical values for a TLB
Total size in blocks	250–2000	15,000–50,000	16,000–250,000	40–1024
Total size in kilobytes	16–64	500–4000	1,000,000–1,000,000,000	0.25–16
Block size in bytes	16–64	64–128	4000–64,000	4–32
Miss penalty in clocks	10–25	100–1000	10,000,000–100,000,000	10–1000
Miss rates (global for L2)	2%–5%	0.1%–2%	0.00001%–0.0001%	0.01%–2%

FIGURE 5.29   The key quantitative design parameters that characterize the major elements of memory hierarchy in a computer. These are typical values for these levels as of 2008. Although the range of values is wide, this is partially because many of the values that have shifted over time are related; for example, as caches become larger to overcome larger miss penalties, block sizes also grow.

Question 1: Where Can a Block Be Placed?

We have seen that block placement in the upper level of the hierarchy can use a range of schemes, from direct mapped to set associative to fully associative. As mentioned above, this entire range of schemes can be thought of as variations on a set-associative scheme where the number of sets and the number of blocks per set varies:

Scheme name	Number of sets	Blocks per set
Direct mapped	Number of blocks in cache	1
Set associative	Number of blocks in the cache / Associativity	Associativity (typically 2–16)
Fully associative	1	Number of blocks in the cache

The advantage of increasing the degree of associativity is that it usually decreases the miss rate. The improvement in miss rate comes from reducing misses that compete for the same location. We will examine these in more detail shortly. First, let's look at how much improvement is gained. Figure 5.30 shows the miss rates for several cache sizes as associativity varies from direct mapped to eight-way set associative. The largest gains are obtained in going from direct mapped to two-way set associative, which yields between a 20% and 30% reduction in the miss rate. As cache sizes grow, the relative improvement from associativity increases only slightly; since the overall miss rate of a larger cache is lower, the opportunity for improving the miss rate decreases and the absolute improvement in the miss rate from associativity shrinks significantly. The potential disadvantages of associativity, as we mentioned earlier, are increased cost and slower access time.

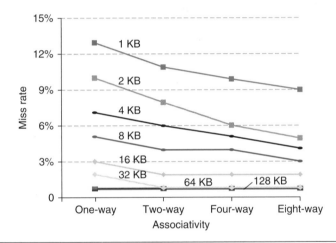

FIGURE 5.30 The data cache miss rates for each of eight cache sizes improve as the associativity increases. While the benefit of going from one-way (direct mapped) to two-way set associative is significant, the benefits of further associativity are smaller (e.g., 1%–10% improvement going from two-way to four-way versus 20%–30% improvement going from one-way to two-way). There is even less improvement in going from four-way to eight-way set associative, which, in turn, comes very close to the miss rates of a fully associative cache. Smaller caches obtain a significantly larger absolute benefit from associativity because the base miss rate of a small cache is larger. Figure 5.15 explains how this data was collected.

Question 2: How Is a Block Found?

The choice of how we locate a block depends on the block placement scheme, since that dictates the number of possible locations. We can summarize the schemes as follows:

Associativity	Location method	Comparisons required
Direct mapped	Index	1
Set associative	Index the set, search among elements	Degree of associativity
Full	Search all cache entries	Size of the cache
	Separate lookup table	0

The choice among direct-mapped, set-associative, or fully associative mapping in any memory hierarchy will depend on the cost of a miss versus the cost of implementing associativity, both in time and in extra hardware. Including the L2 cache on the chip enables much higher associativity, because the hit times are not as critical and the designer does not have to rely on standard SRAM chips as the building blocks. Fully associative caches are prohibitive except for small sizes, where the cost of the comparators is not overwhelming and where the absolute miss rate improvements are greatest.

In virtual memory systems, a separate mapping table—the page table—is kept to index the memory. In addition to the storage required for the table, using an index table requires an extra memory access. The choice of full associativity for page placement and the extra table is motivated by these facts:

1. Full associativity is beneficial, since misses are very expensive.

2. Full associativity allows software to use sophisticated replacement schemes that are designed to reduce the miss rate.

3. The full map can be easily indexed with no extra hardware and no searching required.

Therefore, virtual memory systems almost always use fully associative placement.

Set-associative placement is often used for caches and TLBs, where the access combines indexing and the search of a small set. A few systems have used direct-mapped caches because of their advantage in access time and simplicity. The advantage in access time occurs because finding the requested block does not depend on a comparison. Such design choices depend on many details of the implementation, such as whether the cache is on-chip, the technology used for implementing the cache, and the critical role of cache access time in determining the processor cycle time.

Question 3: Which Block Should Be Replaced on a Cache Miss?

When a miss occurs in an associative cache, we must decide which block to replace. In a fully associative cache, all blocks are candidates for replacement. If the cache is set associative, we must choose among the blocks in the set. Of course, replacement is easy in a direct-mapped cache because there is only one candidate.

There are the two primary strategies for replacement in set-associative or fully associative caches:

- *Random:* Candidate blocks are randomly selected, possibly using some hardware assistance. For example, MIPS supports random replacement for TLB misses.

- *Least recently used* (LRU): The block replaced is the one that has been unused for the longest time.

In practice, LRU is too costly to implement for hierarchies with more than a small degree of associativity (two to four, typically), since tracking the usage information is costly. Even for four-way set associativity, LRU is often approximated—for example, by keeping track of which pair of blocks is LRU (which requires 1 bit), and then tracking which block in each pair is LRU (which requires 1 bit per pair).

For larger associativity, either LRU is approximated or random replacement is used. In caches, the replacement algorithm is in hardware, which means that the scheme should be easy to implement. Random replacement is simple to build in hardware, and for a two-way set-associative cache, random replacement has a miss rate about 1.1 times higher than LRU replacement. As the caches become larger, the miss rate for both replacement strategies falls, and the absolute difference becomes small. In fact, random replacement can sometimes be better than the simple LRU approximations that are easily implemented in hardware.

In virtual memory, some form of LRU is always approximated, since even a tiny reduction in the miss rate can be important when the cost of a miss is enormous. Reference bits or equivalent functionality are often provided to make it easier for the operating system to track a set of less recently used pages. Because misses are so expensive and relatively infrequent, approximating this information primarily in software is acceptable.

Question 4: What Happens on a Write?

A key characteristic of any memory hierarchy is how it deals with writes. We have already seen the two basic options:

- *Write-through:* The information is written to both the block in the cache and the block in the lower level of the memory hierarchy (main memory for a cache). The caches in Section 5.2 used this scheme.

- *Write-back:* The information is written only to the block in the cache. The modified block is written to the lower level of the hierarchy only when it is replaced. Virtual memory systems always use write-back, for the reasons discussed in Section 5.4.

Both write-back and write-through have their advantages. The key advantages of write-back are the following:

- Individual words can be written by the processor at the rate that the cache, rather than the memory, can accept them.

- Multiple writes within a block require only one write to the lower level in the hierarchy.

- When blocks are written back, the system can make effective use of a high-bandwidth transfer, since the entire block is written.

Write-through has these advantages:

- Misses are simpler and cheaper because they never require a block to be written back to the lower level.

- Write-through is easier to implement than write-back, although to be practical, a write-through cache will still need to use a write buffer.

In virtual memory systems, only a write-back policy is practical because of the long latency of a write to the lower level of the hierarchy (disk). The rate at which writes are generated by a processor generally exceed the rate at which the memory system can process them, even allowing for physically and logically wider memories and burst modes for DRAM. Consequently, today lowest-level caches typically use write-back.

The **BIG** Picture

Caches, TLBs, and virtual memory may initially look very different, but they rely on the same two principles of locality, and they can be understood by their answers to four questions:

Question 1: Where can a block be placed?
Answer: One place (direct mapped), a few places (set associative), or any place (fully associative).

Question 2: How is a block found?
Answer: There are four methods: indexing (as in a direct-mapped cache), limited search (as in a set-associative cache), full search (as in a fully associative cache), and a separate lookup table (as in a page table).

Question 3: What block is replaced on a miss?
Answer: Typically, either the least recently used or a random block.

Question 4: How are writes handled?
Answer: Each level in the hierarchy can use either write-through or write-back.

The Three Cs: An Intuitive Model for Understanding the Behavior of Memory Hierarchies

In this section, we look at a model that provides insight into the sources of misses in a memory hierarchy and how the misses will be affected by changes in the hierarchy. We will explain the ideas in terms of caches, although the ideas carry over directly to any other level in the hierarchy. In this model, all misses are classified into one of three categories (the **three Cs**):

- **Compulsory misses**: These are cache misses caused by the first access to a block that has never been in the cache. These are also called **cold-start misses**.

- **Capacity misses**: These are cache misses caused when the cache cannot contain all the blocks needed during execution of a program. Capacity misses occur when blocks are replaced and then later retrieved.

- **Conflict misses**: These are cache misses that occur in set-associative or direct-mapped caches when multiple blocks compete for the same set. Conflict misses are those misses in a direct-mapped or set-associative cache that are eliminated in a fully associative cache of the same size. These cache misses are also called **collision misses**.

Figure 5.31 shows how the miss rate divides into the three sources. These sources of misses can be directly attacked by changing some aspect of the cache design. Since conflict misses arise directly from contention for the same cache block, increasing associativity reduces conflict misses. Associativity, however, may slow access time, leading to lower overall performance.

Capacity misses can easily be reduced by enlarging the cache; indeed, second-level caches have been growing steadily larger for many years. Of course, when we make the cache larger, we must also be careful about increasing the access time, which could lead to lower overall performance. Thus, first-level caches have been growing slowly, if at all.

Because compulsory misses are generated by the first reference to a block, the primary way for the cache system to reduce the number of compulsory misses is to increase the block size. This will reduce the number of references required to touch each block of the program once, because the program will consist of fewer cache blocks. As mentioned above, increasing the block size too much can have a negative effect on performance because of the increase in the miss penalty.

The decomposition of misses into the three Cs is a useful qualitative model. In real cache designs, many of the design choices interact, and changing one cache characteristic will often affect several components of the miss rate. Despite such shortcomings, this model is a useful way to gain insight into the performance of cache designs.

three Cs model A cache model in which all cache misses are classified into one of three categories: compulsory misses, capacity misses, and conflict misses.

compulsory miss Also called cold-start miss. A cache miss caused by the first access to a block that has never been in the cache.

capacity miss A cache miss that occurs because the cache, even with full associativity, cannot contain all the blocks needed to satisfy the request.

conflict miss Also called collision miss. A cache miss that occurs in a set-associative or direct-mapped cache when multiple blocks compete for the same set and that are eliminated in a fully associative cache of the same size.

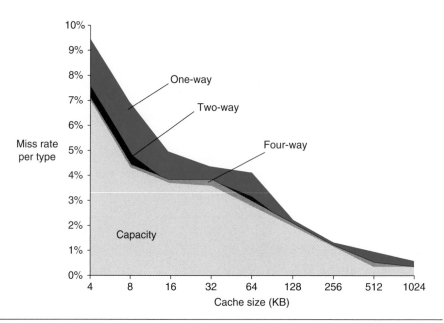

FIGURE 5.31 The miss rate can be broken into three sources of misses. This graph shows the total miss rate and its components for a range of cache sizes. This data is for the SPEC CPU2000 integer and floating-point benchmarks and is from the same source as the data in Figure 5.30. The compulsory miss component is 0.006% and cannot be seen in this graph. The next component is the capacity miss rate, which depends on cache size. The conflict portion, which depends both on associativity and on cache size, is shown for a range of associativities from one-way to eight-way. In each case, the labeled section corresponds to the increase in the miss rate that occurs when the associativity is changed from the next higher degree to the labeled degree of associativity. For example, the section labeled *two-way* indicates the additional misses arising when the cache has associativity of two rather than four. Thus, the difference in the miss rate incurred by a direct-mapped cache versus a fully associative cache of the same size is given by the sum of the sections marked *eight-way, four-way, two-way,* and *one-way.* The difference between eight-way and four-way is so small that it is difficult to see on this graph.

The **BIG** Picture

The challenge in designing memory hierarchies is that every change that potentially improves the miss rate can also negatively affect overall performance, as Figure 5.32 summarizes. This combination of positive and negative effects is what makes the design of a memory hierarchy interesting.

Design change	Effect on miss rate	Possible negative performance effect
Increase cache size	Decreases capacity misses	May increase access time
Increase associativity	Decreases miss rate due to conflict misses	May increase access time
Increase block size	Decreases miss rate for a wide range of block sizes due to spatial locality	Increases miss penalty. Very large block could increase miss rate

FIGURE 5.32 Memory hierarchy design challenges.

Which of the following statements (if any) are generally true?

Check Yourself

1. There is no way to reduce compulsory misses.

2. Fully associative caches have no conflict misses.

3. In reducing misses, associativity is more important than capacity.

5.6 Virtual Machines

An idea related to virtual memory that is almost as old is Virtual Machines (VM). They were first developed in the mid-1960s, and they have remained an important part of mainframe computing over the years. Although largely ignored in the domain of single-user computers in the 1980s and 1990s, they have recently gained popularity due to

- The increasing importance of isolation and security in modern systems

- The failures in security and reliability of standard operating systems

- The sharing of a single computer among many unrelated users

- The dramatic increases in raw speed of processors over the decades, which makes the overhead of VMs more acceptable

The broadest definition of VMs includes basically all emulation methods that provide a standard software interface, such as the Java VM. In this section, we are interested in VMs that provide a complete system-level environment at the binary instruction set architecture (ISA) level. Although some VMs run different ISAs in the VM from the native hardware, we assume they always match the hardware. Such VMs are called (Operating) *System Virtual Machines*. IBM VM/370, VMware ESX Server, and Xen are examples.

System virtual machines present the illusion that the users have an entire computer to themselves, including a copy of the operating system. A single computer runs multiple VMs and can support a number of different operating systems (OSes). On a conventional platform, a single OS "owns" all the hardware resources, but with a VM, multiple OSes all share the hardware resources.

The software that supports VMs is called a *virtual machine monitor* (VMM) or *hypervisor;* the VMM is the heart of virtual machine technology. The underlying hardware platform is called the *host*, and its resources are shared among the *guest* VMs. The VMM determines how to map virtual resources to physical resources: a physical resource may be time-shared, partitioned, or even emulated in software. The VMM is much smaller than a traditional OS; the isolation portion of a VMM is perhaps only 10,000 lines of code.

Although our interest here is in VMs for improving protection, VMs provide two other benefits that are commercially significant:

1. *Managing software.* VMs provide an abstraction that can run the complete software stack, even including old operating systems like DOS. A typical deployment might be some VMs running legacy OSes, many running the current stable OS release, and a few testing the next OS release.

2. *Managing hardware.* One reason for multiple servers is to have each application running with the compatible version of the operating system on separate computers, as this separation can improve dependability. VMs allow these separate software stacks to run independently yet share hardware, thereby consolidating the number of servers. Another example is that some VMMs support migration of a running VM to a different computer, either to balance load or to evacuate from failing hardware.

In general, the cost of processor virtualization depends on the workload. User-level processor-bound programs have zero virtualization overhead, because the OS is rarely invoked, so everything runs at native speeds. I/O-intensive workloads are generally also OS-intensive, executing many system calls and privileged instructions that can result in high virtualization overhead. On the other hand, if the I/O-intensive workload is also *I/O-bound*, the cost of processor virtualization can be completely hidden, since the processor is often idle waiting for I/O.

The overhead is determined by both the number of instructions that must be emulated by the VMM and by how much time each takes to emulate. Hence, when the guest VMs run the same ISA as the host, as we assume here, the goal of the architecture and the VMM is to run almost all instructions directly on the native hardware.

Requirements of a Virtual Machine Monitor

What must a VM monitor do? It presents a software interface to guest software, it must isolate the state of guests from each other, and it must protect itself from guest software (including guest OSes). The qualitative requirements are:

■ Guest software should behave on a VM exactly as if it were running on the native hardware, except for performance-related behavior or limitations of fixed resources shared by multiple VMs.

■ Guest software should not be able to change allocation of real system resources directly.

To "virtualize" the processor, the VMM must control just about everything—access to privileged state, address translation, I/O, exceptions, and interrupts—even though the guest VM and OS currently running are temporarily using them.

For example, in the case of a timer interrupt, the VMM would suspend the currently running guest VM, save its state, handle the interrupt, determine which guest VM to run next, and then load its state. Guest VMs that rely on a timer interrupt are provided with a virtual timer and an emulated timer interrupt by the VMM.

To be in charge, the VMM must be at a higher privilege level than the guest VM, which generally runs in user mode; this also ensures that the execution of any privileged instruction will be handled by the VMM. The basic requirements of system virtual machines are almost identical to those for paged virtual memory listed above:

■ At least two processor modes, system and user

■ A privileged subset of instructions that is available only in system mode, resulting in a trap if executed in user mode; all system resources must be controllable only via these instructions

(Lack of) Instruction Set Architecture Support for Virtual Machines

If VMs are planned for during the design of the ISA, it's relatively easy to reduce both the number of instructions that must be executed by a VMM and improve their emulation speed. An architecture that allows the VM to execute directly on the hardware earns the title *virtualizable*, and the IBM 370 architecture proudly bears that label.

Alas, since VMs have been considered for desktop and PC-based server applications only fairly recently, most instruction sets were created without virtualization in mind. These culprits include x86 and most RISC architectures, including ARM and MIPS.

Because the VMM must ensure that the guest system only interacts with virtual resources, a conventional guest OS runs as a user mode program on top of the VMM. Then, if a guest OS attempts to access or modify information related to hardware resources via a privileged instruction—for example, reading or writing the page table pointer—it will trap to the VMM. The VMM can then effect the appropriate changes to corresponding real resources.

Hence, if any instruction that tries to read or write such sensitive information traps when executed in user mode, the VMM can intercept it and support a virtual version of the sensitive information, as the guest OS expects.

In the absence of such support, other measures must be taken. A VMM must take special precautions to locate all problematic instructions and ensure that they behave correctly when executed by a guest OS, thereby increasing the complexity of the VMM and reducing the performance of running the VM.

Protection and Instruction Set Architecture

Protection is a joint effort of architecture and operating systems, but architects had to modify some awkward details of existing instruction set architectures when virtual memory became popular. For example, to support virtual memory in the IBM 370, architects had to change the successful IBM 360 instruction set architecture that had been announced just six years before. Similar adjustments are being made today to accommodate virtual machines.

For example, the x86 instruction POPF loads the flag registers from the top of the stack in memory. One of the flags is the Interrupt Enable (IE) flag. If you run the POPF instruction in user mode, rather than trap it, it simply changes all the flags except IE. In system mode, it does change the IE. Since a guest OS runs in user mode inside a VM, this is a problem, as it expects to see a changed IE.

Historically, IBM mainframe hardware and VMM took three steps to improve performance of virtual machines:

1. Reduce the cost of processor virtualization

2. Reduce interrupt overhead cost due to the virtualization

3. Reduce interrupt cost by steering interrupts to the proper VM without invoking VMM

In 2006, new proposals by AMD and Intel try to address the first point, reducing the cost of processor virtualization. It will be interesting to see how many generations of architecture and VMM modifications it will take to address all three points, and how long before virtual machines of the 21st century will be as efficient as the IBM mainframes and VMMs of the 1970s.

Elaboration: In addition to virtualizing the instruction set, another challenge is virtualization of virtual memory, as each guest OS in every VM manages its own set of page tables. To make this work, the VMM separates the notions of *real* and *physical memory* (which are often treated synonymously), and makes real memory a separate, intermediate level between virtual memory and physical memory. (Some use the terms *virtual memory, physical memory,* and *machine memory* to name the same three levels.) The guest OS maps virtual memory to real memory via its page tables, and the VMM page tables map the guest's real memory to physical memory. The virtual memory architecture is specified either via page tables, as in IBM VM/370 and the x86, or via the TLB structure, as in MIPS.

Rather than pay an extra level of indirection on every memory access, the VMM maintains a *shadow page table* that maps directly from the guest virtual address space to the physical address space of the hardware. By detecting all modifications to the guest's page table, the VMM can ensure the shadow page table entries being used by the hardware for translations correspond to those of the guest OS environment, with the exception of the correct physical pages substituted for the real pages in the guest tables. Hence, the VMM must trap any attempt by the guest OS to change its page table or to access the page table pointer. This is commonly done by write protecting the guest page tables and trapping any access to the page table pointer by a guest OS. As noted above, the latter happens naturally if accessing the page table pointer is a privileged operation.

The final portion of the architecture to virtualize is I/O. This is by far the most difficult part of system virtualization because of the increasing number of I/O devices attached to the computer *and* the increasing diversity of I/O device types. Another difficulty is the sharing of a real device among multiple VMs, and yet another comes from supporting the myriad of device drivers that are required, especially if different guest OSes are supported on the same VM system. The VM illusion can be maintained by giving each VM generic versions of each type of I/O device driver, and then leaving it to the VMM to handle real I/O.

5.7 Using a Finite-State Machine to Control a Simple Cache

We can now implement control for a cache, just as we implemented control for the single-cycle and pipelined datapaths in Chapter 4. This section starts with a definition of a simple cache and then a description of finite-state machines (FSM). It finishes with the FSM of a controller for this simple cache. Section 5.9 on the CD goes into more depth, showing the cache and controller in a new hardware description language.

A Simple Cache

We're going to design a controller for a simple cache. Here are the key charateristics of the cache:

- Direct-mapped cache

- Write-back using write allocate

- Block size is 4 words (16 bytes or 128 bits)

- Cache size is 16 KB, so it holds 1024 blocks

- 32-bit byte addresses

- The cache includes a valid bit and dirty bit per block

From Section 5.2, we can now calculate the fields of an address for the cache:

- Cache index is 10 bits

- Block offset is 4 bits

- Tag size is $32 - (10 + 4)$ or 18 bits

The signals between the processor to the cache are

- 1-bit Read or Write signal

- 1-bit Valid signal, saying whether there is a cache operation or not

- 32-bit address

- 32-bit data from processor to cache

- 32-bit data from cache to processor

- 1-bit Ready signal, saying the cache operation is complete

Note that this is a blocking cache, in that the processor must wait until the cache has finished the request.

The interface between the memory and the cache has the same fields as between the processor and the cache, except that the data fields are now 128 bits wide. The extra memory width in generally found microprocessors today, which deal with either 32-bit or 64-bit words in the processor while the DRAM controller is often 128 bits. Making the cache block match the width of the DRAM simplified the design. Here are the signals:

- 1-bit Read or Write signal

- 1-bit Valid signal, saying whether there is a memory operation or not

- 32-bit address

- 128-bit data from cache to memory

- 128-bit data from memory to cache

- 1-bit Ready signal, saying the memory operation is complete

Note that the interface to memory is not a fixed number of cycles. We assume a memory controller that will notify the cache via the Ready signal when the memory read or write is finished.

Before describing the cache controller, we need to review finite-state machines, which allow us to control an operation that can take multiple clock cycles.

Finite-State Machines

To design the control unit for the single-cycle datapath, we used a set of truth tables that specified the setting of the control signals based on the instruction class. For a cache, the control is more complex because the operation can be a series of steps. The control for a cache must specify both the signals to be set in any step and the next step in the sequence.

The most common multistep control method is based on **finite-state machines**, which are usually represented graphically. A finite-state machine consists of a set of states and directions on how to change states. The directions are defined by a **next-state function**, which maps the current state and the inputs to a new state. When we use a finite-state machine for control, each state also specifies a set of outputs that are asserted when the machine is in that state. The implementation of a finite-state machine usually assumes that all outputs that are not explicitly asserted are deasserted. Similarly, the correct operation of the datapath depends on the fact that a signal that is not explicitly asserted is deasserted, rather than acting as a don't care.

Multiplexor controls are slightly different, since they select one of the inputs whether they are 0 or 1. Thus, in the finite-state machine, we always specify the setting of all the multiplexor controls that we care about. When we implement the finite-state machine with logic, setting a control to 0 may be the default and thus may not require any gates. A simple example of a finite-state machine appears in ⊙ Appendix C, and if you are unfamiliar with the concept of a finite-state machine, you may want to examine ⊙ Appendix C before proceeding.

A finite-state machine can be implemented with a temporary register that holds the current state and a block of combinational logic that determines both the datapath signals to be asserted and the next state. Figure 5.33 shows how such an implementation might look. ⊙ Appendix D describes in detail how the finite-state machine is implemented using this structure. In ⊙ Section C.3, the combinational control logic for a finite-state machine is implemented both with a ROM (read-only memory) and a PLA (programmable logic array). (Also see ⊙ Appendix C for a description of these logic elements.)

finite-state machine A sequential logic function consisting of a set of inputs and outputs, a next-state function that maps the current state and the inputs to a new state, and an output function that maps the current state and possibly the inputs to a set of asserted outputs.

next-state function A combinational function that, given the inputs and the current state, determines the next state of a finite-state machine.

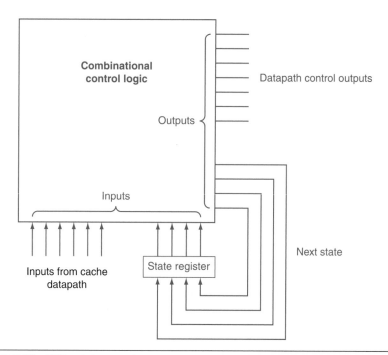

FIGURE 5.33   Finite-state machine controllers are typically implemented using a block of combinational logic and a register to hold the current state. The outputs of the combinational logic are the next-state number and the control signals to be asserted for the current state. The inputs to the combinational logic are the current state and any inputs used to determine the next state. In this case, the inputs are the instruction register opcode bits. Notice that in the finite-state machine used in this chapter, the outputs depend only on the current state, not on the inputs. The *Elaboration* explains this in more detail.

Elaboration: The style of finite-state machine in this book is called a Moore machines, after Edward Moore. Its identifying characteristic is that the output depends only on the current state. For a Moore machine, the box labeled combinational control logic can be split into two pieces. One piece has the control output and only the state input, while the other has only the next-state output.

An alternative style of machine is a Mealy machine, named after George Mealy. The Mealy machine allows both the input and the current state to be used to determine the output. Moore machines have potential implementation advantages in speed and size of the control unit. The speed advantages arise because the control outputs, which are needed early in the clock cycle, do not depend on the inputs, but only on the current state. In ⊙ **Appendix C**, when the implementation of this finite-state machine is taken down to logic gates, the size advantage can be clearly seen. The potential disadvantage of a Moore machine is that it may require additional states. For example, in situations where there is a one-state difference between two sequences of states, the Mealy machine may unify the states by making the outputs depend on the inputs.

FSM for a Simple Cache Controller

Figure 5.34 shows the four states of our simple cache controller:

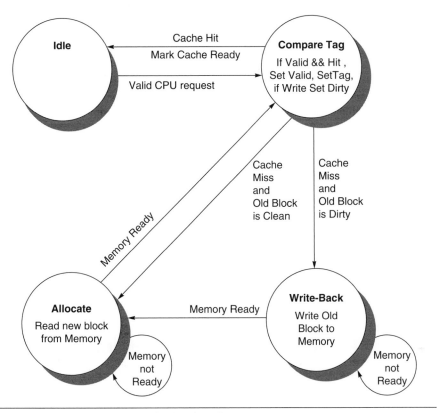

FIGURE 5.34   Four states of the simple controller.

- *Idle:* This state waits for a valid read or write request from the processor, which moves the FSM to the Compare Tag state.

- *Compare Tag:* As the name suggests, this state tests to see if the requested read or write is a hit or a miss. The index portion of the address selects the tag to be compared. If the data in the cache block referred to by the index portion of the address is valid and the tag portion of the address matches the tag, then the requested read or write is a hit. Either the data is read from the selected word or the written to the selected word, and then the Cache Ready signal is set. If it is a write, the dirty bit is set to 1. Note that a write hit also sets the valid bit and the tag field; while it seems unnecessary, it is included because the tag is a single memory, so to change the dirty bit we also need to change the valid and tag fields. If it is a hit and the block is valid, the FSM returns to the idle state. A miss first updates the cache tag and then goes either to the Write-Back state, if the block at this location has dirty bit value of 1, or to the Allocate state if it is 0.

- *Write-Back:* This state writes the 128-bit block to memory using the address composed from the tag and cache index. We remain in this state waiting for the Ready signal from memory. When the memory write is complete, the FSM goes to the Allocate state.

- *Allocate:* The new block is fetched from memory. We remain in this state waiting for the Ready signal from memory. When the memory read is complete, the FSM goes to the Compare Tag state. Although we could have gone to a new state to complete the operation instead of reusing the Compare Tag state, there is a good deal of overlap, including the update of the appropriate word in the block if the access was a write.

This simple model could easily be extended with more states to try to improve performance. For example, the Compare Tag state does both the compare and the read or write of the cache data in a single clock cycle. Often the compare and cache access are done in separate states to try to improve the clock cycle time. Another optimization would be to add a write buffer so that we could save the dirty block and then read the new block first so that the processor doesn't have to wait for two memory accesses on a dirty miss. The cache would then write the dirty block from the write buffer while the processor is operating on the requested data.

⊙ Section 5.9, on the CD, goes into more detail about the FSM, showing the full controller in a hardware description language and a block diagram of this simple cache.

5.8 Parallelism and Memory Hierarchies: Cache Coherence

Given that a multicore multiprocessor means multiple processors on a single chip, these processors very likely share a common physical address space. Caching shared data introduces a new problem, because the view of memory held by two different processors is through their individual caches, which, without any additional precautions, could end up seeing two different values. Figure 5.35 illustrates the problem and shows how two different processors can have two different values for the same location. This difficulty is generally referred to as the *cache coherence problem.*

Informally, we could say that a memory system is coherent if any read of a data item returns the most recently written value of that data item. This definition, although intuitively appealing, is vague and simplistic; the reality is much more complex. This simple definition contains two different aspects of memory system behavior, both of which are critical to writing correct shared memory programs. The first aspect, called *coherence,* defines *what values* can be returned by a read.

Time step	Event	Cache contents for CPU A	Cache contents for CPU B	Memory contents for location X
0				0
1	CPU A reads X	0		0
2	CPU B reads X	0	0	0
3	CPU A stores 1 into X	1	0	1

FIGURE 5.35 The cache coherence problem for a single memory location (X), read and written by two processors (A and B). We initially assume that neither cache contains the variable and that X has the value 0. We also assume a write-through cache; a write-back cache adds some additional but similar complications. After the value of X has been written by A, A's cache and the memory both contain the new value, but B's cache does not, and if B reads the value of X, it will receive 0!

The second aspect, called *consistency,* determines *when* a written value will be returned by a read.

Let's look at coherence first. A memory system is coherent if

1. A read by a processor P to a location X that follows a write by P to X, with no writes of X by another processor occurring between the write and the read by P, always returns the value written by P. Thus, in Figure 5.35 above, if CPU A were to read X after time step 3, it should see the value 1.

2. A read by a processor to location X that follows a write by another processor to X returns the written value if the read and write are sufficiently separated in time and no other writes to X occur between the two accesses. Thus, in Figure 5.35, we need a mechanism so that the value 0 in the cache of CPU B is replaced by the value 1 after CPU A stores 1 into memory at address X in time step 3.

3. Writes to the same location are *serialized*; that is, two writes to the same location by any two processors are seen in the same order by all processors. For example, if CPU B stores 2 into memory at address X after time step 3, processors can never read the value at location X as 2 and then later read it as 1.

The first property simply preserves program order—we certainly expect this property to be true in uniprocessors, for example. The second property defines the notion of what it means to have a coherent view of memory: if a processor could continuously read an old data value, we would clearly say that memory was incoherent.

The need for *write serialization* is more subtle, but equally important. Suppose we did not serialize writes, and processor P1 writes location X followed by P2 writing location X. Serializing the writes ensures that every processor will see the write done by P2 at some point. If we did not serialize the writes, it might be the case that some processor could see the write of P2 first and then see the write of P1, maintaining the value written by P1 indefinitely. The simplest way to avoid such difficulties is to ensure that all writes to the same location are seen in the same order; this property is called *write serialization*.

Basic Schemes for Enforcing Coherence

In a cache coherent multiprocessor, the caches provide both *migration* and *replication* of shared data items:

- *Migration:* A data item can be moved to a local cache and used there in a transparent fashion. Migration reduces both the latency to access a shared data item that is allocated remotely and the bandwidth demand on the shared memory.

- *Replication:* When shared data are being simultaneously read, the caches make a copy of the data item in the local cache. Replication reduces both latency of access and contention for a read shared data item.

Supporting this migration and replication is critical to performance in accessing shared data, so many multiprocessors introduce a hardware protocol to maintain coherent caches. The protocols to maintain coherence for multiple processors are called *cache coherence protocols*. Key to implementing a cache coherence protocol is tracking the state of any sharing of a data block.

The most popular cache coherence protocol is *snooping*. Every cache that has a copy of the data from a block of physical memory also has a copy of the sharing status of the block, but no centralized state is kept. The caches are all accessible via some broadcast medium (a bus or network), and all cache controllers monitor or *snoop* on the medium to determine whether or not they have a copy of a block that is requested on a bus or switch access.

In the following section we explain snooping-based cache coherence as implemented with a shared bus, but any communication medium that broadcasts cache misses to all processors can be used to implement a snooping-based coherence scheme. This broadcasting to all caches makes snooping protocols simple to implement but also limits their scalability.

Snooping Protocols

One method of enforcing coherence is to ensure that a processor has exclusive access to a data item before it writes that item. This style of protocol is called a *write invalidate protocol* because it invalidates copies in other caches on a write. Exclusive access ensures that no other readable or writable copies of an item exist when the write occurs: all other cached copies of the item are invalidated.

Figure 5.36 shows an example of an invalidation protocol for a snooping bus with write-back caches in action. To see how this protocol ensures coherence, consider a write followed by a read by another processor: since the write requires exclusive access, any copy held by the reading processor must be invalidated (hence the protocol name). Thus, when the read occurs, it misses in the cache, and the cache is forced to fetch a new copy of the data. For a write, we require that the writing processor have exclusive access, preventing any other processor from being able to write simultaneously. If two processors do attempt to write the same data simultaneously, one of them wins the race, causing the other processor's copy to be invalidated. For the other processor to complete its write, it must obtain a new copy of the data, which must now contain the updated value. Therefore, this protocol also enforces write serialization.

Processor activity	Bus activity	Contents of CPU A's cache	Contents of CPU B's cache	Contents of memory location X
				0
CPU A reads X	Cache miss for X	0		0
CPU B reads X	Cache miss for X	0	0	0
CPU A writes a 1 to X	Invalidation for X	1		0
CPU B reads X	Cache miss for X	1	1	1

FIGURE 5.36 An example of an invalidation protocol working on a snooping bus for a single cache block (X) with write-back caches. We assume that neither cache initially holds X and that the value of X in memory is 0. The CPU and memory contents show the value after the processor and bus activity have both completed. A blank indicates no activity or no copy cached. When the second miss by B occurs, CPU A responds with the value canceling the response from memory. In addition, both the contents of B's cache and the memory contents of X are updated. This update of memory, which occurs when a block becomes shared, simplifies the protocol, but it is possible to track the ownership and force the write-back only if the block is replaced. This requires the introduction of an additional state called "owner," which indicates that a block may be shared, but the owning processor is responsible for updating any other processors and memory when it changes the block or replaces it.

Hardware/ Software Interface

One insight is that block size plays an important role in cache coherency. For example, take the case of snooping on a cache with a block size of eight words, with a single word alternatively written and read by two processors. Most protocols exchange full blocks between processors, thereby increasing coherency bandwidth demands.

Large blocks can also cause what is called **false sharing**: when two unrelated shared variables are located in the same cache block, the full block is exchanged between processors even though the processors are accessing different variables. Programmers and compilers should lay out data carefully to avoid false sharing.

false sharing When two unrelated shared variables are located in the same cache block and the full block is exchanged between processors even though the processors are accessing different variables.

Elaboration: Although the three properties on page 535 are sufficient to ensure coherence, the question of when a written value will be seen is also important. To see why, observe that we cannot require that a read of X in Figure 5.35 instantaneously sees the value written for X by some other processor. If, for example, a write of X on one processor precedes a read of X on another processor very shortly beforehand, it may be impossible to ensure that the read returns the value of the data written, since the written data may not even have left the processor at that point. The issue of exactly *when* a written value must be seen by a reader is defined by a *memory consistency model*.

We make the following two assumptions. First, a write does not complete (and allow the next write to occur) until all processors have seen the effect of that write. Second, the processor does not change the order of any write with respect to any other memory access. These two conditions mean that if a processor writes location X followed by location Y, any processor that sees the new value of Y must also see the new value of X. These restrictions allow the processor to reorder reads, but forces the processor to finish a write in program order.

Elaboration: Since input can change memory behind the caches and since output could need the latest value in a write back cache, there is also a cache coherency problem for I/O with the caches of a single processor as well as just between caches of multiple processors. The cache coherence problem for multiprocessors and I/O (see Chapter 6), although similar in origin, has different characteristics that affect the appropriate solution. Unlike I/O, where multiple data copies are a rare event—one to be avoided whenever possible—a program running on multiple processors will normally have copies of the same data in several caches.

Elaboration: In addition to the snooping cache coherence protocol where the status of shared blocks is distributed, a *directory-based* cache coherence protocol keeps the sharing status of a block of physical memory in just one location, called the *directory*. Directory-based coherence has slightly higher implementation overhead than snooping, but it can reduce traffic between caches and thus scale to larger processor counts.

5.9 Advanced Material: Implementing Cache Controllers

This section on the CD shows how to implement control for a cache, just as we implemented control for the single-cycle and pipelined datapaths in Chapter 4. This section starts with a description of finite-state machines and the implementation of a cache controller for a simple data cache, including a description of the cache controller in a hardware description language. It then goes into details of an example cache coherence protocol and the difficulties in implementing such a protocol.

5.10   Real Stuff: the AMD Opteron X4 (Barcelona) and Intel Nehalem Memory Hierarchies

In this section, we will look at the memory hierarchy in two modern microprocessors: the AMD Opteron X4 (Barcelona) processor and the Intel Nehalem. Figure 5.37 shows the Intel Nehalem die photo, and Figure 1.9 in Chapter 1 shows the AMD Opteron X4 die photo. Both have secondary and tertiary caches on the main processor die. Such integration reduces access time to the lower-level caches and also reduces the number of pins on the chip, since there is no need for a bus to an external secondary cache. Both have on-chip memory controllers, which reduces the latency to main memory.

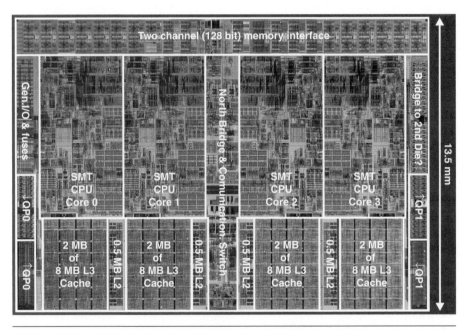

FIGURE 5.37   An Intel Nehalem die processor photo with the components labeled. This 13.5 by 19.6 mm die has 731 million transistors. It contains four processors that each have private 32-KB instruction and 32-LKB instruction caches and a 512-KB L2 cache. The four cores share an 8-MB L3 cache. The two 128-bit memory channels are to DDR3 DRAM. Each core also has a two-level TLB. The memory controller is now on the die, so there is no separate north bridge chip as in Intel Clovertown.

The Memory Hierarchies of the Nehalem and Opteron

Figure 5.38 summarizes the address sizes and TLBs of the two processors. Note that the AMD Opteron X4 (Barcelona) has four TLBs and that the virtual and physical addresses do not have to match the word size. The X4 implements only 48 of the potential 64 bits of its virtual space and 48 of the potential 64 bits of its physical address space. Nehalem has three TLBs, and the virtual address is 48 bits and the physical address is 44 bits.

Characteristic	Intel Nehalem	AMD Opteron X4 (Barcelona)
Virtual address	48 bits	48 bits
Physical address	44 bits	48 bits
Page size	4 KB, 2/4 MB	4 KB, 2/4 MB
TLB organization	1 TLB for instructions and 1 TLB for data per core	1 L1 TLB for instructions and 1 L1 TLB for data per core
	Both L1 TLBs are four-way set associative, LRU replacement	Both L1 TLBs fully associative, LRU replacement
	The L2 TLB is four-way set associative, LRU replacement	1 L2 TLB for instructions and 1 L2 TLB for data per core
	L1 I-TLB has 128 entries for small pages, 7 per thread for large pages	Both L2 TLBs are four-way set associative, round-robin
	L1 D-TLB has 64 entries for small pages, 32 for large pages	Both L1 TLBs have 48 entries
	The L2 TLB has 512 entries	Both L2 TLBs have 512 entries
	TLB misses handled in hardware	TLB misses handled in hardware

FIGURE 5.38   Address translation and TLB hardware for the Intel Nehalem and AMD Opteron X4. The word size sets the maximum size of the virtual address, but a processor need not use all bits. Both processors provide support for large pages, which are used for things like the operating system or mapping a frame buffer. The large-page scheme avoids using a large number of entries to map a single object that is always present. Nehalem supports two hardware-supported threads per core (see Section 7.5 in Chapter 7).

Figure 5.39 shows their caches. Each processor in the X4 has its own L1 64-KB instruction and data caches and its own 512-KB L2 cache. The four processors share a single 2-MB L3 cache. Nehalem has a similar structure, with each processor having its own L1 32-KB instruction and data caches and its own 512-KB L2 cache, and the four processors share a single 8-MB L3 cache.

Figure 5.40 shows the CPI, miss rates per thousand instructions for the L1 and L2 caches, and DRAM accesses per thousand instructions for Opteron X4 running the SPECint 2006 benchmarks. Note that the CPI and cache miss rates are highly correlated. The correlation coefficient of the set of CPIs and the set of L1 misses per 1000 instructions is 0.97. Although we don't have the actual L3 misses, we can infer the effectiveness of L3 by the reduction in DRAM accesses versus L2 misses. While a few programs benefit significantly from the 2-MB L3 cache—h264avc, hmmer, and bzip2—most do not.

Characteristic	Intel Nehalem	AMD Opteron X4 (Barcelona)
L1 cache organization	Split instruction and data caches	Split instruction and data caches
L1 cache size	32 KB each for instructions/data per core	64 KB each for instructions/data per core
L1 cache associativity	4-way (I), 8-way (D) set associative	2-way set associative
L1 replacement	Approximated LRU replacement	LRU replacement
L1 block size	64 bytes	64 bytes
L1 write policy	Write-back, Write-allocate	Write-back, Write-allocate
L1 hit time (load-use)	Not Available	3 clock cycles
L2 cache organization	Unified (instruction and data) per core	Unified (instruction and data) per core
L2 cache size	256 KB (0.25 MB)	512 KB (0.5 MB)
L2 cache associativity	8-way set associative	16-way set associative
L2 replacement	Approximated LRU replacement	Approximated LRU replacement
L2 block size	64 bytes	64 bytes
L2 write policy	Write-back, Write-allocate	Write-back, Write-allocate
L2 hit time	Not Available	9 clock cycles
L3 cache organization	Unified (instruction and data)	Unified (instruction and data)
L3 cache size	8192 KB (8 MB), shared	2048 KB (2 MB), shared
L3 cache associativity	16-way set associative	32-way set associative
L3 replacement	Not Available	Evict block shared by fewest cores
L3 block size	64 bytes	64 bytes
L3 write policy	Write-back, Write-allocate	Write-back, Write-allocate
L3 hit time	Not Available	38 (?)clock cycles

FIGURE 5.39 First-level, second-level, and third-level caches in the Intel Nehalem and AMD Opteron X4 2356 (Barcelona).

Techniques to Reduce Miss Penalties

Both the Nehalem and the Opteron X4 have additional optimizations that allow them to reduce the miss penalty. The first of these is the return of the requested word first on a miss, as described in the *Elaboration* on page 473. Both allow the processor to continue to execute instructions that access the data cache during a cache miss. This technique, called a **nonblocking cache**, is commonly used by designers who are attempting to hide the cache miss latency by using out-of-order processors. They implement two flavors of nonblocking. *Hit under miss* allows additional cache hits during a miss, while *miss under miss* allows multiple outstanding cache misses. The aim of the first of these two is hiding some miss latency with other work, while the aim of the second is overlapping the latency of two different misses.

Overlapping a large fraction of miss times for multiple outstanding misses requires a high-bandwidth memory system capable of handling multiple misses in parallel. In desktop systems, the memory may only be able to take limited advantage of this capability, but large servers and multiprocessors often have memory systems capable of handling more than one outstanding miss in parallel.

nonblocking cache A cache that allows the processor to make references to the cache while the cache is handling an earlier miss.

Name	CPI	L1 D cache misses/1000 instr	L2 D cache misses/1000 instr	DRAM accesses/1000 instr
perl	0.75	3.5	1.1	1.3
bzip2	0.85	11.0	5.8	2.5
gcc	1.72	24.3	13.4	14.8
mcf	10.00	106.8	88.0	88.5
go	1.09	4.5	1.4	1.7
hmmer	0.80	4.4	2.5	0.6
sjeng	0.96	1.9	0.6	0.8
libquantum	1.61	33.0	33.1	47.7
h264avc	0.80	8.8	1.6	0.2
omnetpp	2.94	30.9	27.7	29.8
astar	1.79	16.3	9.2	8.2
xalancbmk	2.70	38.0	15.8	11.4
Median	1.35	13.6	7.5	5.4

FIGURE 5.40 CPI, miss rates, and DRAM accesses for the Opteron model X4 2356 (Barcelona) memory hierarchy running SPECint2006. Alas, the L3 miss counters did not work on this chip, so we only have DRAM accesses to infer the effectiveness of the L3 cache. Note that this figure is for the same systems and benchmarks as Figure 1.20 in Chapter 1.

Both microprocessors prefetch instructions and have a built-in hardware prefetch mechanism for data accesses. They look at a pattern of data misses and use this information to try to predict the next address to start fetching the data before the miss occurs. Such techniques generally work best when accessing arrays in loops.

A significant challenge facing cache designers is to support processors like the Nehalem and Opteron X4, which can execute more than one memory instruction per clock cycle. Multiple requests can be supported in the first-level cache by two different techniques. The cache can be multiported, allowing more than one simultaneous access to the same cache block. Multiported caches, however, are often too expensive, since the RAM cells in a multiported memory must be much larger than single-ported cells. The alternative scheme is to break the cache into banks and allow multiple, independent accesses, provided the accesses are to different banks. The technique is similar to interleaved main memory (see Figure 5.11). The Opteron X4 L1 data cache supports two 128-bit reads per clock cycle and has eight banks.

Nehalem and most other processors follow the policy of *inclusion* in their memory hierarchy. This means that a copy of all data in the higher level caches can also be found in the lower-level caches. In contrast, the AMD processors follow the policy of *exclusion* in their first- and second-level cache, meaning that a cache block can only be found in the first- or second-level caches, but not both. Hence, on an L1 miss when a block is fetched from L2 to L1, the block replaced is sent back to the L2 cache.

The sophisticated memory hierarchies of these chips and the large fraction of the dies dedicated to caches and TLBs show the significant design effort expended to try to close the gap between processor cycle times and memory latency.

Elaboration: The shared L3 cache of Opteron X4 does not always follow exclusion. Since the data blocks can be shared between several processors in the L3 cache, it only removes the cache block from L3 if no other processors are sharing it. Hence, the L3 cache protocol recognizes whether or not the cache block is being shared or only used by a single processor.

Elaboration: Just as Opteron X4 does not follow the conventional inclusion property, it also has a novel relationship between the levels of the memory hierarchy. Instead of the memory feeding the L2 cache that in turn feeds the L1 cache, the L2 cache only holds data that has been evicted from the L1 cache. Thus, the L2 cache can be called a *victim cache*, since it only holds blocks displaced from L1 ("victims"). Similarly, L3 cache is a victim cache for the L2 cache, only containing blocks that spill over from L2. If an L1 miss is not found in the L2 cache but found in the L3 cache, the L3 cache supplies the data directly to L1 cache. Hence, an L1 miss can be serviced by an L2 hit or an L3 hit or memory.

5.11 Fallacies and Pitfalls

As one of the most naturally quantitative aspects of computer architecture, the memory hierarchy would seem to be less vulnerable to fallacies and pitfalls. Not only have there been many fallacies propagated and pitfalls encountered, but some have led to major negative outcomes. We start with a pitfall that often traps students in exercises and exams.

> *Pitfall: Forgetting to account for byte addressing or the cache block size in simulating a cache.*

When simulating a cache (by hand or by computer), we need to make sure we account for the effect of byte addressing and multiword blocks in determining into which cache block a given address maps. For example, if we have a 32-byte direct-mapped cache with a block size of 4 bytes, the byte address 36 maps into block 1 of the cache, since byte address 36 is block address 9 and (9 modulo 8) = 1.

On the other hand, if address 36 is a word address, then it maps into block (36 mod 8) = 4. Make sure the problem clearly states the base of the address.

In like fashion, we must account for the block size. Suppose we have a cache with 256 bytes and a block size of 32 bytes. Into which block does the byte address 300 fall? If we break the address 300 into fields, we can see the answer:

31	30	29	...	...	...	11	10	9	8	7	6	5	4	3	2	1	0
0	0	0	...	...	...	0	0	0	1	0	0	1	0	1	1	0	0

Cache block number / Block offset

Block address

Byte address 300 is block address

$$\left\lfloor \frac{300}{32} \right\rfloor = 9$$

The number of blocks in the cache is

$$\left\lfloor \frac{256}{32} \right\rfloor = 8$$

Block number 9 falls into cache block number (9 modulo 8) = 1.

This mistake catches many people, including the authors (in earlier drafts) and instructors who forget whether they intended the addresses to be in words, bytes, or block numbers. Remember this pitfall when you tackle the exercises.

Pitfall: Ignoring memory system behavior when writing programs or when generating code in a compiler.

This could easily be written as a fallacy: "Programmers can ignore memory hierarchies in writing code." We illustrate with an example using matrix multiply, to complement the sort comparison in Figure 5.18.

Here is the inner loop of the version of matrix multiply from Chapter 3:

```
for (i=0; i!=500; i=i+1)
    for (j=0; j!=500; j=j+1)
        for (k=0; k!=500; k=k+1)
            x[i][j] = x[i][j] + y[i][k] * z[k][j];
```

When run with inputs that are 500 × 500 double precision matrices, the CPU runtime of the above loop on a MIPS CPU with a 1-MB secondary cache was about half the speed compared to when the loop order is changed to k,j,i (so i is innermost)! The only difference is how the program accesses memory and the ensuing effect on the memory hierarchy. Further compiler optimizations, using a technique called *blocking*, can result in a runtime that is another four times faster for this code!

Pitfall: Having less set associativity for a shared cache than the number of cores or threads sharing that cache.

Without extra care, a parallel program running on 2^n processors or threads can easily allocate data structures to addresses that would map to the same set of a shared L2 cache. If the cache is at least 2^n-way associative, then these accidental conflicts are hidden by the hardware from the program. If not, programmers could face apparently mysterious performance bugs—actually due to L2 conflict misses—when migrating from, say, a 16-core design to 32-core design if both use 16-way associative L2 caches.

Pitfall: Using average memory access time to evaluate the memory hierarchy of an out-of-order processor.

If a processor stalls during a cache miss, then you can separately calculate the memory-stall time and the processor execution time, and hence evaluate the memory hierarchy independently using average memory access time (see page 478).

If the processor continues to execute instructions, and may even sustain more cache misses during a cache miss, then the only accurate assessment of the memory hierarchy is to simulate the out-of-order processor along with the memory hierarchy.

Pitfall: Extending an address space by adding segments on top of an unsegmented address space.

During the 1970s, many programs grew so large that not all the code and data could be addressed with just a 16-bit address. Computers were then revised to offer 32-bit addresses, either through an unsegmented 32-bit address space (also called a *flat address space*) or by adding 16 bits of segment to the existing 16-bit address. From a marketing point of view, adding segments that were programmer-visible and that forced the programmer and compiler to decompose programs into segments could solve the addressing problem. Unfortunately, there is trouble any time a programming language wants an address that is larger than one segment, such as indices for large arrays, unrestricted pointers, or reference parameters. Moreover, adding segments can turn every address into two words—one for the segment number and one for the segment offset—causing problems in the use of addresses in registers.

Pitfall: Implementing a virtual machine monitor on an instruction set architecture that wasn't designed to be virtualizable.

Many architects in the 1970s and 1980s weren't careful to make sure that all instructions reading or writing information related to hardware resource information were privileged. This *laissez-faire* attitude causes problems for VMMs for all of these architectures, including the x86, which we use here as an example.

Figure 5.41 describes the 18 instructions that cause problems for virtualization [Robin and Irvine, 2000]. The two broad classes are instructions that

- Read control registers in user mode that reveals that the guest operating system is running in a virtual machine (such as POPF, mentioned earlier)

- Check protection as required by the segmented architecture but assume that the operating system is running at the highest privilege level

Problem category	Problem x86 instructions
Access sensitive registers without trapping when running in user mode	Store global descriptor table register (SGDT) Store local descriptor table register (SLDT) Store interrupt descriptor table register (SIDT) Store machine status word (SMSW) Push flags (PUSHF, PUSHFD) Pop flags (POPF, POPFD)
When accessing virtual memory mechanisms in user mode, instructions fail the x86 protection checks	Load access rights from segment descriptor (LAR) Load segment limit from segment descriptor (LSL) Verify if segment descriptor is readable (VERR) Verify if segment descriptor is writable (VERW) Pop to segment register (POP CS, POP SS, . . .) Push segment register (PUSH CS, PUSH SS, . . .) Far call to different privilege level (CALL) Far return to different privilege level (RET) Far jump to different privilege level (JMP) Software interrupt (INT) Store segment selector register (STR) Move to/from segment registers (MOVE)

FIGURE 5.41 Summary of 18 x86 instructions that cause problems for virtualization [Robin and Irvine, 2000]. The first five instructions in the top group allow a program in user mode to read a control register, such as a descriptor table registers, without causing a trap. The pop flags instruction modifies a control register with sensitive information but fails silently when in user mode. The protection checking of the segmented architecture of the x86 is the downfall of the bottom group, as each of these instructions checks the privilege level implicitly as part of instruction execution when reading a control register. The checking assumes that the OS must be at the highest privilege level, which is not the case for guest VMs. Only the Move to segment register tries to modify control state, and protection checking foils it as well.

To simplify implementations of VMMs on the x86, both AMD and Intel have proposed extensions to the architecture via a new mode. Intel's VT-x provides a new execution mode for running VMs, an architected definition of the VM state, instructions to swap VMs rapidly, and a large set of parameters to select the circumstances where a VMM must be invoked. Altogether, VT-x adds 11 new instructions for the x86. AMD's Pacifica makes similar proposals.

An alternative to modifying the hardware is to make small modifications to the operating system to avoid using the troublesome pieces of the architecture. This technique is called *paravirtualization*, and the open source Xen VMM is a good example. The Xen VMM provides a guest OS with a virtual machine abstraction that uses only the easy-to-virtualize parts of the physical x86 hardware on which the VMM runs.

5.12   Concluding Remarks

The difficulty of building a memory system to keep pace with faster processors is underscored by the fact that the raw material for main memory, DRAMs, is essentially the same in the fastest computers as it is in the slowest and cheapest.

It is the principle of locality that gives us a chance to overcome the long latency of memory access—and the soundness of this strategy is demonstrated at all levels of the memory hierarchy. Although these levels of the hierarchy look quite different in quantitative terms, they follow similar strategies in their operation and exploit the same properties of locality.

Multilevel caches make it possible to use more cache optimizations more easily for two reasons. First, the design parameters of a lower-level cache are different from a first-level cache. For example, because a lower-level cache will be much larger, it is possible to use larger block sizes. Second, a lower-level cache is not constantly being used by the processor, as a first-level cache is. This allows us to consider having the lower-level cache do something when it is idle that may be useful in preventing future misses.

Another trend is to seek software help. Efficiently managing the memory hierarchy using a variety of program transformations and hardware facilities is a major focus of compiler enhancements. Two different ideas are being explored. One idea is to reorganize the program to enhance its spatial and temporal locality. This approach focuses on loop-oriented programs that use large arrays as the major data structure; large linear algebra problems are a typical example. By restructuring the loops that access the arrays, substantially improved locality—and, therefore, cache performance—can be obtained. The discussion on page 544 showed how effective even a simple change of loop structure could be.

Another approach is **prefetching**. In prefetching, a block of data is brought into the cache before it is actually referenced. Many microprocessors use hardware prefetching to try to predict accesses that may be difficult for software to notice.

A third approach is special cache-aware instructions that optimize memory transfer. For example, the microprocessors in Section 7.10 in Chapter 7 use an optimization that does not fetch the contents of a block from memory on a write miss because the program is going to write the full block. This optimization significantly reduces memory traffic for one kernel.

prefetching A technique in which data blocks needed in the future are brought into the cache early by the use of special instructions that specify the address of the block.

As we will see in Chapter 7, memory systems are a central design issue for parallel processors. The growing importance of the memory hierarchy in determining system performance means that this important area will continue to be a focus of both designers and researchers for some years to come.

5.13   Historical Perspective and Further Reading

This history section gives an overview of memory technologies, from mercury delay lines to DRAM, the invention of the memory hierarchy, protection mechanisms, and virtual machines, and concludes with a brief history of operating systems, including CTSS, MULTICS, UNIX, BSD UNIX, MS-DOS, Windows, and Linux.

5.14   Exercises

Contributed by Jichuan Chang, Jacob Leverich, Kevin Lim, and Parthasarathy Ranganathan (all of Hewlett-Packard)

Exercise 5.1

In this exercise we consider memory hierarchies for various applications, listed in the following table.

a.	Software version control
b.	Making phone calls

5.1.1 [10] <5.1> Assuming both client and server are involved in the process, first name the client and server systems. Where can caches be placed to speed up the process?

5.1.2 [10] <5.1> Design a memory hierarchy for the system. Show the typical size and latency at various levels of the hierarchy. What is the relationship between cache size and its access latency?

5.1.3 [15] <5.1> What are the units of data transfers between hierarchies? What is the relationship between the data location, data size, and transfer latency?

5.1.4 [10] <5.1, 5.2> Communication bandwidth and server processing bandwidth are two important factors to consider when designing a memory hierarchy. How can the bandwidths be improved? What is the cost of improving them?

5.1.5 [5] <5.1, 5.8> Now consider multiple clients simultaneously accessing the server. Will such scenarios improve the spatial and temporal locality?

5.1.6 [10] <5.1, 5.8> Give an example of where the cache can provide out-of-date data. How should the cache be designed to mitigate or avoid such issues?

Exercise 5.2

In this exercise we look at memory locality properties of matrix computation. The following code is written in C, where elements within the same row are stored contiguously.

a.	```for (I=0; I<8; I++) for (J=0; J<8000; J++) A[I][J]=B[I][0]+A[J][I];```
b.	```for (J=0; J<8000; J++) for (I=0; I<8; I++) A[I][J]=B[I][0]+A[J][I];```

5.2.1 [5] <5.1> How many 32-bit integers can be stored in a 16-byte cache line?

5.2.2 [5] <5.1> References to which variables exhibit temporal locality?

5.2.3 [5] <5.1> References to which variables exhibit spatial locality?

Locality is affected by both the reference order and data layout. The same computation can also be written below in Matlab, which differs from C by contiguously storing matrix elements within the same column.

a.	```for I=1:8 for J=1:8000 A(I,J)=B(I,0)+A(J,I); end end```
b.	```for J=1:8000 for I=1:8 A(I,J)=B(I,0)+A(J,I); end end```

5.2.4 [10] <5.1> How many 16-byte cache lines are needed to store all 32-bit matrix elements being referenced?

5.2.5 [5] <5.1> References to which variables exhibit temporal locality?

5.2.6 [5] <5.1> References to which variables exhibit spatial locality?

Exercise 5.3

Caches are important to providing a high-performance memory hierarchy to processors. Below is a list of 32-bit memory address references, given as word addresses.

a.	3, 180, 43, 2, 191, 88, 190, 14, 181, 44, 186, 253
b.	21, 166, 201, 143, 61, 166, 62, 133, 111, 143, 144, 61

5.3.1 [10] <5.2> For each of these references, identify the binary address, the tag, and the index given a direct-mapped cache with 16 one-word blocks. Also list if each reference is a hit or a miss, assuming the cache is initially empty.

5.3.2 [10] <5.2> For each of these references, identify the binary address, the tag, and the index given a direct-mapped cache with two-word blocks and a total size of 8 blocks. Also list if each reference is a hit or a miss, assuming the cache is initially empty.

5.3.3 [20] <5.2, 5.3> You are asked to optimize a cache design for the given references. There are three direct-mapped cache designs possible, all with a total of 8 words of data: C1 has 1-word blocks, C2 has 2-word blocks, and C3 has 4-word blocks. In terms of miss rate, which cache design is the best? If the miss stall time is 25 cycles, and C1 has an access time of 2 cycles, C2 takes 3 cycles, and C3 takes 5 cycles, which is the best cache design?

There are many different design parameters that are important to a cache's overall performance. The table below lists parameters for different direct-mapped cache designs.

	Cache Data Size	Cache Block Size	Cache Access Time
a.	32 KB	2 words	1 cycle
b.	32 KB	4 words	2 cycle

5.3.4 [15] <5.2> Calculate the total number of bits required for the cache listed in the table, assuming a 32-bit address. Given that total size, find the total size of the closest direct-mapped cache with 16-word blocks of equal size or greater. Explain why the second cache, despite its larger data size, might provide slower performance than the first cache.

5.3.5 [20] <5.2, 5.3> Generate a series of read requests that have a lower miss rate on a 2 KB 2-way set associative cache than the cache listed in the table. Identify one possible solution that would make the cache listed in the table have an equal or lower miss rate than the 2 KB cache. Discuss the advantages and disadvantages of such a solution.

5.3.6 [15] <5.2> The formula shown on page 457 shows the typical method to index a direct-mapped cache, specifically (Block address) modulo (Number of blocks in the cache). Assuming a 32-bit address and 1024 blocks in the cache, consider a different indexing function, specifically (Block address[31:27] XOR Block address[26:22]). Is it possible to use this to index a direct-mapped cache? If so, explain why and discuss any changes that might need to be made to the cache. If it is not possible, explain why.

Exercise 5.4

For a direct-mapped cache design with a 32-bit address, the following bits of the address are used to access the cache.

	Tag	Index	Offset
a.	31–10	9–5	4–0
b.	31–12	11–6	5–0

5.4.1 [5] <5.2> What is the cache line size (in words)?

5.4.2 [5] <5.2> How many entries does the cache have?

5.4.3 [5] <5.2> What is the ratio between total bits required for such a cache implementation over the data storage bits?

Starting from power on, the following byte-addressed cache references are recorded.

Address	0	4	16	132	232	160	1024	30	140	3100	180	2180

5.4.4 [10] <5.2> How many blocks are replaced?

5.4.5 [10] <5.2> What is the hit ratio?

5.4.6 [20] <5.2> List the final state of the cache, with each valid entry represented as a record of <index, tag, data>.

Exercise 5.5

Recall that we have two write policies and write allocation policies, and their combinations can be implemented either in L1 or L2 cache.

	L1	L2
a.	Write through, non-write allocate	Write back, write allocate
b.	Write through, write allocate	Write back, write allocate

5.5.1 [5] <5.2, 5.5> Buffers are employed between different levels of memory hierarchy to reduce access latency. For this given configuration, list the possible buffers needed between L1 and L2 caches, as well as L2 cache and memory.

5.5.2 [20] <5.2, 5.5> Describe the procedure of handling an L1 write-miss, considering the component involved and the possibility of replacing a dirty block.

5.5.3 [20] <5.2, 5.5> For a multilevel exclusive cache (a block can only reside in one of the L1 and L2 caches), configuration, describe the procedure of handling an L1 write-miss, considering the component involved and the possibility of replacing a dirty block.

Consider the following program and cache behaviors.

	Data Reads per 1000 Instructions	Data Writes per 1000 Instructions	Instruction Cache Miss Rate	Data Cache Miss Rate	Block Size (byte)
a.	250	100	0.30%	2%	64
b.	200	100	0.30%	2%	64

5.5.4 [5] <5.2, 5.5> For a write-through, write-allocate cache, what are the minimum read and write bandwidths (measured by byte per cycle) needed to achieve a CPI of 2?

5.5.5 [5] <5.2, 5.5> For a write-back, write-allocate cache, assuming 30% of replaced data cache blocks are dirty, what are the minimal read and write bandwidths needed for a CPI of 2?

5.5.6 [5] <5.2, 5.5> What are the minimal bandwidths needed to achieve the performance of CPI=1.5?

Exercise 5.6

Media applications that play audio or video files are part of a class of workloads called "streaming" workloads; i.e., they bring in large amounts of data but do not reuse much of it. Consider a video streaming workload that accesses a 512 KB working set sequentially with the following address stream:

0, 2, 4, 6, 8, 10, 12, 14, 16, …

5.6.1 [5] <5.5, 5.3> Assume a 64 KB direct-mapped cache with a 32-byte line. What is the miss rate for the address stream above? How is this miss rate sensitive to the size of the cache or the working set? How would you categorize the misses this workload is experiencing, based on the 3C model?

5.6.2 [5] <5.5, 5.1> Re-compute the miss rate when the cache line size is 16 bytes, 64 bytes, and 128 bytes. What kind of locality is this workload exploiting?

5.6.3 [10] <5.10> "Prefetching" is a technique that leverages predictable address patterns to speculatively bring in additional cache lines when a particular cache line is accessed. One example of prefetching is a stream buffer that prefetches sequentially adjacent cache lines into a separate buffer when a particular cache line is brought in. If the data is found in the prefetch buffer, it is considered as a hit and moved into the cache and the next cache line is prefetched. Assume a two-entry stream buffer and assume that the cache latency is such that a cache line can be loaded before the computation on the previous cache line is completed. What is the miss rate for the address stream above?

Cache block size (B) can affect both miss rate and miss latency. Assuming a 1-CPI machine with an average of 1.35 references (both instruction and data) per instruction, help find the optimal block size given the following miss rates for various block sizes.

	8	16	32	64	128
a.	4%	3%	2%	1.5%	1%
b.	8%	7%	6%	5%	4%

5.6.4 [10] <5.2> What is the optimal block size for a miss latency of 20×B cycles?

5.6.5 [10] <5.2> What is the optimal block size for a miss latency of 24+B cycles?

5.6.6 [10] <5.2> For constant miss latency, what is the optimal block size?

Exercise 5.7

In this exercise, we will look at the different ways capacity affects overall performance. In general, cache access time is proportional to capacity. Assume that main memory accesses take 70 ns and that memory accesses are 36% of all instructions. The following table shows data for L1 caches attached to each of two processors, P1 and P2.

		L1 Size	L1 Miss Rate	L1 Hit Time
a.	P1	2 KB	8.0%	0.66 ns
	P2	4 KB	6.0%	0.90 ns
b.	P1	16 KB	3.4%	1.08 ns
	P2	32 KB	2.9%	2.02 ns

5.7.1 [5] <5.3> Assuming that the L1 hit time determines the cycle times for P1 and P2, what are their respective clock rates?

5.7.2 [5] <5.3> What is the AMAT for P1 and P2?

5.7.3 [5] <5.3> Assuming a base CPI of 1.0 without any memory stalls, what is the total CPI for P1 and P2? Which processor is faster?

For the next three problems, we will consider the addition of an L2 cache to P1 to presumably make up for its limited L1 cache capacity. Use the L1 cache capacities and hit times from the previous table when solving these problems. The L2 miss rate indicated is its local miss rate.

	L2 Size	L2 Miss Rate	L2 Hit Time
a.	1 MB	95%	5.62 ns
b.	8 MB	68%	23.52 ns

5.7.4 [10] <5.3> What is the AMAT for P1 with the addition of an L2 cache? Is the AMAT better or worse with the L2 cache?

5.7.5 [5] <5.3> Assuming a base CPI of 1.0 without any memory stalls, what is the total CPI for P1 with the addition of an L2 cache?

5.7.6 [10] <5.3> Which processor is faster, now that P1 has an L2 cache? If P1 is faster, what miss rate would P2 need in its L1 cache to match P1's performance? If P2 is faster, what miss rate would P1 need in its L1 cache to match P2's performance?

Exercise 5.8

This exercise examines the impact of different cache designs, specifically comparing associative caches to the direct-mapped caches from Section 5.2. For these exercises, refer to the table of address streams shown in Exercise 5.3.

5.8.1 [10] <5.3> Using the references from Exercise 5.3, show the final cache contents for a three-way set associative cache with two-word blocks and a total size of 24 words. Use LRU replacement. For each reference identify the index bits, the tag bits, the block offset bits, and if it is a hit or a miss.

5.8.2 [10] <5.3> Using the references from Exercise 5.3, show the final cache contents for a fully associative cache with one-word blocks and a total size of 8 words. Use LRU replacement. For each reference identify the index bits, the tag bits, and if it is a hit or a miss.

5.8.3 [15] <5.3> Using the references from Exercise 5.3, what is the miss rate for a fully associative cache with two-word blocks and a total size of 8 words, using LRU replacement? What is the miss rate using MRU (most recently used) replacement? Finally what is the best possible miss rate for this cache, given any replacement policy?

Multilevel caching is an important technique to overcome the limited amount of space that a first level cache can provide while still maintaining its speed. Consider a processor with the following parameters:

	Base CPI, No Memory Stalls	Processor Speed	Main Memory Access Time	First Level Cache Miss Rate per Instruction	Second Level Cache, Direct-Mapped Speed	Global Miss Rate with Second Level Cache, Direct-Mapped	Second Level Cache, Eight-Way Set Associative Speed	Global Miss Rate with Second Level Cache, Eight-Way Set Associative
a.	1.5	2 GHz	100 ns	7%	12 cycles	3.5%	28 cycles	1.5%
b.	1.0	2 GHz	150 ns	3%	15 cycles	5.0%	20 cycles	2.0%

5.8.4 [10] <5.3> Calculate the CPI for the processor in the table using: 1) only a first level cache, 2) a second level direct-mapped cache, and 3) a second level eight-way set associative cache. How do these numbers change if main memory access time is doubled? If it is cut in half?

5.8.5 [10] <5.3> It is possible to have an even greater cache hierarchy than two levels. Given the processor above with a second level, direct-mapped cache, a designer wants to add a third level cache that takes 50 cycles to access and will reduce the global miss rate to 1.3%. Would this provide better performance? In general, what are the advantages and disadvantages of adding a third level cache?

5.8.6 [20] <5.3> In older processors such as the Intel Pentium or Alpha 21264, the second level of cache was external (located on a different chip) from the main processor and the first level cache. While this allowed for large second level caches, the latency to access the cache was much higher, and the bandwidth was typically lower because the second level cache ran at a lower frequency. Assume a 512 KB off-chip second level cache has a global miss rate of 4%. If each additional 512 KB of cache lowered global miss rates by 0.7%, and the cache had a total access time of 50 cycles, how big would the cache have to be to match the performance of the second level direct-mapped cache listed in the table? Of the eight-way set associative cache?

Exercise 5.9

For a high-performance system such as a B-tree index for a database, the page size is determined mainly by the data size and disk performance. Assume that on average a B-tree index page is 70% full with fix-sized entries. The utility of a page is its B-tree depth, calculated as $\log_2$(entries). The following table shows that for 16-byte entries, and a 10-year-old disk with a 10 ms latency and 10 MB/s transfer rate, the optimal page size is 16K.

Page Size (KB)	Page Utility or B-Tree Depth (Number of Disk Accesses Saved)	Index Page Access Cost (ms)	Utility/Cost
2	6.49 (or $\log_2$(2048/16×0.7))	10.2	0.64
4	7.49	10.4	0.72
8	8.49	10.8	0.79
16	9.49	11.6	0.82
32	10.49	13.2	0.79
64	11.49	16.4	0.70
128	12.49	22.8	0.55
256	13.49	35.6	0.38

5.9.1 [10] <5.4> What is the best page size if entries now become 128 bytes?

5.9.2 [10] <5.4> Based on 5.9.1, what is the best page size if pages are half full?

5.9.3 [20] <5.4> Based on 5.9.2, what is the best page size if using a modern disk with a 3 ms latency and 100 MB/s transfer rate? Explain why future servers are likely to have larger pages.

Keeping "frequently used" (or "hot") pages in DRAM can save disk accesses, but how do we determine the exact meaning of "frequently used" for a given system? Data engineers use the cost ratio between DRAM and disk access to quantify the reuse time threshold for hot pages. The cost of a disk access is $Disk /accesses_per_sec, while the cost to keep a page in DRAM is $DRAM_MB/page_size. The typical DRAM and disk costs and typical database page sizes at several time points are listed below:

Year	DRAM Cost ($/MB)	Page Size (KB)	Disk Cost ($/disk)	Disk Access Rate (access/sec)
1987	5000	1	15000	15
1997	15	8	2000	64
2007	0.05	64	80	83

5.9.4 [10] <5.1, 5.4> What are the reuse time thresholds for these three technology generations?

5.9.5 [10] <5.4> What are the reuse time thresholds if we keep using the same 4K page size? What's the trend here?

5.9.6 [20] <5.4> What other factors can be changed to keep using the same page size (thus avoiding software rewrite)? Discuss their likeliness with current technology and cost trends.

Exercise 5.10

As described in Section 5.4, virtual memory uses a page table to track the mapping of virtual addresses to physical addresses. This exercise shows how this table must be updated as addresses are accessed. The following table is a stream of virtual addresses as seen on a system. Assume 4 KB pages, a 4-entry fully associative TLB, and true LRU replacement. If pages must be brought in from disk, increment the next largest page number.

a.	4669, 2227, 13916, 34587, 48870, 12608, 49225
b.	12948, 49419, 46814, 13975, 40004, 12707, 52236

TLB

Valid	Tag	Physical Page Number
1	11	12
1	7	4
1	3	6
0	4	9

Page table

Valid	Physical Page or in Disk
1	5
0	Disk
0	Disk
1	6
1	9
1	11
0	Disk
1	4
0	Disk
0	Disk
1	3
1	12

5.10.1 [10] <5.4> Given the address stream in the table, and the initial TLB and page table states shown above, show the final state of the system. Also list for each reference if it is a hit in the TLB, a hit in the page table, or a page fault.

5.10.2 [15] <5.4> Repeat Exercise 5.10.1, but this time use 16 KB pages instead of 4 KB pages. What would be some of the advantages of having a larger page size? What are some of the disadvantages?

5.10.3 [15] <5.3, 5.4> Show the final contents of the TLB if it is 2-way set associative. Also show the contents of the TLB if it is direct mapped. Discuss the importance of having a TLB to high performance. How would virtual memory accesses be handled if there were no TLB?

There are several parameters that impact the overall size of the page table. Listed below are several key page table parameters.

	Virtual Address Size	Page Size	Page Table Entry Size
a.	32 bits	8 KB	4 bytes
b.	64 bits	8 KB	6 bytes

5.10.4 [5] <5.4> Given the parameters in the table above, calculate the total page table size for a system running 5 applications that utilize half of the memory available.

5.10.5 [10] <5.4> Given the parameters in the table above, calculate the total page table size for a system running 5 applications that utilize half of the memory available, given a two level page table approach with 256 entries. Assume each entry of the main page table is 6 bytes. Calculate the minimum and maximum amount of memory required.

5.10.6 [10] <5.4> A cache designer wants to increase the size of a 4 KB virtually indexed, physically tagged cache. Given the page size listed in the table above, is it possible to make a 16 KB direct-mapped cache, assuming 2 words per block? How would the designer increase the data size of the cache?

Exercise 5.11

In this exercise, we will examine space/time optimizations for page tables. The following table shows parameters of a virtual memory system.

	Virtual Address (bits)	Physical DRAM Installed	Page Size	PTE Size (byte)
a.	43	16 GB	4 KB	4
b.	38	8 GB	16 KB	4

5.11.1 [10] <5.4> For a single-level page table, how many page table entries (PTEs) are needed? How much physical memory is needed for storing the page table?

5.11.2 [10] <5.4> Using a multilevel page table can reduce the physical memory consumption of page tables, by only keeping active PTEs in physical memory. How many levels of page tables will be needed in this case? And how many memory references are needed for address translation if missing in TLB?

5.11.3 [15] <5.4> An inverted page table can be used to further optimize space and time. How many PTEs are needed to store the page table? Assuming a hash table implementation, what are the common case and worst case numbers of memory references needed for servicing a TLB miss?

The following table shows the contents of a 4-entry TLB.

Entry-ID	Valid	VA Page	Modified	Protection	PA Page
1	1	140	1	RW	30
2	0	40	0	RX	34
3	1	200	1	RO	32
4	1	280	0	RW	31

5.11.4 [5] <5.4> Under what scenarios would entry 2's valid bit be set to zero?

5.11.5 [5] <5.4> What happens when an instruction writes to VA page 30? When would a software managed TLB be faster than a hardware managed TLB?

5.11.6 [5] <5.4> What happens when an instruction writes to VA page 200?

Exercise 5.12

In this exercise, we will examine how replacement policies impact miss rate. Assume a 2-way set associative cache with 4 blocks. You may find it helpful to draw a table like those found on page 482 to solve the problems in this exercise, as demonstrated below on the address sequence "0, 1, 2, 3, 4."

Address of Memory Block Accessed	Hit or Miss	Evicted Block	Contents of Cache Blocks after Reference			
			Set 0	Set 0	Set 1	Set 1
0	Miss		Mem[0]			
1	Miss		Mem[0]		Mem[1]	
2	Miss		Mem[0]	Mem[2]	Mem[1]	
3	Miss		Mem[0]	Mem[2]	Mem[1]	Mem[3]
4	Miss	0	Mem[4]	Mem[2]	Mem[1]	Mem[3]
...						

The following table shows address sequences.

	Address Sequence
a.	0, 2, 4, 8, 10, 12, 14, 16, 0
b.	1, 3, 5, 1, 3, 1, 3, 5, 3

5.12.1 [5] <5.3, 5.5> Assuming an LRU replacement policy, how many hits does this address sequence exhibit?

5.12.2 [5] <5.3, 5.5> Assuming an MRU (most recently used) replacement policy, how many hits does this address sequence exhibit?

5.12.3 [5] <5.3, 5.5> Simulate a random replacement policy by flipping a coin. For example, "heads" means to evict the first block in a set and "tails" means to evict the second block in a set. How many hits does this address sequence exhibit?

5.12.4 [10] <5.3, 5.5> Which address should be evicted at each replacement to maximize the number of hits? How many hits does this address sequence exhibit if you follow this "optimal" policy?

5.12.5 [10] <5.3, 5.5> Describe why it is difficult to implement a cache replacement policy that is optimal for all address sequences.

5.12.6 [10] <5.3, 5.5> Assume you could make a decision upon each memory reference whether or not you want the requested address to be cached. What impact could this have on miss rate?

Exercise 5.13

To support multiple virtual machines, two levels of memory virtualization are needed. Each virtual machine still controls the mapping of virtual address (VA) to physical address (PA), while the hypervisor maps the physical address (PA) of each virtual machine to the actual machine address (MA). To accelerate such mappings, a software approach called "shadow paging" duplicates each virtual machine's page tables in the hypervisor, and intercepts VA to PA mapping changes to keep both copies consistent. To remove the complexity of shadow page tables, a hardware approach called nested page table (or extended page table) explicitly supports two classes of page tables (VA⇨PA and PA⇨MA) and can walk such tables purely in hardware.

Consider the following sequence of operations:

(1) Create process; (2) TLB miss; (3) page fault; (4) context switch;

5.13.1 [10] <5.4, 5.6> What would happen for the given operation sequence for shadow page table and nested page table, respectively?

5.13.2 [10] <5.4, 5.6> Assuming an x86-based 4-level page table in both guest and nested page table, how many memory references are needed to service a TLB miss for native vs. nested page table?

5.13.3 [15] <5.4, 5.6> Among TLB miss rate, TLB miss latency, page fault rate, and page fault handler latency, which metrics are more important for shadow page table? Which are important for nested page table?

The following table shows parameters for a shadow paging system.

TLB Misses per 1000 Instructions	NPT TLB Miss Latency	Page Faults per 1000 Instructions	Shadowing Page Fault Overhead
0.2	200 cycles	0.001	30,000 cycles

5.13.4 [10] <5.6> For a benchmark with native execution CPI of 1, what are the CPI numbers if using shadow page tables vs. NPT (assuming only page table virtualization overhead)?

5.13.5 [10] <5.6> What techniques can be used to reduce page table shadowing induced overhead?

5.13.6 [10] <5.6> What techniques can be used to reduce NPT induced overhead?

Exercise 5.14

One of the biggest impediments to widespread use of virtual machines is the performance overhead incurred by running a virtual machine. The table below lists various performance parameters and application behavior.

	Base CPI	Priviliged O/S Accesses per 10,000 Instructions	Performance Impact to Trap to the Guest O/S	Performance Impact to Trap to VMM	I/O Accesses per 10,000 Instructions	I/O Access Time (Includes Time to Trap to Guest O/S)
a.	1.5	120	15 cycles	175 cycles	30	1100 cycles
b.	1.75	90	20 cycles	140 cycles	25	1200 cycles

5.14.1 [10] <5.6> Calculate the CPI for the system listed above assuming that there are no accesses to I/O. What is the CPI if the VMM performance impact doubles? If it is cut in half? If a virtual machine software company wishes to obtain a 10% performance degradation, what is the longest possible penalty to trap to the VMM?

5.14.2 [10] <5.6> I/O accesses often have a large impact on overall system performance. Calculate the CPI of a machine using the performance characteristics above, assuming a non-virtualized system. Calculate the CPI again, this time using a virtualized system. How do these CPIs change if the system has half the I/O accesses? Explain why I/O bound applications have a smaller impact from virtualization.

5.14.3 [30] <5.4, 5.6> Compare and contrast the ideas of virtual memory and virtual machines. How do the goals of each compare? What are the pros and cons of each? List a few cases where virtual memory is desired, and a few cases where virtual machines are desired.

5.14.4 [20] <5.6> Section 5.6 discusses virtualization under the assumption that the virtualized system is running the same ISA as the underlying hardware. However, one possible use of virtualization is to emulate non-native ISAs. An example of this is QEMU, which emulates a variety of ISAs such as MIPS, SPARC, and PowerPC. What are some of the difficulties involved in this kind of virtualization? Is it possible for an emulated system to run faster than on its native ISA?

Exercise 5.15

In this exercise, we will explore the control unit for a cache controller for a processor with a write buffer. Use the finite state machine found in Figure 5.34 as a starting point for designing your own finite state machines. Assume that the cache controller is for the simple direct-mapped cache described on page 529, but you will add a write buffer with a capacity of one block.

Recall that the purpose of a write buffer is to serve as temporary storage so that the processor doesn't have to wait for two memory accesses on a dirty miss. Rather than writing back the dirty block before reading the new block, it buffers the dirty block and immediately begins reading the new block. The dirty block can then be written to main memory while the processor is working.

5.15.1 [10] <5.5, 5.7> What should happen if the processor issues a request that *hits* in the cache while a block is being written back to main memory from the write buffer?

5.15.2 [10] <5.5, 5.7> What should happen if the processor issues a request that *misses* in the cache while a block is being written back to main memory from the write buffer?

5.15.3 [30] <5.5, 5.7> Design a finite state machine to enable the use of a write buffer.

Exercise 5.16

Cache coherence concerns the views of multiple processors on a given cache block. The following table shows two processors and their read/write operations on two different words of a cache block X (initially X[0] = X[1] = 0).

	P1	P2
a.	X[0] ++; X[1] = 3;	X[0] = 5; X[1] +=2;
b.	X[0] =10; X[1] = 3;	X[0] = 5; X[1] +=2;

5.16.1 [15] <5.8> List the possible values of the given cache block for a correct cache coherence protocol implementation. List at least one more possible value of the block if the protocol doesn't ensure cache coherency.

5.16.2 [15] <5.8> For a snooping protocol, list a valid operation sequence on each processor/cache to finish the above read/write operations.

5.16.3 [10] <5.8> What are the best-case and worst-case numbers of cache misses needed to execute the listed read/write instructions?

Memory consistency concerns the views of multiple data items. The following table shows two processors and their read/write operations on different cache blocks (A and B initially 0).

	P1	P2
a.	A = 1; B = 2; A+=2; B++;	C = B; D = A;
b.	A = 1; B = 2; A=5; B++;	C = B; D = A;

5.16.4 [15] <5.8> List the possible values of C and D for an implementation that ensures both consistency assumptions on page 538.

5.16.5 [15] <5.8> List at least one more possible pair of values for C and D if such assumptions are not maintained.

5.16.6 [15] <5.2, 5.8> For various combinations of write policies and write allocation policies, which combinations make the protocol implementation simpler?

Exercise 5.17

Both Barcelona and Nehalem are chip multiprocessors (CMPs), having multiple cores and their caches on a single chip. CMP on-chip L2 cache design has interesting trade-offs. The following table shows the miss rates and hit latencies for two benchmarks with private vs. shared L2 cache designs. Assume L1 cache misses once every 32 instructions.

	Private	Shared
Benchmark A misses-per-instruction	0.30%	0.12%
Benchmark B misses-per-instruction	0.06%	0.03%

The next table shows hit latencies.

	Private Cache	Shared Cache	Memory
a.	5	20	180
b.	10	50	120

5.17.1 [15] <5.10> Which cache design is better for each of these benchmarks? Use data to support your conclusion.

5.17.2 [15] <5.10> Shared cache latency increases with the CMP size. Choose the best design if the shared cache latency doubles. Off-chip bandwidth becomes the bottleneck as the number of CMP cores increases. Choose the best design if off-chip memory latency doubles.

5.17.3 [10] <5.10> Discuss the pros and cons of shared vs. private L2 caches for both single-threaded, multi-threaded, and multiprogrammed workloads, and reconsider them if having on-chip L3 caches.

5.17.4 [15] <5.10> Assume both benchmarks have a base CPI of 1 (ideal L2 cache). If having non-blocking cache improves the average number of concurrent L2 misses from 1 to 2, how much performance improvement does this provide over a shared L2 cache? How much improvement can be achieved over private L2?

5.17.5 [10] <5.10> Assume new generations of processors double the number of cores every 18 months. To maintain the same level of per-core performance, how much more off-chip memory bandwidth is needed for a 2012 processor?

5.17.6 [15] <5.10> Consider the entire memory hierarchy. What kinds of optimizations can improve the number of concurrent misses?

Exercise 5.18

In this exercise we show the definition of a web server log and examine code optimizations to improve log processing speed. The data structure for the log is defined as follows:

```
struct entry {
  int  srcIP;    // remote IP address
  char URL[128]; // request URL (e.g., "GET index.html")
  long long refTime;  // reference time
  int  status;   // connection status
  char browser[64]; // client browser name
} log [NUM_ENTRIES];
```

Some processing functions on a log are:

a.	`topK_sourceIP (int hour);`
b.	`browser_histogram (int srcIP); // browsers of a given IP`

5.18.1 [5] <5.11> Which fields in a log entry will be accessed for the given log processing function? Assuming 64-byte cache blocks and no prefetching, how many cache misses per entry does the given function incur on average?

5.18.2 [10] <5.11> How can you reorganize the data structure to improve cache utilization and access locality? Show your structure definition code.

5.18.3 [10] <5.11> Give an example of another log processing function that would prefer a different data structure layout. If both functions are important, how would you rewrite the program to improve the overall performance? Supplement the discussion with code snippet and data.

For the problems below, use data from "Cache Performance for SPEC CPU2000 Benchmarks" (http://www.cs.wisc.edu/multifacet/misc/spec2000cache-data/) for the pairs of benchmarks shown in the following table.

a.	Mesa / gcc
b.	mcf / swim

5.18.4 [10] <5.11> For 64 KB data caches with varying set associativities, what are the miss rates broken down by miss types (cold, capacity, and conflict misses) for each benchmark?

5.18.5 [10] <5.11> Select the set associativity to be used by a 64 KB L1 data cache shared by both benchmarks. If the L1 cache has to be directly mapped, select the set associativity for the 1 MB L2 cache.

5.18.6 [20] <5.11> Give an example in the miss rate table where higher set associativity actually increases miss rate. Construct a cache configuration and reference stream to demonstrate this.

§5.1, page 457: 1 and 4. (3 is false because the cost of the memory hierarchy varies per computer, but in 2008 the highest cost is usually the DRAM.)

§5.2, page 475: 1 and 4: A lower miss penalty can enable smaller blocks, since you don't have that much latency to amortize, yet higher memory bandwidth usually leads to larger blocks, since the miss penalty is only slightly larger.

§5.3, page 491: 1.

§5.4, page 517: 1-a, 2-c, 3-b, 4-d.

§5.5, page 525: 2. (Both large block sizes and prefetching may reduce compulsory misses, so 1 is false.)

Storage and Other I/O Topics

Combining bandwidth and storage . . . enables swift and reliable access to the ever-expanding troves of content on the proliferating disks and . . . repositories of the Internet.

George Gilder
The End Is Drawing Nigh, 2000

The Five Classic Components of a Computer

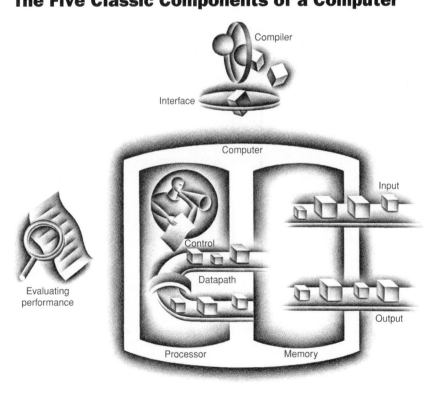

6.1   Introduction

Although users can get frustrated if their computer hangs and must be rebooted, they become apoplectic if their storage system crashes and they lose information. Thus, the standard for dependability is much higher for storage than for computation. Networks also plan for failures in communication, including several mechanisms to detect and recover from such failures. Hence, I/O systems generally place much greater emphasis on dependability and cost, while processors and memory focus on performance and cost.

I/O systems must also plan for expandability and for diversity of devices, which is not a concern for processors. Expandability is related to storage capacity, which is another design parameter for I/O systems; systems may need a lower bound of storage capacity to fulfill their role.

Although performance plays a smaller role for I/O, it is more complex. For example, with some devices we may care primarily about access latency, while

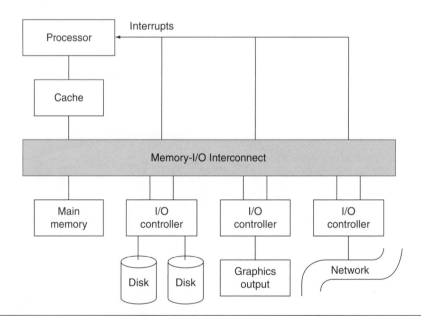

FIGURE 6.1 A typical collection of I/O devices. The connections between the I/O devices, processor, and memory are historically called *buses*, although the term means shared parallel wires and most I/O connections today are closer to dedicated serial lines. Communication among the devices and the processor uses both interrupts and protocols on the interconnect, as we will see in this chapter. Figure 6.9 shows the organization for a desktop PC.

with others throughput is crucial. Furthermore, performance depends on many aspects of the system: the device characteristics, the connection between the device and the rest of the system, the memory hierarchy, and the operating system. All of the components, from the individual I/O devices to the processor to the system software, will affect the dependability, expandability, and performance of tasks that include I/O. Figure 6.1 shows the structure of a simple system with its I/O.

I/O devices are incredibly diverse. Three characteristics are useful in organizing this wide variety:

- *Behavior:* Input (read once), output (write only, cannot be read), or storage (can be reread and usually rewritten).

- *Partner:* Either a human or a machine is at the other end of the I/O device, either feeding data on input or reading data on output.

- *Data rate:* The peak rate at which data can be transferred between the I/O device and the main memory or processor. It is useful to know the maximum demand the device may generate when designing an I/O system.

For example, a keyboard is an *input* device used by a *human* with a *peak data rate* of about 10 bytes per second. Figure 6.2 shows some of the I/O devices connected to computers.

Device	Behavior	Partner	Data rate (Mbit/sec)
Keyboard	Input	Human	0.0001
Mouse	Input	Human	0.0038
Voice input	Input	Human	0.2640
Sound input	Input	Machine	3.0000
Scanner	Input	Human	3.2000
Voice output	Output	Human	0.2640
Sound output	Output	Human	8.0000
Laser printer	Output	Human	3.2000
Graphics display	Output	Human	800.0000–8000.0000
Cable modem	Input or output	Machine	0.1280–6.0000
Network/LAN	Input or output	Machine	100.0000–10000.0000
Network/wireless LAN	Input or output	Machine	11.0000–54.0000
Optical disk	Storage	Machine	80.0000–220.0000
Magnetic tape	Storage	Machine	5.0000–120.0000
Flash memory	Storage	Machine	32.0000–200.0000
Magnetic disk	Storage	Machine	800.0000–3000.0000

FIGURE 6.2   The diversity of I/O devices. I/O devices can be distinguished by whether they serve as input, output, or storage devices; their communication partner (people or other computers); and their peak communication rates. The data rates span eight orders of magnitude. Note that a network can be an input or an output device, but cannot be used for storage. Transfer rates for devices are always quoted in base 10, so that 10 Mbit/sec = 10,000,000 bits/sec.

In Chapter 1, we briefly discussed four important I/O devices: mice, graphics displays, disks, and networks. In this chapter we go into much more depth on storage and related items. On the CD, there is an advanced topics section on networks, which are well covered in other books.

How we should assess I/O performance often depends on the application. In some environments, we may care primarily about system throughput. In these cases, I/O bandwidth will be most important. Even I/O bandwidth can be measured in two different ways:

1. How much data can we move through the system in a certain time?

2. How many I/O operations can we do per unit of time?

Which performance measurement is best may depend on the environment. For example, in many multimedia applications, most I/O requests are for long streams of data, and transfer bandwidth is the important characteristic. In another environment, we may wish to process a large number of small, unrelated accesses to an I/O device. An example of such an environment might be a tax-processing office of the U.S. National Income Tax Service (NITS). NITS mostly cares about processing a large number of forms in a given time; each tax form is stored separately and is fairly small. A system oriented toward large file transfer may be satisfactory, but an I/O system that can support the simultaneous transfer of many small files may be cheaper and faster for processing millions of tax forms.

I/O requests Reads or writes to I/O devices.

In other applications, we care primarily about response time, which you will recall is the total elapsed time to accomplish a particular task. If the **I/O requests** are extremely large, response time will depend heavily on bandwidth, but in many environments, most accesses will be small, and the I/O system with the lowest latency per access will deliver the best response time. On single-user machines such as desktop computers and laptops, response time is the key performance characteristic.

A large number of applications, especially in the vast commercial market for computing, require both high throughput and short response times. Examples include automatic teller machines (ATMs), order entry and inventory tracking systems, file servers, and Web servers. In such environments, we care about both how long each task takes *and* how many tasks we can process in a second. The number of ATM requests you can process per hour doesn't matter if each one takes 15 minutes—you won't have any customers left! Similarly, if you can process each ATM request quickly but can only handle a small number of requests at once, you won't be able to support many ATMs, or the cost of the computer per ATM will be very high.

In summary, the three classes of desktop, server, and embedded computers are sensitive to I/O dependability and cost. Desktop and embedded systems are more focused on response time and diversity of I/O devices, while server systems are more focused on throughput and expandability of I/O devices.

6.2 | Dependability, Reliability, and Availability

Users crave dependable storage, but how do you define it? In the computer industry, it is harder than looking it up in the dictionary. After considerable debate, the following is considered the standard definition [Laprie, 1985]:

> *Computer system dependability is the quality of delivered service such that reliance can justifiably be placed on this service. The service delivered by a system is its observed actual behavior as perceived by other system(s) interacting with this system's users. Each module also has an ideal specified behavior, where a service specification is an agreed description of the expected behavior. A system failure occurs when the actual behavior deviates from the specified behavior.*

Thus, you need a reference specification of expected behavior to be able to determine dependability. Users can then see a system alternating between two states of delivered service with respect to the service specification:

1. *Service accomplishment*, where the service is delivered as specified

2. *Service interruption*, where the delivered service is different from the specified service

Transitions from state 1 to state 2 are caused by *failures*, and transitions from state 2 to state 1 are called *restorations*. Failures can be permanent or intermittent. The latter is the more difficult case; it is harder to diagnose the problem when a system oscillates between the two states. Permanent failures are far easier to diagnose. This definition leads to two related terms: reliability and availability.

Reliability is a measure of the continuous service accomplishment—or, equivalently, of the time to failure—from a reference point. Hence, the *mean time to failure (MTTF)* of disks in Figure 6.5 below is a reliability measure. A related term is *annual failure rate* (AFR), which is just the percentage of devices that would be expected to fail in a year for a given MTTF. Service interruption is measured as *mean time to repair (MTTR)*. *Mean time between failures* (MTBF) is simply the sum of MTTF + MTTR. Although MTBF is widely used, MTTF is often the more appropriate term.

Availability is a measure of service accomplishment with respect to the alternation between the two states of accomplishment and interruption. Availability is statistically quantified as

$$\text{Availability} = \frac{\text{MTTF}}{(\text{MTTF} + \text{MTTR})}$$

Note that reliability and availability are actually quantifiable measures, rather than just synonyms for dependability.

What is the cause of failures? Figure 6.3 summarizes many papers that have collected data on reasons for computer systems and telecommunications systems to fail. Clearly, human operators are a significant source of failures.

Operator	Software	Hardware	System	Year data collected
42%	25%	18%	Datacenter (Tandem)	1985
15%	55%	14%	Datacenter (Tandem)	1989
18%	44%	39%	Datacenter (DEC VAX)	1985
50%	20%	30%	Datacenter (DEC VAX)	1993
50%	14%	19%	U.S. public telephone network	1996
54%	7%	30%	U.S. public telephone network	2000
60%	25%	15%	Internet services	2002

FIGURE 6.3 Summary of studies of reasons for failures. Although it is difficult to collect data to determine whether operators are the cause of errors, since operators often record the reasons for failures, these studies did capture that data. There were often other categories, such as environmental reasons for outages, but they were generally small. The top two rows come from a classic paper by Jim Gray [1990], which is still widely quoted almost 20 years after the data was collected. The next two rows are from a paper by Murphy and Gent, who studied causes of outages in VAX systems over time ["Measuring system and software reliability using an automated data collection process," *Quality and Reliability Engineering International* 11:5, September–October 1995, 341–53]. The fifth and sixth rows are studies of FCC failure data about the U.S. public switched telephone network by Kuhn ["Sources of failure in the public switched telephone network," *IEEE Computer* 30:4, April 1997, 31–36] and by Patty Enriquez. The study of three Internet services is from Oppenheimer, Ganapath, and Patterson [2003].

To increase MTTF, you can improve the quality of the components or design systems to continue operation in the presence of components that have failed. Hence, failure needs to be defined with respect to a context. A failure in a component may not lead to a failure of the system. To make this distinction clear, the term *fault* is used to mean failure of a component. Here are three ways to improve MTTF:

1. *Fault avoidance:* Preventing fault occurrence by construction.

2. *Fault tolerance:* Using redundancy to allow the service to comply with the service specification despite faults occurring, which applies primarily to hardware faults. Section 6.9 describes the RAID approaches to making storage dependable via fault tolerance.

3. *Fault forecasting:* Predicting the presence and creation of faults, which applies to hardware and software faults, allowing the component to be replaced before it fails.

Shrinking MTTR can help availability as much as increasing MTTF. For example, tools for fault detection, diagnosis, and repair can help reduce the time to repair faults by people, software, and hardware.

Which of the following are true about dependability?

Check Yourself

1. If a system is up, then all its components are accomplishing their expected service.

2. Availability is a quantitative measure of the percentage of time a system is accomplishing its expected service.

3. Reliability is a quantitative measure of continuous service accomplishment by a system.

4. The major source of outages today is software.

6.3 Disk Storage

As mentioned in Chapter 1, magnetic disks rely on a rotating platter coated with a magnetic surface and use a moveable read/write head to access the disk. Disk storage is **nonvolatile**—the data remains even when power is removed. A magnetic disk consists of a collection of platters (1–4), each of which has two recordable disk surfaces. The stack of platters is rotated at 5400 to 15,000 RPM and has a diameter from 1-inch to just over 3.5 inches. Each disk surface is divided into concentric circles, called **tracks**. There are typically 10,000 to 50,000 tracks per surface. Each track is in turn divided into **sectors** that contain the information; each track may have 100 to 500 sectors. Sectors are typically 512 bytes in size, although there is an initiative to increase the sector size to 4096 bytes. The sequence recorded on the magnetic media is a sector number, a gap, the information for that sector including error correction code (see ⊙ **Appendix C**, page C-66), a gap, the sector number of the next sector, and so on.

Originally, all tracks had the same number of sectors and hence the same number of bits. With the introduction of zone bit recording (ZBR) in the early 1990s, disk drives changed to a varying number of sectors (and hence bits) per track, instead keeping the spacing between bits constant. ZBR increases the number of bits on the outer tracks and thus increases the drive capacity.

As we saw in Chapter 1, to read and write information the read/write heads must be moved so that they are over the correct location. The disk heads for each surface are connected together and move in conjunction, so that every head is over the same track of every surface. The term *cylinder* is used to refer to all the tracks under the heads at a given point on all surfaces.

To access data, the operating system must direct the disk through a three-stage process. The first step is to position the head over the proper track. This operation is called a **seek**, and the time to move the head to the desired track is called the *seek time*.

nonvolatile Storage device where data retains its value even when power is removed.

track One of thousands of concentric circles that makes up the surface of a magnetic disk.

sector One of the segments that make up a track on a magnetic disk; a sector is the smallest amount of information that is read or written on a disk.

seek The process of positioning a read/write head over the proper track on a disk.

Disk manufacturers report minimum seek time, maximum seek time, and average seek time in their manuals. The first two are easy to measure, but the average is open to wide interpretation because it depends on the seek distance. The industry has decided to calculate average seek time as the sum of the time for all possible seeks divided by the number of possible seeks. Average seek times are usually advertised as 3 ms to 13 ms, but, depending on the application and scheduling of disk requests, the actual average seek time may be only 25% to 33% of the advertised number because of locality of disk references. This locality arises both because of successive accesses to the same file and because the operating system tries to schedule such accesses together.

rotational latency Also called **rotational delay**. The time required for the desired sector of a disk to rotate under the read/write head; usually assumed to be half the rotation time.

Once the head has reached the correct track, we must wait for the desired sector to rotate under the read/write head. This time is called the **rotational latency** or **rotational delay**. The average latency to the desired information is halfway around the disk. Because the disks rotate at 5400 RPM to 15,000 RPM, the average rotational latency is between

$$\text{Average rotational latency} = \frac{0.5 \text{ rotation}}{5400 \text{ RPM}} = \frac{0.5 \text{ rotation}}{5400 \text{ RPM}/\left(60 \dfrac{\text{seconds}}{\text{minute}}\right)}$$

$$= 0.0056 \text{ seconds} = 5.6 \text{ ms}$$

and

$$\text{Average rotational latency} = \frac{0.5 \text{ rotation}}{15{,}000 \text{ RPM}} = \frac{0.5 \text{ rotation}}{15{,}000 \text{ RPM}/\left(60 \dfrac{\text{seconds}}{\text{minute}}\right)}$$

$$= 0.0020 \text{ seconds} = 2.0 \text{ ms}$$

The last component of a disk access, *transfer time,* is the time to transfer a block of bits. The transfer time is a function of the sector size, the rotation speed, and the recording density of a track. Transfer rates in 2008 were between 70 and 125 MB/sec. The one complication is that most disk controllers have a built-in cache that stores sectors as they are passed over; transfer rates from the cache are typically higher and may be up to 375 MB/sec (3 Gbit/sec) in 2008. Today, most disk transfers are multiple sectors in length.

A *disk controller* usually handles the detailed control of the disk and the transfer between the disk and the memory. The controller adds the final component of disk access time, *controller time,* which is the overhead the controller imposes in performing an I/O access. The average time to perform an I/O operation will consist of these four times plus any wait time incurred because other processes are using the disk.

Disk Read Time

What is the average time to read or write a 512-byte sector for a typical disk rotating at 15,000 RPM? The advertised average seek time is 4 ms, the transfer rate is 100 MB/sec, and the controller overhead is 0.2 ms. Assume that the disk is idle so that there is no waiting time.

EXAMPLE

Average disk access time is equal to average seek time + average rotational delay + transfer time + controller overhead. Using the advertised average seek time, the answer is

ANSWER

$$4.0 \text{ ms} + \frac{0.5 \text{ rotation}}{15,000 \text{ RPM}} + \frac{0.5 \text{ KB}}{100 \text{ MB/sec}} + 0.2 \text{ ms} = 4.0 + 2.0 + 0.005 + 0.2 = 6.2 \text{ ms}$$

If the measured average seek time is 25% of the advertised average time, the answer is

$$1.0 \text{ ms} + 2.0 \text{ ms} + 0.005 \text{ ms} + 0.2 \text{ ms} = 3.2 \text{ ms}$$

Notice that when we consider measured average seek time, as opposed to advertised average seek time, the rotational latency can be the largest component of the access time.

Disk densities have continued to increase for more than 50 years. The impact of this compounded improvement in density and the reduction in physical size of a disk drive has been amazing, as Figure 6.4 shows. The aims of different disk designers have led to a wide variety of drives being available at any particular time. Figure 6.5 shows the characteristics of four magnetic disks. In 2008, these disks from a single manufacturer cost between $0.30 and $5.00 per gigabyte. In the broader market, prices generally range between $0.20 and $2.00 per gigabyte, depending on size, interface, and performance.

While disks will remain viable for the foreseeable future, the conventional wisdom about where block numbers are found has not. The assumptions of the sector-track-cylinder model are that nearby blocks are on the same track, blocks in the same cylinder take less time to access since there is no seek time, and some tracks are closer than others. The reason for the breakdown was the raising of the level of the interfaces. Higher-level intelligent interfaces like **ATA** and **SCSI** required a microprocessor inside a disk, which lead to performance optimizations.

To speed-up sequential transfers, these higher-level interfaces organize disks more like tapes than like random access devices. The logical blocks are ordered in serpentine fashion across a single surface, trying to capture all the sectors that are recorded at the same bit density. Hence, sequential blocks may be on different tracks. We will see an example in Figure 6.19 of the pitfall of assuming the conventional sector-track-cylinder model.

Advanced Technology Attachment (ATA) A command set used as a standard for I/O devices that is popular in the PC.

Small Computer Systems Interface (SCSI) A command set used as a standard for I/O devices.

FIGURE 6.4   Six magnetic disks, varying in diameter from 14 inches down to 1.8 inches.
The pictured disks were introduced over more than 15 years ago and hence are not intended to be representative of the best capacity of modern disks of these diameters. This photograph does, however, accurately portray their relative physical sizes. The widest disk is the DEC R81, containing four 14-inch diameter platters and storing 456 MB. It was manufactured in 1985. The 8-inch diameter disk comes from Fujitsu, and this 1984 disk stores 130 MB on six platters. The Micropolis RD53 has five 5.25-inch platters and stores 85 MB. The IBM 0361 also has five platters, but these are just 3.5 inches in diameter. This 1988 disk holds 320 MB. In 2008, the most dense 3.5-inch disk had 2 platters and held 1 TB in the same space, yielding an increase in density of about 3000 times! The Conner CP 2045 has two 2.5-inch platters containing 40 MB and was made in 1990. The smallest disk in this photograph is the Integral 1820. This single 1.8-inch platter contains 20 MB and was made in 1992.

Elaboration: These high-level interfaces let disk controllers add caches, which allow for fast access to data that was recently read between transfers requested by the processor. They use write-through and do not update on a write miss, and often also include prefetch algorithms to try to anticipate demand. Controllers also use a command queue that allow the disk to decide in what order to perform the commands to maximize performance while maintaining correct behavior. Of course, such capabilities complicate the measurement of disk performance and increase the importance of workload choice when comparing disks.

Characteristics	Seagate ST33000655SS	Seagate ST31000340NS	Seagate ST973451SS	Seagate ST9160821AS
Disk diameter (inches)	3.50	3.50	2.50	2.50
Formatted data capacity (GB)	147	1000	73	160
Number of disk surfaces (heads)	2	4	2	2
Rotation speed (RPM)	15,000	7200	15,000	5400
Internal disk cache size (MB)	16	32	16	8
External interface, bandwidth (MB/sec)	SAS, 375	SATA, 375	SAS, 375	SATA, 150
Sustained transfer rate (MB/sec)	73–125	105	79–112	44
Minimum seek (read/write) (ms)	0.2/0.4	0.8/1.0	0.2/0.4	1.5/2.0
Average seek read/write (ms)	3.5/4.0	8.5/9.5	2.9/3.3	12.5/13.0
Mean time to failure (MTTF) (hours)	1,400,000 @ 25°C	1,200,000 @ 25°C	1,600,000 @ 25°C	—
Annual failure rate (AFR) (percent)	0.62%	0.73%	0.55%	—
Contact start-stop cycles	—	50,000	—	>600,000
Warranty (years)	5	5	5	5
Nonrecoverable read errors per bits read	<1 sector per 10^{16}	<1 sector per 10^{15}	<1 sector per 10^{16}	<1 sector per 10^{14}
Temperature, shock (operating)	5°–55°C, 60 G	5°–55°C, 63 G	5°–55°C, 60 G	0°–60°C, 350 G
Size: dimensions (in.), weight (pounds)	1.0" × 4.0" × 5.8", 1.5 lbs	1.0" × 4.0" × 5.8", 1.4 lbs	0.6" × 2.8" × 3.9", 0.5 lbs	0.4" × 2.8" × 3.9", 0.2 lbs
Power: operating/idle/standby (watts)	15/11/—	11/8/1	8/5.8/—	1.9/0.6/0.2
GB/cu. in., GB/watt	6 GB/cu.in., 10 GB/W	43 GB/cu.in., 91 GB/W	11 GB/cu.in., 9 GB/W	37 GB/cu.in., 84 GB/W
Price in 2008, $/GB	~ $250, ~ $1.70/GB	~ $275, ~ $0.30/GB	~ $350, ~ $5.00/GB	~ $100, ~ $0.60/GB

FIGURE 6.5 Characteristics of four magnetic disks by a single manufacturer in 2008. The three leftmost drives are for servers and desktops while the rightmost drive is for laptops. Note that the third drive is only 2.5 inches in diameter, but it is a high performance drive with the highest reliability and fastest seek time. The disks shown here are either serial versions of the interface to SCSI (SAS), a standard I/O bus for many systems, or serial version of ATA (SATA), a standard I/O bus for PCs. The transfer rates from the caches is 3–5 times faster than the transfer rate from the disk surface. The much lower cost per gigabyte of the SATA 3.5-inch drive is primarily due to the hyper-competitive PC market, although there are differences in performance in I/Os per second due to faster rotation and faster seek times for SAS. The service life for these disks is five years. Note that the quoted MTTF assumes nominal power and temperature. Disk lifetimes can be much shorter if temperature and vibration are not controlled. See the link to Seagate at *www.seagate.com* for more information on these drives.

Which of the following are true about disk drives?   **Check Yourself**

1. 3.5-inch disks perform more IOs per second than 2.5-inch disks.

2. 2.5-inch disks offer the highest gigabytes per watt.

3. It takes hours to read the contents of a high capacity disk sequentially.

4. It takes months to read the contents of a high capacity disk using random 512-byte sectors.

6.4   Flash Storage

Many have tried to invent a technology to replace disks, and many have failed: CCD memory, bubble memory, and holographic memory were all found wanting. By the time a new technology would ship, disks made advances as predicted earlier, costs dropped accordingly, and the challenging product would be unattractive in the marketplace.

The first credible challenger is flash memory. This semiconductor memory is nonvolatile like disks, but latency is 100–1000 times faster than disk, and it is smaller, more power efficient, and more shock resistant. Equally important, because of the popularity of flash memory in cell phones, digital cameras, and MP3 players, there is a large market to pay for the investment in improving flash memory technology. Recently, flash memory cost per gigabyte has been falling 50% per year. In 2008, the price per gigabyte of flash was $4 to $10 per gigabyte, or about 2 to 40 times higher than disk and 5 to 10 times lower than DRAM. Figure 6.6 compares three flash-based products.

Characteristics	Kingston SecureDigital (SD) SD4/8 GB	Transend Type I CompactFlash TS16GCF133	RiDATA Solid State Disk 2.5 inch SATA
Formatted data capacity (GB)	8	16	32
Bytes per sector	512	512	512
Data transfer rate (read/write MB/sec)	4	20/18	68/50
Power operating/standby (W)	0.66/0.15	0.66/0.15	2.1/—
Size: height × width × depth (inches)	0.94 × 1.26 × 0.08	1.43 × 1.68 × 0.13	0.35 × 2.75 × 4.00
Weight in grams (454 grams/pound)	2.5	11.4	52
Mean time between failures (hours)	> 1,000,000	> 1,000,000	> 4,000,000
GB/cu. in., GB/watt	84 GB/cu.in., 12 GB/W	51 GB/cu.in., 24 GB/W	8 GB/cu.in., 16 GB/W
Best price (2008)	~ $30	~ $70	~ $300

FIGURE 6.6 Characteristics of three flash storage products. The CompactFlash standard package was proposed by Sandisk Corporation in 1994 for the PCMCIA-ATA cards of portable PCs. Because it follows the ATA interface, it simulates a disk interface, including seek commands, logical tracks, and so on. The RiDATA product imitates an SATA 2.5-inch disk interface.

Although its cost per gigabyte is higher than disks, flash memory is popular in mobile devices in part because it comes in smaller capacities. As a result, the 1-inch diameter hard disks are disappearing from some embedded markets. For example, in 2008 the Apple iPod Shuffle MP3 player sold for $50 and held 1 GB, while the smallest disk holds 4 GB and sells for more than the whole MP3 player.

Flash memory is a type of electrically erasable programmable read-only memory (*EEPROM*). The first flash memory, called *NOR flash* because of the similarity of the storage cell to a standard NOR gate, was a direct competitor with other EEPROMs and is randomly addressable like any memory. A few years later, *NAND flash* memory offered greater storage density, but memory could only be read and written in blocks as wiring needed for random accesses was removed. NAND flash is much less expensive per gigabyte and much more popular than NOR flash; all of the products in Figure 6.6 use NAND flash. Figure 6.7 compares the key characteristics of NOR versus NAND flash memory.

Characteristics	NOR Flash Memory	NAND Flash Memory
Typical use	BIOS memory	USB key
Minimum access size (bytes)	512 bytes	2048 bytes
Read time (microseconds)	0.08	25
Write time (microseconds)	10.00	1500 to erase + 250
Read bandwidth (MBytes/second)	10	40
Write bandwidth (MBytes/second)	0.4	8
Wearout (writes per cell)	100,000	10,000 to 100,000
Best price/GB (2008)	$65	$4

FIGURE 6.7 **Characteristics of NOR versus NAND flash memory in 2008.** These devices can read bytes and 16-bit words despite their large access sizes.

Unlike disks and DRAM, but like other EEPROM technologies, flash memory bits wear out (see Figure 6.7). To cope with such limits, most NAND flash products include a controller to spread the writes by remapping blocks that have been written many times to less trodden blocks. This technique is called *wear leveling*. With wear leveling, consumer products like cell phones, digital cameras, MP3 players, or memory keys are very unlikely to exceed the write limits in the flash. Such controllers lower the potential performance of flash, but they are needed unless higher-level software monitors block wear. However, controllers can also improve yield by mapping out memory cells that were manufactured incorrectly.

Write limits are one reason flash memory is not popular in desktop and server computers. However, in 2008 the first laptops are being sold with flash memory instead of hard disks at a considerable price premium to offer faster boot times, smaller size, and longer battery life. There are also flash memories available in standard disk form factors, as Figure 6.6 shows. Combining both ideas, *hybrid hard disks* include, say, a gigabyte of flash memory so that laptops can boot more quickly and save energy by allowing the disks to remain idle more frequently.

In the coming years, it appears that flash will compete successfully with hard disks for many battery-operated devices. As capacity increases and the cost per gigabyte continues to decline, it will be interesting to see whether the higher performance and energy efficiency of flash memory will yield opportunities in the desktop and server markets as well.

Which of the following are true about flash memory?

1. Like DRAM, flash is a semiconductor memory.

2. Like disks, flash does not lose information if it loses power.

3. The read access time of NOR flash is similar to DRAM.

4. The read bandwidth of NAND flash is similar to disk.

6.5   Connecting Processors, Memory, and I/O Devices

In a computer system, the various subsystems must have interfaces to one another. For example, the memory and processor need to communicate, as do the processor and the I/O devices. For many years, this has been done with a *bus*. A bus is a shared communication link, which uses one set of wires to connect multiple subsystems. The two major advantages of the bus organization are versatility and low cost. By defining a single connection scheme, new devices can easily be added, and peripherals can even be moved between computer systems that use the same kind of bus. Furthermore, buses are cost-effective, because a single set of wires is shared in multiple ways.

The major disadvantage of a bus is that it creates a communication bottleneck, possibly limiting the maximum I/O throughput. When I/O must pass through a single bus, the bandwidth of that bus limits the maximum I/O throughput. Designing a bus system capable of meeting the demands of the processor as well as connecting large numbers of I/O devices to the machine presents a major challenge.

processor-memory bus A bus that connects processor and memory and that is short, generally high speed, and matched to the memory system so as to maximize memory-processor bandwidth.

backplane bus A bus that is designed to allow processors, memory, and I/O devices to coexist on a single bus.

Buses are traditionally classified as **processor-memory buses** or *I/O buses*. Processor-memory buses are short, generally high speed, and matched to the memory system so as to maximize memory-processor bandwidth. I/O buses, by contrast, can be lengthy, can have many types of devices connected to them, and often have a wide range in the data bandwidth of the devices connected to them. I/O buses do not typically interface directly to the memory but use either a processor-memory or a **backplane bus** to connect to memory. Other buses with different characteristics have emerged for special functions, such as graphics buses.

One reason bus design is so difficult is that the maximum bus speed is largely limited by physical factors: the length of the bus and the number of devices. These physical limits prevent us from running the bus arbitrarily fast. In addition, the need to support a range of devices with widely varying latencies and data transfer rates also makes bus design challenging.

As it became difficult to run many parallel wires at high speed due to clock skew and reflection (see ◉ **Appendix C**), the industry transitioned from parallel shared buses to high-speed serial point-to-point interconnections with switches. Thus, such I/O networks have generally replaced I/O buses in our systems.

As a result of this transition, this section has been revised in this edition to emphasize the general problem of connecting I/O devices, processors, and memory, rather than focusing exclusively on buses.

Connection Basics

Let's consider a typical **I/O transaction**. A transaction includes two parts: sending the address and receiving or sending the data. Bus transactions are typically defined by what they do to memory. A *read* transaction transfers data *from* memory (to either the processor or an I/O device), and a *write* transaction writes data *to* the memory. Clearly, this terminology is confusing. To avoid this, we'll try to use the terms *input* and *output*, which are always defined from the perspective of the processor: an input operation is inputting data from the device to memory, where the processor can read it, and an output operation is outputting data to a device from memory where the processor wrote it.

The I/O interconnect serves as a way of expanding the machine and connecting new peripherals. To make this easier, the computer industry has developed several standards. The standards serve as a specification for the computer manufacturer and for the peripheral manufacturer. A standard assures the computer designer that peripherals will be available for a new machine, and it ensures the peripheral builder that users will be able to hook up their new equipment. Figure 6.8 summarizes the key characteristics of the five popular I/O standards: Firewire, USB, PCI Express (PCIe), Serial ATA (SATA), and Serial Attached SCSI (SAS). They connect a variety of devices to the desktop computer, from keyboards to cameras to disks.

Traditional buses are **synchronous**. That means the bus includes a clock in the control lines and a fixed protocol for communicating that is relative to the clock. For example, for performing a read from memory, we might have a protocol that transmits the address and read command on the first clock cycle, using the control lines to indicate the type of request. The memory might then be required to respond with the data word on the fifth clock. This type of protocol can be implemented easily in a small finite-state machine. Because the protocol is predetermined and involves little logic, the bus can run fast, and the interface logic will be small. Synchronous buses have two major disadvantages, however. First, every device on the bus must run at the same clock rate. Second, because of clock skew problems, synchronous buses cannot be long if they are fast (see ◉ Appendix C).

These problems led to **asynchronous** interconnects, which are not clocked. Because they are not clocked, asynchronous interconnects can accommodate a wide variety of devices, and the bus can be lengthened without worrying about

I/O transaction A sequence of operations over the interconnect that includes a request and may include a response, either of which may carry data. A transaction is initiated by a single request and may take many individual bus operations.

synchronous bus A bus that includes a clock in the control lines and a fixed protocol for communicating that is relative to the clock.

asynchronous interconnect Uses a handshaking protocol for coordinating usage rather than a clock; can accommodate a wide variety of devices of differing speeds.

Characteristic	Firewire (1394)	USB 2.0	PCI Express	Serial ATA	Serial Attached SCSI
Intended use	External	External	Internal	Internal	External
Devices per channel	63	127	1	1	4
Basic data width (signals)	4	2	2 per lane	4	4
Theoretical peak bandwidth	50 MB/sec (Firewire 400) or 100 MB/sec (Firewire 800)	0.2 MB/sec (low speed), 1.5 MB/sec (full speed), or 60 MB/sec (high speed)	250 MB/sec per lane (1x); PCIe cards come as 1x, 2x, 4x, 8x, 16x, or 32x	300 MB/sec	300 MB/sec
Hot pluggable	Yes	Yes	Depends on form factor	Yes	Yes
Maximum bus length (copper wire)	4.5 meters	5 meters	0.5 meters	1 meter	8 meters
Standard name	IEEE 1394, 1394b	USB Implementors Forum	PCI-SIG	SATA-IO	T10 committee

FIGURE 6.8   Key characteristics of five dominant I/O standards. The intended use column indicates whether it is designed to be used with cables external to the computer or just inside the computer with short cables or wire on printed circuit boards. PCIe can support simultaneous reads and writes, so some publications double the bandwidth per lane assuming a 50/50 split of read versus write bandwidth.

clock skew or synchronization problems. All the examples in Figure 6.8 are asynchronous.

To coordinate the transmission of data between sender and receiver, an asynchronous bus uses a **handshaking protocol**. A handshaking protocol consists of a series of steps in which the sender and receiver proceed to the next step only when both parties agree. The protocol is implemented with an additional set of control lines.

handshaking protocol A series of steps used to coordinate asynchronous bus transfers in which the sender and receiver proceed to the next step only when both parties agree that the current step has been completed.

The I/O Interconnects of the x86 Processors

Figure 6.9 shows the I/O system of a traditional PC. The processor connects to peripherals via two main chips. The chip next to the processor is the memory controller hub, commonly called the *north bridge*, and the one connected to it is the I/O controller hub, called the *south bridge*.

The north bridge is basically a DMA controller, connecting the processor to memory, possibly a graphics card, and the south bridge chip. The south bridge connects the north bridge to a cornucopia of I/O buses. Intel, AMD, NVIDIA, and others offer a wide variety of these chip sets to connect the processor to the outside world.

Figure 6.10 shows three examples of the chip sets. Note that AMD swallowed the north bridge chip in the Opteron and later products, thereby reducing the chip count and the latency to memory and graphics cards by skipping a chip crossing.

As Moore's law continues, an increasing number of I/O controllers that were formerly available as optional cards that connected to I/O buses have been co-opted into these chip sets. For example, the AMD Opteron X4 and the Intel Nehalem

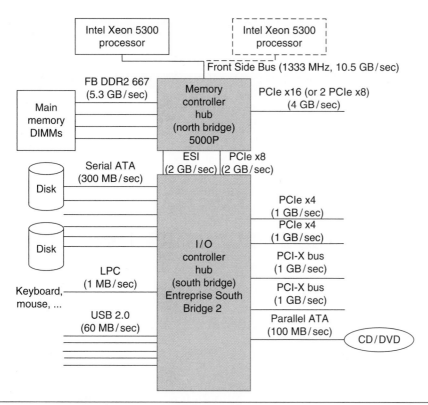

FIGURE 6.9 Organization of the I/O system on an Intel server using the Intel 5000P chip set. If you assume reads and writes are each half the traffic, you can double the bandwidth per link for PCIe.

include the north bridge inside the microprocessor, and the south bridge chip of the Intel 975 includes a RAID controller (see Section 6.9).

These I/O interconnects provide electrical connectivity among I/O devices, processors, and memory, and also define the lowest-level protocol for communication. Above this basic level, we must define hardware and software protocols for controlling data transfers between I/O devices and memory, and for the processor to specify commands to the I/O devices. These topics are covered in the next section.

Both networks and buses connect components together. Which of the following are true about them?

Check Yourself

1. I/O networks and I/O buses are almost always standardized.

2. I/O networks and I/O buses are almost always synchronous.

	Intel 5000P chip set	**Intel 975X chip set**	**AMD 580X CrossFire**
Target segment	Server	Performance PC	Server/Performance PC
Front Side Bus (64 bit)	1066/1333 MHz	800/1066 MHz	—
Memory controller hub ("north bridge")			
Product name	Blackbird 5000P MCH	975X MCH	
Pins	1432	1202	
Memory type, speed	DDR2 FBDIMM 667/533	DDR2 800/667/533	
Memory buses, widths	4 × 72	1 × 72	
Number of DIMMs, DRAM/DIMM	16, 1 GB/2 GB/4 GB	4, 1 GB/2 GB	
Maximum memory capacity	64 GB	8 GB	
Memory error correction available?	Yes	No	
PCIe/External Graphics Interface	1 PCIe x16 or 2 PCIe x	1 PCIe x16 or 2 PCIe x8	
South bridge interface	PCIe x8, ESI	PCIe x8	
I/O controller hub ("south bridge")			
Product name	6321 ESB	ICH7	580X CrossFire
Package size, pins	1284	652	549
PCI-bus: width, speed	Two 64-bit, 133 MHz	32-bit, 33 MHz, 6 masters	—
PCI Express ports	Three PCIe x4		Two PCIe x16, Four PCI x1
Ethernet MAC controller, interface	—	1000/100/10 Mbit	—
USB 2.0 ports, controllers	6	8	10
ATA ports, speed	One 100	Two 100	One 133
Serial ATA ports	6	2	4
AC-97 audio controller, interface	—	Yes	Yes
I/O management	SMbus 2.0, GPIO	SMbus 2.0, GPIO	ASF 2.0, GPIO

FIGURE 6.10   Two I/O chip sets from Intel and one from AMD. Note that the north bridge functions are included on the AMD microprocessor, as they are on the more recent Intel Nehalem.

6.6 Interfacing I/O Devices to the Processor, Memory, and Operating System

A bus or network protocol defines how a word or block of data should be communicated on a set of wires. This still leaves several other tasks that must be performed to actually cause data to be transferred from a device and into the memory address space of some user program. This section focuses on these tasks and will answer such questions as the following:

- How is a user I/O request transformed into a device command and communicated to the device?

- How is data actually transferred to or from a memory location?

- What is the role of the operating system?

As we will see in answering these questions, the operating system plays a major role in handling I/O, acting as the interface between the hardware and the program that requests I/O.

The responsibilities of the operating system arise from three characteristics of I/O systems:

1. Multiple programs using the processor share the I/O system.

2. I/O systems often use interrupts (externally generated exceptions) to communicate information about I/O operations. Because interrupts cause a transfer to kernel or supervisor mode, they must be handled by the operating system (OS).

3. The low-level control of an I/O device is complex, because it requires managing a set of concurrent events and because the requirements for correct device control are often very detailed.

The three characteristics of I/O systems above lead to several different functions the OS must provide:

Hardware/ Software Interface

- The OS guarantees that a user's program accesses only the portions of an I/O device to which the user has rights. For example, the OS must not allow a program to read or write a file on disk if the owner of the file has not granted access to this program. In a system with shared I/O devices, protection could not be provided if user programs could perform I/O directly.

- The OS provides abstractions for accessing devices by supplying routines that handle low-level device operations.

- The OS handles the interrupts generated by I/O devices, just as it handles the exceptions generated by a program.

- The OS tries to provide equitable access to the shared I/O resources, as well as schedule accesses to enhance system throughput.

To perform these functions on behalf of user programs, the operating system must be able to communicate with the I/O devices and to prevent the user program from communicating with the I/O devices directly. Three types of communication are required

1. The OS must be able to give commands to the I/O devices. These commands include not only operations like read and write, but also other operations to be done on the device, such as a disk seek.

2. The device must be able to notify the OS when the I/O device has completed an operation or has encountered an error. For example, when a disk completes a seek, it will notify the OS.

3. Data must be transferred between memory and an I/O device. For example, the block being read on a disk read must be moved from disk to memory.

In the next few subsections, we will see how these communications are performed.

Giving Commands to I/O Devices

memory-mapped I/O
An I/O scheme in which portions of address space are assigned to I/O devices, and reads and writes to those addresses are interpreted as commands to the I/O device.

To give a command to an I/O device, the processor must be able to address the device and to supply one or more command words. Two methods are used to address the device: memory-mapped I/O and special I/O instructions. In **memory-mapped I/O**, portions of the address space are assigned to I/O devices. Reads and writes to those addresses are interpreted as commands to the I/O device.

For example, a write operation can be used to send data to an I/O device where the data will be interpreted as a command. When the processor places the address and data on the memory bus, the memory system ignores the operation because the address indicates a portion of the memory space used for I/O. The device controller, however, sees the operation, records the data, and transmits it to the device as a command. User programs are prevented from issuing I/O operations directly, because the OS does not provide access to the address space assigned to the I/O devices, and thus the addresses are protected by the address translation. Memory-mapped I/O can also be used to transmit data by writing or reading to select addresses. The device uses the address to determine the type of command, and the data may be provided by a write or obtained by a read. In any event, the address encodes both the device identity and the type of transmission between processor and device.

Actually performing a read or write of data to fulfill a program request usually requires several separate I/O operations. Furthermore, the processor may have to interrogate the status of the device between individual commands to determine whether the command completed successfully. For example, a simple printer has two I/O device registers—one for status information and one for data to be printed. The Status register contains a *done bit*, set by the printer when it has printed a character, and an *error bit*, indicating that the printer is jammed or out of paper. Each byte of data to be printed is put into the Data register. The processor must then wait until the printer sets the done bit before it can place another character in the buffer. The processor must also check the error bit to determine if a problem has occurred. Each of these operations requires a separate I/O device access.

Elaboration: The alternative to memory-mapped I/O is to use dedicated **I/O instructions** in the processor. These I/O instructions can specify both the device number and the command word (or the location of the command word in memory). The processor communicates the device address via a set of wires normally included as part of the I/O bus. The actual command can be transmitted over the data lines in the bus. Examples of computers with I/O instructions are the Intel x86 and the IBM 370 computers. By making the I/O instructions illegal to execute when not in kernel or supervisor mode, user programs can be prevented from accessing the devices directly.

I/O instruction
A dedicated instruction that is used to give a command to an I/O device and that specifies both the device number and the command word (or the location of the command word in memory).

Communicating with the Processor

The process of periodically checking status bits to see if it is time for the next I/O operation, as in the previous example, is called **polling**. Polling is the simplest way for an I/O device to communicate with the processor. The I/O device simply puts the information in a Status register, and the processor must come and get the information. The processor is totally in control and does all the work.

Polling can be used in several different ways. Real-time embedded applications poll the I/O devices, since the I/O rates are predetermined and it makes I/O overhead more predictable, which is helpful for real time. As we will see, this allows polling to be used even when the I/O rate is somewhat higher.

The disadvantage of polling is that it can waste a lot of processor time, because processors are so much faster than I/O devices. The processor may read the Status register many times, only to find that the device has not yet completed a comparatively slow I/O operation, or that the mouse has not budged since the last time it was polled. When the device completes an operation, we must still read the status to determine whether it was successful.

The overhead in a polling interface was recognized long ago, leading to the invention of interrupts to notify the processor when an I/O device requires attention from the processor. **Interrupt-driven I/O**, which is used by almost all systems for at least some devices, employs I/O interrupts to indicate to the processor that an I/O device needs attention. When a device wants to notify the processor that it has completed some operation or needs attention, it causes the processor to be interrupted.

An I/O interrupt is just like the exceptions we saw in Chapters 4 and 5, with two important distinctions:

1. An I/O interrupt is asynchronous with respect to the instruction execution. That is, the interrupt is not associated with any instruction and does not prevent the instruction completion. This is very different from either page fault exceptions or exceptions such as arithmetic overflow. Our control unit need only check for a pending I/O interrupt at the time it starts a new instruction.

polling The process of periodically checking the status of an I/O device to determine the need to service the device.

interrupt-driven I/O An I/O scheme that employs interrupts to indicate to the processor that an I/O device needs attention.

2. In addition to the fact that an I/O interrupt has occurred, we would like to convey further information, such as the identity of the device generating the interrupt. Furthermore, the interrupts represent devices that may have different priorities and whose interrupt requests have different urgencies associated with them.

To communicate information to the processor, such as the identity of the device raising the interrupt, a system can use either vectored interrupts or an exception Cause register. When the processor recognizes the interrupt, the device can send either the vector address or a status field to place in the Cause register. As a result, when the OS gets control, it knows the identity of the device that caused the interrupt and can immediately interrogate the device. An interrupt mechanism eliminates the need for the processor to poll the device and instead allows the processor to focus on executing programs.

Interrupt Priority Levels

To deal with the different priorities of the I/O devices, most interrupt mechanisms have several levels of priority; UNIX operating systems use four to six levels. These priorities indicate the order in which the processor should process interrupts. Both internally generated exceptions and external I/O interrupts have priorities; typically, I/O interrupts have lower priority than internal exceptions. There may be multiple I/O interrupt priorities, with high-speed devices associated with the higher priorities.

To support priority levels for interrupts, MIPS provides the primitives that let the operating system implement the policy, similar to the way that MIPS handles TLB misses. Figure 6.11 shows the key registers, and Section B.7 in Appendix B gives more details.

The Status register determines who can interrupt the computer. If the interrupt enable bit is 0, then none can interrupt. A more refined blocking of interrupts is available in the interrupt mask field. There is a bit in the mask corresponding to each bit in the pending interrupt field of the Cause register. To enable the corresponding interrupt, there must be a 1 in the mask field at that bit position. Once an interrupt occurs, the operating system can find the reason in the exception code field of the Status register: 0 means an interrupt occurred, with other values for the exceptions mentioned in Chapter 5.

Here are the steps that must occur in handling an interrupt:

1. Logically AND the pending interrupt field and the interrupt mask field to see which enabled interrupts could be the culprit. Copies are made of these two registers using the `mfc0` instruction.

2. Select the higher priority of these interrupts. The software convention is that the leftmost is the highest priority.

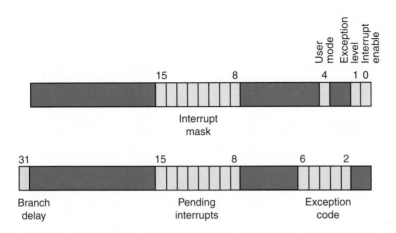

FIGURE 6.11 The Cause and Status registers. This version of the Cause register corresponds to the MIPS-32 architecture. The earlier MIPS I architecture had three nested sets of kernel/user and interrupt enable bits to support nested interrupts. Section B.7 in Appendix B has more details about these registers.

3. Save the interrupt mask field of the Status register.

4. Change the interrupt mask field to disable all interrupts of equal or lower priority.

5. Save the processor state needed to handle the interrupt.

6. To allow higher-priority interrupts, set the interrupt enable bit of the Cause register to 1.

7. Call the appropriate interrupt routine.

8. Before restoring state, set the interrupt enable bit of the Cause register to 0. This allows you to restore the interrupt mask field.

Appendix B shows an exception handler for a simple I/O task on pages B-36 to B-37.

How do the *interrupt priority levels* (IPLs) correspond to these mechanisms? The IPL is an operating system invention. It is stored in the memory of the process, and every process is given an IPL. At the lowest IPL, all interrupts are permitted. Conversely, at the highest IPL, all interrupts are blocked. Raising and lowering the IPL involves changes to the interrupt mask field of the Status register.

Elaboration: The two least significant bits of the pending interrupt and interrupt mask fields are for software interrupts, which are lower priority. These are typically used by higher-priority interrupts to leave work for lower-priority interrupts to do once the immediate reason for the interrupt is handled. Once the higher-priority interrupt is finished, the lower-priority tasks will be noticed and handled.

Transferring the Data between a Device and Memory

We have seen two different methods that enable a device to communicate with the processor. These two techniques—polling and I/O interrupts—form the basis for two methods of implementing the transfer of data between the I/O device and memory. Both these techniques work best with lower-bandwidth devices, where we are more interested in reducing the cost of the device controller and interface than in providing a high-bandwidth transfer. Both polling and interrupt-driven transfers put the burden of moving data and managing the transfer on the processor. After looking at these two schemes, we will examine a scheme more suitable for higher-performance devices or collections of devices.

We can use the processor to transfer data between a device and memory based on polling. In real-time applications, the processor loads data from I/O device registers and stores them into memory.

An alternative mechanism is to make the transfer of data interrupt driven. In this case, the OS would still transfer data in small numbers of bytes from or to the device. But because the I/O operation is interrupt driven, the OS simply works on other tasks while data is being read from or written to the device. When the OS recognizes an interrupt from the device, it reads the status to check for errors. If there are none, the OS can supply the next piece of data, for example, by a sequence of memory-mapped writes. When the last byte of an I/O request has been transmitted and the I/O operation is completed, the OS can inform the program. The processor and OS do all the work in this process, accessing the device and memory for each data item transferred.

Interrupt-driven I/O relieves the processor from having to wait for every I/O event, although if we used this method for transferring data from or to a hard disk, the overhead could still be intolerable, since it could consume a large fraction of the processor when the disk was transferring. For high-bandwidth devices like hard disks, the transfers consist primarily of relatively large blocks of data (hundreds to thousands of bytes). Thus, computer designers invented a mechanism for offloading the processor and having the device controller transfer data directly to or from the memory without involving the processor. This mechanism is called **direct memory access** (DMA). The interrupt mechanism is still used by the device to communicate with the processor, but only on completion of the I/O transfer or when an error occurs.

direct memory access (DMA) A mechanism that provides a device controller with the ability to transfer data directly to or from the memory without involving the processor.

DMA is implemented with a specialized controller that transfers data between an I/O device and memory independent of the processor. The DMA controller becomes the **master** and directs the reads or writes between itself and memory. There are three steps in a DMA transfer:

master A unit on the I/O interconnect that can initiate transfer requests.

1. The processor sets up the DMA by supplying the identity of the device, the operation to perform on the device, the memory address that is the source or destination of the data to be transferred, and the number of bytes to transfer.

2. The DMA starts the operation on the device and arbitrates for the interconnect. When the data is available (from the device or memory), it transfers the data. The DMA device supplies the memory address for the read or the write. If the request requires more than one transfer, the DMA unit generates the next memory address and initiates the next transfer. Using this mechanism, a DMA unit can complete an entire transfer, which may be thousands of bytes in length, without bothering the processor. Many DMA controllers contain some memory to allow them to deal flexibly either with delays in transfer or with those incurred while waiting to become the master.

3. Once the DMA transfer is complete, the controller interrupts the processor, which can then determine by interrogating the DMA device or examining memory whether the entire operation completed successfully.

There may be multiple DMA devices in a computer system. For example, in a system with a single processor-memory bus and multiple I/O buses, each I/O bus controller will often contain a DMA processor that handles any transfers between a device on the I/O bus and the memory.

Unlike either polling or interrupt-driven I/O, DMA can be used to interface a hard disk without consuming all the processor cycles for a single I/O. Of course, if the processor is also contending for memory, it will be delayed when the memory is busy doing a DMA transfer. By using caches, the processor can avoid having to access memory most of the time, thereby leaving most of the memory bandwidth free for use by I/O devices.

Elaboration: To further reduce the need to interrupt the processor and occupy it in handling an I/O request that may involve doing several actual operations, the I/O controller can be made more intelligent. Intelligent controllers are often called *I/O processors* (as well as *I/O controllers* or *channel controllers*). These specialized processors basically execute a series of I/O operations, called an *I/O program*. The program may be stored in the I/O processor, or it may be stored in memory and fetched by the I/O processor. When using an I/O processor, the operating system typically sets up an I/O program that indicates the I/O operations to be done as well as the size and transfer address for any reads or writes. The I/O processor then takes the operations from the I/O program and interrupts the processor only when the entire program is completed. DMA processors are essentially special-purpose processors (usually single-chip and nonprogrammable), while I/O processors are often implemented with general-purpose microprocessors, which run a specialized I/O program.

Direct Memory Access and the Memory System

When DMA is incorporated into an I/O system, the relationship between the memory system and processor changes. Without DMA, all accesses to the memory system come from the processor and thus proceed through address translation and cache access as if the processor generated the references. With DMA, there is another path to the memory system—one that does not go through the address translation mechanism or the cache hierarchy. This difference generates some problems in both virtual memory systems and systems with caches. These problems are usually solved with a combination of hardware techniques and software support.

The difficulties in having DMA in a virtual memory system arise because pages have both a physical and a virtual address. DMA also creates problems for systems with caches, because there can be two copies of a data item: one in the cache and one in memory. Because the DMA processor issues memory requests directly to the memory rather than through the processor cache, the value of a memory location seen by the DMA unit and the processor may differ. Consider a read from disk that the DMA unit places directly into memory. If some of the locations into which the DMA writes are in the cache, the processor will receive the old value when it does a read. Similarly, if the cache is write-back, the DMA may read a value directly from memory when a newer value is in the cache, and the value has not been written back. This is called the *stale data problem* or *coherence problem* (see Chapter 5).

We have looked at three different methods for transferring data between an I/O device and memory. In moving from polling to an interrupt-driven to a DMA interface, we shift the burden for managing an I/O operation from the processor to a progressively more intelligent I/O controller. These methods have the advantage of freeing up processor cycles. Their disadvantage is that they increase the cost of the I/O system. Because of this, a given computer system can choose which point along this spectrum is appropriate for the I/O devices connected to it.

Before discussing the design of I/O systems, let's look briefly at performance measures of them in the next section.

Check Yourself

In ranking the three ways of doing I/O, which statements are true?

1. If we want the lowest latency for an I/O operation to a single I/O device, the order is polling, DMA, and interrupt driven.

2. In terms of lowest impact on processor utilization from a single I/O device, the order is DMA, interrupt driven, and polling.

In a system with virtual memory, should DMA work with virtual addresses or physical addresses? The obvious problem with virtual addresses is that the DMA unit will need to translate the virtual addresses to physical addresses. The major problem with the use of a physical address in a DMA transfer is that the transfer cannot easily cross a page boundary. If an I/O request crossed a page boundary, then the memory locations to which it was being transferred would not necessarily be contiguous in the virtual memory. Consequently, if we use physical addresses, we must constrain all DMA transfers to stay within one page.

One method to allow the system to initiate DMA transfers that cross page boundaries is to make the DMA work on virtual addresses. In such a system, the DMA unit has a small number of map entries that provide virtual-to-physical mapping for a transfer. The operating system provides the mapping when the I/O is initiated. By using this mapping, the DMA unit need not worry about the location of the virtual pages involved in the transfer.

Another technique is for the operating system to break the DMA transfer into a series of transfers, each confined within a single physical page. The transfers are then *chained* together and handed to an I/O processor or intelligent DMA unit that executes the entire sequence of transfers; alternatively, the operating system can individually request the transfers.

Whichever method is used, the operating system must still cooperate by not remapping pages while a DMA transfer involving that page is in progress.

Hardware/ Software Interface

The coherency problem for I/O data is avoided by using one of three major techniques. One approach is to route the I/O activity through the cache. This ensures that reads see the latest value while writes update any data in the cache. Routing all I/O through the cache is expensive and potentially has a large negative performance impact on the processor, since the I/O data is rarely used immediately and may displace useful data that a running program needs. A second choice is to have the OS selectively invalidate the cache for an I/O read or force write-backs to occur for an I/O write (often called cache *flushing*). This approach requires some small amount of hardware support and is probably more efficient if the software can perform the function easily and efficiently. Because this flushing of large parts of the cache need only happen on DMA block accesses, it will be relatively infrequent. The third approach is to provide a hardware mechanism for selectively flushing (or invalidating) cache entries. Hardware invalidation to ensure cache coherence is typical in multiprocessor systems, and the same technique can be used for I/O; Chapter 5 discusses this topic in detail.

Hardware/ Software Interface

6.7   I/O Performance Measures: Examples from Disk and File Systems

How should we compare I/O systems? This is a complex question, because I/O performance depends on many aspects of the system, and different applications stress different aspects of the I/O system. Furthermore, a design can make complex tradeoffs between response time and throughput, making it impossible to measure just one aspect in isolation. For example, handling a request as early as possible generally minimizes response time, although greater throughput can be achieved if we try to handle related requests together. Accordingly, we may increase throughput on a disk by grouping requests that access locations that are close together. Such a policy will increase the response time for some requests, probably leading to a larger variation in response time. Although throughput will be higher, some benchmarks constrain the maximum response time to any request, making such optimizations potentially problematic.

In this section, we give some examples of measurements proposed for determining the performance of storage systems. These benchmarks are affected by a variety of system features, including the disk technology, the way disks are connected, the memory system, the processor, and the file system provided by the operating system.

Before we discuss these benchmarks, we need to address a confusing point about terminology and units. The performance of I/O systems depends on the rate at which the system transfers data. The transfer rate depends on the clock rate, which is typically given in GHz = 10^9 cycles per second. The transfer rate is usually quoted in GB/sec. In I/O systems, GBs are measured using base 10 (i.e., 1 GB = 10^9 = 1,000,000,000 bytes), unlike main memory where base 2 is used (i.e., 1 GB = 2^{30} = 1,073,741,824 bytes). In addition to adding confusion, this difference introduces the need to convert between base 10 (1K = 1000) and base 2 (1K = 1024), because many I/O accesses are for data blocks that have a size that is a power of 2. Rather than complicate all our examples by accurately converting one of the two measurements, we make note here of this distinction and the fact that treating the two measures as if the units were identical introduces a small error. We illustrate this error in Section 6.12.

Transaction Processing I/O Benchmarks

Transaction processing (TP) applications involve both a response time requirement and a performance measurement based on throughput. Furthermore, most of the I/O accesses are small. Because of this, TP applications are chiefly concerned with **I/O rate**, measured as the number of accesses per second, as opposed to **data rate**, measured as bytes of data per second. TP applications generally involve changes to a large database, with the system meeting some response time requirements

---

transaction processing A type of application that involves handling small short operations (called transactions) that typically require both I/O and computation. Transaction processing applications typically have both response time requirements and a performance measurement based on the throughput of transactions.

I/O rate Performance measure of I/Os per unit time, such as reads per second.

data rate Performance measure of bytes per unit time, such as GB/second.

as well as gracefully handling certain types of failures. These applications are extremely critical and cost-sensitive. For example, banks normally use TP systems because they are concerned about a range of characteristics. These include making sure transactions aren't lost, handling transactions quickly, and minimizing the cost of processing each transaction. Although dependability in the face of failure is an absolute requirement in such systems, both response time and throughput are critical to building cost-effective systems.

A number of transaction processing benchmarks have been developed. The best-known set of benchmarks is a series developed by the Transaction Processing Council (TPC).

TPC-C, initially created in 1992, simulates a complex query environment. TPC-H models ad hoc decision support—the queries are unrelated, and knowledge of past queries cannot be used to optimize future queries; the result is that query execution times can be very long. TPC-W is a Web-based transaction benchmark that simulates the activities of a business-oriented transactional Web server. It exercises the database system as well as the underlying Web server software. TPC-App is an application server and Web services benchmark. The most recent is TPC-E, which simulates the transaction processing workload of a brokerage firm. The TPC benchmarks are described at *www.tpc.org*.

All the TPC benchmarks measure performance in transactions per second. In addition, they include a response time requirement, so that throughput performance is measured only when the response time limit is met. To model real-world systems, higher transaction rates are also associated with larger systems, both in terms of users and the size of the database to which the transactions are applied. Hence, storage capacity must scale with performance. Finally, the system cost for a benchmark system must also be included, allowing accurate comparisons of cost/performance.

File System and Web I/O Benchmarks

In addition to processor benchmarks, SPEC offers both a file server benchmark (SPECSFS) and a Web server benchmark (SPECWeb). SPECSFS is a benchmark for measuring NFS (Network File System) performance using a script of file server requests; it tests the performance of the I/O system, including both disk and network I/O, as well as the processor. SPECSFS is a throughput-oriented benchmark but with important response time requirements. SPECWeb is a Web server benchmark that simulates multiple clients requesting both static and dynamic pages from a server, as well as clients posting data to the server (see Chapter 1).

The most recent SPEC effort is to measure power. SPECPower measures power and performance characteristics of small servers.

Sun recently announced *filebench*, a file system benchmark framework. Instead of a standard workload, it provides a language that lets you describe the workload you'd like to run on your file systems. However, there are examples of file workloads that are supposed to emulate common applications of file systems.

Check Yourself

Are the following true or false? Unlike processor benchmarks, I/O benchmarks

1. concentrate on throughput rather than latency

2. can require that the data set scale in size or number of users to achieve performance milestones

3. often report cost performance

6.8   Designing an I/O System

There are two primary types of specifications that designers encounter in I/O systems: latency constraints and bandwidth constraints. In both cases, knowledge of the traffic pattern affects the design and analysis.

Latency constraints involve ensuring that the latency to complete an I/O operation is bounded by a certain amount. In the simple case, the system may be unloaded, and the designer must ensure that some latency bound is met either because it is critical to the application or because the device must receive certain guaranteed service to prevent errors. Likewise, determining the latency on an unloaded system is relatively easy, since it involves tracing the path of the I/O operation and summing the individual latencies.

Finding the average latency (or distribution of latency) under a load is much harder. Such problems are tackled either by queuing theory (when the behavior of the workload requests and I/O service times can be approximated by simple distributions) or by simulation (when the behavior of I/O events is complex). Both topics are beyond the limits of this text.

Designing an I/O system to meet a set of bandwidth constraints given a workload is the other typical problem designers face. Alternatively, the designer may be given a partially configured I/O system and be asked to balance the system to maintain the maximum bandwidth achievable, as dictated by the preconfigured portion of the system. This latter design problem is a simplified version of the first.

The general approach to designing such a system is as follows:

1. Find the weakest link in the I/O system, which is the component in the I/O path that will constrain the design. Depending on the workload, this component can be anywhere, including the processors, the memory system, the I/O controllers, or the devices. Both the workload and configuration limits may dictate where the weakest link is located.

2. Configure this component to sustain the required bandwidth.

3. Determine the requirements for the rest of the system and configure them to support this bandwidth.

The easiest way to understand this methodology is with an example. We'll do a simple analysis of the I/O system of the Sun Fire x4150 server in Section 6.10 to show how this methodology works.

6.9 Parallelism and I/O: Redundant Arrays of Inexpensive Disks

Amdahl's law in Chapter 1 reminds us that neglecting I/O in this parallel revolution is foolhardy. A simple example demonstrates this.

Impact of I/O on System Performance

Suppose we have a benchmark that executes in 100 seconds of elapsed time, of which 90 seconds is CPU time and the rest is I/O time. Suppose the number of processors doubles every two years, but the processors remain the same speed, and I/O time doesn't improve. How much faster will our program run at the end of six years?

EXAMPLE

We know that

$$\text{Elapsed time} = \text{CPU time} + \text{I/O time}$$

$$100 = 90 + \text{I/O time}$$

$$\text{I/O time} = 10 \text{ seconds}$$

ANSWER

The new CPU times and the resulting elapsed times are computed in the following table.

After *n* years	CPU time	I/O time	Elapsed time	% I/O time
0 years	90 seconds	10 seconds	100 seconds	10%
2 years	$\frac{90}{2}$ = 45 seconds	10 seconds	55 seconds	18%
4 years	$\frac{45}{2}$ = 23 seconds	10 seconds	33 seconds	31%
6 years	$\frac{23}{2}$ = 11 seconds	10 seconds	21 seconds	47%

The improvement in CPU performance after six years is

$$\frac{90}{11} = 8$$

However, the improvement in elapsed time is only

$$\frac{100}{21} = 4.7$$

and the I/O time has increased from 10% to 47% of the elapsed time.

Hence, the parallel revolution needs to come to I/O as well as to computation, or the effort spent in parallelizing could be squandered whenever programs do I/O, which they all must do.

Accelerating I/O performance was the original motivation of disk arrays (see ⊙ Section 6.14 on the CD). In the late 1980s, the high performance storage of choice was large, expensive disks, such as the larger ones in Figure 6.4. The argument was that by replacing a few large disks with many small disks, performance would improve because there would be more read heads. This shift is a good match for multiple processors as well, since many read/write heads mean the storage system could support many more independent accesses as well as large transfers spread across many disks. That is, you could get both high I/Os per second and high data transfer rates. In addition to higher performance, there could be advantages in cost, power, and floor space, since smaller disks are generally more efficient per gigabyte than larger disks.

The flaw in the argument was that disk arrays could make reliability much worse. These smaller, inexpensive drives had lower MTTF ratings than the large drives, but more importantly, by replacing a single drive with, say, 50 small drives, the failure rate would go up by at least a factor of 50!

The solution was to add redundancy so that the system could cope with disk failures without losing information. By having many small disks, the cost of extra redundancy to improve dependability is small, relative to the solutions for a few large disks. Thus, dependability was more affordable if you constructed a redundant array of inexpensive disks. This observation led to its name: **redundant arrays of inexpensive disks**, abbreviated **RAID**.

redundant arrays of inexpensive disks (RAID) An organization of disks that uses an array of small and inexpensive disks so as to increase both performance and reliability.

In retrospect, although its invention was motivated by performance, dependability was the key reason for the widespread popularity of RAID. The parallel revolution has resurfaced the original performance side of the argument for RAID. The rest of this section surveys the options for dependability and their impacts on cost and performance.

How much redundancy do you need? Do you need extra information to find the faults? Does it matter how you organize the data and the extra check information on these disks? The paper that coined the term gave an evolutionary answer to these questions, starting with the simplest but most expensive solution.

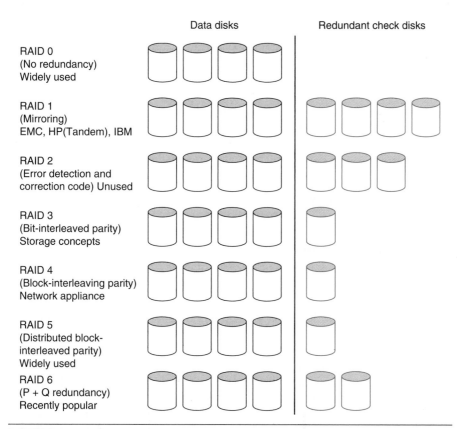

Data disks   Redundant check disks

RAID 0
(No redundancy)
Widely used

RAID 1
(Mirroring)
EMC, HP(Tandem), IBM

RAID 2
(Error detection and
correction code) Unused

RAID 3
(Bit-interleaved parity)
Storage concepts

RAID 4
(Block-interleaving parity)
Network appliance

RAID 5
(Distributed block-
interleaved parity)
Widely used

RAID 6
(P + Q redundancy)
Recently popular

FIGURE 6.12   RAID for an example of four data disks showing extra check disks per RAID level and companies that use each level. Figures 6.13 and 6.14 explain the difference between RAID 3, RAID 4, and RAID 5.

Figure 6.12 shows the evolution and example cost in number of extra check disks. To keep track of the evolution, the authors numbered the stages of RAID, and they are still used today.

No Redundancy (RAID 0)

Simply spreading data over multiple disks, called **striping**, automatically forces accesses to several disks. Striping across a set of disks makes the collection appear to software as a single large disk, which simplifies storage management. It also improves performance for large accesses, since many disks can operate at once. Video-editing systems, for example, often stripe their data and may not worry about dependability as much as, say, databases.

RAID 0 is something of a misnomer, as there is no redundancy. However, RAID levels are often left to the operator to set when creating a storage system, and RAID 0 is often listed as one of the options. Hence, the term RAID 0 has become widely used.

> **striping** Allocation of logically sequential blocks to separate disks to allow higher performance than a single disk can deliver.

Mirroring (RAID 1)

mirroring Writing the
identical data to multiple
disks to increase data
availability.

This traditional scheme for tolerating disk failure, called **mirroring** or *shadowing*, uses twice as many disks as does RAID 0. Whenever data is written to one disk, that data is also written to a redundant disk, so that there are always two copies of the information. If a disk fails, the system just goes to the "mirror" and reads its contents to get the desired information. Mirroring is the most expensive RAID solution, since it requires the most disks.

Error Detecting and Correcting Code (RAID 2)

RAID 2 borrows an error detection and correction scheme most often used for memories (see ⊙ **Appendix C**). Since RAID 2 has fallen into disuse, we'll not describe it here.

Bit-Interleaved Parity (RAID 3)

protection group The
group of data disks
or blocks that share a
common check disk or
block.

The cost of higher availability can be reduced to $1/n$, where n is the number of disks in a **protection group**. Rather than have a complete copy of the original data for each disk, we need only add enough redundant information to restore the lost information on a failure. Reads or writes go to all disks in the group, with one extra disk to hold the check information in case there is a failure. RAID 3 is popular in applications with large data sets, such as multimedia and some scientific codes.

Parity is one such scheme. Readers unfamiliar with parity can think of the redundant disk as having the sum of all the data in the other disks. When a disk fails, then you subtract all the data in the good disks from the parity disk; the remaining information must be the missing information. Parity is simply the sum modulo two.

Unlike RAID 1, many disks must be read to determine the missing data. The assumption behind this technique is that taking longer to recover from failure but spending less on redundant storage is a good tradeoff.

Block-Interleaved Parity (RAID 4)

RAID 4 uses the same ratio of data disks and check disks as RAID 3, but they access data differently. The parity is stored as blocks and associated with a set of data blocks.

In RAID 3, every access went to all disks. However, some applications prefer smaller accesses, allowing independent accesses to occur in parallel. That is the purpose of the RAID levels 4 to 6. Since error detection information in each sector is checked on reads to see if the data is correct, such "small reads" to each disk can occur independently as long as the minimum access is one sector. In the RAID context, a small access goes to just one disk in a protection group while a large access goes to all the disks in a protection group.

Writes are another matter. It would seem that each small write would demand that all other disks be accessed to read the rest of the information needed to

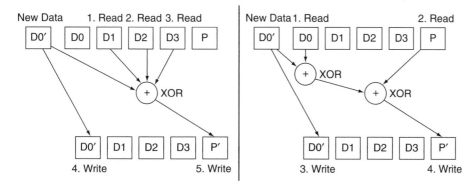

FIGURE 6.13 Small write update on RAID 4. This optimization for small writes reduces the number of disk accesses as well as the number of disks occupied. This figure assumes we have four blocks of data and one block of parity. The naive RAID 4 parity calculation in the left of the figure reads blocks D1, D2, and D3 before adding block D0′ to calculate the new parity P′. (In case you were wondering, the new data D0′ comes directly from the CPU, so disks are not involved in reading it.) The RAID 4 shortcut on the right reads the old value D0 and compares it to the new value D0′ to see which bits will change. You then read the old parity P and then change the corresponding bits to form P′. The logical function exclusive OR does exactly what we want. This example replaces three disk reads (D1, D2, D3) and two disk writes (D0′, P′) involving all the disks for two disk reads (D0, P) and two disk writes (D0′, P′), which involve just two disks. Increasing the size of the parity group increases the savings of the shortcut. RAID 5 uses the same shortcut.

recalculate the new parity, as in the left in Figure 6.13. A "small write" would require reading the old data and old parity, adding the new information, and then writing the new parity to the parity disk and the new data to the data disk.

The key insight to reduce this overhead is that parity is simply a sum of information; by watching which bits change when we write the new information, we need only change the corresponding bits on the parity disk. The right of Figure 6.13 shows the shortcut. We must read the old data from the disk being written, compare old data to the new data to see which bits change, read the old parity, change the corresponding bits, then write the new data and new parity. Thus, the small write involves four disk accesses to two disks instead of accessing all disks. This organization is RAID 4.

Distributed Block-Interleaved Parity (RAID 5)

RAID 4 efficiently supports a mixture of large reads, large writes, and small reads, plus it allows small writes. One drawback to the system is that the parity disk must be updated on every write, so the parity disk is the bottleneck for back-to-back writes.

To fix the parity-write bottleneck, the parity information can be spread throughout all the disks so that there is no single bottleneck for writes. The distributed parity organization is RAID 5.

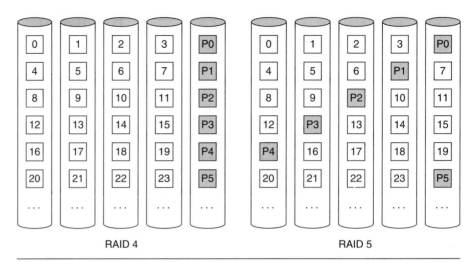

FIGURE 6.14   Block-interleaved parity (RAID 4) versus distributed block-interleaved parity (RAID 5). By distributing parity blocks to all disks, some small writes can be performed in parallel.

Figure 6.14 shows how data is distributed in RAID 4 versus RAID 5. As the organization on the right shows, in RAID 5 the parity associated with each row of data blocks is no longer restricted to a single disk. This organization allows multiple writes to occur simultaneously as long as the parity blocks are not located on the same disk. For example, a write to block 8 on the right must also access its parity block P2, thereby occupying the first and third disks. A second write to block 5 on the right, implying an update to its parity block P1, accesses the second and fourth disks and thus could occur concurrently with the write to block 8. Those same writes to the organization on the left result in changes to blocks P1 and P2, both on the fifth disk, which is a bottleneck.

P + Q Redundancy (RAID 6)

Parity-based schemes protect against a single self-identifying failure. When a single failure correction is not sufficient, parity can be generalized to have a second calculation over the data and another check disk of information. This second check block allows recovery from a second failure. Thus, the storage overhead is twice that of RAID 5. The small write shortcut of Figure 6.13 works as well, except now there are six disk accesses instead of four to update both P and Q information.

RAID Summary

RAID 1 and RAID 5 are widely used in servers; one estimate is that 80% of disks in servers are found in a RAID organization.

One weakness of the RAID systems is repair. First, to avoid making the data unavailable during repair, the array must be designed to allow the failed disks to be replaced without having to turn off the system. RAIDs have enough redundancy to allow continuous operation, but **hot-swapping** disks place demands on the physical and electrical design of the array and the disk interfaces. Second, another failure could occur during repair, so the repair time affects the chances of losing data: the longer the repair time, the greater the chances of another failure that will lose data. Rather than having to wait for the operator to bring in a good disk, some systems include **standby spares** so that the data can be reconstructed immediately upon discovery of the failure. The operator can then replace the failed disks in a more leisurely fashion. Note that a human operator ultimately determines which disks to remove. As Figure 6.3 shows, operators are only human, so they occasionally remove the good disk instead of the broken disk, leading to an unrecoverable disk failure.

hot-swapping Replacing a hardware component while the system is running.

standby spares Reserve hardware resources that can immediately take the place of a failed component.

In addition to designing the RAID system for repair, there are questions about how disk technology changes over time. Although disk manufacturers quote very high MTTF for their products, those numbers are under nominal conditions. If a particular disk array has been subject to temperature cycles due to, say, the failure of the air conditioning system, or to shaking due to a poor rack design, construction, or installation, the failure rates can be three to six times higher (see the fallacy on page 613). The calculation of RAID reliability assumes independence between disk failures, but disk failures could be correlated, because such damage due to the environment would likely happen to all the disks in the array. Another concern is that since disk bandwidth is growing more slowly than disk capacity, the time to repair a disk in a RAID system is increasing, which in turn increases the chances of a second failure. For example, a 1000 GB SATA disk could take almost three hours to read sequentially, assuming no interference. Given that the damaged RAID is likely to continue to serve data, reconstruction could be stretched considerably. Besides increasing that time, another concern is that reading much more data during reconstruction means increasing the chance of an uncorrectable read media failure, which would result in data loss. Other arguments for concern about simultaneous multiple failures are the increasing number of disks in arrays and the use of SATA disks, which are slower and have higher capacity than traditional enterprise disks.

Hence, these trends have led to a growing interest in protecting against more than one failure, and so RAID 6 is increasingly being offered as an option and being used in the field.

Which of the following are true about RAID levels 1, 3, 4, 5, and 6?

1. RAID systems rely on redundancy to achieve high availability.

2. RAID 1 (mirroring) has the highest check disk overhead.

3. For small writes, RAID 3 (bit-interleaved parity) has the worst throughput.

4. For large writes, RAID 3, 4, and 5 have the same throughput.

Check Yourself

Elaboration: One issue is how mirroring interacts with striping. Suppose you had, say, four disks' worth of data to store and eight physical disks to use. Would you create four pairs of disks—each organized as RAID 1—and then stripe data across the four RAID 1 pairs? Alternatively, would you create two sets of four disks—each organized as RAID 0—and then mirror writes to both RAID 0 sets? The RAID terminology has evolved to call the former RAID 1 + 0 or RAID 10 ("striped mirrors") and the latter RAID 0 + 1 or RAID 01 ("mirrored stripes").

6.10   Real Stuff: Sun Fire x4150 Server

In addition to the revolution in how microprocessors are constructed, we are seeing a revolution in how software is delivered. Instead of the traditional model of software sold on a CD or shipped over the Internet to be installed in your computer, the alternative is *software as a service.* That is, you go over the Internet to do your work on a computer that runs the software you want to use to provide the service that you desire. The most popular example is likely Web searching, but there are services for photo editing and storage, document processing, database storage, virtual worlds, and so on. If you looked hard, you can probably find service version of almost every program you use on your desktop computer.

This shift has led to the construction of large data centers to hold the computers and disks to run the services used by millions of external users. What should computers look like if they are designed to be placed in these large data centers? They certainly all don't need displays and keyboards. Clearly, space efficiency and power efficiency will be important if you have 10,000 of them in a datacenter, in addition to the traditional concerns of cost and performance.

The related question is what should storage look like in a datacenter? While there are many options, one popular version is to include disks with the processor and memory, and make this whole unit the building block. To overcome concerns about reliability, the application itself makes redundant copies and is responsible for keeping them consistent and recovering from failures.

The IT industry has largely agreed to some standards in the physical design of computers for the datacenter, specifically the rack used to hold the computers in the datacenter. The most popular is the 19-inch rack, which is 19 inches wide (482.6 mm). Computers designed for the rack are labeled, naturally enough, *rack mount*, but are also called a *subrack* or simply a *shelf*. Because the traditional placement of holes in which to attach the shelves is 1.75 inches (44.45 mm) apart, this distance is commonly called a *rack unit* or simply *unit* (*U*). The most popular 19-inch rack is 42 U high, which is 42 x 1.75 or 73.5 inches high. The depth of the shelf varies.

FIGURE 6.15 A standard 19-inch rack populated with 42 1U servers. This rack has 42 1U "pizza box" servers. Source: http://gchelpdesk.ualberta.ca/news/07mar06/cbhd_news_07mar06.php.

Hence, the smallest rack mount computer is 19 inches wide and 1.75 inches tall, often called 1U computers or 1U servers. Because of their dimensions, they have earned the nickname *pizza boxes*. Figure 6.15 shows an example of a standard rack populated with 42 1U servers.

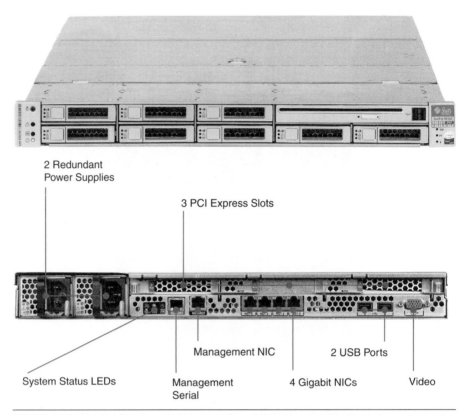

2 Redundant
Power Supplies

3 PCI Express Slots

Management NIC

2 USB Ports

System Status LEDs

Management
Serial

4 Gigabit NICs

Video

FIGURE 6.16 The front and rear of the Sun Fire x4150 1U server. The dimensions are 1.75 inches high by 19 inches wide. The eight 2.5-inch disks drives can be replaced from the front. In the upper right is a DVD and two USB ports. The picture below labels the items at the rear of the server. It has redundant power supplies and fans to allow the server to continue operating despite failures of one of these components.

Figure 6.16 shows the Sun Fire x4150, an example of a 1U server. Maximally configured, this 1U box contains:

- 8 2.66 GHz processors, spread across two sockets (2 Intel Xeon 5345)
- 64 GB of DDR2-667 DRAM, spread across 16 4GB FBDIMMs
- 8 15,000 RPM 73 GB SAS 2.5-inch disk drives
- 1 RAID controller (Supporting RAID 0, RAID 1, RAID 5, and RAID 6)
- 4 10/100/1000 Ethernet ports
- 3 PCI Express x8 ports
- 4 external and 1 internal USB 2.0 ports

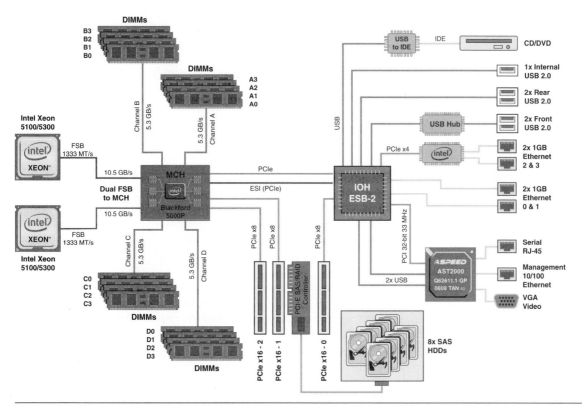

FIGURE 6.17   Logical connections and bandwidths of components in the Sun Fire x4150. The three PCIe connectors allow x16 boards to be plugged in, but it only provides eight lanes of bandwidth to the MCH. Source: Figure 5 of "SUN FIRE™ X4150 AND X4450. SERVER ARCHITECTURE" (see www.sun.com/servers/x64/x4150/).

Figure 6.17 shows the connectivity and bandwidths of the chips on the motherboard. Figures 6.9 and 6.10 describe the I/O chip set for the Intel 5345, and Figure 6.5 describes the SAS disks in the Sun Fire x4150.

To clarify the advice on designing an I/O system in Section 6.8, let's perform a simple performance evaluation to see where the bottlenecks might be for a hypothetical application.

I/O System Design

EXAMPLE

Make the following assumptions about the Sun Fire x4150:

- The user program uses 200,000 instructions per I/O operation
- The operating system averages 100,000 instructions per I/O operation

- The workload consists of 64 KB reads
- Each processor sustains 1 billion instructions per second

Find the maximum sustainable I/O rate for a fully loaded Sun Fire x4150 for random reads and sequential reads. Assume that the reads can always be done on an idle disk if one exists (i.e., ignore disk conflicts) and that the RAID controller is not the bottleneck.

ANSWER

Let's first find the I/O rate of a single processor. Each I/O takes 200,000 user instructions and 100,000 OS instructions, so

Maximum I/O rate of 1 processor =

$$\frac{\text{Instruction execution rate}}{\text{Instructions per I/O}} = \frac{1 \times 10^9}{(200 + 100) \times 10^3} = 3{,}333 \frac{\text{I/Os}}{\text{second}}$$

As a single Intel 5345 socket has four processors, it can perform 13,333 IOPS. Two sockets with eight processors can perform 26,667 IOPS.

Let's determine IOPS per disks for random and sequential reads for the 2.5-inch SAS disk described in Figure 6.5. Rather than use the average seek time from the disk manufacturer, let's assume that it is only a quarter of that time, as is often the case (see Section 6.3). The time per random read of a single disk:

$$\text{Time per I/O at disk} = \text{Seek} + \text{rotational time} + \text{Transfer time}$$

$$= \frac{2.9}{4} \text{ ms} + 2.0 \text{ ms} + \frac{64 \text{ KB}}{112 \text{ MB/sec}} = 3.3 \text{ ms}$$

Thus, each disk can complete 1000 ms/3.3 ms or 303 I/Os per second, and eight disks perform 2424 random reads per second.

For sequential reads, it's just the transfer size divided by the disk bandwidth:

$$\frac{112 \text{ MB/sec}}{64 \text{ KB}} = 1750 \text{ IOPS}$$

Eight disks can perform 14,000 sequential 64 KB reads.

We need to see if the paths from the disks to memory and the processors are a bottleneck. Let's start with the PCI Express interconnect from the RAID card to the north bridge chip. Each lane of a PCIe is 250 MB/second, so eight lanes can perform 2 GB/second.

$$\text{Max I/O rate of PCIe x8} = \frac{\text{PCI bandwidth}}{\text{Bytes per I/O}} = \frac{2 \times 10^9}{64 \times 10^3} = 31{,}250 \frac{\text{I/Os}}{\text{second}}$$

Even eight disks transferring sequentially use less than half the PCIe x8 link.

Once the data gets to the MCB, it needs to be written into the DRAM. The bandwidth of a DDR2 667 MHz FBDIMM is 5336 MB/second. A single DIMM can perform

$$\frac{5336 \text{ MB/sec}}{64 \text{ KB}} = 83{,}375 \text{ IOPS}$$

The memory is not a bottleneck even with one DIMM, and we have 16 in a fully configured Sun Fire x4150.

The final link in the chain is the Front Side Bus that connects north bridge hub to the Intel 5345 socket. Its peak bandwidth is 10.6 GB/sec, but Section 7.10 suggests you get no more than half peak. Each I/O transfers 64 KB, so

$$\text{Max I/O rate of FSB} = \frac{\text{Bus bandwidth}}{\text{Bytes per I/O}} = \frac{5.3 \times 10^9}{64 \times 10^3} = 81{,}540 \frac{\text{I/Os}}{\text{second}}$$

There is one Front Side Bus per socket, so the dual FSB peak is over 150,000 IOPS, and once again, the FSB is not a bottleneck.

Hence, a fully configured Sun Fire x4150 can sustain the peak bandwidth of the eight disks, which is 2424 random reads per second or 14,000 sequential reads per second.

Notice the significant number of simplifying assumptions that are needed to do this example. In practice, many of these simplifications might not hold for critical I/O-intensive applications. For this reason, running a realistic workload or relevant benchmark is often the only plausible way to evaluate I/O performance.

As mention at the beginning of this section, these new datacenters are concerned about power and space as well as cost and performance. Figure 6.18 shows the idle and peak power required by a fully configured Sun Fire x4150, with a breakdown by each component. Let's look at the alternative configurations of the Sun Fire x4150 to conserve power.

I/O System Power Evaluation

Reconfigure a Sun Fire x4150 to minimize power, assuming that the workload in the example above is the only activity on this 1U server.

EXAMPLE

To achieve the 2424 random 64 KB reads per second from the prior example, we need all eight disks and the PCI RAID controller. From the calculations above, a single DIMM can support over 80,000 IOPS, so we can save power in memory. The Sun Fire x4150 minimum memory is two DIMMs, so we can

ANSWER

Item	Components			System			
	Idle	Peak	Number	Idle		Peak	
Single Intel 2.66 GHz E5345 socket, Intel 5000 MCB/IOH chip set, Ethernet controllers, power supplies, fans, . . .	154 W	215 W	1	154 W	37%	215 W	39%
Additional Intel 2.66 GHz E5345 socket	22 W	79 W	1	22 W	5%	79 W	14%
4 GB DDR2-667 5300 FBDIMM	10 W	11 W	16	160 W	39%	176 W	32%
73 GB SAS 15K Disk drives	8 W	8 W	8	64 W	15%	64 W	12%
PCIe x8 RAID Disk controller	15 W	15 W	1	15 W	4%	15 W	3%
Total	—	—	—	415 W	100%	549 W	100%

FIGURE 6.18   Idle and peak power of a fully configured Sun Fire x4150. These experiments came while running SPECJBB with 29 different configurations, so the peak power could be different when running different applications (source: www.sun.com/servers/x64/x4150/calc).

save the power (and cost) of 14 4GB DIMMs. A single socket can support 13,333 IOPS, so we can also reduce the number of Intel E5345 sockets by one. Using the numbers in Figure 6.18, the total system power is now:

$$\text{Idle Power}_{\text{random reads}} = 154 + 2 \times 10 + 8 \times 8 + 15 = 253 \text{ watts}$$

$$\text{Peak Power}_{\text{random reads}} = 215 + 2 \times 11 + 8 \times 8 + 15 = 316 \text{ watts}$$

or a reduction in power by a factor of 1.6 to 1.7.

The original system can performance 14,000 64 KB sequential reads per second. We still need all the disks and the disk controller, and the same number of DIMMs can handle this higher load. This workload exceeds a processing power of the single Intel E5345 socket, so we need to add a second one.

$$\text{Idle Power}_{\text{sequential reads}} = 154 + 22 + 2 \times 10 + 8 \times 8 + 15 = 275 \text{ watts}$$

$$\text{Peak Power}_{\text{sequential reads}} = 215 + 79 + 2 \times 11 + 8 \times 8 + 15 = 395 \text{ watts}$$

or a reduction in power by a factor of 1.4 to 1.5.

6.11 Advanced Topics: Networks

Networks are growing in popularity over time, and unlike other I/O devices, there are many books and courses on them. For readers who have not taken courses or read books on networking, ⊚ Section 6.11 on the CD gives a quick overview of the topics and terminology, including Internetworking, the OSI model, protocol families such as TCP/IP, long-haul networks such as ATM, local area networks such as Ethernet, and wireless networks such as IEEE 802.11.

6.12   Fallacies and Pitfalls

Fallacy: The rated mean time to failure of disks is 1,200,000 hours or almost 140 years, so disks practically never fail.

Marketing practices of disk manufacturers have misled users. How is such an MTTF calculated? Early in the process, manufacturers will put thousands of disks in a room, run them for a few months, and count the number that fail. They compute MTTF as the total number of hours that the disks were cumulatively available divided by the number that failed.

One problem is that this number far exceeds the lifetime of a disk, which is commonly assumed to be five years or 43,800 hours. For this large MTTF to make some sense, disk manufacturers argue that the calculation corresponds to a user who buys a disk, and then keeps replacing the disk every five years—the planned lifetime of the disk. The claim is that if many customers (and their great-grandchildren) did this for the next century, on average they would replace a disk 27 times before a failure, or about 140 years.

A more useful measure would be percentage of disks that fail in a year, called annual failure rate (AFR). Assume 1000 disks with a 1,200,000-hour MTTF and that the disks are used 24 hours a day. If you replaced failed disks with a new one having the same reliability characteristics, the number that would fail per year (8,760 hours) is

$$\text{Failed disks} = \frac{1000 \text{ drives} \times 8760 \text{ hours/drive}}{1{,}200{,}000 \text{ hours/failure}} = 7.3$$

Stated alternatively, the AFR is 0.73%. Disk manufacturers are starting to quote AFR as well as MTTB to give users better intuition about what to expect about their products.

Fallacy: Disk failure rates in the field match their specifications.

Two recent studies evaluated large collections of disks to check the relationship between results in the field compared to specifications. One study was of almost 100,000 ATA and SCSI disks that had quoted MTTF of 1,000,000 to 1,500,000 hours, or AFR of 0.6% to 0.8%. They found AFRs of 2% to 4% to be common, often three to five times higher than the specified rates [Schroeder and Gibson, 2007].

A second study of more than 100,000 ATA disks, which had a quoted AFR of about 1.5%, saw failure rates of 1.7% for drives in their first year rise to 8.6% for drives in their third year, or about five to six times the specified rate [Pinheiro, Weber, and Barroso, 2007].

Fallacy: A GB/sec interconnect can transfer 1 GB of data in 1 second.

First, you generally cannot use 100% of any computer resource. For a bus, you would be fortunate to get 70% to 80% of the peak bandwidth. Time to send the address, time to acknowledge the signals, and stalls while waiting to use a busy bus are among the reasons you cannot use 100% of a bus.

Second, the definition of a gigabyte of storage and a gigabyte per second of bandwidth do not agree. As we discussed on page 596, I/O bandwidth measures are usually quoted in base 10 (i.e., 1 GB/sec = 10^9 bytes/sec), while 1 GB of data is typically a base 2 measure (i.e., 1 GB = 2^{30} bytes). How significant is this distinction? If we could use 100% of the bus for data transfer, the time to transfer 1 GB of data on a 1 GB/sec interconnect is actually

$$\frac{2^{30}}{10^9} = \frac{1,073,741,824}{1,000,000,000} = 1.073741824 \approx 1.07 \text{ seconds}$$

Pitfall: Trying to provide features only within the network versus end to end.

The concern is providing at a lower-level features that can only be accomplished at the highest level, thus only partially satisfying the communication demand. Saltzer, Reed, and Clark [1984] give the *end-to-end argument,* as follows:

> *The function in question can completely and correctly be specified only with the knowledge and help of the application standing at the endpoints of the communication system. Therefore, providing that questioned function as a feature of the communication system itself is not possible.*

Their example of the pitfall was a network at MIT that used several gateways, each of which added a checksum from one gateway to the next. The programmers of the application assumed the checksum guaranteed accuracy, incorrectly believing that the message was protected while stored in the memory of each gateway. One gateway developed a transient failure that swapped one pair of bytes per million bytes transferred. Over time the source code of one operating system was repeatedly passed through the gateway, thereby corrupting the code. The only solution was to correct the infected source files by comparing to paper listings and repairing the code by hand! Had the checksums been calculated and checked by the application running on the end systems, safety would have been assured.

There is a useful role for intermediate checks, however, provided that end-to-end checking is available. End-to-end checking may show that *something* is broken between two nodes, but it doesn't point to where the problem is. Intermediate checks can discover *which component* is broken. You need both for repair.

Pitfall: Moving functions from the CPU to the I/O processor, expecting to improve performance without a careful analysis.

There are many examples of this pitfall trapping people, although I/O processors, when properly used, can certainly enhance performance. A frequent instance of this fallacy is the use of intelligent I/O interfaces, which, because of the higher overhead to set up an I/O request, can turn out to have worse latency than a processor-directed I/O activity (although if the processor is freed up sufficiently, system throughput may still increase). Frequently, performance falls when the I/O processor has much lower performance than the main processor. Consequently, a small amount of main processor time is replaced with a larger amount of I/O processor time. Workstation designers have seen both these phenomena repeatedly.

Myer and Sutherland [1968] wrote a classic paper on the tradeoff of complexity and performance in I/O controllers. Borrowing the religious concept of the "wheel of reincarnation," they eventually noticed they were caught in a loop of continuously increasing the power of an I/O processor until it needed its own simpler coprocessor:

We approached the task by starting with a simple scheme and then adding commands and features that we felt would enhance the power of the machine. Gradually the [display] processor became more complex . . . . Finally the display processor came to resemble a full-fledged computer with some special graphics features. And then a strange thing happened. We felt compelled to add to the processor a second, subsidiary processor, which, itself, began to grow in complexity. It was then that we discovered the disturbing truth. Designing a display processor can become a never-ending cyclical process. In fact, we found the process so frustrating that we have come to call it the "wheel of reincarnation."

Pitfall: Using magnetic tapes to back up disks.

This is both a fallacy and a pitfall. Magnetic tapes have been part of computer systems as long as disks because they use similar technology as disks, and hence historically have followed the same density improvements. The historic cost/performance difference between disks and tapes is based on a sealed, rotating disk having lower access time than sequential tape access; but removable spools of magnetic tape mean many tapes can be used per reader, and they can be very long and so have high capacity. Hence, in the past a single magnetic tape could hold the contents of many disks, and since it was 10 to 100 times cheaper per gigabyte than disks, it was a useful backup medium.

The claim was that magnetic tapes must track disks since innovations in disks must help tapes. This claim was important because tapes were a small market and could not afford a separate large research and development effort. One reason the market is small is that desktop owners generally do not back up disks onto tape, and so while desktops are by far the largest market for disks, desktops are a small market for tapes.

Alas, the larger market has led disks to improve much more quickly than tapes. Starting in 2000 to 2002, the largest popular disk was larger than the largest popular tape. In that same time frame, the price per gigabyte of ATA disks dropped below that of tapes. Tape advocates claim that tapes have compatibility requirements that are not imposed on disks; tape readers must read or write the current and previous generation of tapes, and must read the last four generations of tapes. As disks are closed systems, disk heads need only read the platters enclosed with them, and this advantage explains why disks are improving much more rapidly.

Today, some organizations have dropped tapes altogether, using networks and remote disks to replicate the data geographically. Indeed, many companies offering software as a service use inexpensive components but replicate data at an application level across multiples sites. The sites are picked so that disasters would not take out both sites, enabling instantaneous recovery time. (Long recovery time for site disasters is another serious drawback to the serial nature of magnetic tapes.) Such a solution depends on advances in disk capacity and network bandwidth to make economic sense, but these two are getting much greater investment and hence have better recent records of accomplishment than tape.

Fallacy: Operating systems are the best place to schedule disk accesses.

As mentioned in Section 6.3, higher-level interfaces like ATA and SCSI offer logical block addresses to the host operating system. Given this high-level abstraction, the best an OS can do to try to help performance is to sort the logical block addresses into increasing order. However, since the disk knows the actual mapping of the logical addresses onto the physical geometry of sectors, tracks, and surfaces, it can reduce the rotational and seek latencies by rescheduling.

For example, suppose the workload is four reads [Anderson, 2003]:

Operation	Starting LBA	Length
Read	724	8
Read	100	16
Read	9987	1
Read	26	128

The host might reorder the four reads into logical block order:

Operation	Starting LBA	Length
Read	26	128
Read	100	16
Read	724	8
Read	9987	1

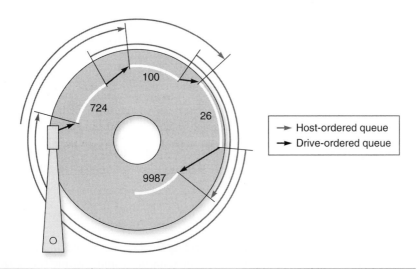

FIGURE 6.19   Example showing OS versus disk schedule accesses, labeled host-ordered versus drive-ordered. The former takes three revolutions to complete the four reads, while the latter completes them in just three-fourths of a revolution (from Anderson [2003]).

Depending on the relative location of the data on the disk, reordering could make it worse, as Figure 6.19 shows. The disk-scheduled reads complete in three-quarters of a disk revolution, but the OS-scheduled reads take three revolutions.

Pitfall: Using the peak transfer rate of a portion of the I/O system to make performance projections or performance comparisons.

Many of the components of an I/O system, from the devices to the controllers to the buses, are specified using their peak bandwidths. In practice, these peak bandwidth measurements are often based on unrealistic assumptions about the system or are unattainable because of other system limitations. For example, in quoting bus performance, the peak transfer rate is sometimes specified using a memory system that is impossible to build. For networked systems, the software overhead of initiating communication is ignored.

The 32-bit, 33MHz PCI bus has a peak bandwidth of about 133 MB/sec. In practice, even for long transfers, it is difficult to sustain more than about 80 MB/sec for realistic memory systems.

Amdahl's law also reminds us that the throughput of an I/O system will be limited by the lowest-performance component in the I/O path.

6.13   Concluding Remarks

I/O systems are evaluated on several different characteristics: dependability; the variety of I/O devices supported; the maximum number of I/O devices; cost; and performance, measured both in latency and in throughput. These goals lead to widely varying schemes for interfacing I/O devices. In the low-end and midrange systems, buffered DMA is likely to be the dominant transfer mechanism. In the high-end systems, latency and bandwidth may both be important, and cost may be secondary. Multiple paths to I/O devices with limited buffering often characterize high-end I/O systems. Typically, being able to access the data on an I/O device at any time (high availability) becomes more important as systems grow. As a result, redundancy and error correction mechanisms become more and more prevalent as we enlarge the system.

Storage and networking demands are growing at unprecedented rates, in part because of increasing demands for all information to be at your fingertips. One estimate is that the amount of information created in 2002 was 5 exabytes—equivalent to 500,000 copies of the text in the U.S. Library of Congress—and that the total amount of information in the world was doubling every three years [Lyman and Varian, 2003].

Future directions of I/O include expanding the reach of wired and wireless networks, with nearly every device potentially having an IP address, and the expanding role of flash memory in storage systems.

Understanding Program Performance

The performance of an I/O system, whether measured by bandwidth or latency, depends on all the elements in the path between the device and memory, including the operating system that generates the I/O commands. The bandwidth of the interconnect, the memory, and the device determine the maximum transfer rate from or to the device. Similarly, the latency depends on the device latency, together with any latency imposed by the memory system or buses. The effective bandwidth and response latency also depend on other I/O requests that may cause contention for some resource in the path. Finally, the operating system is a bottleneck. In some cases, the OS takes a long time to deliver an I/O request from a user program to an I/O device, leading to high latency. In other cases, the operating system effectively limits the I/O bandwidth because of limitations in the number of concurrent I/O operations it can support.

Keep in mind that while performance can help sell an I/O system, users overwhelmingly demand capacity and dependability from their I/O systems.

6.14 Historical Perspective and Further Reading

The history of I/O systems is a fascinating one. ◎ Section 6.14 gives a brief history of magnetic disks, RAID, flash memory, databases, the Internet, the World Wide Web, and how Ethernet continues to triumph over its challengers.

6.15 Exercises

Contributed by Perry Alexander of the University of Kansas

Exercise 6.1

Figure 6.2 describes numerous I/O devices in terms of their behavior, partner, and data rate. However, these classifications often do not provide a complete picture of data flow within a system. Explore device classifications for the following devices.

a.	Auto Pilot
b.	Automated Thermostat

6.1.1 [5] <6.1> For the devices listed in the table, identify I/O interfaces and classify them in terms of their behavior and partner.

6.1.2 [5] <6.1> For the interfaces identified in the previous problem, estimate their data rate.

6.1.3 [5] <6.1> For the interfaces identified in the previous problem, determine whether data rate or operation rate is the best performance measurement.

Exercise 6.2

Mean Time Between Failures (MTBF), Mean Time To Replacement (MTTR), and Mean Time To Failure (MTTF) are useful metrics for evaluating the reliability and availability of a storage resource. Explore these concepts by answering the questions about devices with the following metrics.

	MTTF	MTTR
a.	3 Years	1 Day
b.	7 Years	3 Days

6.2.1 [5] <6.1, 6.2> Calculate the MTBF for each of the devices in the table.

6.2.2 [5] <6.1, 6.2> Calculate the availability for each of the devices in the table.

6.2.3 [5] <6.1, 6.2> What happens to availability as the MTTR approaches 0? Is this a realistic situation?

6.2.4 [5] <6.1, 6.2> What happens to availability as the MTTR gets very high, i.e., a device is difficult to repair? Does this imply the device has low availability?

Exercise 6.3

Average and minimum times for reading and writing to storage devices are common measurements used to compare devices. Using techniques from Chapter 6, calculate values related to read and write time for disks with the following characteristics.

	Average Seek Time	RPM	Disk Transfer Rate	Controller Transfer Rate
a.	10 ms	7500	90 MB/s	100 MB/s
b.	7 ms	10,000	40 MB/s	200 MB/s

6.3.1 [10] <6.2, 6.3> Calculate the average time to read or write a 1024-byte sector for each disk listed in the table.

6.3.2 [10] <6.2, 6.3> Calculate the minimum time to read or write a 2048-byte sector for each disk listed in the table.

6.3.3 [10] <6.2, 6.3> For each disk in the table, determine the dominant factor for performance. Specifically, if you could make an improvement to any aspect of the disk, what would you choose? If there is no dominant factor, explain why.

Exercise 6.4

Ultimately, storage system design requires consideration of usage scenarios as well as disk parameters. Different situations require different metrics. Let's try to systematically evaluate disk systems. Explore differences in how storage systems should be evaluated by answering the questions about the following applications.

a.	Aircraft Control System
b.	Phone Switch

6.4.1 [5] <6.2, 6.3> For each application, would decreasing the sector size during reads and writes improve performance? Explain your answer.

6.4.2 [5] <6.2, 6.3> For each application, would increasing disk rotation speed improve performance? Explain your answer.

6.4.3 [5] <6.2, 6.3> For each application, would increasing disk rotation speed improve system performance given that MTTF is decreased? Explain your answer.

Exercise 6.5

FLASH memory is one of the first true competitors for traditional disk drives. Explore the implications of FLASH memory by answering questions about the following applications.

a.	Aircraft Control System
b.	Phone Switch

6.5.1 [5] <6.2, 6.3, 6.4> As we move towards solid state drives constructed from FLASH memory, what will change about disk read times assuming that the data transfer rate stays constant?

6.5.2 [10] <6.2, 6.3, 6.4> Would each application benefit from a solid state FLASH drive given that cost is a design factor?

6.5.3 [10] <6.2, 6.3, 6.4> Would each application be inappropriate for a solid state FLASH drive given that cost is NOT a design factor?

Exercise 6.6

Explore the nature of FLASH memory by answering the questions related to performance for FLASH memories with the following characteristics.

	Data Transfer Rate	Controller Transfer Rate
a.	120 MB/s	100 MB/s
b.	100 MB/s	90 MB/s

6.6.1 [10] <6.2, 6.3, 6.4> Calculate the average time to read or write a 1024-byte sector for each FLASH memory listed in the table.

6.6.2 [10] <6.2, 6.3, 6.4> Calculate the minimum time to read or write a 512-byte sector for each FLASH memory listed in the table.

6.6.3 [5] <6.2, 6.3, 6.4> Figure 6.6 shows that FLASH memory read and write access times increase as FLASH memory gets larger. Is this unexpected? What factors cause this?

Exercise 6.7

I/O can be performed either synchronously or asynchronously. Explore the differences by answering performance questions about the following peripherals.

a.	Printer
b.	Scanner

6.7.1 [5] <6.5> What would be the most appropriate bus type (synchronous or asynchronous) for handling communications between a CPU and the peripherals listed in the table?

6.7.2 [5] <6.5> What problems would long, synchronous busses cause for connections between a CPU and the peripherals listed in the table?

6.7.3 [5] <6.5> What problems would asynchronous busses cause for connections between a CPU and the peripherals listed in the table?

Exercise 6.8

Among the most common bus types used in practice today are FireWire (IEEE 1394), USB, PCI, and SATA. Although all four are asynchronous, they are implemented in different ways giving them different characteristics. Explore different bus structures by answering questions about the busses and the following peripherals.

a.	Mouse
b.	Graphics Coprocessor

6.8.1 [5] <6.5> Select an appropriate bus (FireWire, USB, PCI, or SATA) for the peripherals listed in the table. Explain why the bus selected is appropriate. (See Figure 6.8 for key characteristics of each bus.)

6.8.2 [20] <6.5> Use online or library resources and summarize the communication structure for each bus type. Identify what the bus controller does and where the control physically is.

6.8.3 [15] <6.5> Outline limitations of each of the bus types. Explain why those limitations must be taken into consideration when using the bus.

Exercise 6.9

Communicating with I/O devices is achieved using combinations of polling, interrupt handling, memory mapping, and special I/O commands. Answer the questions about communicating with I/O subsystems for the following applications using combinations of these techniques.

a.	Auto Pilot
b.	Automated Thermostat

6.9.1 [5] <6.6> Describe device polling. Would each application in the table be appropriate for communication using polling techniques? Explain.

6.9.2 [5] <6.6> Describe interrupt driven communication. For each application in the table, if polling is inappropriate, explain how interrupt driven techniques could be used.

6.9.3 [10] <6.6> For the applications listed in the table, outline a design for memory mapped communication. Identify reserved memory locations and outline their contents.

6.9.4 [10] <6.6> For the applications listed in the table, outline a design for commands implementing command driven communication. Identify commands and their interaction with the device.

6.9.5 [5] <6.6> Does it make sense to define I/O subsystems that use a combination of memory mapping and command driven communication? Explain your answer.

Exercise 6.10

Section 6.6 defines an eight-step process for handling interrupts. The Cause and Status registers together provide information on the cause of the interrupt and the status of the interrupt handling system. Explore interrupt handling by answering the questions about the following combinations of interrupts.

a.	Ethernet Controller Data	Mouse Controller	Reboot
b.	Mouse Controller	Power Down	Overheat

6.10.1 [5] <6.6> When an interrupt is detected, the Status register is saved and all but the highest priority interrupt is disabled. Why are low-priority interrupts disabled? Why is the status register saved prior to disabling interrupts?

6.10.2 [10] <6.6> Prioritize interrupts from the devices listed in each table row.

6.10.3 [10] <6.6> Outline how an interrupt from each of the devices listed in the table would be handled.

6.10.4 [5] <6.6> What happens if the interrupt enable bit of the Cause register is not set when handling an interrupt? What value could the interrupt mask value take to accomplish the same thing?

6.10.5 [5] <6.6> Most interrupt handling systems are implemented in the operating system. What hardware support could be added to make interrupt handling more efficient? Contrast your solution to potential hardware support for function calls.

6.10.6 [5] <6.6> In some interrupt handling implementations, an interrupt causes an immediate jump to an interrupt vector. Instead of a Cause register where each interrupt sets a bit, each interrupt has its own interrupt vector. Can the same priority interrupt system be implemented using this approach? Is there any advantage to this approach?

Exercise 6.11

Direct Memory Access (DMA) allows devices to access memory directly rather than working through the CPU. This can dramatically speed up the performance of peripherals, but adds complexity to memory system implementations. Explore DMA implications by answering the questions about the following peripherals.

a.	Mouse Controller
b.	Ethernet Controller

6.11.1 [5] <6.6> Does the CPU relinquish control of memory when DMA is active? For example, can a peripheral simply communicate with memory directly, avoiding the CPU completely?

6.11.2 [10] <6.6> Of the peripherals listed in the table, which would benefit from DMA? What criteria determine if DMA is appropriate?

6.11.3 [10] <6.6> Of the peripherals listed in the table, which could cause coherency problems with cache contents? What criteria determine if coherency issues must be addressed?

6.11.4 [5] <6.6> Describe what problems could occur when mixing DMA and virtual memory. Which of the peripherals in the table could introduce such problems? How can they be avoided?

Exercise 6.12

Metrics for I/O performance may vary dramatically from application to application. Where the number of transactions processed dominates performance in some situations, data throughput dominates in others. Explore I/O performance evaluation by answering the questions for the following applications.

a.	Mathematical Computations
b.	Online Chat

6.12.1 [10] <6.7> For each application in the table, does I/O performance dominate system performance?

6.12.2 [10] <6.7> For each application in the table, is I/O performance best measured using raw data throughput?

6.12.3 [5] <6.7> For each application in the table, is I/O performance best measured using the number of transactions processed?

6.12.4 [5] <6.7> Is there a relationship between the performance measures from the previous two problems and choosing whether to use polling or interrupt driven communication? What about the choice of using memory mapped or command driven I/O?

Exercise 6.13

Benchmarks play an important role in evaluating and selecting peripheral devices. For benchmarks to be useful, they must exhibit properties similar to those experienced by a device under normal use. Explore benchmarks and device selection by answering questions about the following applications.

a.	Mathematical Computations
b.	Online Chat

6.13.1 [5] <6.7> For each application in the table, define characteristics that a set of benchmarks should exhibit when evaluating an I/O subsystem.

6.13.2 [15] <6.7> Using online or library resources, identify a set of standard benchmarks for applications in the table. Why do standard benchmarks help?

6.13.3 [5] <6.7> Does it make sense to evaluate an I/O subsystem outside the larger system it is a part of? How about evaluating a CPU?

Exercise 6.14

RAID is among the most popular approaches to parallelism and redundancy in storage systems. The name Redundant Arrays of Inexpensive Disks implies several things about RAID arrays that we will explore in the context of the following activities.

a.	High-Performance Mathematical Computations
b.	Online Video Services

6.14.1 [10] <6.9> RAID 0 uses striping to force parallel access among many disks. Why does striping improve disk performance? For each of the activities listed in the table, will striping help better achieve their goals?

6.14.2 [5] <6.9> RAID 1 mirrors data among several disks. Assuming that inexpensive disks have lower MTBF than expensive disks, how can redundancy using inexpensive disks result in a system with lower MTBF? Use the mathematical definition of MTBF to explain your answer. For each of the activities listed in the table, will RAID 1 help better achieve their goals?

6.14.3 [5] <6.9> Like RAID 1, RAID 3 provides higher data availability. Explain the trade-off between RAID 1 and RAID 3. Would each of the applications listed in the table benefit from RAID 3 over RAID 1?

Exercise 6.15

RAID 3, RAID 4, and RAID 5 all use parity system to protect blocks of data. Specifically, a parity block is associated with a collection of data blocks. Each row in the following table shows the values of the data and parity blocks, as described in Figure 6.13.

	New D0	**D0**	**D1**	**D2**	**D3**	**P**
a.	7453	AB9C	AABB	0098	549C	2FFF
b.	F245	7453	DD25	AABB	FEFE	FEFF

6.15.1 [10] <6.9> Calculate the new RAID 3 parity value P' for data in lines a and b in the table.

6.15.2 [10] <6.9> Calculate the new RAID 4 parity value P' for data in lines a and b in the table.

6.15.3 [5] <6.9> Is RAID 3 or RAID 4 more efficient? Are there reasons why RAID 3 would be preferable to RAID 4?

6.15.4 [5] <6.9> RAID 4 and RAID 5 use roughly the same mechanism to calculate and store parity for data blocks. How does RAID 5 differ from RAID 4 and for what applications would RAID 5 be more efficient?

6.15.5 [5] <6.9> RAID 4 and RAID 5 speed improvements grow with respect to RAID 3 as the size of the protected block grows. Why is this the case? Is there a situation where RAID 4 and RAID 5 would be no more efficient than RAID 3?

Exercise 6.16

The emergence of web servers for ecommerce, online storage, and communication has made disk servers critical applications. Availability and speed are well-known metrics for disk servers, but power consumption is becoming increasingly important. Answer the questions about configuration and evaluation of disk servers with the following parameters.

	Program Instructions/ I/O Operation	OS Instructions/ I/O Operation	Workload (KB reads)	Processor Speed (Instructions/ Second)
a.	100,000	150,000	64	2 Billion
b.	200,000	200,000	128	3 Billion

6.16.1 [10] <6.8, 6.10> Find the maximum sustained I/O rate for random reads and writes. Ignore disk conflicts and assume the RAID controller is not the bottleneck. Follow the same approach as outlined in Section 6.10 making similar assumptions where necessary.

6.16.2 [10] <6.8, 6.10> Assume we are configuring a Sun Fire x4150 server as described in Section 6.10. Determine if a configuration of 8 disks presents an I/O bottleneck. Repeat for configurations of 16, 4, and 2 disks.

6.16.3 [10] <6.8, 6.10> Determine if the PCI bus, DIMM, or the Front Side Bus presents an I/O bottleneck. Use the same parameters and assumptions used in Section 6.10.

6.16.4 [5] <6.8, 6.10> Explain why real systems tend to use benchmarks or real applications to assess actual performance.

Exercise 6.17

Determining the performance of a single server with relatively complete data is an easy task. However, when comparing servers from different vendors providing different data, choosing among alternatives can be difficult. Explore the process of finding and evaluating servers by answering questions about the following application.

Database Server

6.17.1 [15] <6.8, 6.10> For the application listed above, identify runtime characteristics for an operational system. Choose characteristics that will support evaluation similar to that performed for Exercise 6.16.

6.17.2 [15] <6.8, 6.10> For the application listed above, find a server available in the marketplace that you feel would be appropriate for running the application. Before evaluating the server, identify reasons why it was selected.

6.17.3 [20] <6.8, 6.10> Using metrics similar to those used in Chapter 6 and Exercise 6.16, assess the server you identified in 6.17.2 in comparison to the Sun Fire x4150 server evaluated in Exercise 6.16. Which would you choose? Did the results of your analysis surprise you? Specifically, would you choose differently?

6.17.4 [15] <6.8, 6.10> Identify a standard benchmark set that would be useful for comparing the server you identified in 6.17.2 with the Sun Fire x4150.

Exercise 6.18

Measurements and statistics provided by storage vendors must be carefully interpreted to gain meaningful predictions about their system behavior. The following table provides data for various disk drives.

	# of Drives	Hours/Drive	Hours/Failure
a.	1000	10,512	1,200,000
b.	1250	8760	1,200,000

6.18.1 [10] <6.12> Calculate annual failure rate (AFR) for disks in the table.

6.18.2 [10] <6.12> Assume that annual failure rate varies over the lifetime of disks in the previous table. Specifically, assume that AFR is three times as high in the 1st month of operation and doubles every year starting in the 5th year. How many disks would be replaced after 7 years of operation? What about 10 years?

6.18.3 [10] <6.12> Assume that disks with lower failure rates are more expensive. Specifically, disks are available at a higher cost that will start doubling their failure rate in year 8 rather than year 5. How much more would you pay for disks if your intent is to keep them for 7 years? What about 10 years?

Exercise 6.19

For disks in the table in Exercise 6.18, assume that your vendor offers a RAID 0 configuration that will increase storage system throughput by 70% and a RAID 1 configuration that will drop AFR of disk pairs by 2. Assume that the cost of each solution is 1.6 times the original solution cost.

6.19.1 [5] <6.9, 6.12> Given only the original problem parameters, would you recommend upgrading to either RAID 0 or RAID 1 assuming individual disk parameters remain the same in the previous table?

6.19.2 [5] <6.9, 6.12> Given that your company operates a global search engine with a large disk farm, does upgrading to either RAID 0 or RAID 1 make economic sense given that your income model is based on the number of advertisements served?

6.19.3 [5] <6.9, 6.12> Repeat 6.19.2 for a large disk farm operated by an online backup company. Does upgrading to either RAID 0 or RAID 1 make economic sense given that your income model is based on the availability of your server?

Exercise 6.20

Day-to-day evaluation and maintenance of operational computer systems involves many of the concepts discussed in Chapter 6. Explore the intricacies of evaluating systems by exploring the following questions.

6.20.1 [20] <6.10, 6.12> Configure the Sun Fire x4150 to provide 10 terabytes of storage for a processor array of 1000 processors running bioinformatics simulations. Your configuration should minimize power consumption while addressing throughput and availability concerns for the disk array. Make sure you consider the properties of large simulations when performing your configuration.

6.20.2 [20] <6.10, 6.12> Recommend a backup and data archiving system for the disk array from 6.20.1. Compare and contrast disk, tape, and online backup capabilities. Use Internet and library resources to identify potential servers. Assess cost and suitability for the application using parameters described in Chapter 6. Select parameters for comparison using properties of the application as well as specified requirements.

6.20.3 [15] <6.10, 6.12> Competing vendors for the systems you identified in 6.20.2 have offered to allow you to evaluate their systems on site. Identify the benchmarks you will use to determine which system is best for your application. Determine how long it will take you to gather enough data to make your determination.

§6.2, page 575: 2 and 3 are true.
§6.3, page 579: 3 and 4 are true.
§6.4, page 582: All are true (assuming 40 MB/s is comparable to 100 MB/s).
§6.5, page 585: 1 is true.
§6.6, page 594: 1 and 2.
§6.7, page 598: 1 and 2. 3 is false, since most TPC benchmarks include cost.
§6.9, page 605: All are true.

**Answers to
Check Yourself**

Multicores, Multiprocessors, and Clusters

There are finer fish in the sea than have ever been caught.

Irish proverb

Multiprocessor or Cluster Organization

Computer

Computer

Network

Computer

Computer

multiprocessor A computer system with at least two processors. This is in contrast to a **uniprocessor**, which has one.

job-level parallelism or **process-level parallelism** Utilizing multiple processors by running independent programs simultaneously.

parallel processing program A single program that runs on multiple processors simultaneously.

cluster A set of computers connected over a local area network (LAN) that functions as a single large multiprocessor.

multicore microprocessor A microprocessor containing multiple processors ("**cores**") in a single integrated circuit.

7.1 Introduction

Computer architects have long sought the El Dorado of computer design: to create powerful computers simply by connecting many existing smaller ones. This golden vision is the fountainhead of **multiprocessors**. Ideally, customers order as many processors as they can afford and receive a commensurate amount of performance. Thus, multiprocessor software must be designed to work with a variable number of processors. As mentioned in Chapter 1, power has become the overriding issue for both datacenters and microprocessors. Replacing large inefficient processors with many smaller, efficient processors can deliver better performance per watt or per joule both in the large and in the small, if software can efficiently use them. Thus, improved power efficiency joins scalable performance in the case for multiprocessors.

Since multiprocessor software must scale, some designs support operation in the presence of broken hardware; that is, if a single processor fails in a multiprocessor with n processors, these system would continue to provide service with $n - 1$ processors. Hence, multiprocessors can also improve availability (see Chapter 6).

High performance can mean high throughput for independent jobs, called **job-level parallelism** or **process-level parallelism**. These parallel jobs are independent applications, and they are an important and popular use of parallel computers. This approach is in contrast to running a single job on multiple processors. We use the term **parallel processing program** to refer to a single program that runs on multiple processors simultaneously.

There have long been scientific problems that have needed much faster computers, and this class of problems has been used to justify many novel parallel computers over the past decades. We will cover several of them in this chapter. Some of these problems can be handled simply, using a **cluster** composed of microprocessors housed in many independent servers or PCs. In addition, clusters can serve equally demanding applications outside the sciences, such as search engines, Web servers, email servers, and databases.

As described in Chapter 1, multiprocessors have been shoved into the spotlight because the power problem means that future increases in performance will apparently come from more processors per chip rather than higher clock rates and improved CPI. They are called **multicore microprocessors** instead of multiprocessor microprocessors, presumably to avoid redundancy in naming. Hence, processors are often called **cores** in a multicore chip. The number of cores is expected to double every two years. Thus, programmers who care about performance must become parallel programmers, for sequential programs mean slow programs.

The tall challenge facing the industry is to create hardware and software that will make it easy to write correct parallel processing programs that will execute efficiently in performance and power as the number of cores per chip scales geometrically.

This sudden shift in microprocessor design has caught many off guard, so there is a great deal of confusion about the terminology and what it means. Figure 7.1 tries to clarify the terms serial, parallel, sequential, and concurrent. The columns of this figure represent the software, which is either inherently sequential or concurrent. The rows of the figure represent the hardware, which is either serial or parallel. For example, the programmers of compilers think of them as sequential programs: the steps are lexical analysis, parsing, code generation, optimization, and so on. In contrast, the programmers of operating systems normally think of them as concurrent programs: cooperating processes handling I/O events due to independent jobs running on a computer.

		Software	
		Sequential	**Concurrent**
Hardware	Serial	Matrix Multiply written in MatLab running on an Intel Pentium 4	Windows Vista Operating System running on an Intel Pentium 4
	Parallel	Matrix Multiply written in MATLAB running on an Intel Xeon e5345 (Clovertown)	Windows Vista Operating System running on an Intel Xeon e5345 (Clovertown)

FIGURE 7.1 Hardware/software categorization and examples of application perspective on concurrency versus hardware perspective on parallelism.

The point of these two axes of Figure 7.1 is that concurrent software can run on serial hardware, such as operating systems for the Intel Pentium 4 uniprocessor, or on parallel hardware, such as an OS on the more recent Intel Xeon e5345 (Clovertown). The same is true for sequential software. For example, the MATLAB programmer writes a matrix multiply thinking about it sequentially, but it could run serially on Pentium 4 hardware or in parallel on Xeon e5345 hardware. You might guess that the only challenge of the parallel revolution is figuring out how to make naturally sequential software have high performance on parallel hardware, but it is also to make concurrent programs have high performance on multiprocessors as the number of processors increases. With this distinction made, in the rest of this chapter we will use *parallel processing program* or *parallel software* to mean either sequential or concurrent software running on parallel hardware.

The next section describes why it is hard to create efficient parallel processing programs. Sections 7.3 and 7.4 describe the two alternatives of a fundamental parallel hardware characteristic, which is whether or not all the processors in the systems rely upon a single physical address. The two popular versions of these alternatives are called *shared memory multiprocessors* and *clusters*. Section 7.5 then describes *multithreading*, a term often confused with multiprocessing, in part because it relies upon similar concurrency in programs. Section 7.6 describes an older classification scheme than in Figure 7.1. In addition, it describes two styles of instruction set architectures that support running of sequential applications on parallel hardware, namely *SIMD* and *vector*. Section 7.7 describes a relatively new style of computer from the graphics hardware community, called a *graphics processing unit* (*GPU*). Appendix A describes GPUs in more detail. We next discuss the difficulty of finding parallel benchmarks in Section 7.9. This section is followed by a description of a new, simple, yet insightful performance model that helps in the design of applications as well as architectures. We use this model in Section 7.11 to evaluate four recent multicore computers on two application kernels. We close with fallacies and pitfalls and our conclusions for parallelism.

Before proceeding further down the path to parallelism, don't forget our initial incursions from the prior chapters:

- Chapter 2, Section 2.11: Parallelism and Instructions: Synchronization

- Chapter 3, Section 3.6: Parallelism and Computer Arithmetic: Associativity

- Chapter 4, Section 4.10: Parallelism and Advanced Instruction-Level Parallelism

- Chapter 5, Section 5.8: Parallelism and Memory Hierarchies: Cache Coherence

- Chapter 6, Section 6.9: Parallelism and I/O: Redundant Arrays of Inexpensive Disks

Check Yourself   True or false: To benefit from a multiprocessor, an application must be concurrent.

7.2   The Difficulty of Creating Parallel Processing Programs

The difficulty with parallelism is not the hardware; it is that too few important application programs have been rewritten to complete tasks sooner on multiprocessors. It is difficult to write software that uses multiple processors to complete one task faster, and the problem gets worse as the number of processors increases.

Why has this been so? Why have parallel processing programs been so much harder to develop than sequential programs?

The first reason is that you *must* get better performance and efficiency from a parallel processing program on a multiprocessor; otherwise, you would just use a sequential program on a uniprocessor, as programming is easier. In fact, uniprocessor design techniques such as superscalar and out-of-order execution take advantage of instruction-level parallelism (see Chapter 4), normally without the involvement of the programmer. Such innovations reduced the demand for rewriting programs for multiprocessors, since programmers could do nothing and yet their sequential programs would run faster on new computers.

Why is it difficult to write parallel processing programs that are fast, especially as the number of processors increases? In Chapter 1, we used the analogy of eight reporters trying to write a single story in hopes of doing the work eight times faster. To succeed, the task must be broken into eight equal-sized pieces, because otherwise some reporters would be idle while waiting for the ones with larger pieces to finish. Another performance danger would be that the reporters would spend too much time communicating with each other instead of writing their pieces of the story. For both this analogy and parallel programming, the challenges include scheduling, load balancing, time for synchronization, and overhead for communication between the parties. The challenge is stiffer with the more reporters for a newspaper story and the more processors for parallel programming.

Our discussion in Chapter 1 reveals another obstacle, namely Amdahl's law. It reminds us that even small parts of a program must be parallelized if the program is to make good use of many cores.

Speed-up Challenge

Suppose you want to achieve a speed-up of 90 times faster with 100 processors. What percentage of the original computation can be sequential?

EXAMPLE

ANSWER

Amdahl's law (Chapter 1) says

Execution time after improvement =

$$\frac{\text{Execution time affected by improvement}}{\text{Amount of improvement}} + \text{Execution time unaffected}$$

We can reformulate Amdahl's in terms of speed-up versus the original execution time:

$$\text{Speed-up} = \frac{\text{Execution time before}}{(\text{Execution time before} - \text{Execution time affected}) + \dfrac{\text{Execution time affected}}{100}}$$

This formula is usually rewritten assuming that the execution time before is 1 for some unit of time, and the execution time affected by improvement is considered the fraction of the original execution time:

$$\text{Speed-up} = \frac{1}{(1 - \text{Fraction time affected}) + \dfrac{\text{Fraction time affected}}{100}}$$

Substituting for the goal of a speed-up of 90 into the formula above:

$$90 = \frac{1}{(1 - \text{Fraction time affected}) + \dfrac{\text{Fraction time affected}}{100}}$$

Then simplifying the formula and solving for fraction time affected:

$$90 \times (1 - 0.99 \times \text{Fraction time affected}) = 1$$

$$90 - (90 \times 0.99 \times \text{Fraction time affected}) = 1$$

$$90 - 1 = 90 \times 0.99 \times \text{Fraction time affected}$$

$$\text{Fraction time affected} = 89/89.1 = 0.999$$

Thus, to achieve a speed-up of 90 from 100 processors, the sequential percentage can only be 0.1%.

Yet, there are applications with substantial parallelism.

Speed-up Challenge: Bigger Problem

EXAMPLE

Suppose you want to perform two sums: one is a sum of 10 scalar variables, and one is a matrix sum of a pair of two-dimensional arrays, with dimensions 10 by 10. What speed-up do you get with 10 versus 100 processors? Next, calculate the speed-ups assuming the matrices grow to 100 by 100.

ANSWER

If we assume performance is a function of the time for an addition, t, then there are 10 additions that do not benefit from parallel processors and 100 additions that do. If the time for a single processor is $110t$, the execution time for 10 processors is

$$\text{Execution time after improvement} =$$

$$\frac{\text{Execution time affected by improvement}}{\text{Amount of improvement}} + \text{Execution time unaffected}$$

$$\text{Execution time affected improvement} = \frac{100t}{10} + 10t = 20t$$

so the speed-up with 10 processors is $110t/20t = 5.5$. The execution time for 100 processors is

$$\text{Execution time after improvement} = \frac{100t}{100} + 10t = 11t$$

so the speed-up with 100 processors is $110t/11t = 10$.

Thus, for this problem size, we get about 55% of the potential speed-up with 10 processors, but only 10% with 100. Look what happens when we increase the matrix. The sequential program now takes $10t + 10,000t = 10,010t$. The execution time for 10 processors is

$$\text{Execution time after improvement} = \frac{10,000t}{10} + 10t = 1010t$$

so the speed-up with 10 processors is $10,010t/1010t = 9.9$. The execution time for 100 processors is

$$\text{Execution time after improvement} = \frac{10,000t}{100} + 10t = 110t$$

so the speed-up with 100 processors is $10,010t/110t = 91$. Thus, for this larger problem size, we get about 99% of the potential speed-up with 10 processors and more than 90% with 100.

These examples show that getting good speed-up on a multiprocessor while keeping the problem size fixed is harder than getting good speed-up by increasing the size of the problem. This allows us to introduce two terms that describe ways to scale up. **Strong scaling** means measuring speed-up while keeping the problem size fixed. **Weak scaling** means that the program size grows proportionally to the increase in the number of processors. Let's assume that the size of the problem, M, is the working set in main memory, and we have P processors. Then the memory per processor for strong scaling is approximately M/P, and for weak scaling, it is approximately M.

Depending on the application, you can argue for either scaling approach. For example, the TPC-C debit-credit database benchmark (Chapter 6) requires that you scale up the number of customer accounts to achieve higher transactions per minute. The argument is that it's nonsensical to think that a given customer base is suddenly going to start using ATMs 100 times a day just because the bank gets a faster computer. Instead, if you're going to demonstrate a system that can perform 100 times the numbers of transactions per minute, you should run the experiment with 100 times as many customers.

This final example shows the importance of load balancing.

strong scaling Speed-up achieved on a multiprocessor without increasing the size of the problem.

weak scaling Speed-up achieved on a multiprocessor while increasing the size of the problem proportionally to the increase in the number of processors.

Speed-up Challenge: Balancing Load

To achieve the speed-up of 91 on the previous larger problem with 100 processors, we assumed the load was perfectly balanced. That is, each of the 100 processors had 1% of the work to do. Instead, show the impact on speed-up if one processor's load is higher than all the rest. Calculate at 2% and 5%.

EXAMPLE

ANSWER

If one processor has 2% of the parallel load, then it must do 2% × 10,000 or 200 additions, and the other 99 will share the remaining 9800. Since they are operating simultaneously, we can just calculate the execution time as a maximum

$$\text{Execution time after improvement} = \text{Max}\left(\frac{9800t}{99}, \frac{200t}{1}\right) + 10t = 210t$$

The speed-up drops to $10{,}010t/210t = 48$. If one processor has 5% of the load, it must perform 500 additions:

$$\text{Execution time after improvement} = \text{Max}\left(\frac{9500t}{99}, \frac{500t}{1}\right) + 10t = 510t$$

The speed-up drops even further to $10{,}010t/510t = 20$. This example demonstrates the value of balancing load, for just a single processor with twice the load of the others cuts speed-up almost in half, and five times the load on one processor reduces the speed-up by almost a factor of five.

Check Yourself

True or false: Strong scaling is not bound by Amdahl's law.

7.3   **Shared Memory Multiprocessors**

Given the difficulty of rewriting old programs to run well on parallel hardware, a natural question is what computer designers can do to simplify the task. One answer was to provide a single physical address space that all processors can share, so that programs need not concern themselves with where they are run, merely that they may be executed in parallel. In this approach, all variables of a program can be made available at any time to any processor. The alternative is to have a separate address space per processor that requires that sharing must be explicit; we'll describe this option in the next section. When the physical address space is common—which is usually the case for multicore chips—then the hardware typically provides cache coherence to give a consistent view of the shared memory (see Section 5.8 of Chapter 5).

A **shared memory multiprocessor** (SMP) is one that offers the programmer a *single physical address space* across all processors, although a more accurate term would have been shared-*address* multiprocessor. Note that such systems can still run independent jobs in their own virtual address spaces, even if they all share a physical address space. Processors communicate through shared variables in memory, with all processors capable of accessing any memory location via loads and stores. Figure 7.2 shows the classic organization of an SMP.

Single address space multiprocessors come in two styles. The first takes about the same time to access main memory no matter which processor requests it and no matter which word is requested. Such machines are called **uniform memory access (UMA)** multiprocessors. In the second style, some memory accesses are

shared memory multiprocessor (SMP) A parallel processor with a single address space, implying implicit communication with loads and stores.

uniform memory access (UMA) A multiprocessor in which accesses to main memory take about the same amount of time no matter which processor requests the access and no matter which word is asked.

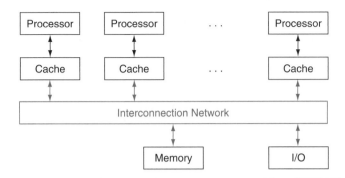

FIGURE 7.2 Classic organization of a shared memory multiprocessor.

much faster than others, depending on which processor asks for which word. Such machines are called **nonuniform memory access (NUMA)** multiprocessors. As you might expect, the programming challenges are harder for a NUMA multiprocessor than for a UMA multiprocessor, but NUMA machines can scale to larger sizes and NUMAs can have lower latency to nearby memory.

As processors operating in parallel will normally share data, they also need to coordinate when operating on shared data; otherwise, one processor could start working on data before another is finished with it. This coordination is called **synchronization**. When sharing is supported with a single address space, there must be a separate mechanism for synchronization. One approach uses a **lock** for a shared variable. Only one processor at a time can acquire the lock, and other processors interested in shared data must wait until the original processor unlocks the variable. Section 2.11 of Chapter 2 describes the instructions for locking in MIPS.

nonuniform memory access (NUMA) A type of single address space multiprocessor in which some memory accesses are much faster than others depending on which processor asks for which word.

synchronization The process of coordinating the behavior of two or more processes, which may be running on different processors.

lock A synchronization device that allows access to data to only one processor at a time.

A Simple Parallel Processing Program for a Shared Address Space

Suppose we want to sum 100,000 numbers on a shared memory multiprocessor computer with uniform memory access time. Let's assume we have 100 processors.

EXAMPLE

The first step again would be to split the set of numbers into subsets of the same size. We do not allocate the subsets to a different memory space, since there is a single memory space for this machine; we just give different starting addresses to each processor. Pn is the number that identifies the processor, between 0 and 99. All processors start the program by running a loop that sums their subset of numbers:

ANSWER

```
sum[Pn] = 0;
for (i = 1000*Pn; i < 1000*(Pn+1); i = i + 1)
    sum[Pn] = sum[Pn] + A[i]; /* sum the assigned areas*/
```

reduction A function
that processes a data
structure and returns
a single value.

The next step is to add these many partial sums. This step is called a **reduction**. We divide to conquer. Half of the processors add pairs of partial sums, and then a quarter add pairs of the new partial sums, and so on until we have the single, final sum. Figure 7.3 illustrates the hierarchical nature of this reduction.

In this example, the two processors must synchronize before the "consumer" processor tries to read the result from the memory location written by the "producer" processor; otherwise, the consumer may read the old value of the data. We want each processor to have its own version of the loop counter variable i, so we must indicate that it is a "private" variable. Here is the code (half is private also):

```
half = 100; /* 100 processors in multiprocessor*/
repeat
        synch(); /* wait for partial sum completion*/
        if (half%2 != 0 && Pn == 0)
            sum[0] = sum[0] + sum[half-1];
            /* Conditional sum needed when half is
               odd; Processor0 gets missing element */
        half = half/2; /* dividing line on who sums */
        if (Pn < half) sum[Pn] = sum[Pn] + sum[Pn+half];
until (half == 1); /* exit with final sum in Sum[0] */
```

Check Yourself

True or false: Shared memory multiprocessors cannot take advantage of job-level parallelism.

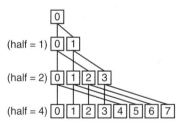

FIGURE 7.3   The last four levels of a reduction that sums results from each processor, from bottom to top. For all processors whose number i is less than half, add the sum produced by processor number (i + half) to its sum.

Elaboration: An alternative to sharing the physical address space would be to have separate physical address spaces but share a common virtual address space, leaving it up to the operating system to handle communication. This approach has been tried, but it has too high an overhead to offer a practical shared memory abstraction to the programmer.

Clusters and Other Message-Passing Multiprocessors

The alternative approach to sharing an address space is for the processors to each have their own private physical address space. Figure 7.4 shows the classic organization of a multiprocessor with multiple private address spaces. This alternative multiprocessor must communicate via explicit **message passing**, which traditionally is the name of such style of computers. Provided the system has routines to **send** and **receive messages**, coordination is built in with message passing, since one processor knows when a message is sent, and the receiving processor knows when a message arrives. If the sender needs confirmation that the message has arrived, the receiving processor can then send an acknowledgment message back to the sender.

message passing
Communicating between multiple processors by explicitly sending and receiving information.

send message routine
A routine used by a processor in machines with private memories to pass to another processor.

receive message routine A routine used by a processor in machines with private memories to accept a message from another processor.

Processor	Processor	. . .	Processor
Cache	Cache	. . .	Cache
Memory	Memory	. . .	Memory

Interconnection Network

FIGURE 7.4   Classic organization of a multiprocessor with multiple private address spaces, traditionally called a message-passing multiprocessor. Note that unlike the SMP in Figure 7.2, the interconnection network is not between the caches and memory but is instead between processor-memory nodes.

Some concurrent applications run well on parallel hardware, independent of whether it offers shared addresses or message passing. In particular, job-level parallelism and applications with little communication—like Web search, mail servers, and file servers—do not require shared addressing to run well.

There were several attempts to build high-performance computers based on high-performance message-passing networks, and they did offer better absolute communication performance than clusters built using local area networks. The problem was that they were much more expensive. Few applications could justify the higher communication performance, given the much higher costs. Hence, **clusters** have become the most widespread example today of the message-passing parallel computer. Clusters are generally collections of commodity computers that are connected to each other over their I/O interconnect via standard network switches and cables. Each runs a distinct copy of the operating system. Virtually every Internet service relies on clusters of commodity servers and switches.

clusters Collections of computers connected via I/O over standard network switches to form a message-passing multiprocessor.

One drawback of clusters has been that the cost of administering a cluster of n machines is about the same as the cost of administering n independent machines, while the cost of administering a shared memory multiprocessor with n processors is about the same as administering a single machine.

This weakness is one of the reasons for the popularity of virtual machines (Chapter 5), since VMs make clusters easier to administer. For example, VMs make it possible to stop or start programs atomically, which simplifies software upgrades. VMs can even migrate a program from one computer in a cluster to another without stopping the program, allowing a program to migrate from failing hardware.

Another drawback to clusters is that the processors in a cluster are usually connected using the I/O interconnect of each computer, whereas the cores in a multiprocessor are usually connected on the memory interconnect of the computer. The memory interconnect has higher bandwidth and lower latency, allowing much better communication performance.

A final weakness is the overhead in the division of memory: a cluster of n machines has n independent memories and n copies of the operating system, but a shared memory multiprocessor allows a single program to use almost all the memory in the computer, and it only needs a single copy of the OS.

EXAMPLE

Memory Efficiency

Suppose a single shared memory processor has 20 GB of main memory, five clustered computers each have 4 GB, and the OS occupies 1 GB. How much more space is there for users with shared memory?

ANSWER

The ratio of memory available for user programs on the shared memory computer versus the cluster would be

$$\frac{20-1}{5\times(4-1)}=\frac{19}{15}\approx 1.25$$

so shared memory computers have about 25% more space.

Let's redo the summing example from the prior section to see the impact of multiple private memories and explicit communication.

A Simple Parallel Processing Program for Message Passing

EXAMPLE

Suppose we want to sum 100,000 numbers in a message-passing multiprocessor with 100 processors, each with multiple private memories.

Since this computer has multiple address spaces, the first step is distributing the 100 subsets to each of the local memories. The processor containing the 100,000 numbers sends the subsets to each of the 100 processor-memory nodes.

ANSWER

The next step is to get the sum of each subset. This step is simply a loop that every processor follows: read a word from local memory and add it to a local variable:

```
sum = 0;
for (i = 0; i<1000; i = i + 1) /* loop over each array */
 sum = sum + AN[i];  /* sum the local arrays */
```

The last step is the reduction that adds these 100 partial sums. The hard part is that each partial sum is located in a different processor. Hence, we must use the interconnection network to send partial sums to accumulate the final sum. Rather than sending all the partial sums to a single processor, which would result in sequentially adding the partial sums, we again divide to conquer.

First, half of the processors send their partial sums to the other half of the processors, where two partial sums are added together. Then one-quarter of the processors (half of the half) send this new partial sum to the other quarter of the processors (the remaining half of the half) for the next round of sums. This halving, sending, and receiving continue until there is a single sum of all numbers. Let Pn represent the number of the processor, send(x,y) be a routine that sends over the interconnection network to processor number x the value y, and receive() be a function that accepts a value from the network for this processor. Here is the code:

```
limit = 100; half = 100;/* 100 processors */
repeat
  half = (half+1)/2; /* send vs. receive dividing line*/
  if (Pn >= half && Pn < limit) send(Pn - half, sum);
  if (Pn < (limit/2)) sum = sum + receive();
  limit = half; /* upper limit of senders */
until (half == 1); /* exit with final sum */
```

This code divides all processors into senders or receivers, and each receiving processor gets only one message, so we can presume that a receiving processor will stall until it receives a message. Thus, send and receive can be used as primitives for synchronization as well as for communication, as the processors are aware of the transmission of data.

If there is an odd number of nodes, the middle node does not participate in send/receive. The limit is then set so that this node is the highest node in the next iteration.

Elaboration: This example assumes implicitly that message passing is about as fast as addition. In reality, message sending and receiving is much slower. An optimization to better balance computation and communication might be to have fewer nodes receive many sums from other processors.

Hardware/ Software Interface

Computers that rely on message passing for communication rather than cache-coherent shared memory are much easier for hardware designers (see Section 5.8 of Chapter 5). The advantage for programmers is that communication is explicit, which means there are fewer performance surprises than with the implicit communication in cache-coherent shared memory computers. The downside for programmers is that it's harder to port a sequential program to a message-passing computer, since every communication must be identified in advance or the program doesn't work. Cache-coherent shared memory allows the hardware to figure out what data needs to be communicated, which makes porting easier. There are differences of opinion as to which is the shortest path to high performance, given the pros and cons of implicit communication.

A weakness of separate memories for user memory turns into a strength in system availability. Since a cluster consists of independent computers connected through a local area network, it is much easier to replace a machine without bringing down the system in a cluster than in an SMP. Fundamentally, the shared address means that it is difficult to isolate a processor and replace a processor without heroic work by the operating system. Since the cluster software is a layer that runs on top of local operating systems running on each computer, it is much easier to disconnect and replace a broken machine.

Given that clusters are constructed from whole computers and independent, scalable networks, this isolation also makes it easier to expand the system without bringing down the application that runs on top of the cluster.

Lower cost, high availability, improved power efficiency, and rapid, incremental expandability make clusters attractive to service providers for the World Wide Web. The search engines that millions of us use every day depend upon this technology. eBay, Google, Microsoft, Yahoo, and others all have multiple datacenters each with clusters of tens of thousands of processors. Clearly, the use of multiple processors in Internet service companies has been hugely successful.

Elaboration: Another form of large scale computing is *grid computing*, where the computers are spread across large areas, and then the programs that run across them must communicate via long haul networks. The most popular and unique form of grid computing was pioneered by the SETI@home project. It was observed that millions of PCs are idle at any one time doing nothing useful, and they could be harvested and put to good uses if someone developed software that could run on those computers and then gave each PC an independent piece of the problem to work on. The first example was the Search for ExtraTerrestrial Intelligence (SETI). Over 5 million computer users in more than 200 countries have signed up for SETI@home and have collectively contributed over 19 billion hours of computer processing time. By the end of 2006, the SETI@home grid operated at 257 TeraFLOPS.

Check Yourself

1. True or false: Like SMPs, message-passing computers rely on locks for synchronization.

2. True or false: Unlike SMPs, message-passing computers need multiple copies of the parallel processing program and the operating system.

7.5 Hardware Multithreading

Hardware multithreading allows multiple threads to share the functional units of a single processor in an overlapping fashion. To permit this sharing, the processor must duplicate the independent state of each thread. For example, each thread would have a separate copy of the register file and the PC. The memory itself can be shared through the virtual memory mechanisms, which already support multiprogramming. In addition, the hardware must support the ability to change to a different thread relatively quickly. In particular, a thread switch should be much more efficient than a process switch, which typically requires hundreds to thousands of processor cycles while a thread switch can be instantaneous.

There are two main approaches to hardware multithreading. **Fine-grained multithreading** switches between threads on each instruction, resulting in interleaved execution of multiple threads. This interleaving is often done in a round-robin fashion, skipping any threads that are stalled at that time. To make fine-grained multithreading practical, the processor must be able to switch threads on every clock cycle. One key advantage of fine-grained multithreading is that it can hide the throughput losses that arise from both short and long stalls, since instructions from other threads can be executed when one thread stalls. The primary disadvantage of fine-grained multithreading is that it slows down the execution of the individual threads, since a thread that is ready to execute without stalls will be delayed by instructions from other threads.

Coarse-grained multithreading was invented as an alternative to fine-grained multithreading. Coarse-grained multithreading switches threads only on costly stalls, such as second-level cache misses. This change relieves the need to have thread switching be essentially free and is much less likely to slow down the execution of an individual thread, since instructions from other threads will only be issued when a thread encounters a costly stall. Coarse-grained multithreading suffers, however, from a major drawback: it is limited in its ability to overcome

hardware multithreading Increasing utilization of a processor by switching to another thread when one thread is stalled.

fine-grained multithreading A version of hardware multithreading that suggests switching between threads after every instruction.

coarse-grained multithreading A version of hardware multithreading that suggests switching between threads only after significant events, such as a cache miss.

throughput losses, especially from shorter stalls. This limitation arises from the pipeline start-up costs of coarse-grained multithreading. Because a processor with coarse-grained multithreading issues instructions from a single thread, when a stall occurs, the pipeline must be emptied or frozen. The new thread that begins executing after the stall must fill the pipeline before instructions will be able to complete. Due to this start-up overhead, coarse-grained multithreading is much more useful for reducing the penalty of high-cost stalls, where pipeline refill is negligible compared to the stall time.

simultaneous multithreading (SMT) A version of multithreading that lowers the cost of multithreading by utilizing the resources needed for multiple issue, dynamically schedule microarchitecture.

Simultaneous multithreading (SMT) is a variation on hardware multithreading that uses the resources of a multiple-issue, dynamically scheduled processor to exploit thread-level parallelism at the same time it exploits instruction-level parallelism. The key insight that motivates SMT is that multiple-issue processors often have more functional unit parallelism available than a single thread can effectively use. Furthermore, with register renaming and dynamic scheduling, multiple instructions from independent threads can be issued without regard to the dependences among them; the resolution of the dependences can be handled by the dynamic scheduling capability.

Since you are relying on the existing dynamic mechanisms, SMT does not switch resources every cycle. Instead, SMT is always executing instructions from multiple threads, leaving it up to the hardware to associate instruction slots and renamed registers with their proper threads.

Figure 7.5 conceptually illustrates the differences in a processor's ability to exploit superscalar resources for the following processor configurations. The top portion shows how four threads would execute independently on a superscalar with no multithreading support. The bottom portion shows how the four threads could be combined to execute on the processor more efficiently using three multithreading options:

- A superscalar with coarse-grained multithreading

- A superscalar with fine-grained multithreading

- A superscalar with simultaneous multithreading

In the superscalar without hardware multithreading support, the use of issue slots is limited by a lack of instruction-level parallelism. In addition, a major stall, such as an instruction cache miss, can leave the entire processor idle.

In the coarse-grained multithreaded superscalar, the long stalls are partially hidden by switching to another thread that uses the resources of the processor. Although this reduces the number of completely idle clock cycles, the pipeline start-up overhead still leads to idle cycles, and limitations to ILP means all issue slots will not be used. In the fine-grained case, the interleaving of threads mostly eliminates fully empty slots. Because only a single thread issues instructions in a given clock cycle, however, limitations in instruction-level parallelism still lead to idle slots within some clock cycles.

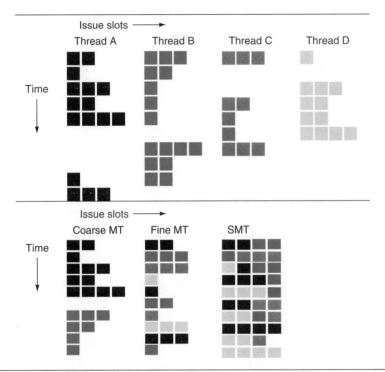

FIGURE 7.5 How four threads use the issue slots of a superscalar processor in different approaches. The four threads at the top show how each would execute running alone on a standard superscalar processor without multithreading support. The three examples at the bottom show how they would execute running together in three multithreading options. The horizontal dimension represents the instruction issue capability in each clock cycle. The vertical dimension represents a sequence of clock cycles. An empty (white) box indicates that the corresponding issue slot is unused in that clock cycle. The shades of gray and color correspond to four different threads in the multithreading processors. The additional pipeline start-up effects for coarse multithreading, which are not illustrated in this figure, would lead to further loss in throughput for coarse multithreading.

In the SMT case, thread-level parallelism and instruction-level parallelism are both exploited, with multiple threads using the issue slots in a single clock cycle. Ideally, the issue slot usage is limited by imbalances in the resource needs and resource availability over multiple threads. In practice, other factors can restrict how many slots are used. Although Figure 7.5 greatly simplifies the real operation of these processors, it does illustrate the potential performance advantages of multithreading in general and SMT in particular. For example, the recent Intel Nehalem multicore supports SMT with two threads to improve core utilization.

Let us conclude with three observations. First, from Chapter 1, we know that the power wall is forcing a design toward simpler and more power-efficient processors on a chip. It may well be that the under-utilized resources of out-of-order processors may be reduced, and so simpler forms of multithreading will be used. For example, the Sun UltraSPARC T2 (Niagara 2) microprocessor in Section 7.11 is an example of a return to simpler microarchitectures and hence the use of fine-grained multithreading.

Second, a key performance challenge is tolerating latency due to cache misses. Fine-grained computers like the UltraSPARC T2 switch to another thread on a miss, which is probably more effective in hiding memory latency than trying to fill unused issue slots as in SMT.

A third observation is that the goal of hardware multithreading is to use hardware more efficiently by sharing components between different tasks. Multicore designs share resources as well. For example, two processors might share a floating-point unit or an L3 cache. Such sharing reduces some of the benefits of multithreading compared with providing more non-multithreaded cores.

Check Yourself

1. True or false: Both multithreading and multicore rely on parallelism to get more efficiency from a chip.

2. True or false: Simultaneous multithreading uses threads to improve resource utilization of a dynamically scheduled, out-of-order processor.

7.6   SISD, MIMD, SIMD, SPMD, and Vector

Another categorization of parallel hardware proposed in the 1960s is still used today. It was based on the number of instruction streams and the number of data streams. Figure 7.6 shows the categories. Thus, a conventional uniprocessor has a single instruction stream and single data stream, and a conventional multiprocessor has multiple instruction streams and multiple data streams. These two categories are abbreviated **SISD** and **MIMD**, respectively.

SISD or Single Instruction stream, Single Data stream. A uniprocessor.

MIMD or Multiple Instruction streams, Multiple Data streams. A multiprocessor.

		Data Streams	
		Single	**Multiple**
Instruction Streams	Single	SISD: Intel Pentium 4	SIMD: SSE instructions of x86
	Multiple	MISD: No examples today	MIMD: Intel Xeon e5345 (Clovertown)

FIGURE 7.6   Hardware categorization and examples based on number of instruction streams and data streams: SISD, SIMD, MISD, and MIMD.

SPMD Single Program, Multiple Data streams. The conventional MIMD programming model, where a single program runs across all processors.

While it is possible to write separate programs that run on different processors on a MIMD computer and yet work together for a grander, coordinated goal, programmers normally write a single program that runs on all processors of an MIMD computer, relying on conditional statements when different processors should execute different sections of code. This style is called **Single Program Multiple Data (SPMD)**, but it is just the normal way to program a MIMD computer.

While it is hard to provide examples of useful computers that would be classified as multiple instruction streams and single data stream (MISD), the inverse makes much more sense. **SIMD** computers operate on vectors of data. For example, a single SIMD instruction might add 64 numbers by sending 64 data streams to 64 ALUs to form 64 sums within a single clock cycle.

The virtues of SIMD are that all the parallel execution units are synchronized and they all respond to a single instruction that emanates from a single program counter (PC). From a programmer's perspective, this is close to the already familiar SISD. Although every unit will be executing the same instruction, each execution unit has its own address registers, and so each unit can have different data addresses. Thus, in terms of Figure 7.1, a sequential application might be compiled to run on serial hardware organized as a SISD or in parallel hardware that was organized as an SIMD.

The original motivation behind SIMD was to amortize the cost of the control unit over dozens of execution units. Another advantage is the reduced size of program memory—SIMD needs only one copy of the code that is being simultaneously executed, while message-passing MIMDs may need a copy in every processor, and shared memory MIMD will need multiple instruction caches.

SIMD works best when dealing with arrays in *for* loops. Hence, for parallelism to work in SIMD, there must be a great deal of identically structured data, which is called **data-level parallelism**. SIMD is at its weakest in *case* or *switch* statements, where each execution unit must perform a different operation on its data, depending on what data it has. Execution units with the wrong data are disabled so that units with proper data may continue. Such situations essentially run at $1/n$th performance, where n is the number of cases.

The so-called array processors that inspired the SIMD category faded into history (see ◉ **Section 7.14** on the CD), but two current interpretations of SIMD remain active today.

SIMD or Single Instruction stream, Multiple Data streams. A multiprocessor. The same instruction is applied to many data streams, as in a vector processor or array processor.

data-level parallelism Parallelism achieved by operating on independent data.

SIMD in x86: Multimedia Extensions

The most widely used variation of SIMD is found in almost every microprocessor today, and is the basis of the hundreds of MMX and SSE instructions of the x86 microprocessor (see Chapter 2). They were added to improve performance of multimedia programs. These instructions allow the hardware to have many ALUs operate simultaneously or, equivalently, to partition a single, wide ALU into many parallel smaller ALUs that operate simultaneously. For example, you could consider a single hardware component to be one 64-bit ALU or two 32-bit ALUs or four 16-bit ALUs or eight 8-bit ALUs. Loads and stores are simply as wide as the widest ALU, so the programmer can think of the same data transfer instruction as transferring either a single 64-bit data element or two 32-bit data elements or four 16-bit data elements or eight 8-bit data elements.

This very low cost parallelism for narrow integer data was the original inspiration of the MMX instructions of the x86. As Moore's law continued, more hardware was added to these multimedia extensions, and now SSE2 supports the simultaneous execution of a pair of 64-bit floating-point numbers.

The width of the operation and the registers is encoded in the opcode of these multimedia instructions. As the data width of the registers and operations grew, the number of opcodes for multimedia instructions exploded, and now there are hundreds of SSE instructions to perform the useful combinations (see Chapter 2).

Vector

An older and more elegant interpretation of SIMD is called a vector architecture, which has been closely identified with Cray Computers. It is again a great match to problems with lots of data-level parallelism. Rather than having 64 ALUs perform 64 additions simultaneously, like the old array processors, the vector architectures pipelined the ALU to get good performance at lower cost. The basic philosophy of vector architecture is to collect data elements from memory, put them in order into a large set of registers, operate on them sequentially in registers, and then write the results back to memory. A key feature of vector architectures is a set of vector registers. Thus, a vector architecture might have 32 vector registers, each with 64 64-bit elements.

EXAMPLE

Comparing Vector to Conventional Code

Suppose we extend the MIPS instruction set architecture with vector instructions and vector registers. Vector operations use the same names as MIPS operations, but with the letter "V" appended. For example, addv.d adds two double-precision vectors. The vector instructions take as their input either a pair of vector registers (addv.d) or a vector register and a scalar register (addvs.d). In the latter case, the value in the scalar register is used as the input for all operations—the operation addvs.d will add the contents of a scalar register to each element in a vector register. The names lv and sv denote vector load and vector store, and they load or store an entire vector of double-precision data. One operand is the vector register to be loaded or stored; the other operand, which is a MIPS general-purpose register, is the starting address of the vector in memory. Given this short description, show the conventional MIPS code versus the vector MIPS code for

$$Y = a \times X + Y$$

where X and Y are vectors of 64 double precision floating-point numbers, initially resident in memory, and a is a scalar double precision variable. (This example is the so-called DAXPY loop that forms the inner loop of the Linpack benchmark; DAXPY stands for double precision $a \times X$ plus Y.). Assume that the starting addresses of X and Y are in $s0 and $s1, respectively.

Here is the conventional MIPS code for DAXPY:

```
        l.d    $f0,a($sp)     ;load scalar a
        addiu  r4,$s0,#512    ;upper bound of what to load
loop:   l.d    $f2,0($s0)     ;load x(i)
        mul.d  $f2,$f2,$f0    ;a × x(i)
        l.d    $f4,0($s1)     ;load y(i)
        add.d  $f4,$f4,$f2    ;a × x(i) + y(i)
        s.d    $f4,0($s1)     ;store into y(i)
        addiu  $s0,$s0,#8     ;increment index to x
        addiu  $s1,$s1,#8     ;increment index to y
        subu   $t0,r4,$s0     ;compute bound
        bne    $t0,$zero,loop ;check if done
```

Here is the vector MIPS code for DAXPY:

```
        l.d     $f0,a($sp)     ;load scalar a
        lv      $v1,0($s0)     ;load vector x
        mulvs.d $v2,$v1,$f0    ;vector-scalar multiply
        lv      $v3,0($s1)     ;load vector y
        addv.d  $v4,$v2,$v3    ;add y to product
        sv      $v4,0($s1)     ;store the result
```

There are some interesting comparisons between the two code segments in this example. The most dramatic is that the vector processor greatly reduces the dynamic instruction bandwidth, executing only six instructions versus almost 600 for MIPS. This reduction occurs both because the vector operations work on 64 elements and because the overhead instructions that constitute nearly half the loop on MIPS are not present in the vector code. As you might expect, this reduction in instructions fetched and executed saves power.

Another important difference is the frequency of pipeline hazards (Chapter 4). In the straightforward MIPS code, every add.d must wait for a mul.d, and every s.d must wait for the add.d. On the vector processor, each vector instruction will only stall for the first element in each vector, and then subsequent elements will flow smoothly down the pipeline. Thus, pipeline stalls are required only once per vector operation, rather than once per vector element. In this example, the pipeline stall frequency on MIPS will be about 64 times higher than it is on VMIPS. The pipeline stalls can be reduced on MIPS by using loop-unrolling (see Chapter 4). However, the large difference in instruction bandwidth cannot be reduced.

Elaboration: The loop in the example above exactly matched the vector length. When loops are shorter, vector architectures use a register that reduces the length of vector operations. When loops are larger, we add bookkeeping code to iterate full-length vector operations and to handle the leftovers. This latter process is called *strip mining*.

Vector versus Scalar

Vector instructions have several important properties compared to conventional instruction set architectures, which are called *scalar architectures* in this context:

- A single vector instruction specifies a great deal of work—it is equivalent to executing an entire loop. The instruction fetch and decode bandwidth needed is dramatically reduced.

- By using a vector instruction, the compiler or programmer indicates that the computation of each result in the vector is independent of the computation of other results in the same vector, so hardware does not have to check for data hazards within a vector instruction.

- Vector architectures and compilers have a reputation of making it much easier than MIMD multiprocessors to write efficient applications when they contain data-level parallelism.

- Hardware need only check for data hazards between two vector instructions once per vector operand, not once for every element within the vectors. Reduced checking can save power as well.

- Vector instructions that access memory have a known access pattern. If the vector's elements are all adjacent, then fetching the vector from a set of heavily interleaved memory banks works very well. Thus, the cost of the latency to main memory is seen only once for the entire vector, rather than once for each word of the vector.

- Because an entire loop is replaced by a vector instruction whose behavior is predetermined, control hazards that would normally arise from the loop branch are nonexistent.

- The savings in instruction bandwidth and hazard checking plus the efficient use of memory bandwidth give vector architectures advantages in power and energy versus scalar architectures.

For these reasons, vector operations can be made faster than a sequence of scalar operations on the same number of data items, and designers are motivated to include vector units if the application domain can use them frequently.

Vector versus Multimedia Extensions

Like multimedia extensions found in the x86 SSE instructions, a vector instruction specifies multiple operations. However, multimedia extensions typically specify a few operations while vector specifies dozens of operations. Unlike multimedia extensions, the number of elements in a vector operation is not in the opcode but in a separate register. This means different versions of the vector architecture can be implemented with a different number of elements just by changing the contents of that register and hence retain binary compatibility. In contrast, a new large set of opcodes is added each time the "vector" length changes in the multimedia extension architecture of the x86.

Also unlike multimedia extensions, the data transfers need not be contiguous. Vectors support both strided accesses, where the hardware loads every nth data element in memory, and indexed accesses, where hardware finds the addresses of the items to be loaded in a vector register.

Like multimedia extensions, vector easily captures the flexibility in data widths, so it is easy to make an operation work on 32 64-bit data elements or 64 32-bit data elements or 128 16-bit data elements or 256 8-bit data elements.

Generally, vector architectures are a very efficient way to execute data parallel processing programs; they are better matches to compiler technology than multimedia extensions; and they are easier to evolve over time than the multimedia extensions to the x86 architecture.

True or false: As exemplified in the x86, multimedia extensions can be thought of as a vector architecture with short vectors that supports only sequential vector data transfers.

Check Yourself

Elaboration: Given the advantages of vector, why aren't they more popular outside high-performance computing? There were concerns about the larger state for vector registers increasing context switch time and the difficulty of handling page faults in vector loads and stores, and SIMD instructions achieved some of the benefits of vector instructions. However, recent announcements from Intel suggest that vectors will play a bigger role. Intel's *Advanced Vector Instructions* (*AVI*), to arrive in 2010, will expand the width of the SSE registers from 128 bits to 256 bits immediately and allow eventual expansion to 1024 bits. This latter width is equivalent to 16 double-precision floating-point numbers. Whether there will be vector load and store instructions are unclear. In addition, Intel's entry into the discrete GPU market for 2010—code named "Larrabee"—is reputed to have vector instructions.

Elaboration: Another advantage of vector and multimedia extensions is that it is relatively easy to extend a scalar instruction set architecture with these instructions to improve performance of data parallel operations.

7.7   Introduction to Graphics Processing Units

A major justification for adding SIMD instructions to existing architectures was that many microprocessors were connected to graphics displays in PCs and workstations, so an increasing fraction of processing time was used for graphics. Hence, as Moore's law increased the number of transistors available to microprocessors, it made sense to improve graphics processing.

Just as Moore's law allowed the CPU to improve graphics processing, it also enabled video graphics controller chips to add functions to accelerate 2D and 3D graphics. Moreover, at the very high end were expensive graphics cards typically from Silicon Graphics, that could be added to workstations, to enable the creation of photographic quality images. These high-end graphics cards were popular for creating computer-generated images that later found their way into television advertisements and then into movies. Thus, video graphics controllers had a target to shoot for as processing resources increased, much as supercomputers provided a rich resource of ideas for microprocessors to borrow in the quest for greater performance.

A major driving force for improving graphics processing was the computer game industry, both on PCs and in dedicated game consoles such as the Sony PlayStation. The rapidly growing game market encouraged many companies to make increasing investments in developing faster graphics hardware, and this positive feedback led graphics processing to improve at a faster rate than general-purpose processing in mainstream microprocessors.

Given that the graphics and game community had different goals than the microprocessor development community, it evolved its own style of processing and terminology. As the graphics processors increased in power, they earned the name *Graphics Processing Units* or *GPUs* to distinguish themselves from CPUs. Here are some of the key characteristics as to how GPUs vary from CPUs:

- GPUs are accelerators that supplement a CPU, so they do not need be able to perform all the tasks of a CPU. This role allows them to dedicate all their resources to graphics. It's fine for GPUs to perform some tasks poorly or not at all, given that in a system with both a CPU and a GPU, the CPU can do them if needed. Thus, the CPU-GPU combination is one example of *heterogeneous multiprocessing*, where not all the processors are identical. (Another example is the IBM Cell architecture in Section 7.11, which was also designed to accelerate 2D and 3D graphics.)

- The programming interfaces to GPUs are high-level application programming interfaces (APIs), such as OpenGL and Microsoft's DirectX, coupled with high-level graphics shading languages, such as NVIDIA's C for Graphics (Cg) and Microsoft's High Level Shader Language (HLSL).

The language compilers target industry-standard intermediate languages instead of machine instructions. GPU driver software generates optimized GPU-specific machine instructions. While these APIs and languages evolve rapidly to embrace new GPU resources enabled by Moore's law, the freedom from backward binary instruction compatibility enables GPU designers to explore new architectures without the fear that they will be saddled with implementing failed experiments forever. This environment leads to more rapid innovation in GPUs than in CPUs.

- Graphics processing involves drawing vertices of 3D geometry primitives such as lines and triangles and *shading* or rendering pixel fragments of geometric primitives. Video games, for example, draw 20 to 30 times as many pixels as vertices.

- Each vertex can be drawn independently, and each pixel fragment can be rendered independently. To render millions of pixels per frame rapidly, the GPU evolved to execute many threads from vertex and pixel shader programs in parallel.

- The graphics data types are vertices, consisting of (x, y, z, w) coordinates, and pixels, consisting of (red, green, blue, alpha) color components. (See Appendix A to learn more about vertices and pixels.) GPUs represent each vertex component as a 32-bit floating-point number. Each of the four pixel components was originally an 8-bit unsigned integer, but recent GPUs now represent each component as single-precision floating-point number between 0.0 and 1.0.

- The working set can be hundreds of megabytes, and it does not show the same temporal locality as data does in mainstream applications. Moreover, there is a great deal of data-level parallelism in these tasks.

These differences led to different styles of architecture:

- Perhaps the biggest difference is that GPUs do not rely on multilevel caches to overcome the long latency to memory, as do CPUs. Instead, GPUs rely on having enough threads to hide the latency to memory. That is, between the time of a memory request and the time that data arrives, the GPU executes hundreds or thousands of threads that are independent of that request.

- GPUs rely on extensive parallelism to obtain high performance, implementing many parallel processors and many concurrent threads.

- The GPU main memory is thus oriented toward bandwidth rather than latency. There are even separate DRAM chips for GPUs that are wider and have higher bandwidth than DRAM chips for CPUs. In addition, GPU memories have traditionally had smaller main memories than conventional microprocessors. In 2008, GPUs typically have 1 GB or less, while CPUs have

2 to 32 GB. Finally, keep in mind that for general-purpose computation, you must include the time to transfer the data between CPU memory and GPU memory, since the GPU is a coprocessor.

■ Given the reliance on many threads to deliver good memory bandwidth, GPUs can accommodate many parallel processors as well as many threads. Hence, each GPU processor is highly multithreaded.

■ In the past, GPUs relied on heterogeneous special purpose processors to deliver the performance needed for graphics applications. Recent GPUs are heading toward identical general-purpose processors to give more flexibility in programming, making them more like the multicore designs found in mainstream computing.

■ Given the four-element nature of the graphics data types, GPUs historically have SIMD instructions, like CPUs. However, recent GPUs are focusing more on scalar instructions to improve programmability and efficiency.

■ Unlike CPUs, there has been no support for double precision floating-point arithmetic, since there has been no need for it in the graphics applications. In 2008, the first GPUs to support double precision in hardware were announced. Nevertheless, single precision operations will still be eight to ten times faster than double precision, even on these new GPUs, while the difference in performance for CPUs is limited to benefits in transferring fewer bytes in the memory system due to using narrow data.

Although GPUs were designed for a narrower set of applications, some programmers wondered if they could specify their applications in a form that would let them tap the high potential performance of GPUs. To distinguish this style of using GPUs, some called it *General Purpose GPUs* or *GPGPUs*. After tiring of trying to specify their problems using the graphics APIs and graphics shading languages, they developed C-inspired programming languages to allow them to write programs directly for the GPUs. An example is Brook, a streaming language for GPUs. The next step in programmability of both the hardware and the programming language is NVIDIA's CUDA (Compute Unified Device Architecture), which enables the programmer to write C programs to execute on GPUs, albeit with some restrictions. The use of GPUs for parallel computing is growing with their increasing programmability.

An Introduction to the NVIDIA GPU Architecture

Appendix A goes into much more depth on GPUs and presents in detail the most recent NVIDIA GPU architecture, called Tesla. Since GPUs evolved in their own environment, they not only have different architectures, as suggested above, but they also have a different set of terms. Once you learn the GPU terms, you will see the similarities to approaches presented in prior sections, such as fine-grained multithreading and vectors.

To help you with that transition to the new vocabulary, we present a quick introduction to the terms and ideas in the Tesla GPU architecture and the CUDA programming environment.

A discrete GPU chip sits on a separate card that plugs into a standard PC over the PCI-Express interconnect. So-called motherboard GPUs are integrated into the motherboard chip set, such as a north bridge or a south bridge (Chapter 6).

GPUs are generally offered as a family of chips at different price performance points, with all being software compatible. Tesla-based GPUs chips are offered with between 1 and 16 nodes, which NVIDIA calls *multiprocessors*. In early 2008, the largest version is called the GeForce 8800 GTX, which has 16 multiprocessors and a clock rate of 1.35 GHz. Each multiprocessor contains eight multithreaded single-precision floating-point units and integer processing units, which NVIDIA calls *streaming processors*.

Since the architecture includes a single-precision floating-point multiply-add instruction, the peak single precision multiply-add performance of the 8800 GTX chip is:

$$16 \text{ MPs} \times \frac{8 \text{ SPs}}{\text{MP}} \times \frac{2 \text{ FLOPs/instr}}{\text{SP}} \times \frac{1 \text{ instr}}{\text{clock}} \times \frac{1.35 \times 10^9 \text{ clocks}}{\text{second}}$$

$$= \frac{16 \times 8 \times 2 \times 1.35 \text{ GFLOPs}}{\text{second}}$$

$$= \frac{345.6 \text{ GFLOPs}}{\text{second}}$$

Each of the 16 multiprocessors of the GeForce 8800 GTX has a software-managed local store with a capacity of 16 KB plus 8192 32-bit registers. The memory system of the 8800 GTX consists of six partitions of 900 MHz Graphics DDR3 DRAM, each 8 bytes wide and with 128 MB of capacity. The total memory size is thus 768 MB. The peak GDDR3 memory bandwidth is

$$6 \times \frac{8 \text{ Bytes}}{\text{transfer}} \times \frac{2 \text{ transfers}}{\text{clock}} \times \frac{0.9 \times 10^9 \text{ clocks}}{\text{second}} = \frac{6 \times 8 \times 2 \times 0.9 \text{GB}}{\text{second}} = \frac{86.4 \text{ GB}}{\text{second}}$$

To hide memory latency, each streaming processor has hardware-supported threads. Each group of 32 threads is called a *warp*. A warp is the unit of scheduling, and the active threads in a warp—up to 32—execute in parallel in SIMD fashion. The multithreaded architecture copes with conditions, however, by allowing threads to take different branch paths. When threads of a warp take diverging paths, the warp sequentially executes both code paths with some inactive threads, which makes the active threads run more slowly. The hardware joins the threads back into a fully active warp as soon as the conditional paths are completed. To get the best performance, all 32 threads of a warp need to execute together in parallel. In similar style, the hardware also looks at the address streams coming from the different threads to try to merge the individual requests into fewer but larger memory block transfers to increase memory performance.

Figure 7.7 combines all these features together and compares a Tesla multiprocessor to a Sun UltraSPARC T2 core, which is described in Sections 7.5 and 7.11. Both are hardware multithreaded by scheduling threads over time, shown on the vertical axis. Each Tesla multiprocessor consists of eight streaming processors, which execute eight parallel threads per clock showing horizontally. As mentioned above, the best performance comes when all 32 threads of a warp execute together in a SIMD-like fashion, which the Tesla architecture calls single-instruction multiple-thread (SIMT). SIMT dynamically discovers which threads of a warp can execute the same instruction together, and which independent threads are idle that cycle. The T2 core contains just a single multithreaded processor. Each cycle it executes one instruction for one thread.

The Tesla multiprocessor uses fine-grained hardware multithreading to schedule 24 warps over time, which are shown vertically in blocks of four clock cycles. Similarly, the UltraSPARC T2 schedules eight hardware-supported threads over time, one thread per cycle, shown vertically. Thus, just as the T2 hardware switches between threads to keep the T2 core busy, the Tesla hardware switches between warps to keep the Tesla multiprocessor busy. The major difference is that the T2 core has one processor that can switch threads every clock cycle, while the minimum unit of switching warps in the Tesla microprocessor is two clock cycles across eight streaming cores. Since Tesla is aimed at programs with a great deal of data-level parallelism, the designers believed there is little performance difference between

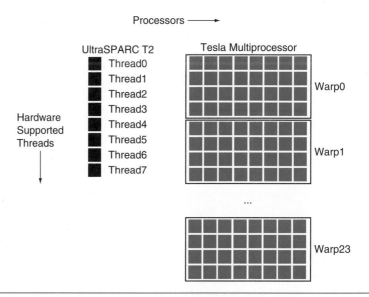

FIGURE 7.7   Comparing single core of a Sun UltraSPARC T2 (Niagara 2) to a single Tesla multiprocessor. The T2 core is a single processor and uses hardware multithreading with eight threads (although there are some restrictions scheduling threads to pipelines). The Tesla multiprocessor contains eight streaming processors and uses hardware-supported multithreading with 24 warps of 32 threads (eight processors times four clock cycles). The T2 can switch every clock cycle, while the Tesla can switch only every two or four clock cycles. One way to compare the two is that the T2 can only multithread the processor over time, while Tesla can multithread over time and over space; that is, across the eight streaming processors as well as segments of four clock cycles.

switching every two or four clock cycles versus every clock cycle, and the hardware was much simpler by restricting the frequency of switching.

The CUDA programming environment has its own terminology as well. A CUDA program is a unified C/C++ program for a heterogeneous CPU and GPU system. It executes on the CPU and dispatches parallel work to the GPU. This work consists of a data transfer from main memory and a *thread dispatch*. A thread is a piece of the program for the GPU. Programmers specify the number of threads in a *thread block*, and the number of thread blocks they wish to start executing on the GPU. The reason the programmers care about thread blocks is that all the threads in the thread block are scheduled to run on the same multiprocessor so they all share the same local memory. Thus, they can communicate via loads and stores instead of messages. The CUDA compiler allocates registers to each thread, under the constraint that the registers per thread times threads per thread block does not exceed the 8192 registers per multiprocessor.

A thread block can be up to 512 threads. Each group of 32 threads in a thread block is packed into warps. Large thread blocks have better efficiency than small ones, and they can be as small as a single thread. As mentioned above, thread blocks and warps with fewer than 32 threads operate less efficiently than full ones.

A hardware scheduler tries to schedule multiple thread blocks per multiprocessor when possible. If it does, the scheduler also partitions the 16 KB local store dynamically between the different thread blocks.

Putting GPUs into Perspective

GPUs like the NVIDIA Tesla architecture do not fit neatly into prior classifications of computers, such Figure 7.6 on page 648. Clearly, the GeForce 8800 GTX, with 16 Tesla multiprocessors, is an MIMD. The question is how to classify each of the Tesla multiprocessors and the eight streaming processors that make up a Tesla multiprocessor.

Recall that we earlier said that SIMD was at its best with for loops and was at its weakest in case and switch statements. Tesla aims at the high performance for data-level parallelism while making it easy for programmers to deal with independent thread-level parallel cases. Tesla allows the programmer to think the multiprocessor is a multithreaded MIMD of eight streaming processors, but the hardware tries to gang together the eight streaming processors to act in SIMT fashion when multiple threads of the same warp can execute together. When the threads do operate independently and follow an independent execution path, they execute more slowly than in SIMT fashion, for all 32 threads of a warp share a single instruction fetch unit. If all 32 threads of a warp were executing independent instructions, each thread would operate at 1/16th the peak performance of a full warp of 32 threads executing on eight streaming processors over four clocks.

Thus, each independent thread has its own effective PC, so programmers can think of the Tesla multiprocessor as MIMD, but programmers need to take care to write control flow statements that allow the SIMT hardware to execute CUDA programs in SIMD fashion to deliver the desired performance.

In contrast to vector architectures, which rely on a vectorizing compiler to recognize data-level parallelism at compile time and generate vector instructions, hardware implementations of Tesla architecture discovers data-level parallelism among threads at runtime. Thus, Tesla GPUs do not need vectorizing compilers, and they make it easier for the programmer to handle the portions of the program that do not have data-level parallelism. To put this unique approach into perspective, Figure 7.8 places GPUs in a classification that looks at instruction-level parallelism versus data-level parallelism and whether it is discovered at compile time or runtime. This categorization is one indication that the Tesla GPU is breaking new ground in computer architecture.

	Static: Discovered at Compile Time	Dynamic: Discovered at Runtime
Instruction-Level Parallelism	VLIW	Superscalar
Data-Level Parallelism	SIMD or Vector	Tesla Multiprocessor

FIGURE 7.8   Hardware categorization of processor architectures and examples based on static versus dynamic and ILP versus DLP.

Check Yourself   True or false: GPUs rely on graphics DRAM chips to reduce memory latency and thereby increase performance on graphics applications.

7.8 Introduction to Multiprocessor Network Topologies

Multicore chips require networks on chips to connect cores together. This section reviews the pros and cons of different multiprocessor networks.

Network costs include the number of switches, the number of links on a switch to connect to the network, the width (number of bits) per link, and length of the links when the network is mapped into chip. For example, some cores may be adjacent and others may be on the other side of the chip. Network performance is multifaceted as well. It includes the latency on an unloaded network to send and receive a message, the throughput in terms of the maximum number of messages that can be transmitted in a given time period, delays caused by contention for a portion of the network, and variable performance depending on the pattern of communication. Another obligation of the network may be fault tolerance, since systems may be required to operate in the presence of broken components. Finally, in this era of power-limited chips, the power efficiency of different organizations may trump other concerns.

Networks are normally drawn as graphs, with each arc of the graph representing a link of the communication network. The processor-memory node is shown as a black square, and the switch is shown as a colored circle. In this section, all links are *bidirectional;* that is, information can flow in either direction. All networks consist of *switches* whose links go to processor-memory nodes and to other switches. The first improvement over a bus is a network that connects a sequence of nodes together:

This topology is called a *ring.* Since some nodes are not directly connected, some messages will have to hop along intermediate nodes until they arrive at the final destination.

Unlike a bus, a ring is capable of many simultaneous transfers. Because there are numerous topologies to choose from, performance metrics are needed to distinguish these designs. Two are popular. The first is *total* **network bandwidth**, which is the bandwidth of each link multiplied by the number of links. This represents the very best case. For the ring network above, with P processors, the total network bandwidth would be P times the bandwidth of one link; the total network bandwidth of a bus is just the bandwidth of that bus, or two times the bandwidth of that link.

To balance this best case, we include another metric that is closer to the worst case: the **bisection bandwidth**. This is calculated by dividing the machine into two parts, each with half the nodes. Then you sum the bandwidth of the links that cross that imaginary dividing line. The bisection bandwidth of a ring is two times the link bandwidth, and it is one times the link bandwidth for the bus. If a single link is as fast as the bus, the ring is only twice as fast as a bus in the worst case, but it is P times faster in the best case.

Since some network topologies are not symmetric, the question arises of where to draw the imaginary line when bisecting the machine. This is a worst-case metric, so the answer is to choose the division that yields the most pessimistic network performance. Stated alternatively, calculate all possible bisection bandwidths and pick the smallest. We take this pessimistic view because parallel programs are often limited by the weakest link in the communication chain.

At the other extreme from a ring is a **fully connected network**, where every processor has a bidirectional link to every other processor. For fully connected networks, the total network bandwidth is $P \times (P - 1)/2$, and the bisection bandwidth is $(P/2)^2$.

The tremendous improvement in performance of fully connected networks is offset by the tremendous increase in cost. This inspires engineers to invent new topologies that are between the cost of rings and the performance of fully connected networks. The evaluation of success depends in large part on the nature of the communication in the workload of parallel programs run on the machine.

The number of different topologies that have been discussed in publications would be difficult to count, but only a handful have been used in commercial parallel processors. Figure 7.9 illustrates two of the popular topologies. Real machines

network bandwidth Informally, the peak transfer rate of a network; can refer to the speed of a single link or the collective transfer rate of all links in the network.

bisection bandwidth The bandwidth between two equal parts of a multiprocessor. This measure is for a worst case split of the multiprocessor.

fully connected network A network that connects processor-memory nodes by supplying a dedicated communication link between every node.

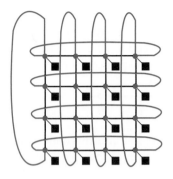

a. 2-D grid or mesh of 16 nodes   b. *n*-cube tree of 8 nodes ($8 = 2^3$ so $n = 3$)

FIGURE 7.9 Network topologies that have appeared in commercial parallel processors.
The colored circles represent switches and the black squares represent processor-memory nodes. Even though a switch has many links, generally only one goes to the processor. The Boolean *n*-cube topology is an *n*-dimensional interconnect with 2^n nodes, requiring *n* links per switch (plus one for the processor) and thus *n* nearest-neighbor nodes. Frequently, these basic topologies have been supplemented with extra arcs to improve performance and reliability.

multistage network
A network that supplies a small switch at each node.

fully connected network
A network that connects processor-memory nodes by supplying a dedicated communication link between every node.

crossbar network
A network that allows any node to communicate with any other node in one pass through the network.

frequently add extra links to these simple topologies to improve performance and reliability.

An alternative to placing a processor at every node in a network is to leave only the switch at some of these nodes. The switches are smaller than processor-memory-switch nodes, and thus may be packed more densely, thereby lessening distance and increasing performance. Such networks are frequently called **multistage networks** to reflect the multiple steps that a message may travel. Types of multistage networks are as numerous as single-stage networks; Figure 7.10 illustrates two of the popular multistage organizations. A **fully connected** or **crossbar network** allows any node to communicate with any other node in one pass through the network. An *Omega network* uses less hardware than the crossbar network ($2n \log_2 n$ versus n^2 switches), but contention can occur between messages, depending on the pattern of communication. For example, the Omega network in Figure 7.10 cannot send a message from P_0 to P_6 at the same time that it sends a message from P_1 to P_7.

Implementing Network Topologies

This simple analysis of all the networks in this section ignores important practical considerations in the construction of a network. The distance of each link affects the cost of communicating at a high clock rate—generally, the longer the distance, the more expensive it is to run at a high clock rate. Shorter distances also make

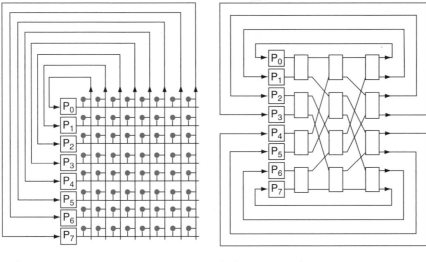

a. Crossbar   b. Omega network

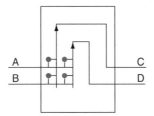

c. Omega network switch box

FIGURE 7.10 Popular multistage network topologies for eight nodes. The switches in these drawings are simpler than in earlier drawings because the links are unidirectional; data comes in at the bottom and exits out the right link. The switch box in c can pass A to C and B to D or B to C and A to D. The crossbar uses n^2 switches, where n is the number of processors, while the Omega network uses $2n \log_2 n$ of the large switch boxes, each of which is logically composed of four of the smaller switches. In this case, the crossbar uses 64 switches versus 12 switch boxes, or 48 switches, in the Omega network. The crossbar, however, can support any combination of messages between processors, while the Omega network cannot.

it easier to assign more wires to the link, as the power to drive many wires from a chip is less if the wires are short. Shorter wires are also cheaper than longer wires. Another practical limitation is that the three-dimensional drawings must be mapped onto chips that are essentially two-dimensional media. The final concern is power. Power concerns may force multicore chips to rely on simple grid topologies, for example. The bottom line is that topologies that appear elegant when sketched on the blackboard may be impractical when constructed in silicon.

7.9   **Multiprocessor Benchmarks**

As we saw in Chapter 1, benchmarking systems is always a sensitive topic, because it is a highly visible way to try to determine which system is better. The results affect not only the sales of commercial systems, but also the reputation of the designers of those systems. Hence, the participants want to win the competition, but they also want to be sure that if someone else wins, they deserve to win because they have a genuinely better system. This desire leads to rules to ensure that the benchmark results are not simply engineering tricks for that benchmark, but are instead advances that improve performance of real applications.

To avoid possible tricks, a typical rule is that you can't change the benchmark. The source code and data sets are fixed, and there is a single proper answer. Any deviation from those rules makes the results invalid.

Many multiprocessor benchmarks follow these traditions. A common exception is to be able to increase the size of the problem so that you can run the benchmark on systems with a widely different number of processors. That is, many benchmarks allow weak scaling rather than require strong scaling, even though you must take care when comparing results for programs running different problem sizes.

Figure 7.11 is a summary of several parallel benchmarks, also described below:

- *Linpack* is a collection of linear algebra routines, and the routines for performing Gaussian elimination constitute what is known as the Linpack benchmark. The DAXPY routine in the example on page 650 represents a small fraction of the source code of the Linpack benchmark, but it accounts for most of the execution time for the benchmark. It allows weak scaling, letting the user pick any size problem. Moreover, it allows the user to rewrite Linpack in any form and in any language, as long as it computes the proper result. Twice a year, the 500 computers with the fastest Linpack performance are published at www.top500.org. The first on this list is considered by the press to be the world's fastest computer.

- *SPECrate* is a throughput metric based on the SPEC CPU benchmarks, such as SPEC CPU 2006 (see Chapter 1). Rather than report performance of the individual programs, SPECrate runs many copies of the program simultaneously. Thus, it measures job-level parallelism, as there is no communication between the jobs. You can run as many copies of the programs as you want, so this is again a form of weak scaling.

- *SPLASH* and *SPLASH 2* (Stanford Parallel Applications for Shared Memory) were efforts by researchers at Stanford University in the 1990s to put together

Benchmark	Scaling?	Reprogram?	Description
Linpack	Weak	Yes	Dense matrix linear algebra [Dongarra, 1979]
SPECrate	Weak	No	Independent job parallelism [Henning, 2007]
Stanford Parallel Applications for Shared Memory SPLASH 2 [Woo et al., 1995]	Strong (although offers two problem sizes)	No	Complex 1D FFT Blocked LU Decomposition Blocked Sparse Cholesky Factorization Integer Radix Sort Barnes-Hut Adaptive Fast Multipole Ocean Simulation Hierarchical Radiosity Ray Tracer Volume Renderer Water Simulation with Spatial Data Structure Water Simulation without Spatial Data Structure
NAS Parallel Benchmarks [Bailey et al., 1991]	Weak	Yes (C or Fortran only)	EP: embarrassingly parallel MG: simplified multigrid CG: unstructured grid for a conjugate gradient method FT: 3-D partial differential equation solution using FFTs IS: large integer sort
PARSEC Benchmark Suite [Bienia et al., 2008]	Weak	No	Blackscholes—Option pricing with Black-Scholes PDE Bodytrack—Body tracking of a person Canneal—Simulated cache-aware annealing to optimize routing Dedup—Next-generation compression with data deduplication Facesim—Simulates the motions of a human face Ferret—Content similarity search server Fluidanimate—Fluid dynamics for animation with SPH method Freqmine—Frequent itemset mining Streamcluster—Online clustering of an input stream Swaptions—Pricing of a portfolio of swaptions Vips—Image processing x264—H.264 video encoding
Berkeley Design Patterns [Asanovic et al., 2006]	Strong or Weak	Yes	Finite-State Machine Combinational Logic Graph Traversal Structured Grid Dense Matrix Sparse Matrix Spectral Methods (FFT) Dynamic Programming N-Body MapReduce Backtrack/Branch and Bound Graphical Model Inference Unstructured Grid

FIGURE 7.11 Examples of parallel benchmarks.

a parallel benchmark suite similar in goals to the SPEC CPU benchmark suite. It includes both kernels and applications, including many from the high-performance computing community. This benchmark requires strong scaling, although it comes with two data sets.

■ The *NAS (NASA Advanced Supercomputing) parallel benchmarks* were another attempt from the 1990s to benchmark multiprocessors. Taken from computational fluid dynamics, they consist of five kernels. They allow weak scaling by defining a few data sets. Like Linpack, these benchmarks can be rewritten, but the rules require that the programming language can only be C or Fortran.

■ The recent *PARSEC (Princeton Application Repository for Shared Memory Computers) benchmark suite* consists of multithreaded programs that use **Pthreads** (POSIX threads) and **OpenMP** (Open MultiProcessing). They focus on emerging markets and consist of nine applications and three kernels. Eight rely on data parallelism, three rely on pipelined parallelism, and one on unstructured parallelism.

Pthreads A UNIX API for creating and manipulating threads. It comes with a library.

OpenMP An API for shared memory multiprocessing in C, C++, or Fortran that runs on UNIX and Microsoft platforms. It includes compiler directives, a library, and runtime directives.

The downside of such traditional restrictions to benchmarks is that innovation is chiefly limited to the architecture and compiler. Better data structures, algorithms, programming languages, and so on often can not be used, since that would give a misleading result. The system could win because of, say, the algorithm, and not because of the hardware or the compiler.

While these guidelines are understandable when the foundations of computing are relatively stable—as they were in the 1990s and the first half of this decade—they are undesirable at the beginning of a revolution. For this revolution to succeed, we need to encourage innovation at all levels.

One recent approach has been advocated by researchers at the University of California at Berkeley. They have identified 13 design patterns that they claim will be part of applications of the future. These design patterns are implemented by frameworks or kernels. Examples are sparse matrices, structured grid, finite-state machines, map reduce, and graph traversal. By keeping the definitions at a high level, they hope to encourage innovations at any level of the system. Thus, the system with the fastest sparse matrix solver is welcome to use any data structure, algorithm, and programming language, in addition to novel architectures and compilers. We'll see examples of such benchmarks in Section 7.11.

Check Yourself

True or false: The main drawback with conventional approaches to benchmarks for parallel computers is that the rules that ensure fairness also suppress innovation.

7.10 Roofline: A Simple Performance Model

This section is based on a paper by Williams and Patterson [2008]. In the recent past, conventional wisdom in computer architecture led to similar microprocessor designs. Nearly every desktop and server computer used caches, pipelining, superscalar instruction issue, branch prediction, and out-of-order execution. The instruction sets varied, but the microprocessors were all from the same school of design.

The switch to multicore likely means that microprocessors will become more diverse, since there is no conventional wisdom as to which architecture will make it easiest to write correct parallel processing programs that run efficiently and scale as the number of cores increases over time. Moreover, as the number of cores per chip does increase, a single manufacturer will likely offer different numbers of cores per chip at different price points at the same time.

Given the increasing diversity, it would be especially helpful if we had a simple model that offered insights into the performance of different designs. It need not be perfect, just insightful.

The 3Cs model from Chapter 5 is an analogy. It is not a perfect model, since it ignores potentially important factors like block size, block allocation policy, and block replacement policy. Moreover, it has quirks. For example, a miss can be ascribed due to capacity in one design and to a conflict miss in another cache of the same size. Yet 3Cs model has been popular for 20 years, because it offers insight into the behavior of programs, helping both architects and programmers improve their creations based on insights from that model.

To find such a model, let's start with the 13 Berkeley design patterns in Figure 7.9. The idea of the design patterns is that the performance of a given application is really the weighted sum of several kernels that implement those design patterns. We'll evaluate individual kernels here, but keep in mind that real applications are combinations of many kernels.

While there are versions with different data types, floating point is popular in several implementations. Hence, peak floating-point performance is a limit on the speed of such kernels on a given computer. For multicore chips, peak floating-point performance is the collective peak performance of all the cores on the chip. If there were multiple microprocessors in the system, you would multiply the peak per chip by the total number of chips.

The demands on the memory system can be estimated by dividing this peak floating-point performance by the average number of floating-point operations per byte accessed:

$$\frac{\text{Floating-Point Operations/Sec}}{\text{Floating-Point Operations/Byte}} = \text{Bytes/Sec}$$

arithmetic intensity
The ratio of floating-point operations in a program to the number of data bytes accessed by a program from main memory.

The ratio of floating-point operations per byte of memory accessed is called the **arithmetic intensity**. It can be calculated by taking the total number of floating-point operations for a program divided by the total number of data bytes transferred to main memory during program execution. Figure 7.12 shows the arithmetic intensity of several of the Berkeley design patterns from Figure 7.11.

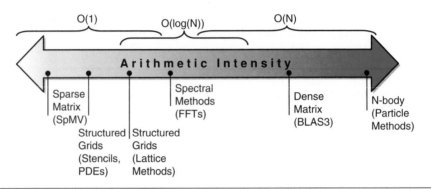

FIGURE 7.12   Arithmetic intensity, specified as the number of float-point operations to run the program divided by the number of bytes accessed in main memory [Williams, Patterson, 2008]. Some kernels have an arithmetic intensity that scales with problem size, such as Dense Matrix, but there are many kernels with arithmetic intensities independent of problem size. For kernels in this former case, weak scaling can lead to different results, since it puts much less demand on the memory system.

The Roofline Model

The proposed simple model ties floating-point performance, arithmetic intensity, and memory performance together in a two-dimensional graph [Williams, Patterson, 2008]. Peak floating-point performance can be found using the hardware specifications mentioned above. The working set of the kernels we consider here do not fit in on-chip caches, so peak memory performance may be defined by the memory system behind the caches. One way to find the peak memory performance is the Stream benchmark. (See the *Elaboration* on page 473 in Chapter 5).

Figure 7.13 shows the model, which is done once for a computer, not for each kernel. The vertical Y-axis is achievable floating-point performance from 0.5 to 64.0 GFLOPs/second. The horizontal X-axis is arithmetic intensity, varying from 1/8 FLOPs/DRAM byte accessed to 16 FLOPs/DRAM byte accessed. Note that the graph is a log-log scale.

For a given kernel, we can find a point on the X-axis based on its arithmetic intensity. If we drew a vertical line through that point, the performance of the kernel on that computer must lie somewhere along that line. We can plot a horizontal line showing peak floating-point performance of the computer. Obviously, the

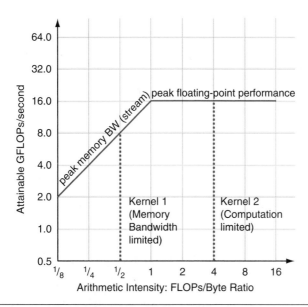

FIGURE 7.13   Roofline Model [Williams, Patterson, 2008]. This example has a peak floating-point performance of 16 GFLOPS/sec and a peak memory bandwidth of 16 GB/sec from the Stream benchmark. (Since stream is actually four measurements, this line is the average of the four.) The dotted vertical line in color on the left represents Kernel 1, which has an arithmetic intensity of 0.5 FLOPs/byte. It is limited by memory bandwidth to no more than 8 GFLOPS/sec on this Opteron X2. The dotted vertical line to the right represents Kernel 2, which has an arithmetic intensity of 4 FLOPs/byte. It is limited only computationally to 16 GFLOPS/s. (This data is based on the AMD Opteron X2 (Revision F) using dual cores running at 2 GHz in a dual socket system.)

actual floating-point performance can be no higher than the horizontal line, since that is a hardware limit.

How could we plot the peak memory performance? Since X-axis is FLOPs/ byte and the Y-axis is FLOPs/second, bytes/second is just a diagonal line at a 45-degree angle in this figure. Hence, we can plot a third line that gives the maximum floating-point performance that the memory system of that computer can support for a given arithmetic intensity. We can express the limits as a formula to plot the line in the graph in Figure 7.13:

$$\text{Attainable GFLOPs/sec} = \text{Min (Peak Memory BW} \times \text{Arithmetic Intensity,}$$
$$\text{Peak Floating-Point Performance)}$$

The horizontal and diagonal lines give this simple model its name and indicates its value. The "roofline" sets an upper bound on performance of a kernel depending on its arithmetic intensity. If we think of arithmetic intensity as a pole that hits the roof, either it hits the flat part of the roof, which means performance is computationally limited, or it hits the slanted part of the roof, which means performance is ultimately limited by memory bandwidth. In Figure 7.13, kernel 2 is an example of the former and kernel 1 is an example of the latter. Given a roofline of a computer, you can apply it repeatedly, since it doesn't vary by kernel.

Note that the "ridge point," where the diagonal and horizontal roofs meet, offers an interesting insight into the computer. If it is far to the right, then only kernels with very high arithmetic intensity can achieve the maximum performance of that computer. If it is far to the left, then almost any kernel can potentially hit the maximum performance. We'll see examples of both shortly.

Comparing Two Generations of Opterons

The AMD Opteron X4 (Barcelona) with four cores is the successor to the Opteron X2 with two cores. To simplify board design, they use the same socket. Hence, they have the same DRAM channels and thus the same peak memory bandwidth. In addition to doubling the number of cores, the Opteron X4 also has twice the peak floating-point performance per core: Opteron X4 cores can issue two floating-point SSE2 instructions per clock cycle, while Opteron X2 cores issue at most one. As the two systems we're comparing have similar clock rates—2.2 GHz for Opteron X2 versus 2.3 GHz for Opteron X4—the Opteron X4 has more than four times the peak floating-point performance of the Opteron X2 with the same DRAM bandwidth. The Opteron X4 also has a 2MB L3 cache, which is not found in the Opteron X2.

Figure 7.14 compares the roofline models for both systems. As we would expect, the ridge point moves from 1 in the Opteron X2 to 5 in the Opteron X4. Hence, to see a performance gain in the next generation, kernels need an arithmetic intensity higher than 1 or their working sets must fit in the caches of the Opteron X4.

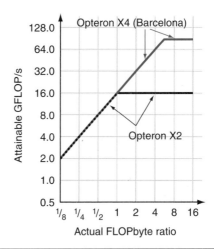

FIGURE 7.14   Roofline models of two generations of Opterons. The Opteron X2 roofline, which is the same as Figure 7.11, is in black, and the Opteron X4 roofline is in color. The bigger ridge point of Opteron X4 means that kernels that where computationally bound on the Opteron X2 could be memory-performance bound on the Opteron X4.

The roofline model gives an upper bound to performance. Suppose your program is far below that bound. What optimizations should you perform, and in what order?

To reduce computational bottlenecks, the following two optimizations can help almost any kernel:

1. *Floating-point operation mix.* Peak floating-point performance for a computer typically requires an equal number of nearly simultaneous additions and multiplications. That balance is necessary either because the computer supports a fused multiply-add instruction (see the *Elaboration* on page 268 in Chapter 3) or because the floating-point unit has an equal number of floating-point adders and floating-point multipliers. The best performance also requires that a significant fraction of the instruction mix is floating-point operations and not integer instructions.

2. *Improve instruction-level parallelism and apply SIMD.* For superscalar architectures, the highest performance comes when fetching, executing, and committing three to four instructions per clock cycle (see Chapter 4). The goal here is to improve the code from the compiler to increase ILP. One way is by unrolling loops. For the x86 architectures, a single SIMD instruction can operate on pairs of double precision operands, so they should be used whenever possible.

To reduce memory bottlenecks, the following two optimizations can help:

1. *Software prefetching.* Usually the highest performance requires keeping many memory operations in flight, which is easier to do by performing software prefetch instructions rather than waiting until the data is required by the computation.

2. *Memory affinity.* Most microprocessors today include a memory controller on the same chip with the microprocessor. If the system has multiple chips, this means that some addresses go to the DRAM that is local to one chip, and the rest require accesses over the chip interconnect to access the DRAM that is local to another chip. The latter case lowers performance. This optimization tries to allocate data and the threads tasked to operate on that data to the same memory-processor pair, so that the processors rarely have to access the memory of the other chips.

The roofline model can help decide which of these optimizations to perform and the order in which to perform them. We can think of each of these optimizations as a "ceiling" below the appropriate roofline, meaning that you cannot break through a ceiling without performing the associated optimization.

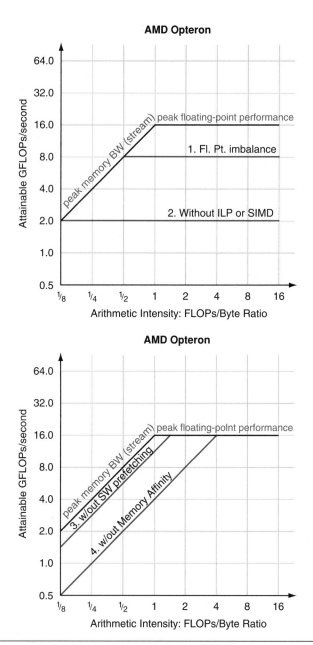

FIGURE 7.15 Roofline model with ceilings. The top graph shows the computational "ceilings" of 8 GFLOPs/sec if the floating-point operation mix is imbalanced and 2 GFLOPs/sec if the optimizations to increase ILP and SIMD are also missing. The bottom graph shows the memory bandwidth ceilings of 11 GB/sec without software prefetching and 4.8 GB/sec if memory affinity optimizations are also missing.

The computational roofline can be found from the manuals, and the memory roofline can be found from running the stream benchmark. The computational ceilings, such as floating-point balance, also come from the manuals for that computer. The memory ceiling requires running experiments on each computer to determine the gap between them. The good news is that this process only need be done once per computer, for once someone characterizes a computer's ceilings, everyone can use the results to prioritize their optimizations for that computer.

Figure 7.15 adds ceilings to the roofline model in Figure 7.13, showing the computational ceilings in the top graph and the memory bandwidth ceilings on the bottom graph. Although the higher ceilings are not labeled with both optimizations, that is implied in this figure; to break through the highest ceiling, you need to have already broken through all the ones below.

The thickness of the gap between the ceiling and the next higher limit is the reward for trying that optimization. Thus, Figure 7.15 suggests that optimization 2, which improves ILP, has a large benefit for improving computation on that computer, and optimization 4, which improves memory affinity, has a large benefit for improving memory bandwidth on that computer.

Figure 7.16 combines the ceilings of Figure 7.15 into a single graph. The arithmetic intensity of a kernel determines the optimization region, which in turn suggests which optimizations to try. Note that the computational optimizations and the memory bandwidth optimizations overlap for much of the arithmetic intensity. Three regions are shaded differently in Figure 7.16 to indicate the different optimization strategies. For example, Kernel 2 falls in the blue trapezoid on the right, which suggests working only on the computational optimizations. Kernel 1 falls in the blue-gray parallelogram in the middle, which suggests trying both types of optimizations. Moreover, it suggests starting with optimizations 2 and 4. Note that the Kernel 1 vertical lines fall below the floating-point imbalance optimization, so optimization 1 may be unnecessary. If a kernel fell in the gray triangle on the lower left, it would suggest trying just memory optimizations.

Thus far, we have been assuming that the arithmetic intensity is fixed, but that is not really the case. First, there are kernels where the arithmetic intensity increases with problem size, such as for Dense Matrix and N-body problems (see Figure 7.12). Indeed, this can be a reason that programmers have more success with weak scaling than with strong scaling. Second, caches affect the number of accesses that go to memory, so optimizations that improve cache performance also improve arithmetic intensity. One example is improving temporal locality by unrolling loops and then grouping together statements with similar addresses. Many computers have special cache instructions that allocate data in a cache but do not first fill the data from memory at that address, since it will soon be overwritten. Both these optimizations reduce memory traffic, thereby moving the arithmetic intensity pole to the right by a factor of, say, 1.5. This shift right could put the kernel in a different optimization region.

The next section uses the roofline model to demonstrate the difference for four recent multicore microprocessors for two real application kernels. While the examples above show how to help programmers improve performance, the model can also be used by architects to decide where they optimize hardware to improve performance of the kernels that they think will be important.

Elaboration: The ceilings are ordered so that lower ceilings are easier to optimize. Clearly, a programmer can optimize in any order, but following this sequence reduces the chances of wasting effort on an optimization that has no benefit due to other constraints. Like the 3Cs model, as long as the roofline model delivers on insights, a model can have quirks. For example, it assumes the program is load balanced between all processors.

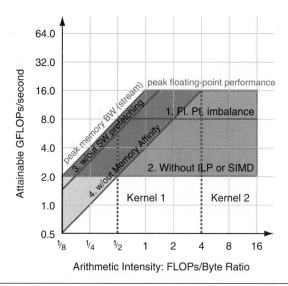

FIGURE 7.16 Roofline model with ceilings, overlapping areas shaded, and the two kernels from Figure 7.13. Kernels whose arithmetic intensity land in the blue trapezoid on the right should focus on computation optimizations, and kernels whose arithmetic intensity land in the gray triangle in the lower left should focus on memory bandwidth optimizations. Those that land in the blue-gray parallelogram in the middle need to worry about both. As Kernel 1 falls in the parallelogram in the middle, try optimizing ILP and SIMD, memory affinity, and software prefetching. Kernel 2 falls in the trapezoid on the right, so try optimizing ILP and SIMD and the balance of floating-point operations.

Elaboration: An alternative to the Stream benchmark is to use the raw DRAM bandwidth as the roofline. While the DRAMs definitely set a hard bound, actual memory performance is often so far from that boundary that it's not that useful as an upper bound. That is, no program can go close to that bound. The downside to using Stream is that very careful programming may exceed the Stream results, so the memory roofline may not be as hard a limit as the computational roofline. We stick with Stream because few programmers will be able to deliver more memory bandwidth than Stream discovers.

Elaboration: The two axes used above were floating-point operations per second and arithmetic intensity of accesses to main memory. The roofline model could be used for other kernels and computers where the performance was a function of different performance metrics.

For example, if the working set fits in the L2 cache of the computer, the bandwidth plotted on the diagonal roofline could be L2 cache bandwidth instead of main memory bandwidth, and the arithmetic intensity on the X-axis would be based on FLOPs per L2 cache byte accessed. The diagonal L2 performance line would move up, and the ridge point would likely move to the left.

As a second example, if the kernel was sort, records sorted per second could replace floating-point operations per instruction on the Y-axis and arithmetic intensity would become records per DRAM byte accessed.

The roofline model could even work for an I/O intensive kernel. The Y-axis would be I/O operations per second, the X-axis would be the average number of instructions per I/O operation, and the roofline would show peak I/O bandwidth.

Elaboration: Although the roofline model shown is for multicore processors, it clearly would work for a uniprocessor as well.

7.11   Real Stuff: Benchmarking Four Multicores Using the Roofline Model

Given the uncertainty about the best way to proceed in this parallel revolution, it's not surprising that we see as many different designs as there are multicore chips. In this section, we'll examine four multicore systems for two kernels of the design patterns in Figure 7.11: sparse matrix and structured grid. (The information in this section is from [Williams, Oliker, et al., 2007], [Williams, Carter, et al., 2008], [Williams and Patterson, 2008].)

Four Multicore Systems

Figure 7.17 shows the basic organization of the four systems, and Figure 7.18 lists the key characteristics of the examples of this section. These are all dual socket systems. Figure 7.19 shows the roofline performance model for each system.

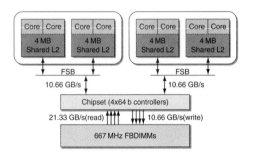

(a) Intel Xeon e5345 (Clovertown)

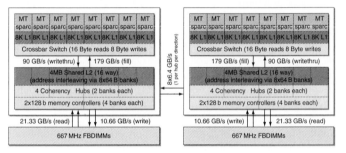

(c) Sun UltraSPARC T2 5140 (Niagara 2)

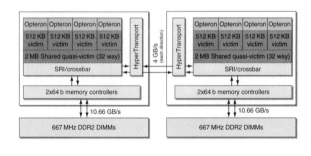

(b) AMD Opteron X4 2356 (Barcelona)

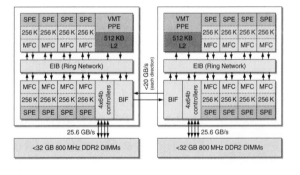

(d) IBM Cell QS20

FIGURE 7.17 Four recent multiprocessors, each using two sockets for the processors. Starting from the upper left hand corner, the computers are: (a) Intel Xeon e5345 (Clovertown), (b) AMD Opteron X4 2356 (Barcelona), (c) Sun UltraSPARC T2 5140 (Niagara 2), and (d) IBM Cell QS20. Note that the Intel Xeon e5345 (Clovertown) has a separate north bridge chip not found in the other microprocessors.

MPU Type	ISA	Number Threads	Number Cores	Number Sockets	Clock GHz	Peak GFLOP/s	DRAM: Peak GB/s, Clock Rate, Type	
Intel Xeon e5345 (Clovertown)	x86/64	8	8	2	2.33	75	FSB: 2 x 10.6	667 MHz FBDIMM
AMD Opteron X4 2356 (Barcelona)	x86/64	8	8	2	2.30	74	2 x 10.6	667 MHz DDR2
Sun UltraSPARC T2 5140 (Niagara 2)	Sparc	128	16	2	1.17	22	2 x 21.3 (read) 2 x 10.6 (write)	667 MHz FBDIMM
IBM Cell QS20	Cell	16	16	2	3.20	29	2 x 25.6	XDR

FIGURE 7.18 Characteristics of the four recent multicores. Although the Xeon e5345 and Opteron X4 have the same speed DRAMs, the Stream benchmark shows a higher practical memory bandwidth due to the inefficiencies of the front side bus on the Xeon e5345.

The Intel Xeon e5345 (code-named "Clovertown") contains four cores per socket by packaging two dual core chips into a single socket. These two chips share a front side bus that is attached to a separate north bridge chip set (see Chapter 6). This north bridge chip set supports two front side buses and hence two sockets. It includes the memory controller for the 667 MHz Fully Buffered DRAM DIMMs (FBDIMMs). This dual-socket system uses a processor clock rate of 2.33 GHz and has the highest peak performance of the four examples: 75 GFLOPS. However, the roofline model in Figure 7.19 shows that this can be achieved only with arithmetic intensities of 8 and above. The reason is that the dual front side buses interfere with each other, yielding relatively low memory bandwidth to programs.

The AMD Opteron X4 2356 (Barcelona) contains four cores per chip, and each socket has a single chip. Each chip has a memory controller on board and its own path to 667 MHz DDR2 DRAM. These two sockets communicate over separate, dedicated Hypertransport links, which makes it possible to build a "glueless" multichip system. This dual-socket system uses a processor clock rate of 2.30 GHz and has a peak performance of about 74 GFLOPS. Figure 7.19 shows that the ridge point in the roofline model is to the left of the Xeon e5345 (Clovertown), at an arithmetic intensity of about 5 FLOPS per byte.

The Sun UltraSPARC T2 5140 (code named "Niagara 2") is quite different from the two x86 microarchitectures. It uses eight relatively simple cores per chip with a much lower clock rate. It also provides fine-grained multithreading with eight threads per core. A single chip has four memory controllers that could drive four sets of 667 MHz FBDIMMs. To join two UltraSPARC T2 chips together, two of the four memory channels are connected, leaving two memory channels per chip. This dual-socket system has a peak performance of about 22 GFLOPS, and the ridge point is an amazingly low arithmetic intensity of just 1/3 FLOPS per byte.

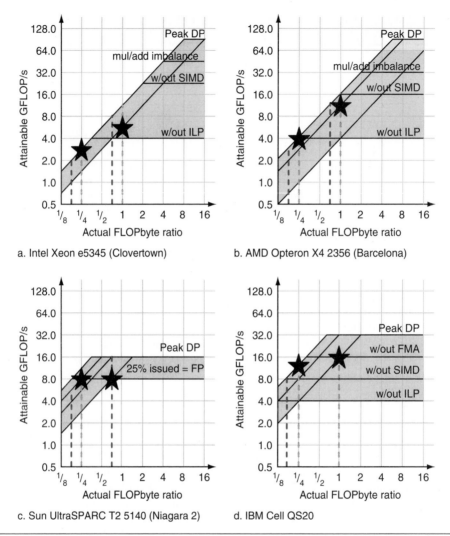

FIGURE 7.19   Roofline model for multicore multiprocessors in Figure 7.15. The ceilings are the same as in Figure 7.13. Starting from the upper left hand corner, the computers are: (a) Intel Xeon e5345 (Clovertown), (b) AMD Opteron X4 2356 (Barcelona), (c) Sun UltraSPARC T2 5140 (Niagara 2), and (d) IBM Cell QS20. Note the ridge points for the four microprocessors intersect the X-axis at the arithmetic intensities of 6, 4, 1/3, and 3/4, respectively. The dashed vertical lines are for the two kernels of this section and the stars mark the performance achieved for these kernels after all the optimizations. SpMV is the pair of dashed vertical lines on the left. It has two lines because its arithmetic intensity improved from 0.166 to 0.255 based on register blocking optimizations. LBHMD is the dashed vertical lines on the right. It has a pair of lines in (a) and (b) because a cache optimization skips filling the cache block on a miss when the processor would write new data into the entire block. That optimization increases the arithmetic intensity from 0.70 to 1.07. It's a single line in (c) at 0.70 because UltraSPARC T2 does not offer the cache optimization. It is a single line at 1.07 in (d) because Cell has local store loaded by DMA, so the program doesn't fetch unnecessary data as do caches.

The IBM Cell QS20 is again different from the two x86 microarchitectures and from UltraSPARC T2. It is a heterogeneous design, with a relatively simple PowerPC core and with eight SPEs (Synergistic Processing Elements) that have their own unique SIMD-style instruction set. Each SPE also has its own local memory instead of a cache. An SPE must transfer data from main memory into the local memory to operate on it and then back to main memory when it is completed. It uses DMA, which has some similarity to software prefetching. The two sockets are connected via links dedicated to multichip communications. The clock rate of this system is highest of the four multicores at 3.2 GHz, and it uses XDR DRAM chips, which are typically found in game consoles. They have high bandwidth but low capacity. Given that the Cell's main application was graphics, it has much higher single precision performance than double precision performance. The peak double precision performance of the SPEs in the dual socket system is 29 GFLOPS, and the ridge point of arithmetic intensity is 0.75 FLOPs per byte.

While the two x86 architectures have many fewer cores per chip than the IBM and Sun offerings in early 2008, that is just where they are today. As the number of cores is expected to double every technology generation, it will be interesting to see whether the x86 architectures will close the "core gap" or if IBM and Sun can sustain a larger number of cores, given that their primary focus is on servers versus the desktop.

Note that these machines take very different approaches to the memory system. The Xeon e5345 uses a conventional private L1 cache and then pairs of processors each share an L2 cache. These are connected through an off-chip memory controller to a common memory over two buses. In contrast, Opteron X4 has a separate memory controller and memory per chip, and each core has private L1 and L2 caches. UltraSPARC T2 has the memory controller on-chip and four separate DRAM channels per chip, and the cores all share the L2 cache, which has four banks to improve bandwidth. Its fine-grained multithreading on top of its multicore design allows it to keep many memory accesses in flight. The most radical is the Cell. It has local private memories per SPE and uses DMA to transfer data between the DRAM attached to each chip and local memory. It sustains many memory accesses in flight by having many cores and then many DMA transfers per core.

Let's see how these four contrasting multicores perform on two kernels.

Sparse Matrix

The first example kernel of the Sparse Matrix computational design pattern is Sparse Matrix-Vector multiply (SpMV). SpMV is popular in scientific computing, economic modeling, and information retrieval. Alas, conventional implementations often run at less than 10% of peak performance of uniprocessors. One reason is the irregular access to memory, which you might expect from a kernel working with sparse matrices. The computation is

$$y = A \times x$$

where A is a sparse matrix and x and y are dense vectors. Fourteen sparse matrices taken from a variety of real applications were used to evaluate SpMV performance, but only the median performance is reported here. The arithmetic intensity varies from 0.166 before a register blocking optimization to 0.250 FLOPS per byte afterward.

The code was first parallelized to utilize all the cores. Given that the low arithmetic intensity of SpMV was below the ridge point of all four multicores in Figure 7.19, most of the optimizations involved the memory system:

- *Prefetching.* To get the most out of the memory systems, both software and hardware prefetching were used.

- *Memory Affinity.* This optimization reduces accesses to the DRAM memory connected to the other socket in the three systems that have local DRAM memory.

- *Compressing Data Structures.* Since memory bandwidth likely limits performance, this optimization uses smaller data structures to increase performance—for example, using a 16-bit index instead of a 32-bit index, and using more space efficient representations of the nonzeros in the rows of a sparse matrix.

Figure 7.20 shows the performance on SpMV for the four systems versus the number of cores. (The same results are found in Figure 7.19, but it's hard to compare performance when on a log scale.) Note that despite having the highest peak performance in Figure 7.18 and the highest single core performance, the Intel Xeon e5345 has the lowest delivered performance of the four multicores. Opteron X4 doubles its performance. The Xeon e5345 bottleneck is the dual front side buses. Despite the lowest clock rate, the larger number of simple cores of the Sun UltraSPARC T2 outperforms the two x86 processors. The IBM Cell has the highest performance of the four. Note that all but the Xeon e5345 scale well with the number of cores, although the Opteron X4 scales more slowly with four or more cores.

Structured Grid

The second kernel is an example of the structured grid design pattern. Lattice-Boltzmann Magneto-Hydrodynamics (LBMHD) is popular for computational fluid dynamics; it is a structured grid code with a series of time steps.

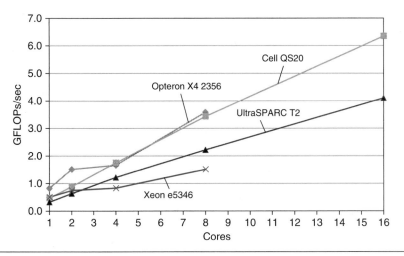

FIGURE 7.20 **Performance of SpMV on the four multicores.**

Each point involves reading and writing about 75 double precision floating-point numbers and about 1300 floating-point operations. Like SpMV, LBMHD tends to get a small fraction of peak performance on uniprocessors because of the complexity of the data structures and the irregularity of memory access patterns. The FLOPS to byte ratio is a much higher 0.70 versus less than 0.25 in SpMV. By not filling the cache block from memory on a write miss when the program is going to overwrite the whole block, the intensity rises to 1.07. All multicores but UltraSPARC T2 (Niagara 2) offer this cache optimization.

Figure 7.19 shows that the arithmetic intensity of LBMHD is high enough that both computational and memory bandwidth optimizations make sense on all multicores but UltraSPARC T2, whose roofline ridge point is below that of LBMHD. UltraSPARC T2 can reach the roofline using only the computational optimizations.

In addition to parallelizing the code so that it could use all the cores, the following optimizations were used for LBMHD:

- *Memory Affinity:* This optimization is again useful for the same reasons mentioned above.

- *TLB Miss Minimization:* To reduce TLB misses significantly in LBMHD, use a structure of arrays and combine some loops together rather than the conventional approach of using an array of structures.

- *Loop Unrolling and Reordering:* To expose sufficient parallelism and improve cache utilization, the loops were unrolled and then reordered to group statements with similar addresses.

- *"SIMD-ize":* The compilers of the two x86 systems could not generate good SSE code, so these had to be written by hand in assembly language.

Figure 7.21 shows the performance for the four systems versus the number of cores for LBMHD. Like the SpMV, the Intel Xeon e5345 has the worst scalability. This time the more powerful cores of Opteron X4 outperform the simple cores of UltraSPARC T2 despite having half the number of cores. Once again, the IBM Cell is the fastest system. All but Xeon e5345 scale with the number of cores, although T2 and Cell scale more smoothly than the Opteron X4.

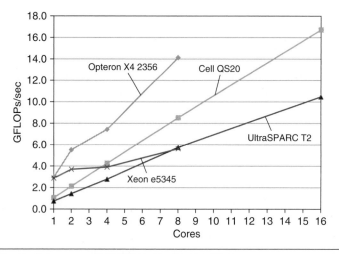

FIGURE 7.21   Performance of LBMHD on the four multicores.

Productivity

In addition to performance, another important issue for the parallel computing revolution is productivity, or the programming difficulty of achieving performance. To illustrate the differences, Figure 7.22 compares naïve performance to fully optimized performance for the four cores on the two kernels.

MPU Type	Kernel	Base GFLOPs/s	Optimized GFLOPs/s	Naïve % of Optimized
Intel Xeon e5345	SpMV	1.0	1.5	64%
(Clovertown)	LBMHD	4.6	5.6	82%
AMD Opteron X4 2356	SpMV	1.4	3.6	38%
(Barcelona)	LBMHD	7.1	14.1	50%
Sun UltraSPARC T2	SpMV	3.5	4.1	86%
(Niagara 2)	LBMHD	9.7	10.5	93%
IBM Cell QS20	SpMV	-	6.4	0%
	LBMHD	-	16.7	0%

FIGURE 7.22 Base versus fully optimized performance of the four cores on the two kernels.
Note the high fraction of fully optimized performance delivered by the Sun UltraSPARC T2 (Niagara 2). There is no base performance column for the IBM Cell because there is no way to port the code to the SPEs without caches. While you could run the code on the Power core, it has an order of magnitude lower performance than the SPES, so we ignore it in this figure.

The easiest was UltraSPARC T2, due to its large memory bandwidth and its easy-to-understand cores. The advice for these two kernels in UltraSPARC T2 is simply to try to get good performing code from the compiler and then use as many threads as possible. The one caution for other kernels is that UltraSPARC T2 can come afoul of the pitfall about making sure set associativity matches the number of hardware threads (see page 545 of Chapter 5). Each chip supports 64 hardware threads, while the L2 cache is four-way set associative. This mismatch can require restructuring loops to reduce conflict misses.

The Xeon e5346 was difficult because it was hard to understand the memory behavior of the dual front side buses, it was hard to understand how hardware prefetching worked, and it was difficult to get good SIMD code from the compiler. The C code for it and for the Opteron X4 are liberally sprinkled with intrinsic statements involving SIMD instructions to get good performance.

The Opteron X4 benefited from the most types of optimizations, so it needed more effort than the Xeon e5345, although the memory behavior of the Opteron X4 was easier to understand than that of the Xeon e5345.

Cell provided two types of challenges. First, the SIMD instructions of the SPE were awkward to compile for, so at times you needed to help the compiler by inserting intrinsic statements with assembly language instructions into the C code. Second, the memory system was more interesting. Since each SPE has local memory in a separate address space, you could not simply port the code and start running on the SPE. Hence, there is no base code column for the IBM Cell in Figure 7.22, and you needed to change the program to issue DMA commands to transfer data back and forth between local store and memory. The good news is that DMA played the role of software prefetch in caches, and DMA is much easier to use and achieve good memory performance. Cell was able to deliver almost 90% of the memory bandwidth "roofline" to these kernels, compared to 50% or less for the other multicores.

For over a decade prophets have voiced the contention that the organization of a single computer has reached its limits and that truly significant advances can be made only by interconnection of a multiplicity of computers in such a manner as to permit cooperative solution. . . . Demonstration is made of the continued validity of the single processor approach . . .

Gene Amdahl, "Validity of the single processor approach to achieving large scale computing capabilities," Spring Joint Computer Conference, 1967

7.12 Fallacies and Pitfalls

The many assaults on parallel processing have uncovered numerous fallacies and pitfalls. We cover three here.

Fallacy: Amdahl's law doesn't apply to parallel computers.

In 1987, the head of a research organization claimed that Amdahl's law had been broken by a multiprocessor machine. To try to understand the basis of the media reports, let's see the quote that gave us Amdahl's law [1967, p. 483]:

A fairly obvious conclusion which can be drawn at this point is that the effort expended on achieving high parallel processing rates is wasted unless it is accompanied by achievements in sequential processing rates of very nearly the same magnitude.

This statement must still be true; the neglected portion of the program must limit performance. One interpretation of the law leads to the following lemma: portions of every program must be sequential, so there must be an economic upper bound to the number of processors—say, 100. By showing linear speed-up with 1000 processors, this lemma is disproved; hence the claim that Amdahl's law was broken.

The approach of the researchers was to use weak scaling: rather than going 1000 times faster on the same data set, they computed 1000 times more work in comparable time. For their algorithm, the sequential portion of the program was constant, independent of the size of the input, and the rest was fully parallel—hence, linear speed-up with 1000 processors.

Amdahl's law obviously applies to parallel processors. What this research does point out is that one of the main uses of faster computers is to run larger problems, but to beware how the algorithm scales as you increase problem size.

Fallacy: Peak performance tracks observed performance.

For example, Section 7.11 shows that the Intel Xeon e5345, the microprocessor with the highest peak performance, was the slowest of the four multicore microprocessors for two kernels.

The supercomputer industry used this metric in marketing, and the fallacy is exacerbated with parallel machines. Not only are marketers using the nearly unattainable peak performance of a uniprocessor node, but also they are then multiplying it by the total number of processors, assuming perfect speed-up! Amdahl's law suggests how difficult it is to reach either peak; multiplying the two together multiplies the sins. The roofline model helps put peak performance in perspective.

Pitfall: Not developing the software to take advantage of, or optimize for, a multi-processor architecture.

There is a long history of software lagging behind on parallel processors, possibly because the software problems are much harder. We give one example to show the subtlety of the issues, but there are many examples we could choose!

One frequently encountered problem occurs when software designed for a uniprocessor is adapted to a multiprocessor environment. For example, the SGI operating system originally protected the page table with a single lock, assuming that page allocation is infrequent. In a uniprocessor, this does not represent a performance problem. In a multiprocessor, it can become a major performance bottleneck for some programs. Consider a program that uses a large number of pages that are initialized at start-up, which UNIX does for statically allocated pages. Suppose the program is parallelized so that multiple processes allocate the pages. Because page allocation requires the use of the page table, which is locked whenever it is in use, even an OS kernel that allows multiple threads in the OS will be serialized if the processes all try to allocate their pages at once (which is exactly what we might expect at initialization time!).

This page table serialization eliminates parallelism in initialization and has significant impact on overall parallel performance. This performance bottleneck persists even for job-level parallelism. For example, suppose we split the parallel processing program apart into separate jobs and run them, one job per processor, so that there is no sharing between the jobs. (This is exactly what one user did, since he reasonably believed that the performance problem was due to unintended sharing or interference in his application.) Unfortunately, the lock still serializes all the jobs—so even the independent job performance is poor.

This pitfall indicates the kind of subtle but significant performance bugs that can arise when software runs on multiprocessors. Like many other key software components, the OS algorithms and data structures must be rethought in a multi-processor context. Placing locks on smaller portions of the page table effectively eliminates the problem.

We are dedicating all of our future product development to multicore designs. We believe this is a key inflection point for the industry. ... This is not a race. This is a sea change in computing..."

Paul Otellini, Intel President, Intel Developers Forum, 2004.

7.13   Concluding Remarks

The dream of building computers by simply aggregating processors has been around since the earliest days of computing. Progress in building and using effective and efficient parallel processors, however, has been slow. This rate of progress has been limited by difficult software problems as well as by a long process of evolving the architecture of multiprocessors to enhance usability and improve efficiency. We have discussed many of the software challenges in this chapter, including the difficulty of writing programs that obtain good speed-up due to Amdahl's law. The wide variety of different architectural approaches and the limited success and short life of many of the parallel architectures of the past have compounded the software difficulties. We discuss the history of the development of these multiprocessors in ⊙ Section 7.14 on the CD.

As we said in Chapter 1, despite this long and checkered past, the information technology industry has now tied its future to parallel computing. Although it is easy to make the case that this effort will fail like many in the past, there are reasons to be hopeful:

software as a service Rather than selling software that is installed and run on customers own computers, software is run at a remote site and made available over the Internet typically via a Web interface to customers. Customers are charged based on use.

- Clearly, **software as a service** is growing in importance, and clusters have proven to be a very successful way to deliver such services. By providing redundancy at a higher-level, including geographically distributed datacenters, such services have delivered $24 \times 7 \times 365$ availability for customers around the world. It's hard not to imagine that both the number of servers per datacenter and the number of datacenters will continue to grow. Certainly, such datacenters will embrace multicore designs, since they can already use thousands of processors in their applications.

- The use of parallel processing in domains such as scientific and engineering computation is popular. This application domain has an almost limitless thirst for more computation. It also has many applications that have lots of natural concurrency. Once again, clusters dominate this application area. For example, using the 2007 Linpack report, clusters represent more than 80% of the 500 fastest computers. Nonetheless, it has not been easy: programming parallel processors even for these applications remains challenging. Yet this group too will surely embrace multicore chips, since again they have experience with hundreds to thousand of processors.

- All desktop and server microprocessor manufacturers are building multiprocessors to achieve higher performance, so unlike the past, there is no easy path to higher performance for sequential applications. Hence, programmers who need higher performance must parallelize their codes or write new parallel processing programs.

■ Multiple processors on the same chip allow a very different speed of communication than multiple chip designs, offering both much lower latency and much higher bandwidth. These improvements may make it easier to deliver good performance.

■ In the past, microprocessors and multiprocessors were subject to different definitions of success. When scaling uniprocessor performance, microprocessor architects were happy if single thread performance went up by the square root of the increased silicon area. Thus, they were happy with sublinear performance in terms of resources. Multiprocessor success used to be defined as linear speed-up as a function of the number of processors, assuming that the cost of purchase or cost of administration of n processors was n times as much as one processor. Now that parallelism is happening on-chip via multicore, we can use the traditional microprocessor of being successful with sublinear performance improvement.

■ The success of just-in-time runtime compilation makes it feasible to think of software adapting itself to take advance of the increasing number of cores per chip, which provides flexibility that is not available when limited to static compilers.

■ Unlike in the past, the open source movement has become a critical portion of the software industry. This movement is a meritocracy, where better engineering solutions can win the mind share of the developers over legacy concerns. It also embraces innovation, inviting change to old software and welcoming new languages and software products. Such an open culture could be extremely helpful in this time of rapid change.

This revolution in the hardware/software interface is perhaps the greatest challenge facing the field in the last 50 years. It will provide many new research and business opportunities inside and outside the IT field, and the companies that dominate the multicore era may not be the same ones that dominated the uniprocessor era. Perhaps you will be one of the innovators who will seize the opportunities that are sure to appear in the uncertain times ahead.

Historical Perspective and Further Reading

This section on the CD gives the rich and often disastrous history of multiprocessors over the last 50 years.

Exercises

Contributed by David Kaeli of Northeastern University

Exercise 7.1

First, write down a list of your daily activities that you typically do on a weekday. For instance, you might get out of bed, take a shower, get dressed, eat breakfast, dry your hair, brush your teeth, etc. Make sure to break down your list so you have a minimum of 10 activities.

7.1.1 [5] <7.2> Now consider which of these activities is already exploiting some form of parallelism (e.g., brushing multiple teeth at the same time, versus one at a time, carrying one book at a time to school, versus loading them all into your backpack and then carry them "in parallel"). For each of your activities, discuss if they are already working in parallel, but if not, why they are not.

7.1.2 [5] <7.2> Next, consider which of the activities could be carried out concurrently (e.g., eating breakfast and listening to the news). For each of your activities, describe which other activity could be paired with this activity.

7.1.3 [5] <7.2> For 7.1.2, what could we change about current systems (e.g., showers, clothes, TVs, cars) so that we could perform more tasks in parallel?

7.1.4 [5] <7.2> Estimate how much shorter time it would take to carry out these activities if you tried to carry out as many tasks in parallel as possible.

Exercise 7.2

Many computer applications involve searching through a set of data and sorting the data. A number of efficient searching and sorting algorithms have been devised in order to reduce the runtime of these tedious tasks. In this problem we will consider how best to parallelize these tasks.

7.2.1 [10] <7.2> Consider the following binary search algorithm (a classic divide and conquer algorithm) that searches for a value X in an sorted N-element array A and returns the index of matched entry:

```
BinarySearch(A[0..N-1], X) {
      low = 0
      high = N - 1
      while (low <= high) {
          mid = (low + high) / 2
          if (A[mid] > X)
              high = mid - 1
          else if (A[mid] < X)
              low = mid + 1
          else
              return mid // found
      }
      return -1 // not found
}
```

Assume that you have Y cores on a multi-core processor to run BinarySearch. Assuming that Y is much smaller than N, express the speedup factor you might expect to obtain for values of Y and N. Plot these on a graph.

7.2.2 [5] <7.2> Next, assume that Y is equal to N. How would this affect your conclusions in your previous answer? If you were tasked with obtaining the best speedup factor possible (i.e., strong scaling), explain how you might change this code to obtain it.

Exercise 7.3

Consider the following piece of C code:

```
for (j=2;j<1000;j++)
    D[j] = D[j-1]+D[j-2];
```

The MIPS code corresponding to the above fragment is:

```
          DADDIU  r2,r2,999
loop:     L.D     f1, -16(f1)
          L.D     f2, -8(f1)
          ADD.D   f3, f1, f2
          S.D     f3, 0(r1)
          DADDIU  r1, r1, 8
          BNE     r1, r2, loop
```

Instructions have the following associated latencies (in cycles):

ADD.D	L.D	S.D	DADDIU
4	6	1	2

7.3.1 [10] <7.2> How many cycles does it take for all instructions in a single iteration of the above loop to execute?

7.3.2 [10] <7.2> When an instruction in a later iteration of a loop depends upon a data value produced in an earlier iteration of the same loop, we say that there is a *loop carried dependence* between iterations of the loop. Identify the loop-carried dependences in the above code. Identify the dependent program variable and assembly-level registers. You can ignore the loop induction variable j.

7.3.3 [10] <7.2> Loop unrolling was described in Chapter 4. Apply loop unrolling to this loop and then consider running this code on a 2-node distributed memory message passing system. Assume that we are going to use message passing as described in Section 7.4, where we introduce a new operation send (x, y) that sends to node x the value y, and an operation receive( ) that waits for the value being sent to it. Assume that send operations take a cycle to issue (i.e., later instructions on the same node can proceed on the next cycle), but take 10 cycles be received on the receiving node. Receive instructions stall execution on the node where they are executed until they receive a message. Produce a schedule for the two nodes assuming an unroll factor of 4 for the loop body (i.e., the loop body will appear 4 times). Compute the number of cycles it will take for the loop to run on the message passing system.

7.3.4 [10] <7.2> The latency of the interconnect network plays a large role in the efficiency of message passing systems. How fast does the interconnect need to be in order to obtain any speedup from using the distributed system described in 7.3.3?

Exercise 7.4

Consider the following recursive mergesort algorithm (another classic divide and conquer algorithm). Mergesort was first described by John Von Neumann in 1945. The basic idea is to divide an unsorted list x of m elements into two sublists of about half the size of the original list. Repeat this operation on each sublist, and continue until we have lists of size 1 in length. Then starting with sublists of length 1, "merge" the two sublists into a single sorted list.

```
Mergesort(m)
    var list left, right, result
    if length(m) ≤ 1
        return m
```

```
else
    var middle = length(m) / 2
    for each x in m up to middle
        add x to left
    for each x in m after middle
        add x to right
    left = Mergesort(left)
    right = Mergesort(right)
    result = Merge(left, right)
    return result
```

The merge step is carried out by the following code:

```
Merge(left,right)
    var list result
    while length(left) > 0 and length(right) > 0
        if first(left) ≤ first(right)
            append first(left) to result
            left = rest(left)
        else
            append first(right) to result
            right = rest(right)
    if length(left) > 0
        append rest(left) to result
    if length(right) > 0
        append rest(right) to result
    return result
```

7.4.1 [10] <7.2> Assume that you have Y cores on a multi-core processor to run MergeSort. Assuming that Y is much smaller than length(m), express the speedup factor you might expect to obtain for values of Y and length(m). Plot these on a graph.

7.4.2 [10] <7.2> Next, assume that Y is equal to length(m). How would this affect your conclusions your previous answer? If you were tasked with obtaining the best speedup factor possible (i.e., strong scaling), explain how you might change this code to obtain it.

Exercise 7.5

You are trying to bake 3 blueberry pound cakes. Cake ingredients are as follows:

1 cup butter, softened
1 cup sugar

4 large eggs
1 teaspoon vanilla extract
1/2 teaspoon salt
1/4 teaspoon nutmeg
1 1/2 cups flour
1 cup blueberries

The recipe for a single cake is as follows:

> Step 1: Preheat oven to 325°F (160°C). Grease and flour your cake pan.

> Step 2: In large bowl, beat together with a mixer butter and sugar at medium speed until light and fluffy. Add eggs, vanilla, salt and nutmeg. Beat until thoroughly blended. Reduce mixer speed to low and add flour, 1/2 cup at a time, beating just until blended.

> Step 3: Gently fold in blueberries. Spread evenly in prepared baking pan. Bake for 60 minutes.

7.5.1 [5] <7.2> Your job is to cook 3 cakes as efficiently as possible. Assuming that you only have one oven large enough to hold one cake, one large bowl, one cake pan, and one mixer, come up with a schedule to make three cakes as quickly as possible. Identify the bottlenecks in completing this task.

7.5.2 [5] <7.2> Assume now that you have three bowls, 3 cake pans and 3 mixers. How much faster is the process now that you have additional resources?

7.5.3 [5] <7.2> Assume now that you have two friends that will help you cook, and that you have a large oven that can accommodate all three cakes. How will this change the schedule you arrived at in 7.5.1 above?

7.5.4 [5] <7.2> Compare the cake-making task to computing 3 iterations of a loop on a parallel computer. Identify data-level parallelism and task-level parallelism in the cake-making loop.

Exercise 7.6

Matrix multiplication plays an important role in a number of applications. Two matrices can only be multiplied if the number of columns of the first matrix is equal to the number of rows in the second.

Let's assume we have an $m \times n$ matrix A and we want to multiply it by an $n \times p$ matrix B. We can express their product as an $m \times p$ matrix denoted by AB (or $A \cdot B$). If we assign $C = AB$, and $c_{i,j}$ denotes the entry in C at position (i, j), then

$$c_{i,j} = \sum_{r=1}^{n} a_{i,r} b_{r,j} = a_{i,1} b_{1,j} + a_{i,2} b_{2,j} + \cdots + a_{i,n} b_{n,j}$$

for each element i and j with $1 \leq i \leq m$ and $1 \leq j \leq p$. Now we want to see if we can parallelize the computation of C. Assume that matrices are laid out in memory sequentially as follows: $a_{1,1}$, $a_{2,1}$, $a_{3,1}$, $a_{4,1}$, ..., etc..

7.6.1 [10] <7.3> Assume that we are going to compute C on both a single core shared memory machine and a 4-core shared-memory machine. Compute the speedup we would expect to obtain on the 4-core machine, ignoring any memory issues.

7.6.2 [10] <7.3> Repeat 7.6.1, assuming that updates to C incur a cache miss due to false sharing when consecutive elements are in a row (i.e., index i) are updated.

7.6.3 [10] <7.3> How would you fix the false sharing issue that can occur?

Exercise 7.7

Consider the following portions of two different programs running at the same time on four processors in a symmetric multi-core processor (SMP). Assume that before this code is run, both x and y are 0.

Core 1: x = 2;

Core 2: y = 2;

Core 3: w = x + y + 1;

Core 4: z = x + y;

7.7.1 [10] <7.3> What are all the possible resulting values of w, x, y, and z? For each possible outcome, explain how we might arrive at those values. You will need to examine all possible interleavings of instructions.

7.7.2 [5] <7.3> How could you make the execution more deterministic so that only one set of values is possible?

Exercise 7.8

In a CC-NUMA shared memory system, CPUs and physical memory are divided across compute nodes. Each CPU has local caches. To maintain the coherency of memory, we can add status bits into each cache block, or we can introduce dedicated memory directories. Using directories, each node provides a dedicated hardware table for managing the status of every block of memory that is "local" to that node. The size of each directory is a function of the size of the CC-NUMA shared space (an entry is provided for each block of memory local to a node). If we store coherency information in the cache, we add this information to every cache in every system (i.e., the amount of storage space is a function of the number of cache lines available in all caches).

In the following proplems, assume that all nodes have the same number of CPUs and the same amount memory (i.e., CPUs and memory are evenly divided between the nodes of the CC-NUMA machine).

7.8.1 [15] <7.3> If we have P CPU in the system, with T nodes in the CC-NUMA system, with each CPU having C memory blocks stored in it, and we maintain a byte of coherency information in each cache line, provide an equation that expresses the amount of memory that will be present in the caches in a single node of the system to maintain coherency. Do not include the actual data storage space consumed in this equation, only account for space used to store coherency information.

7.8.2 [15] <7.3>If each directory entry maintains a byte of information for each CPU, if our CC-NUMA system has S memory blocks, and the system has T nodes, provide an equation that expresses the amount of memory that will be present in each directory.

Exercise 7.9

Considering the CC-NUMA system described in the Exercise 7.8, assume that the system has 4 nodes, each with a single-core CPU (each CPU has its own L1 data cache and L2 data cache). The L1 data cache is store-through, though the L2 data cache is write-back. Assume that system has a workload where one CPU writes to an address, and the other CPUs all read that data that is written. Also assume that the address written to is initially only in memory and not in any local cache. Also, after the write, assume that the updated block is only present in the L1 cache of the core performing the write.

7.9.1 [10] <7.3> For a system that maintains coherency using cache-based block status, describe the inter-node traffic that will be generated as each of the 4 cores writes to a unique address, after which each address written to is read from by each of the remaining 3 cores.

7.9.2 [10] <7.3> For a directory-based coherency mechanism, describe the inter-node traffic generated when executing the same code pattern.

7.9.3 [20] <7.3> Repeat 7.9.1 and 7.9.2 assuming that each CPU is now a multi-core CPU, with 4 cores per CPU, each maintaining an L1 data cache, but provided with a shared L2 data cache across the 4 cores. Each core will perform the write, followed by reads by each of the 15 other cores.

7.9.4 [10] <7.3> Consider the system described in 7.9.3, now assuming that each core writes to byte stored in the same cache block. How does this impact bus traffic? Explain.

Exercise 7.10

On a CC-NUMA system, the cost of accessing non-local memory can limit our ability to utilize multiprocessing effectively. The following table shows the costs associated with access data in local memory versus non-local memory and the locality of our application expresses as the proportion of access that are local.

Local load/store (cycle)	Non-local load/store (cycles)	% local accesses
25	200	20

Answer the following questions. Assume that memory accesses are evenly distributed through the application. Also, assume that only a single memory operation can be active during any cycle. State all assumptions about the ordering of local versus non-local memory operations.

7.10.1 [10] <7.3> If on average we need to access memory once every 75 cycles, what is impact on our application?

7.10.2 [10] <7.3> If on average we need to access memory once every 50 cycles, what is impact on our application?

7.10.3 [10] <7.3> If on average we need to access memory once every 100 cycles, what is impact on our application?

Exercise 7.11

The dining philosopher's problem is a classic problem of synchronization and concurrency. The general problem is stated as philosophers sitting at a round table doing one of two things: eating or thinking. When they are eating, they are not thinking, and when they are thinking, they are not eating. There is a bowl of pasta in the center. A fork is placed in between each philosopher. The result is that each philosopher has one fork to her left and one fork to her right. Given the nature of eating pasta, the philosopher needs two forks to eat, and can only use the forks on her immediate left and right. The philosophers do not speak to one another.

7.11.1 [10] <7.4> Describe the scenario where none of philosophers ever eats (i.e., starvation). What is the sequence of events that happen that lead up to this problem?

7.11.2 [10] <7.4> Describe how we can solve this problem by introducing the concept of a priority? But can we guarantee that we will treat all the philosophers fairly? Explain.

Now assume we hire a waiter who is in charge of assigning forks to philosophers. Nobody can pick up a fork until the waiter says they can. The waiter has global knowledge of all forks. Further, if we impose the policy that philosophers will always request to pick up their left fork before requesting to pick up their right fork, then we can guarantee to avoid deadlock.

7.11.3 [10] <7.4> We can implement requests to the waiter as either a queue of requests or as a periodic retry of a request. With a queue, requests are handled in the order they are received. The problem with using the queue is that we may not always be able to service the philosopher whose request is at the head of the queue (due to the unavailability of resources). Describe a scenario with 5 philosophers where a queue is provided, but service is not granted even though there are forks available for another philosopher (whose request is deeper in the queue) to eat.

7.11.4 [10] <7.4> If we implement requests to the waiter by periodically repeating our request until the resources become available, will this solve the problem described in 7.11.3? Explain.

Exercise 7.12

Consider the following three CPU organizations:

CPU SS: A 2-core superscalar microprocessor that provides out-of-order issue capabilities on 2 function units (FUs). Only a single thread can run on each core at a time.

CPU MT: A fine-grained multithreaded processor that allows instructions from 2 threads to be run concurrently (i.e., there are two functional units), though only instructions from a single thread can be issued on any cycle.

CPU SMT: An SMT processor that allows instructions from 2 threads to be run concurrently (i.e., there are two functional units), and instructions from either or both threads can be issued to run on any cycle.

Assume we have two threads X and Y to run on these CPUs that include the following operations:

Thread X	Thread Y
A1 – takes 3 cycles to execute	B1 – take 2 cycles to execute
A2 – no dependencies	B2 – conflicts for a functional unit with B1
A3 – conflicts for a functional unit with A1	B3 – depends on the result of B2
A4 – depends on the result of A3	B4 – no dependencies and takes 2 cycles to execute

Assume all instructions take a single cycle to execute unless noted otherwise or they encounter a hazard.

7.12.1 [10] <7.5> Assume that you have 1 SS CPU. How many cycles will it take to execute these two threads? How many issue slots are wasted due to hazards?

7.12.2 [10] <7.5> Now assume you have 2 SS CPUs. How many cycles will it take to execute these two threads? How many issue slots are wasted due to hazards?

7.12.3 [10] <7.5> Assume that you have 1 MT CPU. How many cycles will it take to execute these two threads? How many issue slots are wasted due to hazards?

Exercise 7.13

Virtualization software is being aggressively deployed to reduce the costs of managing today's high performance servers. Companies like VMWare, Microsoft and IBM have all developed a range of virtualization products. The general concept, described in Chapter 5, is that a hypervisor layer can be introduced between the hardware and the operating system to allow multiple operating systems to share the same physical hardware. The hypervisor layer is then responsible for allocating CPU and memory resources, as well as handling services typically handled by the operating system (e.g., I/O).

Virtualization provides an abstract view of the underlying hardware to the hosted operating system and application software. This will require us to rethink how multi-core and multiprocessor systems will be designed in the future to support the sharing of CPUs and memories by a number of operating systems concurrently.

7.13.1 [30] <7.5> Select two hypervisors on the market today, and compare and contrast how they virtualize and manage the underlying hardware (CPUs and memory).

7.13.2 [15] <7.5> Discuss what changes may be necessary in future multi-core CPU platforms in order to better match the resource demands placed on these systems. For instance, can multi-threading play an effective role in alleviating the competition for computing resources?

Exercise 7.14

We would like to execute the loop below as efficiently as possible. We have two different machines, a MIMD machine and a SIMD machine.

```
for (i=0; i < 2000; i++)
  for (j=0; j<3000; j++)
      X_array[i][j] = Y_array[j][i] + 200;
```

7.14.1 [10] <7.6> For a 4 CPU MIMD machine, show the sequence of MIPS instructions that you would execute on each CPU. What is the speedup for this MIMD machine?

7.14.2 [20] <7.6> For an 8-wide SIMD machine (i.e., 8 parallel SIMD functional units), write an assembly program in using your own SIMD extensions to MIPS to execute the loop. Compare the number of instructions executed on the SIMD machine to the MIMD machine.

Exercise 7.15

A systolic array is an example of an MISD machine. A systolic array is a pipeline network or "wavefront" of data processing elements. Each of these elements does not need a program counter since execution is triggered by the arrival of data. Clocked systolic arrays compute in "lock-step" with each processor undertaking alternate compute and communication phases.

7.15.1 [10] <7.6> Consider proposed implementations of a systolic array (you can find these in on the Internet or in technical publications). Then attempt to program the loop provided in Exercise 7.14 using this MISD model. Discuss any difficulties you encounter.

7.15.2 [10] <7.6> Discuss the similarities and differences between an MISD and SIMD machine. Answer this question in terms of data-level parallelism.

Exercise 7.16

Assume we want to execute the DAXP loop show on page 651 in MIPS assembly on the NVIDIA 8800 GTX GPU described in this Chapter. In this problem, we will assume that all math operations are performed on single-precision floating-point numbers (we will rename the loop SAXP). Assume that instructions take the following number of cycles to execute.

Loads	Stores	Add.S	Mult.S
5	2	3	4

7.16.1 [20] <7.7> Describe how you will constructs warps for the SAXP loop to exploit the 8 cores provided in a single multiprocessor.

Exercise 7.17

Download the CUDA Toolkit and SDK from http://www.nvidia.com/object/cuda_get.html. Make sure to use the "emurelease" (Emulation Mode) version of the code (you will not need actual NVIDIA hardware for this assignment). Build the example programs provided in the SDK, and confirm that they run on the emulator.

7.17.1 [90] <7.7> Using the "template" SDK sample as a starting point, write a CUDA program to perform the following vector operations:

1) $a - b$ (vector-vector subtraction)

2) a · b (vector dot product)

The dot product of two vectors $a = [a_1, a_2, \ldots, a_n]$ and $b = [b_1, b_2, \ldots, b_n]$ is defined as:

$$a \cdot b = \sum_{i=1}^{n} a_i b_i = a_1 b_1 + a_2 b_2 + \cdots + a_n b_n$$

Submit code for each program that demonstrates each operation and verifies the correctness of the results.

7.17.2 [90] <7.7> If you have GPU hardware available, complete a performance analysis your program, examining the computation time for the GPU and a CPU version of your program for a range of vector sizes. Explain any results you see.

Exercise 7.18

AMD has recently announced that they will be integrating a graphics processing unit with their X86 cores in a single package, though with different clocks for each of the cores. This is an example of a heterogeneous multiprocessor system which we expect to see produced commericially in the near future. One of the key design points will be to allow for fast data communication between the CPU and the GPU. Presently communications must be performed between discrete CPU and GPU chips. But this is changing in AMDs Fusion architecture. Presently the plan is to use multiple (at least 16) PCI express channels for facilitate intercommunication. Intel is also jumping into this arena with their Larrabee chip. Intel is considering to use their QuickPath interconnect technology.

7.18.1 [25] <7.7> Compare the bandwidth and latency associated with these two interconnect technologies.

Exercise 7.19

Refer to Figure 7.7b that shows an n-cube interconnect topology of order 3 that interconnects 8 nodes. One attractive feature of an n-cube interconnection network topology is its ability to sustain broken links and still provide connectivity.

7.19.1 [10] <7.8> Develop an equation that computes how many links in the n-cube (where n is the order of the cube) can fail and we can still guarantee an unbroken link will exist to connect any node in the n-cube.

7.19.2 [10] <7.8> Compare the resiliency to failure of n-cube to a fully-connected interconnection network. Plot a comparison of reliability as a function of the added number of links for the two topologies.

Exercise 7.20

Benchmarking is field of study that involves identifying representative workloads to run on specific computing platforms in order to be able to objectively compare performance of one system to another. In this exercise we will compare two classes of benchmarks: the Whetstone CPU benchmark and the PARSEC Benchmark suite. Select one program from PARSEC. All programs should be freely available on the Internet. Consider running multiple copies of Whetstone versus running the PARSEC Benchmark on any of systems described in Section 7.11.

7.20.1 [60] <7.9> What is inherently different between these two classes of workload when run on these multi-core systems?

7.20.2 [60] <7.9, 7.10> In terms of the Roofline Model, how dependent will the results you obtain when running these benchmarks be on the amount of sharing and synchronization present in the workload used?

Exercise 7.21

When performing computations on sparse matrices, latency in the memory hierarchy becomes much more of a factor. Sparse matrices lack the spatial locality in the data stream typically found in matrix operations. As a result, new matrix representations have been proposed.

One the earliest sparse matrix representations is the Yale Sparse Matrix Format. It stores an initial sparse $m{\times}n$ matrix, M in row form using three one-dimensional arrays. Let R be the number of nonzero entries in M. We construct an array A of length R that contains all nonzero entries of M (in left-to-right top-to-bottom order). We also construct a second array IA of length $m + 1$ (i.e., one entry per row, plus one). $IA(i)$ contains the index in A of the first nonzero element of row i. Row i of the original matrix extends from $A(IA(i))$ to $A(IA(i+1)-1)$. The third array, JA, contains the column index of each element of A, so it also is of length R.

7.21.1 [15] <7.9> Consider the sparse matrix X below and write C code that would store this code in Yale Sparse Matrix Format.

```
Row 1 [1, 2, 0, 0, 0, 0]
Row 2 [0, 0, 1, 1, 0, 0]
Row 3 [0, 0, 0, 0, 9, 0]
Row 4 [2, 0, 0, 0, 0, 2]
Row 5 [0, 0, 3, 3, 0, 7]
Row 6 [1, 3, 0, 0, 0, 1]
```

7.21.2 [10] <7.9> In terms of storage space, assuming that each element in matrix X is single precision floating point, compute the amount of storage used to store the Matrix above in Yale Sparse Matrix Format.

7.21.3 [15] <7.9> Perform matrix multiplication of Matrix X by Matrix Y shown below.

    [2, 4, 1, 99, 7, 2]

Put this computation in a loop, and time its execution. Make sure to increase the number of times this loop is executed to get good resolution in your timing measurement. Compare the runtime of using a naïve representation of the matrix, and the Yale Sparse Matrix Format.

7.21.4 [15] <7.9> Can you find a more efficient sparse matrix representation (in terms of space and computational overhead)?

Exercise 7.22

In future systems, we expect to see heterogeneous computing platforms constructed out of heterogeneous CPUs. We have begun to see some appear in the embedded processing market in systems that contain both floating point DSPs and a microcontroller CPUs in a multichip module package.

Assume that you have three classes of CPU:

CPU A—A moderate speed multi-core CPU (with a floating point unit) that can execute multiple instructions per cycle.

CPU B—A fast single-core integer CPU (i.e., no floating point unit) that can execute a single instruction per cycle.

CPU C—A slow vector CPU (with floating point capability) that can execute multiple copies of the same instruction per cycle.

Assume that our processors run at the following frequencies:

CPU A	CPU B	CPU C
1 GHz	3 GHz	250 MHz

CPU A can execute 2 instructions per cycle, CPU B can execute 1 instruction per cycle, and CPU C can execute 8 instructions (though the same instruction) per cycle. Assume all operations can complete execution in a single cycle of latency without any hazards.

All three CPUs have the ability to perform integer arithmetic, though CPU B cannot perform floating point arithmetic. CPU A and B have an instruction set similar to a MIPS processor. CPU C can only perform floating point add and subtract operations, as well as memory loads and stores. Assume all CPUs have access to shared memory and that synchronization has zero cost.

The task at hand is to compare two matrices X and Y that each contain 1024×1024 floating point elements. The output should be a count of the number indices where the value in X was larger or equal to the value in Y.

7.22.1 [10] <7.11> Describe how you would partition the problem on the 3 different CPUs to obtain the best performance.

7.22.2 [10] <7.11> What kind of instruction would you add to the vector CPU C to obtain better performance?

Exercise 7.23

Assume a quad-core computer system can process database queries at a steady state rate of requests per second. Also assume that each transaction takes, on average, a fixed amount of time to process. The following table shows pairs of transaction latency and processing rate.

Average Transaction Latency	Maximum transaction processing rate
1 ms	5000/sec
2 ms	5000/sec
1 ms	10,000/sec
2 ms	10,000/sec

For each of the pairs in the table, answer the following questions:

7.23.1 [10] <7.11> On average, how many requests are being processed at any given instant?

7.23.2 [10] <7.11> If move to an 8-core system, ideally, what will happen to the system throughput (i.e., how many queries/second will the computer process)?

7.22.3 [10] <7.11> Discuss why we rarely obtain this kind of speedup by simply increasing the number of cores.

§7.1, page 634: False. Job-level parallelism can help sequential applications and sequential applications can be made to run on parallel hardware, although it is more challenging.

§7.2, page 638: False. *Weak* scaling can compensate for a serial portion of the program that would otherwise limit scalability.

§7.3, page 640: False. Since the shared address is a *physical* address, multiple jobs each in their own *virtual* address spaces can run well on a shared memory multi-processor.

§7.4, page 645: 1. False. Sending and receiving a message is an implicit synchronization, as well as a way to share data. 2. True.

§7.5, page 648: 1. True. 2. True.

§7.6, page 653: True.

§7.7, page 660: False. Graphics DRAM DIMMs are prized for their higher bandwidth.

§7.9, page 666: True. We likely need innovation at all levels of the hardware and software stack to win the industry's bet on parallel computing.

**Answers to
Check Yourself**

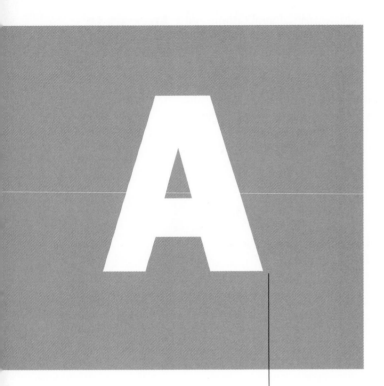

APPENDIX

Graphics and Computing GPUs

Imagination is more important than knowledge.

Albert Einstein
On Science, 1930s

John Nickolls
Director of Architecture
NVIDIA

David Kirk
Chief Scientist
NVIDIA

A.1   Introduction

This appendix focuses on the **GPU**—the ubiquitous **graphics processing unit** in every PC, laptop, desktop computer, and workstation. In its most basic form, the GPU generates 2D and 3D graphics, images, and video that enable window-based operating systems, graphical user interfaces, video games, visual imaging applications, and video. The modern GPU that we describe here is a highly parallel, highly multithreaded multiprocessor optimized for **visual computing**. To provide real-time visual interaction with computed objects via graphics, images, and video, the GPU has a unified graphics and computing architecture that serves as both a programmable graphics processor and a scalable parallel computing platform. PCs and game consoles combine a GPU with a CPU to form **heterogeneous systems**.

graphics processing unit (GPU) A processor optimized for 2D and 3D graphics, video, visual computing, and display.

visual computing A mix of graphics processing and computing that lets you visually interact with computed objects via graphics, images, and video.

heterogeneous system A system combining different processor types. A PC is a heterogeneous CPU–GPU system.

A Brief History of GPU Evolution

Fifteen years ago, there was no such thing as a GPU. Graphics on a PC were performed by a video graphics array (VGA) controller. A VGA controller was simply a memory controller and display generator connected to some DRAM. In the 1990s, semiconductor technology advanced sufficiently that more functions could be added to the VGA controller. By 1997, VGA controllers were beginning to incorporate some three-dimensional (3D) acceleration functions, including hardware for triangle setup and rasterization (dicing triangles into individual pixels) and texture mapping and shading (applying "decals" or patterns to pixels and blending colors).

In 2000, the single chip graphics processor incorporated almost every detail of the traditional high-end workstation graphics pipeline and therefore, deserved a new name beyond VGA controller. The term GPU was coined to denote that the graphics device had become a processor.

Over time, GPUs became more programmable, as programmable processors replaced fixed function dedicated logic while maintaining the basic 3D graphics pipeline organization. In addition, computations became more precise over time, progressing from indexed arithmetic, to integer and fixed point, to single precision floating-point, and recently to double precision floating-point. GPUs have become massively parallel programmable processors with hundreds of cores and thousands of threads.

Recently, processor instructions and memory hardware were added to support general purpose programming languages, and a programming environment was created to allow GPUs to be programmed using familiar languages, including C and C++. This innovation makes a GPU a fully general-purpose, programmable, manycore processor, albeit still with some special benefits and limitations.

GPU Graphics Trends

application programming interface (API) A set of function and data structure definitions providing an interface to a library of functions.

GPUs and their associated drivers implement the OpenGL and DirectX models of graphics processing. OpenGL is an open standard for 3D graphics programming available for most computers. DirectX is a series of Microsoft multimedia programming interfaces, including Direct3D for 3D graphics. Since these **application programming interfaces (APIs)** have well-defined behavior, it is possible to build effective hardware acceleration of the graphics processing functions defined by the APIs. This is one of the reasons (in addition to increasing device density) that new GPUs are being developed every 12 to 18 months that double the performance of the previous generation on existing applications.

Frequent doubling of GPU performance enables new applications that were not previously possible. The intersection of graphics processing and parallel computing invites a new paradigm for graphics, known as visual computing. It replaces large sections of the traditional sequential hardware graphics pipeline model with programmable elements for geometry, vertex, and pixel programs. Visual computing in a modern GPU combines graphics processing and parallel computing in novel ways that permit new graphics algorithms to be implemented, and open the door to entirely new parallel processing applications on pervasive high-performance GPUs.

Heterogeneous System

Although the GPU is arguably the most parallel and most powerful processor in a typical PC, it is certainly not the only processor. The CPU, now multicore and soon to be manycore, is a complementary, primarily serial processor companion to the massively parallel manycore GPU. Together, these two types of processors comprise a heterogeneous multiprocessor system.

The best performance for many applications comes from using both the CPU and the GPU. This appendix will help you understand how and when to best split the work between these two increasingly parallel processors.

GPU Evolves into Scalable Parallel Processor

GPUs have evolved functionally from hardwired, limited capability VGA controllers to programmable parallel processors. This evolution has proceeded by changing the logical (API-based) graphics pipeline to incorporate programmable elements and also by making the underlying hardware pipeline stages less specialized and more programmable. Eventually, it made sense to merge disparate programmable pipeline elements into one unified array of many programmable processors.

In the GeForce 8-series generation of GPUs, the geometry, vertex, and pixel processing all run on the same type of processor. This unification allows for dramatic scalability. More programmable processor cores increase the total system throughput. Unifying the processors also delivers very effective load balancing, since any processing function can use the whole processor array. At the other end of the spectrum, a processor array can now be built with very few processors, since all of the functions can be run on the same processors.

Why CUDA and GPU Computing?

This uniform and scalable array of processors invites a new model of programming for the GPU. The large amount of floating-point processing power in the GPU processor array is very attractive for solving nongraphics problems. Given the large degree of parallelism and the range of scalability of the processor array for graphics applications, the programming model for more general computing must express the massive parallelism directly, but allow for scalable execution.

GPU computing is the term coined for using the GPU for computing via a parallel programming language and API, without using the traditional graphics API and graphics pipeline model. This is in contrast to the earlier **General Purpose computation on GPU (GPGPU)** approach, which involves programming the GPU using a graphics API and graphics pipeline to perform nongraphics tasks.

Compute Unified Device Architecture (CUDA) is a scalable parallel programming model and software platform for the GPU and other parallel processors that allows the programmer to bypass the graphics API and graphics interfaces of the GPU and simply program in C or C++. The CUDA programming model has an SPMD (single-program multiple data) software style, in which a programmer writes a program for one thread that is instanced and executed by many threads in parallel on the multiple processors of the GPU. In fact, CUDA also provides a facility for programming multiple CPU cores as well, so CUDA is an environment for writing parallel programs for the entire heterogeneous computer system.

GPU computing Using a GPU for computing via a parallel programming language and API.

GPGPU Using a GPU for general-purpose computation via a traditional graphics API and graphics pipeline.

CUDA A scalable parallel programming model and language based on C/C++. It is a parallel programming platform for GPUs and multicore CPUs.

GPU Unifies Graphics and Computing

With the addition of CUDA and GPU computing to the capabilities of the GPU, it is now possible to use the GPU as both a graphics processor and a computing processor at the same time, and to combine these uses in visual computing applications. The underlying processor architecture of the GPU is exposed in two ways: first, as implementing the programmable graphics APIs, and second, as a massively parallel processor array programmable in C/C++ with CUDA.

Although the underlying processors of the GPU are unified, it is not necessary that all of the SPMD thread programs are the same. The GPU can run graphics shader programs for the graphics aspect of the GPU, processing geometry, vertices, and pixels, and also run thread programs in CUDA.

The GPU is truly a versatile multiprocessor architecture, supporting a variety of processing tasks. GPUs are excellent at graphics and visual computing as they were specifically designed for these applications. GPUs are also excellent at many general-purpose throughput applications that are "first cousins" of graphics, in that they perform a lot of parallel work, as well as having a lot of regular problem structure. In general, they are a good match to data-parallel problems (see Chapter 7), particularly large problems, but less so for less regular, smaller problems.

GPU Visual Computing Applications

Visual computing includes the traditional types of graphics applications plus many new applications. The original purview of a GPU was "anything with pixels," but it now includes many problems without pixels but with regular computation and/or data structure. GPUs are effective at 2D and 3D graphics, since that is the purpose for which they are designed. Failure to deliver this application performance would be fatal. 2D and 3D graphics use the GPU in its "graphics mode," accessing the processing power of the GPU through the graphics APIs, OpenGL^{TM}, and DirectX^{TM}. Games are built on the 3D graphics processing capability.

Beyond 2D and 3D graphics, image processing and video are important applications for GPUs. These can be implemented using the graphics APIs or as computational programs, using CUDA to program the GPU in computing mode. Using CUDA, image processing is simply another data-parallel array program. To the extent that the data access is regular and there is good locality, the program will be efficient. In practice, image processing is a very good application for GPUs. Video processing, especially encode and decode (compression and decompression according to some standard algorithms) is quite efficient.

The greatest opportunity for visual computing applications on GPUs is to "break the graphics pipeline." Early GPUs implemented only specific graphics APIs, albeit at very high performance. This was wonderful if the API supported the operations that you wanted to do. If not, the GPU could not accelerate your task, because early GPU functionality was immutable. Now, with the advent of GPU computing and CUDA, these GPUs can be programmed to implement a different virtual pipeline by simply writing a CUDA program to describe the computation and data flow that is desired. So, all applications are now possible, which will stimulate new visual computing approaches.

A.2 GPU System Architectures

In this section, we survey GPU system architectures in common use today. We discuss system configurations, GPU functions and services, standard programming interfaces, and a basic GPU internal architecture.

Heterogeneous CPU–GPU System Architecture

A heterogeneous computer system architecture using a GPU and a CPU can be described at a high level by two primary characteristics: first, how many functional subsystems and/or chips are used and what are their interconnection technologies and topology; and second, what memory subsystems are available to these functional subsystems. See Chapter 6 for background on the PC I/O systems and chip sets.

The Historical PC (circa 1990)

Figure A.2.1 is a high-level block diagram of a legacy PC, circa 1990. The north bridge (see Chapter 6) contains high-bandwidth interfaces, connecting the CPU, memory, and PCI bus. The south bridge contains legacy interfaces and devices: ISA bus (audio, LAN), interrupt controller; DMA controller; time/counter. In this system, the display was driven by a simple framebuffer subsystem known

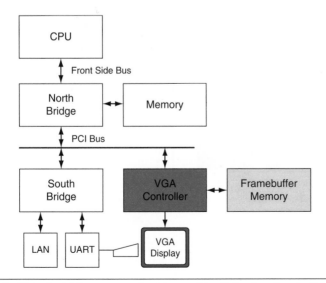

FIGURE A.2.1 Historical PC. VGA controller drives graphics display from framebuffer memory.

PCI-Express (PCIe)
A standard system I/O
interconnect that uses
point-to-point links.
Links have a configurable
number of lanes and
bandwidth.

as a VGA (video graphics array) which was attached to the PCI bus. Graphics subsystems with built-in processing elements (GPUs) did not exist in the PC landscape of 1990.

Figure A.2.2 illustrates two configurations in common use today. These are characterized by a separate GPU (discrete GPU) and CPU with respective memory subsystems. In Figure A.2.2a, with an Intel CPU, we see the GPU attached via a 16-lane **PCI-Express** 2.0 link to provide a peak 16 GB/s transfer rate, (peak of 8 GB/s in each direction). Similarly, in Figure A.2.2b, with an AMD CPU, the GPU

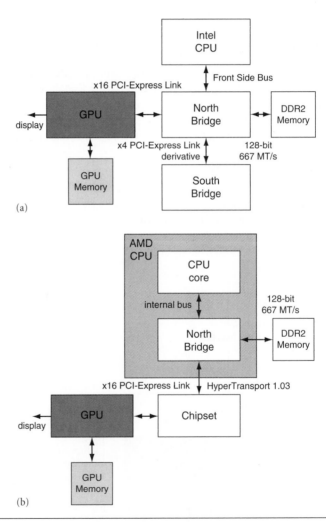

FIGURE A.2.2 Contemporary PCs with Intel and AMD CPUs. See Chapter 6 for an explanation of the components and interconnects in this figure.

is attached to the chipset, also via PCI-Express with the same available bandwidth. In both cases, the GPUs and CPUs may access each other's memory, albeit with less available bandwidth than their access to the more directly attached memories. In the case of the AMD system, the north bridge or memory controller is integrated into the same die as the CPU.

A low-cost variation on these systems, a **unified memory architecture (UMA)** system, uses only CPU system memory, omitting GPU memory from the system. These systems have relatively low performance GPUs, since their achieved performance is limited by the available system memory bandwidth and increased latency of memory access, whereas dedicated GPU memory provides high bandwidth and low latency.

A high performance system variation uses multiple attached GPUs, typically two to four working in parallel, with their displays daisy-chained. An example is the NVIDIA SLI (scalable link interconnect) multi-GPU system, designed for high performance gaming and workstations.

The next system category integrates the GPU with the north bridge (Intel) or chipset (AMD) with and without dedicated graphics memory.

Chapter 5 explains how caches maintain coherence in a shared address space. With CPUs and GPUs, there are multiple address spaces. GPUs can access their own physical local memory and the CPU system's physical memory using virtual addresses that are translated by an MMU on the GPU. The operating system kernel manages the GPU's page tables. A system physical page can be accessed using either coherent or noncoherent PCI-Express transactions, determined by an attribute in the GPU's page table. The CPU can access GPU's local memory through an address range (also called aperture) in the PCI-Express address space.

unified memory architecture (UMA) A system architecture in which the CPU and GPU share a common system memory.

Game Consoles

Console systems such as the Sony PlayStation 3 and the Microsoft Xbox 360 resemble the PC system architectures previously described. Console systems are designed to be shipped with identical performance and functionality over a lifespan that can last five years or more. During this time, a system may be reimplemented many times to exploit more advanced silicon manufacturing processes and thereby to provide constant capability at ever lower costs. Console systems do not need to have their subsystems expanded and upgraded the way PC systems do, so the major internal system buses tend to be customized rather than standardized.

GPU Interfaces and Drivers

In a PC today, GPUs are attached to a CPU via PCI-Express. Earlier generations used **AGP**. Graphics applications call OpenGL [Segal and Akeley, 2006] or Direct3D [Microsoft DirectX Specification] API functions that use the GPU as a coprocessor. The APIs send commands, programs, and data to the GPU via a graphics device driver optimized for the particular GPU.

AGP An extended version of the original PCI I/O bus, which provided up to eight times the bandwidth of the original PCI bus to a single card slot. Its primary purpose was to connect graphics subsystems into PC systems.

Graphics Logical Pipeline

The graphics logical pipeline is described in Section A.3. Figure A.2.3 illustrates the major processing stages, and highlights the important programmable stages (vertex, geometry, and pixel shader stages).

FIGURE A.2.3   Graphics logical pipeline. Programmable graphics shader stages are blue, and fixed-function blocks are white.

Mapping Graphics Pipeline to Unified GPU Processors

Figure A.2.4 shows how the logical pipeline comprising separate independent programmable stages is mapped onto a physical distributed array of processors.

Basic Unified GPU Architecture

Unified GPU architectures are based on a parallel array of many programmable processors. They unify vertex, geometry, and pixel shader processing and parallel computing on the same processors, unlike earlier GPUs which had separate processors dedicated to each processing type. The programmable processor array is tightly integrated with fixed function processors for texture filtering, rasterization, raster operations, anti-aliasing, compression, decompression, display, video decoding, and high-definition video processing. Although the fixed-function processors significantly outperform more general programmable processors in terms of absolute performance constrained by an area, cost, or power budget, we will focus on the programmable processors here.

Compared with multicore CPUs, manycore GPUs have a different architectural design point, one focused on executing many parallel threads efficiently on many

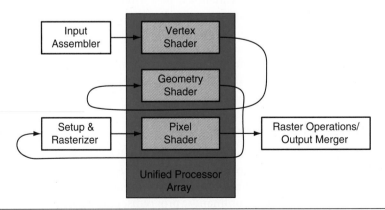

FIGURE A.2.4   Logical pipeline mapped to physical processors. The programmable shader stages execute on the array of unified processors, and the logical graphics pipeline dataflow recirculates through the processors.

processor cores. By using many simpler cores and optimizing for data-parallel behavior among groups of threads, more of the per-chip transistor budget is devoted to computation, and less to on-chip caches and overhead.

Processor Array

A unified GPU processor array contains many processor cores, typically organized into multithreaded multiprocessors. Figure A.2.5 shows a GPU with an array of 112 streaming processor (SP) cores, organized as 14 multithreaded streaming multiprocessors (SM). Each SP core is highly multithreaded, managing 96 concurrent threads and their state in hardware. The processors connect with four 64-bit-wide DRAM partitions via an interconnection network. Each SM has eight SP cores, two special function units (SFUs), instruction and constant caches, a multithreaded instruction unit, and a shared memory. This is the basic Tesla architecture implemented by the NVIDIA GeForce 8800. It has a unified architecture in which the traditional graphics programs for vertex, geometry, and pixel shading run on the unified SMs and their SP cores, and computing programs run on the same processors.

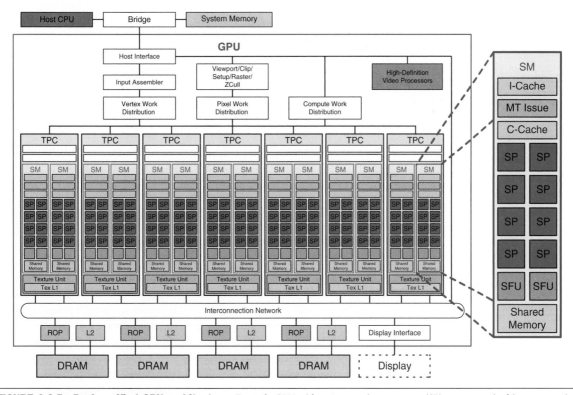

FIGURE A.2.5 Basic unified GPU architecture. Example GPU with 112 streaming processor (SP) cores organized in 14 streaming multiprocessors (SMs); the cores are highly multithreaded. It has the basic Tesla architecture of an NVIDIA GeForce 8800. The processors connect with four 64-bit-wide DRAM partitions via an interconnection network. Each SM has eight SP cores, two special function units (SFUs), instruction and constant caches, a multithreaded instruction unit, and a shared memory.

The processor array architecture is scalable to smaller and larger GPU configurations by scaling the number of multiprocessors and the number of memory partitions. Figure A.2.5 shows seven clusters of two SMs sharing a texture unit and a texture L1 cache. The texture unit delivers filtered results to the SM given a set of coordinates into a texture map. Because filter regions of support often overlap for successive texture requests, a small streaming L1 texture cache is effective to reduce the number of requests to the memory system. The processor array connects with raster operation (ROP) processors, L2 texture caches, external DRAM memories, and system memory via a GPU-wide interconnection network. The number of processors and number of memories can scale to design balanced GPU systems for different performance and market segments.

 Programming GPUs

Programming multiprocessor GPUs is qualitatively different than programming other multiprocessors like multicore CPUs. GPUs provide two to three orders of magnitude more thread and data parallelism than CPUs, scaling to hundreds of processor cores and tens of thousands of concurrent threads in 2008. GPUs continue to increase their parallelism, doubling it about every 12 to 18 months, enabled by Moore's law [1965] of increasing integrated circuit density and by improving architectural efficiency. To span the wide price and performance range of different market segments, different GPU products implement widely varying numbers of processors and threads. Yet users expect games, graphics, imaging, and computing applications to work on any GPU, regardless of how many parallel threads it executes or how many parallel processor cores it has, and they expect more expensive GPUs (with more threads and cores) to run applications faster. As a result, GPU programming models and application programs are designed to scale transparently to a wide range of parallelism.

The driving force behind the large number of parallel threads and cores in a GPU is real-time graphics performance—the need to render complex 3D scenes with high resolution at interactive frame rates, at least 60 frames per second. Correspondingly, the scalable programming models of graphics shading languages such as Cg (C for graphics) and HLSL (high-level shading language) are designed to exploit large degrees of parallelism via many independent parallel threads and to scale to any number of processor cores. The CUDA scalable parallel programming model similarly enables general parallel computing applications to leverage large numbers of parallel threads and scale to any number of parallel processor cores, transparently to the application.

In these scalable programming models, the programmer writes code for a single thread, and the GPU runs myriad thread instances in parallel. Programs thus scale transparently over a wide range of hardware parallelism. This simple paradigm arose from graphics APIs and shading languages that describe how to shade one vertex or one pixel. It has remained an effective paradigm as GPUs have rapidly increased their parallelism and performance since the late 1990s.

This section briefly describes programming GPUs for real-time graphics applications using graphics APIs and programming languages. It then describes programming GPUs for visual computing and general parallel computing applications using the C language and the CUDA programming model.

Programming Real-Time Graphics

APIs have played an important role in the rapid, successful development of GPUs and processors. There are two primary standard graphics APIs: **OpenGL** and **Direct3D**, one of the Microsoft DirectX multimedia programming interfaces. OpenGL, an open standard, was originally proposed and defined by Silicon Graphics Incorporated. The ongoing development and extension of the OpenGL standard [Segal and Akeley, 2006], [Kessenich, 2006] is managed by Khronos, an industry consortium. Direct3D [Blythe, 2006], a de facto standard, is defined and evolved forward by Microsoft and partners. OpenGL and Direct3D are similarly structured, and continue to evolve rapidly with GPU hardware advances. They define a logical graphics processing pipeline that is mapped onto the GPU hardware and processors, along with programming models and languages for the programmable pipeline stages.

OpenGL An open-standard graphics API.

Direct3D A graphics API defined by Microsoft and partners.

Logical Graphics Pipeline

Figure A.3.1 illustrates the Direct3D 10 logical graphics pipeline. OpenGL has a similar graphics pipeline structure. The API and logical pipeline provide a streaming dataflow infrastructure and plumbing for the programmable shader stages, shown in blue. The 3D application sends the GPU a sequence of vertices grouped into geometric primitives—points, lines, triangles, and polygons. The input assembler collects vertices and primitives. The vertex shader program executes per-vertex processing,

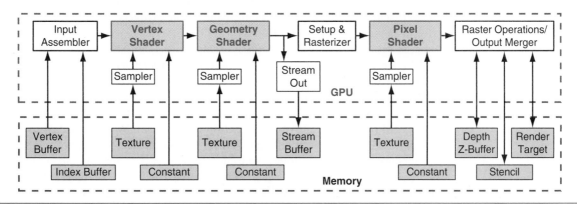

FIGURE A.3.1   Direct3D 10 graphics pipeline. Each logical pipeline stage maps to GPU hardware or to a GPU processor. Programmable shader stages are blue, fixed-function blocks are white, and memory objects are grey. Each stage processes a vertex, geometric primitive, or pixel in a streaming dataflow fashion.

including transforming the vertex 3D position into a screen position and lighting the vertex to determine its color. The geometry shader program executes per-primitive processing and can add or drop primitives. The setup and rasterizer unit generates pixel fragments (fragments are potential contributions to pixels) that are covered by a geometric primitive. The pixel shader program performs per-fragment processing, including interpolating per-fragment parameters, texturing, and coloring. Pixel shaders make extensive use of sampled and filtered lookups into large 1D, 2D, or 3D arrays called **textures**, using interpolated floating-point coordinates. Shaders use texture accesses for maps, functions, decals, images, and data. The raster operations processing (or output merger) stage performs Z-buffer depth testing and stencil testing, which may discard a hidden pixel fragment or replace the pixel's depth with the fragment's depth, and performs a color blending operation that combines the fragment color with the pixel color and writes the pixel with the blended color.

The graphics API and graphics pipeline provide input, output, memory objects, and infrastructure for the shader programs that process each vertex, primitive, and pixel fragment.

texture A 1D, 2D, or 3D array that supports sampled and filtered lookups with interpolated coordinates.

Graphics Shader Programs

shader A program that operates on graphics data such as a vertex or a pixel fragment.

shading language A graphics rendering language, usually having a dataflow or streaming programming model.

Real-time graphics applications use many different **shader** programs to model how light interacts with different materials and to render complex lighting and shadows. **Shading languages** are based on a dataflow or streaming programming model that corresponds with the logical graphics pipeline. Vertex shader programs map the position of triangle vertices onto the screen, altering their position, color, or orientation. Typically a vertex shader thread inputs a floating-point (x, y, z, w) vertex position and computes a floating-point (x, y, z) screen position. Geometry shader programs operate on geometric primitives (such as lines and triangles) defined by multiple vertices, changing them or generating additional primitives. Pixel fragment shaders each "shade" one pixel, computing a floating-point red, green, blue, alpha (RGBA) color contribution to the rendered image at its pixel sample (x, y) image position. Shaders (and GPUs) use floating-point arithmetic for all pixel color calculations to eliminate visible artifacts while computing the extreme range of pixel contribution values encountered while rendering scenes with complex lighting, shadows, and high dynamic range. For all three types of graphics shaders, many program instances can be run in parallel, as independent parallel threads, because each works on independent data, produces independent results, and has no side effects. Independent vertices, primitives, and pixels further enable the same graphics program to run on differently sized GPUs that process different numbers of vertices, primitives, and pixels in parallel. Graphics programs thus scale transparently to GPUs with different amounts of parallelism and performance.

Users program all three logical graphics threads with a common targeted high-level language. HLSL (high-level shading language) and Cg (C for graphics) are commonly used. They have C-like syntax and a rich set of library functions for matrix operations, trigonometry, interpolation, and texture access and filtering, but are far from general computing languages: they currently lack general memory access, pointers, file I/O, and recursion. HLSL and Cg assume that programs live within a logical graphics pipeline, and thus I/O is implicit. For example, a pixel fragment shader may expect the geometric normal and multiple texture coordinates to have been interpolated from vertex values by upstream fixed-function stages and can simply assign a value to the COLOR output parameter to pass it downstream to be blended with a pixel at an implied (x, y) position.

The GPU hardware creates a new independent thread to execute a vertex, geometry, or pixel shader program for every vertex, every primitive, and every pixel fragment. In video games, the bulk of threads execute pixel shader programs, as there are typically 10 to 20 times or more pixel fragments than vertices, and complex lighting and shadows require even larger ratios of pixel to vertex shader threads. The graphics shader programming model drove the GPU architecture to efficiently execute thousands of independent fine-grained threads on many parallel processor cores.

Pixel Shader Example

Consider the following Cg pixel shader program that implements the "environment mapping" rendering technique. For each pixel thread, this shader is passed five parameters, including 2D floating-point texture image coordinates needed to sample the surface color, and a 3D floating-point vector giving the reflection of the view direction off the surface. The other three "uniform" parameters do not vary from one pixel instance (thread) to the next. The shader looks up color in two texture images: a 2D texture access for the surface color, and a 3D texture access into a cube map (six images corresponding to the faces of a cube) to obtain the external world color corresponding to the reflection direction. Then the final four-component (red, green, blue, alpha) floating-point color is computed using a weighted average called a "lerp" or linear interpolation function.

```
void reflection(
    float2          texCoord        : TEXCOORD0,
    float3          reflection_dir  : TEXCOORD1,
    out float4      color           : COLOR,
    uniform float       shiny,
    uniform sampler2D   surfaceMap,
    uniform samplerCUBE envMap)
{
// Fetch the surface color from a texture
    float4 surfaceColor = tex2D(surfaceMap, texCoord);

// Fetch reflected color by sampling a cube map
    float4 reflectedColor = texCUBE(environmentMap, reflection_dir);

// Output is weighted average of the two colors
    color = lerp(surfaceColor, reflectedColor, shiny);
}
```

Although this shader program is only three lines long, it activates a lot of GPU hardware. For each texture fetch, the GPU texture subsystem makes multiple memory accesses to sample image colors in the vicinity of the sampling coordinates, and then interpolates the final result with floating-point filtering arithmetic. The multithreaded GPU executes thousands of these lightweight Cg pixel shader threads in parallel, deeply interleaving them to hide texture fetch and memory latency.

Cg focuses the programmer's view to a single vertex or primitive or pixel, which the GPU implements as a single thread; the shader program transparently scales to exploit thread parallelism on the available processors. Being application-specific, Cg provides a rich set of useful data types, library functions, and language constructs to express diverse rendering techniques.

Figure A.3.2 shows skin rendered by a fragment pixel shader. Real skin appears quite different from flesh-color paint because light bounces around a lot before re-emerging. In this complex shader, three separate skin layers, each with unique subsurface scattering behavior, are modeled to give the skin a visual depth and translucency. Scattering can be modeled by a blurring convolution in a flattened "texture" space, with red being blurred more than green, and blue blurred less.

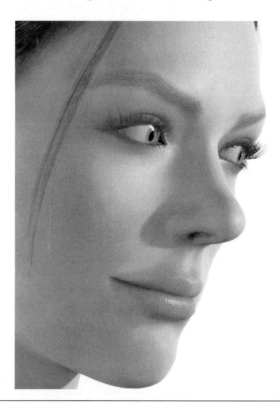

FIGURE A.3.2   GPU-rendered image. To give the skin visual depth and translucency, the pixel shader program models three separate skin layers, each with unique subsurface scattering behavior. It executes 1400 instructions to render the red, green, blue, and alpha color components of each skin pixel fragment.

The compiled Cg shader executes 1400 instructions to compute the color of one skin pixel.

As GPUs have evolved superior floating-point performance and very high streaming memory bandwidth for real-time graphics, they have attracted highly parallel applications beyond traditional graphics. At first, access to this power was available only by couching an application as a graphics-rendering algorithm, but this GPGPU approach was often awkward and limiting. More recently, the CUDA programming model has provided a far easier way to exploit the scalable high-performance floating-point and memory bandwidth of GPUs with the C programming language.

Programming Parallel Computing Applications

CUDA, Brook, and CAL are programming interfaces for GPUs that are focused on data parallel computation rather than on graphics. CAL (Compute Abstraction Layer) is a low-level assembler language interface for AMD GPUs. Brook is a streaming language adapted for GPUs by Buck, et. al. [2004]. CUDA, developed by NVIDIA [2007], is an extension to the C and C++ languages for scalable parallel programming of manycore GPUs and multicore CPUs. The CUDA programming model is described below, adapted from an article by Nickolls, Buck, Garland, and Skadron [2008].

With the new model the GPU excels in data parallel and throughput computing, executing high performance computing applications as well as graphics applications.

Data Parallel Problem Decomposition

To map large computing problems effectively to a highly parallel processing architecture, the programmer or compiler decomposes the problem into many small problems that can be solved in parallel. For example, the programmer partitions a large result data array into blocks and further partitions each block into elements, such that the result blocks can be computed independently in parallel, and the elements within each block are computed in parallel. Figure A.3.3 shows a decomposition of a result data array into a 3×2 grid of blocks, where each block is further decomposed into a 5×3 array of elements. The two-level parallel decomposition maps naturally to the GPU architecture: parallel multiprocessors compute result blocks, and parallel threads compute result elements.

The programmer writes a program that computes a sequence of result data grids, partitioning each result grid into coarse-grained result blocks that can be computed independently in parallel. The program computes each result block with an array of fine-grained parallel threads, partitioning the work among threads so that each computes one or more result elements.

Scalable Parallel Programming with CUDA

The CUDA scalable parallel programming model extends the C and C++ languages to exploit large degrees of parallelism for general applications on highly parallel multiprocessors, particularly GPUs. Early experience with CUDA shows

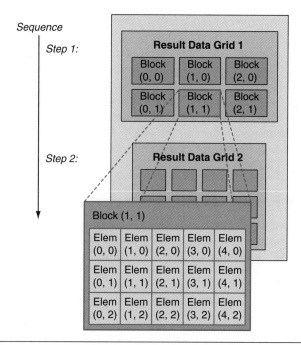

FIGURE A.3.3   Decomposing result data into a grid of blocks of elements to be computed in parallel.

that many sophisticated programs can be readily expressed with a few easily understood abstractions. Since NVIDIA released CUDA in 2007, developers have rapidly developed scalable parallel programs for a wide range of applications, including seismic data processing, computational chemistry, linear algebra, sparse matrix solvers, sorting, searching, physics models, and visual computing. These applications scale transparently to hundreds of processor cores and thousands of concurrent threads. NVIDIA GPUs with the Tesla unified graphics and computing architecture (described in sections A.4 and A.7) run CUDA C programs, and are widely available in laptops, PCs, workstations, and servers. The CUDA model is also applicable to other shared memory parallel processing architectures, including multicore CPUs [Stratton, 2008].

CUDA provides three key abstractions—a *hierarchy of thread groups, shared memories,* and *barrier synchronization*—that provide a clear parallel structure to conventional C code for one thread of the hierarchy. Multiple levels of threads, memory, and synchronization provide fine-grained data parallelism and thread parallelism, nested within coarse-grained data parallelism and task parallelism. The abstractions guide the programmer to partition the problem into coarse subproblems that can be solved independently in parallel, and then into finer pieces that can be solved in parallel. The programming model scales transparently to large numbers of processor cores: a compiled CUDA program executes on any number of processors, and only the runtime system needs to know the physical processor count.

The CUDA Paradigm

CUDA is a minimal extension of the C and C++ programming languages. The programmer writes a serial program that calls parallel **kernels**, which may be simple functions or full programs. A kernel executes in parallel across a set of parallel threads. The programmer organizes these threads into a hierarchy of thread blocks and grids of thread blocks. A **thread block** is a set of concurrent threads that can cooperate among themselves through barrier synchronization and through shared access to a memory space private to the block. A **grid** is a set of thread blocks that may each be executed independently and thus may execute in parallel.

When invoking a kernel, the programmer specifies the number of threads per block and the number of blocks comprising the grid. Each thread is given a unique *thread ID* number `threadIdx` within its thread block, numbered `0, 1, 2, ..., blockDim-1`, and each thread block is given a unique *block ID* number `blockIdx` within its grid. CUDA supports thread blocks containing up to 512 threads. For convenience, thread blocks and grids may have 1, 2, or 3 dimensions, accessed via `.x`, `.y`, and `.z` index fields.

As a very simple example of parallel programming, suppose that we are given two vectors x and y of n floating-point numbers each and that we wish to compute the result of $y = ax + y$ for some scalar value a. This is the so-called `SAXPY` kernel defined by the BLAS linear algebra library. Figure A.3.4 shows C code for performing this computation on both a serial processor and in parallel using CUDA.

The `__global__` declaration specifier indicates that the procedure is a kernel entry point. CUDA programs launch parallel kernels with the extended function call syntax:

```
kernel<<<dimGrid, dimBlock>>>(... parameter list ...);
```

where `dimGrid` and `dimBlock` are three-element vectors of type `dim3` that specify the dimensions of the grid in blocks and the dimensions of the blocks in threads, respectively. Unspecified dimensions default to one.

In Figure A.3.4, we launch a grid of n threads that assigns one thread to each element of the vectors and puts 256 threads in each block. Each individual thread computes an element index from its thread and block IDs and then performs the desired calculation on the corresponding vector elements. Comparing the serial and parallel versions of this code, we see that they are strikingly similar. This represents a fairly common pattern. The serial code consists of a loop where each iteration is independent of all the others. Such loops can be mechanically transformed into parallel kernels: each loop iteration becomes an independent thread. By assigning a single thread to each output element, we avoid the need for any synchronization among threads when writing results to memory.

The text of a CUDA kernel is simply a C function for one sequential thread. Thus, it is generally straightforward to write and is typically simpler than writing parallel code for vector operations. Parallelism is determined clearly and explicitly by specifying the dimensions of a grid and its thread blocks when launching a kernel.

kernel A program or function for one thread, designed to be executed by many threads.

thread block A set of concurrent threads that execute the same thread program and may cooperate to compute a result.

grid A set of thread blocks that execute the same kernel program.

Computing y = ax + y with a serial loop:

```
void saxpy_serial(int n, float alpha, float *x, float *y)
{
    for(int i = 0; i<n; ++i)
        y[i] = alpha*x[i] + y[i];
}

// Invoke serial SAXPY kernel
saxpy_serial(n, 2.0, x, y);
```

Computing y = ax + y in parallel using CUDA:

```
__global__
void saxpy_parallel(int n, float alpha, float *x, float *y)
{

    int i = blockIdx.x*blockDim.x + threadIdx.x;

    if( i<n )  y[i] = alpha*x[i] + y[i];
}

// Invoke parallel SAXPY kernel (256 threads per block)
int nblocks = (n + 255) / 256;
saxpy_parallel<<<nblocks, 256>>>(n, 2.0, x, y);
```

FIGURE A.3.4   Sequential code (top) in C versus parallel code (bottom) in CUDA for SAXPY (see Chapter 7). CUDA parallel threads replace the C serial loop—each thread computes the same result as one loop iteration. The parallel code computes *n* results with *n* threads organized in blocks of 256 threads.

synchronization barrier
Threads wait at a synchronization barrier until all threads in the thread block arrive at the barrier.

Parallel execution and thread management is automatic. All thread creation, scheduling, and termination is handled for the programmer by the underlying system. Indeed, a Tesla architecture GPU performs all thread management directly in hardware. The threads of a block execute concurrently and may synchronize at a **synchronization barrier** by calling the __syncthreads() intrinsic. This guarantees that no thread in the block can proceed until all threads in the block have reached the barrier. After passing the barrier, these threads are also guaranteed to see all writes to memory performed by threads in the block before the barrier. Thus, threads in a block may communicate with each other by writing and reading per-block shared memory at a synchronization barrier.

Since threads in a block may share memory and synchronize via barriers, they will reside together on the same physical processor or multiprocessor. The number of thread blocks can, however, greatly exceed the number of processors. The CUDA thread programming model virtualizes the processors and gives the programmer the flexibility to parallelize at whatever granularity is most convenient. Virtualization into threads and thread blocks allows intuitive problem decompositions, as the number of blocks can be dictated by the size of the data being processed rather than by the number of processors in the system. It also allows the same CUDA program to scale to widely varying numbers of processor cores.

To manage this processing element virtualization and provide scalability, CUDA requires that thread blocks be able to execute independently. It must be possible to execute blocks in any order, in parallel or in series. Different blocks have no means of direct communication, although they may *coordinate* their activities using **atomic memory operations** on the global memory visible to all threads—by atomically incrementing queue pointers, for example. This independence requirement allows thread blocks to be scheduled in any order across any number of cores, making the CUDA model scalable across an arbitrary number of cores as well as across a variety of parallel architectures. It also helps to avoid the possibility of deadlock. An application may execute multiple grids either independently or dependently. Independent grids may execute concurrently, given sufficient hardware resources. Dependent grids execute sequentially, with an implicit interkernel barrier between them, thus guaranteeing that all blocks of the first grid complete before any block of the second, dependent grid begins.

atomic memory operation A memory read, modify, write operation sequence that completes without any intervening access.

Threads may access data from multiple memory spaces during their execution. Each thread has a private **local memory**. CUDA uses local memory for thread-private variables that do not fit in the thread's registers, as well as for stack frames and register spilling. Each thread block has a **shared memory**, visible to all threads of the block, which has the same lifetime as the block. Finally, all threads have access to the same **global memory**. Programs declare variables in shared and global memory with the __shared__ and __device__ type qualifiers. On a Tesla architecture GPU, these memory spaces correspond to physically separate memories: per-block shared memory is a low-latency on-chip RAM, while global memory resides in the fast DRAM on the graphics board.

local memory Per-thread local memory private to the thread.

shared memory Per-block memory shared by all threads of the block.

global memory Per-application memory shared by all threads.

Shared memory is expected to be a low-latency memory near each processor, much like an L1 cache. It can therefore provide high-performance communication and data sharing among the threads of a thread block. Since it has the same lifetime as its corresponding thread block, kernel code will typically initialize data in shared variables, compute using shared variables, and copy shared memory results to global memory. Thread blocks of sequentially dependent grids communicate via global memory, using it to read input and write results.

Figure A.3.5 diagrams the nested levels of threads, thread blocks, and grids of thread blocks. It further shows the corresponding levels of memory sharing: local, shared, and global memories for per-thread, per-thread-block, and per-application data sharing.

A program manages the global memory space visible to kernels through calls to the CUDA runtime, such as cudaMalloc() and cudaFree(). Kernels may execute on a physically separate device, as is the case when running kernels on the GPU. Consequently, the application must use cudaMemcpy() to copy data between the allocated space and the host system memory.

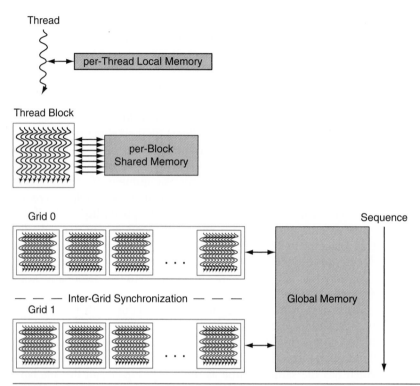

FIGURE A.3.5   Nested granularity levels—thread, thread block, and grid—have corresponding memory sharing levels—local, shared, and global. Per-thread local memory is private to the thread. Per-block shared memory is shared by all threads of the block. Per-application global memory is shared by all threads.

single-program multiple data (SPMD) A style of parallel programming model in which all threads execute the same program. SPMD threads typically coordinate with barrier synchronization.

The CUDA programming model is similar in style to the familiar single-program multiple data (**SPMD**) model—it expresses parallelism explicitly, and each kernel executes on a fixed number of threads. However, CUDA is more flexible than most realizations of SPMD, because each kernel call dynamically creates a new grid with the right number of thread blocks and threads for that application step. The programmer can use a convenient degree of parallelism for each kernel, rather than having to design all phases of the computation to use the same number of threads. Figure A.3.6 shows an example of an SPMD-like CUDA code sequence. It first instantiates kernelF on a 2D grid of 3 × 2 blocks where each 2D thread block consists of 5 × 3 threads. It then instantiates kernelG on a 1D grid of four 1D thread blocks with six threads each. Because kernelG depends on the results of kernelF, they are separated by an interkernel synchronization barrier.

The concurrent threads of a thread block express fine-grained data parallelism and thread parallelism. The independent thread blocks of a grid express

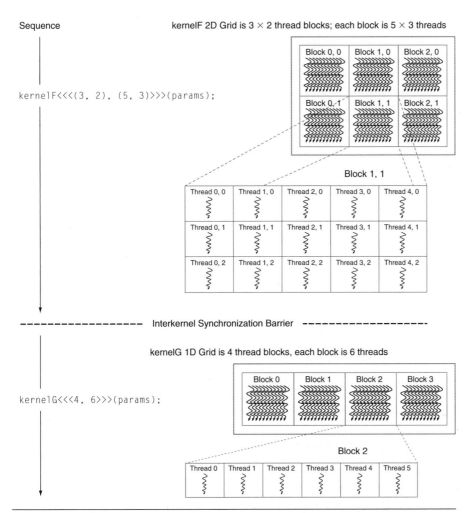

Sequence   kernelF 2D Grid is 3 × 2 thread blocks; each block is 5 × 3 threads

kernelF<<<(3, 2), (5, 3)>>>(params);

Interkernel Synchronization Barrier

kernelG 1D Grid is 4 thread blocks, each block is 6 threads

kernelG<<<4, 6>>>(params);

FIGURE A.3.6   Sequence of kernel _F_ instantiated on a 2D grid of 2D thread blocks, an interkernel synchronization barrier, followed by kernel _G_ on a 1D grid of 1D thread blocks.

coarse-grained data parallelism. Independent grids express coarse-grained task parallelism. A kernel is simply C code for one thread of the hierarchy.

Restrictions

For efficiency, and to simplify its implementation, the CUDA programming model has some restrictions. Threads and thread blocks may only be created by invoking a parallel kernel, not from within a parallel kernel. Together with the required independence of thread blocks, this makes it possible to execute CUDA programs with a simple scheduler that introduces minimal runtime overhead. In fact, the Tesla GPU architecture implements *hardware* management and scheduling of threads and thread blocks.

Task parallelism can be expressed at the thread block level but is difficult to express within a thread block because thread synchronization barriers operate on all the threads of the block. To enable CUDA programs to run on any number of processors, dependencies among thread blocks within the same kernel grid are not allowed—blocks must execute independently. Since CUDA requires that thread blocks be independent and allows blocks to be executed in any order, combining results generated by multiple blocks must in general be done by launching a second kernel on a new grid of thread blocks (although thread blocks may *coordinate* their activities using atomic memory operations on the global memory visible to all threads—by atomically incrementing queue pointers, for example).

Recursive function calls are not currently allowed in CUDA kernels. Recursion is unattractive in a massively parallel kernel, because providing stack space for the tens of thousands of threads that may be active would require substantial amounts of memory. Serial algorithms that are normally expressed using recursion, such as quicksort, are typically best implemented using nested data parallelism rather than explicit recursion.

To support a heterogeneous system architecture combining a CPU and a GPU, each with its own memory system, CUDA programs must copy data and results between host memory and device memory. The overhead of CPU–GPU interaction and data transfers is minimized by using DMA block transfer engines and fast interconnects. Compute-intensive problems large enough to need a GPU performance boost amortize the overhead better than small problems.

Implications for Architecture

The parallel programming models for graphics and computing have driven GPU architecture to be different than CPU architecture. The key aspects of GPU programs driving GPU processor architecture are:

- *Extensive use of fine-grained data parallelism:* Shader programs describe how to process a single pixel or vertex, and CUDA programs describe how to compute an individual result.

- *Highly threaded programming model:* A shader thread program processes a single pixel or vertex, and a CUDA thread program may generate a single result. A GPU must create and execute millions of such thread programs per frame, at 60 frames per second.

- *Scalability:* A program must automatically increase its performance when provided with additional processors, without recompiling.

- *Intensive floating-point (or integer) computation.*

- *Support of high throughput computations.*

A.4 Multithreaded Multiprocessor Architecture

To address different market segments, GPUs implement scalable numbers of multiprocessors—in fact, GPUs are multiprocessors composed of multiprocessors. Furthermore, each multiprocessor is highly multithreaded to execute many fine-grained vertex and pixel shader threads efficiently. A quality basic GPU has two to four multiprocessors, while a gaming enthusiast's GPU or computing platform has dozens of them. This section looks at the architecture of one such multithreaded multiprocessor, a simplified version of the NVIDIA Tesla streaming multiprocessor (SM) described in Section A.7.

Why use a multiprocessor, rather than several independent processors? The parallelism within each multiprocessor provides localized high performance and supports extensive multithreading for the fine-grained parallel programming models described in Section A.3. The individual threads of a thread block execute together within a multiprocessor to share data. The multithreaded multiprocessor design we describe here has eight scalar processor cores in a tightly coupled architecture, and executes up to 512 threads (the SM described in Section A.7 executes up to 768 threads). For area and power efficiency, the multiprocessor shares large complex units among the eight processor cores, including the instruction cache, the multithreaded instruction unit, and the shared memory RAM.

Massive Multithreading

GPU processors are highly multithreaded to achieve several goals:

- Cover the latency of memory loads and texture fetches from DRAM
- Support fine-grained parallel graphics shader programming models
- Support fine-grained parallel computing programming models
- Virtualize the physical processors as threads and thread blocks to provide transparent scalability
- Simplify the parallel programming model to writing a serial program for one thread

Memory and texture fetch latency can require hundreds of processor clocks, because GPUs typically have small streaming caches rather than large working-set caches like CPUs. A fetch request generally requires a full DRAM access latency plus interconnect and buffering latency. Multithreading helps cover the latency with useful computing—while one thread is waiting for a load or texture fetch to complete, the processor can execute another thread. The fine-grained parallel programming models provide literally thousands of independent threads that can keep many processors busy despite the long memory latency seen by individual threads.

A graphics vertex or pixel shader program is a program for a single thread that processes a vertex or a pixel. Similarly, a CUDA program is a C program for a single thread that computes a result. Graphics and computing programs instantiate many parallel threads to render complex images and compute large result arrays. To dynamically balance shifting vertex and pixel shader thread workloads, each multiprocessor concurrently executes multiple different thread programs and different types of shader programs.

To support the independent vertex, primitive, and pixel programming model of graphics shading languages and the single-thread programming model of CUDA C/C++, each GPU thread has its own private registers, private per-thread memory, program counter, and thread execution state, and can execute an independent code path. To efficiently execute hundreds of concurrent lightweight threads, the GPU multiprocessor is hardware multithreaded—it manages and executes hundreds of concurrent threads in hardware without scheduling overhead. Concurrent threads within thread blocks can synchronize at a barrier with a single instruction. Lightweight thread creation, zero-overhead thread scheduling, and fast barrier synchronization efficiently support very fine-grained parallelism.

Multiprocessor Architecture

A unified graphics and computing multiprocessor executes vertex, geometry, and pixel fragment shader programs, and parallel computing programs. As Figure A.4.1 shows, the example multiprocessor consists of eight scalar processor (SP) cores each with a large multithreaded register file (RF), two special function units (SFU), a multithreaded instruction unit, an instruction cache, a read-only constant cache, and a shared memory.

The 16 KB shared memory holds graphics data buffers and shared computing data. CUDA variables declared as __shared__ reside in the shared memory. To map the logical graphics pipeline workload through the multiprocessor multiple times, as shown in Section A.2, vertex, geometry, and pixel threads have independent input and output buffers, and workloads arrive and depart independently of thread execution.

Each SP core contains scalar integer and floating-point arithmetic units that execute most instructions. The SP is hardware multithreaded, supporting up to 64 threads. Each pipelined SP core executes one scalar instruction per thread per clock, which ranges from 1.2 GHz to 1.6 GHz in different GPU products. Each SP core has a large register file (RF) of 1024 general-purpose 32-bit registers, partitioned among its assigned threads. Programs declare their register demand, typically 16 to 64 scalar 32-bit registers per thread. The SP can concurrently run many threads that use a few registers or fewer threads that use more registers. The compiler optimizes register allocation to balance the cost of spilling registers versus the cost of fewer threads. Pixel shader programs often use 16 or fewer registers, enabling each SP to run up to 64 pixel shader threads to cover long-latency texture fetches. Compiled CUDA programs often need 32 registers per thread, limiting each SP to 32 threads, which limits such a kernel program to 256 threads per thread block on this example multiprocessor, rather than its maximum of 512 threads.

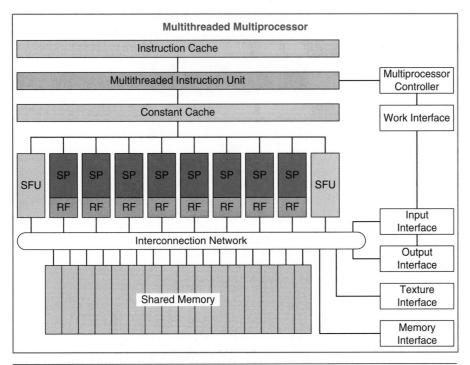

FIGURE A.4.1 Multithreaded multiprocessor with eight scalar processor (SP) cores. The eight SP cores each have a large multithreaded register file (RF) and share an instruction cache, multithreaded instruction issue unit, constant cache, two special function units (SFUs), interconnection network, and a multibank shared memory.

The pipelined SFUs execute thread instructions that compute special functions and interpolate pixel attributes from primitive vertex attributes. These instructions can execute concurrently with instructions on the SPs. The SFU is described later.

The multiprocessor executes texture fetch instructions on the texture unit via the texture interface, and uses the memory interface for external memory load, store, and atomic access instructions. These instructions can execute concurrently with instructions on the SPs. Shared memory access uses a low-latency interconnection network between the SP processors and the shared memory banks.

Single-Instruction Multiple-Thread (SIMT)

To manage and execute hundreds of threads running several different programs efficiently, the multiprocessor employs a **single-instruction multiple-thread (SIMT)** architecture. It creates, manages, schedules, and executes concurrent threads in groups of parallel threads called *warps*. The term **warp** originates from weaving, the first parallel thread technology. The photograph in Figure A.4.2 shows a warp of parallel threads emerging from a loom. This example multiprocessor uses a SIMT warp size of 32 threads, executing four threads in each of the eight

single-instruction multiple-thread (SIMT) A processor architecture that applies one instruction to multiple independent threads in parallel.

warp The set of parallel threads that execute the same instruction together in a SIMT architecture.

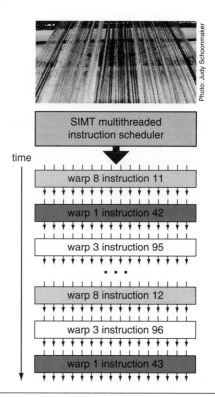

FIGURE A.4.2   SIMT multithreaded warp scheduling. The scheduler selects a ready warp and issues an instruction synchronously to the parallel threads composing the warp. Because warps are independent, the scheduler may select a different warp each time.

SP cores over four clocks. The Tesla SM multiprocessor described in Section A.7 also uses a warp size of 32 parallel threads, executing four threads per SP core for efficiency on plentiful pixel threads and computing threads. Thread blocks consist of one or more warps.

This example SIMT multiprocessor manages a pool of 16 warps, a total of 512 threads. Individual parallel threads composing a warp are the same type and start together at the same program address, but are otherwise free to branch and execute independently. At each instruction issue time, the SIMT multithreaded instruction unit selects a warp that is ready to execute its next instruction, then issues that instruction to the active threads of that warp. A SIMT instruction is broadcast synchronously to the active parallel threads of a warp; individual threads may be inactive due to independent branching or predication. In this multiprocessor, each SP scalar processor core executes an instruction for four individual threads of a warp using four clocks, reflecting the 4:1 ratio of warp threads to cores.

SIMT processor architecture is akin to single-instruction multiple data (SIMD) design, which applies one instruction to multiple data lanes, but differs in that SIMT applies one instruction to multiple independent threads in parallel, not just to multiple data lanes. An instruction for a SIMD processor controls a vector of multiple data lanes together, whereas an instruction for a SIMT processor controls an individual thread, and the SIMT instruction unit issues an instruction to a warp of independent parallel threads for efficiency. The SIMT processor finds data-level parallelism among threads at runtime, analogous to the way a superscalar processor finds instruction-level parallelism among instructions at runtime.

A SIMT processor realizes full efficiency and performance when all threads of a warp take the same execution path. If threads of a warp diverge via a data-dependent conditional branch, execution serializes for each branch path taken, and when all paths complete, the threads converge to the same execution path. For equal length paths, a divergent if-else code block is 50% efficient. The multiprocessor uses a branch synchronization stack to manage independent threads that diverge and converge. Different warps execute independently at full speed regardless of whether they are executing common or disjoint code paths. As a result, SIMT GPUs are dramatically more efficient and flexible on branching code than earlier GPUs, as their warps are much narrower than the SIMD width of prior GPUs.

In contrast with SIMD vector architectures, SIMT enables programmers to write thread-level parallel code for individual independent threads, as well as data-parallel code for many coordinated threads. For program correctness, the programmer can essentially ignore the SIMT execution attributes of warps; however, substantial performance improvements can be realized by taking care that the code seldom requires threads in a warp to diverge. In practice, this is analogous to the role of cache lines in traditional codes: cache line size can be safely ignored when designing for correctness but must be considered in the code structure when designing for peak performance.

SIMT Warp Execution and Divergence

The SIMT approach of scheduling independent warps is more flexible than the scheduling of previous GPU architectures. A warp comprises parallel threads of the same type: vertex, geometry, pixel, or compute. The basic unit of pixel fragment shader processing is the 2-by-2 pixel quad implemented as four pixel shader threads. The multiprocessor controller packs the pixel quads into a warp. It similarly groups vertices and primitives into warps, and packs computing threads into a warp. A thread block comprises one or more warps. The SIMT design shares the instruction fetch and issue unit efficiently across parallel threads of a warp, but requires a full warp of active threads to get full performance efficiency.

This unified multiprocessor schedules and executes multiple warp types concurrently, allowing it to concurrently execute vertex and pixel warps. Its warp scheduler operates at less than the processor clock rate, because there are four thread lanes per processor core. During each scheduling cycle, it selects a warp to execute a SIMT warp instruction, as shown in Figure A.4.2. An issued warp-instruction executes as four sets of eight threads over four processor cycles of throughput. The processor pipeline uses several clocks of latency to complete each instruction. If the number of active warps times the clocks per warp exceeds the pipeline latency, the programmer can ignore the pipeline latency. For this multiprocessor, a round-robin schedule of eight warps has a period of 32 cycles between successive instructions for the same warp. If the program can keep 256 threads active per multiprocessor, instruction latencies up to 32 cycles can be hidden from an individual sequential thread. However, with few active warps, the processor pipeline depth becomes visible and may cause processors to stall.

A challenging design problem is implementing zero-overhead warp scheduling for a dynamic mix of different warp programs and program types. The instruction scheduler must select a warp every four clocks to issue one instruction per clock per thread, equivalent to an IPC of 1.0 per processor core. Because warps are independent, the only dependencies are among sequential instructions from the same warp. The scheduler uses a register dependency scoreboard to qualify warps whose active threads are ready to execute an instruction. It prioritizes all such ready warps and selects the highest priority one for issue. Prioritization must consider warp type, instruction type, and the desire to be fair to all active warps.

Managing Threads and Thread Blocks

The multiprocessor controller and instruction unit manage threads and thread blocks. The controller accepts work requests and input data and arbitrates access to shared resources, including the texture unit, memory access path, and I/O paths. For graphics workloads, it creates and manages three types of graphics threads concurrently: vertex, geometry, and pixel. Each of the graphics work types have independent input and output paths. It accumulates and packs each of these input work types into SIMT warps of parallel threads executing the same thread program. It allocates a free warp, allocates registers for the warp threads, and starts warp execution in the multiprocessor. Every program declares its per-thread register demand; the controller starts a warp only when it can allocate the requested register count for the warp threads. When all the threads of the warp exit, the controller unpacks the results and frees the warp registers and resources.

The controller creates **cooperative thread arrays (CTAs)** which implement CUDA thread blocks as one or more warps of parallel threads. It creates a CTA when it can create all CTA warps and allocate all CTA resources. In addition to threads and registers, a CTA requires allocating shared memory and barriers. The program declares the required capacities, and the controller waits until it can allocate those amounts before launching the CTA. Then it creates CTA warps at the warp scheduling rate, so that a CTA program starts executing immediately at full multiprocessor performance. The controller monitors when all threads of a CTA have exited, and frees the CTA shared resources and its warp resources.

cooperative thread array (CTA) A set of concurrent threads that executes the same thread program and may cooperate to compute a result. A GPU CTA implements a CUDA thread block.

Thread Instructions

The SP thread processors execute scalar instructions for individual threads, unlike earlier GPU vector instruction architectures, which executed four-component vector instructions for each vertex or pixel shader program. Vertex programs generally compute (x, y, z, w) position vectors, while pixel shader programs compute (red, green, blue, alpha) color vectors. However, shader programs are becoming longer and more scalar, and it is increasingly difficult to fully occupy even two components of a legacy GPU four-component vector architecture. In effect, the SIMT architecture parallelizes across 32 independent pixel threads, rather than parallelizing the four vector components within a pixel. CUDA C/C++ programs have predominantly scalar code per thread. Previous GPUs employed vector packing (e.g., combining subvectors of work to gain efficiency) but that complicated the scheduling hardware as well as the compiler. Scalar instructions are simpler and compiler friendly. Texture instructions remain vector based, taking a source coordinate vector and returning a filtered color vector.

To support multiple GPUs with different binary microinstruction formats, high-level graphics and computing language compilers generate intermediate assembler-level instructions (e.g., Direct3D vector instructions or PTX scalar instructions), which are then optimized and translated to binary GPU microinstructions. The NVIDIA PTX (parallel thread execution) instruction set definition [2007] provides a stable target ISA for compilers, and provides compatibility over several generations of GPUs with evolving binary microinstruction-set architectures. The optimizer readily expands Direct3D vector instructions to multiple scalar binary microinstructions. PTX scalar instructions translate nearly one to one with scalar binary microinstructions, although some PTX instructions expand to multiple binary microinstructions, and multiple PTX instructions may fold into one binary microinstruction. Because the intermediate assembler-level instructions use virtual registers, the optimizer analyzes data dependencies and allocates real registers. The optimizer eliminates dead code, folds instructions together when feasible, and optimizes SIMT branch diverge and converge points.

Instruction Set Architecture (ISA)

The thread ISA described here is a simplified version of the Tesla architecture PTX ISA, a register-based scalar instruction set comprising floating-point, integer, logical, conversion, special functions, flow control, memory access, and texture operations. Figure A.4.3 lists the basic PTX GPU thread instructions; see the NVIDIA PTX specification [2007] for details. The instruction format is:

```
opcode.type d, a, b, c;
```

where d is the destination operand, a, b, c are source operands, and .type is one of:

Type	.type Specifier
Untyped bits 8, 16, 32, and 64 bits	.b8, .b16, .b32, .b64
Unsigned integer 8, 16, 32, and 64 bits	.u8, .u16, .u32, .u64
Signed integer 8, 16, 32, and 64 bits	.s8, .s16, .s32, .s64
Floating-point 16, 32, and 64 bits	.f16, .f32, .f64

Basic PTX GPU Thread Instructions

Group	Instruction	Example	Meaning	Comments
Arithmetic	arithmetic .*type* = .s32, .u32, .f32, .s64, .u64, .f64			
	add.*type*	add.f32 d, a, b	d = a + b;	
	sub.*type*	sub.f32 d, a, b	d = a - b;	
	mul.*type*	mul.f32 d, a, b	d = a * b;	
	mad.*type*	mad.f32 d, a, b, c	d = a * b + c;	multiply-add
	div.*type*	div.f32 d, a, b	d = a / b;	multiple microinstructions
	rem.*type*	rem.u32 d, a, b	d = a % b;	integer remainder
	abs.*type*	abs.f32 d, a	d = |a|;	
	neg.*type*	neg.f32 d, a	d = 0 - a;	
	min.*type*	min.f32 d, a, b	d = (a < b)? a:b;	floating selects non-NaN
	max.*type*	max.f32 d, a, b	d = (a > b)? a:b;	floating selects non-NaN
	setp.*cmp.type*	setp.lt.f32 p, a, b	p = (a < b);	compare and set predicate
	numeric .*cmp* = eq, ne, lt, le, gt, ge; unordered *cmp* = equ, neu, ltu, leu, gtu, geu, num, nan			
	mov.*type*	mov.b32 d, a	d = a;	move
	selp.*type*	selp.f32 d, a, b, p	d = p? a: b;	select with predicate
	cvt.dtype.atype	cvt.f32.s32 d, a	d = convert(a);	convert atype to dtype
Special Function	special .*type* = .f32 (some .f64)			
	rcp.*type*	rcp.f32 d, a	d = 1/a;	reciprocal
	sqrt.*type*	sqrt.f32 d, a	d = sqrt(a);	square root
	rsqrt.*type*	rsqrt.f32 d, a	d = 1/sqrt(a);	reciprocal square root
	sin.*type*	sin.f32 d, a	d = sin(a);	sine
	cos.*type*	cos.f32 d, a	d = cos(a);	cosine
	lg2.*type*	lg2.f32 d, a	d = log(a)/log(2)	binary logarithm
	ex2.*type*	ex2.f32 d, a	d = 2 ** a;	binary exponential
Logical	logic.*type* = .pred,.b32, .b64			
	and.*type*	and.b32 d, a, b	d = a & b;	
	or.*type*	or.b32 d, a, b	d = a | b;	
	xor.*type*	xor.b32 d, a, b	d = a ^ b;	
	not.*type*	not.b32 d, a, b	d = ~a;	one's complement
	cnot.*type*	cnot.b32 d, a, b	d = (a==0)? 1:0;	C logical not
	shl.*type*	shl.b32 d, a, b	d = a << b;	shift left
	shr.*type*	shr.s32 d, a, b	d = a >> b;	shift right
Memory Access	memory .*space* = .global, .shared, .local, .const; .*type* = .b8, .u8, .s8, .b16, .b32, .b64			
	ld.*space.type*	ld.global.b32 d, [a+off]	d = *(a+off);	load from memory *space*
	st.*space.type*	st.shared.b32 [d+off], a	*(d+off) = a;	store to memory *space*
	tex.*nd.dtyp.btype*	tex.2d.v4.f32.f32 d, a, b	d = tex2d(a, b);	texture lookup
	atom.*spc.op.type*	atom.global.add.u32 d,[a], b atom.global.cas.b32 d,[a], b, c	atomic { d = *a; *a = op(*a, b); }	atomic read-modify-write operation
	atom .*op* = and, or, xor, add, min, max, exch, cas; .*spc* = .global; .*type* = .b32			
Control Flow	branch	@p bra target	if (p) goto target;	conditional branch
	call	call (ret), func, (params)	ret = func(params);	call function
	ret	ret	return;	return from function call
	bar.sync	bar.sync d	wait for threads	barrier synchronization
	exit	exit	exit;	terminate thread execution

FIGURE A.4.3   Basic PTX GPU thread instructions.

Source operands are scalar 32-bit or 64-bit values in registers, an immediate value, or a constant; predicate operands are 1-bit Boolean values. Destinations are registers, except for store to memory. Instructions are predicated by prefixing them with @p or @!p, where p is a predicate register. Memory and texture instructions transfer scalars or vectors of two to four components, up to 128 bits total. PTX instructions specify the behavior of one thread.

The PTX arithmetic instructions operate on 32-bit and 64-bit floating-point, signed integer, and unsigned integer types. Recent GPUs support 64-bit double precision floating-point; see Section A.6. On current GPUs, PTX 64-bit integer and logical instructions are translated to two or more binary microinstructions that perform 32-bit operations. The GPU special function instructions are limited to 32-bit floating-point. The thread control flow instructions are conditional branch, function call and return, thread exit, and bar.sync (barrier synchronization). The conditional branch instruction @p bra target uses a predicate register p (or !p) previously set by a compare and set predicate setp instruction to determine whether the thread takes the branch or not. Other instructions can also be predicated on a predicate register being true or false.

Memory Access Instructions

The tex instruction fetches and filters texture samples from 1D, 2D, and 3D texture arrays in memory via the texture subsystem. Texture fetches generally use interpolated floating-point coordinates to address a texture. Once a graphics pixel shader thread computes its pixel fragment color, the raster operations processor blends it with the pixel color at its assigned (x, y) pixel position and writes the final color to memory.

To support computing and C/C++ language needs, the Tesla PTX ISA implements memory load/store instructions. They use integer byte addressing with register plus offset address arithmetic to facilitate conventional compiler code optimizations. Memory load/store instructions are common in processors, but are a significant new capability in the Tesla architecture GPUs, as prior GPUs provided only the texture and pixel accesses required by the graphics APIs.

For computing, the load/store instructions access three read/write memory spaces that implement the corresponding CUDA memory spaces in Section A.3:

- Local memory for per-thread private addressable temporary data (implemented in external DRAM)

- Shared memory for low-latency access to data shared by cooperating threads in the same CTA/thread block (implemented in on-chip SRAM)

- Global memory for large data sets shared by all threads of a computing application (implemented in external DRAM)

The memory load/store instructions ld.global, st.global, ld.shared, st.shared, ld.local, and st.local access the global, shared, and local memory spaces. Computing programs use the fast barrier synchronization instruction bar.sync to synchronize threads within a CTA/thread block that communicate with each other via shared and global memory.

To improve memory bandwidth and reduce overhead, the local and global load/ store instructions coalesce individual parallel thread requests from the same SIMT warp together into a single memory block request when the addresses fall in the same block and meet alignment criteria. Coalescing memory requests provides a significant performance boost over separate requests from individual threads. The multiprocessor's large thread count, together with support for many outstanding load requests, helps cover load-to-use latency for local and global memory implemented in external DRAM.

The latest Tesla architecture GPUs also provide efficient atomic memory operations on memory with the atom.op.u32 instructions, including integer operations add, min, max, and, or, xor, exchange, and cas (compare-and-swap) operations, facilitating parallel reductions and parallel data structure management.

Barrier Synchronization for Thread Communication

Fast barrier synchronization permits CUDA programs to communicate frequently via shared memory and global memory by simply calling __syncthreads(); as part of each interthread communication step. The synchronization intrinsic function generates a single bar.sync instruction. However, implementing fast barrier synchronization among up to 512 threads per CUDA thread block is a challenge.

Grouping threads into SIMT warps of 32 threads reduces the synchronization difficulty by a factor of 32. Threads wait at a barrier in the SIMT thread scheduler so they do not consume any processor cycles while waiting. When a thread executes a bar.sync instruction, it increments the barrier's thread arrival counter and the scheduler marks the thread as waiting at the barrier. Once all the CTA threads arrive, the barrier counter matches the expected terminal count, and the scheduler releases all the threads waiting at the barrier and resumes executing threads.

Streaming Processor (SP)

The multithreaded streaming processor (SP) core is the primary thread instruction processor in the multiprocessor. Its register file (RF) provides 1024 scalar 32-bit registers for up to 64 threads. It executes all the fundamental floating-point operations, including add.f32, mul.f32, mad.f32 (floating multiply-add), min.f32, max.f32, and setp.f32 (floating compare and set predicate). The floating-point add and multiply operations are compatible with the IEEE 754 standard for single precision FP numbers, including not-a-number (NaN) and infinity values. The SP core also implements all of the 32-bit and 64-bit integer arithmetic, comparison, conversion, and logical PTX instructions in Figure A.4.3.

The floating-point add and mul operations employ IEEE round-to-nearest-even as the default rounding mode. The mad.f32 floating-point multiply-add operation performs a multiplication with truncation, followed by an addition with round-to-nearest-even. The SP flushes input denormal operands to sign-preserved-zero. Results that underflow the target output exponent range are flushed to sign-preserved-zero after rounding.

Special Function Unit (SFU)

Certain thread instructions can execute on the SFUs, concurrently with other thread instructions executing on the SPs. The SFU implements the special function instructions of Figure A.4.3, which compute 32-bit floating-point approximations to reciprocal, reciprocal square root, and key transcendental functions. It also implements 32-bit floating-point planar attribute interpolation for pixel shaders, providing accurate interpolation of attributes such as color, depth, and texture coordinates.

Each pipelined SFU generates one 32-bit floating-point special function result per cycle; the two SFUs per multiprocessor execute special function instructions at a quarter the simple instruction rate of the eight SPs. The SFUs also execute the `mul.f32` multiply instruction concurrently with the eight SPs, increasing the peak computation rate up to 50% for threads with a suitable instruction mixture.

For functional evaluation, the Tesla architecture SFU employs quadratic interpolation based on enhanced minimax approximations for approximating the reciprocal, reciprocal square-root, $\log_2 x$, 2^x, and sin/cos functions. The accuracy of the function estimates ranges from 22 to 24 mantissa bits. See Section A.6 for more details on SFU arithmetic.

Comparing with Other Multiprocessors

Compared with SIMD vector architectures such as x86 SSE, the SIMT multiprocessor can execute individual threads independently, rather than always executing them together in synchronous groups. SIMT hardware finds data parallelism among independent threads, whereas SIMD hardware requires the software to express data parallelism explicitly in each vector instruction. A SIMT machine executes a warp of 32 threads synchronously when the threads take the same execution path, yet can execute each thread independently when they diverge. The advantage is significant because SIMT programs and instructions simply describe the behavior of a single independent thread, rather than a SIMD data vector of four or more data lanes. Yet the SIMT multiprocessor has SIMD-like efficiency, spreading the area and cost of one instruction unit across the 32 threads of a warp and across the eight streaming processor cores. SIMT provides the performance of SIMD together with the productivity of multithreading, avoiding the need to explicitly code SIMD vectors for edge conditions and partial divergence.

The SIMT multiprocessor imposes little overhead because it is hardware multithreaded with hardware barrier synchronization. That allows graphics shaders and CUDA threads to express very fine-grained parallelism. Graphics and CUDA programs use threads to express fine-grained data parallelism in a per-thread program, rather than forcing the programmer to express it as SIMD vector instructions. It is simpler and more productive to develop scalar single-thread code than vector code, and the SIMT multiprocessor executes the code with SIMD-like efficiency.

Coupling eight streaming processor cores together closely into a multiprocessor and then implementing a scalable number of such multiprocessors makes a two-level multiprocessor composed of multiprocessors. The CUDA programming model exploits the two-level hierarchy by providing individual threads for fine-grained parallel computations, and by providing grids of thread blocks for coarse-grained parallel operations. The same thread program can provide both fine-grained and coarse-grained operations. In contrast, CPUs with SIMD vector instructions must use two different programming models to provide fine-grained and coarse-grained operations: coarse-grained parallel threads on different cores, and SIMD vector instructions for fine-grained data parallelism.

Multithreaded Multiprocessor Conclusion

The example GPU multiprocessor based on the Tesla architecture is highly multithreaded, executing a total of up to 512 lightweight threads concurrently to support fine-grained pixel shaders and CUDA threads. It uses a variation on SIMD architecture and multithreading called SIMT (single-instruction multiple-thread) to efficiently broadcast one instruction to a warp of 32 parallel threads, while permitting each thread to branch and execute independently. Each thread executes its instruction stream on one of the eight streaming processor (SP) cores, which are multithreaded up to 64 threads.

The PTX ISA is a register-based load/store scalar ISA that describes the execution of a single thread. Because PTX instructions are optimized and translated to binary microinstructions for a specific GPU, the hardware instructions can evolve rapidly without disrupting compilers and software tools that generate PTX instructions.

A.5   Parallel Memory System

Outside of the GPU itself, the memory subsystem is the most important determiner of the performance of a graphics system. Graphics workloads demand very high transfer rates to and from memory. Pixel write and blend (read-modify-write) operations, depth buffer reads and writes, and texture map reads, as well as command and object vertex and attribute data reads, comprise the majority of memory traffic.

Modern GPUs are highly parallel, as shown in Figure A.2.5. For example, the GeForce 8800 can process 32 pixels per clock, at 600 MHz. Each pixel typically requires a color read and write and a depth read and write of a 4-byte pixel. Usually an average of two or three texels of four bytes each are read to generate the pixel's color. So for a typical case, there is a demand of 28 bytes times 32 pixels = 896 bytes per clock. Clearly the bandwidth demand on the memory system is enormous.

To supply these requirements, GPU memory systems have the following characteristics:

- They are wide, meaning there are a large number of pins to convey data between the GPU and its memory devices, and the memory array itself comprises many DRAM chips to provide the full total data bus width.

- They are fast, meaning aggressive signaling techniques are used to maximize the data rate (bits/second) per pin.

- GPUs seek to use every available cycle to transfer data to or from the memory array. To achieve this, GPUs specifically do not aim to minimize latency to the memory system. High throughput (utilization efficiency) and short latency are fundamentally in conflict.

- Compression techniques are used, both lossy, of which the programmer must be aware, and lossless, which is invisible to the application and opportunistic.

- Caches and work coalescing structures are used to reduce the amount of off-chip traffic needed and to ensure that cycles spent moving data are used as fully as possible.

DRAM Considerations

GPUs must take into account the unique characteristics of DRAM. DRAM chips are internally arranged as multiple (typically four to eight) banks, where each bank includes a power-of-2 number of rows (typically around 16,384), and each row contains a power-of-2 number of bits (typically 8192). DRAMs impose a variety of timing requirements on their controlling processor. For example, dozens of cycles are required to activate one row, but once activated, the bits within that row are randomly accessible with a new column address every four clocks. Double-data rate (DDR) synchronous DRAMs transfer data on both rising and falling edges of the interface clock (see Chapter 5). So a 1 GHz clocked DDR DRAM transfers data at 2 gigabits per second per data pin. Graphics DDR DRAMs usually have 32 bidirectional data pins, so eight bytes can be read or written from the DRAM per clock.

GPUs internally have a large number of generators of memory traffic. Different stages of the logical graphics pipeline each have their own request streams: command and vertex attribute fetch, shader texture fetch and load/store, and pixel depth and color read-write. At each logical stage, there are often multiple independent units to deliver the parallel throughput. These are each independent memory requestors. When viewed at the memory system, there are an enormous number of uncorrelated requests in flight. This is a natural mismatch to the reference pattern preferred by the DRAMs. A solution is for the GPU's memory controller to maintain separate heaps of traffic bound for different DRAM banks, and wait until enough traffic for a particular DRAM row is pending before activating that row and transferring all the traffic at once. Note that accumulating pending requests, while good for DRAM row locality and thus efficient use of the data bus, leads to longer average latency as seen by the requestors whose requests spend time waiting for others. The design must take care that no particular request waits too long, otherwise some processing units can starve waiting for data and ultimately cause neighboring processors to become idle.

GPU memory subsystems are arranged as multiple *memory partitions*, each of which comprises a fully independent memory controller and one or two DRAM devices that are fully and exclusively owned by that partition. To achieve the best load balance and therefore approach the theoretical performance of *n* partitions, addresses are finely interleaved evenly across all memory partitions. The partition interleaving stride is typically a block of a few hundred bytes. The number of memory partitions is designed to balance the number of processors and other memory requesters.

Caches

GPU workloads typically have very large working sets—on the order of hundreds of megabytes to generate a single graphics frame. Unlike with CPUs, it is not practical to construct caches on chips large enough to hold anything close to the full working set of a graphics application. Whereas CPUs can assume very high cache hit rates (99.9% or more), GPUs experience hit rates closer to 90% and must therefore cope with many misses in flight. While a CPU can reasonably be designed to halt while waiting for a rare cache miss, a GPU needs to proceed with misses and hits intermingled. We call this a *streaming cache architecture.*

GPU caches must deliver very high-bandwidth to their clients. Consider the case of a texture cache. A typical texture unit may evaluate two bilinear interpolations for each of four pixels per clock cycle, and a GPU may have many such texture units all operating independently. Each bilinear interpolation requires four separate texels, and each texel might be a 64-bit value. Four 16-bit components are typical. Thus, total bandwidth is $2 \times 4 \times 4 \times 64 = 2048$ bits per clock. Each separate 64-bit texel is independently addressed, so the cache needs to handle 32 unique addresses per clock. This naturally favors a multibank and/or multiport arrangement of SRAM arrays.

MMU

Modern GPUs are capable of translating virtual addresses to physical addresses. On the GeForce 8800, all processing units generate memory addresses in a 40-bit virtual address space. For computing, load and store thread instructions use 32-bit byte addresses, which are extended to a 40-bit virtual address by adding a 40-bit offset. A memory management unit performs virtual to physical address translation; hardware reads the page tables from local memory to respond to misses on behalf of a hierarchy of translation lookaside buffers spread out among the processors and rendering engines. In addition to physical page bits, GPU page table entries specify the compression algorithm for each page. Page sizes range from 4 to 128 kilobytes.

Memory Spaces

As introduced in Section A.3, CUDA exposes different memory spaces to allow the programmer to store data values in the most performance-optimal way. For the following discussion, NVIDIA Tesla architecture GPUs are assumed.

Global memory

Global memory is stored in external DRAM; it is not local to any one physical streaming multiprocessor (SM) because it is meant for communication among different CTAs (thread blocks) in different grids. In fact, the many CTAs that reference a location in global memory may not be executing in the GPU at the same time; by design, in CUDA a programmer does not know the relative order in which CTAs are executed. Because the address space is evenly distributed among all memory partitions, there must be a read/write path from any streaming multiprocessor to any DRAM partition.

Access to global memory by different threads (and different processors) is not guaranteed to have sequential consistency. Thread programs see a relaxed memory ordering model. Within a thread, the order of memory reads and writes to the same address is preserved, but the order of accesses to different addresses may not be preserved. Memory reads and writes requested by different threads are unordered. Within a CTA, the barrier synchronization instruction bar.sync can be used to obtain strict memory ordering among the threads of the CTA. The membar thread instruction provides a memory barrier/fence operation that commits prior memory accesses and makes them visible to other threads before proceeding. Threads can also use the atomic memory operations described in Section A.4 to coordinate work on memory they share.

Shared memory

Per-CTA shared memory is only visible to the threads that belong to that CTA, and shared memory only occupies storage from the time a CTA is created to the time it terminates. Shared memory can therefore reside on-chip. This approach has many benefits. First, shared memory traffic does not need to compete with limited off-chip bandwidth needed for global memory references. Second, it is practical to build very high-bandwidth memory structures on-chip to support the read/write demands of each streaming multiprocessor. In fact, the shared memory is closely coupled to the streaming multiprocessor.

Each streaming multiprocessor contains eight physical thread processors. During one shared memory clock cycle, each thread processor can process two threads' worth of instructions, so 16 threads' worth of shared memory requests must be handled in each clock. Because each thread can generate its own addresses, and the addresses are typically unique, the shared memory is built using 16 independently addressable SRAM banks. For common access patterns, 16 banks are sufficient to maintain throughput, but pathological cases are possible; for example, all 16 threads might happen to access a different address on one SRAM bank. It must be possible to route a request from any thread lane to any bank of SRAM, so a 16-by-16 interconnection network is required.

Local Memory

Per-thread local memory is private memory visible only to a single thread. Local memory is architecturally larger than the thread's register file, and a program can compute addresses into local memory. To support large allocations of local memory (recall the total allocation is the per-thread allocation times the number of active threads), local memory is allocated in external DRAM.

Although global and per-thread local memory reside off-chip, they are well-suited to being cached on-chip.

Constant Memory

Constant memory is read-only to a program running on the SM (it can be written via commands to the GPU). It is stored in external DRAM and cached in the SM. Because commonly most or all threads in a SIMT warp read from the same address in constant memory, a single address lookup per clock is sufficient. The constant cache is designed to broadcast scalar values to threads in each warp.

Texture Memory

Texture memory holds large read-only arrays of data. Textures for computing have the same attributes and capabilities as textures used with 3D graphics. Although textures are commonly two-dimensional images (2D arrays of pixel values), 1D (linear) and 3D (volume) textures are also available.

A compute program references a texture using a `tex` instruction. Operands include an identifier to name the texture, and 1, 2, or 3 coordinates based on the texture dimensionality. The floating-point coordinates include a fractional portion that specifies a sample location often in between texel locations. Noninteger coordinates invoke a bilinear weighted interpolation of the four closest values (for a 2D texture) before the result is returned to the program.

Texture fetches are cached in a streaming cache hierarchy designed to optimize throughput of texture fetches from thousands of concurrent threads. Some programs use texture fetches as a way to cache global memory.

Surfaces

Surface is a generic term for a one-dimensional, two-dimensional, or three-dimensional array of pixel values and an associated format. A variety of formats are defined; for example, a pixel may be defined as four 8-bit RGBA integer components, or four 16-bit floating-point components. A program kernel does not need to know the surface type. A `tex` instruction recasts its result values as floating-point, depending on the surface format.

Load/Store Access

Load/store instructions with integer byte addressing enable the writing and compiling of programs in conventional languages like C and C++. CUDA programs use load/store instructions to access memory.

To improve memory bandwidth and reduce overhead, the local and global load/store instructions coalesce individual parallel thread requests from the same warp together into a single memory block request when the addresses fall in the same block and meet alignment criteria. Coalescing individual small memory requests into large block requests provides a significant performance boost over separate requests. The large thread count, together with support for many outstanding load requests, helps cover load-to-use latency for local and global memory implemented in external DRAM.

ROP

As shown in Figure A.2.5, NVIDIA Tesla architecture GPUs comprise a scalable streaming processor array (SPA), which performs all of the GPU's programmable calculations, and a scalable memory system, which comprises external DRAM control and fixed function Raster Operation Processors (ROPs) that perform color and depth framebuffer operations directly on memory. Each ROP unit is paired with a specific memory partition. ROP partitions are fed from the SMs via an interconnection network. Each ROP is responsible for depth and stencil tests and updates, as well as color blending. The ROP and memory controllers cooperate to implement lossless color and depth compression (up to 8:1) to reduce external bandwidth demand. ROP units also perform atomic operations on memory.

A.6 Floating-point Arithmetic

GPUs today perform most arithmetic operations in the programmable processor cores using IEEE 754–compatible single precision 32-bit floating-point operations (see Chapter 3). The fixed-point arithmetic of early GPUs was succeeded by 16-bit, 24-bit, and 32-bit floating-point, then IEEE 754–compatible 32-bit floating-point.

Some fixed-function logic within a GPU, such as texture-filtering hardware, continues to use proprietary numeric formats. Recent GPUs also provide IEEE 754 compatible double precision 64-bit floating-point instructions.

Supported Formats

half precision A 16-bit binary floating-point format, with 1 sign bit, 5-bit exponent, 10-bit fraction, and an implied integer bit.

The IEEE 754 standard for floating-point arithmetic [2008] specifies basic and storage formats. GPUs use two of the basic formats for computation, 32-bit and 64-bit binary floating-point, commonly called single precision and double precision. The standard also specifies a 16-bit binary storage floating-point format, **half precision**. GPUs and the Cg shading language employ the narrow 16-bit half data format for efficient data storage and movement, while maintaining high dynamic range. GPUs perform many texture filtering and pixel blending computations at half precision within the texture filtering unit and the raster operations unit. The OpenEXR high dynamic-range image file format developed by Industrial Light and Magic [2003] uses the identical half format for color component values in computer imaging and motion picture applications.

Basic Arithmetic

multiply-add (MAD) A single floating-point instruction that performs a compound operation: multiplication followed by addition.

Common single precision floating-point operations in GPU programmable cores include addition, multiplication, **multiply-add**, minimum, maximum, compare, set predicate, and conversions between integer and floating-point numbers. Floating-point instructions often provide source operand modifiers for negation and absolute value.

The floating-point addition and multiplication operations of most GPUs today are compatible with the IEEE 754 standard for single precision FP numbers, including not-a-number (NaN) and infinity values. The FP addition and multiplication operations use IEEE round-to-nearest-even as the default rounding mode. To increase floating-point instruction throughput, GPUs often use a compound multiply-add instruction (`mad`). The multiply-add operation performs FP multiplication with truncation, followed by FP addition with round-to-nearest-even. It provides two floating-point operations in one issuing cycle, without requiring the instruction scheduler to dispatch two separate instructions, but the computation is not fused and truncates the product before the addition. This makes it different from the fused multiply-add instruction discussed in Chapter 3 and later in this section. GPUs typically flush denormalized source operands to sign-preserved zero, and they flush results that underflow the target output exponent range to sign-preserved zero after rounding.

Specialized Arithmetic

GPUs provide hardware to accelerate special function computation, attribute interpolation, and texture filtering. Special function instructions include cosine,

sine, binary exponential, binary logarithm, reciprocal, and reciprocal square root. Attribute interpolation instructions provide efficient generation of pixel attributes, derived from plane equation evaluation. The **special function unit (SFU)** introduced in Section A.4 computes special functions and interpolates planar attributes [Oberman and Siu, 2005].

Several methods exist for evaluating special functions in hardware. It has been shown that quadratic interpolation based on Enhanced Minimax Approximations is a very efficient method for approximating functions in hardware, including reciprocal, reciprocal square-root, $\log_2 x$, 2^x, sin, and cos.

We can summarize the method of SFU quadratic interpolation. For a binary input operand X with *n*-bit significand, the significand is divided into two parts: X_u is the upper part containing *m* bits, and X_l is the lower part containing *n-m* bits. The upper *m* bits X_u are used to consult a set of three lookup tables to return three finite-word coefficients C_0, C_1, and C_2. Each function to be approximated requires a unique set of tables. These coefficients are used to approximate a given function f(X) in the range $X_u <= X < X_u + 2^{-m}$ by evaluating the expression:

$$f(X) = C_0 + C_1 X_l + C_2 X_l^2$$

The accuracy of each of the function estimates ranges from 22 to 24 significand bits. Example function statistics are shown in Figure A.6.1.

The IEEE 754 standard specifies exact-rounding requirements for division and square root, however, for many GPU applications, exact compliance is not required. Rather, for those applications, higher computational throughput is more important than last-bit accuracy. For the SFU special functions, the CUDA math library provides both a full accuracy function and a fast function with the SFU instruction accuracy.

Another specialized arithmetic operation in a GPU is attribute interpolation. Key *attributes* are usually specified for vertices of primitives that make up a scene to be rendered. Example attributes are color, depth, and texture coordinates. These attributes must be interpolated in the (x, y) screen space as needed to determine the

special function unit (SFU) A hardware unit that computes special functions and interpolates planar attributes.

Function	Input interval	Accuracy (good bits)	ULP[*] error	% exactly rounded	Monotonic
$1/x$	[1, 2)	24.02	0.98	87	Yes
$1/\text{sqrt}(x)$	[1, 4)	23.40	1.52	78	Yes
2^x	[0, 1)	22.51	1.41	74	Yes
$\log_2 x$	[1, 2)	22.57	N/A[**]	N/A	Yes
sin/cos	[0, π/2)	22.47	N/A	N/A	No

[*]ULP: unit in the last place. [**]N/A: not applicable.

FIGURE A.6.1 Special function approximation statistics. For the NVIDIA GeForce 8800 special function unit (SFU).

values of the attributes at each pixel location. The value of a given attribute U in an (x, y) plane can be expressed using plane equations of the form:

$$U(x, y) = A_u x + B_u y + C_u$$

where A, B, and C are interpolation parameters associated with each attribute U. The interpolation parameters A, B, and C are all represented as single precision floating-point numbers.

Given the need for both a function evaluator and an attribute interpolator in a pixel shader processor, a single SFU that performs both functions for efficiency can be designed. Both functions use a sum of products operation to interpolate results, and the number of terms to be summed in both functions is very similar.

Texture Operations

Texture mapping and filtering is another key set of specialized floating-point arithmetic operations in a GPU. The operations used for texture mapping include:

1. Receive texture address (s, t) for the current screen pixel (x, y), where s and t are single precision floating-point numbers.

2. Compute the level of detail to identify the correct texture **MIP-map** level.

3. Compute the trilinear interpolation fraction.

4. Scale texture address (s, t) for the selected MIP-map level.

5. Access memory and retrieve desired texels (texture elements).

6. Perform filtering operation on texels.

MIP-map A Latin phrase *multum in parvo*, or much in a small space. A MIP-map contains precalculated images of different resolutions, used to increase rendering speed and reduce artifacts.

Texture mapping requires a significant amount of floating-point computation for full-speed operation, much of which is done at 16-bit half precision. As an example, the GeForce 8800 Ultra delivers about 500 GFLOPS of proprietary format floating-point computation for texture mapping instructions, in addition to its conventional IEEE single precision floating-point instructions. For more details on texture mapping and filtering, see Foley and van Dam [1995].

Performance

The floating-point addition and multiplication arithmetic hardware is fully pipelined, and latency is optimized to balance delay and area. While pipelined, the throughput of the special functions is less than the floating-point addition and multiplication operations. Quarter-speed throughput for the special functions is typical performance in modern GPUs, with one SFU shared by four SP cores. In contrast, CPUs typically have significantly lower throughput for similar functions, such as division and square root, albeit with more accurate results. The attribute interpolation hardware is typically fully pipelined to enable full-speed pixel shaders.

Double precision

Newer GPUs such as the Tesla T10P also support IEEE 754 64-bit double precision operations in hardware. Standard floating-point arithmetic operations in double precision include addition, multiplication, and conversions between different floating-point and integer formats. The 2008 IEEE 754 floating-point standard includes specification for the fused-multiply-add operation (FMA), as discussed in Chapter 3. The FMA operation performs a floating-point multiplication followed by an addition, with a single rounding. The fused multiplication and addition operations retain full accuracy in intermediate calculations. This behavior enables more accurate floating-point computations involving the accumulation of products, including dot products, matrix multiplication, and polynomial evaluation. The FMA instruction also enables efficient software implementations of exactly rounded division and square root, removing the need for a hardware division or square root unit.

A double precision hardware FMA unit implements 64-bit addition, multiplication, conversions, and the FMA operation itself. The architecture of a double

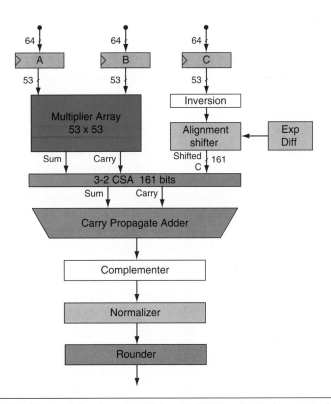

FIGURE A.6.2 Double precision fused-multiply-add (FMA) unit. Hardware to implement floating-point $A \times B + C$ for double precision.

precision FMA unit enables full-speed denormalized number support on both inputs and outputs. Figure A.6.2 shows a block diagram of an FMA unit.

As shown in Figure A.6.2, the significands of A and B are multiplied to form a 106-bit product, with the results left in carry-save form. In parallel, the 53-bit addend C is conditionally inverted and aligned to the 106-bit product. The sum and carry results of the 106-bit product are summed with the aligned addend through a 161-bit-wide carry-save adder (CSA). The carry-save output is then summed together in a carry-propagate adder to produce an unrounded result in nonredundant, two's complement form. The result is conditionally recomplemented, so as to return a result in sign-magnitude form. The complemented result is normalized, and then it is rounded to fit within the target format.

A.7   Real Stuff: The NVIDIA GeForce 8800

The NVIDIA GeForce 8800 GPU, introduced in November 2006, is a unified vertex and pixel processor design that also supports parallel computing applications written in C using the CUDA parallel programming model. It is the first implementation of the Tesla unified graphics and computing architecture described in Section A.4 and in Lindholm, Nickolls, Oberman, and Montrym [2008]. A family of Tesla architecture GPUs addresses the different needs of laptops, desktops, workstations, and servers.

Streaming Processor Array (SPA)

The GeForce 8800 GPU shown in Figure A.7.1 contains 128 streaming processor (SP) cores organized as 16 streaming multiprocessors (SMs). Two SMs share a texture unit in each texture/processor cluster (TPC). An array of eight TPCs makes up the streaming processor array (SPA), which executes all graphics shader programs and computing programs.

The host interface unit communicates with the host CPU via the PCI-Express bus, checks command consistency, and performs context switching. The input assembler collects geometric primitives (points, lines, triangles). The work distribution blocks dispatch vertices, pixels, and compute thread arrays to the TPCs in the SPA. The TPCs execute vertex and geometry shader programs and computing programs. Output geometric data is sent to the viewport/clip/setup/raster/zcull block to be rasterized into pixel fragments that are then redistributed back into the SPA to execute pixel shader programs. Shaded pixels are sent across the interconnection network for processing by the ROP units. The network also routes texture memory read requests from the SPA to DRAM and reads data from DRAM through a level-2 cache back to the SPA.

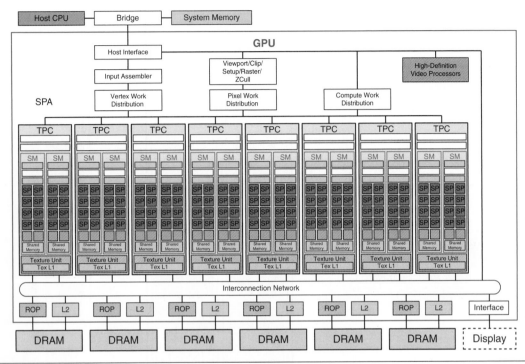

FIGURE A.7.1   NVIDIA Tesla unified graphics and computing GPU architecture. This GeForce 8800 has 128 streaming processor (SP) cores in 16 streaming multiprocessors (SM), arranged in eight texture/processor clusters (TPC). The processors connect with six 64-bit-wide DRAM partitions via an interconnection network. Other GPUs implementing the Tesla architecture vary the number of SP cores, SMs, DRAM partitions, and other units.

Texture/Processor Cluster (TPC)

Each TPC contains a geometry controller, an SM controller (SMC), two streaming multiprocessors (SMs), and a texture unit as shown in Figure A.7. 2.

The geometry controller maps the logical graphics vertex pipeline into recirculation on the physical SMs by directing all primitive and vertex attribute and topology flow in the TPC.

The SMC controls multiple SMs, arbitrating the shared texture unit, load/store path, and I/O path. The SMC serves three graphics workloads simultaneously: vertex, geometry, and pixel.

The texture unit processes a texture instruction for one vertex, geometry, or pixel quad, or four compute threads per cycle. Texture instruction sources are texture coordinates, and the outputs are weighted samples, typically a four-component (RGBA) floating-point color. The texture unit is deeply pipelined. Although it

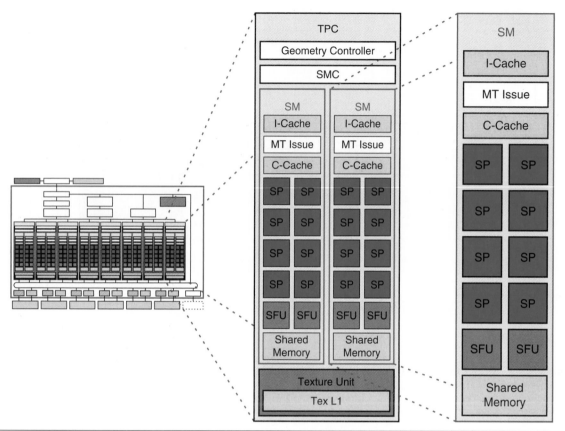

FIGURE A.7.2   Texture/processor cluster (TPC) and a streaming multiprocessor (SM). Each SM has eight streaming processor (SP) cores, two SFUs, and a shared memory.

contains a streaming cache to capture filtering locality, it streams hits mixed with misses without stalling.

Streaming Multiprocessor (SM)

The SM is a unified graphics and computing multiprocessor that executes vertex, geometry, and pixel-fragment shader programs and parallel computing programs. The SM consists of eight SP thread processor cores, two SFUs, a multithreaded instruction fetch and issue unit (MT issue), an instruction cache, a read-only constant cache, and a 16 KB read/write shared memory. It executes scalar instructions for individual threads.

The GeForce 8800 Ultra clocks the SP cores and SFUs at 1.5 GHz, for a peak of 36 GFLOPS per SM. To optimize power and area efficiency, some SM nondatapath units operate at half the SP clock rate.

To efficiently execute hundreds of parallel threads while running several different programs, the SM is hardware multithreaded. It manages and executes up to 768 concurrent threads in hardware with zero scheduling overhead. Each thread has its own thread execution state and can execute an independent code path.

A warp consists of up to 32 threads of the same type—vertex, geometry, pixel, or compute. The SIMT design, previously described in Section A.4, shares the SM instruction fetch and issue unit efficiently across 32 threads but requires a full warp of active threads for full performance efficiency.

The SM schedules and executes multiple warp types concurrently. Each issue cycle, the scheduler selects one of the 24 warps to execute a SIMT warp instruction. An issued warp instruction executes as four sets of 8 threads over four processor cycles. The SP and SFU units execute instructions independently, and by issuing instructions between them on alternate cycles, the scheduler can keep both fully occupied. A scoreboard qualifies each warp for issue each cycle. The instruction scheduler prioritizes all ready warps and selects the one with highest priority for issue. Prioritization considers warp type, instruction type, and "fairness" to all warps executing in the SM.

The SM executes cooperative thread arrays (CTAs) as multiple concurrent warps which access a shared memory region allocated dynamically for the CTA.

Instruction Set

Threads execute scalar instructions, unlike previous GPU vector instruction architectures. Scalar instructions are simpler and compiler friendly. Texture instructions remain vector based, taking a source coordinate vector and returning a filtered color vector.

The register-based instruction set includes all the floating-point and integer arithmetic, transcendental, logical, flow control, memory load/store, and texture instructions listed in the PTX instruction table of Figure A.4.3. Memory load/store instructions use integer byte addressing with register-plus-offset address arithmetic. For computing, the load/store instructions access three read-write memory spaces: local memory for per-thread, private, temporary data; shared memory for low-latency per-CTA data shared by the threads of the CTA; and global memory for data shared by all threads. Computing programs use the fast barrier synchronization bar.sync instruction to synchronize threads within a CTA that communicate with each other via shared and global memory. The latest Tesla architecture GPUs implement PTX atomic memory operations, which facilitate parallel reductions and parallel data structure management.

Streaming Processor (SP)

The multithreaded SP core is the primary thread processor, as introduced in Section A.4. Its register file provides 1024 scalar 32-bit registers for up to 96 threads (more threads than the example SP of Section A.4). Its floating-point add and multiply operations are compatible with the IEEE 754 standard for single precision FP numbers, including not-a-number (NaN) and infinity. The add and multiply operations use IEEE round-to-nearest-even as the default rounding mode. The SP core also implements all of the 32-bit and 64-bit integer arithmetic, comparison, conversion, and logical PTX instructions in Figure A.4.3. The processor is fully pipelined, and latency is optimized to balance delay and area.

Special Function Unit (SFU)

The SFU supports computation of both transcendental functions and planar attribute interpolation. As described in Section A.6, it uses quadratic interpolation based on enhanced minimax approximations to approximate the reciprocal, reciprocal square root, $\log_2 x$, 2^x, and sin/cos functions at one result per cycle. The SFU also supports pixel attribute interpolation such as color, depth, and texture coordinates at four samples per cycle.

Rasterization

Geometry primitives from the SMs go in their original round-robin input order to the viewport/clip/setup/raster/zcull block. The viewport and clip units clip the primitives to the view frustum and to any enabled user clip planes, and then transform the vertices into screen (pixel) space.

Surviving primitives then go to the setup unit, which generates edge equations for the rasterizer. A coarse-rasterization stage generates all pixel tiles that are at least partially inside the primitive. The zcull unit maintains a hierarchical z surface, rejecting pixel tiles if they are conservatively known to be occluded by previously drawn pixels. The rejection rate is up to 256 pixels per clock. Pixels that survive zcull then go to a fine-rasterization stage that generates detailed coverage information and depth values.

The depth test and update can be performed ahead of the fragment shader, or after, depending on current state. The SMC assembles surviving pixels into warps to be processed by an SM running the current pixel shader. The SMC then sends surviving pixel and associated data to the ROP.

Raster Operations Processor (ROP) and Memory System

Each ROP is paired with a specific memory partition. For each pixel fragment emitted by a pixel shader program, ROPs perform depth and stencil testing and updates, and in parallel, color blending and updates. Lossless color compression (up to 8:1) and depth compression (up to 8:1) are used to reduce DRAM bandwidth. Each ROP has a peak rate of four pixels per clock and supports 16-bit floating-point and 32-bit floating-point HDR formats. ROPs support double-rate-depth processing when color writes are disabled.

Antialiasing support includes up to 16× multisampling and supersampling. The coverage-sampling antialiasing (CSAA) algorithm computes and stores Boolean coverage at up to 16 samples and compresses redundant color, depth, and stencil information into the memory footprint and a bandwidth of four or eight samples for improved performance.

The DRAM memory data bus width is 384 pins, arranged in six independent partitions of 64 pins each. Each partition supports double-data-rate DDR2 and graphics-oriented GDDR3 protocols at up to 1.0 GHz, yielding a bandwidth of about 16 GB/s per partition, or 96 GB/s.

The memory controllers support a wide range of DRAM clock rates, protocols, device densities, and data bus widths. Texture and load/store requests can occur between any TPC and any memory partition, so an interconnection network routes requests and responses.

Scalability

The Tesla unified architecture is designed for scalability. Varying the number of SMs, TPCs, ROPs, caches, and memory partitions provides the right balance for different performance and cost targets in GPU market segments. Scalable link interconnect (SLI) connects multiple GPUs, providing further scalability.

Performance

The GeForce 8800 Ultra clocks the SP thread processor cores and SFUs at 1.5 GHz, for a theoretical operation peak of 576 GFLOPS. The GeForce 8800 GTX has a 1.35 GHz processor clock and a corresponding peak of 518 GFLOPS.

The following three sections compare the performance of a GeForce 8800 GPU with a multicore CPU on three different applications—dense linear algebra, fast Fourier transforms, and sorting. The GPU programs and libraries are compiled CUDA C code. The CPU code uses the single precision multithreaded Intel MKL 10.0 library to leverage SSE instructions and multiple cores.

Dense Linear Algebra Performance

Dense linear algebra computations are fundamental in many applications. Volkov and Demmel [2008] present GPU and CPU performance results for single precision dense matrix-matrix multiplication (the SGEMM routine) and LU, QR, and Cholesky matrix factorizations. Figure A.7.3 compares GFLOPS rates on SGEMM dense matrix-matrix multiplication for a GeForce 8800 GTX GPU with a quad-core CPU. Figure A.7.4 compares GFLOPS rates on matrix factorization for a GPU with a quad-core CPU.

Because SGEMM matrix-matrix multiply and similar BLAS3 routines are the bulk of the work in matrix factorization, their performance sets an upper bound on factorization rate. As the matrix order increases beyond 200 to 400, the factorization

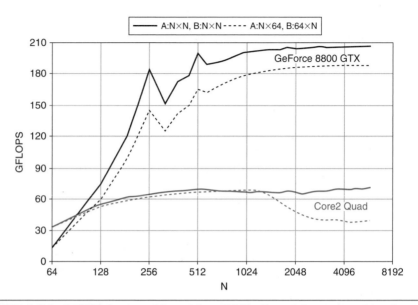

FIGURE A.7.3   SGEMM dense matrix-matrix multiplication performance rates. The graph shows single precision GFLOPS rates achieved in multiplying square N×N matrices (solid lines) and thin N×64 and 64×N matrices (dashed lines). Adapted from Figure 6 of Volkov and Demmel [2008]. The black lines are a 1.35 GHz GeForce 8800 GTX using Volkov's SGEMM code (now in NVIDIA CUBLAS 2.0) on matrices in GPU memory. The blue lines are a quad-core 2.4 GHz Intel Core2 Quad Q6600, 64-bit Linux, Intel MKL 10.0 on matrices in CPU memory.

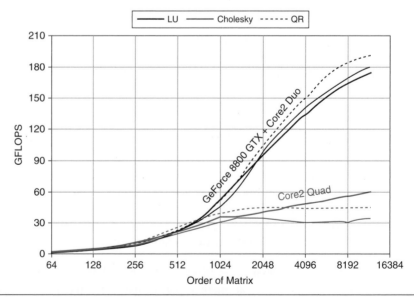

FIGURE A.7.4   Dense matrix factorization performance rates. The graph shows GFLOPS rates achieved in matrix factorizations using the GPU and using the CPU alone. Adapted from Figure 7 of Volkov and Demmel [2008]. The black lines are a 1.35 GHz NVIDIA GeForce 8800 GTX, CUDA 1.1, Windows XP attached to a 2.67 GHz Intel Core2 Duo E6700 Windows XP, including all CPU–GPU data transfer times. The blue lines are a quad-core 2.4 GHz Intel Core2 Quad Q6600, 64-bit Linux, Intel MKL 10.0.

problem becomes large enough that SGEMM can leverage the GPU parallelism and overcome the CPU–GPU system and copy overhead. Volkov's SGEMM matrix-matrix multiply achieves 206 GFLOPS, about 60% of the GeForce 8800 GTX peak multiply-add rate, while the QR factorization reached 192 GFLOPS, about 4.3 times the quad-core CPU.

FFT Performance

Fast Fourier Transforms are used in many applications. Large transforms and multidimensional transforms are partitioned into batches of smaller 1D transforms.

Figure A.7.5 compares the in-place 1D complex single precision FFT performance of a 1.35 GHz GeForce 8800 GTX (dating from late 2006) with a 2.8 GHz quad-Core Intel Xeon E5462 series (code named "Harpertown," dating from late 2007). CPU performance was measured using the Intel Math Kernel Library (MKL) 10.0 FFT with four threads. GPU performance was measured using the NVIDIA CUFFT 2.1 library and batched 1D radix-16 decimation-in-frequency FFTs. Both CPU and GPU throughput performance was measured using batched FFTs, batch size was $2^{24}/n$, where n is the transform size. Thus, the workload for every transform size was 128 MB. To determine GFLOPS rate, the number of operations per transform was taken as $5n \log_2 n$.

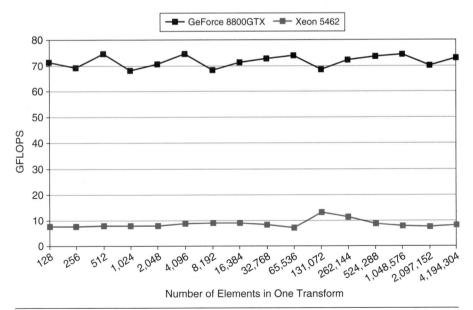

FIGURE A.7.5 Fast Fourier Transform throughput performance. The graph compares the performance of batched one-dimensional in-place complex FFTs on a 1.35 GHz GeForce 8800 GTX with a quad-core 2.8 GHz Intel Xeon E5462 series (code named "Harpertown"), 6MB L2 Cache, 4GB Memory, 1600 FSB, Red Hat Linux, Intel MKL 10.0.

Sorting Performance

In contrast to the applications just discussed, sort requires far more substantial coordination among parallel threads, and parallel scaling is correspondingly harder to obtain. Nevertheless, a variety of well-known sorting algorithms can be efficiently parallelized to run well on the GPU. Satish, et al. [2008] detail the design of sorting algorithms in CUDA, and the results they report for radix sort are summarized below.

Figure A.7.6 compares the parallel sorting performance of a GeForce 8800 Ultra with an 8-core Intel Clovertown system, both of which date to early 2007. The CPU cores are distributed between two physical sockets. Each socket contains a multichip module with twin Core2 chips, and each chip has a 4MB L2 cache. All sorting routines were designed to sort key-value pairs where both keys and values are 32-bit integers. The primary algorithm being studied is radix sort, although the quicksort-based `parallel_sort()` procedure provided by Intel's Threading Building Blocks is also included for comparison. Of the two CPU-based radix sort codes, one was implemented using only the scalar instruction set and the other utilizes carefully hand-tuned assembly language routines that take advantage of the SSE2 SIMD vector instructions.

The graph itself shows the achieved sorting rate—defined as the number of elements sorted divided by the time to sort—for a range of sequence sizes. It is apparent

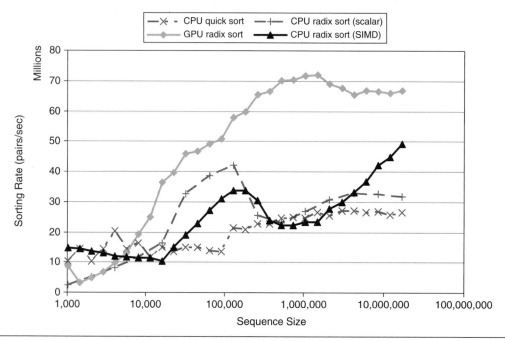

FIGURE A.7.6   Parallel sorting performance. This graph compares sorting rates for parallel radix sort implementations on a 1.5 GHz GeForce 8800 Ultra and an 8-core 2.33 GHz Intel Core2 Xeon E5345 system.

from this graph that the GPU radix sort achieved the highest sorting rate for all sequences of 8K-elements and larger. In this range, it is on average 2.6 times faster than the quicksort-based routine and roughly 2 times faster than the radix sort routines, all of which were using the eight available CPU cores. The CPU radix sort performance varies widely, likely due to poor cache locality of its global permutations.

A.8 Real Stuff: Mapping Applications to GPUs

The advent of multicore CPUs and manycore GPUs means that mainstream processor chips are now parallel systems. Furthermore, their parallelism continues to scale with Moore's law. The challenge is to develop mainstream visual computing and high-performance computing applications that transparently scale their parallelism to leverage the increasing number of processor cores, much as 3D graphics applications transparently scale their parallelism to GPUs with widely varying numbers of cores.

This section presents examples of mapping scalable parallel computing applications to the GPU using CUDA.

Sparse Matrices

A wide variety of parallel algorithms can be written in CUDA in a fairly straightforward manner, even when the data structures involved are not simple regular grids. Sparse matrix-vector multiplication (SpMV) is a good example of an important numerical building block that can be parallelized quite directly using the abstractions provided by CUDA. The kernels we discuss below, when combined with the provided CUBLAS vector routines, make writing iterative solvers such as the conjugate gradient method straightforward.

A sparse $n \times n$ matrix is one in which the number of nonzero entries m is only a small fraction of the total. Sparse matrix representations seek to store only the nonzero elements of a matrix. Since it is fairly typical that a sparse $n \times n$ matrix will contain only $m = O(n)$ nonzero elements, this represents a substantial savings in storage space and processing time.

One of the most common representations for general unstructured sparse matrices is the compressed sparse row (CSR) representation. The m nonzero elements of the matrix A are stored in row-major order in an array Av. A second array Aj records the corresponding column index for each entry of Av. Finally, an array Ap of $n + 1$ elements records the extent of each row in the previous arrays; the entries for row i in Aj and Av extend from index Ap[i] up to, but not including, index Ap[i + 1]. This implies that Ap[0] will always be 0 and Ap[n] will always be the number of nonzero elements in the matrix. Figure A.8.1 shows an example of the CSR representation of a simple matrix.

$$A = \begin{bmatrix} 3 & 0 & 1 & 0 \\ 0 & 0 & 0 & 0 \\ 0 & 2 & 4 & 1 \\ 1 & 0 & 0 & 1 \end{bmatrix}$$

```
                       Row 0    Row 2    Row 3
Av[7] =  { 3  1    2  4  1    1  1  }

Aj[7] =  { 0  2    1  2  3    0  3  }

Ap[5] =  { 0   2   2   5   7          }
```

a. Sample matrix *A*   b. CSR representation of matrix

FIGURE A.8.1   Compressed sparse row (CSR) matrix.

```
float multiply_row(unsigned int rowsize,
                   unsigned int *Aj, // column indices for row
                   float *Av,        // nonzero entries for row
                   float *x)         // the RHS vector
{
    float sum = 0;

    for(unsigned int column=0; column<rowsize; ++column)
        sum += Av[column] * x[Aj[column]];

    return sum;
}
```

FIGURE A.8.2   Serial C code for a single row of sparse matrix-vector multiply.

Given a matrix A in CSR form and a vector x, we can compute a single row of the product $y = Ax$ using the `multiply_row()` procedure shown in Figure A.8.2. Computing the full product is then simply a matter of looping over all rows and computing the result for that row using `multiply_row()`, as in the serial C code shown in Figure A.8.3.

This algorithm can be translated into a parallel CUDA kernel quite easily. We simply spread the loop in `csrmul_serial()` over many parallel threads. Each thread will compute exactly one row of the output vector y. The code for this kernel is shown in Figure A.8.4. Note that it looks extremely similar to the serial loop used in the `csrmul_serial()` procedure. There are really only two points of difference. First, the `row` index for each thread is computed from the block and thread indices assigned to each thread, eliminating the for-loop. Second, we have a conditional that only evaluates a row product if the row index is within the bounds of the matrix (this is necessary since the number of rows n need not be a multiple of the block size used in launching the kernel).

```
void csrmul_serial(unsigned int *Ap, unsigned int *Aj,
                   float *Av, unsigned int num_rows,
                   float *x, float *y)
{
    for(unsigned int row=0; row<num_rows; ++row)
    {
        unsigned int row_begin = Ap[row];
        unsigned int row_end   = Ap[row+1];

        y[row] = multiply_row(row_end-row_begin, Aj+row_begin,
                              Av+row_begin, x);
    }
}
```

FIGURE A.8.3   Serial code for sparse matrix-vector multiply.

```
__global__
void csrmul_kernel(unsigned int *Ap, unsigned int *Aj,
                   float *Av, unsigned int num_rows,
                   float *x, float *y)
{
    unsigned int row = blockIdx.x*blockDim.x + threadIdx.x;

    if( row<num_rows )
    {
        unsigned int row_begin = Ap[row];
        unsigned int row_end   = Ap[row+1];

        y[row] = multiply_row(row_end-row_begin, Aj+row_begin,
                              Av+row_begin, x);
    }
}
```

FIGURE A.8.4   CUDA version of sparse matrix-vector multiply.

Assuming that the matrix data structures have already been copied to the GPU device memory, launching this kernel will look like:

```
unsigned int blocksize = 128;  // or any size up to 512
unsigned int nblocks   = (num_rows + blocksize - 1) / blocksize;
csrmul_kernel<<<nblocks,blocksize>>>(Ap, Aj, Av, num_rows, x, y);
```

The pattern that we see here is a very common one. The original serial algorithm is a loop whose iterations are independent of each other. Such loops can be parallelized quite easily by simply assigning one or more iterations of the loop to each parallel thread. The programming model provided by CUDA makes expressing this type of parallelism particularly straightforward.

This general strategy of decomposing computations into blocks of independent work, and more specifically breaking up independent loop iterations, is not unique to CUDA. This is a common approach used in one form or another by various parallel programming systems, including OpenMP and Intel's Threading Building Blocks.

Caching in Shared memory

The SpMV algorithms outlined above are fairly simplistic. There are a number of optimizations that can be made in both the CPU and GPU codes that can improve performance, including loop unrolling, matrix reordering, and register blocking. The parallel kernels can also be reimplemented in terms of data parallel *scan* operations presented by Sengupta, et al. [2007].

One of the important architectural features exposed by CUDA is the presence of the per-block shared memory, a small on-chip memory with very low latency. Taking advantage of this memory can deliver substantial performance improvements. One common way of doing this is to use shared memory as a software-managed cache to hold frequently reused data. Modifications using shared memory are shown in Figure A.8.5.

In the context of sparse matrix multiplication, we observe that several rows of *A* may use a particular array element x[i]. In many common cases, and particularly when the matrix has been reordered, the rows using x[i] will be rows near row *i*. We can therefore implement a simple caching scheme and expect to achieve some performance benefit. The block of threads processing rows *i* through *j* will load x[i] through x[j] into its shared memory. We will unroll the multiply_row() loop and fetch elements of x from the cache whenever possible. The resulting code is shown in Figure A.8.5. Shared memory can also be used to make other optimizations, such as fetching Ap[row+1] from an adjacent thread rather than refetching it from memory.

Because the Tesla architecture provides an explicitly managed on-chip shared memory, rather than an implicitly active hardware cache, it is fairly common to add this sort of optimization. Although this can impose some additional development burden on the programmer, it is relatively minor, and the potential performance benefits can be substantial. In the example shown above, even this fairly simple use of shared memory returns a roughly 20% performance improvement on representative matrices derived from 3D surface meshes. The availability of an explicitly managed memory in lieu of an implicit cache also has the advantage that caching and prefetching policies can be specifically tailored to the application needs.

```
__global__
void csrmul_cached(unsigned int *Ap, unsigned int *Aj,
                   float *Av, unsigned int num_rows,
                   const float *x, float *y)
{
    // Cache the rows of x[] corresponding to this block.
    __shared__ float cache[blocksize];

    unsigned int block_begin = blockIdx.x * blockDim.x;
    unsigned int block_end   = block_begin + blockDim.x;
    unsigned int row         = block_begin + threadIdx.x;

    // Fetch and cache our window of x[].
    if( row<num_rows)  cache[threadIdx.x] = x[row];
    __syncthreads();

    if( row<num_rows )
    {
        unsigned int row_begin = Ap[row];
        unsigned int row_end   = Ap[row+1];
        float sum = 0, x_j;

        for(unsigned int col=row_begin; col<row_end; ++col)
        {
            unsigned int j = Aj[col];

            // Fetch x_j from our cache when possible
            if( j>=block_begin && j<block_end )
                x_j = cache[j-block_begin];
            else
                x_j = x[j];

            sum += Av[col] * x_j;
        }

        y[row] = sum;
    }
}
```

FIGURE A.8.5   Shared memory version of sparse matrix-vector multiply.

These are fairly simple kernels whose purpose is to illustrate basic techniques in writing CUDA programs, rather than how to achieve maximal performance. Numerous possible avenues for optimization are available, several of which are explored by Williams, et al. [2007] on a handful of different multicore architectures. Nevertheless, it is still instructive to examine the comparative performance of even these simplistic kernels. On a 2 GHz Intel Core2 Xeon E5335 processor, the `csrmul_serial()` kernel runs at roughly 202 million nonzeros processed per second, for a collection of Laplacian matrices derived from 3D triangulated surface meshes. Parallelizing this kernel with the `parallel_for` construct provided by Intel's Threading Building Blocks produces parallel speed-ups of 2.0, 2.1, and 2.3 running on two, four, and eight cores of the machine, respectively. On a GeForce 8800 Ultra, the `csrmul_kernel()` and `csrmul_cached()` kernels achieve processing rates of roughly 772 and 920 million nonzeros per second, corresponding to parallel speed-ups of 3.8 and 4.6 times over the serial performance of a single CPU core.

Scan and Reduction

Parallel *scan*, also known as parallel *prefix sum*, is one of the most important building blocks for data-parallel algorithms [Blelloch, 1990]. Given a sequence a of n elements:

$$[a_0, a_1, \ldots, a_{n-1}]$$

and a binary associative operator $\oplus$, the `scan` function computes the sequence:

$$\mathrm{scan}(a, \oplus) = [a_0, (a_0 \oplus a_1), \ldots, (a_0 \oplus a_1 \oplus \ldots \oplus a_{n-1})]$$

As an example, if we take $\oplus$ to be the usual addition operator, then applying scan to the input array

$$a = [3\ 1\ 7\ 0\ 4\ 1\ 6\ 3]$$

will produce the sequence of partial sums:

$$\mathrm{scan}(a, +) = [3\ 4\ 11\ 11\ 15\ 16\ 22\ 25]$$

This scan operator is an *inclusive* scan, in the sense that element i of the output sequence incorporates element a_i of the input. Incorporating only previous elements would yield an *exclusive* scan operator, also known as a *prefix-sum* operation.

The serial implementation of this operation is extremely simple. It is simply a loop that iterates once over the entire sequence, as shown in Figure A.8.6.

At first glance, it might appear that this operation is inherently serial. However, it can actually be implemented in parallel efficiently. The key observation is that

```
template<class T>
__host__ T plus_scan(T *x, unsigned int n)
{
    for(unsigned int i=1; i<n; ++i)
        x[i] = x[i-1] + x[i];
}
```

FIGURE A.8.6 Template for serial plus-scan.

```
template<class T>
__device__ T plus_scan(T *x)
{
    unsigned int i = threadIdx.x;
    unsigned int n = blockDim.x;

    for(unsigned int offset=1; offset<n; offset *= 2)
    {
        T t;

        if(i>=offset)   t = x[i-offset];
        __syncthreads();

        if(i>=offset)   x[i] = t + x[i];
        __syncthreads();
    }
    return x[i];
}
```

FIGURE A.8.7 CUDA template for parallel plus-scan.

because addition is associative, we are free to change the order in which elements are added together. For instance, we can imagine adding pairs of consecutive elements in parallel, and then adding these partial sums, and so on.

One simple scheme for doing this is from Hillis and Steele [1989]. An implementation of their algorithm in CUDA is shown in Figure A.8.7. It assumes that the input array x[] contains exactly one element per thread of the thread block. It performs $\log_2 n$ iterations of a loop collecting partial sums together.

To understand the action of this loop, consider Figure A.8.8, which illustrates the simple case for $n = 8$ threads and elements. Each level of the diagram represents one step of the loop. The lines indicate the location from which the data is being fetched. For each element of the output (i.e., the final row of the diagram) we are building a summation tree over the input elements. The edges highlighted in blue show the form of this summation tree for the final element. The leaves of this tree are all the initial elements. Tracing back from any output element shows that it incorporates all input values up to and including itself.

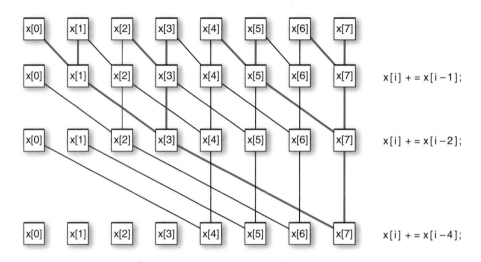

FIGURE A.8.8   Tree-based parallel scan data references.

While simple, this algorithm is not as efficient as we would like. Examining the serial implementation, we see that it performs $O(n)$ additions. The parallel implementation, in contrast, performs $O(n \log n)$ additions. For this reason, it is not *work efficient*, since it does more work than the serial implementation to compute the same result. Fortunately, there are other techniques for implementing scan that are work efficient. Details on more efficient implementation techniques and the extension of this per-block procedure to multiblock arrays are provided by Sengupta, et al. [2007].

In some instances, we may only be interested in computing the sum of all elements in an array, rather than the sequence of all prefix sums returned by scan. This is the *parallel reduction* problem. We could simply use a scan algorithm to perform this computation, but reduction can generally be implemented more efficiently than scan.

Figure A.8.9 shows the code for computing a reduction using addition. In this example, each thread simply loads one element of the input sequence (i.e., it initially sums a subsequence of length 1). At the end of the reduction, we want thread 0 to hold the sum of all elements initially loaded by the threads of its block. The loop in this kernel implicitly builds a summation tree over the input elements, much like the scan algorithm above.

At the end of this loop, thread 0 holds the sum of all the values loaded by this block. If we want the final value of the location pointed to by total to contain the total of all elements in the array, we must combine the partial sums of all the blocks in the grid. One strategy to do this would be to have each block write its partial sum into a second array and then launch the reduction kernel again, repeating the process until we had reduced the sequence to a single value. A more attractive alternative supported by the Tesla GPU architecture is to use the atomicAdd()

```
__global__
void plus_reduce(int *input, unsigned int N, int *total)
{
    unsigned int tid = threadIdx.x;
    unsigned int i   = blockIdx.x*blockDim.x + threadIdx.x;

    // Each block loads its elements into shared memory, padding
    // with 0 if N is not a multiple of blocksize
    __shared__ int x[blocksize];
    x[tid] = (i<N) ? input[i] : 0;
    __syncthreads();

    // Every thread now holds 1 input value in x[]
    //
    // Build summation tree over elements.
    for(int s=blockDim.x/2; s>0; s=s/2)
    {
        if(tid < s)  x[tid] += x[tid + s];
        __syncthreads();
    }

    // Thread 0 now holds the sum of all input values
    // to this block. Have it add that sum to the running total
    if( tid == 0 )  atomicAdd(total, x[tid]);
}
```

FIGURE A.8.9 CUDA implementation of plus-reduction.

primitive, an efficient atomic read-modify-write primitive supported by the memory subsystem. This eliminates the need for additional temporary arrays and repeated kernel launches.

Parallel reduction is an essential primitive for parallel programming and highlights the importance of per-block shared memory and low-cost barriers in making cooperation among threads efficient. This degree of data shuffling among threads would be prohibitively expensive if done in off-chip global memory.

Radix Sort

One important application of scan primitives is in the implementation of sorting routines. The code in Figure A.8.10 implements a radix sort of integers across a single thread block. It accepts as input an array values containing one 32-bit integer for each thread of the block. For efficiency, this array should be stored in per-block shared memory, but this is not required for the sort to behave correctly.

This is a fairly simple implementation of radix sort. It assumes the availability of a procedure partition_by_bit() that will partition the given array such that

```
__device__ void radix_sort(unsigned int *values)
{
    for(int bit=0; bit<32; ++bit)
    {
        partition_by_bit(values, bit);
        __syncthreads();
    }
}
```

FIGURE A.8.10   CUDA code for radix sort.

```
__device__ void partition_by_bit(unsigned int *values,
                                 unsigned int bit)
{
    unsigned int i    = threadIdx.x;
    unsigned int size = blockDim.x;
    unsigned int x_i  = values[i];
    unsigned int p_i  = (x_i >> bit) & 1;

    values[i] = p_i;
    __syncthreads();

    // Compute number of T bits up to and including p_i.
    // Record the total number of F bits as well.
    unsigned int T_before = plus_scan(values);
    unsigned int T_total  = values[size-1];
    unsigned int F_total  = size - T_total;
    __syncthreads();

    // Write every x_i to its proper place
    if( p_i )
        values[T_before-1 + F_total] = x_i;
    else
        values[i - T_before] = x_i;
}
```

FIGURE A.8.11   CUDA code to partition data on a bit-by-bit basis, as part of radix sort.

all values with a 0 in the designated bit will come before all values with a 1 in that bit. To produce the correct output, this partitioning must be stable.

Implementing the partitioning procedure is a simple application of scan. Thread i holds the value x_i and must calculate the correct output index at which to write this value. To do so, it needs to calculate (1) the number of threads $j < i$ for which the designated bit is 1 and (2) the total number of bits for which the designated bit is 0. The CUDA code for partition_by_bit() is shown in Figure A.8.11.

A similar strategy can be applied for implementing a radix sort kernel that sorts an array of large length, rather than just a one-block array. The fundamental step remains the scan procedure, although when the computation is partitioned across multiple kernels, we must double-buffer the array of values rather than doing the partitioning in place. Details on performing radix sorts on large arrays efficiently are provided by Satish, Harris, and Garland [2008].

N-Body Applications on a GPU[1]

Nyland, Harris, and Prins [2007] describe a simple yet useful computational kernel with excellent GPU performance—the *all-pairs N-body* algorithm. It is a time-consuming component of many scientific applications. N-body simulations calculate the evolution of a system of bodies in which each body continuously interacts with every other body. One example is an astrophysical simulation in which each body represents an individual star, and the bodies gravitationally attract each other. Other examples are protein folding, where N-body simulation is used to calculate electrostatic and van der Waals forces; turbulent fluid flow simulation; and global illumination in computer graphics.

The all-pairs N-body algorithm calculates the total force on each body in the system by computing each pair-wise force in the system, summing for each body. Many scientists consider this method to be the most accurate, with the only loss of precision coming from the floating-point hardware operations. The drawback is its $O(n^2)$ computational complexity, which is far too large for systems with more than 10^6 bodies. To overcome this high cost, several simplifications have been proposed to yield $O(n \log n)$ and $O(n)$ algorithms; examples are the Barnes-Hut algorithm, the Fast Multipole Method and Particle-Mesh-Ewald summation. All of the *fast* methods still rely on the all-pairs method as a kernel for accurate computation of short-range forces; thus it continues to be important.

N-Body Mathematics

For gravitational simulation, calculate the body-body force using elementary physics. Between two bodies indexed by i and j, the 3D force vector is:

$$\mathbf{f}_{ij} = G \frac{m_i m_j}{\|\mathbf{r}_{ij}\|^2} \times \frac{\mathbf{r}_{ij}}{\|\mathbf{r}_{ij}\|}$$

The force magnitude is calculated in the left term, while the direction is computed in the right (unit vector pointing from one body to the other).

Given a list of interacting bodies (an entire system or a subset), the calculation is simple: for all pairs of interactions, compute the force and sum for each body. Once the total forces are calculated, they are used to update each body's position and velocity, based on the previous position and velocity. The calculation of the forces has complexity $O(n^2)$, while the update is $O(n)$.

---

[1] Adapted from Nyland, Harris and Prins [2007], "Fast N-Body Simulation with CUDA," Chapter 31 of *GPU Gems 3*.

The serial force-calculation code uses two nested for-loops iterating over pairs of bodies. The outer loop selects the body for which the total force is being calculated, and the inner loop iterates over all the bodies. The inner loop calls a function that computes the pair-wise force, then adds the force into a running sum.

To compute the forces in parallel, we assign one thread to each body, since the calculation of force on each body is independent of the calculation on all other bodies. Once all of the forces are computed, the positions and velocities of the bodies can be updated.

The code for the serial and parallel versions is shown in Figure A.8.12 and Figure A.8.13. The serial version has two nested for-loops. The conversion to CUDA, like many other examples, converts the serial outer loop to a per-thread kernel where each thread computes the total force on a single body. The CUDA kernel computes a global thread ID for each thread, replacing the iterator variable of the serial outer loop. Both kernels finish by storing the total acceleration in a global array used to compute the new position and velocity values in a subsequent step.

```
void accel_on_all_bodies()
{
    int i, j;
    float3 acc(0.0f, 0.0f, 0.0f);

    for (i = 0; i < N; i++) {
        for (j = 0; j < N; j++) {
            acc = body_body_interaction(acc, body[i], body[j]);
        }
        accel[i] = acc;
    }
}
```

FIGURE A.8.12   Serial code to compute all pair-wise forces on N bodies.

```
__global__ void accel_on_one_body()
{
    int i = threadIdx.x + blockDim.x * blockIdx.x;
    int j;
    float3 acc(0.0f, 0.0f, 0.0f);

    for (j = 0; j < N; j++) {
        acc = body_body_interaction(acc, body[i], body[j]);
    }
    accel[i] = acc;
}
```

FIGURE A.8.13   CUDA thread code to compute the total force on a single body.

The outer loop is replaced by a CUDA kernel grid that launches *N* threads, one for each body.

Optimization for GPU Execution

The CUDA code shown is functionally correct, but is not efficient, as it ignores key architectural features. Better performance can be achieved with three main optimizations. First, shared memory can be used to avoid identical memory reads between threads. Second, using multiple threads per body improves performance for small values of *N*. Third, loop unrolling reduces loop overhead.

Using Shared memory

Shared memory can hold a subset of body positions, much like a cache, eliminating redundant global memory requests between threads. We optimize the code shown above to have each of *p* threads in a thread-block load *one* position into shared memory (for a total of *p* positions). Once all the threads have loaded a value into shared memory, ensured by __syncthreads(), each thread can then perform *p* interactions (using the data in shared memory). This is repeated *N/p* times to complete the force calculation for each body, which reduces the number of requests to memory by a factor of *p* (typically in the range 32–128).

The function called accel_on_one_body() requires a few changes to support this optimization. The modified code is shown in Figure A.8.14.

```
__shared__ float4 shPosition[256];
...
__global__ void accel_on_one_body()
{
    int i = threadIdx.x + blockDim.x * blockIdx.x;
    int j, k;
    int p = blockDim.x;
    float3 acc(0.0f, 0.0f, 0.0f);
    float4 myBody = body[i];

    for (j = 0; j < N; j += p) {   // Outer loops jumps by p each time
        shPosition[threadIdx.x] = body[j+threadIdx.x];
        __syncthreads();
        for (k = 0; k < p; k++) { // Inner loop accesses p positions
            acc = body_body_interaction(acc, myBody, shPosition[k]);
        }
        __syncthreads();
    }
    accel[i] = acc;
}
```

FIGURE A.8.14   CUDA code to compute the total force on each body, using shared memory to improve performance.

The loop that formerly iterated over all bodies now jumps by the block dimension p. Each iteration of the outer loop loads p successive positions into shared memory (one position per thread). The threads synchronize, and then p force calculations are computed by each thread. A second synchronization is required to ensure that new values are not loaded into shared memory prior to all threads completing the force calculations with the current data.

Using shared memory reduces the memory bandwidth required to less than 10% of the total bandwidth that the GPU can sustain (using less than 5 GB/s). This optimization keeps the application busy performing computation rather than waiting on memory accesses, as it would have without the use of shared memory. The performance for varying values of N is shown in Figure A.8.15.

Using Multiple Threads per Body

Figure A.8.15 shows performance degradation for problems with small values of N ($N < 4096$) on the GeForce 8800 GTX. Many research efforts that rely on N-body calculations focus on small N (for long simulation times), making it a target of our optimization efforts. Our presumption to explain the lower performance was that there was simply not enough work to keep the GPU busy when N is small. The solution is to allocate more threads per body. We change the thread-block dimensions from $(p, 1, 1)$ to $(p, q, 1)$, where q threads divide the work of a single body into equal parts. By allocating the additional threads within the same thread block, partial results can be stored in shared memory. When all the force calculations are

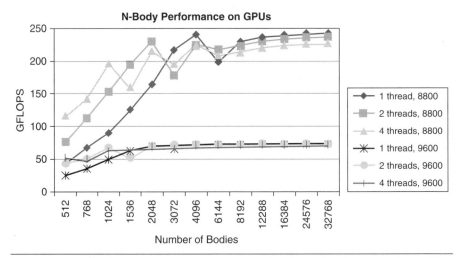

FIGURE A.8.15   Performance measurements of the N-body application on a GeForce 8800 GTX and a GeForce 9600. The 8800 has 128 stream processors at 1.35 GHz, while the 9600 has 64 at 0.80 GHz (about 30% of the 8800). The peak performance is 242 GFLOPS. For a GPU with more processors, the problem needs to be bigger to achieve full performance (the 9600 peak is around 2048 bodies, while the 8800 doesn't reach its peak until 16,384 bodies). For small N, more than one thread per body can significantly improve performance, but eventually incurs a performance penalty as N grows.

done, the q partial results can be collected and summed to compute the final result. Using two or four threads per body leads to large improvements for small N.

As an example, the performance on the 8800 GTX jumps by 110% when $N = 1024$ (one thread achieves 90 GFLOPS, where four achieve 190 GFLOPS). Performance degrades slightly on large N, so we only use this optimization for N smaller than 4096. The performance increases are shown in Figure A.8.15 for a GPU with 128 processors and a smaller GPU with 64 processors clocked at two-thirds the speed.

Performance Comparison

The performance of the N-body code is shown in Figure A.8.15 and Figure A.8.16. In Figure A.8.15, performance of high- and medium-performance GPUs is shown, along with the performance improvements achieved by using multiple threads per body. The performance on the faster GPU ranges from 90 to just under 250 GFLOPS.

Figure A.8.16 shows nearly identical code (C++ versus CUDA) running on Intel Core2 CPUs. The CPU performance is about 1% of the GPU, in the range of 0.2 to 2 GFLOPS, remaining nearly constant over the wide range of problem sizes.

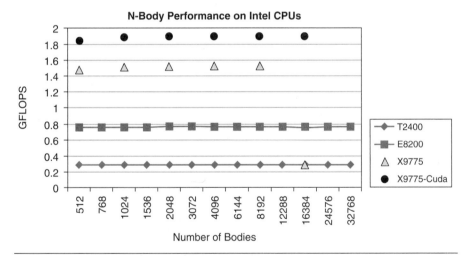

FIGURE A.8.16   Performance measurements on the N-body code on a CPU. The graph shows single precision N-body performance using Intel Core2 CPUs, denoted by their CPU model number. Note the dramatic reduction in GFLOPS performance (shown in GFLOPS on the *y*-axis), demonstrating how much faster the GPU is compared to the CPU. The performance on the CPU is generally independent of problem size, except for an anomalously low performance when N=16,384 on the X9775 CPU. The graph also shows the results of running the CUDA version of the code (using the CUDA-for-CPU compiler) on a single CPU core, where it outperforms the C++ code by 24%. As a programming language, CUDA exposes parallelism and locality that a compiler can exploit. The Intel CPUs are a 3.2 GHz Extreme X9775 (code named "Penryn"), a 2.66 GHz E8200 (code named "Wolfdale"), a desktop, pre-Penryn CPU, and a 1.83 GHz T2400 (code named "Yonah"), a 2007 laptop CPU. The Penryn version of the Core 2 architecture is particularly interesting for N-body calculations with its 4-bit divider, allowing division and square root operations to execute four times faster than previous Intel CPUs.

The graph also shows the results of compiling the CUDA version of the code for a CPU, where the performance improves by 24%. CUDA, as a programming language, exposes parallelism, allowing the compiler to make better use of the SSE vector unit on a single core. The CUDA version of the N-body code naturally maps to multicore CPUs as well (with grids of blocks), where it achieves nearly perfect scaling on an eight-core system with N = 4096 (ratios of 2.0, 3.97, and 7.94 on two, four, and eight cores, respectively).

Results

With a modest effort, we developed a computational kernel that improves GPU performance over multicore CPUs by a factor of up to 157. Execution time for the N-body code running on a recent CPU from Intel (Penryn X9775 at 3.2 GHz, single core) took more than 3 seconds per frame to run the same code that runs at a 44 Hz frame rate on a GeForce 8800 GPU. On pre-Penryn CPUs, the code requires 6–16 seconds, and on older Core2 processors and Pentium IV processor, the time is about 25 seconds. We must divide the apparent increase in performance in half, as the CPU requires only half as many calculations to compute the same result (using the optimization that the forces on a pair of bodies are equal in strength and opposite in direction).

How can the GPU speed up the code by such a large amount? The answer requires inspecting architectural details. The pair-wise force calculation requires 20 floating-point operations, comprised mostly of addition and multiplication instructions (some of which can be combined using a multiply-add instruction), but there are also division and square root instructions for vector normalization. Intel CPUs take many cycles for single precision division and square root instructions,[2] although this has improved in the latest Penryn CPU family with its faster 4-bit divider.[3] Additionally, the limitations in register capacity leads to many MOV instructions in the x86 code (presumably to/from L1 cache). In contrast, the GeForce 8800 executes a reciprocal square-root thread instruction in four clocks; see Section A.6 for special function accuracy. It has a larger register file (per thread) and shared memory that can be accessed as an instruction operand. Finally, the CUDA compiler emits 15 instructions for one iteration of the loop, compared with more than 40 instructions from a variety of x86 CPU compilers. Greater parallelism, faster execution of complex instructions, more register space, and an efficient compiler all combine to explain the dramatic performance improvement of the N-body code between the CPU and the GPU.

---

[2] The x86 SSE instructions reciprocal-square-root (RSQRT*) and reciprocal (RCP*) were not considered, as their accuracy is too low to be comparable.

[3] Intel Corporation, *Intel 64 and IA-32 Architectures Optimization Reference Manual*. November 2007. Order Number: 248966-016. Also available at www3.intel.com/design/processor/manuals/248966.pdf.

On a GeForce 8800, the all-pairs N-body algorithm delivers more than 240 GFLOPS of performance, compared to less than 2 GFLOPS on recent sequential processors. Compiling and executing the CUDA version of the code on a CPU demonstrates that the problem scales well to multicore CPUs, but is still significantly slower than a single GPU.

We coupled the GPU N-body simulation with a graphical display of the motion, and can interactively display 16K bodies interacting at 44 frames per second. This allows astrophysical and biophysical events to be displayed and navigated at interactive rates. Additionally, we can parameterize many settings, such as noise reduction, damping, and integration techniques, immediately displaying their effects on the dynamics of the system. This provides scientists with stunning visual imagery, boosting their insights on otherwise invisible systems (too large or small, too fast or too slow), allowing them to create better models of physical phenomena.

Figure A.8.17 shows a time-series display of an astrophysical simulation of 16K bodies, with each body acting as a galaxy. The initial configuration is a

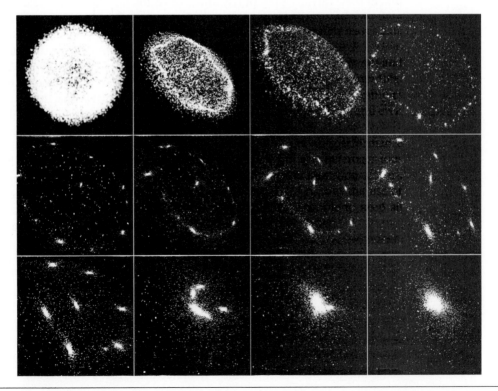

FIGURE A.8.17   12 images captured during the evolution of an N-body system with 16,384 bodies.

spherical shell of bodies rotating about the z-axis. One phenomenon of interest to astrophysicists is the clustering that occurs, along with the merging of galaxies over time. For the interested reader, the CUDA code for this application is available in the CUDA SDK from www.nvidia.com/CUDA.

 A.9 **Fallacies and Pitfalls**

GPUs have evolved and changed so rapidly that many fallacies and pitfalls have arisen. We cover a few here.

Fallacy: GPUs are just SIMD vector multiprocessors. It is easy to draw the false conclusion that GPUs are simply SIMD vector multiprocessors. GPUs do have a SPMD-style programming model, in that a programmer can write a single program that is executed in multiple thread instances with multiple data. The execution of these threads is not purely SIMD or vector, however; it is single-instruction multiple-thread (SIMT), described in Section A.4. Each GPU thread has its own scalar registers, thread private memory, thread execution state, thread ID, independent execution and branch path, and effective program counter, and can address memory independently. Although a group of threads (e.g., a warp of 32 threads) executes more efficiently when the PCs for the threads are the same, this is not necessary. So, the multiprocessors are not purely SIMD. The thread execution model is MIMD with barrier synchronization and SIMT optimizations. Execution is more efficient if individual thread load/store memory accesses can be coalesced into block accesses, as well. However, this is not strictly necessary. In a purely SIMD vector architecture, memory/register accesses for different threads must be aligned in a regular vector pattern. A GPU has no such restriction for register or memory accesses; however, execution is more efficient if warps of threads access local blocks of data.

In a further departure from a pure SIMD model, an SIMT GPU can execute more than one warp of threads concurrently. In graphics applications, there may be multiple groups of vertex programs, pixel programs, and geometry programs running in the multiprocessor array concurrently. Computing programs may also execute different programs concurrently in different warps.

Fallacy: GPU performance cannot grow faster than Moore's law. Moore's law is simply a rate. It is not a "speed of light" limit for any other rate. Moore's law describes an expectation that over time, as semiconductor technology advances and transistors become smaller, the manufacturing cost per transistor will decline exponentially. Put another way, given a constant manufacturing cost, the number of transistors will increase exponentially. Gordon Moore [1965] predicted that this progression would provide roughly two times the number of transistors for the same manufacturing cost every year, and later revised it to doubling every two years. Although Moore made the initial prediction in 1965 when there were just 50 components per integrated circuit, it has proved remarkably consistent. The reduction of transistor size has historically had other benefits, such as lower power per transistor and faster clock speeds at constant power.

This increasing bounty of transistors is used by chip architects to build processors, memory, and other components. For some time, CPU designers have used the extra transistors to increase processor performance at a rate similar to Moore's law, so much so that many people think that processor performance growth of two times every 18–24 months is Moore's law. In fact, it is not.

Microprocessor designers spend some of the new transistors on processor cores, improving the architecture and design, and pipelining for more clock speed. The rest of the new transistors are used for providing more cache, to make memory access faster. In contrast, GPU designers use almost none of the new transistors to provide more cache; most of the transistors are used for improving the processor cores and adding more processor cores.

GPUs get faster by four mechanisms. First, GPU designers reap the Moore's law bounty directly by applying exponentially more transistors to building more parallel, and thus faster, processors. Second, GPU designers can improve on the architecture over time, increasing the efficiency of the processing. Third, Moore's law assumes constant cost, so the Moore's law rate can clearly be exceeded by spending more for larger chips with more transistors. Fourth, GPU memory systems have increased their effective bandwidth at a pace nearly comparable to the processing rate, by using faster memories, wider memories, data compression, and better caches. The combination of these four approaches has historically allowed GPU performance to double regularly, roughly every 12 to 18 months. This rate, exceeding the rate of Moore's law, has been demonstrated on graphics applications for approximately ten years and shows no sign of significant slowdown. The most challenging rate limiter appears to be the memory system, but competitive innovation is advancing that rapidly too.

Fallacy: GPUs only render 3D graphics; they can't do general computation.
GPUs are built to render 3D graphics as well as 2D graphics and video. To meet the demands of graphics software developers as expressed in the interfaces and performance/feature requirements of the graphics APIs, GPUs have become massively parallel programmable floating-point processors. In the graphics domain, these processors are programmed through the graphics APIs and with arcane graphics programming languages (GLSL, Cg, and HLSL, in OpenGL and Direct3D).

However, there is nothing preventing GPU architects from exposing the parallel processor cores to programmers without the graphics API or the arcane graphics languages.

In fact, the Tesla architecture family of GPUs exposes the processors through a software environment known as CUDA, which allows programmers to develop general application programs using the C language and soon C++. GPUs are Turing-complete processors, so they can run any program that a CPU can run, although perhaps less well. And perhaps faster.

Fallacy: GPUs cannot run double precision floating-point programs fast. In the past, GPUs could not run double precision floating-point programs at all, except through software emulation. And that's not very fast at all. GPUs have made the progression from indexed arithmetic representation (lookup tables for colors) to 8-bit integers per color component, to fixed-point arithmetic, to single precision floating-point, and recently added double precision. Modern GPUs perform virtually all calculations in single precision IEEE floating-point arithmetic, and are beginning to use double precision in addition.

For a small additional cost, a GPU can support double precision floating-point as well as single precision floating-point. Today, double precision runs more slowly than the single precision speed, about five to ten times slower. For incremental additional cost, double precision performance can be increased relative to single precision in stages, as more applications demand it.

Fallacy: GPUs don't do floating-point correctly. GPUs, at least in the Tesla architecture family of processors, perform single precision floating-point processing at a level prescribed by the IEEE 754 floating-point standard. So, in terms of accuracy, GPUs are the equal of any other IEEE 754–compliant processors.

Today, GPUs do not implement some of the specific features described in the standard, such as handling denormalized numbers and providing precise floating-point exceptions. However, the recently introduced Tesla T10P GPU provides full IEEE rounding, fused-multiply-add, and denormalized number support for double precision.

Pitfall: Just use more threads to cover longer memory latencies. CPU cores are typically designed to run a single thread at full speed. To run at full speed, every instruction and its data need to be available when it is time for that instruction to run. If the next instruction is not ready or the data required for that instruction is not available, the instruction cannot run and the processor stalls. External memory is distant from the processor, so it takes many cycles of wasted execution to fetch data from memory. Consequently, CPUs require large local caches to keep running without stalling. Memory latency is long, so it is avoided by striving to run in the cache. At some point, program working set demands may be larger than any cache. Some CPUs have used multithreading to tolerate latency, but the number of threads per core has generally been limited to a small number.

The GPU strategy is different. GPU cores are designed to run many threads concurrently, but only one instruction from any thread at a time. Another way to say this is that a GPU runs each thread slowly, but in aggregate runs the threads efficiently. Each thread can tolerate some amount of memory latency, because other threads can run.

The downside of this is that multiple—many multiple threads—are required to cover the memory latency. In addition, if memory accesses are scattered or not correlated among threads, the memory system will get progressively slower in responding to each individual request. Eventually, even the multiple threads will not be able to cover the latency. So, the pitfall is that for the "just use more threads" strategy to work for covering latency, you have to have enough threads, and the threads have to be well-behaved in terms of locality of memory access.

Fallacy: O(n) algorithms are difficult to speed up. No matter how fast the GPU is at processing data, the steps of transferring data to and from the device may limit the performance of algorithms with O(n) complexity (with a small amount of work per datum). The highest transfer rate over the PCIe bus is approximately 48 GB/second when DMA transfers are used, and slightly less for nonDMA transfers. The CPU, in contrast, has typical access speeds of 8–12 GB/second to system memory. Example problems, such as vector addition, will be limited by the transfer of the inputs to the GPU and the returning output from the computation.

There are three ways to overcome the cost of transferring data. First, try to leave the data on the GPU for as long as possible, instead of moving the data back and forth for different steps of a complicated algorithm. CUDA deliberately leaves data alone in the GPU between launches to support this.

Second, the GPU supports the concurrent operations of copy-in, copy-out and computation, so data can be streamed in and out of the device while it is computing. This model is useful for any data stream that can be processed as it arrives. Examples are video processing, network routing, data compression/decompression, and even simpler computations such as large vector mathematics.

The third suggestion is to use the CPU and GPU together, improving performance by assigning a subset of the work to each, treating the system as a heterogeneous computing platform. The CUDA programming model supports allocation of work to one or more GPUs along with continued use of the CPU without the use of threads (via asynchronous GPU functions), so it is relatively simple to keep all GPUs and a CPU working concurrently to solve problems even faster.

A.10 Concluding Remarks

GPUs are massively parallel processors and have become widely used, not only for 3D graphics, but also for many other applications. This wide application was made possible by the evolution of graphics devices into programmable processors. The graphics application programming model for GPUs is usually an API such as DirectX™ or OpenGL™. For more general-purpose computing, the CUDA programming model uses an SPMD (single-program multiple data) style, executing a program with many parallel threads.

GPU parallelism will continue to scale with Moore's law, mainly by increasing the number of processors. Only the parallel programming models that can readily scale to hundreds of processor cores and thousands of threads will be successful in supporting manycore GPUs and CPUs. Also, only those applications that have many largely independent parallel tasks will be accelerated by massively parallel manycore architectures.

Parallel programming models for GPUs are becoming more flexible, for both graphics and parallel computing. For example, CUDA is evolving rapidly in the direction of full C/C++ functionality. Graphics APIs and programming models will likely adapt parallel computing capabilities and models from CUDA. Its SPMD-style threading model is scalable, and is a convenient, succinct, and easily learned model for expressing large amounts of parallelism.

Driven by these changes in the programming models, GPU architecture is in turn becoming more flexible and more programmable. GPU fixed-function units are becoming accessible from general programs, along the lines of how CUDA programs already use texture intrinsic functions to perform texture lookups using the GPU texture instruction and texture unit.

GPU architecture will continue to adapt to the usage patterns of both graphics and other application programmers. GPUs will continue to expand to include more processing power through additional processor cores, as well as increasing the thread and memory bandwidth available for programs. In addition, the programming models must evolve to include programming heterogeneous manycore systems including both GPUs and CPUs.

Acknowledgments

This appendix is the work of several authors at NVIDIA. We gratefully acknowledge the significant contributions of Michael Garland, John Montrym, Doug Voorhies, Lars Nyland, Erik Lindholm, Paulius Micikevicius, Massimiliano Fatica, Stuart Oberman, and Vasily Volkov.

A.11 Historical Perspective and Further Reading

This section, which appears on the CD, surveys the history of programmable real-time graphics processing units (GPUs) from the early 1980s through today as they declined in price by two orders of magnitude and increased in performance by two orders of magnitude. It traces the evolution of the GPU from fixed function pipelines to programmable graphics processors, with perspectives on GPU computing, unified graphics and computing processors, visual computing, and scalable GPUs.

Assemblers, Linkers, and the SPIM Simulator

Fear of serious injury cannot alone justify suppression of free speech and assembly.

Louis Brandeis
Whitney v. California, 1927

James R. Larus
Microsoft Research
Microsoft

B.1   Introduction

Encoding instructions as binary numbers is natural and efficient for computers. Humans, however, have a great deal of difficulty understanding and manipulating these numbers. People read and write symbols (words) much better than long sequences of digits. Chapter 2 showed that we need not choose between numbers and words, because computer instructions can be represented in many ways. Humans can write and read symbols, and computers can execute the equivalent binary numbers. This appendix describes the process by which a human-readable program is translated into a form that a computer can execute, provides a few hints about writing assembly programs, and explains how to run these programs on SPIM, a simulator that executes MIPS programs. UNIX, Windows, and Mac OS X versions of the SPIM simulator are available on the CD.

Assembly language is the symbolic representation of a computer's binary encoding—the **machine language**. Assembly language is more readable than machine language, because it uses symbols instead of bits. The symbols in assembly language name commonly occurring bit patterns, such as opcodes and register specifiers, so people can read and remember them. In addition, assembly language

machine language
Binary representation used for communication within a computer system.

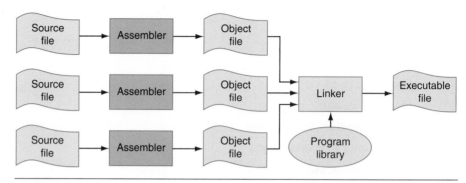

FIGURE B.1.1   The process that produces an executable file. An assembler translates a file of assembly language into an object file, which is linked with other files and libraries into an executable file.

assembler A program that translates a symbolic version of instruction into the binary version.

macro A pattern-matching and replacement facility that provides a simple mechanism to name a frequently used sequence of instructions.

unresolved reference A reference that requires more information from an outside source to be complete.

linker Also called **link editor**. A systems program that combines independently assembled machine language programs and resolves all undefined labels into an executable file.

permits programmers to use *labels* to identify and name particular memory words that hold instructions or data.

A tool called an **assembler** translates assembly language into binary instructions. Assemblers provide a friendlier representation than a computer's 0s and 1s, which simplifies writing and reading programs. Symbolic names for operations and locations are one facet of this representation. Another facet is programming facilities that increase a program's clarity. For example, **macros**, discussed in Section B.2, enable a programmer to extend the assembly language by defining new operations.

An assembler reads a single assembly language *source file* and produces an *object file* containing machine instructions and bookkeeping information that helps combine several object files into a program. Figure B.1.1 illustrates how a program is built. Most programs consist of several files—also called *modules*—that are written, compiled, and assembled independently. A program may also use prewritten routines supplied in a *program library*. A module typically contains *references* to subroutines and data defined in other modules and in libraries. The code in a module cannot be executed when it contains **unresolved references** to labels in other object files or libraries. Another tool, called a **linker**, combines a collection of object and library files into an *executable file*, which a computer can run.

To see the advantage of assembly language, consider the following sequence of figures, all of which contain a short subroutine that computes and prints the sum of the squares of integers from 0 to 100. Figure B.1.2 shows the machine language that a MIPS computer executes. With considerable effort, you could use the opcode and instruction format tables in Chapter 2 to translate the instructions into a symbolic program similar to that shown in Figure B.1.3. This form of the routine is much

```
00100111101111011111111111100000
10101111110111111000000000010100
10101111110100100000000000100000
10101111101001010000000000100100
10101111101000000000000000011000
10101111101000000000000000011100
10001111101011100000000000011100
10001111101110000000000000011000
00000001110011100000000000011001
00100101110010000000000000000001
00101001000000010000000001100101
10101111110101000000000000011100
00000000000000000111100000010010
00000011000011111100100000100001
00010100001000001111111111110111
10101111110111001000000000011000
00111100000001000001000000000000
10001111101001010000000000011000
00001100000100000000000011101100
00100100100001000000010000110000
10001111101111110000000000010100
00100111101111101000000000100000
00000011111000000000000000001000
00000000000000000001000000100001
```

FIGURE B.1.2 **MIPS machine language code for a routine to compute and print the sum of the squares of integers between 0 and 100.**

easier to read, because operations and operands are written with symbols rather than with bit patterns. However, this assembly language is still difficult to follow, because memory locations are named by their address rather than by a symbolic label.

Figure B.1.4 shows assembly language that labels memory addresses with mnemonic names. Most programmers prefer to read and write this form. Names that begin with a period, for example .data and .globl, are **assembler directives** that tell the assembler how to translate a program but do not produce machine instructions. Names followed by a colon, such as str: or main:, are labels that name the next memory location. This program is as readable as most assembly language programs (except for a glaring lack of comments), but it is still difficult to follow, because many simple operations are required to accomplish simple tasks and because assembly language's lack of control flow constructs provides few hints about the program's operation.

By contrast, the C routine in Figure B.1.5 is both shorter and clearer, since variables have mnemonic names and the loop is explicit rather than constructed with branches. In fact, the C routine is the only one that we wrote. The other forms of the program were produced by a C compiler and assembler.

In general, assembly language plays two roles (see Figure B.1.6). The first role is the output language of compilers. A *compiler* translates a program written in a

assembler directive An operation that tells the assembler how to translate a program but does not produce machine instructions; always begins with a period.

```
addiu      $29, $29, -32
sw         $31, 20($29)
sw         $4,  32($29)
sw         $5,  36($29)
sw         $0,  24($29)
sw         $0,  28($29)
lw         $14, 28($29)
lw         $24, 24($29)
multu      $14, $14
addiu      $8,  $14, 1
slti       $1,  $8, 101
sw         $8,  28($29)
mflo       $15
addu       $25, $24, $15
bne        $1,  $0, -9
sw         $25, 24($29)
lui        $4,  4096
lw         $5,  24($29)
jal        1048812
addiu      $4,  $4, 1072
lw         $31, 20($29)
addiu      $29, $29, 32
jr         $31
move       $2,  $0
```

FIGURE B.1.3   The same routine written in assembly language. However, the code for the routine does not label registers or memory locations nor include comments.

source language The
high-level language
in which a program is
originally written.

high-level language (such as C or Pascal) into an equivalent program in machine or assembly language. The high-level language is called the **source language**, and the compiler's output is its *target language*.

Assembly language's other role is as a language in which to write programs. This role used to be the dominant one. Today, however, because of larger main memories and better compilers, most programmers write in a high-level language and rarely, if ever, see the instructions that a computer executes. Nevertheless, assembly language is still important to write programs in which speed or size is critical or to exploit hardware features that have no analogues in high-level languages.

Although this appendix focuses on MIPS assembly language, assembly programming on most other machines is very similar. The additional instructions and address modes in CISC machines, such as the VAX, can make assembly programs shorter but do not change the process of assembling a program or provide assembly language with the advantages of high-level languages, such as type-checking and structured control flow.

```
        .text
        .align  2
        .globl  main
main:
        subu    $sp, $sp, 32
        sw      $ra, 20($sp)
        sd      $a0, 32($sp)
        sw      $0,  24($sp)
        sw      $0,  28($sp)
loop:
        lw      $t6, 28($sp)
        mul     $t7, $t6, $t6
        lw      $t8, 24($sp)
        addu    $t9, $t8, $t7
        sw      $t9, 24($sp)
        addu    $t0, $t6, 1
        sw      $t0, 28($sp)
        ble     $t0, 100, loop
        la      $a0, str
        lw      $a1, 24($sp)
        jal     printf
        move    $v0, $0
        lw      $ra, 20($sp)
        addu    $sp, $sp, 32
        jr      $ra


        .data
        .align  0
str:
        .asciiz "The sum from 0 .. 100 is %d\n"
```

FIGURE B.1.4 The same routine written in assembly language with labels, but no comments. The commands that start with periods are assembler directives (see pages B-47–49). .text indicates that succeeding lines contain instructions. .data indicates that they contain data. .align n indicates that the items on the succeeding lines should be aligned on a 2^n byte boundary. Hence, .align 2 means the next item should be on a word boundary. .globl main declares that main is a global symbol that should be visible to code stored in other files. Finally, .asciiz stores a null-terminated string in memory.

When to Use Assembly Language

The primary reason to program in assembly language, as opposed to an available high-level language, is because the speed or size of a program is critically important. For example, consider a computer that controls a piece of machinery, such as a car's brakes. A computer that is incorporated in another device, such as a car, is called an *embedded computer*. This type of computer needs to respond rapidly and predictably to events in the outside world. Because a compiler introduces

```
    #include <stdio.h>

int
main (int argc, char *argv[])
{
    int i;
    int sum = 0;

    for (i = 0; i <= 100; i = i + 1) sum = sum + i * i;
    printf ("The sum from 0 .. 100 is %d\n", sum);
}
```

FIGURE B.1.5   The routine written in the C programming language.

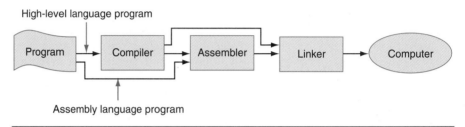

FIGURE B.1.6   Assembly language either is written by a programmer or is the output of a compiler.

uncertainty about the time cost of operations, programmers may find it difficult to ensure that a high-level language program responds within a definite time interval—say, 1 millisecond after a sensor detects that a tire is skidding. An assembly language programmer, on the other hand, has tight control over which instructions execute. In addition, in embedded applications, reducing a program's size, so that it fits in fewer memory chips, reduces the cost of the embedded computer.

A hybrid approach, in which most of a program is written in a high-level language and time-critical sections are written in assembly language, builds on the strengths of both languages. Programs typically spend most of their time executing a small fraction of the program's source code. This observation is just the principle of locality that underlies caches (see Section 5.1 in Chapter 5).

Program profiling measures where a program spends its time and can find the time-critical parts of a program. In many cases, this portion of the program can be made faster with better data structures or algorithms. Sometimes, however, significant performance improvements only come from recoding a critical portion of a program in assembly language.

This improvement is not necessarily an indication that the high-level language's compiler has failed. Compilers typically are better than programmers at producing uniformly high-quality machine code across an entire program. Programmers, however, understand a program's algorithms and behavior at a deeper level than a compiler and can expend considerable effort and ingenuity improving small sections of the program. In particular, programmers often consider several procedures simultaneously while writing their code. Compilers typically compile each procedure in isolation and must follow strict conventions governing the use of registers at procedure boundaries. By retaining commonly used values in registers, even across procedure boundaries, programmers can make a program run faster.

Another major advantage of assembly language is the ability to exploit specialized instructions—for example, string copy or pattern-matching instructions. Compilers, in most cases, cannot determine that a program loop can be replaced by a single instruction. However, the programmer who wrote the loop can replace it easily with a single instruction.

Currently, a programmer's advantage over a compiler has become difficult to maintain as compilation techniques improve and machines' pipelines increase in complexity (Chapter 4).

The final reason to use assembly language is that no high-level language is available on a particular computer. Many older or specialized computers do not have a compiler, so a programmer's only alternative is assembly language.

Drawbacks of Assembly Language

Assembly language has many disadvantages that strongly argue against its widespread use. Perhaps its major disadvantage is that programs written in assembly language are inherently machine-specific and must be totally rewritten to run on another computer architecture. The rapid evolution of computers discussed in Chapter 1 means that architectures become obsolete. An assembly language program remains tightly bound to its original architecture, even after the computer is eclipsed by new, faster, and more cost-effective machines.

Another disadvantage is that assembly language programs are longer than the equivalent programs written in a high-level language. For example, the C program in Figure B.1.5 is 11 lines long, while the assembly program in Figure B.1.4 is 31 lines long. In more complex programs, the ratio of assembly to high-level language (its *expansion factor*) can be much larger than the factor of three in this example. Unfortunately, empirical studies have shown that programmers write roughly the same number of lines of code per day in assembly as in high-level languages. This means that programmers are roughly x times more productive in a high-level language, where x is the assembly language expansion factor.

To compound the problem, longer programs are more difficult to read and understand, and they contain more bugs. Assembly language exacerbates the problem because of its complete lack of structure. Common programming idioms, such as *if-then* statements and loops, must be built from branches and jumps. The resulting programs are hard to read, because the reader must reconstruct every higher-level construct from its pieces and each instance of a statement may be slightly different. For example, look at Figure B.1.4 and answer these questions: What type of loop is used? What are its lower and upper bounds?

Elaboration: Compilers can produce machine language directly instead of relying on an assembler. These compilers typically execute much faster than those that invoke an assembler as part of compilation. However, a compiler that generates machine language must perform many tasks that an assembler normally handles, such as resolving addresses and encoding instructions as binary numbers. The tradeoff is between compilation speed and compiler simplicity.

Elaboration: Despite these considerations, some embedded applications are written in a high-level language. Many of these applications are large and complex programs that must be extremely reliable. Assembly language programs are longer and more difficult to write and read than high-level language programs. This greatly increases the cost of writing an assembly language program and makes it extremely difficult to verify the correctness of this type of program. In fact, these considerations led the Department of Defense, which pays for many complex embedded systems, to develop Ada, a new high-level language for writing embedded systems.

B.2   Assemblers

An assembler translates a file of assembly language statements into a file of binary machine instructions and binary data. The translation process has two major parts. The first step is to find memory locations with labels so that the relationship between symbolic names and addresses is known when instructions are translated. The second step is to translate each assembly statement by combining the numeric equivalents of opcodes, register specifiers, and labels into a legal instruction. As shown in Figure B.1.1, the assembler produces an output file, called an *object file*, which contains the machine instructions, data, and bookkeeping information.

An object file typically cannot be executed, because it references procedures or data in other files. A **label** is **external** (also called **global**) if the labeled object can

external label Also called global label. A label referring to an object that can be referenced from files other than the one in which it is defined.

be referenced from files other than the one in which it is defined. A label is *local* if the object can be used only within the file in which it is defined. In most assemblers, labels are local by default and must be explicitly declared global. Subroutines and global variables require external labels since they are referenced from many files in a program. **Local labels** hide names that should not be visible to other modules—for example, static functions in C, which can only be called by other functions in the same file. In addition, compiler-generated names—for example, a name for the instruction at the beginning of a loop—are local so that the compiler need not produce unique names in every file.

local label A label referring to an object that can be used only within the file in which it is defined.

Local and Global Labels

Consider the program in Figure B.1.4. The subroutine has an external (global) label `main`. It also contains two local labels—`loop` and `str`—that are only visible with this assembly language file. Finally, the routine also contains an unresolved reference to an external label `printf`, which is the library routine that prints values. Which labels in Figure B.1.4 could be referenced from another file?

EXAMPLE

Only global labels are visible outside a file, so the only label that could be referenced from another file is `main`.

ANSWER

Since the assembler processes each file in a program individually and in isolation, it only knows the addresses of local labels. The assembler depends on another tool, the linker, to combine a collection of object files and libraries into an executable file by resolving external labels. The assembler assists the linker by providing lists of labels and unresolved references.

However, even local labels present an interesting challenge to an assembler. Unlike names in most high-level languages, assembly labels may be used before they are defined. In the example, in Figure B.1.4, the label `str` is used by the `la` instruction before it is defined. The possibility of a **forward reference**, like this one, forces an assembler to translate a program in two steps: first find all labels and then produce instructions. In the example, when the assembler sees the `la` instruction, it does not know where the word labeled `str` is located or even whether `str` labels an instruction or datum.

forward reference A label that is used before it is defined.

An assembler's first pass reads each line of an assembly file and breaks it into its component pieces. These pieces, which are called *lexemes*, are individual words, numbers, and punctuation characters. For example, the line

```
ble    $t0, 100, loop
```

contains six lexemes: the opcode `ble`, the register specifier `$t0`, a comma, the number `100`, a comma, and the symbol `loop`.

symbol table A table that matches names of labels to the addresses of the memory words that instructions occupy.

If a line begins with a label, the assembler records in its **symbol table** the name of the label and the address of the memory word that the instruction occupies. The assembler then calculates how many words of memory the instruction on the current line will occupy. By keeping track of the instructions' sizes, the assembler can determine where the next instruction goes. To compute the size of a variable-length instruction, like those on the VAX, an assembler has to examine it in detail. However, fixed-length instructions, like those on MIPS, require only a cursory examination. The assembler performs a similar calculation to compute the space required for data statements. When the assembler reaches the end of an assembly file, the symbol table records the location of each label defined in the file.

The assembler uses the information in the symbol table during a second pass over the file, which actually produces machine code. The assembler again examines each line in the file. If the line contains an instruction, the assembler combines the binary representations of its opcode and operands (register specifiers or memory address) into a legal instruction. The process is similar to the one used in Section 2.5 in Chapter 2. Instructions and data words that reference an external symbol defined in another file cannot be completely assembled (they are unresolved), since the symbol's address is not in the symbol table. An assembler does not complain about unresolved references, since the corresponding label is likely to be defined in another file.

The BIG Picture

Assembly language is a programming language. Its principal difference from high-level languages such as BASIC, Java, and C is that assembly language provides only a few, simple types of data and control flow. Assembly language programs do not specify the type of value held in a variable. Instead, a programmer must apply the appropriate operations (e.g., integer or floating-point addition) to a value. In addition, in assembly language, programs must implement all control flow with *go to*s. Both factors make assembly language programming for any machine—MIPS or x86—more difficult and error-prone than writing in a high-level language.

Elaboration: If an assembler's speed is important, this two-step process can be done in one pass over the assembly file with a technique known as **backpatching**. In its pass over the file, the assembler builds a (possibly incomplete) binary representation of every instruction. If the instruction references a label that has not yet been defined, the assembler records the label and instruction in a table. When a label is defined, the assembler consults this table to find all instructions that contain a forward reference to the label. The assembler goes back and corrects their binary representation to incorporate the address of the label. Backpatching speeds assembly because the assembler only reads its input once. However, it requires an assembler to hold the entire binary representation of a program in memory so instructions can be backpatched. This requirement can limit the size of programs that can be assembled. The process is complicated by machines with several types of branches that span different ranges of instructions. When the assembler first sees an unresolved label in a branch instruction, it must either use the largest possible branch or risk having to go back and readjust many instructions to make room for a larger branch.

backpatching A method for translating from assembly language to machine instructions in which the assembler builds a (possibly incomplete) binary representation of every instruction in one pass over a program and then returns to fill in previously undefined labels.

Object File Format

Assemblers produce object files. An object file on UNIX contains six distinct sections (see Figure B.2.1):

- The *object file header* describes the size and position of the other pieces of the file.

- The **text segment** contains the machine language code for routines in the source file. These routines may be unexecutable because of unresolved references.

- The **data segment** contains a binary representation of the data in the source file. The data also may be incomplete because of unresolved references to labels in other files.

- The **relocation information** identifies instructions and data words that depend on **absolute addresses**. These references must change if portions of the program are moved in memory.

- The *symbol table* associates addresses with external labels in the source file and lists unresolved references.

- The *debugging information* contains a concise description of the way the program was compiled, so a debugger can find which instruction addresses correspond to lines in a source file and print the data structures in readable form.

The assembler produces an object file that contains a binary representation of the program and data and additional information to help link pieces of a program.

text segment The segment of a UNIX object file that contains the machine language code for routines in the source file.

data segment The segment of a UNIX object or executable file that contains a binary representation of the initialized data used by the program.

relocation information The segment of a UNIX object file that identifies instructions and data words that depend on absolute addresses.

absolute address A variable's or routine's actual address in memory.

Object file header	Text segment	Data segment	Relocation information	Symbol table	Debugging information

FIGURE B.2.1   Object file. A UNIX assembler produces an object file with six distinct sections.

This relocation information is necessary because the assembler does not know which memory locations a procedure or piece of data will occupy after it is linked with the rest of the program. Procedures and data from a file are stored in a contiguous piece of memory, but the assembler does not know where this memory will be located. The assembler also passes some symbol table entries to the linker. In particular, the assembler must record which external symbols are defined in a file and what unresolved references occur in a file.

Elaboration: For convenience, assemblers assume each file starts at the same address (for example, location 0) with the expectation that the linker will *relocate* the code and data when they are assigned locations in memory. The assembler produces *relocation information*, which contains an entry describing each instruction or data word in the file that references an absolute address. On MIPS, only the subroutine call, load, and store instructions reference absolute addresses. Instructions that use PC-relative addressing, such as branches, need not be relocated.

Additional Facilities

Assemblers provide a variety of convenience features that help make assembler programs shorter and easier to write, but do not fundamentally change assembly language. For example, *data layout directives* allow a programmer to describe data in a more concise and natural manner than its binary representation.

In Figure B.1.4, the directive

```
.asciiz "The sum from 0 .. 100 is %d\n"
```

stores characters from the string in memory. Contrast this line with the alternative of writing each character as its ASCII value (Figure 2.15 in Chapter 2 describes the ASCII encoding for characters):

```
.byte 84, 104, 101, 32, 115, 117, 109, 32
.byte 102, 114, 111, 109, 32, 48, 32, 46
.byte 46, 32, 49, 48, 48, 32, 105, 115
.byte 32, 37, 100, 10, 0
```

The .asciiz directive is easier to read because it represents characters as letters, not binary numbers. An assembler can translate characters to their binary representation much faster and more accurately than a human can. Data layout directives specify data in a human-readable form that the assembler translates to binary. Other layout directives are described in Section B.10.

String Directive

Define the sequence of bytes produced by this directive:

```
.asciiz "The quick brown fox jumps over the lazy dog"
```

EXAMPLE

```
.byte 84,  104, 101, 32,  113, 117, 105, 99
.byte 107, 32,  98,  114, 111, 119, 110, 32
.byte 102, 111, 120, 32,  106, 117, 109, 112
.byte 115, 32,  111, 118, 101, 114, 32,  116
.byte 104, 101, 32,  108, 97,  122, 121, 32
.byte 100, 111, 103, 0
```

ANSWER

Macro is a pattern-matching and replacement facility that provides a simple mechanism to name a frequently used sequence of instructions. Instead of repeatedly typing the same instructions every time they are used, a programmer invokes the macro and the assembler replaces the macro call with the corresponding sequence of instructions. Macros, like subroutines, permit a programmer to create and name a new abstraction for a common operation. Unlike subroutines, however, macros do not cause a subroutine call and return when the program runs, since a macro call is replaced by the macro's body when the program is assembled. After this replacement, the resulting assembly is indistinguishable from the equivalent program written without macros.

Macros

As an example, suppose that a programmer needs to print many numbers. The library routine `printf` accepts a format string and one or more values to print as its arguments. A programmer could print the integer in register $7 with the following instructions:

EXAMPLE

```
        .data
int_str: .asciiz "%d"
        .text
        la   $a0, int_str # Load string address
                          # into first arg
```

```
        mov    $a1, $7   # Load value into
                         # second arg
        jal    printf    # Call the printf routine
```

The .data directive tells the assembler to store the string in the program's data segment, and the .text directive tells the assembler to store the instructions in its text segment.

However, printing many numbers in this fashion is tedious and produces a verbose program that is difficult to understand. An alternative is to introduce a macro, print_int, to print an integer:

```
            .data
int_str:.asciiz "%d"
            .text
            .macro print_int($arg)
            la $a0, int_str # Load string address into
                            # first arg
            mov $a1, $arg   # Load macro's parameter
                            # ($arg) into second arg
            jal printf      # Call the printf routine
            .end_macro
    print_int($7)
```

formal parameter
A variable that is the argument to a procedure or macro; replaced by that argument once the macro is expanded.

The macro has a **formal parameter**, $arg, that names the argument to the macro. When the macro is expanded, the argument from a call is substituted for the formal parameter throughout the macro's body. Then the assembler replaces the call with the macro's newly expanded body. In the first call on print_int, the argument is $7, so the macro expands to the code

```
la  $a0, int_str
mov $a1, $7
jal printf
```

In a second call on print_int, say, print_int($t0), the argument is $t0, so the macro expands to

```
la  $a0, int_str
mov $a1, $t0
jal printf
```

What does the call print_int($a0) expand to?

```
la  $a0, int_str
mov $a1, $a0
jal printf
```

This example illustrates a drawback of macros. A programmer who uses this macro must be aware that print_int uses register $a0 and so cannot correctly print the value in that register.

Some assemblers also implement *pseudoinstructions,* which are instructions provided by an assembler but not implemented in hardware. Chapter 2 contains many examples of how the MIPS assembler synthesizes pseudoinstructions and addressing modes from the spartan MIPS hardware instruction set. For example, Section 2.7 in Chapter 2 describes how the assembler synthesizes the blt instruction from two other instructions: slt and bne. By extending the instruction set, the MIPS assembler makes assembly language programming easier without complicating the hardware. Many pseudoinstructions could also be simulated with macros, but the MIPS assembler can generate better code for these instructions because it can use a dedicated register ($at) and is able to optimize the generated code.

Hardware/ Software Interface

Elaboration: Assemblers *conditionally assemble* pieces of code, which permits a programmer to include or exclude groups of instructions when a program is assembled. This feature is particularly useful when several versions of a program differ by a small amount. Rather than keep these programs in separate files—which greatly complicates fixing bugs in the common code—programmers typically merge the versions into a single file. Code particular to one version is conditionally assembled, so it can be excluded when other versions of the program are assembled.

If macros and conditional assembly are useful, why do assemblers for UNIX systems rarely, if ever, provide them? One reason is that most programmers on these systems write programs in higher-level languages like C. Most of the assembly code is produced by compilers, which find it more convenient to repeat code rather than define macros. Another reason is that other tools on UNIX—such as cpp, the C preprocessor, or m4, a general macro processor—can provide macros and conditional assembly for assembly language programs.

B.3   Linkers

separate compilation
Splitting a program across
many files, each of which
can be compiled without
knowledge of what is in
the other files.

Separate compilation permits a program to be split into pieces that are stored in different files. Each file contains a logically related collection of subroutines and data structures that form a *module* in a larger program. A file can be compiled and assembled independently of other files, so changes to one module do not require recompiling the entire program. As we discussed above, separate compilation necessitates the additional step of linking to combine object files from separate modules and fix their unresolved references.

The tool that merges these files is the *linker* (see Figure B.3.1). It performs three tasks:

- Searches the program libraries to find library routines used by the program

- Determines the memory locations that code from each module will occupy and relocates its instructions by adjusting absolute references

- Resolves references among files

A linker's first task is to ensure that a program contains no undefined labels. The linker matches the external symbols and unresolved references from a program's files. An external symbol in one file resolves a reference from another file if both refer to a label with the same name. Unmatched references mean a symbol was used but not defined anywhere in the program.

Unresolved references at this stage in the linking process do not necessarily mean a programmer made a mistake. The program could have referenced a library routine whose code was not in the object files passed to the linker. After matching symbols in the program, the linker searches the system's program libraries to find predefined subroutines and data structures that the program references. The basic libraries contain routines that read and write data, allocate and deallocate memory, and perform numeric operations. Other libraries contain routines to access a database or manipulate terminal windows. A program that references an unresolved symbol that is not in any library is erroneous and cannot be linked. When the program uses a library routine, the linker extracts the routine's code from the library and incorporates it into the program text segment. This new routine, in turn, may depend on other library routines, so the linker continues to fetch other library routines until no external references are unresolved or a routine cannot be found.

If all external references are resolved, the linker next determines the memory locations that each module will occupy. Since the files were assembled in isolation,

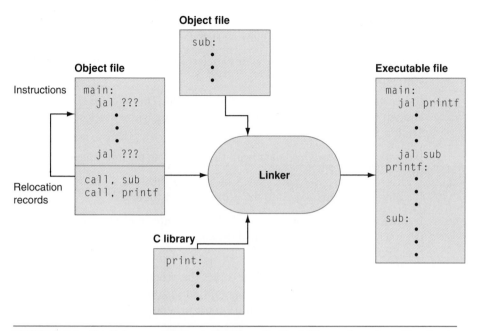

FIGURE B.3.1 The linker searches a collection of object files and program libraries to find nonlocal routines used in a program, combines them into a single executable file, and resolves references between routines in different files.

the assembler could not know where a module's instructions or data would be placed relative to other modules. When the linker places a module in memory, all absolute references must be *relocated* to reflect its true location. Since the linker has relocation information that identifies all relocatable references, it can efficiently find and backpatch these references.

The linker produces an executable file that can run on a computer. Typically, this file has the same format as an object file, except that it contains no unresolved references or relocation information.

B.4 Loading

A program that links without an error can be run. Before being run, the program resides in a file on secondary storage, such as a disk. On UNIX systems, the operating system kernel brings a program into memory and starts it running. To start a program, the operating system performs the following steps:

1. It reads the executable file's header to determine the size of the text and data segments.

2. It creates a new address space for the program. This address space is large enough to hold the text and data segments, along with a stack segment (see Section B.5).

3. It copies instructions and data from the executable file into the new address space.

4. It copies arguments passed to the program onto the stack.

5. It initializes the machine registers. In general, most registers are cleared, but the stack pointer must be assigned the address of the first free stack location (see Section B.5).

6. It jumps to a start-up routine that copies the program's arguments from the stack to registers and calls the program's main routine. If the main routine returns, the start-up routine terminates the program with the exit system call.

B.5   Memory Usage

The next few sections elaborate the description of the MIPS architecture presented earlier in the book. Earlier chapters focused primarily on hardware and its relationship with low-level software. These sections focus primarily on how assembly language programmers use MIPS hardware. These sections describe a set of conventions followed on many MIPS systems. For the most part, the hardware does not impose these conventions. Instead, they represent an agreement among programmers to follow the same set of rules so that software written by different people can work together and make effective use of MIPS hardware.

Systems based on MIPS processors typically divide memory into three parts (see Figure B.5.1). The first part, near the bottom of the address space (starting at address 400000_{hex}), is the *text segment*, which holds the program's instructions.

The second part, above the text segment, is the *data segment*, which is further divided into two parts. **Static data** (starting at address 10000000_{hex}) contains objects whose size is known to the compiler and whose lifetime—the interval during which a program can access them—is the program's entire execution. For example, in C, global variables are statically allocated, since they can be referenced

static data The portion of memory that contains data whose size is known to the compiler and whose lifetime is the program's entire execution.

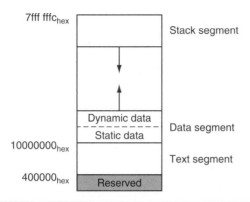

FIGURE B.5.1   Layout of memory.

anytime during a program's execution. The linker both assigns static objects to locations in the data segment and resolves references to these objects.

Immediately above static data is *dynamic data*. This data, as its name implies, is allocated by the program as it executes. In C programs, the malloc library routine

---

Because the data segment begins far above the program at address 10000000_{hex}, load and store instructions cannot directly reference data objects with their 16-bit offset fields (see Section 2.5 in Chapter 2). For example, to load the word in the data segment at address 10010020_{hex} into register $v0 requires two instructions:

Hardware/ Software Interface

```
lui  $s0, 0x1001 # 0x1001 means 1001 base 16
lw   $v0, 0x0020($s0) # 0x10010000 + 0x0020 = 0x10010020
```

(The *0x* before a number means that it is a hexadecimal value. For example, 0x8000 is 8000_{hex} or $32,768_{ten}$.)

To avoid repeating the lui instruction at every load and store, MIPS systems typically dedicate a register ($gp) as a *global pointer* to the static data segment. This register contains address 10008000_{hex}, so load and store instructions can use their signed 16-bit offset fields to access the first 64 KB of the static data segment. With this global pointer, we can rewrite the example as a single instruction:

```
lw $v0, 0x8020($gp)
```

Of course, a global pointer register makes addressing locations 10000000_{hex}– 10010000_{hex} faster than other heap locations. The MIPS compiler usually stores *global variables* in this area, because these variables have fixed locations and fit better than other global data, such as arrays.

finds and returns a new block of memory. Since a compiler cannot predict how much memory a program will allocate, the operating system expands the dynamic data area to meet demand. As the upward arrow in the figure indicates, malloc expands the dynamic area with the sbrk system call, which causes the operating system to add more pages to the program's virtual address space (see Section 5.4 in Chapter 5) immediately above the dynamic data segment.

stack segment The portion of memory used by a program to hold procedure call frames.

The third part, the program **stack segment**, resides at the top of the virtual address space (starting at address 7fffffff$_{hex}$). Like dynamic data, the maximum size of a program's stack is not known in advance. As the program pushes values on to the stack, the operating system expands the stack segment down toward the data segment.

This three-part division of memory is not the only possible one. However, it has two important characteristics: the two dynamically expandable segments are as far apart as possible, and they can grow to use a program's entire address space.

B.6   Procedure Call Convention

Conventions governing the use of registers are necessary when procedures in a program are compiled separately. To compile a particular procedure, a compiler must know which registers it may use and which registers are reserved for other procedures. Rules for using registers are called **register use** or **procedure call conventions**. As the name implies, these rules are, for the most part, conventions followed by software rather than rules enforced by hardware. However, most compilers and programmers try very hard to follow these conventions because violating them causes insidious bugs.

register use convention Also called **procedure call convention.** A software protocol governing the use of registers by procedures.

The calling convention described in this section is the one used by the gcc compiler. The native MIPS compiler uses a more complex convention that is slightly faster.

The MIPS CPU contains 32 general-purpose registers that are numbered 0–31. Register $0 always contains the hardwired value 0.

- Registers $at (1), $k0 (26), and $k1 (27) are reserved for the assembler and operating system and should not be used by user programs or compilers.

- Registers $a0–$a3 (4–7) are used to pass the first four arguments to routines (remaining arguments are passed on the stack). Registers $v0 and $v1 (2, 3) are used to return values from functions.

- Registers $t0–$t9 (8–15, 24, 25) are **caller-saved registers** that are used to hold temporary quantities that need not be preserved across calls (see Section 2.8 in Chapter 2).

- Registers $s0–$s7 (16–23) are **callee-saved registers** that hold long-lived values that should be preserved across calls.

- Register $gp (28) is a global pointer that points to the middle of a 64K block of memory in the static data segment.

- Register $sp (29) is the stack pointer, which points to the last location on the stack. Register $fp (30) is the frame pointer. The jal instruction writes register $ra (31), the return address from a procedure call. These two registers are explained in the next section.

caller-saved register A register saved by the routine being called.

callee-saved register A register saved by the routine making a procedure call.

The two-letter abbreviations and names for these registers—for example $sp for the stack pointer—reflect the registers' intended uses in the procedure call convention. In describing this convention, we will use the names instead of register numbers. Figure B.6.1 lists the registers and describes their intended uses.

Procedure Calls

This section describes the steps that occur when one procedure (the *caller*) invokes another procedure (the *callee*). Programmers who write in a high-level language (like C or Pascal) never see the details of how one procedure calls another, because the compiler takes care of this low-level bookkeeping. However, assembly language programmers must explicitly implement every procedure call and return.

Most of the bookkeeping associated with a call is centered around a block of memory called a **procedure call frame**. This memory is used for a variety of purposes:

- To hold values passed to a procedure as arguments

- To save registers that a procedure may modify, but which the procedure's caller does not want changed

- To provide space for variables local to a procedure

procedure call frame A block of memory that is used to hold values passed to a procedure as arguments, to save registers that a procedure may modify but that the procedure's caller does not want changed, and to provide space for variables local to a procedure.

In most programming languages, procedure calls and returns follow a strict last-in, first-out (LIFO) order, so this memory can be allocated and deallocated on a stack, which is why these blocks of memory are sometimes called stack frames.

Figure B.6.2 shows a typical stack frame. The frame consists of the memory between the frame pointer ($fp), which points to the first word of the frame, and the stack pointer ($sp), which points to the last word of the frame. The stack grows down from higher memory addresses, so the frame pointer points above the

Register name	Number	Usage
$zero	0	constant 0
$at	1	reserved for assembler
$v0	2	expression evaluation and results of a function
$v1	3	expression evaluation and results of a function
$a0	4	argument 1
$a1	5	argument 2
$a2	6	argument 3
$a3	7	argument 4
$t0	8	temporary (not preserved across call)
$t1	9	temporary (not preserved across call)
$t2	10	temporary (not preserved across call)
$t3	11	temporary (not preserved across call)
$t4	12	temporary (not preserved across call)
$t5	13	temporary (not preserved across call)
$t6	14	temporary (not preserved across call)
$t7	15	temporary (not preserved across call)
$s0	16	saved temporary (preserved across call)
$s1	17	saved temporary (preserved across call)
$s2	18	saved temporary (preserved across call)
$s3	19	saved temporary (preserved across call)
$s4	20	saved temporary (preserved across call)
$s5	21	saved temporary (preserved across call)
$s6	22	saved temporary (preserved across call)
$s7	23	saved temporary (preserved across call)
$t8	24	temporary (not preserved across call)
$t9	25	temporary (not preserved across call)
$k0	26	reserved for OS kernel
$k1	27	reserved for OS kernel
$gp	28	pointer to global area
$sp	29	stack pointer
$fp	30	frame pointer
$ra	31	return address (used by function call)

FIGURE B.6.1   MIPS registers and usage convention.

stack pointer. The executing procedure uses the frame pointer to quickly access values in its stack frame. For example, an argument in the stack frame can be loaded into register $v0 with the instruction

```
lw $v0, 0($fp)
```

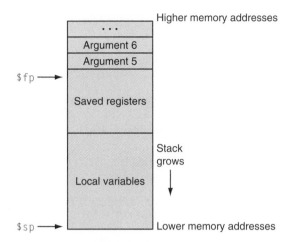

FIGURE B.6.2 Layout of a stack frame. The frame pointer ($fp) points to the first word in the currently executing procedure's stack frame. The stack pointer ($sp) points to the last word of the frame. The first four arguments are passed in registers, so the fifth argument is the first one stored on the stack.

A stack frame may be built in many different ways; however, the caller and callee must agree on the sequence of steps. The steps below describe the calling convention used on most MIPS machines. This convention comes into play at three points during a procedure call: immediately before the caller invokes the callee, just as the callee starts executing, and immediately before the callee returns to the caller. In the first part, the caller puts the procedure call arguments in standard places and invokes the callee to do the following:

1. Pass arguments. By convention, the first four arguments are passed in registers $a0–$a3. Any remaining arguments are pushed on the stack and appear at the beginning of the called procedure's stack frame.

2. Save caller-saved registers. The called procedure can use these registers ($a0–$a3 and $t0–$t9) without first saving their value. If the caller expects to use one of these registers after a call, it must save its value before the call.

3. Execute a jal instruction (see Section 2.8 of Chapter 2), which jumps to the callee's first instruction and saves the return address in register $ra.

Before a called routine starts running, it must take the following steps to set up its stack frame:

1. Allocate memory for the frame by subtracting the frame's size from the stack pointer.

2. Save callee-saved registers in the frame. A callee must save the values in these registers ($s0–$s7, $fp, and $ra) before altering them, since the caller expects to find these registers unchanged after the call. Register $fp is saved by every procedure that allocates a new stack frame. However, register $ra only needs to be saved if the callee itself makes a call. The other callee-saved registers that are used also must be saved.

3. Establish the frame pointer by adding the stack frame's size minus 4 to $sp and storing the sum in register $fp.

Hardware/ Software Interface

The MIPS register use convention provides callee- and caller-saved registers, because both types of registers are advantageous in different circumstances. Callee-saved registers are better used to hold long-lived values, such as variables from a user's program. These registers are only saved during a procedure call if the callee expects to use the register. On the other hand, caller-saved registers are better used to hold short-lived quantities that do not persist across a call, such as immediate values in an address calculation. During a call, the callee can also use these registers for short-lived temporaries.

Finally, the callee returns to the caller by executing the following steps:

1. If the callee is a function that returns a value, place the returned value in register $v0.

2. Restore all callee-saved registers that were saved upon procedure entry.

3. Pop the stack frame by adding the frame size to $sp.

4. Return by jumping to the address in register $ra.

recursive procedures
Procedures that call themselves either directly or indirectly through a chain of calls.

Elaboration: A programming language that does not permit **recursive procedures**—procedures that call themselves either directly or indirectly through a chain of calls—need not allocate frames on a stack. In a nonrecursive language, each procedure's frame may be statically allocated, since only one invocation of a procedure can be active at a time. Older versions of Fortran prohibited recursion, because statically allocated frames produced faster code on some older machines. However, on load store architectures like MIPS, stack frames may be just as fast, because a frame pointer register points directly to the active stack frame, which permits a single load or store instruction to access values in the frame. In addition, recursion is a valuable programming technique.

Procedure Call Example

As an example, consider the C routine

```
main ()
{
    printf ("The factorial of 10 is %d\n", fact (10));
}

int fact (int n)
{
    if (n < 1)
        return (1);
    else
        return (n * fact (n - 1));
}
```

which computes and prints 10! (the factorial of 10, $10! = 10 \times 9 \times \ldots \times 1$). fact is a recursive routine that computes $n!$ by multiplying n times $(n-1)!$. The assembly code for this routine illustrates how programs manipulate stack frames.

Upon entry, the routine main creates its stack frame and saves the two callee-saved registers it will modify: $fp and $ra. The frame is larger than required for these two register because the calling convention requires the minimum size of a stack frame to be 24 bytes. This minimum frame can hold four argument registers ($a0–$a3) and the return address $ra, padded to a double-word boundary (24 bytes). Since main also needs to save $fp, its stack frame must be two words larger (remember: the stack pointer is kept doubleword aligned).

```
        .text
        .globl main
main:
        subu  $sp,$sp,32     # Stack frame is 32 bytes long
        sw    $ra,20($sp)    # Save return address
        sw    $fp,16($sp)    # Save old frame pointer
        addiu $fp,$sp,28     # Set up frame pointer
```

The routine main then calls the factorial routine and passes it the single argument 10. After fact returns, main calls the library routine printf and passes it both a format string and the result returned from fact:

```
li      $a0,10          # Put argument (10) in $a0
jal     fact            # Call factorial function

la      $a0,$LC         # Put format string in $a0
move    $a1,$v0         # Move fact result to $a1
jal     printf          # Call the print function
```

Finally, after printing the factorial, main returns. But first, it must restore the registers it saved and pop its stack frame:

```
lw      $ra,20($sp)     # Restore return address
lw      $fp,16($sp)     # Restore frame pointer
addiu   $sp,$sp,32      # Pop stack frame
jr      $ra             # Return to caller

        .rdata
$LC:
        .ascii  "The factorial of 10 is %d\n\000"
```

The factorial routine is similar in structure to main. First, it creates a stack frame and saves the callee-saved registers it will use. In addition to saving $ra and $fp, fact also saves its argument ($a0), which it will use for the recursive call:

```
        .text
fact:
    subu    $sp,$sp,32      # Stack frame is 32 bytes long
    sw      $ra,20($sp)     # Save return address
    sw      $fp,16($sp)     # Save frame pointer
    addiu   $fp,$sp,28      # Set up frame pointer
    sw      $a0,0($fp)      # Save argument (n)
```

The heart of the fact routine performs the computation from the C program. It tests whether the argument is greater than 0. If not, the routine returns the value 1. If the argument is greater than 0, the routine recursively calls itself to compute fact(n-1) and multiplies that value times *n:*

```
    lw      $v0,0($fp)      # Load n
    bgtz    $v0,$L2         # Branch if n > 0
    li      $v0,1           # Return 1
    jr      $L1             # Jump to code to return

$L2:
    lw      $v1,0($fp)      # Load n
    subu    $v0,$v1,1       # Compute n - 1
    move    $a0,$v0         # Move value to $a0
```

```
jal      fact            # Call factorial function

lw       $v1,0($fp)      # Load n
mul      $v0,$v0,$v1     # Compute fact(n-1) * n
```

Finally, the factorial routine restores the callee-saved registers and returns the value in register $v0:

```
$L1:                     # Result is in $v0
    lw       $ra, 20($sp) # Restore $ra
    lw       $fp, 16($sp) # Restore $fp
    addiu    $sp, $sp, 32 # Pop stack
    jr       $ra          # Return to caller
```

Stack in Recursive Procedure

Figure B.6.3 shows the stack at the call fact(7). main runs first, so its frame is deepest on the stack. main calls fact(10), whose stack frame is next on the stack. Each invocation recursively invokes fact to compute the next-lowest factorial. The stack frames parallel the LIFO order of these calls. What does the stack look like when the call to fact(10) returns?

EXAMPLE

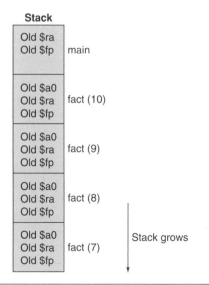

FIGURE B.6.3 Stack frames during the call of fact(7)**.**

ANSWER

Elaboration: The difference between the MIPS compiler and the gcc compiler is that the MIPS compiler usually does not use a frame pointer, so this register is available as another callee-saved register, $s8. This change saves a couple of instructions in the procedure call and return sequence. However, it complicates code generation, because a procedure must access its stack frame with $sp, whose value can change during a procedure's execution if values are pushed on the stack.

Another Procedure Call Example

As another example, consider the following routine that computes the tak function, which is a widely used benchmark created by Ikuo Takeuchi. This function does not compute anything useful, but is a heavily recursive program that illustrates the MIPS calling convention.

```
int tak (int x, int y, int z)
{
    if (y < x)
        return 1+ tak (tak (x - 1, y, z),
            tak (y - 1, z, x),
            tak (z - 1, x, y));
    else
        return z;
}

int main ()
{
    tak(18, 12, 6);
}
```

The assembly code for this program is shown below. The tak function first saves its return address in its stack frame and its arguments in callee-saved registers, since the routine may make calls that need to use registers $a0–$a2 and $ra. The function uses callee-saved registers, since they hold values that persist over the lifetime of the function, which includes several calls that could potentially modify registers.

```
        .text
        .globl   tak

tak:
        subu     $sp, $sp, 40
        sw       $ra, 32($sp)

        sw       $s0, 16($sp)       # x
        move     $s0, $a0
        sw       $s1, 20($sp)       # y
        move     $s1, $a1
        sw       $s2, 24($sp)       # z
        move     $s2, $a2
        sw       $s3, 28($sp)       # temporary
```

The routine then begins execution by testing if $y < x$. If not, it branches to label L1, which is shown below.

```
        bge      $s1, $s0, L1       # if (y < x)
```

If $y < x$, then it executes the body of the routine, which contains four recursive calls. The first call uses almost the same arguments as its parent:

```
        addiu    $a0, $s0, -1
        move     $a1, $s1
        move     $a2, $s2
        jal      tak                # tak (x - 1, y, z)
        move     $s3, $v0
```

Note that the result from the first recursive call is saved in register $s3, so that it can be used later.

The function now prepares arguments for the second recursive call.

```
        addiu    $a0, $s1, -1
        move     $a1, $s2
        move     $a2, $s0
        jal      tak                # tak (y - 1, z, x)
```

In the instructions below, the result from this recursive call is saved in register $s0. But first we need to read, for the last time, the saved value of the first argument from this register.

```
addiu      $a0, $s2, -1
move       $a1, $s0
move       $a2, $s1
move       $s0, $v0
jal        tak                    # tak (z - 1, x, y)
```

After the three inner recursive calls, we are ready for the final recursive call. After the call, the function's result is in $v0 and control jumps to the function's epilogue.

```
move       $a0, $s3
move       $a1, $s0
move       $a2, $v0
jal        tak                    # tak (tak(...), tak(...), tak(...))
addiu      $v0, $v0, 1
j          L2
```

This code at label L1 is the consequent of the *if-then-else* statement. It just moves the value of argument z into the return register and falls into the function epilogue.

```
L1:
      move       $v0, $s2
```

The code below is the function epilogue, which restores the saved registers and returns the function's result to its caller.

```
L2:
      lw         $ra, 32($sp)
      lw         $s0, 16($sp)
      lw         $s1, 20($sp)
      lw         $s2, 24($sp)
      lw         $s3, 28($sp)
      addiu      $sp, $sp, 40
      jr         $ra
```

The main routine calls the tak function with its initial arguments, then takes the computed result (7) and prints it using SPIM's system call for printing integers.

```
      .globl     main
main:
      subu       $sp, $sp, 24
      sw         $ra, 16($sp)

      li         $a0, 18
      li         $a1, 12
```

```
li      $a2, 6
jal     tak                     # tak(18, 12, 6)

move    $a0, $v0
li      $v0, 1                  # print_int syscall
syscall

lw      $ra, 16($sp)
addiu   $sp, $sp, 24
jr      $ra
```

B.7   Exceptions and Interrupts

Section 4.9 of Chapter 4 describes the MIPS exception facility, which responds both to exceptions caused by errors during an instruction's execution and to external interrupts caused by I/O devices. This section describes exception and **interrupt handling** in more detail.[1] In MIPS processors, a part of the CPU called *coprocessor 0* records the information the software needs to handle exceptions and interrupts. The MIPS simulator SPIM does not implement all of coprocessor 0's registers, since many are not useful in a simulator or are part of the memory system, which SPIM does not implement. However, SPIM does provide the following coprocessor 0 registers:

interrupt handler A piece of code that is run as a result of an exception or an interrupt.

Register name	Register number	Usage
BadVAddr	8	memory address at which an offending memory reference occurred
Count	9	timer
Compare	11	value compared against timer that causes interrupt when they match
Status	12	interrupt mask and enable bits
Cause	13	exception type and pending interrupt bits
EPC	14	address of instruction that caused exception
Config	16	configuration of machine

---

1. This section discusses exceptions in the MIPS-32 architecture, which is what SPIM implements in Version 7.0 and later. Earlier versions of SPIM implemented the MIPS-1 architecture, which handled exceptions slightly differently. Converting programs from these versions to run on MIPS-32 should not be difficult, as the changes are limited to the Status and Cause register fields and the replacement of the rfe instruction by the eret instruction.

These seven registers are part of coprocessor 0's register set. They are accessed by the mfc0 and mtc0 instructions. After an exception, register EPC contains the address of the instruction that was executing when the exception occurred. If the exception was caused by an external interrupt, then the instruction will not have started executing. All other exceptions are caused by the execution of the instruction at EPC, except when the offending instruction is in the delay slot of a branch or jump. In that case, EPC points to the branch or jump instruction and the BD bit is set in the Cause register. When that bit is set, the exception handler must look at EPC + 4 for the offending instruction. However, in either case, an exception handler properly resumes the program by returning to the instruction at EPC.

If the instruction that caused the exception made a memory access, register BadVAddr contains the referenced memory location's address.

The Count register is a timer that increments at a fixed rate (by default, every 10 milliseconds) while SPIM is running. When the value in the Count register equals the value in the Compare register, a hardware interrupt at priority level 5 occurs.

Figure B.7.1 shows the subset of the Status register fields implemented by the MIPS simulator SPIM. The interrupt mask field contains a bit for each of the six hardware and two software interrupt levels. A mask bit that is 1 allows interrupts at that level to interrupt the processor. A mask bit that is 0 disables interrupts at that level. When an interrupt arrives, it sets its interrupt pending bit in the Cause register, even if the mask bit is disabled. When an interrupt is pending, it will interrupt the processor when its mask bit is subsequently enabled.

The user mode bit is 0 if the processor is running in kernel mode and 1 if it is running in user mode. On SPIM, this bit is fixed at 1, since the SPIM processor does not implement kernel mode. The exception level bit is normally 0, but is set to 1 after an exception occurs. When this bit is 1, interrupts are disabled and the EPC is not updated if another exception occurs. This bit prevents an exception handler from being disturbed by an interrupt or exception, but it should be reset when the handler finishes. If the interrupt enable bit is 1, interrupts are allowed. If it is 0, they are disabled.

Figure B.7.2 shows the subset of Cause register fields that SPIM implements. The branch delay bit is 1 if the last exception occurred in an instruction executed in the delay slot of a branch. The interrupt pending bits become 1 when an interrupt

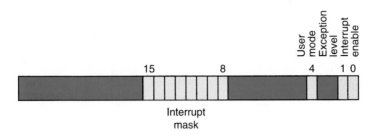

FIGURE B.7.1   The Status register.

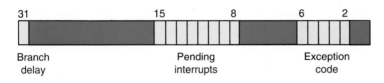

FIGURE B.7.2   The Cause register.

is raised at a given hardware or software level. The exception code register describes the cause of an exception through the following codes:

Number	Name	Cause of exception
0	Int	interrupt (hardware)
4	AdEL	address error exception (load or instruction fetch)
5	AdES	address error exception (store)
6	IBE	bus error on instruction fetch
7	DBE	bus error on data load or store
8	Sys	syscall exception
9	Bp	breakpoint exception
10	RI	reserved instruction exception
11	CpU	coprocessor unimplemented
12	Ov	arithmetic overflow exception
13	Tr	trap
15	FPE	floating point

Exceptions and interrupts cause a MIPS processor to jump to a piece of code, at address 80000180_{hex} (in the kernel, not user address space), called an *exception handler*. This code examines the exception's cause and jumps to an appropriate point in the operating system. The operating system responds to an exception either by terminating the process that caused the exception or by performing some action. A process that causes an error, such as executing an unimplemented instruction, is killed by the operating system. On the other hand, other exceptions such as page faults are requests from a process to the operating system to perform a service, such as bringing in a page from disk. The operating system processes these requests and resumes the process. The final type of exceptions are interrupts from external devices. These generally cause the operating system to move data to or from an I/O device and resume the interrupted process.

The code in the example below is a simple exception handler, which invokes a routine to print a message at each exception (but not interrupts). This code is similar to the exception handler (exceptions.s) used by the SPIM simulator.

EXAMPLE

Exception Handler

The exception handler first saves register $at, which is used in pseudo-instructions in the handler code, then saves $a0 and $a1, which it later uses to pass arguments. The exception handler cannot store the old values from these registers on the stack, as would an ordinary routine, because the cause of the exception might have been a memory reference that used a bad value (such as 0) in the stack pointer. Instead, the exception handler stores these registers in an exception handler register ($k1, since it can't access memory without using $at) and two memory locations (save0 and save1). If the exception routine itself could be interrupted, two locations would not be enough since the second exception would overwrite values saved during the first exception. However, this simple exception handler finishes running before it enables interrupts, so the problem does not arise.

```
.ktext 0x80000180
mov $k1, $at    # Save $at register
sw  $a0, save0  # Handler is not re-entrant and can't use
sw  $a1, save1  # stack to save $a0, $a1
                # Don't need to save $k0/$k1
```

The exception handler then moves the Cause and EPC registers into CPU registers. The Cause and EPC registers are not part of the CPU register set. Instead, they are registers in coprocessor 0, which is the part of the CPU that handles exceptions. The instruction mfc0 $k0, $13 moves coprocessor 0's register 13 (the Cause register) into CPU register $k0. Note that the exception handler need not save registers $k0 and $k1, because user programs are not supposed to use these registers. The exception handler uses the value from the Cause register to test whether the exception was caused by an interrupt (see the preceding table). If so, the exception is ignored. If the exception was not an interrupt, the handler calls print_excp to print a message.

```
mfc0    $k0, $13        # Move Cause into $k0

srl     $a0, $k0, 2     # Extract ExcCode field
andi    $a0, $a0, 0xf

bgtz    $a0, done       # Branch if ExcCode is Int (0)

mov     $a0, $k0        # Move Cause into $a0
mfco    $a1, $14        # Move EPC into $a1
jal     print_excp      # Print exception error message
```

Before returning, the exception handler clears the Cause register; resets the Status register to enable interrupts and clear the EXL bit, which allows subsequent exceptions to change the EPC register; and restores registers $a0, $a1, and $at. It then executes the eret (exception return) instruction, which returns to the instruction pointed to by EPC. This exception handler returns to the instruction following the one that caused the exception, so as to not re-execute the faulting instruction and cause the same exception again.

```
done:   mfc0    $k0, $14        # Bump EPC
        addiu   $k0, $k0, 4     # Do not re-execute
                                # faulting instruction
        mtc0    $k0, $14        # EPC

        mtc0    $0, $13         # Clear Cause register

        mfc0    $k0, $12        # Fix Status register
        andi    $k0, 0xfffd     # Clear EXL bit
        ori     $k0, 0x1        # Enable interrupts
        mtc0    $k0, $12

        lw      $a0, save0      # Restore registers
        lw      $a1, save1
        mov     $at, $k1

        eret                    # Return to EPC

        .kdata
save0:  .word 0
save1:  .word 0
```

Elaboration: On real MIPS processors, the return from an exception handler is more complex. The exception handler cannot always jump to the instruction following EPC. For example, if the instruction that caused the exception was in a branch instruction's delay slot (see Chapter 4), the next instruction to execute may not be the following instruction in memory.

B.8   Input and Output

SPIM simulates one I/O device: a memory-mapped console on which a program can read and write characters. When a program is running, SPIM connects its own terminal (or a separate console window in the X-window version xspim or the Windows version PCSpim) to the processor. A MIPS program running on SPIM can read the characters that you type. In addition, if the MIPS program writes characters to the terminal, they appear on SPIM's terminal or console window. One exception to this rule is control-C: this character is not passed to the program, but instead causes SPIM to stop and return to command mode. When the program stops running (for example, because you typed control-C or because the program hit a breakpoint), the terminal is reconnected to SPIM so you can type SPIM commands.

To use memory-mapped I/O (see below), spim or xspim must be started with the -mapped_io flag. PCSpim can enable memory-mapped I/O through a command line flag or the "Settings" dialog.

The terminal device consists of two independent units: a *receiver* and a *transmitter*. The receiver reads characters from the keyboard. The transmitter displays characters on the console. The two units are completely independent. This means, for example, that characters typed at the keyboard are not automatically echoed on the display. Instead, a program echoes a character by reading it from the receiver and writing it to the transmitter.

A program controls the terminal with four memory-mapped device registers, as shown in Figure B.8.1. "Memory-mapped" means that each register appears as a special memory location. The *Receiver Control register* is at location ffff0000$_{hex}$. Only two of its bits are actually used. Bit 0 is called "ready": if it is 1, it means that a character has arrived from the keyboard but has not yet been read from the Receiver Data register. The ready bit is read-only: writes to it are ignored. The ready bit changes from 0 to 1 when a character is typed at the keyboard, and it changes from 1 to 0 when the character is read from the Receiver Data register.

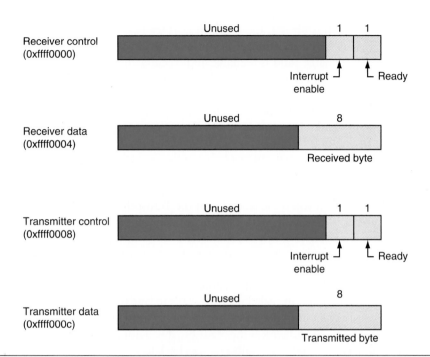

FIGURE B.8.1 The terminal is controlled by four device registers, each of which appears as a memory location at the given address. Only a few bits of these registers are actually used. The others always read as 0s and are ignored on writes.

Bit 1 of the Receiver Control register is the keyboard "interrupt enable." This bit may be both read and written by a program. The interrupt enable is initially 0. If it is set to 1 by a program, the terminal requests an interrupt at hardware level 1 whenever a character is typed, and the ready bit becomes 1. However, for the interrupt to affect the processor, interrupts must also be enabled in the Status register (see Section B.7). All other bits of the Receiver Control register are unused.

The second terminal device register is the *Receiver Data register* (at address ffff0004$_\text{hex}$). The low-order eight bits of this register contain the last character typed at the keyboard. All other bits contain 0s. This register is read-only and changes only when a new character is typed at the keyboard. Reading the Receiver Data register resets the ready bit in the Receiver Control register to 0. The value in this register is undefined if the Receiver Control register is 0.

The third terminal device register is the *Transmitter Control register* (at address ffff0008$_\text{hex}$). Only the low-order two bits of this register are used. They behave much like the corresponding bits of the Receiver Control register. Bit 0 is called "ready" and is read-only. If this bit is 1, the transmitter is ready to accept a new character for output. If it is 0, the transmitter is still busy writing the previous character. Bit 1 is "interrupt enable" and is readable and writable. If this bit is set to 1, then the terminal requests an interrupt at hardware level 0 whenever the transmitter is ready for a new character, and the ready bit becomes 1.

The final device register is the *Transmitter Data register* (at address ffff000c$_{hex}$). When a value is written into this location, its low-order eight bits (i.e., an ASCII character as in Figure 2.15 in Chapter 2) are sent to the console. When the Transmitter Data register is written, the ready bit in the Transmitter Control register is reset to 0. This bit stays 0 until enough time has elapsed to transmit the character to the terminal; then the ready bit becomes 1 again. The Transmitter Data register should only be written when the ready bit of the Transmitter Control register is 1. If the transmitter is not ready, writes to the Transmitter Data register are ignored (the write appears to succeed but the character is not output).

Real computers require time to send characters to a console or terminal. These time lags are simulated by SPIM. For example, after the transmitter starts to write a character, the transmitter's ready bit becomes 0 for a while. SPIM measures time in instructions executed, not in real clock time. This means that the transmitter does not become ready again until the processor executes a fixed number of instructions. If you stop the machine and look at the ready bit, it will not change. However, if you let the machine run, the bit eventually changes back to 1.

B.9 SPIM

SPIM is a software simulator that runs assembly language programs written for processors that implement the MIPS-32 architecture, specifically Release 1 of this architecture with a fixed memory mapping, no caches, and only coprocessors 0 and 1.[2] SPIM's name is just MIPS spelled backwards. SPIM can read and immediately execute assembly language files. SPIM is a self-contained system for running

---

2. Earlier versions of SPIM (before 7.0) implemented the MIPS-1 architecture used in the original MIPS R2000 processors. This architecture is almost a proper subset of the MIPS-32 architecture, with the difference being the manner in which exceptions are handled. MIPS-32 also introduced approximately 60 new instructions, which are supported by SPIM. Programs that ran on the earlier versions of SPIM and did not use exceptions should run unmodified on newer versions of SPIM. Programs that used exceptions will require minor changes.

MIPS programs. It contains a debugger and provides a few operating system–like services. SPIM is much slower than a real computer (100 or more times). However, its low cost and wide availability cannot be matched by real hardware!

An obvious question is, "Why use a simulator when most people have PCs that contain processors that run significantly faster than SPIM?" One reason is that the processor in PCs are Intel 80x86s, whose architecture is far less regular and far more complex to understand and program than MIPS processors. The MIPS architecture may be the epitome of a simple, clean RISC machine.

In addition, simulators can provide a better environment for assembly programming than an actual machine because they can detect more errors and provide a better interface than an actual computer.

Finally, simulators are useful tools in studying computers and the programs that run on them. Because they are implemented in software, not silicon, simulators can be examined and easily modified to add new instructions, build new systems such as multiprocessors, or simply collect data.

Simulation of a Virtual Machine

The basic MIPS architecture is difficult to program directly because of delayed branches, delayed loads, and restricted address modes. This difficulty is tolerable since these computers were designed to be programmed in high-level languages and present an interface designed for compilers rather than assembly language programmers. A good part of the programming complexity results from delayed instructions. A *delayed branch* requires two cycles to execute (see the *Elaborations* on pages 343 and 381 of Chapter 4). In the second cycle, the instruction immediately following the branch executes. This instruction can perform useful work that normally would have been done before the branch. It can also be a nop (no operation) that does nothing. Similarly, *delayed loads* require two cycles to bring a value from memory, so the instruction immediately following a load cannot use the value (see Section 4.2 of Chapter 4).

MIPS wisely chose to hide this complexity by having its assembler implement a **virtual machine.** This virtual computer appears to have nondelayed branches and loads and a richer instruction set than the actual hardware. The assembler *reorganizes* (rearranges) instructions to fill the delay slots. The virtual computer also provides *pseudoinstructions*, which appear as real instructions in assembly language programs. The hardware, however, knows nothing about pseudoinstructions, so the assembler must translate them into equivalent sequences of actual machine instructions. For example, the MIPS hardware only provides instructions to branch when a register is equal to or not equal to 0. Other conditional branches, such as one that branches when one register is greater than another, are synthesized by comparing the two registers and branching when the result of the comparison is true (nonzero).

virtual machine A virtual computer that appears to have nondelayed branches and loads and a richer instruction set than the actual hardware.

By default, SPIM simulates the richer virtual machine, since this is the machine that most programmers will find useful. However, SPIM can also simulate the delayed branches and loads in the actual hardware. Below, we describe the virtual machine and only mention in passing features that do not belong to the actual hardware. In doing so, we follow the convention of MIPS assembly language programmers (and compilers), who routinely use the extended machine as if it was implemented in silicon.

Getting Started with SPIM

The rest of this appendix introduces SPIM and the MIPS R2000 Assembly language. Many details should never concern you; however, the sheer volume of information can sometimes obscure the fact that SPIM is a simple, easy-to-use program. This section starts with a quick tutorial on using SPIM, which should enable you to load, debug, and run simple MIPS programs.

SPIM comes in different versions for different types of computer systems. The one constant is the simplest version, called spim, which is a command-line-driven program that runs in a console window. It operates like most programs of this type: you type a line of text, hit the return key, and spim executes your command. Despite its lack of a fancy interface, spim can do everything that its fancy cousins can do.

There are two fancy cousins to spim. The version that runs in the X-windows environment of a UNIX or Linux system is called xspim. xspim is an easier program to learn and use than spim, because its commands are always visible on the screen and because it continually displays the machine's registers and memory. The other fancy version is called PCspim and runs on Microsoft Windows. The UNIX and Windows versions of **SPIM** ⊚ are on the CD (click on Tutorials). Tutorials on xspim, pcSpim, spim, and **SPIM command-line options** ⊚ are on the CD (click on Software).

If you are going to run SPIM on a PC running Microsoft Windows, you should first look at the tutorial on **PCSpim** ⊚ on the CD. If you are going to run SPIM on a computer running UNIX or Linux, you should read the tutorial on **xspim** ⊚ (click on Tutorials).

Surprising Features

Although SPIM faithfully simulates the MIPS computer, SPIM is a simulator, and certain things are not identical to an actual computer. The most obvious differences are that instruction timing and the memory systems are not identical. SPIM does not simulate caches or memory latency, nor does it accurately reflect floating-point operation or multiply and divide instruction delays. In addition, the floating-point instructions do not detect many error conditions, which would cause exceptions on a real machine.

Another surprise (which occurs on the real machine as well) is that a pseudo-instruction expands to several machine instructions. When you single-step or examine memory, the instructions that you see are different from the source program. The correspondence between the two sets of instructions is fairly simple, since SPIM does not reorganize instructions to fill delay slots.

Byte Order

Processors can number bytes within a word so the byte with the lowest number is either the leftmost or rightmost one. The convention used by a machine is called its *byte order*. MIPS processors can operate with either *big-endian* or *little-endian* byte order. For example, in a big-endian machine, the directive .byte 0, 1, 2, 3 would result in a memory word containing

Byte #			
0	1	2	3

while in a little-endian machine, the word would contain

Byte #			
3	2	1	0

SPIM operates with both byte orders. SPIM's byte order is the same as the byte order of the underlying machine that runs the simulator. For example, on an Intel 80x86, SPIM is little-endian, while on a Macintosh or Sun SPARC, SPIM is big-endian.

System Calls

SPIM provides a small set of operating system–like services through the system call (syscall) instruction. To request a service, a program loads the system call code (see Figure B.9.1) into register $v0 and arguments into registers $a0–$a3 (or $f12 for floating-point values). System calls that return values put their results in register $v0 (or $f0 for floating-point results). For example, the following code prints "the answer = 5":

```
        .data
str:
        .asciiz "the answer = "
        .text
```

Service	System call code	Arguments	Result
print_int	1	$a0 = integer	
print_float	2	$f12 = float	
print_double	3	$f12 = double	
print_string	4	$a0 = string	
read_int	5		integer (in $v0)
read_float	6		float (in $f0)
read_double	7		double (in $f0)
read_string	8	$a0 = buffer, $a1 = length	
sbrk	9	$a0 = amount	address (in $v0)
exit	10		
print_char	11	$a0 = char	
read_char	12		char (in $v0)
open	13	$a0 = filename (string), $a1 = flags, $a2 = mode	file descriptor (in $a0)
read	14	$a0 = file descriptor, $a1 = buffer, $a2 = length	num chars read (in $a0)
write	15	$a0 = file descriptor, $a1 = buffer, $a2 = length	num chars written (in $a0)
close	16	$a0 = file descriptor	
exit2	17	$a0 = result	

FIGURE B.9.1   System services.

```
li      $v0, 4      # system call code for print_str
la      $a0, str    # address of string to print
syscall             # print the string

li      $v0, 1      # system call code for print_int
li      $a0, 5      # integer to print
syscall             # print it
```

The print_int system call is passed an integer and prints it on the console. print_float prints a single floating-point number; print_double prints a double precision number; and print_string is passed a pointer to a null-terminated string, which it writes to the console.

The system calls read_int, read_float, and read_double to read an entire line of input up to and including the newline. Characters following the number are ignored. read_string has the same semantics as the UNIX library routine fgets. It reads up to $n - 1$ characters into a buffer and terminates the string with a null byte. If fewer than $n - 1$ characters are on the current line, read_string reads up to and including the newline and again null-terminates the string.

Warning: Programs that use these syscalls to read from the terminal should not use memory-mapped I/O (see Section B.8).

sbrk returns a pointer to a block of memory containing *n* additional bytes. exit stops the program SPIM is running. exit2 terminates the SPIM program, and the argument to exit2 becomes the value returned when the SPIM simulator itself terminates.

print_char and read_char write and read a single character. open, read, write, and close are the standard UNIX library calls.

B.10   MIPS R2000 Assembly Language

A MIPS processor consists of an integer processing unit (the CPU) and a collection of coprocessors that perform ancillary tasks or operate on other types of data, such as floating-point numbers (see Figure B.10.1). SPIM simulates two coprocessors. Coprocessor 0 handles exceptions and interrupts. Coprocessor 1 is the floating-point unit. SPIM simulates most aspects of this unit.

Addressing Modes

MIPS is a load store architecture, which means that only load and store instructions access memory. Computation instructions operate only on values in registers. The bare machine provides only one memory-addressing mode: c(rx), which uses the sum of the immediate c and register rx as the address. The virtual machine provides the following addressing modes for load and store instructions:

Format	Address computation
(register)	contents of register
imm	immediate
imm (register)	immediate + contents of register
label	address of label
label ± imm	address of label + or – immediate
label ± imm (register)	address of label + or – (immediate + contents of register)

Most load and store instructions operate only on aligned data. A quantity is *aligned* if its memory address is a multiple of its size in bytes. Therefore, a halfword

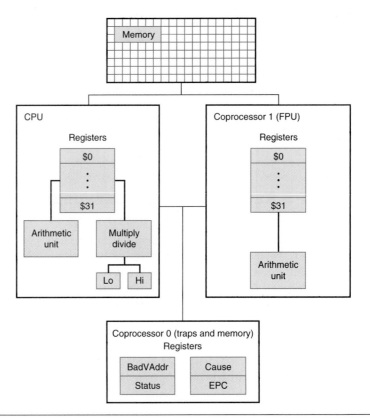

FIGURE B.10.1   MIPS R2000 CPU and FPU.

object must be stored at even addresses, and a full word object must be stored at addresses that are a multiple of four. However, MIPS provides some instructions to manipulate unaligned data (lwl, lwr, swl, and swr).

Elaboration: The MIPS assembler (and SPIM) synthesizes the more complex addressing modes by producing one or more instructions before the load or store to compute a complex address. For example, suppose that the label table referred to memory location 0×10000004 and a program contained the instruction

```
ld $a0, table + 4($a1)
```

The assembler would translate this instruction into the instructions

```
lui $at, 4096
addu $at, $at, $a1
lw $a0, 8($at)
```

The first instruction loads the upper bits of the label's address into register $at, which is the register that the assembler reserves for its own use. The second instruction adds the contents of register $a1 to the label's partial address. Finally, the load instruction uses the hardware address mode to add the sum of the lower bits of the label's address and the offset from the original instruction to the value in register $at.

Assembler Syntax

Comments in assembler files begin with a sharp sign (#). Everything from the sharp sign to the end of the line is ignored.

Identifiers are a sequence of alphanumeric characters, underbars (_), and dots (.) that do not begin with a number. Instruction opcodes are reserved words that *cannot* be used as identifiers. Labels are declared by putting them at the beginning of a line followed by a colon, for example:

```
        .data
item:   .word 1
        .text
        .globl  main      # Must be global
main:   lw          $t0, item
```

Numbers are base 10 by default. If they are preceded by *0x*, they are interpreted as hexadecimal. Hence, 256 and 0x100 denote the same value.

Strings are enclosed in double quotes ("). Special characters in strings follow the C convention:

- newline   \n

- tab   \t

- quote   \"

SPIM supports a subset of the MIPS assembler directives:

.align n	Align the next datum on a 2^n byte boundary. For example, .align 2 aligns the next value on a word boundary. .align 0 turns off automatic alignment of .half, .word, .float, and .double directives until the next .data or .kdata directive.
.ascii str	Store the string *str* in memory, but do not null-terminate it.

`.asciiz str`	Store the string *str* in memory and null-terminate it.
`.byte b1,..., bn`	Store the *n* values in successive bytes of memory.
`.data <addr>`	Subsequent items are stored in the data segment. If the optional argument *addr* is present, subsequent items are stored starting at address *addr*.
`.double d1,..., dn`	Store the *n* floating-point double precision numbers in successive memory locations.
`.extern sym size`	Declare that the datum stored at *sym* is *size* bytes large and is a global label. This directive enables the assembler to store the datum in a portion of the data segment that is efficiently accessed via register $gp.
`.float f1,..., fn`	Store the *n* floating-point single precision numbers in successive memory locations.
`.globl sym`	Declare that label *sym* is global and can be referenced from other files.
`.half h1,..., hn`	Store the *n* 16-bit quantities in successive memory halfwords.
`.kdata <addr>`	Subsequent data items are stored in the kernel data segment. If the optional argument *addr* is present, subsequent items are stored starting at address *addr*.
`.ktext <addr>`	Subsequent items are put in the kernel text segment. In SPIM, these items may only be instructions or words (see the `.word` directive below). If the optional argument *addr* is present, subsequent items are stored starting at address *addr*.
`.set noat and .set at`	The first directive prevents SPIM from complaining about subsequent instructions that use register $at. The second directive re-enables the warning. Since pseudoinstructions expand into code that uses register $at, programmers must be very careful about leaving values in this register.
`.space n`	Allocates *n* bytes of space in the current segment (which must be the data segment in SPIM).

`.text <addr>`	Subsequent items are put in the user text segment. In SPIM, these items may only be instructions or words (see the `.word` directive below). If the optional argument *addr* is present, subsequent items are stored starting at address *addr*.
`.word w1,..., wn`	Store the *n* 32-bit quantities in successive memory words.

SPIM does not distinguish various parts of the data segment (`.data`, `.rdata`, and `.sdata`).

Encoding MIPS Instructions

Figure B.10.2 explains how a MIPS instruction is encoded in a binary number. Each column contains instruction encodings for a field (a contiguous group of bits) from an instruction. The numbers at the left margin are values for a field. For example, the `j` opcode has a value of 2 in the opcode field. The text at the top of a column names a field and specifies which bits it occupies in an instruction. For example, the `op` field is contained in bits 26–31 of an instruction. This field encodes most instructions. However, some groups of instructions use additional fields to distinguish related instructions. For example, the different floating-point instructions are specified by bits 0–5. The arrows from the first column show which opcodes use these additional fields.

Instruction Format

The rest of this appendix describes both the instructions implemented by actual MIPS hardware and the pseudoinstructions provided by the MIPS assembler. The two types of instructions are easily distinguished. Actual instructions depict the fields in their binary representation. For example, in

Addition (with overflow)

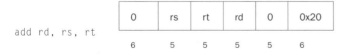

the `add` instruction consists of six fields. Each field's size in bits is the small number below the field. This instruction begins with six bits of 0s. Register specifiers begin with an *r*, so the next field is a 5-bit register specifier called `rs`. This is the same register that is the second argument in the symbolic assembly at the left of this line. Another common field is imm_{16}, which is a 16-bit immediate number.

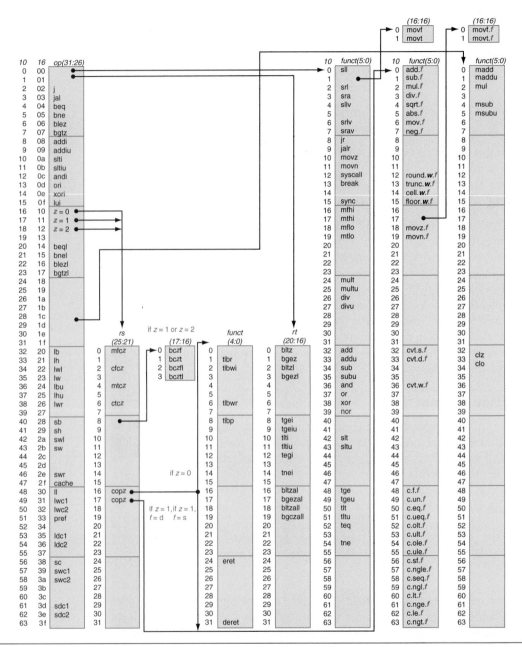

FIGURE B.10.2 MIPS opcode map. The values of each field are shown to its left. The first column shows the values in base 10, and the second shows base 16 for the op field (bits 31 to 26) in the third column. This op field completely specifies the MIPS operation except for six op values: 0, 1, 16, 17, 18, and 19. These operations are determined by other fields, identified by pointers. The last field (funct) uses "f" to mean "s" if rs = 16 and op = 17 or "d" if rs = 17 and op = 17. The second field (rs) uses "z" to mean "0", "1", "2", or "3" if op = 16, 17, 18, or 19, respectively. If rs = 16, the operation is specified elsewhere: if $z = 0$, the operations are specified in the fourth field (bits 4 to 0); if $z = 1$, then the operations are in the last field with f = s. If rs = 17 and $z = 1$, then the operations are in the last field with f = d.

Pseudoinstructions follow roughly the same conventions, but omit instruction encoding information. For example:

Multiply (without overflow)

```
mul rdest, rsrc1, src2       pseudoinstruction
```

In pseudoinstructions, `rdest` and `rsrc1` are registers and `src2` is either a register or an immediate value. In general, the assembler and SPIM translate a more general form of an instruction (e.g., add $v1, $a0, 0x55) to a specialized form (e.g., addi $v1, $a0, 0x55).

Arithmetic and Logical Instructions

Absolute value

```
abs rdest, rsrc       pseudoinstruction
```

Put the absolute value of register `rsrc` in register `rdest`.

Addition (with overflow)

```
add rd, rs, rt
```

0	rs	rt	rd	0	0x20
6	5	5	5	5	6

Addition (without overflow)

```
addu rd, rs, rt
```

0	rs	rt	rd	0	0x21
6	5	5	5	5	6

Put the sum of registers `rs` and `rt` into register `rd`.

Addition immediate (with overflow)

```
addi rt, rs, imm
```

8	rs	rt	imm
6	5	5	16

Addition immediate (without overflow)

```
addiu rt, rs, imm
```

9	rs	rt	imm
6	5	5	16

Put the sum of register `rs` and the sign-extended immediate into register `rt`.

AND

and rd, rs, rt

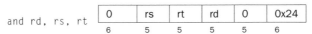

Put the logical AND of registers rs and rt into register rd.

AND immediate

andi rt, rs, imm

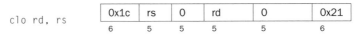

Put the logical AND of register rs and the zero-extended immediate into register rt.

Count leading ones

clo rd, rs

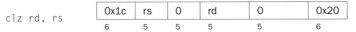

Count leading zeros

clz rd, rs

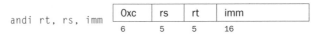

Count the number of leading ones (zeros) in the word in register rs and put the result into register rd. If a word is all ones (zeros), the result is 32.

Divide (with overflow)

div rs, rt

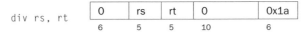

Divide (without overflow)

divu rs, rt

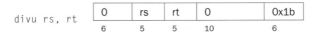

Divide register rs by register rt. Leave the quotient in register lo and the remainder in register hi. Note that if an operand is negative, the remainder is unspecified by the MIPS architecture and depends on the convention of the machine on which SPIM is run.

Divide (with overflow)

```
div rdest, rsrc1, src2       pseudoinstruction
```

Divide (without overflow)

```
divu rdest, rsrc1, src2      pseudoinstruction
```

Put the quotient of register rsrc1 and src2 into register rdest.

Multiply

```
mult rs, rt
```

0	rs	rt	0	0x18
6	5	5	10	6

Unsigned multiply

```
multu rs, rt
```

0	rs	rt	0	0x19
6	5	5	10	6

Multiply registers rs and rt. Leave the low-order word of the product in register lo and the high-order word in register hi.

Multiply (without overflow)

```
mul rd, rs, rt
```

0x1c	rs	rt	rd	0	2
6	5	5	5	5	6

Put the low-order 32 bits of the product of rs and rt into register rd.

Multiply (with overflow)

```
mulo rdest, rsrc1, src2              pseudoinstruction
```

Unsigned multiply (with overflow)

```
mulou rdest, rsrc1, src2             pseudoinstruction
```

Put the low-order 32 bits of the product of register rsrc1 and src2 into register rdest.

Multiply add

madd rs, rt

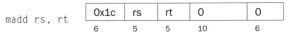

0x1c	rs	rt	0	0
6	5	5	10	6

Unsigned multiply add

maddu rs, rt

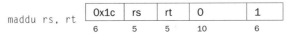

0x1c	rs	rt	0	1
6	5	5	10	6

Multiply registers rs and rt and add the resulting 64-bit product to the 64-bit value in the concatenated registers lo and hi.

Multiply subtract

msub rs, rt

0x1c	rs	rt	0	4
6	5	5	10	6

Unsigned multiply subtract

msub rs, rt

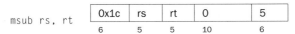

0x1c	rs	rt	0	5
6	5	5	10	6

Multiply registers rs and rt and subtract the resulting 64-bit product from the 64-bit value in the concatenated registers lo and hi.

Negate value (with overflow)

neg rdest, rsrc   *pseudoinstruction*

Negate value (without overflow)

negu rdest, rsrc   *pseudoinstruction*

Put the negative of register rsrc into register rdest.

NOR

nor rd, rs, rt

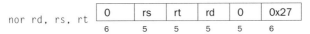

0	rs	rt	rd	0	0x27
6	5	5	5	5	6

Put the logical NOR of registers rs and rt into register rd.

NOT

```
not rdest, rsrc                    pseudoinstruction
```

Put the bitwise logical negation of register `rsrc` into register `rdest`.

OR

```
or rd, rs, rt
```

0	rs	rt	rd	0	0x25
6	5	5	5	5	6

Put the logical OR of registers `rs` and `rt` into register `rd`.

OR immediate

```
ori rt, rs, imm
```

0xd	rs	rt	imm
6	5	5	16

Put the logical OR of register `rs` and the zero-extended immediate into register `rt`.

Remainder

```
rem rdest, rsrc1, rsrc2            pseudoinstruction
```

Unsigned remainder

```
remu rdest, rsrc1, rsrc2           pseudoinstruction
```

Put the remainder of register `rsrc1` divided by register `rsrc2` into register `rdest`. Note that if an operand is negative, the remainder is unspecified by the MIPS architecture and depends on the convention of the machine on which SPIM is run.

Shift left logical

```
sll rd, rt, shamt
```

0	rs	rt	rd	shamt	0
6	5	5	5	5	6

Shift left logical variable

```
sllv rd, rt, rs
```

0	rs	rt	rd	0	4
6	5	5	5	5	6

Shift right arithmetic

sra rd, rt, shamt

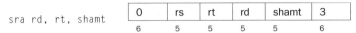

0	rs	rt	rd	shamt	3
6	5	5	5	5	6

Shift right arithmetic variable

srav rd, rt, rs

0	rs	rt	rd	0	7
6	5	5	5	5	6

Shift right logical

srl rd, rt, shamt

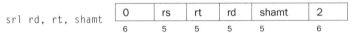

0	rs	rt	rd	shamt	2
6	5	5	5	5	6

Shift right logical variable

srlv rd, rt, rs

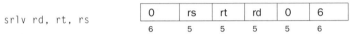

0	rs	rt	rd	0	6
6	5	5	5	5	6

Shift register rt left (right) by the distance indicated by immediate shamt or the register rs and put the result in register rd. Note that argument rs is ignored for sll, sra, and srl.

Rotate left

rol rdest, rsrc1, rsrc2   *pseudoinstruction*

Rotate right

ror rdest, rsrc1, rsrc2   *pseudoinstruction*

Rotate register rsrc1 left (right) by the distance indicated by rsrc2 and put the result in register rdest.

Subtract (with overflow)

sub rd, rs, rt

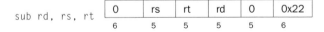

0	rs	rt	rd	0	0x22
6	5	5	5	5	6

Subtract (without overflow)

subu rd, rs, rt

0	rs	rt	rd	0	0x23
6	5	5	5	5	6

Put the difference of registers rs and rt into register rd.

Exclusive OR

xor rd, rs, rt

0	rs	rt	rd	0	0x26
6	5	5	5	5	6

Put the logical XOR of registers rs and rt into register rd.

XOR immediate

xori rt, rs, imm

0xe	rs	rt	Imm
6	5	5	16

Put the logical XOR of register rs and the zero-extended immediate into register rt.

Constant-Manipulating Instructions

Load upper immediate

lui rt, imm

0xf	0	rt	imm
6	5	5	16

Load the lower halfword of the immediate imm into the upper halfword of register rt. The lower bits of the register are set to 0.

Load immediate

li rdest, imm   *pseudoinstruction*

Move the immediate imm into register rdest.

Comparison Instructions

Set less than

slt rd, rs, rt

0	rs	rt	rd	0	0x2a
6	5	5	5	5	6

Set less than unsigned

sltu rd, rs, rt

0	rs	rt	rd	0	0x2b
6	5	5	5	5	6

Set register rd to 1 if register rs is less than rt, and to 0 otherwise.

Set less than immediate

slti rt, rs, imm

0xa	rs	rt	imm
6	5	5	16

Set less than unsigned immediate

sltiu rt, rs, imm

0xb	rs	rt	imm
6	5	5	16

Set register rt to 1 if register rs is less than the sign-extended immediate, and to 0 otherwise.

Set equal

seq rdest, rsrc1, rsrc2   *pseudoinstruction*

Set register rdest to 1 if register rsrc1 equals rsrc2, and to 0 otherwise.

Set greater than equal

sge rdest, rsrc1, rsrc2   *pseudoinstruction*

Set greater than equal unsigned

sgeu rdest, rsrc1, rsrc2   *pseudoinstruction*

Set register rdest to 1 if register rsrc1 is greater than or equal to rsrc2, and to 0 otherwise.

Set greater than

sgt rdest, rsrc1, rsrc2   *pseudoinstruction*

Set greater than unsigned

```
sgtu rdest, rsrc1, rsrc2          pseudoinstruction
```

Set register rdest to 1 if register rsrc1 is greater than rsrc2, and to 0 otherwise.

Set less than equal

```
sle rdest, rsrc1, rsrc2           pseudoinstruction
```

Set less than equal unsigned

```
sleu rdest, rsrc1, rsrc2          pseudoinstruction
```

Set register rdest to 1 if register rsrc1 is less than or equal to rsrc2, and to 0 otherwise.

Set not equal

```
sne rdest, rsrc1, rsrc2           pseudoinstruction
```

Set register rdest to 1 if register rsrc1 is not equal to rsrc2, and to 0 otherwise.

Branch Instructions

Branch instructions use a signed 16-bit instruction *offset* field; hence, they can jump $2^{15} - 1$ *instructions* (not bytes) forward or 2^{15} instructions backward. The *jump* instruction contains a 26-bit address field. In actual MIPS processors, branch instructions are delayed branches, which do not transfer control until the instruction following the branch (its "delay slot") has executed (see Chapter 4). Delayed branches affect the offset calculation, since it must be computed relative to the address of the delay slot instruction (PC + 4), which is when the branch occurs. SPIM does not simulate this delay slot, unless the -bare or -delayed_branch flags are specified.

In assembly code, offsets are not usually specified as numbers. Instead, an instructions branch to a label, and the assembler computes the distance between the branch and the target instructions.

In MIPS-32, all actual (not pseudo) conditional branch instructions have a "likely" variant (for example, beq's likely variant is beql), which does *not* execute the instruction in the branch's delay slot if the branch is not taken. Do not use these instructions; they may be removed in subsequent versions of the architecture. SPIM implements these instructions, but they are not described further.

Branch instruction

    b label   *pseudoinstruction*

Unconditionally branch to the instruction at the label.

Branch coprocessor false

    bclf cc label

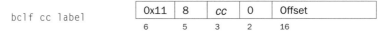

0x11	8	cc	0	Offset
6	5	3	2	16

Branch coprocessor true

    bclt cc label

0x11	8	cc	1	Offset
6	5	3	2	16

Conditionally branch the number of instructions specified by the offset if the floating-point coprocessor's condition flag numbered *cc* is false (true). If *cc* is omitted from the instruction, condition code flag 0 is assumed.

Branch on equal

    beq rs, rt, label

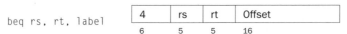

4	rs	rt	Offset
6	5	5	16

Conditionally branch the number of instructions specified by the offset if register rs equals rt.

Branch on greater than equal zero

    bgez rs, label

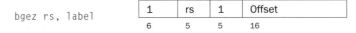

1	rs	1	Offset
6	5	5	16

Conditionally branch the number of instructions specified by the offset if register rs is greater than or equal to 0.

Branch on greater than equal zero and link

bgezal rs, label

1	rs	0x11	Offset
6	5	5	16

Conditionally branch the number of instructions specified by the offset if register rs is greater than or equal to 0. Save the address of the next instruction in register 31.

Branch on greater than zero

bgtz rs, label

7	rs	0	Offset
6	5	5	16

Conditionally branch the number of instructions specified by the offset if register rs is greater than 0.

Branch on less than equal zero

blez rs, label

6	rs	0	Offset
6	5	5	16

Conditionally branch the number of instructions specified by the offset if register rs is less than or equal to 0.

Branch on less than and link

bltzal rs, label

1	rs	0x10	Offset
6	5	5	16

Conditionally branch the number of instructions specified by the offset if register rs is less than 0. Save the address of the next instruction in register 31.

Branch on less than zero

bltz rs, label

1	rs	0	Offset
6	5	5	16

Conditionally branch the number of instructions specified by the offset if register rs is less than 0.

Branch on not equal

bne rs, rt, label

5	rs	rt	Offset
6	5	5	16

Conditionally branch the number of instructions specified by the offset if register rs is not equal to rt.

Branch on equal zero

beqz rsrc, label   *pseudoinstruction*

Conditionally branch to the instruction at the label if rsrc equals 0.

Branch on greater than equal

bge rsrc1, rsrc2, label   *pseudoinstruction*

Branch on greater than equal unsigned

bgeu rsrc1, rsrc2, label   *pseudoinstruction*

Conditionally branch to the instruction at the label if register rsrc1 is greater than or equal to rsrc2.

Branch on greater than

bgt rsrc1, src2, label   *pseudoinstruction*

Branch on greater than unsigned

bgtu rsrc1, src2, label   *pseudoinstruction*

Conditionally branch to the instruction at the label if register rsrc1 is greater than src2.

Branch on less than equal

ble rsrc1, src2, label   *pseudoinstruction*

Branch on less than equal unsigned

```
bleu rsrc1, src2, label
```
             pseudoinstruction

Conditionally branch to the instruction at the label if register `rsrc1` is less than or equal to `src2`.

Branch on less than

```
blt rsrc1, rsrc2, label
```
             pseudoinstruction

Branch on less than unsigned

```
bltu rsrc1, rsrc2, label
```
             pseudoinstruction

Conditionally branch to the instruction at the label if register `rsrc1` is less than `rsrc2`.

Branch on not equal zero

```
bnez rsrc, label
```
             pseudoinstruction

Conditionally branch to the instruction at the label if register `rsrc` is not equal to 0.

Jump Instructions

Jump

`j target`

2	target
6	26

Unconditionally jump to the instruction at target.

Jump and link

`jal target`

3	target
6	26

Unconditionally jump to the instruction at target. Save the address of the next instruction in register $ra.

Jump and link register

jalr rs, rd

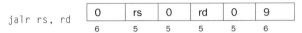

0	rs	0	rd	0	9
6	5	5	5	5	6

Unconditionally jump to the instruction whose address is in register rs. Save the address of the next instruction in register rd (which defaults to 31).

Jump register

jr rs

0	rs	0	8
6	5	15	6

Unconditionally jump to the instruction whose address is in register rs.

Trap Instructions

Trap if equal

teq rs, rt

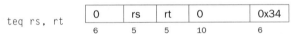

0	rs	rt	0	0x34
6	5	5	10	6

If register rs is equal to register rt, raise a Trap exception.

Trap if equal immediate

teqi rs, imm

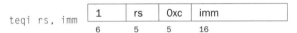

1	rs	0xc	imm
6	5	5	16

If register rs is equal to the sign-extended value imm, raise a Trap exception.

Trap if not equal

teq rs, rt

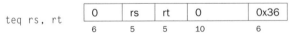

0	rs	rt	0	0x36
6	5	5	10	6

If register rs is not equal to register rt, raise a Trap exception.

Trap if not equal immediate

teqi rs, imm

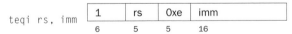

1	rs	0xe	imm
6	5	5	16

If register rs is not equal to the sign-extended value imm, raise a Trap exception.

Trap if greater equal

tge rs, rt

0	rs	rt	0	0x30
6	5	5	10	6

Unsigned trap if greater equal

tgeu rs, rt

0	rs	rt	0	0x31
6	5	5	10	6

If register rs is greater than or equal to register rt, raise a Trap exception.

Trap if greater equal immediate

tgei rs, imm

1	rs	8	imm
6	5	5	16

Unsigned trap if greater equal immediate

tgeiu rs, imm

1	rs	9	imm
6	5	5	16

If register rs is greater than or equal to the sign-extended value imm, raise a Trap exception.

Trap if less than

tlt rs, rt

0	rs	rt	0	0x32
6	5	5	10	6

Unsigned trap if less than

tltu rs, rt

0	rs	rt	0	0x33
6	5	5	10	6

If register rs is less than register rt, raise a Trap exception.

Trap if less than immediate

tlti rs, imm

1	rs	a	imm
6	5	5	16

Unsigned trap if less than immediate

tltiu rs, imm

1	rs	b	imm
6	5	5	16

If register rs is less than the sign-extended value imm, raise a Trap exception.

Load Instructions

Load address

la rdest, address   *pseudoinstruction*

Load computed *address*—not the contents of the location—into register rdest.

Load byte

lb rt, address

0x20	rs	rt	Offset
6	5	5	16

Load unsigned byte

lbu rt, address

0x24	rs	rt	Offset
6	5	5	16

Load the byte at *address* into register rt. The byte is sign-extended by lb, but not by lbu.

Load halfword

lh rt, address

0x21	rs	rt	Offset
6	5	5	16

Load unsigned halfword

lhu rt, address

0x25	rs	rt	Offset
6	5	5	16

Load the 16-bit quantity (halfword) at *address* into register rt. The halfword is sign-extended by lh, but not by lhu.

Load word

lw rt, address

0x23	rs	rt	Offset
6	5	5	16

Load the 32-bit quantity (word) at *address* into register rt.

Load word coprocessor 1

lwcl ft, address

0x31	rs	rt	Offset
6	5	5	16

Load the word at *address* into register ft in the floating-point unit.

Load word left

lwl rt, address

0x22	rs	rt	Offset
6	5	5	16

Load word right

lwr rt, address

0x26	rs	rt	Offset
6	5	5	16

Load the left (right) bytes from the word at the possibly unaligned *address* into register rt.

Load doubleword

ld rdest, address   *pseudoinstruction*

Load the 64-bit quantity at *address* into registers rdest and rdest + 1.

Unaligned load halfword

ulh rdest, address   *pseudoinstruction*

Unaligned load halfword unsigned

ulhu rdest, address   *pseudoinstruction*

Load the 16-bit quantity (halfword) at the possibly unaligned *address* into register rdest. The halfword is sign-extended by ulh, but not ulhu.

Unaligned load word

ulw rdest, address   *pseudoinstruction*

Load the 32-bit quantity (word) at the possibly unaligned *address* into register rdest.

Load linked

ll rt, address

0x30	rs	rt	Offset
6	5	5	16

Load the 32-bit quantity (word) at *address* into register rt and start an atomic read-modify-write operation. This operation is completed by a store conditional (sc) instruction, which will fail if another processor writes into the block containing the loaded word. Since SPIM does not simulate multiple processors, the store conditional operation always succeeds.

Store Instructions

Store byte

sb rt, address

0x28	rs	rt	Offset
6	5	5	16

Store the low byte from register rt at *address*.

Store halfword

sh rt, address

0x29	rs	rt	Offset
6	5	5	16

Store the low halfword from register rt at *address*.

Store word

sw rt, address

0x2b	rs	rt	Offset
6	5	5	16

Store the word from register rt at *address*.

Store word coprocessor 1

swcl ft, address

0x31	rs	ft	Offset
6	5	5	16

Store the floating-point value in register ft of floating-point coprocessor at *address*.

Store double coprocessor 1

sdcl ft, address

0x3d	rs	ft	Offset
6	5	5	16

Store the doubleword floating-point value in registers ft and ft + 1 of floating-point coprocessor at *address*. Register ft must be even numbered.

Store word left

swl rt, address

0x2a	rs	rt	Offset
6	5	5	16

Store word right

swr rt, address

0x2e	rs	rt	Offset
6	5	5	16

Store the left (right) bytes from register rt at the possibly unaligned *address*.

Store doubleword

sd rsrc, address   *pseudoinstruction*

Store the 64-bit quantity in registers rsrc and rsrc + 1 at *address*.

Unaligned store halfword

        ush rsrc, address   *pseudoinstruction*

Store the low halfword from register rsrc at the possibly unaligned *address*.

Unaligned store word

        usw rsrc, address   *pseudoinstruction*

Store the word from register rsrc at the possibly unaligned *address*.

Store conditional

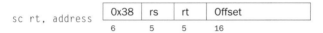

0x38	rs	rt	Offset
6	5	5	16

        sc rt, address

Store the 32-bit quantity (word) in register rt into memory at *address* and complete an atomic read-modify-write operation. If this atomic operation is successful, the memory word is modified and register rt is set to 1. If the atomic operation fails because another processor wrote to a location in the block containing the addressed word, this instruction does not modify memory and writes 0 into register rt. Since SPIM does not simulate multiple processors, the instruction always succeeds.

Data Movement Instructions

Move

        move rdest, rsrc   *pseudoinstruction*

Move register rsrc to rdest.

Move from hi

        mfhi rd

0	0	rd	0	0x10
6	10	5	5	6

Move from lo

mflo rd

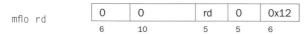

0	0	rd	0	0x12
6	10	5	5	6

The multiply and divide unit produces its result in two additional registers, hi and lo. These instructions move values to and from these registers. The multiply, divide, and remainder pseudoinstructions that make this unit appear to operate on the general registers move the result after the computation finishes.

Move the hi (lo) register to register rd.

Move to hi

mthi rs

0	rs	0	0x11
6	5	15	6

Move to lo

mtlo rs

0	rs	0	0x13
6	5	15	6

Move register rs to the hi (lo) register.

Move from coprocessor 0

mfc0 rt, rd

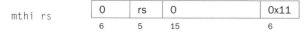

0x10	0	rt	rd	0
6	5	5	5	11

Move from coprocessor 1

mfc1 rt, fs

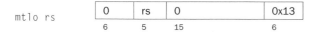

0x11	0	rt	fs	0
6	5	5	5	11

Coprocessors have their own register sets. These instructions move values between these registers and the CPU's registers.

Move register rd in a coprocessor (register fs in the FPU) to CPU register rt. The floating-point unit is coprocessor 1.

Move double from coprocessor 1

```
mfc1.d rdest, frsrc1                    pseudoinstruction
```

Move floating-point registers frsrc1 and frsrc1 + 1 to CPU registers rdest and rdest + 1.

Move to coprocessor 0

mtc0 rd, rt

0x10	4	rt	rd	0
6	5	5	5	11

Move to coprocessor 1

mtc1 rd, fs

0x11	4	rt	fs	0
6	5	5	5	11

Move CPU register rt to register rd in a coprocessor (register fs in the FPU).

Move conditional not zero

movn rd, rs, rt

0	rs	rt	rd	0xb
6	5	5	5	11

Move register rs to register rd if register rt is not 0.

Move conditional zero

movz rd, rs, rt

0	rs	rt	rd	0xa
6	5	5	5	11

Move register rs to register rd if register rt is 0.

Move conditional on FP false

movf rd, rs, cc

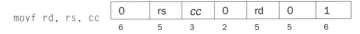

0	rs	cc	0	rd	0	1
6	5	3	2	5	5	6

Move CPU register rs to register rd if FPU condition code flag number *cc* is 0. If *cc* is omitted from the instruction, condition code flag 0 is assumed.

Move conditional on FP true

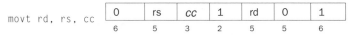

movt rd, rs, cc

0	rs	cc	1	rd	0	1
6	5	3	2	5	5	6

Move CPU register rs to register rd if FPU condition code flag number *cc* is 1. If *cc* is omitted from the instruction, condition code bit 0 is assumed.

Floating-Point Instructions

The MIPS has a floating-point coprocessor (numbered 1) that operates on single precision (32-bit) and double precision (64-bit) floating-point numbers. This coprocessor has its own registers, which are numbered $f0–$f31. Because these registers are only 32 bits wide, two of them are required to hold doubles, so only floating-point registers with even numbers can hold double precision values. The floating-point coprocessor also has eight condition code (*cc*) flags, numbered 0–7, which are set by compare instructions and tested by branch (bclf or bclt) and conditional move instructions.

Values are moved in or out of these registers one word (32 bits) at a time by lwc1, swc1, mtc1, and mfc1 instructions or one double (64 bits) at a time by ldc1 and sdc1, described above, or by the l.s, l.d, s.s, and s.d pseudoinstructions described below.

In the actual instructions below, bits 21–26 are 0 for single precision and 1 for double precision. In the pseudoinstructions below, fdest is a floating-point register (e.g., $f2).

Floating-point absolute value double

abs.d fd, fs

0x11	1	0	fs	fd	5
6	5	5	5	5	6

Floating-point absolute value single

abs.s fd, fs

0x11	0	0	fs	fd	5

Compute the absolute value of the floating-point double (single) in register fs and put it in register fd.

Floating-point addition double

add.d fd, fs, ft

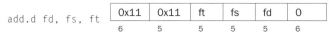

0x11	0x11	ft	fs	fd	0
6	5	5	5	5	6

Floating-point addition single

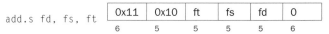

add.s fd, fs, ft

0x11	0x10	ft	fs	fd	0
6	5	5	5	5	6

Compute the sum of the floating-point doubles (singles) in registers fs and ft and put it in register fd.

Floating-point ceiling to word

ceil.w.d fd, fs

0x11	0x11	0	fs	fd	0xe
6	5	5	5	5	6

ceil.w.s fd, fs

0x11	0x10	0	fs	fd	0xe
6	5	5	5	5	6

Compute the ceiling of the floating-point double (single) in register fs, convert to a 32-bit fixed-point value, and put the resulting word in register fd.

Compare equal double

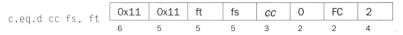

c.eq.d cc fs, ft

0x11	0x11	ft	fs	cc	0	FC	2
6	5	5	5	3	2	2	4

Compare equal single

c.eq.s cc fs, ft

0x11	0x10	ft	fs	cc	0	FC	2
6	5	5	5	3	2	2	4

Compare the floating-point double (single) in register fs against the one in ft and set the floating-point condition flag cc to 1 if they are equal. If cc is omitted, condition code flag 0 is assumed.

Compare less than equal double

c.le.d cc fs, ft

0x11	0x11	ft	fs	cc	0	FC	0xe
6	5	5	5	3	2	2	4

Compare less than equal single

c.le.s cc fs, ft

0x11	0x10	ft	fs	cc	0	FC	0xe
6	5	5	5	3	2	2	4

Compare the floating-point double (single) in register fs against the one in ft and set the floating-point condition flag *cc* to 1 if the first is less than or equal to the second. If *cc* is omitted, condition code flag 0 is assumed.

Compare less than double

c.lt.d cc fs, ft

0x11	0x11	ft	fs	*cc*	0	FC	0xc
6	5	5	5	3	2	2	4

Compare less than single

c.lt.s cc fs, ft

0x11	0x10	ft	fs	*cc*	0	FC	0xc
6	5	5	5	3	2	2	4

Compare the floating-point double (single) in register fs against the one in ft and set the condition flag *cc* to 1 if the first is less than the second. If *cc* is omitted, condition code flag 0 is assumed.

Convert single to double

cvt.d.s fd, fs

0x11	0x10	0	fs	fd	0x21
6	5	5	5	5	6

Convert integer to double

cvt.d.w fd, fs

0x11	0x14	0	fs	fd	0x21
6	5	5	5	5	6

Convert the single precision floating-point number or integer in register fs to a double (single) precision number and put it in register fd.

Convert double to single

cvt.s.d fd, fs

0x11	0x11	0	fs	fd	0x20
6	5	5	5	5	6

Convert integer to single

cvt.s.w fd, fs

0x11	0x14	0	fs	fd	0x20
6	5	5	5	5	6

Convert the double precision floating-point number or integer in register fs to a single precision number and put it in register fd.

Convert double to integer

cvt.w.d fd, fs

0x11	0x11	0	fs	fd	0x24
6	5	5	5	5	6

Convert single to integer

cvt.w.s fd, fs

0x11	0x10	0	fs	fd	0x24
6	5	5	5	5	6

Convert the double or single precision floating-point number in register fs to an integer and put it in register fd.

Floating-point divide double

div.d fd, fs, ft

0x11	0x11	ft	fs	fd	3
6	5	5	5	5	6

Floating-point divide single

div.s fd, fs, ft

0x11	0x10	ft	fs	fd	3
6	5	5	5	5	6

Compute the quotient of the floating-point doubles (singles) in registers fs and ft and put it in register fd.

Floating-point floor to word

floor.w.d fd, fs

0x11	0x11	0	fs	fd	0xf
6	5	5	5	5	6

floor.w.s fd, fs

0x11	0x10	0	fs	fd	0xf

Compute the floor of the floating-point double (single) in register fs and put the resulting word in register fd.

Load floating-point double

l.d fdest, address   *pseudoinstruction*

Load floating-point single

```
l.s fdest, address              pseudoinstruction
```

Load the floating-point double (single) at `address` into register `fdest`.

Move floating-point double

`mov.d fd, fs`

0x11	0x11	0	fs	fd	6
6	5	5	5	5	6

Move floating-point single

`mov.s fd, fs`

0x11	0x10	0	fs	fd	6
6	5	5	5	5	6

Move the floating-point double (single) from register `fs` to register `fd`.

Move conditional floating-point double false

`movf.d fd, fs, cc`

0x11	0x11	*cc*	0	fs	fd	0x11
6	5	3	2	5	5	6

Move conditional floating-point single false

`movf.s fd, fs, cc`

0x11	0x10	*cc*	0	fs	fd	0x11
6	5	3	2	5	5	6

Move the floating-point double (single) from register `fs` to register `fd` if condition code flag *cc* is 0. If *cc* is omitted, condition code flag 0 is assumed.

Move conditional floating-point double true

`movt.d fd, fs, cc`

0x11	0x11	*cc*	1	fs	fd	0x11
6	5	3	2	5	5	6

Move conditional floating-point single true

`movt.s fd, fs, cc`

0x11	0x10	*cc*	1	fs	fd	0x11
6	5	3	2	5	5	6

Move the floating-point double (single) from register fs to register fd if condition code flag *cc* is 1. If *cc* is omitted, condition code flag 0 is assumed.

Move conditional floating-point double not zero

movn.d fd, fs, rt

0x11	0x11	rt	fs	fd	0x13
6	5	5	5	5	6

Move conditional floating-point single not zero

movn.s fd, fs, rt

0x11	0x10	rt	fs	fd	0x13
6	5	5	5	5	6

Move the floating-point double (single) from register fs to register fd if processor register rt is not 0.

Move conditional floating-point double zero

movz.d fd, fs, rt

0x11	0x11	rt	fs	fd	0x12
6	5	5	5	5	6

Move conditional floating-point single zero

movz.s fd, fs, rt

0x11	0x10	rt	fs	fd	0x12
6	5	5	5	5	6

Move the floating-point double (single) from register fs to register fd if processor register rt is 0.

Floating-point multiply double

mul.d fd, fs, ft

0x11	0x11	ft	fs	fd	2
6	5	5	5	5	6

Floating-point multiply single

mul.s fd, fs, ft

0x11	0x10	ft	fs	fd	2
6	5	5	5	5	6

Compute the product of the floating-point doubles (singles) in registers fs and ft and put it in register fd.

Negate double

neg.d fd, fs

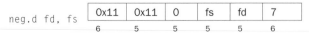

0x11	0x11	0	fs	fd	7
6	5	5	5	5	6

Negate single

	0x11	0x10	0	fs	fd	7
`neg.s fd, fs`	6	5	5	5	5	6

Negate the floating-point double (single) in register fs and put it in register fd.

Floating-point round to word

	0x11	0x11	0	fs	fd	0xc
`round.w.d fd, fs`	6	5	5	5	5	6

	0x11	0x10	0	fs	fd	0xc
`round.w.s fd, fs`						

Round the floating-point double (single) value in register fs, convert to a 32-bit fixed-point value, and put the resulting word in register fd.

Square root double

	0x11	0x11	0	fs	fd	4
`sqrt.d fd, fs`	6	5	5	5	5	6

Square root single

	0x11	0x10	0	fs	fd	4
`sqrt.s fd, fs`	6	5	5	5	5	6

Compute the square root of the floating-point double (single) in register fs and put it in register fd.

Store floating-point double

`s.d fdest, address`   *pseudoinstruction*

Store floating-point single

`s.s fdest, address`   *pseudoinstruction*

Store the floating-point double (single) in register fdest at *address*.

Floating-point subtract double

	0x11	0x11	ft	fs	fd	1
`sub.d fd, fs, ft`	6	5	5	5	5	6

Floating-point subtract single

sub.s fd, fs, ft

0x11	0x10	ft	fs	fd	1
6	5	5	5	5	6

Compute the difference of the floating-point doubles (singles) in registers fs and ft and put it in register fd.

Floating-point truncate to word

trunc.w.d fd, fs

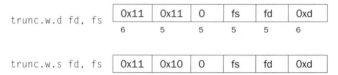

0x11	0x11	0	fs	fd	0xd
6	5	5	5	5	6

trunc.w.s fd, fs

0x11	0x10	0	fs	fd	0xd

Truncate the floating-point double (single) value in register fs, convert to a 32-bit fixed-point value, and put the resulting word in register fd.

Exception and Interrupt Instructions

Exception return

eret

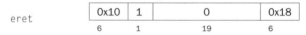

0x10	1	0	0x18
6	1	19	6

Set the EXL bit in coprocessor 0's Status register to 0 and return to the instruction pointed to by coprocessor 0's EPC register.

System call

syscall

0	0	0xc
6	20	6

Register $v0 contains the number of the system call (see Figure B.9.1) provided by SPIM.

Break

break code

0	code	0xd
6	20	6

Cause exception *code*. Exception 1 is reserved for the debugger.

No operation

nop

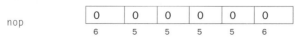

0	0	0	0	0	0
6	5	5	5	5	6

Do nothing.

B.11 Concluding Remarks

Programming in assembly language requires a programmer to trade helpful features of high-level languages—such as data structures, type checking, and control constructs—for complete control over the instructions that a computer executes. External constraints on some applications, such as response time or program size, require a programmer to pay close attention to every instruction. However, the cost of this level of attention is assembly language programs that are longer, more time-consuming to write, and more difficult to maintain than high-level language programs.

Moreover, three trends are reducing the need to write programs in assembly language. The first trend is toward the improvement of compilers. Modern compilers produce code that is typically comparable to the best handwritten code—and is sometimes better. The second trend is the introduction of new processors that are not only faster, but in the case of processors that execute multiple instructions simultaneously, also more difficult to program by hand. In addition, the rapid evolution of the modern computer favors high-level language programs that are not tied to a single architecture. Finally, we witness a trend toward increasingly complex applications, characterized by complex graphic interfaces and many more features than their predecessors. Large applications are written by teams of programmers and require the modularity and semantic checking features provided by high-level languages.

Further Reading

Aho, A., R. Sethi, and J. Ullman [1985]. *Compilers: Principles, Techniques, and Tools*, Reading, MA: Addison-Wesley.

Slightly dated and lacking in coverage of modern architectures, but still the standard reference on compilers.

Sweetman, D. [1999]. *See MIPS Run*, San Francisco, CA: Morgan Kaufmann Publishers.

A complete, detailed, and engaging introduction to the MIPS instruction set and assembly language programming on these machines.

Detailed documentation on the MIPS-32 architecture is available on the Web:

MIPS32™ Architecture for Programmers Volume I: Introduction to the MIPS32™ Architecture
(http://mips.com/content/Documentation/MIPSDocumentation/ProcessorArchitecture/ ArchitectureProgrammingPublicationsforMIPS32/MD00082-2B-MIPS32INT-AFP-02.00.pdf/ getDownload)

MIPS32™ Architecture for Programmers Volume II: The MIPS32™ Instruction Set
(http://mips.com/content/Documentation/MIPSDocumentation/ProcessorArchitecture/ ArchitectureProgrammingPublicationsforMIPS32/MD00086-2B-MIPS32BIS-AFP-02.00.pdf/getDownload)

MIPS32™ Architecture for Programmers Volume III: The MIPS32™ Privileged Resource Architecture
(http://mips.com/content/Documentation/MIPSDocumentation/ProcessorArchitecture/ ArchitectureProgrammingPublicationsforMIPS32/MD00090-2B-MIPS32PRA-AFP-02.00.pdf/getDownload)

B.12   Exercises

B.1 [5] <§B.5> Section B.5 described how memory is partitioned on most MIPS systems. Propose another way of dividing memory that meets the same goals.

B.2 [20] <§B.6> Rewrite the code for fact to use fewer instructions.

B.3 [5] <§B.7> Is it ever safe for a user program to use registers $k0 or $k1?

B.4 [25] <§B.7> Section B.7 contains code for a very simple exception handler. One serious problem with this handler is that it disables interrupts for a long time. This means that interrupts from a fast I/O device may be lost. Write a better exception handler that is interruptable and enables interrupts as quickly as possible.

B.5 [15] <§B.7> The simple exception handler always jumps back to the instruction following the exception. This works fine unless the instruction that causes the exception is in the delay slot of a branch. In that case, the next instruction is the target of the branch. Write a better handler that uses the EPC register to determine which instruction should be executed after the exception.

B.6 [5] <§B.9> Using SPIM, write and test an adding machine program that repeatedly reads in integers and adds them into a running sum. The program should stop when it gets an input that is 0, printing out the sum at that point. Use the SPIM system calls described on pages B-43 and B-45.

B.7 [5] <§B.9> Using SPIM, write and test a program that reads in three integers and prints out the sum of the largest two of the three. Use the SPIM system calls described on pages B-43 and B-45. You can break ties arbitrarily.

B.8 [5] <§B.9> Using SPIM, write and test a program that reads in a positive integer using the SPIM system calls. If the integer is not positive, the program should terminate with the message "Invalid Entry"; otherwise the program should print out the names of the digits of the integers, delimited by exactly one space. For example, if the user entered "728," the output would be "Seven Two Eight."

B.9 [25] <§B.9> Write and test a MIPS assembly language program to compute and print the first 100 prime numbers. A number n is prime if no numbers except 1 and n divide it evenly. You should implement two routines:

■ test_prime (n)   Return 1 if n is prime and 0 if n is not prime.

■ main ()   Iterate over the integers, testing if each is prime. Print the first 100 numbers that are prime.

Test your programs by running them on SPIM.

B.10 [10] <§§B.6, B.9> Using SPIM, write and test a recursive program for solving the classic mathematical recreation, the Towers of Hanoi puzzle. (This will require the use of stack frames to support recursion.) The puzzle consists of three pegs (1, 2, and 3) and n disks (the number n can vary; typical values might be in the range from 1 to 8). Disk 1 is smaller than disk 2, which is in turn smaller than disk 3, and so forth, with disk n being the largest. Initially, all the disks are on peg 1, starting with disk n on the bottom, disk $n - 1$ on top of that, and so forth, up to disk 1 on the top. The goal is to move all the disks to peg 2. You may only move one disk at a time, that is, the top disk from any of the three pegs onto the top of either of the other two pegs. Moreover, there is a constraint: You must not place a larger disk on top of a smaller disk.

The C program below can be used to help write your assembly language program.

```c
/* move n smallest disks from start to finish using
extra */

void hanoi(int n, int start, int finish, int extra){
    if(n != 0){
        hanoi(n-1, start, extra, finish);
        print_string("Move disk");
        print_int(n);
        print_string("from peg");
        print_int(start);
        print_string("to peg");
        print_int(finish);
        print_string(".\n");
        hanoi(n-1, extra, finish, start);
    }
}
main(){
    int n;
    print_string("Enter number of disks>");
    n = read_int();
    hanoi(n, 1, 2, 3);
    return 0;
}
```

Index

CD information is listed by chapter and section number followed by page ranges (CD3.10:6–9). Page references preceded by a single letter refer to appendixes.